Howard Coster

The Rt. Hon. David Lloyd George, O.M., M.P.

WAR MEMOIRS

Volume I, Part 1.

David Lloyd George

Simon Publications
2001

Copyright © 1943 by David Lloyd George

Originally published by Oldhams Press Ltd, London

Library of Congress Control Number: 43018058

ISBN: 1-931541-35-3

Printed by Lightning Source Inc. La Vergne, TN

Published by Simon Publications, P. O. Box 321, Safety Harbor,
FL 34695

FOREWORD

TO

NEW EDITION

I HAVE received many communications expressing a hope that my War Memoirs should be published at a price which would bring them within easier reach of readers of average means.

The publication of a popular edition has afforded me an opportunity for checking the statements published in the first edition in the light of public criticisms, of facts brought to light by subsequent writings, and of the numerous letters written to me by men who took an active part in the events I narrate. After a careful perusal of this fresh material I have not found it necessary to revise or correct any of the assertions I made or opinions I expressed in the original narrative.

I have added a sample of the letters that poured in during the last four or five years from eye-witnesses. I have specially chosen for publication a few of those I received on the Passchendaele episode, as the account I gave of that battle has been regarded as the most direct and detailed arraignment of the military command to which I have committed myself in these pages. A fair representative selection of this correspondence is given as an appendix to my Passchendaele chapter.

I aim to tell the naked truth about War as I saw it from the conning-tower at Downing Street. I saw how the incredible heroism of the common man was being squandered to repair the incompetence of the trained inexperts (for they were actually trained not to be expert in mastering the actualities of modern warfare) in the production of equipment, in transport, in tackling the submarine menace, in the narrow, selfish and unimaginative strategy and in the ghastly butchery of a succession of vain and insane offensives. The last great struggle revealed not only the horrid and squalid aspects of war but its muddles; its futilities; its chanciness; its precariousness; its wastefulness of the lives, the treasure and the virtues of mankind—all that demonstrates the supreme stupidity of committing to such a brutal and blunder-headed tribunal as War the determination of issues upon which the happiness and progress of humanity so largely depend.

When all the people that on earth do dwell are gladly scraping the butter off their own and their children's bread in order to keep the god of war fit and sleek, it is necessary to show them clearly what a fool he really is.

Bron-y-de, Churt.   D. LLOYD GEORGE.
January, 1938.

PREFACE

TO

VOLUME ONE*

MOST of the leading actors in the Great War, both Statesmen and Warriors, have committed to writing the story of the part they played in it. With one or two exceptions they have written their narrative themselves, although the composition of books has been to them as new a venture as it is now to me. With the exception of M. Briand, who never put pen to paper, all the dominant personalities of the War have told their tale of what they did and why they did it; amongst rulers, the Kaiser, the Crown Prince, M. Poincaré, President Wilson (through Mr. Baker); amongst statesmen, M. Clemenceau, Mr. Asquith, Lord Grey, Mr. Churchill, Colonel House, Prince Max of Baden, Von Bülow; amongst the warriors, Foch, Joffre, Hindenburg, Ludendorff, Hofmann, Cadorna, French, Haig (with the aid of another pen), Henry Wilson, Robertson, Pershing, and a host of others. My library shelves groan under the burden of war autobiographies. No wonder I hesitated for years to follow the example set me by those who figured so prominently on the stage where I also occupied a not inconspicuous position. I had almost decided to bequeath the undertaking to those with whom I should leave my papers, when two incidents occurred which influenced me to take up my pencil and relate my own story in my own words.

The first was an illness which released me from the irksome and peculiarly thankless duty of leadership in a political party unhappily poisoned and paralysed by internal dissension amongst its better known members. The other was a visit paid me during my convalescence by an old comrade of the Great War. He entreated me to take advantage of my seclusion from active political warfare to give my account of the events of the War. He reminded me that amongst statesmen I was the only one who went right through it from the declaration of War to the signing of Peace. He urged that the real history of the War might not—and probably would not—be written for another generation, but that the books written to-day by the men—generals and politicians—who had a share either in the

---

* This Preface is the result of the merging by the author of the Prefaces to Volumes I and III of the original edition in six volumes.

fighting or in the direction would constitute the principal material upon which the historian would draw for his facts and impressions. All these books gave the point of view of the individual writer, biased naturally either by limitation of his opportunities or by a controverted theory of events, or, too frequently, by the exigencies of a personal apologia. It was pointed out to me that I was the only person in authority who was in Mr. Britling's position. I " saw it through " from the outbreak of the quarrel to the settlement of the terms. There are multitudes who were better acquainted with certain aspects of the War; there are, or were, a few who for a limited period were in a better position to view the struggle as a whole; but there is no one (and I often recall the fact with horror) who was as intimately acquainted as myself with the war direction during the whole of its rending and tearing course through the vitals of mankind.

To tell the story at all is like repeating what was seen in a nightmare, and I shrank for years from writing my record of the horrifying details. It is not pleasant to remember how men and women devoted energy, intelligence, and zeal for four-and-a-half years to the work of destruction and pain. But it must be told if such a calamity is to be averted in the future. It is better that the real facts should be given. I do not pretend to know them all, but some of them I know better than my contemporaries. These I am doing my best to relate accurately in the following pages. I make my own contribution, not as one who claims to be an experienced author, but as a witness giving evidence on what he remembers of these tremendous transactions.

I have written of men and events as I saw and thought of them. That may involve criticism where others might praise and commendation where others might attach blame. Where I have indulged in any stricture, I have taken the utmost pains to test the accuracy of my recollection by reference to contemporary documents. I have also consulted men who took an active part in episodes I record. But the pathways and boundaries of memory are so obliterated and confused by time, that the most reliable witness often strays, unless the road is marked out with the " writing that remains." Luckily, I have in my possession—thanks to careful secretaries—a vast number of memoranda, minutes and letters concerning the War and Peace, all written at the time.

The only value which these volumes may possess for the future historian of war will depend upon the memories being genuine and upon the extent to which they are fortified by documentary or other contemporary evidence. These documents I have chosen and quoted or used with a full sense of the responsibility resting on every public servant not to reveal or publish anything which may injure the interests of his country. In the exercise of this discretion I owe much to the scrutiny of one of the most efficient and distinguished public servants of his generation—Sir Maurice Hankey. I owe thanks also to a great many kind friends who have assisted me by supplementing and stimulating my memory with their own as to occurrences where I enjoyed their valued co-operation.

The tale is one which does not always give me any pleasure to tell; quite the reverse. There is much of it which I wrote with intense reluctance. For I found it necessary in the interests of a truthful record to relate facts which constitute a severe criticism on the action of men whose memory is honoured by their fellow countrymen for many sterling qualities which they possessed in a remarkable degree. My disinclination for revealing to the public unpleasant truths which reflect on distinguished public servants is naturally enhanced by the fact that some of them are no longer present to defend themselves. For that reason I felt disposed to pass on to others the duty of writing the true history of the occurrences recorded in these volumes. But as all these Great War figures had in their lifetime, either themselves or through the agency of authorised substitutes, already given their version of affairs, in which they did not spare those of whom they disapproved—including myself—I felt I was justified in publishing information at my disposal which corrected wrong impressions. Moreover, I took the view that if you accept the responsibility of writing history, you cannot do so honestly without allocating blame as well as praise, where either is due to the men who take a leading part in the events which make that history. And the right and duty of criticism or approval for their contribution does not cease with their death. Warriors are in that respect in the same category as politicians. Apart from that general consideration, there are at least two imperative reasons why the facts should be told now and not later. It has been sagely remarked by Macaulay that the knowledge of past events "is valuable only as it leads us to form just calculations with respect to the future." The atmosphere of the world—East and West—is charged with the international suspicions, rivalries, ambitions and fears that have always hitherto ended in war. Nations are arming for war. Every nation throughout the world—almost without exception—is increasing its armaments. Every effort to arrest this menacing expansion of the mechanism of wholesale slaughter has failed. Nations with already enormous armaments are increasing and improving them. Formidable nations that were disarmed, are re-arming. Governments are making preparations for war in defiance of treaties they signed, and they are doing so with an urgent anxiety that can only be explained by a general apprehension that war is impending. There is no confidence in any quarter that peace can be long preserved. In these circumstances it is essential first of all that nations should know, before they declare war, to what they are committing themselves. All nations alike enter into a war with an equal confidence in ultimate victory for their banners. Defeat is always a surprise to the vanquished. Elements they had not realised, defects in their own equipment, resources or qualities, or superiority in those of their foes, which they never suspected, mistakes attributable to inferior leadership which threw away good chances—and finally that play of chance and fate, which no genius can forecast or control, all make the issue of a war as doubtful as that of a serious disease. A good physician may pull through a man with a weak constitution—a poor or second-rate doctor may ruin the chances of a patient with the soundest natural physique. A good cause counts in any struggle, but it is by no means decisive in a particular conflict between right and wrong.

I remember forming one of a delegation of British Ministers (which included Mr. Asquith, Lord Kitchener, Mr. Balfour, Sir Edward Grey) which attended an important conference at Paris in 1915. When we left for London, M. Combe ("le petit père Combe") came to the station on behalf of the French Government to see us off. He was a small and vivacious octogenarian whose optimism had not been in the least dimmed by years or by the maledictions of the devout, whom he had offended by his attacks on the Church. As soon as he entered the saloon carriage where we were seated, he started to deliver an oration on the subject of the War and its prospects—all full of hope and confidence. He ended with a peroration about "*Justice, Liberté, le Droit et la Victoire.*" Mr. Balfour regarded the whole performance with ill-concealed disdain and turning to me said: "He must have strangely misread history if he thinks that '*Justice, Liberté et Droit*' are synonymous with '*Victoire.*'"

There is a melancholy justification for this cynicism in the events of the past. Victory may not always go to the big battalions, neither does it invariably incline to the righteous, for it is a historical truism that a just cause often contends in vain against the superior might or efficiency of its opponents or the weakness or greater stupidity of its adherents. Those who entrust the destiny of their country to war therefore incur unforeseeable risks which may be fatal to them and the land they love. No other arbitrament is so costly in its procedure as well as so uncertain in its event. Let those who doubt this read carefully what happened in the Great War and see how reckless and unintelligent handling brought us almost to the rim of catastrophe, and how we were saved largely by the incredible folly of our foes. But you cannot always rely on your opponents making greater mistakes than your own.

The next lesson is one we must not overlook in a world of armed nations—that if mankind should unhappily fail to abolish war from the category of its visitations, then, if we are involved in another, we must take earnest heed that we do not fall into the errors that cost us so dearly last time. That is also my excuse for giving an account, so detailed as to be weighted with dreariness, of the great improvisations which were set up to organise the resources of the nations for war. A study of these is essential to anyone who wishes to learn how a country can be organised to the best advantage either in War or in Peace.

But, whether in exposition, approbation or condemnation, I must emphasise the importance of this precept—that these lessons cannot be learnt unless they are truthfully taught. If out of respect for honoured memories or cherished delusions, the truth be suppressed and defects hidden under a varnish of glorification, then we shall learn nothing, and if there be a next time we may not then escape disaster as we did in the last calamity—by a shuddering breadth.

I regret more than words can express the necessity for telling the bare facts of our bloodstained stagger to victory. But I had to tell them or leave unchallenged the supremacy of misleading and therefore dangerous illusions.

Unfortunately, censure attracts more attention than laudation. I have criticised a few—very few—statesmen and generals. That attracts controversy, and controversy involves a publicity which casts the larger and more important part of the narrative into the shade. If in these pages I have resorted to criticism, I have also recalled with pleasure the great services of many. Bonar Law, Balfour, Churchill, Cecil, Geddes, Maclay, Reading, Smuts, Borden, Hughes, Milner, Northcliffe, Fisher, Ernle, Lee of Fareham, are amongst a multitude of statesmen and administrators to whom praise is due and has been accorded without stint. I have dwelt on the successes of Generals like Plumer, Allenby, Maude, Monash and Cowans, whose triumphs lit up the dismal narrative of military ineptitude displayed by a few others. There were great figures whose shortcomings added to our difficulties. In their case I have also called attention to the exceptional qualities they possessed. And as to the myriads of officers and men whose incredible valour and endurance saved their country from the consequences of every blunder perpetrated, whether by politicians, generals or admirals, if I have failed in bestowing on them the full measure of praise they merit, it is from lack of adequate power to express the emotion to which I am moved by a renewed contemplation of their heroism.

Bron-y-de, Churt.   D. Lloyd George.
    1933-34.

CONTENTS

CONTENTS

CONTENTS

xiv

CONTENTS

LIST OF PLATES

Reginald Haines.

The Rt. Hon. David Lloyd George, M.P., in
the robes of Chancellor of the Exchequer, 1914.

Elliott & Fry.

The Earl of Oxford and Asquith.

Press Portrait Bureau.

Viscount Grey of Fallodon, K.G.

Press Portrait Bureau.

The Lord Cunliffe.

E.N.A.

Count Paul Wolff-Metternich.

M. Albert Thomas (French Minister of Munitions), Sir Douglas Haig and General
Joffre in earnest conversation with Mr. Lloyd George during his visit to the Somme
front.

A SLIGHT DISCREPANCY SOMEWHERE

HASQUITH (*to his pal Jawge*) : " 'Ere ! Not s'much o' your ' Too Late ! ' Wot's the blinkin' good o' me a-'ollerin' aht what I'm a-'ollerin' aht if you go a-'ollerin aht wot you're a-'ollerin' aht ? "

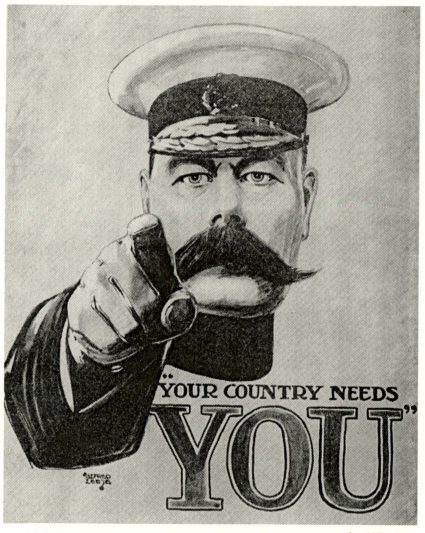

The famous poster placarded throughout the country to help in recruiting Kitchener's Army.

Imperial War Cabinet

Vandyk.

at Downing Street.

G. C. Beresford.

The Earl of Balfour, O.M., K.G.

Press Portrait Bureau.

The Rt. Hon. Sir Eric Geddes, G.C.B.

Russell.

Viscount Haldane, O.M.

Elliott & Fry.

Field-Marshal Sir William Robertson.

The Rt. Hon. Andrew Bonar Law.

President Wilson.

Lord Carson.

The Rt. Hon. George Nicoll Barnes.

The Rt. Hon. Viscount Devonport.   The Rt. Hon. Lord Maclay.

The Rt. Hon. Lord Ernle.   The Rt. Hon. Lord Lee of Fareham.

E. O. Hoppé.

Lord Northcliffe.

Lieut.-Colonel Sir Maurice Hankey,
G.C.B.

E.N.A.

Rasputin.

Vandyk

To a great man from his friend
J. C. Smuts

General the Rt. Hon. J. C. Smuts.

Admiral of the Fleet, Earl Jellicoe, bidding good-bye to Lord Kitchener on board *Hampshire*. Within half an hour of the taking of this photograph *Hampshire* struck a mine and Lord Kitchener was drowned.

WAR MEMOIRS

CHAPTER 1

THE BREWING OF THE STORM

1. FIRST CONTACT WITH FOREIGN AFFAIRS

In the year 1904, on the day when the Anglo-French Entente was announced, I arrived at Dalmeny on a couple of days' visit to the late Lord Rosebery. His first greeting to me was: " Well, I suppose you are just as pleased as the rest of them with this French agreement?" I assured him that I was delighted that our snarling and scratching relations with France had come to an end at last. He replied: "You are all wrong. It means war with Germany in the end! "

About a year after this prophetical utterance I became for the first time a Minister of the Crown. Had anyone then told me that before I ceased to hold office in the British Cabinet I should not only have witnessed a war between Britain and Germany, but have taken an active, and in fact a leading part in its prosecution, I should have treated such a forecast as one of the many wild predictions of good or evil with which every public man is assailed by persons of unbalanced minds.

Before my appointment I took very little part in the discussion of foreign affairs and had no pretence to a greater knowledge of their intricacies than that which is possessed by the average Member of Parliament who has read history, and brings it up to date with such information as is supplied by the leading newspapers and reviews of all Parties. My interests were definitely centred on more domestic matters; on the special concerns of Wales, and on the education controversy, free trade, Home Rule, the land question and social reform. In foreign policy I had always been, as I am to-day, an ardent advocate of the rights of small nationalities, and I had been trained to believe in a peaceable settlement of the differences which arose between the nations of the world. Notwithstanding the sinister growth of armaments and a feverish anxiety to perfect them in all countries, there had been unbroken peace for over forty years between the Great Powers of Western Europe, and this bred a cheerful if illusive hope that the world would ultimately abandon war as a tribunal for adjudicating international disputes. This happy confidence in the gradual and final escape of the world from the perils of war (except against savages) was fostered, as I shall show later, by the extent to which nearly all of us, even Cabinet Ministers, were kept sedulously in the dark about our foreign conversations and commitments.

I was, of course, well aware of the secular antagonism between France and Germany and how that antagonism had been kept alive by the tearing from the side of France of two of her best-beloved provinces. The Franco-Prussian War was a memory of my boyhood. After the fall of the Empire, Radical sentiment tended to be pro-French in sympathy with the democratic institutions of our nearest neighbour, whereas Conservative opinion inclined to be more pro-German.

Inside the Liberal Party the tradition of its more advanced elements ever since the days of Charles James Fox had been one of constant friendliness towards the French Republic; English Conservatism had never quite got over the prejudices and apprehensions roused by the French Revolution and the Napoleonic episode, and Liberal Imperialism was inclined to follow in the track of the Anti-Revolution Whigs.

Mr. Gladstone was passionately pro-French in his general attitude. The Bismarckism of blood and iron never appealed to him. He was essentially a Liberal in foreign affairs. When he visited Caernarvonshire in 1892, I was invited by Sir Edward Watkin to meet him at dinner at the Watkin châlet on the slopes of Snowdon. It was a small party. Apart from the members of the family, the late Tom Ellis and I were the only other guests. Mr. Gladstone did practically all the talking at the dinner-table and afterwards, and the rest of us, only too thrilled to meet and hear this great figure from a past world, were naturally content to listen in silence.

He was 83 years of age, but showed none of the usual symptoms of senility. He was vital. His deep vibrant tones were music to the ear whatever he said. That evening he was at times even gay and merry.

His conversation ranged over a curious variety of topics. He talked for some time on the development of transport in the country and the improvement in the habits of the people who were associated with it; the sodden driver and the drunken ostler of the past against the sober engine driver and railway porter of to-day. To illustrate this theme he told us one or two quite amusing stories of his experiences in the old coaching days. I can only recall one of his tales. When posting from Wales to London he sat on the box seat, and in order to relieve the dreary hours he sought conversation with the driver, who was a fine specimen of what much beef and more beer could produce. Not achieving great success by ordinary conversation he pulled out a handsome watch of which he was proud, opened it, showed the works to the driver and explained to him the function of the various wheels and levers. The only observation he elicited was: " What puzzles me is how you wind that 'ere watch when you get home drunk."

He then gave us a dissertation on corrugated-iron roofing, and the difficulties which had been encountered in keeping buildings of this kind warm in winter and cool in summer. The last subject was suggested by the fact that the châlet was built of this material. He then diverged to other reminiscences. He recalled with regret the prohibitive price of sugar candy when he was a boy and told us with gusto of his delight when he discovered recently, in walking along the streets of some obscure town in Cheshire, how cheaply you could to-day purchase this joy of his departed youth.

He then launched out into a wonderful panegyric on the people of France. I think it arose out of a reference to the Channel tunnel which Sir Edward Watkin was then promoting. Mr. Gladstone made it quite clear that in his judgment the French were a much more enlightened, broadminded and civilised people than those over whose destinies he was at the moment privileged to preside. The Radicals of that day might not have accepted his perfervid eulogies on the superiority of French intelligence, but apart from that his outburst more or less represented the Radical attitude towards the French Republic and its citizens at the time when I came into active politics. On the other hand, Germany, with her militarism, her autocracy and her constitutional devices to enhance the voting power of property and to depress and restrict the power of the worker in the State, and her resolve generally to keep democracy in its proper place, evoked a good deal of sympathetic approval amongst the more Conservative elements in the country.

Lord Rosebery and his friends did not share in these Radical sentiments towards French democracy. Their attitude was one of distrust of France and ill-concealed goodwill towards Germany. During Lord Rosebery's occupation of the Foreign Office in 1892-94, he had once or twice engaged the country in grave disputes with France and brought us to the brink of serious conflict. In the House of Commons his Under-Secretary, Sir Edward Grey,* in alluding to the menace of some French movement towards the British sphere of influence in the Sudan, had characterised it as " an unfriendly act." The Radical supporters of the Government resented the threat implied in the phrase, and they continued to view with great suspicion Sir Edward Grey's attitude towards France.

When the Campbell-Bannerman Administration was formed, it was sharply divided into two sections: the Radical element, of which the Prime Minister was the chief, and the Liberal Imperialists, relics of that element which deserted Fox and backed Palmerston. Chief

---

* The late Viscount Grey of Fallodon.

among them were Mr. Asquith,* Sir Edward Grey and Mr. Haldane.†
There was a perceptible difference of attitude between the two
sections on questions of foreign policy. The old pro-Boers inherited
the pacifist doctrines of Mr. Gladstone. The Liberal League
members of the Cabinet affected a more Palmerstonian attitude in
foreign affairs. The former suspicion of France which characterised
them in pre-Entente days had by this time altogether vanished, even
from the stubborn mind of Sir Edward Grey, but for it was
substituted a worrying distrust of the designs of Germany.

This was by no means confined to the Foreign Secretary.
Germany's naval shipbuilding programme was largely responsible
for this change in the Tory and Liberal Imperialist attitude towards
Germany. The Kaiser frequently boasted that he created the
formidable Navy of Germany, and he was always contemplating and
reviewing it with the pride of a Creator. He saw and said it was
good. What good it brought Germany is not evident, but the
story of evil it wrought will always remain one of the most
poignant chapters in the history not only of Germany but
of mankind. It was partly responsible for the World War. It
undoubtedly helped to range the British Empire amongst the
enemies of Germany and later on it brought America into the war.
Apart from these facts, it contributed to the spirit of arrogant
superiority which dictated the course of German diplomacy, and
consequently to the sense of apprehension which drew other
powerful nations to military and naval understandings. Its creation
undoubtedly helped to stimulate the Kaiser's fatal swagger.

The blustering zeal which he threw into the building of his
redoubtable navy was regarded as a threat not only to Britain's
supremacy at sea but to her actual security. Foolish speeches
delivered by men of no inconsiderable authority and influence in
Germany, hinting a challenge to Britain's fleet, were quoted
in the British Press and caused uneasiness in minds not readily
given to panic. The Radical section of the Cabinet were
just as much alive as their Imperialist colleagues to the menace which
rival warship programmes involved to the good relations they were
anxious to maintain with Germany as well as with all other nations.

I first became directly concerned with this issue when in 1908, on
the death of Sir Henry Campbell-Bannerman and Mr. Asquith's
accession to the Premiership, I left the Board of Trade to succeed
Mr. Asquith as Chancellor of the Exchequer. In this post it became my
duty to find the money for naval programmes, and Anglo-German relations thus became a subject in which I was departmentally interested.

I might here say a word as to the two crises which occurred in the
Asquith Cabinet over shipbuilding programmes submitted by the

* Afterwards Earl of Oxford and Asquith, d. 1928.
† Afterwards Viscount Haldane of Cloan, d. 1928.

Board of Admiralty. The first was in 1908, when Mr. M'Kenna was First Lord of the Admiralty; the second in 1913-14, when Mr. Winston Churchill held that post.

As Chancellor of the Exchequer, I never resisted any addition to the strength of the Navy which would provide a reasonable margin of security against the increases in the German Navy effected by the shipbuilding programme of the German Admiralty. My opposition to the demands of the Board of Admiralty in 1908 and 1913 might be summed up in the fourfold proposition:—

1. The Admiralty demand an extravagant margin which is burdensome and provocative;

2. We ought to concentrate more on small craft for the protection of our trade routes and less on mammoth ships;

3. There is a growing reaction in the world against the burden of increasing armaments, and a general desire for a better understanding between the nations. We ought therefore to concentrate more on seeking an arrangement with Germany as to competitive building than on provocative programmes;

4. During the 1913-14 dispute in the Cabinet over the Admiralty estimates I pointed out that Germany was now devoting her attention to strengthening her Army rather than her Navy.

In my first protest against what I conceived to be panic demands from the Admiralty I received the zealous and energetic support of Mr. Winston Churchill. Unfortunately, by 1913 he had become First Lord of the Admiralty, and his inflammable fancy had been caught by the fascination of the monster ship. The fight against " bloated armaments "—to use the old Disraelian phrase—was weakened by so formidable a defection.

I do not propose to discuss at this point the merits of the controversy, but I would like to mention two or three facts in justification of the attitude adopted by the Radical section of the Cabinet. I have consulted the memoranda and counter-memoranda which were put in during the 1913 discussions. The Treasury, which was not without information from expert naval sources, claimed that even if we proceeded with the old accepted programme, rejecting the new proposals, we should still have in 1917 the following margin of superiority:—

Dreadnoughts .... over 84 per cent.
Pre-Dreadnoughts .... 127 ,, ,,
Armoured Cruisers .... 278 ,, ,,
Light Cruisers .... over 70 ,, ,,
Torpedo Craft .... 60 ,, ,,

This estimate was based, not merely upon numbers, but upon a qualitative comparison which included speed, weight of guns and age.   These figures were not accepted by the Admiralty. The Treasury computation assumed too great a margin of superiority in Dreadnoughts, but the sifted figures showed a secure margin.   There was a further argument advanced by the Treasury and their supporters, viz., that, throughout the whole of the ship-building competition between Germany and ourselves for the past ten years, we had always forced the pace by increasing the size of the ships, the weight of guns, and the speed of our vessels, beginning this fatal competition with the laying down of superiority of strength against any possible combination of foreign fleets.   The laying down of the Dreadnought seemed to many of us a piece of wanton and profligate ostentation.

As to the second Treasury proposition, that we ought to concentrate more on small craft and less on big ships, the experience of the War was a complete vindication of the point of view taken by the Treasury in 1913.   We suffered severely from the shortage of cruisers and torpedo-boat destroyers for the protection of our vessels, mercantile and naval, against submarine attack; and the Admiralty, under the direction of Sir John Fisher, had to work with feverish energy to make up this serious deficiency.   The shortage in itself was created, not so much by the fact that we had not a sufficient number of torpedo-boat destroyers, but because the vulnerability of our great battleships and battle cruisers to torpedo attack was such that we had to detach the best part of our torpedo-boat strength to defend them.

With the third and fourth propositions I shall have to deal in the course of my narrative.

It was of course impossible not to have an uneasy feeling that the German battle fleet was built with the design of challenging British naval supremacy.   Grand-Admiral von Tirpitz in his memoirs is quite explicit about this, and so at times was the Kaiser. I do not say that they deliberately set before themselves as their goal a war with Britain that would destroy our fleet.   They would have been content if their fleet grew so powerful that it frightened Britain into renouncing her supremacy at sea without a fight.   But von Tirpitz, the real creator of the German Navy, avows openly that they would be content with nothing less.

Opposed as I was to inflated armaments, I never hesitated in the view that Britain could not afford and would not allow such a situation to arise.   We had no army large enough to defend our country against the enormous conscript armies of the Continent. Our fleet was still just as much the sole guarantor of our liberties and independence as in the days of Napoleon.   We should therefore have to go on building ship for ship, and three ships to two, against any effort of the Germans.   Our financial resources and shipbuilding equipment were adequate to counter their utmost achievement in naval rivalry. But, this being the position, it was no less obvious that such unrestricted competition would involve quite needless financial exhaustion and growing irritation for both countries, and would only leave them at the end, with empty pockets and burdened backs, in the same position of relative strength as that from which they had started.

As one who had been taught to believe that peace was the only sane and sound basis for human progress, I sought to allay the growing antagonism between the two nations. As Chancellor of the Exchequer, I could not be indifferent to the cost of the useless naval competition. It was an exhausting drain upon resources sadly needed for social amelioration and national development. So I sought some means of reaching an agreement with Germany which would enable us on both sides to slow down the rate and volume of our naval construction.

An opportunity for this seemed to present itself when at the suggestion of Sir Edward Grey in July, 1908, I came into contact with the German Ambassador, Count Metternich. Of our meeting I made some years later a note from memory, which I reproduce here: —

"Soon after I became Chancellor of the Exchequer in 1908, Count Metternich, the German Ambassador, invited me to lunch at the Embassy. I had never met the Ambassador and I had a suspicion that the invitation had some political purpose. After lunch he soon made it clear why I had been asked. He knew that I belonged to the more pacifist group in the Cabinet. He introduced the subject of the growing suspicions between our two countries. I thought it a good opportunity for explaining to him that the real ground for the growing antagonism in this country towards Germany was not jealousy of her rapidly developing commerce, but fear of her growing Navy. I pointed out how completely dependent we were on our overseas supplies for our daily bread, and that any country that wrested from us the supremacy of the seas would be in a position to starve our population into abject surrender in a few months. I also urged that if our sea defences were overwhelmed by a superior naval force, our Army could put up no effective resistance against the huge military machines of the Continent. I thought it well to tell him that on the subject of maintaining the invulnerability of our shores by means of an adequately superior Navy there was no difference of opinion in the Cabinet, and that although I was one of those who were opposed to these huge armaments, I should, if our community were in the least imperilled, be the first to propose even a loan of £100,000,000 if that were necessary to inaugurate a programme for building a Navy adequate to our safety. I said to him, ' If this rival shipbuilding goes on to such an extent as to render our people seriously apprehensive of invasion we shall be driven inevitably to adopt conscription and thus raise an army capable of defending our shores against any invader.' He replied quite curtly, ' Do you think we should wait?'

M. Delcassé had just been driven out of the Quai d'Orsay largely owing to German hostility. He had, however, been well received in London on his visit to this country immediately after his dismissal. I forget how his name cropped up in our conversation. I only remember one passage. When I said, ' You dismissed M. Delcassé from his position of Foreign Secretary in France,' he cut in tartly, ' But evidently not in England!' I proceeded, ' If Germany had demanded the dismissal of the most unpopular Minister in this country he would by that very demand be translated to the highest altitude of popular favour.'

The luncheon party was, I fear, not a success."

Since the above note was written, I have, through the courtesy of the German Foreign Office, been able to study the German Diplomatic Correspondence for the period in question. From this I am reminded that there were, in fact, two interviews with Metternich, separated by an interval of about a fortnight. The first was on 14th July, 1908, when I was invited by Sir Edward Grey to lunch, to meet Count Metternich, and the second was the lunch already referred to at the German Embassy on the 28th. Both of these interviews were reported very fully to Berlin by Metternich, and came before the Kaiser, whose annotations to the reports are highly significant of the German attitude at that time. They are also worth study for the light they throw on the character of the Kaiser—the quick leaps from sense to superciliousness which later on precipitated the world catastrophe. I reproduce the full text of the report on Grey's luncheon party, and extracts from the later interview with myself:—

SECRET.

London, July 16th, 1908.

Marginal Comments by the Kaiser.

The day before yesterday Sir Edward Grey invited me to breakfast* at his house with Mr. Lloyd George. The present Chancellor of the Exchequer has in a short time educated himself from an ultra-radical Welsh lawyer into a leading and esteemed personality in his Party and in the Cabinet. As he thinks imperially he is also respected by the Unionists. If I remember rightly, he allowed himself some years ago as a

* Lunch.

representative of the Opposition to have now and then a dig at Germany in Jingo fashion. As responsible Minister I found him to be of a conciliatory attitude of mind.

When I touched upon the question raised in Parliament regarding espionage, he agreed with me that unfortunately every bit of nonsense was believed here, as soon as it had to do with Germany.

When I remarked that it was a pity that English policy seemed to wish to exchange French friendship for German hostility, and that the Entente policy had called forth the uneasiness in Europe, Sir Edward Grey stated more or less as follows: During the last ten years England had several times very nearly got into warlike complications with France and Russia. Without an amicable arrangement it would probably have come to a war already. There was only an Entente with France. None " yet " with Russia. Against this, Germany had the Triple Alliance. It was incomprehensible how one could speak in this connection of a policy to isolate Germany.

Mr. Lloyd George joined in by saying that it probably was the diplomatic support of France by England which had upset Germany (1). Sir Edward Grey replied that as far as Morocco was concerned, England was pledged to give that support.

(1) *Yes.*

I remarked that France was in an absolutely safe position as long as she recognised the *status quo* in Europe (2). Alone she could not attack this. However, supported by England the idea of revenge might one day come to life again (3). *Avis au lecteur*: The article in the " Temps," which recommended England to have a strong army in order to become qualified for an alliance.

(2) *German Territory !*

(3) *Well said !*

When Mr. Lloyd George expressed the opinion that he did not believe France had intentions of war, although the French had not been able to make up their minds to recognise the pact, I replied that I also did not believe in any such intentions of the French. Also, that I had not the slightest objection to England settling its disputes with other nations. On the other hand, in political journalism the friends and defenders of English foreign policy took care to spread the conviction that here one was not dealing merely with a settling of disputes, but simultaneously with the producing of a bulwark against the German Power. This procedure did not comply with a friendly tendency, and could not be taken as such in Germany, but was bound to call forth uneasiness there, and specially in Europe (4). Sir Edward Grey then remarked that the unpleasant part of the situation was caused by the fact that we mutually blamed each other for having hostile intentions. The belief in an eventual English attack existed in Germany; here, however, one believed that the German Fleet was built to threaten England's position.

Both Ministers were of the opinion that the situation between England and Germany turned round the naval question. The expenditure for the English fleet would as a result of the German naval programme (5) and the speeding up (6) in naval construction increase to such an extent, and at the same time apprehensions of the German danger would increase so in intensity, that relations between the countries could not improve as long as they were getting up against each other in naval rivalry (7). Every Englishman would spend his last penny to preserve their superiority at sea (8), on which depends not only England's position in the world, but also its existence as an independent State. The ruinous expenditure to which the naval rivalry led (9) could not make the relations between the two nations prosper. Anybody who only knew England a little, knew that there was no intention here to threaten (10) Germany with the English fleet or attack Germany at all. Taking into consideration the proportions of the English Army, a landing would be clearly out of the question. Mr. Lloyd George remarked jokingly that Prince Bismarck had said, when on some occasion or other the question of an English landing was discussed, that in a case like that he would leave it to the police to arrest

(4) *Quite right.*

(5) *Wrong ! A result of England's ambitions for world empire and tendency to see phantoms.*

(6) *Has not been speeded up !*

(7) *Does not exist ! Ours is limited by law !*

(8) *See Nauticus, they have it 3 times over already ! ! !*

(9) *Such insolent talk has never been heard from England, not even in the days of acutest tension with Russia about Afghanistan ! It has never ventured to require Russia to withdraw its troops from the border, or to stop the reinforcements of its garrisons.*

(10) *? ! They have done so permanently already.*

the English corps on landing. The conditions to-day were still exactly the same when it was a question of England threatening Germany. To England, on the contrary, a powerful German Fleet (11) with a still more powerful Army in the background, was a real danger (12).

I replied that a German invasion existed only in the imagination of the English. No sensible person was thinking of it in Germany (13). Unfortunately fleet building had become more expensive through the invention of the " Dreadnought " (13), through which England had lost its immense advantage and other seafaring nations had been compelled to adopt the same large types of ships and consequently to high expenditure in connection herewith. But, à qui la faute? During the last few days there had been a discussion in the House of Commons about the introduction of a still larger type of ship, a floating fortress. As long as the English defence policy tended to create uneasiness in Germany, I considered a curtailment in the armaments at sea as being out of the question (13). Sir Edward Grey would first have to introduce a political détente between both countries and through his policy in Central Europe re-establish the belief that his Ententes would not be one day misused against us (14) before the ground would be cleared for a possible discussion about the curtailment of sea armaments (15), not before. Mr. Lloyd George, who took a lively part in the discussion about the naval construction, answered that a slowing down of the tempo in our fleet building (16) would contribute more quickly to reassure public opinion than any political action could. We should find them on this side most ready to meet us half-way in establishing a joint basis for curtailment of the fleet building on both sides (17). The introduction of the Dreadnought type had been a great mistake from the English side. The Government here would give every possible guarantee (18) that no new type should be introduced (19) if we could come to an understanding. He had very much

(11) Will never be powerful compared with England ! and still less of a danger than the already superior English fleet is to us.

(12) That after my speech at the Guildhall is first-class cheek !

(13) Quite right.

(14) Very good.

(15) Wrong ! We will not discuss that ! We shall never be dictated to as to how our armament should be constituted.

(16) We have no fast tempo. Neither are we building SECRET " Dreadnoughts " for other nations—which are then bought by England—or camouflaged as an armoured cruiser, suddenly turn up as battleships.

(17) This unheard-of demand the English Minister should put first to Roosevelt, Clemenceau, Mirabello* or Japan ! The replies would be cheerful ! Why only to us ? Because they believe that my diplomacy is fed up, and is being impressed by their shouting for war.

(18) We don't need it.

(19) Is the same to us.

* Italian Naval Minister.

regretted that the correspondence between His Majesty the Kaiser and Lord Tweedmouth had not been published at the time. From that correspondence the friendly feeling of His Majesty the Kaiser for England would have become clear to the public and he would also have seen in His Majesty's letter a justification for entering into confidential discussion with us about naval expenditure (20). If he had at the time had the responsibility for the State Finances he would indeed have insisted in the Cabinet on the publication of the correspondence (21). A conference at The Hague was not the proper way (22) to reach curtailment in naval expenditure. If, as he fervently hoped, it should ever come to this, it must not be tried in an official manner, such as with an exchange of notes (23). Unofficial confidential discussions which must not be made public at all (24), would, if an understanding between England and ourselves in this matter were at all possible, be more likely to conduce to the desired end (25).

Sir Edward Grey agreed with his colleague except on the point where the latter had recommended the timeliness of the publication of the correspondence.

I told Mr. Lloyd George he was right: that neither a conference at The Hague nor even less an official proposal by way of a note (26) from the English to the German Government, would solve the question of decreasing the fleet expenditure (27); that I even considered an official movement (28) in this direction under the circumstances very dubious (29) and grave and dangerous, but for the rest I would not be moved from the safe ground which I had taken up with my demand: First a policy of reassurance, then we can talk about the fleet (30).

In reporting this discussion I have left out a good deal and have, in order to be brief, only mentioned the most important parts. The incidental things, however, contribute to the right colouring of the whole picture. I allow myself, in order not to be misunderstood, to add the following supplementary final remarks.

Your Highness knows that for a long time the

Marginal notes:

(20) *He would have received a nice reply from me. Would have no result !*

(21) *Aha !*

(22) *Right.*

(23) *I should answer them with bombs.*

(24) *Out of the question ! So that the German people don't rise and smash the windows of the Minister in with bricks !*

(25) *No.*

(26) *That would be a declaration of war !*

(27) *Right.*

(28) *We should look upon that as a declaration of war.*

(29) *Definitely war.*

(30) *No ! There will be no talk about that at all !*

English Government has entertained the wish to come to an agreement with us about naval expenditure (31). Before and during the second Conference at The Hague an abortive attempt was made in this direction. If I have been rightly informed, the fear has already arisen on our side that the English Government might, alone or with others, put an official proposal to us for limitation of our naval programme and that from this an immediate danger of war would result (32). It is my firm belief that the present Government is far (33) from setting before us, through any sort of ultimatum, the issue of either giving in or going to war. She has no sort of intention of putting a threatening question to us (34). She desires much more to prevent later possibilities of war through timely agreement. If I decline somebody's wish, I need not for that reason fight with him at once. This comes only then into consideration when I see that the other one puts on the air of forcing (36) his wish (35) upon me.

(31) *Out of the question! They will first have to achieve this with other great Powers!*

(32) *Yes.*

(33) *??*

(34) *In the conversation of the Ministers lies already a hidden threat! Let them compare themselves first with America. The latter is much stronger than we are!*

(36) *He does that.*

(35) *In our position it is better that such a wish should not be expressed!*

To both Ministers I have made the fulfilment of their wish dependent on one condition, the explanation of which lies in our hands. I would have needlessly constricted future possibilities, and made the position more acute, if I had given them to understand that we never and under no circumstances would be prepared to come to an arrangement with them about naval expenditure. The price which I mentioned for this will certainly not soon be paid to us by Sir Edward Grey.   (*Signed*) P. Metternich.

Final Remarks of the Kaiser:—

Bravo! Metternich! Has done his business very well, except in one point, which is the most important. The Ambassador has overlooked entirely that he was not permitted, even if entirely non-committally and only as a private opinion, to [? agree]* to the insolent demands of the English Ministers to make their peacefulness dependent on the diminution of our sea force. Through that he has put himself on a very dangerous slope. I am sorry for him because of that. It must be pointed out to him that I do *not* wish a good understanding with England at the expense of the extension of the German fleet. If England only intends graciously to hold out her hand to us with the indication

* Word missing in original.

that we should curtail our fleet, then this is an excessive impudence, which contains a great insult for the German people and its Kaiser, and which should be refused *a limine* by the Ambassador!   By the same rights France and Russia could then demand a curtailment of our land force.   As soon as one allows any foreign Power under any pretext whatsoever to have something to say about our own armaments, then one may retire, like Portugal and Spain! The German fleet is not built *against* anybody and not *against* England either?   But according to *our* needs!   This has been said quite clearly in the Navy Law and has remained unchanged for eleven years!   This law is being carried out to the very last tittle: whether the British like it or not does not worry us.   If they want a war, *they* may *start* it, we are not afraid of it!

(Signed) Wilhelm R.I.

Here are the most important passages in the report Count Metternich sent to Berlin of our second conversation—with the Kaiser's marginal notes: —

Kaiser's Marginal Notes.

" . . . On the same day I had a long discussion with the Chancellor of the Exchequer, Mr. Lloyd George. . . . I explained to him why the political course followed by England during the last six years was bound to lead to the present uncomfortable situation: formerly on the side of the Triple Alliance, now on the side of Germany's opponents; Morocco thrown as an apple of discord between Germany and France; France encouraged in the idea of *revanche* through hope of help from England; Entente politics as a bulwark against alleged German expansion and aggressivenesss; spy scares and fears of invasion; a twisting of German intentions in political journalism, a slandering of the motives of German politics, and nothing done

(1) *A very good summary!*

to stop it (1).   Through the unchecked poisoning of public opinion, I said, we are being pushed unwillingly into the perilous position of seeing the spectre of war rising on the horizon—a spectre which Mr. Lloyd George and I are alike convinced that both our Governments as well

(2) *That's not my idea at all! If England wants to have war, just let her start it, we'll give her what for!*

as both our countries wish to expel (2).

The Minister showed an understanding of all this, but, like every one of his countrymen, he sees in the naval question the central point of German-English relations, around which everything turns and of which all other happenings are a result. . . . England, he said, had the money and would strain every nerve to retain supremacy at sea (3). With a race in fleet building (4) the tension would unavoidably be increased, and therewith at the same time the danger of a collision would grow. At the end of the crushing armaments (5) the distance between the two fleets would still be great, and we should not be any nearer to our object (6). We should be playing into the hands of two tendencies here which he was fighting against, and which were not in our interest. With the growth of expenditure for the Navy in the race between Germany and England, new financial sources would have to be found and all thoughts would be turned to the Tariff Party, which promised new receipts at the expense of foreign countries and without further burdening the Englishman. . . . Further: the more the German fleet approached the English in strength (7) the stronger the thought would become that English safety no longer depended on its fleet alone, but that England must also develop an Army. In order to have a really strong Army there was only one means: Conscription. With the quick growth of the German Navy the possibility of an invasion increased—although he did not at all believe in such (8) an intention—and then England would be pushed into the introduction of Conscription (9). The military party and a great number of Conservatives were already anxiously wishing for this. With the approach of the German menace, the great mass of the people, which as yet would not have anything to do with conscription, would soon be won for it (10). . . . I replied that Germany had sufficient means at its disposal to produce a very respectable fleet, apart from its army. . . . Even if the burden were heavy, it would be necessary in view of the international situation. At least ten (11) years' hard work would be necessary to produce an armed country, and an army equal to the Continental pattern. If we saw that England was going over to Conscription, with its eyes on Germany, in order to reach an alliance with France, I did not believe that we should wait

Marginal notes:

(3) *Nobody wants to dispute that !*

(4) *Does not exist at all; only in the English brain !*

(5) *? Not for us !*

(6) *But that is not our object.*

(7) *Absolutely out of the question and has never been attempted.*

(8) *! !*

(9) *It would do them good.*

(10) Tant mieux.

(11) Sancta Simplicitas ! 50 !

B

(12) *We should be totally indifferent.*

(13) *This is unheard of! and is a result of Metternich going into the idea at all.*

(14) *This is talk which until now has been only used against fellows like China or Italy! It is unheard of!*

(15) *We have not got that far yet!*

(16) *! !*

(17) *Bluff!*

(18) *No! Three times no. After the above words NEVER!*

(19) *Bosh!*

patiently for this process to be carried to completion (12). . . . Mr. Lloyd George then returned to his pet idea, the slackening down in the speed of naval construction (13) and exhorted me to make use of the time during which the peace-loving Liberal Government was at the helm. . . . Considering how much greater importance the fleet has for England than it has for Germany, the English fleet must always be a good bit stronger than ours, in order to be able to furnish that feeling of security which England requires from it, and at the same time sufficiently powerful to keep any wanton idea of attack on her from arising on our side (14). The German fleet, however, should be strong enough to give adequate protection for our overseas interests, and at the same time to give the English fleet, despite the latter's necessary superiority, the feeling that it would be risky to pick a quarrel with us (15). The relative strength of 2:3, it seemed to him, would establish the right balance (16) at sea between us. He could not cite the authority of the English Government for this, but only uttered his own personal view; he knew, however, that we should find the greatest friendly response from the Liberal Cabinet (17) if we should be inclined to discuss the slackening down of the speed of naval construction (18). If even we only agreed to build one Dreadnought less every year, this would result in a complete change of the feeling in England towards us (19). . . ."

The above extracts give a fairly good picture of the course of my discussion with Metternich. How the whole report, and in particular my unspeakable impertinence in daring to suggest, on any grounds and for any consideration, that there should be an agreed limit to the German Navy, affected the Kaiser is best seen in his footnote to the report, which I transcribe in full : —

" This sort of conversation as it has been carried on between Lloyd George and Metternich is utterly unworthy and provoking for Germany! I must beg him in future to have nothing to do with that sort of expectoration. Here he has accepted very patiently as a listener the opinions and orders of English statesmen, and has only ventured protests which had no effect at all. He should give these gentlemen, *who do not wish to see ' our wanton ideas of an attack,' realised,* an answer like ' Go to H——,' etc. That would bring these fellows to their senses again. That Lloyd George even dared to come out with an order for defining the speed of OUR building is beyond the limit, but is a result of Metternich putting himself during the first discussions on the dangerous path of *' a possibility not being out of the question.'* The clever British are trying to hook him, and sooner or later they will pull the string and drag him out; despite this ' private talk,' ' non-committal character of expression of opinion,' etc.! He should *ab ovo* refuse everything with such remarks as, ' No country allows itself to be dictated to or admonished by another country about the size and kind of its armaments.' ' I refuse to discuss such a matter.' For the rest, let them read the Navy Law —known for eleven years—and Nauticus!

Metternich should give that sort of fanatic a kick in the ——; he is too soft!"

The luncheon party had a further sequel, of which I was not made aware at the time, and have only recently learned through a perusal of the German Diplomatic papers.

At the time of my interview with Metternich, I was planning to visit Germany in the following month of August, 1908, in order to study on the spot the German systems of industrial insurance, with a view to preparing my own scheme of health and unemployment insurance for this country. Metternich, reporting this to Berlin, had urged that the British Chancellor of the Exchequer, whom he described as " one of the most outstanding personalities in England, and one who most probably would be called upon one day to stand at the head of a Liberal Government," should be treated with the utmost consideration. The Kaiser accordingly arranged that I should be invited to pay him a visit. But in the meantime Metternich came over hurriedly to talk to the German Imperial Chancellor, von Buelow, who had reprimanded him for his incautious conversation with me. I understand that von Buelow was warned that I should certainly discuss the Navy with His Imperial Majesty, and that if Wilhelm used to my face the sort of remark he had noted on Metternich's report, a grave instance of *lèse-majesté* would be liable to ensue. A hasty warning was sent to Court and I never received the Kaiser's suggested invitation.

I was, however, successful in securing an interview with the Vice-Chancellor, von Bethmann-Hollweg, who was in Berlin at the time. He was then in charge of Health Insurance and had a very thorough acquaintance with its working. He was very helpful to me in my investigations on that subject. He was good enough to invite me and my party to be his guests at a big dinner which he gave at the Zoologischer Garten.

Von Bethmann-Hollweg was an attractive but not an arresting personality. He gave me the idea of an intelligent, industrious and eminently sensible bureaucrat, but he did not leave on my mind an impression of having met a man of power who might one day shake destiny. He gave us a good dinner, and at its close great tankards of lager beer were brought round, and von Bethmann-Hollweg grew talkative and combative.

He embarked upon a discussion of the European situation, and was very bitter about what he called " the encirclement of Germany with an iron ring by France, Russia and England." I did my best to assure him that, so far as England was concerned, there was not the slightest desire to enter into any hostile combinations against Germany, and that we were most anxious to live in peace and neighbourliness with his great country. I told him, however, that England was very uneasy about the growth of the German Navy, and felt that it was aimed straight at her heart; and I repeated all that I had said to Count Metternich about our being an island and completely dependent upon the sea for our very existence. He was not very enthusiastic about the German Navy, and I perceived that he was no advocate of a shipbuilding programme that would be regarded as a menace by Great Britain; but he did his best to convince me that the German people had no desire to attack England. The impression he left on my mind was that official Germany was genuinely apprehensive of the *rapprochement* between France and England, and England and Russia. They were quite convinced that King Edward was organising a Confederacy with a hostile purport against Germany. The King was regarded as an inveterate enemy of German might.

This led to one extraordinary outburst in the course of his conversation, when he reverted to the theme of the growing hostility of England, France and Russia against Germany, and the " iron ring " they were pressing round her. " An iron ring! " he repeated violently, shouting out the statement, and waving his arm to the whole assembled company. " England is embracing France. She is making friends with Russia. But it is not that you love each other; it is that you hate Germany! " And he repeated and literally shouted the word " hate " thrice. He became very excited, and his discretion was certainly not under control, for he went on to show a distinct antipathy even to Bavaria, when he contrasted the attachment of the eastern provinces of Prussia, and of Berlin, to the Kaiser, and their readiness to die at a word from him, with the more lukewarm attitude of Bavaria.

Incidentally, he let in a flood of light upon the view of the ordinary German as to the decadence of England. He was clearly of the opinion that we were no longer a hard-working people; he thought that we loved our ease too much, and that we were a nation of week-enders. He gave a description of his own day: how he rose at seven o'clock, and worked until eight; then went for a ride until nine, then had his breakfast; afterwards resumed his daily tasks; worked practically till dinner, and kept going right through the week. He said, " In England, you go to your office at eleven; you have a long luncheon hour; you leave at four; on Thursday you go to the country; you remain there until Tuesday morning, and you call it a week-end!"

It is fair to say that this was after dinner! But I am not at all sure that this revelation of the Continental pre-war idea of English degeneracy had not something to do with the contempt with which military Germany contemplated the possibility of our intervention later on. It was very generally assumed that English fibre had been softened and disintegrated by prosperity. The poor show we had made in the Boer War had confirmed this idea.

What made it more significant was that his personal attitude towards England and Englishmen was extremely friendly, and this was not a mere matter of words, for he had sent his son to Oxford. His view was that the German worker was a better man than the English worker; that the German scientists were easily superior in quality and numbers to the insignificant band of British scientists. On the other hand, he seemed to have a better opinion of the English than of the German upper and middle classes. He attributed the superiority of the German worker to the fact that in his early years he received a stern military training in obedience which taught him habits of discipline and continuity.

I left Berlin gravely disturbed by the expressions of distrust and suspicion I had encountered in so high and friendly a quarter. It seemed to me to be ominously significant of what must be the general opinion at the time in leading German circles.

At the other end of the scale, I was also deeply impressed by a scene I witnessed at Stuttgart during the same tour. On our arrival there we learnt that a " Zeppelin " was about to make an exhibition flight. We went along to the field where the giant airship was moored, to find that by a last-minute accident it had crashed and been wrecked. Of course we were deeply disappointed, but disappointment was a totally inadequate word for the agony of grief and dismay which swept over the massed Germans who witnessed the catastrophe. There was no loss of life to account for it. Hopes and ambitions far wider than those concerned with a scientific and mechanical success appeared to have shared the wreck of the dirigible. Then the crowd swung into the chanting of " Deutschland über Alles " with a fanatic fervour of patriotism. What spearpoint of Imperial advance did this airship portend? These incidents were cracks in the cold surface, through which the hot, seething lava of unrest could be seen stirring uneasily underneath.

After these few glimpses of our foreign problem, I was drawn back during the succeeding years into the anxious preoccupations of domestic affairs. I understood, nevertheless, that there was a growing menace to peace abroad, and social order at home, which we must strive to avert if possible by peaceable methods, though I realised that we could not altogether rule out of account the possibility of a failure of such methods.

2. PLAN FOR A PARTY TRUCE

My observation to Metternich, in the conversation already reported, about the possibility of our being driven to adopt Conscription, was by no means a casual sentence thrown out by me as a debating point in the course of an argument. Still less was it a piece of bald bluff, used in the hope of convincing or impressing the German Ambassador.

I had for some time past been growingly concerned with the precariousness of our position in the event of our naval defence being broken through. We had depended upon it for centuries to protect us against invasion from the Continent. Hitherto it had not failed us, and this immunity had given us a sense of complete security. This feeling was expressed by Sir John Fisher in his famous remark that " We could sleep soundly in our beds because of the invincibility of our Navy." But the rapid march of scientific discovery, constantly revealing the existence of hitherto unsuspected forces, which were capable of the most formidable utilisation for service and disservice to mankind, made me feel that it was quite within the realm of possibility that one day there might be an invention which would neutralise our superiority, and reduce us to equality with, if not inferiority to, our neighbours. Inventions which portended such a menace had already appeared. Whether the peril would come from the air or from under the waters, I knew not; but no one could feel assured that such possibilities were altogether out of the reckoning. In such an event our position would be one of complete helplessness in the face of an invader with a powerful army.

We had two fundamental weaknesses in such a contingency. The first was that our army was too insignificant to stand up against the gigantic forces of the Continent. The second was that we were so overwhelmingly dependent upon overseas supplies for our food, that if these were cut off we should, within a few months, be brought to the very verge of starvation. It was this consideration amongst others that always led me to urge that we ought to devote more thought to the development of the resources of British soil.

I did not agree with Lord Roberts' case that a large force could at that time be landed from the Continent to capture London. In the absence of some invention which had not yet been found, or at least had not yet been developed, our Navy was powerful enough to prevent any emergency of that kind arising. My apprehension was entirely as to what the unknown future had in store for us if science neutralised the efficiency of our warships.

There were ominous clouds gathering over the Continent of Europe and perceptibly thickening and darkening. The submarine and the Zeppelin indicated a possible challenge to the invincibility of our defence. I felt we should be safer if we had in this country a system of training for our young manhood which would fit it for the defence of the Realm in the possible event of an invasion of our shores. I was opposed to conscript armies of the Continental type, and thought them designed rather for aggression than for defence. For the latter purpose it seemed to me that something resembling the Swiss militia system would suffice and might be adopted here.

It was with these thoughts in my mind that I ventured in 1910 to submit to the leaders of both political parties in this country a series of proposals for national co-operation over a period of years, to deal with special matters of urgent importance.

In the year 1910 we were beset by an accumulation of grave issues —rapidly becoming graver. The gravest have not yet been solved. It was becoming evident to discerning eyes that the Party and Parliamentary system was unequal to coping with them. There was a jam at the legislative dock gates and there was no prospect of the growing traffic being able to get through. The shadow of unemployment was rising ominously above the horizon. Our international rivals were forging ahead at a great rate and jeopardising our hold on the markets of the world. There was an arrest in that expansion of our foreign trade which had contributed to the phenomenal prosperity of the previous half-century, and of which we had made such a muddled and selfish use. Our working population, crushed into dingy and mean streets, with no assurance that they would not be deprived of their daily bread by ill-health or trade fluctuations, were becoming sullen with discontent. Whilst we were growing more dependent on overseas supplies for our food, our soil was gradually going out of cultivation. The life of the countryside was wilting away and we were becoming dangerously over-industrialised. Excessive indulgence in alcoholic drinks was undermining the health and efficiency of a considerable section of the population. The Irish controversy was poisoning our relations with the United States of America. A great Constitutional struggle over the House of Lords threatened revolution at home, another threatened civil war at our doors in Ireland. Great nations were arming feverishly for an apprehended struggle into which we might be drawn by some visible or invisible ties, interests, or sympathies. Were we prepared for all the terrifying contingencies?

Moved by this prospect I submitted to Mr. Asquith a Memorandum urging that a truce should be declared between the Parties for the purpose of securing the co-operation of the leading party statesmen in a settlement of our national problems—Second Chamber, Home Rule, the development of our agricultural resources, National Training for Defence, the remedying of social evils, and a fair and judicial enquiry into the working of our fiscal system.

Mr. Asquith regarded the proposal with considerable favour, and it was decided to submit it to four or five members of the Cabinet for their observations. So far as I can recollect, the only Cabinet Ministers who were called into consultation were Lord Crewe, Sir Edward Grey, Lord Haldane, and Mr. Winston Churchill. I cannot recall any criticism in detail from any of them. They all approved of the idea in principle, and it was agreed that the proposal should be submitted to Mr. Balfour, who was still the Leader of the Conservative Party. The only outsiders to whom I showed the document were Mr. F. E. Smith (subsequently Lord Birkenhead) and Mr. Garvin. They were very pleased with the whole conception.

Mr. Balfour was by no means hostile; in fact, he went a long way towards indicating that personally he regarded the proposal with a considerable measure of approval. He was not, however, certain of the reception which would be accorded to it by his party. Unfortunately, at that time he was not very firmly seated in the saddle. The Die-Hard cry against his leadership was getting audibly shriller each day. However, he consulted some of his leading colleagues, and he received from them replies which were by no means discouraging. I understood that Lord Lansdowne, Lord Cawdor, Lord Curzon, Mr. Walter Long, and Mr. Austen Chamberlain favoured the plan. When he came to summon a more formal and general meeting of his colleagues, he again found that the ablest members of the Conservative Party were by no means antipathetic to the idea. So far as I can recollect, the only opposition came from the late Lord Londonderry. But when Mr. Balfour proceeded later on to sound the opinion of less capable and therefore more narrowly partisan members of his party, he encountered difficulties which proved insurmountable. He called upon me one evening at 11, Downing Street to discuss the matter, and I found him then much more hesitant and reluctant. I gathered from him that the chief objection entertained by his colleagues was to my presence in such a combination. I was so completely associated in their minds with extreme radical proposals, I was so much in the front of the offence at that time, and I had said so many wounding things in the scrimmage, that they were more than doubtful whether they could secure the adhesion of their supporters to any Coalition of which I was a member.

I instantly assured him that, as far as I was concerned, I would not make my inclusion in the Ministry a condition of my support. On the contrary, I was quite prepared to keep out of it and give it my whole-hearted and zealous backing as an independent member of the House of Commons, so long as it tackled its job with courage and conviction. He then told me that there was one other man he felt he would have to consult. He said: " You will be surprised when I give you his name." When I heard it, I think I was rather surprised that this individual should still hold such an important and influential position in the councils of the Party, for he had retired from active political life for a good many years: it was Mr. Akers-Douglas, who had formerly been Chief Whip of the Conservative Party, and was then Lord Chilston. I remember one of the last things Mr. Balfour said to me on that occasion. Putting his hand on his forehead, looking down and more or less soliloquising, he said: " I cannot become another Robert Peel in my party!" After a short interval he added: " Although I cannot see where the Disraeli is to come from, unless it be my cousin Hugh, and I cannot quite see him fulfilling that rôle!" Mr. Akers-Douglas, however, turned down the project for co-operation in settling these momentous national issues, and there was an end to it. It very nearly came off. It was not rejected by the real leaders of the Party, but by men who, for some obscure reason best known to political organisations, have great influence inside the councils of a party without possessing any of the capabilities that excite general admiration and confidence outside.

I am not concerned, in these War reminiscences, to examine the possibilities of this project, had it been adopted and carried out, except in so far as it might have altered or modified the international situation. Had it materialised then, there would by 1914 have been a body of trained young men aggregating between a million and one-and-a-half million, fit for incorporation in our armies, shortly after the declaration of war. What is still more important, there would have been rifles and other equipment for them, which it took us over eighteen months to manufacture in the Great War, and the requisite machinery for manufacturing still more for ourselves and our Allies. There would also have been a staff of trained and competent officers fit to lead such an army into the field. Had such a force been in existence when the crisis arose in 1914, and had Germany been conscious of the fact that the British contribution would not be limited to her " contemptible little army " of six divisions, but that there was a large body of trained and equipped men behind that small Expeditionary Force which could soon be made fit to take an effective part in the fighting line, Germany would have hesitated before plunging the world into the disaster of the Great War. The young men who were sent to the trenches during the last two years of the War had received much less training than an application of the Swiss Militia System would have given to those who would have been called to the Colours in 1911, 1912, 1913, and 1914.

Even if the existence of such a formidable force had not influenced the course of events in the direction of peace, the contribution made by it in the earlier stages of the War might well have been decisive and have shortened the term of this devastating struggle.

I have heard it said that, at the battle of Ypres, the troops on both sides were so tired out by the end that the irruption of one fresh division on either side would have achieved victory for the army lucky enough to secure so timely a reinforcement. A number of Territorial battalions, not one of which had received anything like the Swiss training, were thrown into the battle line before the end of the fight, and, according to the testimony of Sir John French, rendered invaluable aid to our exhausted troops. If, instead of 19 battalions of Territorials with able but amateur officers, there had been three or four hundred battalions of more fully trained men, led by thoroughly equipped officers, the battle of Ypres would not have been a stalemate, but a victory which might have liberated Flanders and ended the War.

The same observation applies to the Dardanelles, where the fatal delays in landing troops which enabled the Turks to bring reinforcements were due to the fact that we could not spare the one extra division necessary to make up an Expeditionary Force—not even a spare division—until it was too late to achieve any results. Even from the point of view of filling up the serious gaps in the ranks of our Regular Army, due to the disastrous retreat from Mons, the heavy fighting on the Marne and at Ypres, the possession of a trained Militia would have been invaluable. Young men with an aggregate training of about a year, mixed up with the Regulars, would have been more useful than the Reservists, a large number of whom had been softened and debilitated by years of civilian occupation. All these considerations constantly leapt to my mind during the progress of the campaign, and always brought with them a regret for the " Great Refusal " of 1910.

There is much to be said in favour of the Party system. The open conflict of Parties is better for a country than the squalid intrigues of personal ambitions or of rival interests conducted in the dark. But there are times when it stands seriously in the way of the highest national interests. On these occasions it hinders, delays and thwarts real progress, and in the event the nation suffers heavily. I shall always regard the rejection of the proposals for co-operation in 1910 as a supreme instance of this kind of damage. On the other hand, the ground for co-operation must be one of genuine national well-being. A suspension of party hostilities merely in order to ensure a distribution of patronage and power amongst the leading contestants, degrades and enervates politics.

3. THE AGADIR CRISIS, 1911

As to the part I took in the Agadir incident, it is hardly necessary for me to write at any length. The story has been so fully and fairly told by both Mr. Winston Churchill and Sir Edward Grey that there is little which I need add.

My intervention was due largely to the fear that if things were allowed to drift, we might find ourselves drawn into a great European War on a question in which we were inextricably involved. For the French position in Morocco was part of the Lansdowne Treaty, and Sir Edward Grey in his book, "Twenty-Five Years," makes it clear that he regarded a dispute on anything which constituted a challenge to that settlement as something which we were bound to put in a different category from any dispute which might arise between France and Germany outside the four corners of that arrangement. I still think there is very great force in his contention in that respect.

The situation can be outlined in a few words. France, who had been accorded a zone of influence in Morocco by the Treaty of Algeciras, found it necessary to send an expedition to Fez. Germany, conceiving with some reason that France had annexationist designs, thought she would be entitled to corresponding compensations elsewhere, and promptly took steps to indicate her claim, and opened the negotiations by sending a gunboat to the Moroccan harbour of Agadir. This was a blundering and blustering kind of diplomacy, and when Britain, naturally concerned at its meaning and possible outcome, sent a communication to Berlin on the subject, our letter was left unanswered for weeks, while we learnt from France that the German Government was pressing quite impossible demands upon her as the price of withdrawal from Agadir.

It is hard to say whether there was real danger of war. There is an ominous passage in a dispatch from von Bethmann-Hollweg to the Kaiser, dated 15th July, 1911, when the German silence *vis-à-vis* Britain had already continued for eleven days. The Imperial Chancellor reported that Herr von Kiderlen, the German Foreign Secretary, had gathered from his discussion with the French Ambassador the impression that "in order to reach a favourable result, we shall certainly have to take a very strong line!" To this the Kaiser makes a marginal note: —

"Then I must return home at once. For I can't let my Government take that sort of action without being right on the spot so as to keep a careful watch on the consequences and have them well in hand! Anything else would be unpardonable, and too parliamentary! *Le Roi s'amuse!* And meantime we are steering straight for mobilisation! That must not happen WITHOUT ME!

Besides, our Allies must first be informed about this! For it may draw them in, in sympathy!"

There can be no doubt as to the meaning of those words. The Kaiser clearly contemplated the mobilisation of his armies as a not unlikely result of the diplomatic situation. In 1914 mobilisation made for war—it meant war.

When the rude indifference of the German Government to our communication had lasted for seventeen days—from the 4th to the 21st July—I felt that matters were growing tensely critical and that we were drifting clumsily towards war. It was not merely that by failing even to send a formal acknowledgment of the Foreign Secretary's letter the Germans were treating us with intolerable insolence, but that their silence might well mean that they were blindly ignorant of the sense in which we treated our obligations under the Treaty, and might not realise until too late that we felt bound to stand by France. These reasons prompted me to make the Mansion House speech which has already been so fully dealt with by Sir Edward Grey and Mr. Churchill.

On the 21st July I was due to speak to the Bankers at their annual banquet to the Chancellor of the Exchequer and I decided to take advantage of the occasion to make a statement which would warn Germany of the peril into which her Ministers were rushing her so heedlessly.

I felt that I had no right to intervene in a matter which was in the sphere of the Foreign Office, and to make a declaration which might involve our relations with Germany, without obtaining the consent of both the Prime Minister and Grey. Before delivering it, therefore, I submitted its terms to the Prime Minister. He fully approved, and sent immediately to the Foreign Office to ask Sir Edward Grey to come to the Cabinet Room in order to obtain his views and procure his sanction. My recollection is that when he arrived, he cordially assented to every word of my draft, and I delivered the speech later on to the Bankers at the Mansion House.*

The genesis of that speech is, as I have said, quite correctly recorded by both Grey and Churchill, but I have here given my own confirmation of their narrative, because my public intervention at

---

* The passage of my speech in question was as follows:

"But I am also bound to say this—that I believe it is essential in the highest interests, not merely of this country, but of the world, that Britain should at all hazards maintain her place and her prestige amongst the Great Powers of the world. Her potent influence has many a time been in the past, and may yet be in the future, invaluable to the cause of human liberty. It has more than once in the past redeemed continental nations, who are sometimes too apt to forget that service, from overwhelming disaster, and even from national extinction. I would make great sacrifices to preserve peace. I conceive that nothing would justify a disturbance of international goodwill except questions of the gravest national moment. But if a situation were to be forced upon us in which peace could only be preserved by the surrender of the great and beneficent position Britain has won by centuries of heroism and achievement, by allowing Britain to be treated, where her interests were vitally affected, as if she were of no account in the Cabinet of Nations, then I say emphatically that peace at that price would be a humiliation intolerable for a great country like ours to endure. National honour is no party question. The security of our great international trade is no party question. The peace of the world is much more likely to be secured if all nations realise fairly what the conditions of peace must be. . . ."

that time in the sphere of foreign affairs was so unusual that a rumour gained currency, and even finds place in German and Austrian official diplomatic correspondence, that I was merely acting as a mouthpiece to read out a statement prepared by the Cabinet, and was at most but vaguely aware of its implications. Even E. T. Raymond avers that what I read was a passage carefully prepared for me by Sir Edward Grey. But I have not the least desire to shuffle off my true responsibility in this connection. The initiative in this matter was my own, as was the wording of the statement. Certainly I secured authoritative approval before I made it, but it was not actually submitted to the whole Cabinet in advance.

The effect of the speech was unquestionably to clear the air, and avert any danger of Europe drifting unawares into war. The German Government, naturally, was furious, for its gunboat diplomacy had received a severe and well-merited rebuff. Metternich was instructed to make representations about my speech to the British Foreign Office. He did so in a very stern manner, but found little to cheer him in his reception. He reported to von Kiderlen-Waechter that " with reference to the speech of the Chancellor of the Exchequer, Grey was thoroughly uncompromising, defended it as moderate, and stated that it had been entirely right for this speech to be made." The truth was, of course, that the Wilhelmstrasse had over-reached itself, and taken a course which it was difficult either to explain or to explain away. The Austrian diplomatic correspondence shows that the Kaiser and his Minister thought the Government then in office in France was a weak one and lacked backbone. The German Foreign Office doubtless conceived that a sudden and dramatic rattling of the sabre would terrify this feeble Ministry and that by this means Germany would win substantial concessions in Morocco. But they were not prepared to go to war with both France and England, to make good this gamble.

Von Kiderlen-Waechter described my speech to the Austrian Ambassador at Berlin as " an unfair and colossal bluff." However, it was bluff he was not prepared to call. It was in truth by no means bluff, and if an equally clear statement of our attitude had been made in a July only three years later, it is conceivable that once again the peril of a recklessly incurred war might have been averted.

4. NO CABINET CONSIDERATION OF FOREIGN POLICY

During the eight years that preceded the war, the Cabinet devoted a ridiculously small percentage of its time to a consideration of foreign affairs. This was partly, but not altogether, due to the political conditions under which we worked. The 1906-14 Governments and Parliaments were engaged in a series of controversies on home affairs, each of which raised more passion than any dispute between the rival political parties within living memory.

Education, Temperance, Land Taxation—culminating in the most serious constitutional crisis since the days of the Reform Bill—the Parliament Act, Home Rule, and the Disestablishment of the Church in Wales: these subjects challenged an infinite variety of human interests, sentiment, and emotion, and the partisan warfare that raged round these topics was so fierce that by 1913 this country was brought to the verge of civil war.

Of course, certain aspects of foreign policy were familiar to those Ministers who attended the Committee of Imperial Defence, but apart from that the Cabinet as a whole were never called into genuine consultation upon the fundamental aspects of the foreign situation. There was a reticence and a secrecy which practically ruled out three-fourths of the Cabinet from the chance of making any genuine contribution to the momentous questions then fermenting on the continent of Europe, which ultimately ended in an explosion that almost shattered the civilisation of the world. During the whole of those eight years, when I was a member of the Cabinet, I can recall no such review of the European situation being given to us as that which Sir Edward Grey delivered to the Colonial Conference in 1907, or to the Prime Ministers of the Dominions at the Committee of Imperial Defence in 1911. Even there the information that was withheld was more important than that which was imparted. For instance, nothing was said about our military commitments. There was in the Cabinet an air of " hush hush " about every allusion to our relations with France, Russia and Germany. Direct questions were always answered with civility, but were not encouraged. We were made to feel that, in these matters, we were reaching our hands towards the mysteries, and that we were too young in the priesthood to presume to enter into the sanctuary reserved for the elect. So we confined our inquisitiveness and our counsel to the more mundane affairs in which we had taken part in Opposition during the whole of our political careers. Discussions, if they could be called discussions, on foreign affairs, were confined to the elder statesmen who had seen service in some previous ministerial existence. Apart from the Prime Minister and the Foreign Secretary there were only two or three men such as Lord Loreburn, the Lord Chancellor, Lord Morley, Lord Crewe, and, for a short time, Lord Ripon, who were expected to make any contribution on the infrequent occasions when the Continental situation was brought to our awed attention. As a matter of fact, we were hardly qualified to express any opinion on so important a matter, for we were not privileged to know any more of the essential facts than those which the ordinary newspaper reader could gather from the perusal of his morning journal. I recollect the late Lord Northcliffe, at a dinner at Lord Birkenhead's house, where he was invited to meet a number of Cabinet Ministers in the Liberal Administration, telling us all quite bluntly that the Editor of a great London journal was better informed about what was happening in the capitals of the world than any Cabinet Minister. He maintained that all the information we got was carefully filtered. He might have gone further and said that much of the information essential for forming a sound opinion was deliberately withheld. When a Cabinet Minister first takes office, nothing gives him a greater sense of his personal importance than the stout little leather bag with a specially constructed key which is sent after him every night to any address which he may give. It is supposed to contain communications of the most deadly import and secrecy as to what is happening in Courts and Chancelleries throughout the world. As a matter of fact it is just a series of harmless dispatches from our representatives in every foreign country, great and small. There is not a dispatch which contains anything that the Foreign Office clerks who copied it, and the Foreign Office printers who set the type, and the numerous Private Secretaries who have access to these printed copies, could not read without the danger of any indiscreet revelation by any of them disturbing our relations with the most insignificant Kingdom or Republic in the world. All the things that mattered were conveyed in private and confidential letters from our Diplomatic Representatives abroad to the Foreign Secretary personally, in his private and unpublished replies, and in the interviews which he held with the Ambassadors at the Foreign Office in Downing Street. What mattered just as much, perhaps even more, were the secret arrangements arrived at between the military and naval staffs of Britain, France, and Russia as to the part their respective forces were expected to play in the event of war with Germany. None of these vital communications were placed at the disposal of the Cabinet. They were passed on to the Prime Minister, and perhaps to one or two other Ministers. The rest of us were kept in the dark and were therefore not in a position to assess the realities of the foreign situation. When Lord Ripon* was made leader of the House of Lords, having been in Cabinets since the days of Palmerston he knew from previous experience of the existence of secret interchanges of this character, and he asked Sir Edward Grey for an opportunity of perusing them, as he was leading the House of Lords and could hardly do so with judgment unless he were really informed.

There is no more conspicuous example of this kind of suppression of vital information than the way in which the military arrangements we entered into with France were kept from the Cabinet for six years. They came to my knowledge, first of all, in 1911, during the Agadir crisis, but the Cabinet as a whole were not acquainted with them before the following year. There is abundant evidence that both the French and the Russians regarded these military arrangements

---

* When I first entered the Cabinet, Lord Ripon was the oldest member and I was the youngest.

as practically tantamount to a commitment on our part to
come to the aid of France in the event of her being attacked by
Germany. When the British Government was hesitating at the end
of July, 1914, as to whether it would support France in the event of
a German attack, French statesmen almost reverted to the
" Perfidious Albion " mood, and even the meek M. Paul Cambon
said that the only question was whether the word " honour " was to
be expunged from the British dictionary. On the whole, the view
summarised in that pungent comment is the one I heard expressed
by most supporters and opponents of our intervention in the Great
War; and yet the Cabinet were never informed of these vital arrangements until we were so deeply involved in the details of military and
naval plans that it was too late to repudiate the inference. To
attempt then to set right the impression produced in the minds of our
Allies would have created a new situation, involving a return, in an
aggravated form, of the unpleasant relations with France which the
Lansdowne Agreement of 1904 had, for the time being, brought to
an end. In 1906 both Sir Henry Campbell-Bannerman and Mr.
Asquith expressed grave doubts as to the wisdom of proceeding with
these discussions. They ultimately assented to that course being
pursued under pressure from Sir Edward Grey and Lord Haldane.
When in 1912 (six years after they had been entered into) Sir Edward
Grey communicated these negotiations and arrangements to the
Cabinet the majority of its Members were aghast. Hostility scarcely
represents the strength of the sentiment which the revelation
aroused: it was more akin to consternation. Sir Edward Grey
allayed the apprehensions of his colleagues to some extent by
emphatic assurances that these military arrangements left us quite
free, in the event of war, to decide whether we should or should not
participate in the conflict. The Prime Minister also exercised his
great authority with the Cabinet in the same direction. In spite of
these assurances a number of Cabinet Ministers were not reconciled
to the action taken by the Foreign Office, the War Office and the
Admiralty, and these commitments undoubtedly added a good deal
to the suspicions which made the task of Sir Edward Grey in securing
unanimity in 1914 very much more difficult.

Personally, I was prepared to accept the Foreign Secretary's
assurances that we were not committed. I was strengthened in my
conviction that there was no definite commitment to give military
support to France in her quarrels with Germany by the meetings of
the Committee of Imperial Defence during the Agadir crisis. There
Sir Henry Wilson, with the aid of a pointer and a big map, explained
to us the whole of the arrangements which had been entered into
with the French Foreign Office; they were contingent upon a
German attack upon Belgium, and the march of German divisions
through that country to attack France. In that contingency our

Expeditionary Force was to be taken to the Belgian frontier along the French railways, for the purpose of giving every support to the army which was resisting the invader in that quarter. I never doubted that, if the Germans interfered with the integrity and independence of Belgium, we were in honour bound to discharge our treaty obligations to that country.

CHAPTER II

THE CRASH

1. UNEXPECTED PLUNGE INTO WAR

How was it that the world was so unexpectedly plunged into this terrible conflict? Who was responsible? Not even the astutest and most far-seeing statesman foresaw in the early summer of 1914 that the autumn would find the nations of the world interlocked in the most terrible conflict that had ever been witnessed in the history of mankind; and if you came to the ordinary men and women who were engaged in their daily avocations in all countries there was not one of them who suspected the imminence of such a catastrophe. Of those who, in the first weeks of July, were employed in garnering their hay or corn harvests, either in this country or on the Continent of Europe, it is safe to say that not one ever contemplated the possibility that another month would find them called to the Colours and organised in battle array for a struggle that would end in the violent death of millions of them, and in the mutilation of many more millions. The nations slithered over the brink into the boiling cauldron of war without any trace of apprehension or dismay.

When I first heard the news of the assassination of the Grand Duke Ferdinand, I felt that it was a grave matter, and that it might provoke serious consequences which only the firmest and most skilful handling could prevent from developing into an emergency that would involve nations. But my fears were soon assuaged by the complete calm with which the Rulers and diplomats of the world seemed to regard the event. The Kaiser departed for his usual yachting holiday in the Norwegian fiords. His Chief Minister left for his usual shooting party on his estate in Silesia. The acting Head of the German Foreign Office went off on a honeymoon trip. A still more reassuring fact—the military head of the German Army, von Moltke, left for his cure in a foreign spa. The President of the French Republic and his Prime Minister were on a ceremonial visit to Russia and only arrived back in Paris on July 29th. Our Foreign Office preserved its ordinary tranquillity of demeanour and thought it unnecessary to sound an alarm even in the Cabinet Chamber. I remember that some time in July, an influential Hungarian lady, whose name I have forgotten, called upon me at 11, Downing Street, and told me that we were taking the assassination of the Grand Duke much too quietly;

that it had provoked such a storm throughout the Austrian Empire as she had never witnessed, and that unless something were done immediately to satisfy and appease resentment, it would certainly result in war with Serbia, with the incalculable consequences which such an operation might precipitate in Europe. However, such official reports as came to hand did not seem to justify the alarmist view she took of the situation.

I cannot recall any discussion on the subject in the Cabinet until the Friday evening before the final declaration of war by Germany. We were much more concerned with the threat of imminent civil war in the North of Ireland. The situation there absorbed our thoughts, and constituted the subject-matter for the major part of our deliberations. Mr. Churchill recalls the fact that on that Friday, the 24th of July, we met in the Prime Minister's room in the House of Commons to discuss once more the Irish crisis, which was daily becoming more menacing. When the discussion was over the Cabinet rose, but the Foreign Secretary asked us to remain behind for a few more minutes as he had something to impart to us about the situation in Europe. When we resumed our seats he told us, for the first time, that he thought the position was very grave, but he was hopeful that the conversations which were proceeding between Austria and Russia might lead to a pacific settlement. So we separated upon that assurance. On Saturday Sir Edward Grey left for his fishing lodge in Hampshire, and all other Ministers followed his example and left town. On Sunday came the news of the landing of arms by Nationalists at Howth, near Dublin, and of a conflict with the military which arose out of that incident. The excitement over this event overshadowed, for the time being, the Continental situation. At that very hour Isvolzky, the Russian Ambassador in Paris, who was then at St. Petersburg, and M. Paleologue, the French Ambassador in Russia, both said: " It is war this time "; and later on the same Sunday afternoon, Monsieur Sazonow, the Russian Foreign Minister, made a similar statement to Monsieur Paleologue, and added: " It is too terrible to contemplate." Mr. Harold Nicolson, in his Life of his father, the late Lord Carnock, who was then Permanent Head of the Foreign Office, states that Sir Arthur Nicolson, as he then was, became so alarmed about the situation on this Sunday, that he took immediate steps to bring Sir Edward Grey back to London. War was declared by Austria on Serbia two days later and by Germany and Russia five days later.

Even then I met no responsible Minister who was not convinced that, in one way or another, the calamity of a great European war would somehow be averted.

2 NOBODY WANTED WAR

In looking back upon the incidents of those few eventful days one

feels like recalling a nightmare, and after reading most of the literature explaining why the nations went to war, and who was responsible, the impression left on my mind is one of utter chaos, confusion,
feebleness and futility, especially of a stubborn refusal to look at the
rapidly approaching cataclysm.   The nations backed their machines
over the precipice.   Amongst the rulers and statesmen who alone
could give the final word which caused great armies to spring from
the ground and march to and across frontiers, one can see now clearly
that not one of them wanted war; certainly not on this scale.   The
possible exception is the foolish Berchtold, the Austrian Premier,
upon whom must be fixed the chief personal responsibility for most
of what happened.*   As to the rest, they all shrank from the prospect.
Least of all could it be said that the aged Franz Joseph wanted
war.

The last thing the vainglorious Kaiser wanted was a European
war.   The feeble and simple-minded but sincere Czar of the Russias
certainly did not desire war.   During his reign the occasional outbursts of truculence against strikers, Jews, and revolutionaries, for
which he was held responsible, were not any expression of natural
ferocity on his part.   They always occurred as a result of official
incitement, usually as a means of countering some domestic crisis.
But on this occasion his principal official adviser, Sazonow, displayed
a real horror at the prospect of a great war, and in the Czar's more
intimate circles, even Rasputin warned the Court of the danger to
the Dynasty which would be involved in plunging Russia into a
great conflict with his powerful neighbours.

Austrian and German rulers and statesmen had a hankering desire
for a small war against a tiny neighbour who, standing alone, would
easily and speedily be overwhelmed.   It would soon be over, the
prestige of Austria would be restored by this exhibition of her
irresistible might, and Germany would once more prove herself the
undoubted master of Europe and the unchallengeable arbiter of its
destinies.   But the last thing any of these Rulers and Statesmen wanted
was a prairie fire that would scorch up a whole continent.   Those who
directed affairs amongst the Central Powers only felt that they must
burn out that " wasps' nest," as they called Serbia, and they never
seemed to take cognizance of the fact that the grass on the plains of
Europe at that time was all tinder.   There was no arresting voice

* That Berchtold was prepared if necessary to launch a European war in furtherance
of his projects is evidenced by a dispatch from him on 25th July, 1914, to the Austrian
Ambassador at St. Petersburg, where he gives him the following instructions: —
    " . . . When your Excellency reaches this point in your conversation with Herr
Sazonow, it will be a suitable opportunity for stating in connection with your account
of our motives and intentions, that we—as your Excellency would be already in a
position to make clear—are seeking for no territorial gain, and have no intention
of impairing the sovereignty of the Kingdom (of Serbia) but that on the other hand
we shall go to the utmost limit in carrying through our demands, *and shall not even
recoil from the possibility of European complications.*"   (My italics.)

anywhere to call a halt: no dominant personality to enforce attention or offer acceptable guidance amidst the chaos. The world was exceptionally unfortunate in the quality of its counsellors in this terrible emergency. Had there been a Bismarck in Germany, a Palmerston or a Disraeli in Britain, a Roosevelt in America, or a Clemenceau in authority in Paris, the catastrophe might, and I believe would, have been averted; but there was no one of that quality visible on the bridge in any great State. Von Bethmann-Hollweg, Poincaré, Viviani, Berchtold, Sazonow and Grey were all able, experienced, conscientious and respectable mariners, but distinctly lacking in the force, vision, imagination and resource which alone could have saved the situation. They were all handy men in a well-behaved sea, but helpless in a typhoon.

In Germany, which counted most in this crisis, navigation was complicated by the august presence on the bridge, of a weak, fussy and egotistical personage, who, at critical moments, overawed and overrode all his subordinates. He never contemplated a great war as a possibility when in the early days of July he issued his first directions as to the course of German diplomacy, and then sailed away to the Norwegian fiords, where he depended for his information as to the course of a crisis whose issue was in his hands, upon some local newspaper.* When he came back and realised that he might be involved in a great European struggle, he visibly shrank from the prospect, but he had not the strength to countermand his orders. He was afraid of being taunted with cowardice in the face of danger. So he allowed himself to be dragged into a conflict, for leadership in which he was utterly unfitted by training, talent or temperament.

The picture which the events of the last fateful days present to me is that which you see in an estuary, when a river, which has been gliding steadily along towards the sea for a long distance without any consciousness of the final destiny which awaits it in the direction in which it flows, suddenly finds itself confronted with the immensity of the ocean and the terror of its waves. The confusion and tumult of waters which ensue mean that its reluctance has come too late. If I were on a jury trying any of the men who were in control of affairs at that date, I should bring against most of them a verdict of manslaughter rather than of murder. A brief summary of what

* " . . . My fleet was cruising as usual in the Norwegian fiords, while I was on my summer vacation trip. During my stay at Balholm I received but meagre news from the Foreign Office and was obliged to rely principally on the Norwegian newspapers, from which I received the impression that the situation was growing worse. I telegraphed repeatedly to the Chancellor and the Foreign Office that I considered it advisable to return home, but was asked each time not to interrupt my journey. . . .
" . . . When, after that, however, I learned from the Norwegian newspapers—*not from Berlin*—of the Austrian ultimatum to Serbia, and, immediately after, of the Serbian Note to Austria, I started upon my return journey without further ado. . . ."
(" My Memoirs," 1878-1918, ex-Kaiser Wilhelm II, pp. 241-2.)

happened will give an idea of the aimlessness and muddle that prevailed.

Grey wanted Russia and Austria to talk it out amongst themselves. He then suggested the mediation of Germany with Austria, of France with Russia, and of Russia with Serbia. On the other hand, Germany preferred to leave Austria to talk it out alone with Serbia without any intermediary or intervener. Sazonow leaned towards conversations between Russia and Austria; Germany, later on, but much too late, inclined in the same direction. Grey then cut athwart this idea with his proposal for a conference of Ambassadors in London, but he wished to leave both Austria and Serbia out of this gathering —a fatal omission which undoubtedly led Germany to reject the proposal. In von Bethmann-Hollweg's opinion a Conference so constituted looked too much like a tribunal to try Austria's case, when the country which was arraigned would not even be present to state her defence, and, in any event, all the judges being biased and the majority definitely hostile, would have but one friend on the Bench. Germany still preferred a continuation of the Austro-Russian talks. And, besides, it was quite clear that the Germans did not care for the idea of a meeting in London. England, France, and Russia would be represented there by skilled and experienced diplomatists, rootedly opposed to the Austrian objectives in the Balkans; on the other hand, the German Ambassador had not the full confidence of the German Foreign Office, for many reasons. Amongst others, he was suspected of hesitancy and lukewarmness in his attitude towards the Austrian pretensions. Even Russia was not enthusiastic about the notion of a Conference, preferring to continue direct negotiations with Austria. Sazonow only accepted the proposal of a Conference in the event of these direct negotiations breaking down. The Four-Power Conference was, therefore, turned down. The suggestion had only served to waste invaluable time. It was not wisely framed, and it was not put forward with conviction; it was not pressed home and it was finally dropped; in fact, it was dropped at the first objection. It was a timid and half-hearted approach, and at the first difficulty it encountered it was abandoned by its distracted author. Then came the muddle about mobilisation and semi-mobilisation of the Austrian, Russian, and Serbian Armies. The Willy-Nicky letters followed with the Czar's suggestion of a reference to the Hague, and the Kaiser's counter-suggestion of a cancellation by the Czar of his Decree for mobilising the Russian Army. The letters were written to the tramp of battalions and the rumble of cannon pressing on towards frontiers, and the inevitable clash that was to come. A multitude of moidered Counsellors, by their conflicting advice, now hustled Wisdom into the arms of the bravoes who had for years waited eagerly for this hour, and were standing impatiently outside the Council Chambers ready to strangle their victim.

3. ATTITUDE—MILITARY, POLITICAL AND CIVILIAN—TO WAR

Whilst diplomacy desired peace and worked for it by confused and bewildered methods, there were powerful elements in every community that thirsted for war. The Military Chiefs, high and low, in at least three of the countries principally concerned were not averse from putting their theories, plans, and hopes to the test. All of them believed in the machine they had helped to perfect, and they were confident that if tried it would prove triumphant. In this country this desire did not count in the estimation of a hair! Our overwhelming confidence in the power of our Navy may perhaps have influenced opinion in certain quarters, but that influence was not decisive. In Germany, on the other hand, military sentiment counted a good deal. I am inclined to believe, after a careful perusal of the evidence, that it was a decisive factor. The Kaiser had, owing to certain incidents and indiscretions, lost much of his popularity. His popularity with his Army was definitely on the wane. They realised that he had not the heart of a soldier, and that he was not the man who would lead them into battle—if he could avoid a fight. The Crown Prince was their favourite. The Kaiser was becoming sensitive to this rather contemptuous opinion formed of his courage by the Army he idolised. He knew that any symptom of shrinking or shuddering at the prospect of a great fight would finally forfeit the last remnant of respect for him in the breasts of the soldiers he adored. This he could not face. So the last fatal days before the War present the pitiable spectacle of a man torn between fear, common sense and vanity, the two former pulling him back from the chasm—the latter pushing him relentlessly over the brink. His letter of the 28th of July to von Jagow is a perfect specimen of the distracted state of mind which was produced by this inward struggle. In it he said : —

"That the requests of the Danube Monarchy had been broadly met; the Serbs' few reservations could probably be cleared up by negotiation; the reply amounted to a ' capitulation in the humblest style,' and with it there disappeared *all reason for war*." (The italics were the Kaiser's.)*

This part of the letter is often quoted. What is not so often quoted is the following sentence in the same note in which he stated that he considered that a guarantee was needed for the execution of the demands upon Serbia, and also that as " a visible *satisfaction d'honneur* for Austria the Austrian Army should temporarily occupy Belgrade as a pledge." The letter is a proof of the fatal hesitancy in the Kaiser's will, prompted by conflicting appeals. His subordination of judgment to the will of the Army is further illustrated by his attitude towards the invasion of Belgium. When

* Lutz : "Lord Grey and the World War" (pp. 257-8).

he realised that a march across Belgium without the consent of its Government would bring Britain into the War, he sent for Von Moltke and asked him whether it would not be possible to change the war plan and concentrate on Russia. Von Moltke replied that it was too late, as all the preparations had been made on the assumption that the German Army would immediately march through Belgium and capture Paris in a given time. The Kaiser is stated to have replied: "Your uncle would have given me a different answer." Nevertheless he surrendered.

The "little war" to occupy Belgrade was the bait of the General Staff to land the Great War. Once its hook was in the gills of the Kaiser he was dragged along. The "little war" involved the mobilisation and declaration of war by Austria. That brought on the partial mobilisation of Russia. That drove Germany into the declaration of war against Russia. Then we were already in the World War.

In Austria and Russia the High Command were finally responsible for the War. They insisted on mobilisation whilst not unhopeful negotiations were still going on. Austrian mobilisation led to Russia mobilising her army so as to prevent any surprise movement across the frontier. Austria mobilised to strike at Serbia. Russia mobilised for a counterblow. When the Kaiser, frightened by the thunder clouds, intervened personally with the Czar to avert war, he begged " Nicky " to cancel his Decree which had already gone forth, for the mobilisation of the Russian army. The Czar was willing to accede to this not unreasonable request, but the army leaders assured him that the "technical" difficulties of cancellation and even of partial demobilisation were insuperable. It was thus that the military chiefs in the leading countries of the Continent thrust the nations into war, whilst their impotent statesmen were still fumbling for Peace. Each army believed in its own invincibility and was anxious to demonstrate it.

The belief in the superiority of the German Army was by no means confined to the Germans. I remember two or three years before the War, Lord Kitchener, who was then Sirdar of Egypt, calling upon me at the Treasury in connection with a loan for the development of the Sudan. As it was shortly after the Agadir crisis, we got on to the subject of the Franco-German position. He had a poor opinion of the French Army, and thought the Germans would " walk through them like partridges." Shortly afterwards, there was a banquet at Buckingham Palace to entertain some foreign potentate, and I sat next to a foreign Prince, who was not a German. He also entertained the same opinion of the invincibility of the German Army, and used exactly the same metaphor as Lord Kitchener about the way it would scatter all other armies like partridges.

The French Army, on the other hand, were equally confident of their powers. They believed they had the best gun in the field—the famous *soixante-quinze*—and they were not far wrong. It is not the first time that rapture over the possession of a new military invention has made a nation less averse from war. The French had also great confidence in the training given to their officers and in the fine quality of their troops. They knew their organisation was excellent and they had the inevitable " plan." There never was a time since 1870 when the French Army had less fear of its great rival. The Russians had improved their Army in equipment and organisation since their defeat in Manchuria. They felt infinitely superior to the Austrian Army, and deemed themselves quite a match for what was left of the German Army, after the better half of it had marched to the West. Generals in this frame of mind hungered for war and had no difficulty in manœuvring statesmen who did not know their own minds into positions where war became inevitable. Thus great armaments made war.

But the Army was not the only element that desired war. The populace caught the war fever. In every capital they clamoured for war. The theory which is propagated to-day by pacifist orators of the more cantankerous and less convincing type that the Great War was engineered by elder and middle-aged statesmen who sent younger men to face its horrors, is an invention. The elder statesmen did their feckless best to prevent war, whilst the youth of the rival countries were howling impatiently at their doors for immediate war. I saw it myself during the first four days of August, 1914. I shall never forget the warlike crowds that thronged Whitehall and poured into Downing Street, whilst the Cabinet was deliberating on the alternative of peace or war. On Sunday there was a great crowd. Monday was Bank Holiday, and multitudes of young people concentrated in Westminster demonstrating for war against Germany. We could hear the hum of this surging mass from the Cabinet Chamber. On Monday afternoon I walked with Mr. Asquith to the House of Commons to hear Grey's famous speech. The crowd was so dense that no car could drive through it, and had it not been for police assistance we could not have walked a yard on our way. It was distinctly a pro-war demonstration. I remember observing at the time: " These people are very anxious to send our poor soldiers to face death; how many of them will ever go into battle themselves?" It was an unworthy doubt of the courage and patriotism of the demonstrators. A few days later recruiting stands were set up in the Horse Guards Parade, and that great open space beheld a crowd of young men surging around these stands and pushing their way through to give their names for enlistment in the Kitchener Armies. For days I heard, from the windows of Downing Street and the Treasury, the movement of a myriad feet towards the stands and the shouting of names of eager volunteers by the recruiting sergeants. The War had leapt into popularity between Saturday and Monday. On Saturday the Governor of the Bank of England called on me, as Chancellor of the Exchequer, to inform me on behalf of the City that the financial and trading interests in the City of London were totally opposed to our intervening in the War. By Monday there was a complete change. The threatened invasion of Belgium had set the nation on fire from sea to sea. By then Sir Edward Grey had ample evidence that his stipulation to Monsieur Cambon that we could only come to the aid of France if public opinion demanded it, was completely fulfilled. But Belgium was responsible for the change. Before then the Cabinet was hopelessly divided—fully one third, if not one half, being opposed to our entry into the War. After the German ultimatum to Belgium the Cabinet was almost unanimous. Had Germany without any provocation attacked France, I have no doubt that public sentiment in this country would have demanded that the Government should go to the aid of the victim of such wanton aggression. But it was thoroughly understood that on this occasion France was drawn into the quarrel by her Treaty obligations with Russia, and that if France had stood out of the dispute, Germany would only have been too pleased to leave her alone. The Franco-Russian Alliance was offensive and defensive. France was therefore bound to support Russia, whether she was interested in the *casus belli* or not. But Britain was not in that position. We had given no undertaking to come to the aid of Russia in any dispute, whether in the East or in the West. Russian autocracy was almost as unpopular with the people of these islands as Bolshevism is to-day. It was identified with Siberian prisons for political offenders, and with wholesale pogroms of harmless Jews, and with the massacre of workers whose only crime was the presentation of a petition for the redress of their undoubted wrongs. So long therefore as the war was likely to take the form of a contest between the autocracies of Germany and Austria on the one hand, and of Russia and her Allies on the other, British opinion was definitely opposed to intervention. It is a misfortune that Sir Edward Grey did not play sooner and more boldly this card of our treaty pledges to Belgium. It might have averted war altogether.

The London demonstrations had their counterparts in St. Petersburg, Berlin, Vienna and Paris. Blood was up and blood must flow. The populace and the military were at last of one mind. This combination took decision out of the hands of quivering and hesitant statesmanship, which desired peace but had not the resolution and boldness to do the simple things that could alone ensure it. Mr. Emil Ludwig's description of huge assemblies in the London squares demanding peace, whilst a small mob of French residents in London gathered together to clamour for war, is nonsense—and mischievous nonsense, because such a false picture deludes and misleads the statesmanship of the future as to the real perils against which it has to guard.

There is no better evidence of the change which came over public opinion than the following extracts from the *Daily News*. The great Liberal journal came tardily to the conclusion that war was justifiable. It represented the reluctance with which Liberals throughout the country contemplated the prospect of Britain entering into the War. Its testimony as to the state of public opinion during these eventful days is therefore not biased by any bellicosity. Here is a paragraph which appeared in that paper on the 3rd of August, which gives a very faithful account of the temper of the nation up to and including Sunday: —

" There is no war party in this country. On the contrary, the horrors of war have already seized on the popular imagination, and in the highways and public vehicles in London yesterday, the populace were heard to express their indignation at the swift and tragic movements on the Continent."

Here is an account of the crowds on the following day, after it came to be known that Germany was threatening Belgium: —

" The crowd continued to grow and grow. It extended from Trafalgar Square where it formed a dense mass, right along to the House of Commons, where its greatest number gathered about Downing Street, opposite the War Office. Groups of young men passed along in taxi-cabs singing the ' Marseillaise.' During the earlier part of the day there had been little disposition to demonstrate by the wearing of colours, but the tendency spread, and hundreds were buying Union Jacks. At seven o'clock in the evening, when Mr. Asquith left the subsequent Council Meeting to go to the House of Lords, the crowds cheered him with extraordinary fervour. It was a scene of enthusiasm unprecedented in recent times."

Here follows an extract from the account of the temper of the crowd of the 4th of August, after it had been known that we had delivered out ultimatum to Germany: —

" In anticipation of the receipt of Germany's reply, huge crowds gathered in Whitehall and outside Buckingham Palace, and extraordinary scenes of enthusiasm were witnessed. . . . Ministers entering 10, Downing Street were loudly cheered.

Not for years—since Mafeking night—have such crowds been seen in London, and Whitehall, the Mall, and Trafalgar Square, were all packed with excited throngs."

Then follows an account of the frenzy with which the Declaration of War was received: —

> The enthusiasm culminated outside Buckingham Palace when it became known that war had been declared. The word was passed round by the police that silence was necessary, inasmuch as the King was holding a Council for the signing of the necessary proclamations. . . . The news that war had been declared was received with tremendous cheering which grew into a deafening roar when King George, Queen Mary and the Prince of Wales appeared on the balcony. . . .
>
> Westminster, Charing Cross, and the main thoroughfares round Westminster were thronged all last night with excited throngs, who displayed marked tendencies towards mafficking. Both in numbers and in noisiness it far exceeded the crowds of Monday. Union Jacks were everywhere to be seen, and the air was filled with the sound of patriotic songs; Trafalgar Square was almost impassable.
>
> A hostile crowd assembled outside the German Embassy, and smashed the windows. A special message was sent to Cannon Row, and a force of mounted and unmounted police was quickly on the scene, but had considerable difficulty in restoring order."

In face of these reports, given by a witness whose leaning was definitely against war, what becomes of the suggestion that we entered into the War against the vocal opposition of the people of this country? All wars are popular on the day of their declaration. To quote Walpole's famous observation upon a war into which he had been reluctantly forced: " They are ringing the bells now: soon they will be wringing their hands." But never was there a war so universally acclaimed as that into which Britain entered on the 4th of August, 1914.

4. 4TH AUGUST, 1914

The 4th of August, 1914, is one of the world's fateful dates. The decision taken on that day in the name and on behalf of the British Empire altered the destiny of Europe. It is not too much to say that it gave a different turn or direction to the advance of the human race. The trumpets of war had already sounded in the East and in the West, and colossal armies were hurrying to the slaughter. Millions of men were either on the march or strapping on their armour for the conflict, and roads and railway tracks trembled with the weight of guns and munitions and all the sinister devices and mechanisms of human destruction!

Was there any hope that the great catastrophe could be averted? There were continuous meetings of the Cabinet on Friday, Saturday and Sunday. I experienced much difficulty in attending throughout because of the Conference at the Treasury to deal with the grave financial situation into which we had been plunged by War. But I heard and took part in most of the discussion. It revealed serious differences of opinion on the subject of British intervention in a Russo-German war even although France was forced by her Russian alliance to join in. Grey never definitely put before the Cabinet the proposition that Britain should, in that event, declare war. He never expressed a clear and unequivocal opinion either way and no decision was therefore taken on that point. But it was quite clear from the course of the debate inside the Cabinet and the informal conversations which took place outside during our short adjournments that we were hopelessly divided on the subject of Britain entering the War on the issue as it had developed at that date. Had the question of defending the neutrality and integrity of Belgium been raised there would not have been a dissentient voice on that issue. Lord Morley and John Burns might conceivably have stood out. Of that I am not convinced had a decision on that point alone been reached in time as a means of circumscribing the area of war and possibly of persuading Germany of the futility of waging it at all under conditions which would have been unfavourable to her preconcerted military schemes. But such a proposal was never submitted to our judgment.

The one faint glimmer still visible in the lowering sky was in the direction of Belgium.

The dark clouds were rapidly closing up, but there was still one visible corner of blue. The Germans had signed a treaty not merely to respect, but to protect the neutrality of Belgium. Would they honour their bond? Great Britain was a party to that compact. If anyone broke its terms, Britain was bound to throw in her might against the invader. Would the faith of Prussia, strengthened by the fear of Britain, prevail? If the treaty stood, the situation might yet be saved.

The policy I urged upon my colleagues was not one merely of passive non-intervention in the struggle between Germany and Austria on the one hand and Russia and France on the other. We were not in the position of France. She was bound by Treaty to support Russia in her quarrels with Germany. We were under no such obligation. I proposed, therefore, that we should take immediate steps to increase and strengthen our Army in numbers and equipment, so that when we judged the time had come for intervention, none of the belligerents could afford to disregard our appeal. Had Germany respected the integrity of Belgium, that policy would have been the wisest course to pursue. There would have been plenty of time for passions to exhaust their force and for the sanguine expectations of military enthusiasm to evaporate. The problem of France would have been a different one; the march of events would have been slower. France, instead of having to defend a frontier of over 500 miles, without fortresses or artificial barriers, could have concentrated all her strength on defending a frontier of 250 miles protected by formidable fortresses. An army (including reserves) of 3,000,000 men, holding entrenched positions on this narrow frontier, would have been invincible, and Germany might well have been content merely to defend her frontiers in the West, and throw her armies into Poland. There, difficulties of transport, bad roads, inadequate railways, immense distances, would have postponed decision for weeks if not for months. It took Germany over 12 months' hard fighting to conquer Poland. Even then the Russian Army was still in being and ready to resume the conflict in 1916. British intervention in the cause of peace might then have induced saner counsels. Britain was the one Power in Europe that had never yet been beaten in a European war. With her immunity from attack, with her immense fleet manned by the most skilful seamen in the world, with her enormous resources, she could be reckoned upon to wear down any Power. Had Britain been able to throw into the scale a well-equipped army of a million men to support her fleet, Germany would have hesitated before she rejected terms of peace and thus brought the British Empire into the conflict on the side of her enemies. These were the arguments I advanced in favour of non-intervention in the struggle if the neutrality of Belgium were respected.

The invasion of Belgium put an end to all these possibilities. Then our Treaty obligations were involved. On Sunday, the 2nd of August, the omens were not propitious. There were clear indications that the German forces were massing on the Belgian frontier. Germany had appealed to Belgium for permission to march through her territories to attack France. Belgian Ministers hesitated, but the answer given by Belgium's heroic King constitutes one of the most thrilling pages of history. The British Government, on hearing the news, issued an ultimatum to Germany warning her that unless by twelve o'clock on August 4th assurances were received from Germany that the neutrality of Belgium would be treated as inviolate, Britain would have no alternative but to take steps to enforce that treaty. Would Germany realise what war with Britain meant, arrest the progress of her armies, change her strategy, and perhaps consent to a parley? How much depended upon the answer to these questions! We could suspect then what it meant: we know now. There were many of us who could hardly believe that those responsible for guiding the destiny of Germany would be so fatuous as deliberately to provoke the hostility of the British Empire with its inexhaustible reserves and with its grim tenacity of purpose once it engaged in a struggle.

Amongst those who criticise the intervention of Britain there are two sections. There are those who pretend to believe that this was a war intrigued and organised and dictated by financiers for their own purpose. In Germany and amongst the friends of Germany in other lands there are those who ascribe our action to the irritation produced by a growing jealousy of Germany's strength and prosperity, and British politicians are pictured as eagerly on the pounce for an opportunity to destroy this redoubtable rival. As to both, the tale of these days is a complete answer. I was Chancellor of the Exchequer and, as such, I saw Money before the war; I saw it immediately after the outbreak of war; I lived with it for days, and did my best to steady its nerve, for I knew how much depended on restoring its confidence; and I say that money was a frightened and trembling thing: money shivered at the prospect. It is a foolish and ignorant libel to call this a financiers' war. As to the second form of attack on British action, big businesses everywhere wanted to keep out of it, and as to the rest this narrative will be a reply. Here were no eager men praying for the hour to arrive when they could strike down a great commercial rival.

It was a day full of rumours and reports, throbbing with anxiety. Hour after hour passed, and no sign came from Germany. There were only disturbing rumours of further German movements towards the Belgian line. The evening came. Still no answer. Shortly after nine o'clock I was summoned to the Cabinet Room for an important consultation. There I found Mr. Asquith, Sir Edward Grey, and Mr. Haldane all looking very grave. Mr. M'Kenna arrived soon afterwards. A message from the German Foreign Office to the German Embassy in London had been intercepted. It was not in cipher. It informed the German Ambassador that the British Ambassador in Berlin had asked for his passports at 7 p.m. and declared war. A copy of this message was passed on to me, and I have it still in my possession. A facsimile of this fateful document as it was submitted to us at this solemn conference is reproduced overleaf:

"Time: 9.5 p.m.
Date: Aug. 4th, 1914.

The following message has been intercepted by W.O. Censor:—
To German Ambassador from Berlin.

English Ambassador has just demanded his passport shortly after seven o'clock declaring war.

(Signed) Jagow."

No news had been received from Sir Edward Goschen.*
We were therefore at a loss to know what it meant. It looked

* We learnt subsequently that his telegram to us announcing his action had been held up by the German authorities. It never reached us, and not until Sir Edward Goschen arrived back in Britain some nine days later did we hear of its dispatch and obtain a copy of its text.

opposite:

TELEPHOHE MESSAGES RECEIVED BY CHIEF CENSOR

FROM CHIEF CENSOR. WAR OFFICE.

Time: 9.5 p.m.

Date: August 4th 1914.

The following message has been intercepted by W.O.Censor:-

To:.German.Ambassador.......................

From......Berlin.............................

English Ambassador has just demanded his passport
shortly after seven o'clock declaring war

/Signed/   Jagow

Asst Chief Censor
Cochrane

The British Cabinet's first intimation of the outbreak of War conveyed in
an intercepted telegram from the German Government to the German
Ambassador in London, Prince Lichnowski.

like an attempt on the part of the Germans to anticipate the hour of the declaration of war in order to effect some *coup* either against British ships or British coasts. Should this intercept be treated as the commencement of hostilities, or should we wait until we either heard officially from Germany that our conditions had been rejected, or until the hour of the ultimatum had expired? We sat at the green table in the famous room where so many historic decisions had been taken in the past. It was not then a very well-lighted room, and my recollection is that the lights had not all been turned on, and in the dimness you might imagine the shades of the great British states-men of the past taking part in a conference which meant so much to the Empire, to the building up of which they had devoted their lives—Chatham, Pitt, Fox, Castlereagh, Canning, Peel, Palmerston, Disraeli, Gladstone. In that simple, unadorned, almost dingy room they also had pondered over the problems which had perplexed their day. But never had they been confronted with so tremendous a decision as that with which British Ministers were faced in these early days of August, 1914.

And now came the terrible decision: should we unleash the savage dogs of war at once, or wait until the time limit of the ultimatum had expired, and give peace the benefit of even such a doubt as existed for at least another two hours? We had no difficulty in deciding that the Admiralty was to prepare the fleet against any sudden attack from the German flotillas and to warn our coasts against any possible designs from the same quarter. But should we declare war now, or at midnight? The ultimatum expired at midnight in Berlin. That was midnight according to Central Europe time: it meant eleven o'clock according to Greenwich time. We resolved to wait until eleven. Would any message arrive from Berlin before eleven informing us of the intention of Germany to respect Belgian neutrality? If it came there was still a faint hope that something might be arranged before the marching armies crashed into each other.

As the hour approached a deep and tense solemnity fell on the room. No one spoke. It was like awaiting the signal for the pulling of a lever which would hurl millions to their doom—with just a chance that a reprieve might arrive in time. Our eyes wandered anxiously from the clock to the door, and from the door to the clock, and little was said.

" Boom! " The deep notes of Big Ben rang out into the night the first strokes in Britain's most fateful hour since she arose out of the deep. A shuddering silence fell upon the room. Every face was suddenly contracted in a painful intensity. " Doom! " " Doom! " " Doom! " to the last stroke. The big clock echoed in our ears like the hammer of destiny. What destiny? Who could tell? We had challenged the most powerful military empire the world has yet brought forth. France was too weak alone to challenge its might

c

and Russia was ill-organised, ill-equipped, corrupt. We knew what brunt Britain would have to bear. Could she stand it? There was no doubt or hesitation in any breast. But let it be admitted without shame that a thrill of horror quickened every pulse. Did we know that before peace would be restored to Europe we should have to wade through four years of the most concentrated slaughter, mutilation, suffering, devastation, and savagery which mankind has ever witnessed? That twelve millions of the gallant youth of the nations would be slain, that another twenty millions would be mutilated? That Europe would be crushed under the weight of a colossal war debt? That only one empire would stand the shock? That the three other glittering empires of the world would have been flung to the dust, and shattered beyond repair? That revolution, famine, and anarchy would sweep over half Europe, and that their menace would scorch the rest of this hapless continent?

Has the full tale yet been told? Who can tell? But had we foreseen it all on the 4th of August we could have done no other.

Twenty minutes after the hour Mr. Winston Churchill came in and informed us that the wires had already been sent to the British ships of war in every sea announcing the fact that war had been declared and that they were to act accordingly. Soon afterwards we dispersed. There was nothing more to say that night. To-morrow would bring us novel tasks and new bearings. As I left I felt like a man standing on a planet that had been suddenly wrenched from its orbit by a demoniac hand and that was spinning wildly into the unknown.

On the morrow Ministers woke up to a new and unaccustomed outlook. Hitherto we had been dealing with Britain and the world at peace. Now we were confronted with the problems of Europe, including Britain, plunged into the vortex of war.

Measures which conferred unheard-of powers on the Executive were passed through both Houses of Parliament after a few hours' discussion. Most of them had been carefully thought out during the tranquil years of peace by the numerous sub-committees of the Committee of Imperial Defence. Of what was accomplished by that remarkable body in the years before the War, and of its foresight, nothing has yet been written. Its founder—Earl Balfour—when he set up the Committee of Imperial Defence as an essential part of the organisation of defence, rendered a service to his country which deserves immortality. Under Mr. Asquith it carried on its task and traditions with undiminished vigour and persistence. It therefore came to pass that when war was thrust upon us, plans which played a vital part in our achievement of victory lay at hand in the pigeon-holes of the Committee of Imperial Defence, prepared down to the last detail and ready to be put into execution. Credit must be given to Lord Balfour for the creation and direction of this body and to Mr. Asquith for making the fullest use of its powers and for further developing its area and scope, but above all it is due to three indefatigable secretaries, Sir George Clarke, later Lord Sydenham, Admiral Sir Charles Ottley, and the ablest and most resourceful of them all, Lieutenant-Colonel Sir Maurice Hankey. The War Book, perfected under Mr. Asquith's chairmanship, and the work of Lord Haldane at the War Office—his organisation of the Territorials, creation of a General Staff as a thinking brain for the Army, and the foundation of the Officer's Training Corps—constitute a powerful answer to those who taunt the Liberal Government with being quite unprepared for the contingency of war.

To these instances may be added the preparedness of the Navy, more especially in the matter of capital ships, under the guidance of Lord Tweedmouth, Mr. M'Kenna, and Mr. Winston Churchill.

But the C.I.D. had by no means completed its exhaustive survey of the possibilities and demands of war, when the storm broke upon us. That probably accounts for the fact that two contingencies which turned out to be of vital consequence had not yet been explored. The first was the financial chaos which would inevitably ensue, especially in a country which transacted most of the intricate business of financing international trade.

The second was the enormous expenditure of munitions which would be involved in war under modern conditions. No one had contemplated the construction of earthen fortifications on so gigantic a scale as that which developed in the Great War upon which Europe had now entered. The Torres Vedras lines were a matter of a few miles. So were Todleben's earthen ramparts at Sebastopol. The colossal earthworks of 1914-18 extended over hundreds of miles. The myriads of heavy guns, trench mortars, and machine guns, the millions of projectiles which became an essential part of the equipment of armies engaged in such vast operations, were beyond the contemplation of any student of the exigencies of war. With these two unforeseen emergencies it was my destiny to be called upon to deal.

5. CABINET IGNORANCE OF FRENCH'S STRATEGICAL ADVICE

To weave the events of the War into a consecutive narrative is no part of my undertaking. That task has already been discharged by other and more expert pens than mine. I simply set myself to contribute to the story of the War more or less detached incidents with which I was especially concerned. The Cabinet were told very little about military or naval movements. In so far as there was any civilian consultation it was confined to the Prime Minister, Mr. Winston Churchill, and occasionally Lord Haldane and Sir Edward Grey.

The Cabinet was ignorant of the fact that in the Councils of War held immediately after the declaration, Sir John French was opposed to the Expeditionary Force being taken to the Belgian frontier. The first War Council held after the entry of this country into the War was on 5th August. Ministers were represented by the Prime Minister, Lord Haldane, Sir Edward Grey and Mr. Winston Churchill; the Navy by Prince Louis of Battenberg, and the Army by Lord Kitchener, Lord Roberts, Sir John French, Sir Ian Hamilton, Sir Charles Douglas, Sir H. C. Sclater, Sir John Cowans, Sir Stanley von Donop, Sir Douglas Haig, Sir J. M. Grierson, Sir A. J. Murray and Sir Henry Wilson. At this Council Sir John French said : —

" that the prearranged plan to meet this situation had been that the Expeditionary Force should mobilise simultaneously with the French and concentrate behind the French Army at Maubeuge by the fifteenth day of mobilisation. The intention then had been for it to move eastward towards the Meuse and act on the left of the French Army against the right German flank. It had, however, always been felt that, if we were late in commencing our mobilisation, as had actually happened, we should have to change our plan. Maubeuge, in his opinion, was no longer a safe place at which to concentrate. He suggested that Amiens would now be the safer place at which to concentrate. The general tenor of his opinion was that the Expeditionary Force should be sent to France; a safe place for concentration should be selected, and events should be awaited. He added that, as an alternative, and owing to the existing conditions, he was inclined to consider a landing at Antwerp with a view to co-operation with the Belgians and Dutch. The three forces would form a considerable army, and would necessarily contain a large German force, and they might be able to advance southward. The feasibility of this plan, however, was largely a naval question. As an alternative to a landing at Antwerp, he proposed a landing in France and a movement to Antwerp by the coast route."

He does not seem to have received any support from any quarter for his suggestions and he appears not to have pressed them any further. The general effect of the consultations which took place on that and the following day was that we should conform our strategy with that of the French Army.

Had either of the two courses been adopted, it is clear now that the whole course of events would have been different, and particularly would this have been the case if five British Divisions had occupied Antwerp. There would have been then on the German flank five excellent Divisions of picked troops. This would have provided the necessary stiffening for the Belgian militia. The Germans would not have considered it safe to penetrate as deeply into France as they subsequently did without clearing their flank from this redoubtable menace. They would thus have lost valuable time, and time was the essence of their plan.

This advice given by the Commander-in-Chief of the Expeditionary Forces was withheld from the Cabinet and was therefore never discussed by Ministers. During the three or four weeks that followed the declaration of War the attention of the Cabinet was concentrated upon questions of recruiting, the escape of the *Goeben,* the conjecture as to what Turkey was likely to do, messages from Greece, and occasional obscure reports from the Front, which were delivered to us at the beginning of each sitting by Lord Kitchener in his loud staccato voice, and with that remote look in his eyes, directed at no one in particular, which was a sure indication of his unease amid surroundings with which he was not familiar. He was sitting in council with men, belonging to the profession with which he had wrestled all his life, and for which, in his heart, he had the usual mixture of military contempt and apprehension. His main idea at the Council table was to tell the politicians as little as possible of what was going on and get back to his desk at the War Office as quickly as he could decently escape. Now and again he flashed out an illuminating sentence of information. Just before the first German blow was delivered, I recollect that Lord Kitchener departed from his usual secretiveness so far as to reveal to us what General Joffre's intentions were. The French Commander-in-Chief, according to him, did not believe that the Germans would march through the Central and Western Provinces of Belgium, because it was an industrial area where the roads were not good and not in the least suited to the movement of large bodies of men with transport and artillery. His idea was that the German Army would swing towards the South-Eastern corner of Belgium, and attempt to pierce the Allied defences in the direction of Namur. Lord Kitchener said that Joffre's idea of the French strategy was that of a boxer who covered himself from his antagonist's blows with his left arm whilst he came round with the right and hit an unexpected blow at his antagonist's weakest point. Lord Kitchener informed us that he thought General Joffre's conception of the German plan of operation was all wrong. He was firmly convinced the Germans would march along all the eleven roads that made for the frontier, and would endeavour to outflank the Allied forces at a point much higher up than that indicated by General Joffre. However, he said, Joffre held stubbornly to his view. We were soon to know the result of this fatal miscalculation.

One morning I was engaged in the Treasury disposing of a few urgent financial problems before the meeting of the Cabinet when Mr. Winston Churchill walked into my room with an unusually gloomy mien. He had clearly some grave news to communicate, and as I was surrounded by officials he beckoned me to come outside.

We went into another room, and he then told me what he had just heard from Kitchener: that the Germans had advanced with enormous forces along the upper Belgian roads; had driven our troops from Mons, and that the whole British force was now in full retreat pursued by a German force of overwhelmingly superior strength. Mr. Churchill records that he was " relieved and overjoyed at my response," but I certainly felt, more than ever, that we were up against it, and that nothing but a mobilisation of the whole of our strength could save Europe and the world from an incalculable disaster.

For several days we had no reports as to what was happening. We heard nothing of the great struggle in Lorraine where the French invading army was hurled back across the frontier after a pitched battle in which the Germans won a decisive victory more by a superiority in artillery than in numbers. We heard nothing of the defeat of the French on the Meuse and the advance of the German Army from that direction towards Paris. We were in a complete fog as to the movements and plans of our own little army. All we knew was that they quitted their positions on the Belgian frontier and were pressed—if not pursued—southwards by overwhelming German forces. We were assured, however, day-by-day, that the retreating army had at last taken up a position in which they were prepared to make a stand with every hope of successfully repelling their assailants. And then on the following morning we were informed that they had abandoned this position and resumed their retreat, but were prepared to fight on a more defensible line, which, we observed, was many leagues nearer Paris.

We heard nothing of the hurried crossing of the Somme, the Aisne, the Marne, the Oise, and we were not told for days of the retirement behind the Seine, miles to the south of Paris. The Cabinet was bewildered by the scrappy and incoherent reports given to it each morning by Lord Kitchener. He was pressed to give us a more satisfactory account of what was really happening. But he protested that he had imparted to his colleagues all the information which had been vouchsafed to him from our Headquarters in France. The first intimation we received of the seriousness and the magnitude of the defeat inflicted upon the Allied Armies was a report in *The Times*— published in defiance of the Censor—giving a graphic account of the march of the German troops through Amiens singing the " Wacht am Rheim " along its deserted streets.

The Cabinet ultimately decided to send Lord Kitchener to France to find out. Conflicting accounts of what passed on this occasion between our great Generals have already appeared, and I feel it is no part of my task to reconcile them. It was my first experience of the fallibility of the Military Leaders—the stubborn miscalculation, muddle and lack of co-ordination, which resulted in mowing down the flower of the finest armies ever put in the field by France and England.

I need hardly say that we were surprised and disappointed by a collapse that had not in the least been anticipated by us or our military advisers. But there was no panic. Reinforcements were hastened to France. Soon afterwards the victory of the Marne—one of the great historical battles of the world—checked the German advance. For the moment utter disaster was averted, and we had time to make fresh plans for the future.

From the fighting of the first two months of the War there emerged two facts of supreme importance in their relation to the strategy of the War. Had these facts been fully appreciated by the Allied Generals at the time and had they conformed their plans to this understanding the War would have taken a different course. The first fact was the enormous superiority of the Germans in artillery—not so much in numbers as in weight and the definite advantage enuring to them in this respect. For the first time the heavy gun was treated as a mobile weapon and its superiority in range and destructive effect to the ordinary field gun broke up the French offensive and crumpled up the French plan of campaign.

The second was the difficulty—even with superior gun power—of dislodging a brave and tenacious enemy from prepared positions where the defender operated under cover. The French failed completely in open warfare in Belgium and Lorraine. The longer range and more shattering power of the German artillery broke up their attack, demoralised their troops and forced them to a speedy retreat to save their armies from utter destruction. On the other hand the defeated troops successfully repelled all attacks by the victorious foe on the Grand Couronne of Nancy, although made with the same overwhelming gun superiority. The French dug themselves in on these hills and the Germans were beaten off with great loss in spite of their more powerful artillery.

Marshal Foch in his Memoirs, writing of the lessons taught (but not learnt) by the fighting of August and September, 1914, says:—

" Generally speaking, it seemed proved that the new means of action furnished by automatic weapons and long-range guns enabled the defence to hold up any attempt at breaking through long enough for a counter-attack to be launched with saving effect. The ' pockets,' which resulted from partial attacks which were successful and seemingly even decisive, could not be maintained, in spite of very costly losses, long enough to ensure a definite rupture of the adversary's line. They could be too quickly rendered uninhabitable and useless for the assailant.

When a defensive front has been forced by superior numbers to fall back, it has not thereby been broken. Counter-attacks on the assailant's flank have often consumed the latter's reserves and threatened his communications, to the extent of eventually stopping his partial advance and causing him to retire.

Many new subjects for reflection are offered when we examine the limitations and the weaknesses of an offensive which, while tactically successful at first, is continued in violation of the principles which modern weapons have now imposed; . . ."

When did the Allied Generals come to these wise conclusions? Not before the bloody assaults of Artois and Champagne in 1915— not even by the still more sanguinary battles of the Somme in 1916.

CHAPTER III

SIR EDWARD GREY*

I CANNOT give a fair presentation of the events that led to the War, prolonged its duration, and aggravated and extended its desolation, without a candid picture of the personalities who controlled and directed these events. Their characteristics were responsible for much that happened—for better or for worse. It is a mistaken view of history to assume that its episodes were entirely due to fundamental causes which could not be averted, and that they were not precipitated or postponed by the intervention of personality. The appearance of one dominating individual in a critical position at a decisive moment has often altered the course of events for years and even generations. A gifted and resolute person has often postponed for centuries a catastrophe which appeared imminent and which but for him would have befallen. On the other hand a weak or hesitant person has invited or expedited calamity which but for him might never have happened or which at least could have been long deferred. I cannot therefore tell my tale of the Great War without giving some idea of the men whose qualities either hastened or failed to avert it, or had the effect of prolonging its devastating course once it had started.

I have found it an exceedingly difficult and occasionally disagreeable task to give an accurate account of the prominent figures in the War when so many of them were colleagues with whom I always enjoyed the most pleasant personal relations: some of them men with whom I worked in perfect amity for over a decade; some to whom I owed many personal courtesies and kindnesses; some who accorded help in the kind of attacks which now and again threaten to overwhelm any man who in politics chooses the more controversial role.

These considerations more especially apply to my examination of the attributes of Mr. Asquith, Sir Edward Grey, Mr. Bonar Law, Mr. Churchill and the other distinguished political leaders with whom I was privileged to work for so many years in cordiality and good fellowship.

As Lord Grey (or as he then was, Sir Edward Grey) was among those who played a decisive part in the movements and occurrences

* The late Viscount Grey of Fallodon.

that led to the War, it is necessary to an understanding of my narrative that I should give a frank estimate of his qualities. His tenure of the crucial office of Foreign Secretary constituted an essential part of what happened, and his personality was distinctly one of the elements that contributed to the great catastrophe. I cannot, therefore, leave out my impressions of his character in my tale of events. It would not be worth while doing so—it would not be fair to my readers—unless I gave a frank analysis of the man who strove honestly to avert war but failed, and said something of the characteristics and shortcomings that were largely responsible for that failure. I appreciate the imperative duty of not allowing any irrelevant considerations to influence judgment. For that reason in my character sketches of political personages I have sternly repressed every tendency to partisan bias.

The public know less of Sir Edward Grey than of any conspicuous statesman of his time. His reputation is therefore on a purely conjectural foundation. Sir Edward Grey's position in public life was always entirely different from that which Mr. Asquith established for himself. The latter had neither rank nor wealth to help him along. He won his way to Premiership entirely by superb talent and parliamentary achievement. No Prime Minister in history—with the notable exceptions of Gladstone and Disraeli—possessed a better mental equipment for a political career. Sir Edward Grey had high intelligence but of a more commonplace texture. It was reflected in his speeches, which were clear, correct and orderly, but were characterised by no distinction of phrase or thought. His handling of foreign affairs was of the same conventional type. His influence was derived from other sources. He had qualities, largely of appearance, manner and restraint, which gave the impression of the " strong, silent man " whom the generation brought up on Carlyle earnestly sought, and, when they thought they had discovered him, fervently adored. In the War and post-War days of Clemenceau, Foch, Lenin, Mussolini, Roosevelt and Hitler—all talkers—that legend has become a little mildewed. The strongest men of history have never been silent. One of the strongest—Napoleon—could on occasion even be garrulous. Just before 1914 the vogue of the taciturn was still prevalent and no man profited as much by it as Grey. His striking physiognomy with the thin lips, the firmly closed mouth, and the chiselled features gave the impression of cold hammered steel. Add to this exterior the reticence of speech and the calm level utterance on the rare occasions when he spoke, and you were led to expect imperturbable strength in an emergency. He did not command the flaming phrase that illumines but sometimes also scorches and leaves behind an irritating burn. On the other hand he possessed to perfection that correctitude of phrase and demeanour which passes for—and sometimes is—diplomacy, and that serene flow of unexceptionable diction which is apt to be reckoned as statesmanship until a crisis comes to put these urbanities to the test.

Apart from these attributes, Grey's unique position was due to the care with which he kept almost entirely out of the clash of Party conflicts, and never measured his prowess against the formidable gladiators who held the arena in his time. It is not that he was less contentious than Mr. Asquith: for Mr. Asquith was the least contentious of politicians. He shrank from the combat until duty forced him into it. But he never failed then to play a redoubtable part in the front of the fight whatever the hazard. He was therefore subjected to every kind of assault fair and foul to which all active politicians are liable from exasperated adversaries. On the other hand, although Sir Edward Grey's uneasy attitude towards all his various leaders in turn proved him to be temperamentally fractious, he was fortunate throughout his political career in avoiding any trial of dialectical strength or skill with the deadly swordsmen who held the arena during his political life. Even when he was busily negotiating faction inside his Party he preferred to remain behind the lines, leaving the actual fighting to Lord Rosebery, Mr. Asquith, and Mr. Haldane. He thus succeeded in attaining high position in Party Governments without incurring any of the risks of active engagement in Party struggles. The only office he ever held was by tradition deemed to be immune from the slings and arrows of partisan warfare. In opposition he substantially confined his sparring activities to impartial comments on foreign affairs. His administration in office and his allotted function out of office alike were therefore not subjected to the fierce onslaughts that test the quality of political leaders. His face was never disfigured by any blows received in action, for he consistently shunned the political battlefield. He was specially fitted to discharge the duties of an office administered under such tranquil conditions with a dignity and grace which appealed to all Parties alike. Hence the unique position of immunity from severe criticism which he had always enjoyed.

In the policy which led up to our participation in the War, Sir Edward Grey, amongst British statesmen, played the leading part. His navigation of foreign waters was not seriously challenged. Whether he could have steered Europe clear of the rocks must always be a matter of conjecture and inference from the facts. Men who are at all interested in that aspect of the problem will for some time draw differing conclusions. I am inclined to believe that the verdict of posterity will be adverse to his handling of the situation.

Of one thing there can be no doubt; he failed calamitously in his endeavours to avert the Great War. As to Sir Edward Grey's hesitations during the fateful days when the thunderclouds were deepening and rapidly darkening the sky, I have endeavoured to give an accurate summary of the facts. They tell their own tale of a pilot

c*

whose hand trembled in the palsy of apprehension, unable to grip the levers and manipulate them with a firm and clear purpose. He was pursuing his avowed policy of waiting for public opinion to decide his direction for him. He reminded me of a Chairman of Committees whom I knew in the tumultuous days of the 1892-95 Parliament. It was peculiarly a Parliament that demanded firmness as well as fairness in the occupant of the Chair. Mr. Mellor was an able, cultured and upright man of gentlemanly exterior and demeanour, who would have been acclaimed by all parties as an ideal Chairman in quiet times. But the Home Rule Parliament of 1892-95 was the most tempestuous I have seen, and there Mr. Mellor's suavity and judicial courtesy were a pitiable sight. I can hear him now, rising in his place and looking at neither side lest it be suggested that he was accusing one or other of being responsible, and calling out in an appealing but not compelling voice: " Order, Order! " Sir Edward Grey's impartial but weak and uncompelling appeals to the raging nations of Europe to keep the peace always recall this parliamentary incident to my memory. In the din he was barely heard—he certainly was not heeded. Had he warned Germany in time of the point at which Britain would declare war— and wage it with her whole strength—the issue would have been different. I know it is said that he was hampered by the divisions in the Cabinet. On one question, however, there was no difference of opinion—the invasion of Belgium. He could at any stage of the negotiations have secured substantial unanimity amongst his colleagues on that point. At the very worst there would have been only two resignations, and those would have followed our entry into war, whatever the issue upon which it was fought. The assent of all the Opposition leaders was assured, and thus in the name of a united people he could have intimated to the German Government that if they put into operation their plan of marching through Belgium they would encounter the active hostility of the British Empire. And he could have uttered this warning in sufficient time to leave the German military authorities without any excuse for not changing their dust-laden plans. When the ultimatum was actually delivered, war had already broken out between Germany and her neighbours, and the German staff were able with some show of reason to inform the Kaiser that it was then too late to alter their arrangements without jeopardising the German chance of victory. As a matter of fact, the Kaiser was even then anxious, in order to avoid a conflict with us. to divert his forces from the Belgian frontier, and turn their faces towards the East. Von Moltke gave him the answer which I have already indicated.

It was a temperamental failure. Grey's mind was not made for prompt action. It is reported of the late Sir Hugh Bell, the great northern industrial magnate, who was a colleague of Sir Edward

Grey for years on the N.E. Railway, that he once said of him: " Grey is a good colleague because he never takes any risks: and he is a thoroughly bad colleague for the same reason." That saying explains why he did not take his stand on Belgium in time to give those who dreaded war in Germany a chance of reconsidering their plans in time. He would not take the risk involved in making such a bold declaration. He was still hoping that war could be averted by quieter and more conventional methods. He altogether lacked that quality of audacity which makes a great Minister.

His Arbitration Treaty with America was a notable event. The rest of his big efforts came to naught. His Balkan Settlement in 1913 fell to pieces as soon as it left our shores. His London Convention was luckily rejected, for had it been in operation during the War, it would have deprived us of our most effective weapon against Germany. He failed to keep Turkey, and afterwards Bulgaria, out of the War. His stiff and formal beckonings to them to cross over to our side could only provoke ridicule. There were many obvious expedients—including the sending of a special envoy to Turkey and Bulgaria who would be empowered to promise financial support—that he might have employed to keep both or either out of the War. He resorted to none of them. These last two failures, which a more strenuous or resourceful Foreign Minister would have converted into success prolonged the War by years, and very nearly caused the defeat of the Allies. His advice to Greece in 1914 not to join forces with the Allies was a calamity which cost us the Gallipoli Peninsula, and conduced to the overthrow of Serbia. He hesitated and fumbled in his negotiations to bring Italy into the War. As Luigi Villari says in his interesting and illuminating book, " The War on the Italian Front ": " The negotiations had been shilly-shallying for months." Had it not been that Grey had taken a few weeks' holiday and left Mr. Asquith—who was quite capable of coming to bold decisions—in charge of the Foreign Office in his absence, Italy might have sulked at the cold, critical treatment accorded her advances. In a few days Mr. Asquith brushed aside trivialities and brought the negotiations to a stage that led to a speedy decision. Had he not done so, what would have happened to the Allies? The Austrian Armies could have concentrated their whole strength on Russia, and that great country would have succumbed in 1915 to the joint attack of Germany and Austria. Throughout, Grey mistook correctitude for rectitude.

Sir Edward Grey belonged to the class which, through heredity and tradition, expects to find a place on the magisterial bench to sit in judgment upon and above their fellow-men, before they ever have any opportunity to make themselves acquainted with the tasks and trials of mankind—and some of them preserve those magisterial airs through life. They are remote from the hard work of the community.

They take it for granted.   The men drawn from that class who attained pre-eminence, like Palmerston, Randolph Churchill, Salisbury and Balfour, threw themselves into the arduous conflicts of politics and fought their way to the top, giving and taking on the way the blows that hammer character.   Sir Edward Grey stepped into generalship without ever doing any soldiering—not a good training for facing real danger.   It was all right when things went smoothly, and all you had to do was to put forward a soldierly appearance on parade.   It is a different thing when you are suddenly confronted with the greatest and most deadly diplomatic struggle ever seen between great nations.   The conflicts of politics are as good a discipline and hardening for the troubles of an official career as war is for the military leader.   The veteran who never fought a battle may escape the perils of shot and shell through which his comrades have passed, but he also misses the experience which would be useful to him when at last he finds himself thrown into action.

He was the most insular of our statesmen, and knew less of foreigners through contact with them than any Minister in the Government.   He rarely, if ever, crossed the seas.   Northumberland was good enough for him, and if he could not get there and needed a change, there was his fishing lodge in Hampshire.   This was a weakness—and it was a definite weakness in a Foreign Secretary, and especially in a Foreign Secretary with no imagination—which accounted for some of his most conspicuous failures.   He had no real understanding of foreigners—I am not at all sure that for this purpose he would not include Scotland, Ireland and Wales as foreign parts. Moreover, when a conference in some foreign capital might have saved the situation, his dislike of leaving England stood in the way. When he suggested a Conference of Ambassadors of the Four Powers a few days before the War, he proposed that it should be held in London.   I shall point out later on how this egotistic insularity prevented the summoning of a conference which might, and I think would, at that stage have brought Bulgaria on to the Allied side.   The ideal Foreign Secretary would be a cross between a recluse and a tramp, e.g., between Sir Edward Grey and Mr. Ramsay MacDonald.

A Cabinet which was compelled by political and economic exigencies to concentrate its energies on domestic problems left the whole field of foreign affairs to Sir Edward Grey.   Anyone reading with care and impartiality the record of the way in which he missed his opportunities must come to the conclusion that he lacked the knowledge of foreign countries and the vision, imagination, breadth of mind and that high courage, bordering on audacity, which his immense task demanded.

CHAPTER IV

THE FINANCIAL CRISIS

1. HOW WE SAVED THE CITY

THE political situation naturally did not develop without immediate and violent reaction on the inherently unstable financial equilibrium of the whole world, which is maintained by perhaps the most sensitive organisation devised by man; and the financial crisis which marked the outbreak of the War began some days before hostilities actually commenced. This was inevitable, because finance, or indeed the conduct of business operations of every nature, is based on successful anticipation and the ability to foresee and to discount or prepare for coming conditions. It was in July, 1914, before the Austrian ultimatum was presented, that uneasiness showed itself on the bourses of the world, when Vienna, Berlin, and Paris commenced to sell securities to an unusual extent. These transactions were for the most part effected in New York, where the stream of orders to sell quickly grew into a torrent. On the 27th, after diplomatic relations between Austria-Hungary and Serbia had been broken off, the volume of selling became such that the foreign exchange market in New York gave way under the unprecedented pressure to remit to Europe the proceeds of sales. From New York this breakdown spread to other foreign exchanges generally and was, in fact, the immediate cause of the world financial crisis. It affected this country to a special degree, since London was the financial centre of the world, and more sensitive than any other capital to disturbances in the complex credit system through which international economic relations function. The business of London as a financial centre depends for its smooth working upon the punctual payments by foreign debtors of the money owing to British creditors. This is particularly the case where liability of the debtors arises out of bills of exchange " accepted " on their behalf by the creditors, so much so that mercantile tradition, embodied everywhere in law, insists on the prompt payment of a bill of exchange on maturity. This special obligation, indeed, is considered paramount; and default is looked upon as a deadly sin. And every accepting house which accepts a bill and assumes the obligation implied by it on behalf of a foreign trader does so on the understanding that the latter will provide the necessary funds in good time.

London was not the only but easily the first of all the " accepting " cities of the world. The crackle of a bill on London with the signature of one of the great accepting houses was as good as the ring of gold in any port throughout the civilised world. A long experience maturing into a sure instinct taught these commercial financiers what to endorse and what to reject. When I asked the Governor of the Bank, Sir Walter Cunliffe, how he knew which bills were safe to approve, he replied, " I smell them." When the delicate financial cobweb was likely to be torn into shreds by the rude hand of war, London was inevitably thrown into a panic. The sudden paralysis of the foreign exchanges and of the London money market made it impossible for the very numerous foreign traders whose bills had been accepted in London to acquire money in London—wherewith to meet their obligations of this nature—in exchange for the money which they possessed in their own countries. In the aggregate the liabilities of this type amounted to hundreds of millions of sterling. If there were a general default it followed that the accepting houses would fail to pay bills upon which the whole business of the discount market depended, and which were among the most important assets of the London banks. In the last week of July, therefore, there was every prospect of such a crash in London as had never been known. The position of the banks, upon whose continued operation depends the supply of the means of payment in all business transactions, was also menaced from another direction. So soon as it became possible for the proceeds of the sale of securities to New York to be remitted to Europe, the pressure of sales was diverted to the London Stock Exchange, and there naturally followed a great depreciation in prices of stock all round. Though it was possible for the banks to withstand the depreciation of the investments they themselves owned, it was another matter when the solvency of the very large number of borrowers on the security of stocks was endangered. Thus, during the week, everything contributing, prices continued to move in a vicious circle of depreciation. So far there had been no real panic, the difficult situation which had arisen being due almost entirely to the inability of other nations to meet their liabilities. Though in this particular I do not think the actual course of events had been generally anticipated, something of the kind had been foreseen by the Sub-Committee of the Committee of Imperial Defence which considered the question of Trading with the Enemy in 1911 and 1912, and was referred to in its report.* The declaration of war by Austria precipitated matters. The outlook on that day was so serious that Mr. Montagu, the Financial Secretary to the Treasury, collected together a number of financial and business men to meet me at luncheon to discuss the situation.

* Report of Proceedings of the Standing Sub-Committee of the C.I.D. on Trading with the Enemy, Sept. 1912, pp. 8 and 9.

On Friday, 31st, the London Stock Exchange was closed, all the other stock exchanges except that of New York and the official market in Paris having closed the previous day.

Up to this point the Government, though keeping in close touch with developments in the City and watching events, had refrained from any action. But on Friday the Bank of England, which had this time felt the pressure for several days, found its reserve position seriously weakened and raised the bank rate (which had already been raised from 3 per cent. to 4 per cent.) to 8 per cent. Next day the Governor of the Bank applied to me as Chancellor of the Exchequer for permission to exceed the fiduciary issue of the notes prescribed by the Bank Charter Act 1844. This request was granted in a letter signed by the Prime Minister and myself, modelled on the precedents of 1847, 1857, and 1866, when a similar course was forced on the Government. As permission had, on those occasions, been made conditional upon no discounts or advances being granted at less than 10 per cent., the bank rate was raised to that figure. On this day, though no panic was shown by the public, there were unusual demands for gold on the Bank of England on the part of people seeking to cash the notes supplied to them by their own banks.

It was fully realised, of course, that increasing the issue of notes was a first step to ease the immediate situation in one direction only, and that it did nothing really to relieve the accepting houses or the Stock Exchange. But the two days, Sunday, 2nd, and Monday, 3rd August, which happened to be a Bank Holiday, gave a breathing space, and nearly the whole of Sunday was taken up in conferences at the Treasury, at which the situation was reviewed and a policy formulated. During these discussions, in addition to the help of Sir John Bradbury, the able permanent head of the Treasury, and of other permanent officials, I had the advantage of the advice of Lord Reading and Sir George Paish.

The outcome of our deliberations was a decision that the next step to be taken should be one calculated to relieve the accepting houses; and a proclamation was issued that evening granting a moratorium of one month to the acceptors of bills. This emergency measure obviously afforded no help to the banks or the discount houses. In fact, it ratified and consolidated a position which was detrimental, especially to the latter, in so much as it definitely froze up their chief liquid assets.

Partly in consequence of this, many of the leading representatives of these two financial interests and of trade generally met together to consider the situation from their point of view. After sitting till 2 a.m. on Monday, this conference formulated certain resolutions which were forwarded to the Government. To one of their recommendations effect was given on the 3rd, when it was announced that the 4th, 5th, and 6th August would be additional Bank Holidays.

This was done in order to obtain a further respite and to gain time to devise measures appropriate to the situation; but there was some doubt as to its advisability, owing to the fear that the cash circulated during the holidays might be accumulated by the trading community, and not be passed to the banks where it would be put into circulation again. On the same day an Act was passed through all its stages in both Houses regularising the proclamation in regard to a moratorium and giving the Government power to declare a general moratorium.

These three holidays were some of the busiest and most anxious days I ever spent. I had summoned a conference composed of Ministers and other officials and some of the leading bankers and traders, which sat morning and afternoon under my chairmanship. Ultimate decisions had to be taken by me subject to consent and if necessary revision by the Cabinet in so unprecedented a situation, where a mistake might injure the credit and confidence so essential to full strength and use of " the sinews of war." I resolved to consult every person whose ability, knowledge and experience would assist me in coming to the right conclusion. Mr. (later Sir) Austen Chamberlain, the Chancellor of the Exchequer in the preceding Unionist Government, was, amongst others, invited by me to the Allied War Conferences and assisted in the deliberations. This was an unusual, if not an unprecedented step to take; but the situation warranted any measures that might help, however novel. I well remember Mr. Chamberlain's surprise when I asked him in the House of Commons if he could give us the benefit of his experience and knowledge, and the prompt manner in which he placed himself entirely at our disposal. During the morning of the 5th, indeed, when I was obliged to leave the conference to attend the Cabinet, Mr. Chamberlain took my place as chairman; and so was brought about the unique situation of a member of the Opposition presiding at a Government Conference, a foretaste of the Coalition. I gladly acknowledge the value of the service he rendered in helping to unravel the complexities of the financial crisis and to succour those who had been caught in the tangle. He had that admixture of experience, authority, common sense and courage which is so essential in an emergency. A point which impressed me specially at the beginning of our discussions was the difficulty of reconciling the interests of the different sections of the banking community. Nevertheless, during the whole of our deliberations I was most ably backed up and advised in my position as chairman by all my colleagues, of whom five notable members have since died, i.e., Lord Cunliffe, Governor of the Bank of England, Sir Austen Chamberlain, Sir Edward Holden, Chairman of the London City and Midland Bank, Mr. Huth Jackson, and Lord St. Aldwyn. It was the first time I had been brought into direct contact with the latter since 1891, when as Sir Michael Hicks-Beach he piloted the Tithe Bill

through the House of Commons. The late Sir Samuel Evans and
I fought it for several nights. Sir Michael was a consummate
Parliamentarian. He had a reputation for explosive irascibility in
his private dealings, but in the House of Commons he was a model
of suavity and address. He was chosen by the distracted and specially
vocal financiers as their chief spokesman at these Treasury
Conferences, where he handled his duties with all his old tact and
mastery.

Our labours were not completed till the 6th August, the last day
of the holidays, but we had advanced far enough by the 5th for me,
on that day, to give the House of Commons an interim account of
our activities and recommendations, and after announcing that steps
had already been taken to suspend the Bank Act, to state definitely
that it had been decided not to suspend specie payments. The latter
decision, which marked the main difference between our treatment
of the situation and that adopted by other countries, was one which
in fact did greatly help us to recover financial normality, because
it tended towards a restoration of confidence which was so vitally
necessary at the moment. In accordance with this view, I made an
appeal to the public to refrain on patriotic grounds from attempting
to hoard gold, and accentuated the great part that finance was going
to play in the struggle upon which we were entering. In order to
deal with the need for currency, I explained that the Government
was about to issue Government notes of the value of £1 and 10s., and
that though the preparation and printing of these notes in the short
time available entailed an immense effort, the Treasury officials and
others concerned had made such progress that three million pounds
would be ready at the end of the holidays, after which notes would
be available at the rate of five million pounds a day. Postal orders
were temporarily to be legal tender. Another announcement I was
able to make, which was a sign of the strength of the Bank of England
and would tend to reassure the business community, was that after
the holidays the bank rate would be reduced from 10 per cent. to
6 per cent. I explained the reasons for the limited moratorium
which had already been announced and that a more general
moratorium extending for a month would be proclaimed, during
which period bankers would pass cheques through the clearing
houses as usual, and would supply cash to their customers for the
payment of wages and the normal requirements of daily life. Mr.
Chamberlain also spoke with a view to allaying alarm. As a matter
of fact, the 10 per cent. bank rate was in actual operation on one day
only, Saturday, the 1st August, before the holidays intervened.

In the House next day I introduced the Currency and Bank Notes
Bill legalising the issue of the new currency notes and the suspension
of the Bank Act, and it passed through all its stages in both Houses
during the day. As the conference had by then completed its

deliberations, I was also able to give further details of the extended moratorium, which was announced that day in what was known as the First General Proclamation. Not the least of the numerous anxieties weighing on the Government at this time of general upheaval and stress was this problem of establishing the financial stability of the nation itself, and as the responsible Minister I awaited with great anxiety the moment when business should again start, to learn the outcome of our experiments. It was with great relief, therefore, that on Friday, 7th, I was able, after the banks had reopened, to communicate to the Commons the favourable nature of the reports on the banking situation which had come in from all parts of the country, to the effect that there was no panic and that cash was being freely paid in.

Nevertheless, though much had been done, we had by no means reached the end of our difficulties. As I have said, the moratorium had originally been instituted to save the accepting houses from bankruptcy, but it was no more than a temporary expedient and it did not settle what was going to happen after the month had elapsed —still a real and very urgent question. So long as the accepting houses were threatened with bankruptcy the position of the banks and discount houses which held bills drawn upon them was precarious; and credit remained paralysed. The first remedial measure taken was in the form of an arrangement announced on the 12th August, by which the Bank of England undertook to discount pre-moratorium bills and to relieve the holders of the bills of all liability in respect of them. The bills so discounted amounted during the next few weeks to over a hundred million pounds, and the Bank, of course, could only take them subject to a guarantee against loss, being in reality merely the agent of the Government in the matter. This was a bold and important step, for by it the Government, in order to re-establish the foreign trade situation through the speedy rehabilitation of the discount market, temporarily assumed immense liabilities; and its action was generally approved. But sweeping though the measure was and valuable as was the relief it afforded, it did not accomplish all that was required, since the accepting houses still remained liable for the bills at maturity, and being still uncertain of their own solvency hesitated to enter upon fresh business, the very course which was essential to the re-establishment of the situation. In other words, the normal machinery for financing international trade, which was so vital a factor in our economic existence, was not working. To help the accepting houses, therefore, the Government took a further step. By an arrangement which was made public on the 5th September, the Bank of England, still with the indispensable guarantee, undertook to advance funds to acceptors to pay off the bills at maturity, and to postpone until a year after the end of the War any claim against them for repayment. By this means time was given to the accepting houses to recover the sums due from their clients, and they were enabled to proceed and carry on business free from embarrassment.

Thus at last was the problem of the pre-moratorium bills solved, and the position of the accepting houses consolidated. But we were not yet out of the wood. There were several other sources of danger to be dealt with before the moratorium could be removed. The Courts (Emergency Powers) Acts, passed on the 31st August, relieved the hardships of debtors who could not pay owing to war conditions. Schemes, into details of which I need not here enter, were also devised to meet the difficulties arising out of advances to the Stock Exchange and of debts due from foreign countries to British traders. The next important point was both a grave and difficult one to settle and occasioned long and anxious discussion, for there was room for great difference of opinion. The moratorium had undoubtedly saved the situation during the height of the crisis, but, once it should have served its purpose and helped to restore the normal flow of international business, its continuation could only be detrimental in many ways. The trend of events during August and September, however, had furnished considerable experience upon which to form a judgment, and at the end of the latter month it was decided that the moratorium should come to an end on the 4th November. The adoption of this course, which proved to be the correct one, was very largely due to the advice of Lord Reading and Sir George Paish, by both of whom it was urgently pressed. There was another matter which was of no slight moment to us as Ministers. In the various schemes which had been improvised against time and carried out during the crisis, the guarantee of the Government, it must be remembered, had been given on our sole responsibility. It was imperative, therefore, that Parliamentary authority should at the earliest opportunity be given to our actions. This was done by the Government (War Obligations) Act, which received the Royal Assent on 27 November, and was in essence an act of indemnity for the Ministers.

Thus were matters tided over. During the worst part of it, whether it be regarded as a week or ten days, which covered the period whilst Europe changed from a state of unstable peace definitely to war, the City of London could not guess how near to ruin it was. But it suspected the worst, and many of its leaders were too overwhelmed by the great dangers to which they saw themselves exposed to be able to think with their accustomed composure and to preserve unshaken their wonted touch. Financiers in a fright do not make an heroic picture. One must make allowances, however, for men who were millionaires with an assured credit which seemed as firm as the globe it girdled, and who suddenly found their fortunes scattered by a bomb hurled at random from a reckless hand. The strongest and sturdiest figure amongst them was Sir Edward Holden, with the brogue and stout heart of Lancashire in all his utterances. He stood out amongst all these money barons. Not unnaturally the Ministers and officials, who could afford to take a more detached and impersonal view of the affairs of the country, were better able to perceive what was required from the larger point of view and to act immediately. One great difference between our policy and that of other nations was that we definitely endeavoured as soon as possible to re-establish our economic system on a normal basis, a task which was frankly abandoned by most of the other governments. And this we succeeded to a very great extent in effecting immediately. In fact so successful was our recovery that the pendulum perhaps swung too much in the opposite direction and led on the part of some to the attitude expressed by the catchword " business as usual." This, though valuable at the moment of doubt to help re-establish confidence, later on led to an entire misconception in many quarters of the effort demanded by what proved to be a struggle for our very existence.

Throughout these conferences I found Lord Reading's aid invaluable. His knowledge of finance, his mastery of figures, his dexterity and his calm and sure judgment helped at many turns.

The nation passed through the great financial crisis in a marvellous way. There was no sign of panic on the part of the public in a situation that for us as a nation was unprecedented. In this emergency the main duties of the Government were to keep things going and to restore normality as quickly as possible by prompt and wise and, if necessary, drastic action, and meanwhile to maintain the community as a whole in that state of composure which is barren soil for the breeding of panic. In doing the former the Government and the Treasury were greatly assisted by the steadfast attitude of the Governor of the Bank of England, whose wise, far-sighted and broad point of view on the national aspect of affairs, and whose massive strength were a source of comfort and good counsel. His sense of humour, which he concealed under a dour and almost surly countenance, was an encouragement in those trying days. He was fond of little practical jokes to lighten the dismal anxieties of our common burden. He affected a deep resentment at our issuing the £1 notes as Treasury and not Bank of England Notes. He scoffed at the inferiority of our issue in the quality of its paper and its artistry as compared with the crisp £5 note of the Great Bank over which he presided. (The first issue of Treasury Notes was a temporary one and very rough.) I can see his impressive figure with its rolling gait, coming one morning through the door of the Treasury Board Room. He had a scornful look on his face. He came up to my desk with a mumbled greeting, solemnly opened the portfolio he always carried, and pulled out a bedraggled £1 Treasury Note, dirty and barely legible. He said: " Look at that. It came into the bank yesterday in that condition. I told you the paper was no good —far better to have left it to us." He had scrubbed the note in order to reduce it to this condition of effacement for the pleasure of ragging me. I told him so and he laughed. His manner was not propitiatory to strangers, but when you got to know him he was a genial, kindly man, and I liked him. I relied on his shrewdness, his common sense and instinct.

He was a man of very few words. I cannot recall a single sentence he uttered at any of these numerous conferences. What he said was half whispered in my ear. He accompanied me later on to Paris to meet M. Bark, the Russian Finance Minister, and M. Ribot, the French Finance Minister, at a conference to discuss the subject of financing Russian contracts in America. When a question arose as to a transhipment of gold the Governor of the Bank of France expressed himself with great fluency. I then said: " The Governor of the Bank of England will state the British view on the subject." He rose slowly, and after a few preliminary puffs he said: " We do not mean to part with our gold," and then subsided into his seat.

During his visit we drove to Boulogne to catch the boat. On our way I was anxious to make a detour through Bethune, which I was eager to see. It was occasionally bombarded, but the risk was trifling. However, the Governor would not consent to my proposal. I was surprised, for he was a man of undoubted courage. He said: " A predecessor of mine was killed visiting the trenches at Namur. But he was there on business with the King, and the city said, ' Poor fellow! ' But if I were hit in the stomach at Bethune they would all say, ' D——d fool—what business had he to go there?' " That was conclusive, and I never saw Bethune.

To revert to our financial arrangements in the first few weeks of the war: The risks of every course were undoubtedly great. But decisions had of necessity to be prompt. Panic had to be anticipated at every turn. It was no time for sitting indefinitely in Council in order to evolve the perfect course of action which would reduce to a minimum the eventual cost to the National Exchequer. The possible consequences of delay or of the adoption of inadequate measures, which did not at once restore public confidence, were so appalling that immediate action was imperatively demanded. In the result the Government loss was negligible. We guaranteed about £500,000,000 of securities in respect of debts incurred across the seas—some of these on enemy security. In due course it was all gathered in except a few millions. In this aspect the problem before us was akin to that presented at the same time by the State Insurance of Shipping, though in the latter case it was only necessary to put into operation a scheme, worked out under the auspices of the Committee of Imperial

Defence, and all ready to be applied. I had gratifying proof, indeed, that the share I had taken in the policy of the Government met with the approval and gained the confidence of a section of the business and financial world which had not previously regarded my efforts as Chancellor of the Exchequer with any favour.

Amongst those whose advice I sought was Lord Rothschild. My previous contact with him was not of a propitiatory character. He had led the opposition in the City to my scheme for Old Age Pensions and to my Budget proposals in 1909, and I had assailed him in phrases which were not of the kind to which the head of the great house of Rothschild had hitherto been subjected. My attack was strongly resented by all his friends. However, this was no time to allow political quarrels to intrude into counsel. The nation was in peril. I invited him to the Treasury for a talk. He came promptly. We shook hands. I said, "Lord Rothschild, we have had some political unpleasantness." He interrupted me: "Mr. Lloyd George, this is no time to recall those things. What can I do to help?" I told him. He undertook to do it at once. It was done.

When he died, shortly afterwards, I attended his funeral. On a grey, damp morning the streets to the cemetery were lined with poor Jews who were there to pay their humble tribute of reverence to the great Prince in Israel, who never forgot the poor and the wretched amongst his people.

In the long run not only did the measures undertaken achieve their object, but the liabilities incurred by the Government at that time did not result in appreciable loss. Having, after an interval of eighteen years, carefully considered all the circumstances, I am of opinion that it was the bold policy of the Government, relying on the strength of the national character, which enabled the City of London to recover quickly from the stunning blow at the outbreak of war, and to continue to pulsate and fulfil one of its functions as the economic heart of the whole Empire of which it was the centre.

2. SUPPLEMENTARY BUDGET AND THE FIRST WAR LOAN

On 17th November, 1914, I introduced my first War Budget. Virtually it was my only War Budget, for although on 4th May, 1915, I made the customary Budget statement, shortly before vacating the Exchequer to undertake the office of Minister of Munitions, I did not on that date introduce any new features or modifications of taxation. My reasons were twofold: In the first place, the additional taxes I had already imposed in November, 1914, were only beginning to fructify, and I pointed out that while additions to taxations would be necessary, we should have to wait till the autumn to decide what they should be; and in the second place, the only extra charges I had in mind in May for immediate application, were on alcoholic liquors; and the storm of opposition which these encountered made it impossible to introduce them at that time without raising most violent and undesirable political controversy. This is a story which I deal with more fully in a subsequent section when discussing the drink problem in the War.

The real 1915 Budget was that introduced in September by my successor, Mr. M'Kenna, and it was memorable for the imposition of the M'Kenna Duties, which in subsequent years were to play so important a part in political controversy, and were the prelude to a revolutionary change in our fiscal system.

By November, 1914, it was obvious that the additional expenditure caused by the War would far outrun anything provided for by the peace-time Budget I had introduced in the spring. Already on 8th August the House of Commons had voted the Government a credit of £100,000,000 for War purposes, and it was now necessary to ask it for a further credit of more than twice that amount. If the War were to continue far into 1915, much greater sums still would be required.

The issue before the country, and particularly before myself as Chancellor of the Exchequer, was whether these huge sums should be raised entirely by loans, and added in full to the National Debt, or whether we should aim at paying our way as far as possible by current taxation, and thus reduce the debt burden to be handed on to the next generation.

I took the view that the immense spending of the Government was bound to cause a very considerable inflation of our currency. War-time demands would stimulate our industries to unprecedented activity; and in addition, the closing down of the international commerce of Central Europe and the crippling of the industrial capacities of France and Belgium, would, for the time being, mean that a heavy extra demand for goods by other countries would fall on us. The result would be a much bigger circulation of money here, and it would be far easier to pay for the War while this state of things lasted, than later on, when trade depression supervened and deflation removed our spare cash.

Accordingly, when Parliament reassembled in November, 1914, for an unexpected Autumn Session, and I laid before the House of Commons a proposal for a second vote of credit for £225,000,000, I introduced at the same time a supplementary Budget, with the object of raising a portion of this sum by additional taxation.

The additions were as follows: I doubled the income tax—raising it from 1s. 4d. to 2s. 8d. in the £. I also doubled the super-tax. Already I had in the spring introduced the graduation of this tax, making it range up from 5d. in the £ on income exceeding £3,000, to a maximum of 1s. 4d. on income in excess of £11,000. These charges I now doubled. The beer duty I raised from 7s. 9d. per barrel to 25s., and the tea duty from 5d. to 8d. per lb. On the other hand, as a compensation to publicans for the sharp restrictions on facilities for drinking which were being introduced, I cut down their licence duty—a concession involving about half a million.

The beer and tea duties went on, of course, at once. But the higher income and super-taxes only took effect for the final quarter of the current financial year. Had there been no additional taxation, the revenue realised in 1914-15 would have been below the estimate, through reduced yield of certain taxes and duties. As a result even of the short currency of these added levies, the 1914-15 revenue exceeded my estimate of May, 1914, by about 19½ millions. In a full year these extra taxes would produce upwards of £60,000,000 of additional revenue.

When I decided to frame a supplementary budget, I asked Mr. Austen Chamberlain, who had been Chancellor under the last Conservative administration, to co-operate with me in working out its details, in order that the party truce might be fully preserved in the matter. He accepted my invitation, and we entered on consultations; but before long he resigned his connection with the Government. This was not the outcome of any personal disagreement. Indeed, when making a statement on this matter in the House on 24th November, he declared: —

> " During the confidential conversations I have had with the Chancellor of the Exchequer and his colleagues since he invited me to discuss the details of his Budget with him, I could make no complaint whatever of the spirit with which the Right Honourable gentleman approached the questions with which we dealt, and I desire to state that he has looked on the questions which came before him as revenue questions pure and simple, and that he has not allowed his mind to be diverted by any ulterior object."

But Mr. Austen Chamberlain was in a difficult position when it came to the additional duties I proposed to levy on beer. The links between the Conservative Party and the " Trade " were very strong. As a representative of that party he could not possibly associate it in advance with proposals to more-than-treble the tax on beer. " Even as a compromise," he declared, he could not assume personal responsibility for such a measure.

The House of Commons, however, did not shrink from the beer taxes, and the Budget with its drastic additions to our fiscal imposts was passed speedily into law. Such complaisance may not strike us to-day as very wonderful, faced as we are by annual budgets which in a time of peace are four times as large. But the Britain of 1914 had no experience of such burdens, and would have been aghast at my suggestions had it not been for the moment too elevated by the enthusiasms of its war task.

In the course of my Budget speech of November, 1914, I made a statement which is not without interest to-day. Urging the importance of raising as much as possible of our war expenditure by immediate taxation, in place of leaving it all for repayment in future years, I predicted that immediately after the War there would be a short spell of booming industry, while here and abroad the deficits of goods which had been held up by the War were being made good. " But," I continued, " when that period is over we shall be face to face with one of the most serious industrial situations with which we have ever been confronted. We shall have exhausted an enormous amount of the capital of the world which would otherwise have been available for industries. Our purchasers, both here and abroad, will be crippled. Their purchasing power will have been depressed. Let us make no mistake. Great Britain will be confronted with some of the gravest problems with which it has ever been faced."

Unhappily, the last fifteen years have conspired to verify this prophecy all too thoroughly.

In bringing forward this supplementary Budget, I also announced the issue of the first War Loan. The vote of credit granted in August for the War had been for £100 million, and I was now asking for a fresh credit of £225 million. It was clear that further votes would before long be required. For the present, however, I contented myself with the proposal of a War Loan of a face value of £350,000,000. It was to be 3½ per cent. security, issued at 95, and thus yielding the Government £332½ million of actual cash. Of this total, £45 million were required for loans to our Allies and Dominions. The remainder would be used, along with the yield of the additional taxes imposed, for financing our own immediate war expenditure.

The loan was made redeemable at par in 1925-28. In view of its issue price of 95, its interest yield was approximately 3⅔ per cent. The whole loan was very quickly over-subscribed.

This was the only War Loan for which I was immediately responsible. The second War Loan was that issued on 21st June, 1915, by Mr. M'Kenna. It was for an unspecified amount (with an upper limit of £910 million), and consisted of stock issued at par, bearing interest at 4½ per cent. It brought in about £570 million of new money by the time the list was closed on 10th July, as well as Consols and other Government securities for conversion, to an amount equalling about £276,500,000 of the new War Loan stock.

Looking back, I cannot help regretting that Mr. M'Kenna should have thought it necessary to raise the interest rate of a Government loan to 4½ per cent. Maybe this corresponded to the price that was being offered in the money market for other gilt-edged securities. But in view of the increase in our nominal capital reserves due to war inflation and to the restriction of an overseas market for investment money which was also one of the effects of the War, there can be little doubt that the Government could have continued to obtain as much money as it required by voluntary investment, without raising its interest rate beyond the level of $3\frac{2}{3}$ per cent. at which my first loan had been negotiated. Investors would have had to take this, for lack of an alternative. And if they had been unwilling to do so, there would have been a clear and popular ground for the conscription of capital for war purposes—a step which would have been an appropriate corollary to the conscription of man-power which we were soon to introduce.

As it was, the adoption of the principle that the British Government had to pay the commercial rate for money needed to defend the country had a costly sequel. This principle governed the plans for the Third War Loan, for which arrangements were begun toward the end of 1916, and carried through in January, 1917, by Mr. Bonar Law, who had just replaced Mr. M'Kenna at the Exchequer. That loan was issued at 95, bearing interest at 5 per cent., and over £2,000 million was raised at this penal figure. The same rate governed subsequent borrowings, which by the end of the War had added a further £4,000,000,000 to our National Debt. It cost the country a dozen years of remorseless deflation and concomitant depression to bring interest rates down again to a level that would enable this vast sum to be reconverted to $3\frac{1}{2}$ per cent. Throughout the interval, not only was the country taxing itself to pay a sum ranging at one time as high as £100,000,000 a year more than it would otherwise have done, but the high yield of a gilt-edged Government security kept up rates all round, and made money dearer for all enterprises, industrial, commercial and national. It would be hard to estimate the sum total of the price paid by the nation in every department of affairs for the decision of Mr. M'Kenna in 1915 to increase the rate of interest paid by the Government on its war-time borrowings. His action had, no doubt, the fullest authorisation from the leading circles of banking and finance. But the country has since then had ample evidence that these circles are by no means to be reckoned as infallible advisers.

CHAPTER V

THE FIGHT FOR MUNITIONS

1. INTRODUCTORY

THE outbreak of war found this country totally unprepared for land hostilities on a Continental scale. Our traditional defence force has always been our Navy, and this weapon has been kept efficient and ready at all times. But our Army, mainly used for policing our widely scattered Empire, was a small, highly trained force of professional soldiers, excellent for their normal tasks, but lacking both the numbers and the equipment for large-scale fighting against European armies.

Unhappily, too, the War Office was hampered by a traditional reactionism. Its policy seemed ever to be that of preparing, not for the next war, but for the last one or the last but one. The Boer War found us still in the mentality of the Crimea, and the Great War caught our military thinkers planning for the next war under the conditions of the Alma in so far as these were modified by the irrelevant experiences of the African veldt. Unfortunately, they only remembered the lessons that were better forgotten because they were inapplicable, and forgot all the experiences by which they ought to have profited because they were a foretaste of the methods of future warfare. Todleben's famous earthworks had no meaning for them, nor had the trenches of Magersfontein and the Tugela, where our massed troops were slaughtered by riflemen they never saw. But the thin red line of Inkerman and the glorious charge which sabred the gunners at Balaclava, and the Boer horsemanship which rushed Methuen's camp at Klip's Drift dominated the military mind. Military imagination makes up in retentiveness what it misses in agility.

The man-power needed for our new armies was fortunately not dependent for its production on the unsympathetic organisation of the War Office. Lord Kitchener's outstanding name and fame constituted a great appeal, which was organised with expert efficiency and understanding by the agents of the two great political parties. From farm and village and city street young men thronged into the recruiting offices at the sound of Lord Kitchener's call to arms. The first half-million managed within the first month to press its way through the recruiting stations, and it speedily grew to a million, then to two, then three.   The immortal story has been told and retold, and it is not my business to tell it again.   In the magnitude and grandeur of the response it has no parallel in history.   Considering the fact that there were neither rifles, machine-guns, cannon nor mortars available for training, the dug-out officers and non-commissioned officers achieved wonders in the turning of their material into armies.

The equipment of these armies, however, is another story; and in so far as that equipment included the provision of munitions, that duty was eventually placed upon me.   The story is therefore mine to tell.

The whole business was at the outset jealously retained by the War Office in its own hands, even to the tailoring contracts.   The result was shortage, delays, misfits and muddles.

Happily for the world, the weapons of modern slaughter do not grow naturally.   They have to be designed and manufactured; and although Britain was the leading manufacturing country in the world, its industries were almost entirely concerned with the arts of peace.   It was deficient in machinery for the production of rifles, machine-guns and artillery especially of the heavier calibres.   Armament firms were few, and the methods of the national arsenals were obsolescent and primitive to a degree.   The Army Chiefs were mostly horsemen—Lord French and Sir Douglas Haig were both cavalrymen, and won their reputations as cavalry generals.   Lord Kitchener was a sapper.   His only experiences of war, however, would have left him with the impression that mobility counted more than weight and quantity of shell.

High-explosive shell, which the German forces were using against us with such shattering effect, was regarded up to the outbreak of war by our own Ordnance Department as being merely in the experimental stage, and the problem of a satisfactory filling and fuse for it had not be solved.   It had not been seriously and systematically investigated.   The War Office was obsessed with the importance of shrapnel.   It was the only artillery lesson of the Boer War which they remembered, and in September, 1914, our War Office Generals were still preparing to slug African kopjes with Boers hiding behind bushes or boulders.   It was the most useful shell in Africa.   Why not in Europe?   They had been criticised in 1900 because the supply was inadequate, they were not going to be caught and castigated this time.   Their mental arsenals had no room for anything but shrapnel.

As to heavy artillery, the regular establishment of the Army at the outbreak of war did not provide for anything beyond the 60-pounder.   The 4.7 was considered almost too cumbrous a weapon for the field.   There were a few specimens of six-inch howitzers in existence, of obsolescent pattern, and some six-inch guns, which could be gleaned here and there, partly from coastal forts. There was only one 9.2-inch howitzer just completed. There was very little ammunition for any of these heavy guns. Our old siege train guns were muzzle-loaders! It had been the official view of the General Staff that the tendency of field operations to approximate towards siege warfare, displayed in the Russo-Japanese fighting in Manchuria—the most recent example of modern war—should not be accepted as a general tendency, and they had made no plans or preparations for dealing with such a situation. The Japanese armies walked round the field defences of the Russians without attempting to destroy them or storm then, just as French did with his cavalry at Magersfontein. Why not in France? A trench hundreds of miles long from Switzerland to the sea, which you could not outflank, either on the right or the left, was beyond their limited vision.

Some of our old-fashioned six-inch howitzers arrived in France in time to be used in the battle of the Aisne, but even by the end of January, 1915, the British had only 24 of these weapons in the field, or one battery per corps—one-sixteenth the number that were being used against us by the Germans. And the Germans had shells for their howitzers; we had a very scanty ration for ours. The official allowance of machine-guns to our troops was two per battalion, and even this meagre dole was not available for our new armies during the first months of their service, although they were sent to fight against German forces equipped with 16 machine-guns per battalion. As to shells, the production of shell cases was absurdly inadequate, but such as it was it greatly exceeded the provision for filling the empty cases with explosives or for manufacturing fuses to detonate them. When I paid a visit to Woolwich Arsenal some months after the outbreak of the War, I found stacks of empty shells which were being slowly and tediously filled, one at a time, with ladles by hand from cauldrons of seething fluid. The production of the fuses for detonating the shells was governed by the same lack of imagination, and consequently there was a similar deficiency in output.

It was not so much a question of unpreparedness at the outbreak of war. No one before the War contemplated our raising armies aggregating hundreds of thousands of men for any war in which we were ever likely to be engaged. Our military arrangements with France never went beyond the dispatch of an Expeditionary Force of six divisions to support the French armies on their left flank. When the Cabinet decided to appeal for volunteers they only asked for a recruitment of 100,000. What followed that appeal exceeded the most sanguine anticipation. When the German armies overran Belgium and broke the French front, marching up to gates of Paris, the youth of Britain rolled up in such numbers that the whole idea of our contribution to the War was changed by this uprising of indignant valour. The Cabinet, excited by the spectacle to a fit of audacity, raised the limit of enlistment to 500,000. The flood did not take long to overflow even that limit.

No blame can, therefore, be attached to the War Office or its responsible heads for failing to have in store, at the outbreak of the War, a reserve of equipment and munitions for the hitherto undreamed-of forces we were compelled to raise and put into the field. But they cannot be held guiltless of mental obtuseness in their neglect to keep abreast of modern development in pattern of munitions and machinery for munition production, and still more of a most pitiable breakdown of initiative in facing the new task which confronted them, of bringing munition production up to the standard demanded by the actual conditions of warfare as they soon manifested themselves in the campaign of 1914.

Modern warfare, we discovered, was to a far greater extent than ever before a conflict of chemists and manufacturers. Man-power, it is true, was indispensable, and generalship will always, whatever the conditions, have a vital part to play. But troops, however brave and well led, were powerless under modern conditions unless equipped with adequate and up-to-date artillery (with masses of explosive shell), machine-guns, aircraft and other supplies. Against enemy machine-gun posts and wire entanglements the most gallant and best-led men could only throw away their precious lives in successive waves of heroic martyrdom. Their costly sacrifice could avail nothing for the winning of victory.

This question of munitions supply thus emerged as the crucial issue of the War. Before long it became clear that unless we could solve it, and solve it promptly, we were doomed to certain futility in this War.

2. FINANCE OF PRODUCTION

At the outbreak of the War my only connection with the problem of munitions supply was the responsibility, as Chancellor of the Exchequer, for finding money to pay the bills.

My instruction as to what the actualities of war were likely to be was confined to a visit which the Secretary of State for War (Mr. Haldane) invited me to pay with him to Army manœuvres in the vicinity of Hungerford in the summer of 1908. I was thrilled with the anticipation of viewing a battle, even although it was only a stage fight. I felt that, under such auspices, one would see something of what the terrible reality would be like. There were real soldiers, real rifles, bayonets, swords, cavalry, cannon, commanded by real generals who had fought more than once in real wars. Mr. Haldane and I were perched, with the staff of one of the opposing armies, on a hill which was defended by infantry supported by field guns. When some years later I saw the Messines Ridge and Kemmel

I realised with what prevision the General Staff had chosen the terrain for the military manœuvres of 1908. It was explained to us that the hill was to be attacked by a force not visible at the moment but which was expected soon to deploy from a valley about a mile off. It was an exciting moment when we saw the skirmishers of the enemy emerge from the defile, whence they were followed by masses of infantry spreading and swarming over the plain. The volleys fired by attackers and defenders and the roar of the cannon on both sides were deafening. This must be something like real war! The issue did not tremble long in the balance, for a regiment of cavalry hitherto hidden in the woods dashed out of cover, and, half-concealed by a heavy shower of rain which then fell providentially, galloped along to the foot of the hill, gallantly scrambled up the slopes in the face of shot and shell, reached the parapet, swept over our poor guns and captured the position. I felt then that I knew something of what our Generals expected the next war would be like. When Mr. Haldane asked me afterwards to find out of the Exchequer an additional sum for the provision of light guns I felt they were quite necessary to avert the possibility of such a catastrophe happening in a Continental war when the mounted hordes of the Continental armies attacked our Expeditionary Forces on the hills of Flanders. Machine-guns were too trivial a toy to be included in the schedule of fresh demands on the Exchequer. This interesting military experience came to my mind when eight years later I saw masses of cavalry ride up to the lines to storm the trenched and wired plateau of the Somme above Guinchy. I remembered the Hungerford manœuvres and I understood better than ever that a military obsession, however fantastic it may be, is stronger than death—than many deaths.

Let me state at the outset that neither at the outbreak of war nor at any subsequent period in its course was the provision of munitions hampered by failure to furnish the money for their purchase or production. On the contrary, I repeatedly made it clear that as far as the Treasury was concerned no obstacle would come from that quarter in providing every supply that could possibly aid us to victory. If the choice were between spending gold or British lives, I was ready to take the responsibility of calling on the nation to yield its last coin, provided it were wisely and effectively spent. Nor did the country itself ever hesitate to support this attitude.

On the 5th August, 1914, the day after the declaration of war, the House of Commons was invited by me to vote an initial sum of £100 million towards the cost. I let the War Office know that it could have whatever funds it needed to expedite supplies, and in September I took the further step of definitely setting aside a sum of £20 million and earmarking it as a fund to be drawn on to finance extensions of factories and works for the production of munitions. I must add that

D

the Master-General of Ordnance decided in his wisdom not to inform the trade at first of this provision, as is proved by the following extract from a minute by him, dated 2nd October, 1914: —

> " The Secretary of State told me on 30th September that the Cabinet had decided that day that the various firms supplying munitions of war were to be called upon to increase their plant so as to allow of large orders over and above those already placed to be executed in order that we should be able to obtain additional supplies of guns, rifles, ammunition, etc., in the same time if possible as those already ordered and promised, and that in addition our Allies should also be able to procure the same.
>
> He informed me that the Chancellor of the Exchequer had agreed to place twenty millions sterling at the disposal of the trade for the purpose of increasing their plant. . . .
>
> *It has been considered by me inadvisable at this stage to inform the trade that grants of money will be made,* as hitherto I have received no hint or notice of difficulties of that sort. . . ."

That last sentence illuminates the War Office horror at the thought of adopting to meet this unprecedented emergency any method not sanctioned by " pigeon-holed " tradition wrapped in red tape.

I soon realised that the ordinary methods of Treasury approval for expenditure were inapplicable to the exigencies of war and that to make orders for essential supplies dependent on discussions of every detail between the War Department and Treasury officials would delay and hamper action.

Pointing out that in the present emergency it was not possible to insist on the normal routine and Treasury control in regard to departmental commitments for contracts which now often had to include abnormal financial conditions, I suggested that throughout the War such contracts should be concluded without reference to the Treasury. The departmental heads in the War Office were thus given freedom to take full and immediate responsibility for whatever contracts they held necessary. I assented to this procedure all the more readily because there was installed at the War Office as its financial adviser an able Treasury official—Sir Charles Harris. Not in the whole public service could be found a more faithful and vigilant watchdog for the public money.

3.   RED TAPE AT THE WAR OFFICE

But although a financial *carte blanche* had thus been offered to the responsible authorities for all measures necessary to supply munitions, and although the needs of our troops at the front were urgent and terrible, the shortage of munitions continued and increased. The War Office neglected to utilise to the full its powers to remedy the lamentable shortage from which our armies were suffering so severely.

Admittedly the authorities were faced with an unprecedented situation. To cope with it, measures equally unprecedented were necessary. The gravamen of the charge against them is that they completely failed to show the resource and flexibility of mind requisite to grapple with that situation and to improvise those exceptional measures. The only defence they have been able to produce is the plea that the demands on them were out of all proportion to previous experience; that they strove to meet them through their traditional channels of supply; and that those channels became choked in the effort. But that was obvious from the outset. Their task should have been to increase those sources of supply in original ways available to us as one of the three greatest and most resourceful and adaptable manufacturing countries in the world. Any powers they sought for the purpose would instantly have been accorded to them by Parliament. They not only failed to do this; they put all kinds of obstacles, both at the outset and later on, in the way of everyone who tried to help them, or relieve them of some part of their burden.

Up to the beginning of the War the normal routine was for the Minister of War as the instrument of Government to decide what operations he would sanction. The Commander-in-Chief would notify him of his requirements for carrying out those operations. On the basis of this information the Master-General of Ordnance would decide what stores must be obtained, and would in turn inform the Director of Army Contracts, who would approach the recognised armament firms, and refer their quotations for consideration to the Financial Secretary of the War Office. After due discussion, a contract would eventually be placed.

As soon as the War started, however, the Financial Department, on the suggestion of the Treasury, informed the Director of Army Contracts that he need not refer quotations to them before closing contracts, so long as he let them know of all liabilities incurred. This should have considerably expedited procedure. I am inclined to believe that in practice this relaxation had the effect of increasing the delays. It turned out to be a psychological blunder. The explanation casts an interesting light on the limitations of Departmentalism. As long as the officer ordering the supplies had the check of scrutiny and sanction by the officer of another department, he put forward his requisitions boldly. His responsibility in the event of any accusation of extravagance was by this means shared if not altogether transferred. But now the whole undivided burden of decision was cast upon him. Responsibility to the strong is a stimulus—to the weak it is a palsy. There were many unpleasant memories lingering in the military mind of select committees and commissions appointed in past wars to investigate extravagant orders inefficiently executed. The Master-General of Ordnance hints that he felt most uneasy without the support of his customary financial strait-waistcoat, and complains that it " threw increased responsibility for the expenditure on the shoulders of the Master-General of Ordnance, who, feeling that he had not every item checked as usual before commitment, had to look still closer into each proposal involving expenditure, whether for contracts placed with the Trade for finished war material or for buildings, machinery and staff required for his own department." The Ordnance Department therefore felt constrained by the sense of an unaccustomed responsibility to find good and sufficient excuses for going slowly, and halting and hesitating in front of the munitions problem.

The War Office had always dealt direct with the Government arsenals and a certain small circle of contractors only, and could not bring itself to launch out into dealings with a wider circle. The taking in hand of an array of new and untried firms and the organisation of them for munitions production would beyond question have been a serious and unprecedented responsibility. The Ordnance Department recoiled from that risk.

When, therefore, prominent industrialists all over the country clamoured to be of assistance, and made offers to supply military stores and munitions, the War Office did all it could to keep them at bay. Complaints reached me that they were treated as if they were greedy suppliants for profitable war contracts. The general policy of the War Office was to give these would-be helpers a list of the traditional contracting munition firms, and invite them to approach these firms with offers to sub-contract for supplies. It must be borne in mind that these firms were already working at full pressure, choked with orders from the War Office for not only their maximum output, but for whatever extended output they could hold out any hope of developing. It was obvious that their overworked staffs would neither have the time to organise a large system of subsidiary firms, nor the inclination to spare some of their best skilled men to train workers in other concerns in the processes of munition manufacture; and furthermore, they would naturally be none too eager to teach other firms which might develop into awkward rivals and competitors with themselves in days to come. In peace time there had been between Admiralty, War Office and foreign orders only barely sufficient orders for armaments to go round, and few guessed how long it would be before peace returned.

It was subsequently discovered that not only had some of the armament firms accepted contracts from the British War Office which were far beyond their capacity to execute, but that some of them had undertaken orders on a gigantic scale from the Russian Government. When they accepted these Russian contracts they must have known that they had not the faintest chance of executing them in time if they were to deal fairly with their British orders. Their failure to execute these orders was largely responsible for the disasters which befell the Russian armies in the campaign of 1914-15. War is the harvest of the armament firms. But in all countries they were inclined to over-estimate the capacity of their own fields and barns.

The policy of the War Office relieved it of the dreaded responsibility for the control of work from these outside firms, but at the cost of interposing between the crying needs of our front line on the one hand, and the vast manufacturing capacity of Great Britain on the other, the narrow bottle-neck of a handful of overworked firms, far too busy with their own tasks to undertake the gigantic duty which the War Office sought to thrust upon them, of organising the whole potential productive capacity of the country for munitions manufacture.

The military organisers appear to have been handicapped by that ingrained distrust, misunderstanding and contempt of all business men (not on the War Office register) which was traditionally prevalent in the Services; and doubtless the business men on their side were—to say the least—puzzled by their contact with the military mind and army manners. The Master-General of Ordnance has explained that the method adopted with some of these would-be helpers was to send them down to one of the arsenals to see the work being carried out and form an opinion as to their firm's capabilities of undertaking it; and he adds that while many went, comparatively few returned to say that they could do it. In the light of the subsequent achievements of such men under the direction of the Ministry of Munitions, one has an idea of the sort of encouragement these men must have received at official hands. And it shows that there was a genuine, though mistaken, under-estimate of the capacity, skill and adaptable engineering ability of the nation at large. Doubtless there were many incompetents and exploiters among those eager applicants for orders. But a filter of red tape was ill adapted to sift them out and still retain the really efficient business men, who are often the first to recoil, perplexed and disgruntled, at such treatment. The good men and the rubbish alike failed to squeeze through the fine and resistant mesh. Meantime the War Office, aware that it was not in sight of obtaining the gigantic supplies required by the front line, spent much time begging the soldiers not to use up shells so quickly.

4. FIRST SIGNS OF SHELL SHORTAGE

After the first rapid fluctuations of the War in the retreat from Mons and the advance from the Marne to the Aisne, the battle-front began to settle down, in September and October, 1914, into that long line of deep entrenchments which were to characterise the Western Front up to the end of the War.

The utilisation of the 5.9 howitzer by the Germans as a field gun was a surprise to the French and British alike. Its effect on the nerve of the troops was shattering, and it contributed largely to the break-up of Allied resistance in the early stages of the War.

Already the Allied forces had experienced the immense weight of the German artillery, and the crashing moral effect of the high-explosive shells which they freely employed. The ability of the Germans to use, even when it was a war of movement, heavy guns of a calibre far greater than we had begun to think of as practicable in the field of battle, and the devastation wrought by their " coal-boxes " and " Jack Johnsons," as their giant shells were irreverently nicknamed, had been a revelation to our military chiefs, British and French alike. Such defences as were hastily improvised proved quite inadequate to protect the retreating armies against the attacks of this deadly gun. No trenches had been prepared, and such shallow trenches as were here and there hurriedly scratched in the soil during the retreat offered no shelter from the explosives rained upon them by Germany's heavy artillery. On the other hand, when it came to the German turn to retreat, their engineers dug deep into the earth, and the bombardment by light guns was quite ineffective against such defences. As the War thus passed to the stage of trench warfare, we found that the shrapnel of our field guns was powerless not only to level parapets, to destroy trenches and to obliterate machine-gun emplacements, but even to tear down barbed-wire entanglements, and that the only way to save British lives was to churn up enemy defences with a crashing barrage of high-explosive shells that would smash the machine-guns, level trenches and break lanes through the wire before an attack was attempted.

At that time the War Office was supplying only shrapnel for the field guns, and of the shell even for field howitzers and 60-pounders, 70 per cent. was shrapnel. The few six-inch howitzers and the lonely 9.2-inch howitzer which was sent out in October, fired high explosive, but had only a limited amount of ammunition.*

By the first week in September, 1914, General Headquarters in France were writing to the Master-General of Ordnance, asking for supplies of H.E. (high explosives). The request was emphatically reiterated on the 15th, and by the 21st a definite request for 15 per cent. of H.E. shells for the field guns was made—a proportion raised presently to 25 per cent. and by the 6th of November to 50 per cent. A week later this request was modified to 25 per cent. but raised on 31st December again to 50 per cent. The War Office refused to supply this proportion, on the plea that " the nature of the operations may again alter as they have done in the past." Thus persistent was

* H.E. was first used by 18-pounders on 31/10/14.

the refusal of the War Office to recognise the fact, demonstrated ten years earlier by the Russo-Japanese conflict in Manchuria, that modern warfare tended to become a war of entrenchments and siege operations. I may add that on the 22nd October, 1914, the French General Deville had informed the War Office that the French were giving up shrapnel altogether and concentrating on H.E.

But even more serious than the failure of a supply of H.E. was the general shortage of shells of any kind whatever. By 17th September, Sir John French was wiring for increased supplies of shells for his howitzers, pointing out that the reserves in stock on the lines of communication had fallen dangerously low, and that " in view of the large expenditure of this ammunition now taking place and to be expected, this is a serious matter. No effort should be spared to send out further supplies at once."

The War Office replied that they were sending out what they could—it would increase Sir John French's stock to about ten days' supply at his then rate of expenditure—and warned him that " this will run our stock very low, and we cannot supply at this rate until manufacturers reach their maximum output." The shortage of ammunition for the larger guns became the theme of almost daily telegrams of Sir John French. By 28th September he was writing to draw attention also to a pending shortage of field-gun ammunition. He said: " For 18-pounders the proposal is to dispatch 15,000 rounds a week, or less than 7 rounds per gun a day. This is by far too small an amount. During the last fortnight there has been an average daily expenditure of 14 rounds per gun, notwithstanding the fact that these guns, as a whole, have been, comparatively speaking, but lightly engaged during the action on the Aisne. I need hardly say that a shortage of ammunition for Field Artillery might be attended with the gravest results. It may be thought that the nature of the recent operations have been abnormal, but in my opinion future operations in this campaign will to a great extent be of a similar kind, and in order to maintain the Army in an efficient fighting condition I am compelled to represent that the proposed rate of ammunition supply cannot possibly suffice to meet demands." In its reply, dated 7th October, to this letter, the War Office excused itself in the following terms: " With reference to your letter of 28th September, I am commanded by the Army Council to point out that they have provided in the first instance, and have also sent out, replenishments in almost every case fully up to *the quantities of gun ammunition which were laid down before the War.*" (My italics.) This letter went on to promise increased amounts, and Sir John French answering it on the 10th October, retorted that even this larger rate of supply would provide the army with only 9 rounds per gun per day for the 60-pounders, 11 rounds per day for the 4.5-inch howitzers, and if all the divisions were counted, only 6 rounds per day for the 18-pounder field artillery. Thereafter a series of urgent telegrams came from France for more shells. The tremendous attempt made by the Germans to throw the British Army into the Channel and to capture the ports had just started. The first battle of Ypres, the last fought in the open field on this front, had developed, and in the middle of that terrible struggle the Field-Marshal wired Lord Kitchener: " If the reserve on the lines of communication is not at once made up to at least the authorised scale and maintained on that scale, it is possible that the troops may soon be required to fight without the support of artillery. The great battle which has now lasted for several days still proceeds, and the gravest result will be entailed by a shortage of artillery ammunition." In reply he was told by the Secretary of State for War: " As soon as I can work out the rate you are expending ammunition I will answer the last paragraph. . . . You will of course see that economy is practised. . . ." Three days later, the Master-General of Ordnance wrote to G.H.Q. declaring: " I cannot say what our future supplies will be, as it entirely depends on the promises of the firms to whom we have given large orders being kept up to date." He added that he could not increase supplies of 4.7-inch shell without depleting the equipment of the fresh divisions now being made up. French replied that he had been compelled to reduce supplies for the howitzers to 10 rounds per gun a day, and would shortly have to bring down the 18-pounder field guns to the same ration. He begged for the ammunition which the Master-General of Ordnance was holding up as equipment of batteries not yet sent overseas—" I submit that it is of greater importance to keep the batteries which are already here adequately supplied with ammunition, than it is to retain ammunition in England for the batteries which are to come out later "—and in an urgent postscript added: —

" I *must press* this point: *The offensive is of the last importance during the next two weeks or so!* I wish to emphasise third paragraph of my letter.—J.F." (His own italics.)

Two days later, on the 31st October, French wired repeating his plea, to which the War Office acceded. Kitchener also suggested to him that Joffre ought to send more French guns with a plentiful supply of ammunition. But, as a consequence, when two days later Sir John French asked for another infantry division, he was offered a choice of Stuart Wortley's Territorial Division " without artillery, for which we have not got ammunition," or the incompletely trained VIIIth Division,* with its artillery depleted by the supplies sent out already.

Throughout November and December the shortage of ammunition

* " The Official History of the War: Military Operations, France and Belgium," Vol. II, page 450, notes that the 8th Division " was ' untrained ' according to home standards. . . . The Division assembled at Hursley Park, near Winchester, between the 19th September and 2nd November; it began embarking on the 4th November. There was, therefore, no opportunity for training in brigade and division."

was growing. On the 12th November G.H.Q. wired for more shells for the 4.7-inch guns, and the War Office stated in reply what they had sent in the last week, and added: " We cannot continue to supply at this rate." On the 12th December, Sir John French wired Lord Kitchener: " I am very anxious about our supply of ammunition." Kitchener replied that the output was insufficient for the guns already in the field, and that he doubted the wisdom of sending more batteries to France, as " it is obviously uneconomical to keep batteries in France that cannot be used because of the want of ammunition." On the 31st December French wrote to the War Office: " The present supply of artillery ammunition has been found to be so inadequate as to make offensive operations, even on a small scale, quite out of the question. Recent experience has shown that the ammunition available suffices for scarcely one hour's bombardment of a small portion of the enemy's line, and that even this operation leaves no ammunition to repel a counter-attack or to give the assaulting columns sufficient support. Owing to the nature of the operations in which we are, and shall continue to be, engaged, *the supply of artillery ammunition is the governing factor. . . . It is on the supply of ammunition for artillery that the future operations of the British Army will depend."* (My italics.)

The members of the Cabinet saw none of these letters from Sir John French at the time, and knew nothing of their existence.

5. THE FIRST CABINET COMMITTEE

It was not perhaps obvious at first to everyone how vital this question of munitions was, or how urgent and grave it was to become. The eyes of the nation during those early months were set more upon the spectacular massing of our man-power, and the enrolment of the first million of the new Army. Indeed, this public attitude caused an accentuation of the difficulty, for vast numbers of highly skilled workers, whose technical ability was of the first importance for increasing the output of munitions, were swept by the torrent of public enthusiasm or driven by the undiscriminating taunts of their neighbours into the ranks of these recruits. But it was clear to some of us that the arming and equipment of our forces would be no less essential than their numbers, and far harder to attain. And when the first warning echoes of the shortage in France began to be heard, the rumours of the congestion in our munition firms at home came to our ears, we felt that special action must be taken to deal with the matter.

In September I urged the appointment of a special Committee of the Cabinet to look into the question of guns, shells and rifles. At first, Lord Kitchener resisted so strongly that the Cabinet turned down the proposal. He was held in such awe at this date that his colleagues did not dare challenge his authority. Eventually, however, early in October, I prevailed upon the Cabinet to appoint a Committee to examine the question of our munition supplies, and to advise as to means of increasing production and expediting deliveries. The Committee consisted of the following seven persons: —

The Secretary of State for War (Lord Kitchener).
The Lord Chancellor (Lord Haldane).
The Chancellor of the Exchequer (Mr. Lloyd George).
The First Lord of the Admiralty (Mr. Churchill).
The Home Secretary (Mr. M'Kenna).
The President of the Board of Trade (Mr. Runciman).
The President of the Board of Agriculture (Lord Lucas).*

This Committee met altogether six times between the 12th October, 1914, and the 1st January, 1915, and took the initiative in some of the more important questions of policy and procedure which arose. As the work done by this short-lived Committee formed the basis of later developments for the supply of munitions, I give some brief account of it. At the first meeting on the 12th October, it reviewed the question of the provision of guns for the new armies and recommended that orders should be given for the manufacture of artillery on a much larger scale than had hitherto been contemplated by the War Office. Instructions were given for the ordering of 3,000 18-pounder field guns, to be delivered by May, 1915, instead of the 892 already ordered for delivery in June. I pressed hard that the capacity of the existing armament firms should be extended, that the great engineering capacity of this country outside the armament works should be immediately mobilised for the production of munitions and that the works of large engineering firms should be taken over and converted to that purpose. The Master-General of Ordnance objected on the grounds that the manufacture of guns, rifles and shells was a very delicate operation and needed long experience and trained skill of a high order; that the few firms who possessed the necessary experience and training subcontracted in respect of all work which outside firms were capable of doing; and that by this means all the engineering capacity which could safely be trusted was fully engaged. To go beyond that process and leave the whole production of any munitions of war to inexperienced establishments would be too risky. He dwelt on the dangers arising from faulty shells. The whole of our guns might burst. Such was his case for the existing procedure. There can be no doubt that any great expansion under the pressure of necessity was bound to lead to some defective work, but the sequel proved that the risk was far greater from badly designed fuses—for which the Ordnance Department was responsible—than from the carelessness of British manufacturers. The rifle shortage was also considered. There was no prospect of supplying our recruits with rifles for many months to

* Subsequently killed in action.

come unless special efforts were made to quicken supply. A message was sent to the representative of the War Office in the U.S.A., instructing him to ascertain the maximum output which could be secured from firms capable of manufacturing field guns or rifles to a total of 1,500 18-pounder guns and half a million rifles. I may say that the reply to this inquiry showed that there appeared to be little hope of securing additional output from that source before September, 1915.

On the next day, 13th October, representatives of the Ordnance Factories, and of Messrs. Armstrong, Vickers, the Coventry Ordnance Works, and Beardmore, met our Committee. In regard to finance, I promised the representatives of the armament firms who were called in that the Government could find the capital required to extend the works of the armament firms or those of their sub-contractors, and would compensate them for any resulting loss. Thus encouraged, the contractors engaged to increase their output by every possible means, and as a result of this meeting the commitments of the works represented were raised from 878 guns to 1,608—deliveries in all cases to be completed not later than August, 1915.

It was after this second meeting that I decided to pay a visit to France to inspect methods employed there to expand and quicken production.

At successive meetings on the 20th and 21st October we took up the question of propellent and explosives, which was left to the Secretary of State for War to investigate further, and that of the supply of rifles—it being decided to increase largely the number already ordered for delivery in July, 1915. As a result, big orders were placed in the United States, and grants of money made to firms in this country for the increase of their plant. Then, in regard to the organisation of trade resources, it was decided that a Committee of the armament firms should be formed to distribute the orders to individual firms.

This summary gives some of the main points dealt with during the first four meetings of the Committee in October; but it was not long before I discovered that grants of money, though essential, were not all that was necessary to meet the situation.

The difficulty at this time of increasing the orders for munitions, or of accelerating delivery of existing orders under the War Office procedure, was becoming every week more apparent, for the existing armament workshops were already working to their full capacity, and the War Office seemed unable to organise any effective increase in their capacity or their number. This country was richer than any other in a wide variety of manufacturing plant, a vast amount of which we subsequently found ways and means of adapting to the production of munitions. Labour difficulties were systematically pleaded by the munition firms as an excuse for failure to carry out

D*

their contracts; yet there was still in the country an ampler supply of labour than we enjoyed at any subsequent period of the struggle. The numbers of skilled workmen were dwindling day by day owing to indiscriminate recruiting. The head officials at the War Office, who were responsible for the whole field of munition design and production, made no effort to retain pivotal men in our engineering works, and they clung most tenaciously to their methods of assigning contracts. They refused stubbornly to adopt the only effectual measures for utilising and organising the manufacturing and labour resources of this country in order to secure an adequate output.

In order to obtain a further insight into the possibilities of increasing our munition supply, I decided after the second meeting of the Cabinet Committee to visit France to see what was being done there in the way of expanding production.

On this visit I was accompanied by Lord Reading, then Lord Chief Justice, and by Sir John Simon, then Attorney-General.

Our party—Lord Reading, Sir John Simon and myself—left Newhaven at midnight on October 16th and crossed on a destroyer to Dieppe. It was my first experience of the physical proximity of war. As soon as we left Newhaven the lights were put out, as a German submarine had been seen off Cherbourg that morning. We had to steam out of the ordinary route and hang about a good deal, so that the crossing took twice as long as the ordinary packet boat would have taken.

At Dieppe we were met on behalf of the French Government and were taken to visit some of the battlefields north of Paris. One of the cars which met us was driven by the dramatist Henri Bernstein, who had recently taken a prominent part in denouncing M. Caillaux during his wife's trial. We were taken to Senlis and Beauvais among other places. The lower part of Senlis was a complete ruin after its bombardment by the Germans. That was our first view of the ruin caused by war. At Creil the bridge over the river had been blown up by the French to cover their retreat from the Germans, and we passed over a pontoon bridge. Motoring through a country which seemed in some districts to have been almost abandoned by its inhabitants, for we were on the track of the German march, we reached Paris in the evening. Paris itself looked like a deserted city. All the gaiety, bustle and vivacity had gone. The Government was still at Bordeaux, whither it had fled during the panic of August. The Elysée, the Chamber of Deputies, the Luxembourg and all the Government offices were locked up and left in charge of a few heroic caretakers. The President, the Ministers, the Deputies—almost all except Clemenceau and Briand—had gone. It will be recalled that M. Clemenceau, when asked whether he thought the Government ought to leave Paris as the Germans were almost at the gates, replied: "Yes, Paris is too far from the front!" The young men of Paris were away at the front: older men were outside on guard armed with obsolete rifles with long bayonets. A considerable number of the remaining population, especially in the richer quarters, had sought safety further south when the Germans were approaching with great strides towards the *banlieue*. The hotels were closed, and shops which did not dispense the necessaries of life had neither purchasers nor window-gazers. The sparse population of the streets looked grave and preoccupied. Before the war the dress of the ordinary Parisian women always seemed to me to be sombre, just as the apparel of the average British women gave one the impression of being drab; but on this occasion garments, both male and female, were blacker than ever, for the French army during the terrible battles of September had suffered casualties more appalling than had ever been inflicted on any armies within so short a space of time. It was, indeed, a grim city.

On Sunday morning, at ten o'clock, we achieved the object of our journey, which was to ascertain how far the French Government had organised private industry for the purpose of producing munitions of war, and how far, in view of French experience, similar organisation could be undertaken in the United Kingdom. General St. Clair Deville, the inventor of the famous 75-millimetre gun, had been authorised by the French Government to give us all the information he procured, and he and Captain Cambefort placed their knowledge and experience at our disposal. General Deville struck us as a splendid type of the quiet, thoughtful, and efficient Frenchman. Cambefort spoke English excellently (he was a big merchant and manufacturer at Lyons in times of peace), and knew England well. They explained to us what arrangements the French were making to increase their supplies of guns, shells, etc., and what provision they were making for future development. They explained how the Government, as soon as war broke out, called engineers and manufacturers together in order to make the best available use of all factories and workshops capable of assisting in Government work. The great difficulty was shortage of skilled workmen, because at the mobilisation no thought had been given to this necessity, and all of military service age, not then actually engaged in munition work, had gone to the front. The Government was now doing its utmost to get them back, though this was very difficult, as they were scattered over different regiments and in different parts of the battle front. Still, a number of these skilled men had now been recovered. Munitions were being manufactured by private firms, and private production would rapidly increase.

The return of essential and pivotal skilled men who had been drafted either into the Territorials or Kitchener Armies was not seriously taken in hand in Britain until after the formation of the Ministry of Munitions in May, 1915. By that time many of these workers had already fallen in futile battles, owing largely to lack of guns and ammunition they could have helped to provide. Production suffered seriously from this mistake.

General Deville said that England had such an immense number of splendidly equipped engineering works, with every variety of machines, plant and tools, that our situation was, for the purposes of increasing supplies, better than that of France. He offered to be at the disposition of our Government for advising us on the method of munition production they had evolved. We reported this offer to the War Office, but I never heard that it came to anything. If he repeated to the Ordnance Authorities at home the advice he gave to me it certainly did not fructify.

While in Paris I received a visit from Lord Robert Cecil, who had been on a search for his sister's son, reported missing. He learned as a result of his inquiries that the boy had been badly wounded, and taken with others in the same condition to a French country house. Here their wounds were being attended to when the Germans took possession of the mansion. The men's wounds were only partially dressed, the hæmorrhage in many cases being only temporarily stopped. The doctor who was attending them warned the German officer that to move these men meant their death, but in spite of this the officer insisted on their being bundled into carts and taken away as prisoners. As a result of this they all died. Had they been left behind and recovered, they might have returned to the front and helped to kill German soldiers. Such are the ruthless alternatives of war.

Lord Robert was also arranging for a burial service for the dead British soldiers, who were to be exhumed where that was possible, and buried again with religious rites—a rather gloomy and gruesome task. He was anxious that the British Government should arrange a mission for this purpose. I promised to see to it.

We were privileged to have an interview with General Gallieni, who was Military Governor of Paris. He was certainly a very remarkable person. He was evidently a very ill man; he looked sallow, shrunken, and haunted. Death seemed to be chasing the particles of life out of his veins. Afterwards we learnt that he was suffering from a serious internal disease. He died from this disease in 1916. Still, he was fearless, resolute and confident. He had just made a notable contribution to the victory of the Marne. We discussed with him very fully the whole military position.

Early on Monday morning we left Paris and motored to Amiens, the General Headquarters of the Northern Army of France. On the way we passed through Montdidier. German aeroplanes had just bombed the town and the fragments of their bombs were hardly cold when we arrived. Here I heard, for the first time in my life, the crack of shells fired with murderous intent against human beings, and my first experience of it gave me a shudder. At Amiens we came to the Headquarters of General Castelnau, one of the ablest military leaders in the War. He had already won a great reputation in the fierce battles of the Grand Couronne in front of Nancy, where under his leadership the French repulsed the German efforts to break through on that critical front. His personality created a deep impression on our minds. He was a short man with a high forehead and intelligent dark eyes—quiet and grave in demeanour. I drove with him up to the French lines beyond Doullens. On the road the General explained how the War was progressing and how differently things had turned out from what military staffs on both sides had anticipated and planned. It was clear that neither German nor French generals had foreseen that the War would develop into a siege operation on a colossal scale.

"I imagined," he said, "that we should have had great pitched battles, with a fortnight or so in between for rest and preparation. But here am I—I have marched with my men from Lorraine to Normandy, and they have been fighting incessantly for 79 days and nights—and are still fighting."

He had a habit of giving answers to my questions which were curiously irrelevant, but always striking. On the way up to the front we met an ambulance, and I asked him whether that was carrying the wounded to the hospital behind the lines. His answer was: "The man who is responsible for this war has the soul of a devil!" He discussed the losses, which had been enormous on both sides. The Prussian Guards, he said, had been wiped out, and the French had lost too many brave men. He deplored their loss, and said: "I look at the lists of these dead heroes, and learn how they died, and I weep, and say: 'There is not one of these men who is not a greater man than I'."

Two of his own sons had been on these lists of the killed. He was in the habit of reading out to his staff every morning the names of fallen officers. One morning the list contained the name of his own son. When the name was reached his only sign of emotion was a gulp, a catch in the throat, before the name "Charles Castelnau" passed his lips, and he then proceeded calmly to the end of the list. In commenting on the military position he grew grave when talking of the clutch in which the two armies were locked, and the apparent impossibility of breaking it. I asked how many men were under his command, and he said there were nine army corps. "Well," I remarked, "that is a greater army than Napoleon ever commanded in any single battle."

His answer was a kind of soliloquy. "Ah, Napoleon, Napoleon! If he were here now, he'd have thought of the 'something else'." Asked what he thought of the chances of the War, and whether the French would succeed in driving the enemy out of France, Castelnau's answer was: "*Il le faut!*"

The answers which both General Castelnau and subsequently Generals Foch and Balfourier gave to my questions on the military situation left on me the impression that even the ablest of the French military leaders were, for the time being, completely baffled by the military dilemma presented to them by the unexpected change in the tactics of the German Army. A war of movement had been anticipated and provided for in the equipment and organisation of the Army. A great siege operation where the *soixante-quinze* and the Chasseurs played a subordinate part had clearly not been thought of. They had attempted here and there to penetrate this earthen fortress and had everywhere failed with heavy losses. They were now looking for the " something else." Unfortunately for the Allies they looked for possibilities straight in front of them only and failed to look around and far beyond.

General Castelnau seemed very popular with his men, visiting them in the trenches and cheering them, calling them " *mes infants* " and enquiring whether they had enough to eat. " *Trop!* " said one soldier, who was marching to take his place in the trenches with a yard of the delicious French bread under his arm.

I was told that the men were entirely different in spirit from what they were at the beginning of the War. Then they were terrified of the big shells of the enemy and recoiled in horror from the hideous explosives. It needed a very firm hand to put a stop to the effect of this terror. We heard that General Maud'huy, who had by that time joined our party, and who had the record of being one of the most daring of French Generals, had dealt with his men in a very drastic way. A section of them had broken under the fire of the German artillery. The next day, therefore, the General marched them out again until they were under shell fire, when he ordered them to halt and face about. He then began to put them through their ordinary drills, on the understanding that any man who attempted to run away would be shot immediately. When he thought that they were used to shell fire, he marched them back again. I asked Maud'huy if this story I had heard about him were true. He smiled, and said " Ah, but I gave them their reward afterwards! " " And what was that? " I asked. " *Monsieur*," was the answer, " when we were attacking I permitted them the next time to advance two hundred metres in front of the rest." " Was there any further trouble with their *morale?* " " *Jamais!* " was the reply. The complaint about *morale* arose mainly concerning soldiers drawn from certain French departments remote from the German frontiers and with no memories of any Teutonic invasion in the past; peasants drawn from these areas were inclined to treat the fight as something which more particularly affected the northerners. The spirit of the men from these districts had now been completely established. They all knew that it was a struggle to the death for France to which their devotion was beyond challenge or fear. I observed the countenance of men who had passed through the fiery furnace. Though they were resigned and calm, yet the horror of it all was stamped on some of their faces—a horror that habitude and resignation had not yet been able to smooth out.

We proceeded to General Balfourier's headquarters, and there for the first time saw something of the bombardment of villages by the German artillery. It was continuous but leisurely. There was no serious fighting going on, and I have no doubt that the report on both sides would be: "All quiet on this front!"

I did my best during this visit to inform myself by question directed to General Castelnau and General Balfourier, and everyone I met, as to the real character of the problem with which the Allies were confronted owing to the digging in of the German Army.

This was the first occasion on which I met General Foch. He was a totally different type from General Castelnau. The part he had taken in the recent victory on the Marne added to my eagerness to meet him. He corresponded more with the British idea of what a typical Frenchman is like—vivacious, demonstrative, emphatic and gesticulatory. He talked just as much with his hands and arms as he did with his tongue. But whether he expressed himself with hand or voice he always talked well and to the point. His high broad forehead and his penetrating eye proved him a man of exceptional gifts. I asked him if he had any message for the British Cabinet and he said, "Tell them there will be no more retreats." I asked him whether I could also tell them there would be any more advances. He hesitated and was evidently perplexed by the question. After a perceptible halt he replied: "That depends on the men and material you will be able to throw into the battle line." He said that the Belgians had been obliged to retreat before the German advance, but his advice to them had been, "If you want to keep your country, dig yourselves into it, and hang on to it!"

At the Headquarters of Balfourier's Division we saw a German prisoner who had just been brought in—a Prussian Guard. He was wounded in the arm, and evidently in pain. The Lord Chief Justice spoke to him, and ascertained that he came from Berlin. The prisoner behaved with great dignity, being neither surly nor communicative, but evidently feeling his position keenly. He had every appearance of an educated man. "Well," said the French General, "you need not worry. You will be taken to the hospital, and looked after just as well as our own men." "Your men are well treated by us, too," replied the German. The General shrugged his shoulders. "At any rate," he said, "for you it is now only a question of time. When the war is over you will be free to return to your home." "Ah!" said the prisoner, with weary longing, "home is the only thing that matters in life!"

I inquired of a young French officer who was helping to guide us round the front whether the stories of German cruelty to women were true. "No," he answered. "They leave them alone as a rule." And he added with a cynical shrug, "They do not appreciate women."

At this stage of the War there was not much outward visible sign of its devastation. The hundreds of long-range guns which later on smashed towns and villages and churned up fields had not yet begun their ruinous activities. The country as a whole showed no signs of pillage or destruction. The peasants were in the fields, often working stolidly within range of the German shells. I heard of one old woman who was working in a potato field when a shell burst dangerously near. She stopped for a moment, looked at it and then went on with her work. Everywhere there was a sense of everyone having calmly settled down to an established condition of things which threatened to last for some time. The inhabitants of villages which were being bombarded were leaving the villages during the day and returning at night to sleep. It was early in the morning when we met an old man and woman who had left their home in a bombarded village just for the day. The old woman was carrying under her arm a duck, probably destined for their midday meal. They were engaged in deep conversation, but to all appearances were taking the situation very philosophically.

When we reached the British Headquarters at St. Omer, Sir John French had left for the Menin road where "some fighting" was reported to be going on. It was the beginning of the terrible battle of Ypres.

CHAPTER VI

THE FIGHT FOR MUNITIONS—*continued*

I. A POLICY OF SHORT VIEWS

In spite of the recommendation of the Cabinet Committee that it was advisable to mobilise the engineering resources of this country more fully for the production of munitions, the War Office adhered to its dependence on the established armament firms. Had the War been " over by Christmas," then the official policy might have carried us through. Although Lord Kitchener, on 4th December, 1914, in one of the very few interviews he granted to the Press, spoke of the possibility that the War would last three years, the authorities at the War Office responsible for the supply of munitions were slow to envisage the character and the probable duration of the struggle. This came to light in the course of negotiations for the purchase of rifles from America.

The War Office decided that no more rifles than those already on order should be arranged for unless delivery was promised by 1st May, 1915. In this connection I transcribe a letter I wrote to the Master-General of Ordnance on 23rd November, 1914, relative to the War Office action: —

" Dear General von Donop,—Lord Reading has shown me your letters to him on the subject of further American orders for rifles. I understand that you are of opinion that unless delivery by the 1st of May is promised the Army will not stand in need of additional rifles beyond those which have already been promised to you after that date. I must say this rather surprises me in the face of the figures supplied to the Committee of which I was a member. Unless you have arranged for an enormous addition to the supplies which you then foresaw, we shall certainly be very seriously short even in the month of September. We were then working on the assumption that the Kitchener Armies were limited to the figures which Parliament had then sanctioned. Since then Parliament has ordered the enlistment of another million men. Do the promises received by you from various sources for the delivery of rifles provide for the equipment of this additional million?

I should have thought that as long as you had a responsible firm in America who were prepared to undertake the delivery to you of additional rifles—even although they were only received in substantial numbers late next year—it would have been worth while accepting their services.

Kindly let me know, as I promised to inform Mr. Grenfell definitely what the decision of the War Office is on the point.— Yours sincerely,

D. Ll. GEORGE.

P.S. Further supplies of rifles will be required for the Central Association of Volunteer Corps, which has been quite recently sanctioned by the War Office, in which there are already some 200,000 men and which, according to War Office anticipation, will amount eventually to a million."

I have no record of any reply to this letter, but the Master-General of Ordnance probably spoke to me on the matter when he saw me.

This failure to realise the scale of warfare to which we were committed, and the corresponding scale of armament and munition output that would be required, was characteristic of the War Office during those early months. When it was discovered in December that the deliveries of gun ammunition promised by the main contractors were not coming forward, it was not inferred that the scheme of production was at fault. The contractors' estimates had been too sanguine; the sub-contractors had broken down over unforeseen difficulties. These failures were, indeed, taken by the War Office to be proof of the fundamental soundness of their contention that the technical difficulties of armament work were likely to defeat the inexpert manufacturer, and could only be tackled by the established firms.

Accordingly the War Office enlisted the aid of the Board of Trade for a scheme to transfer skilled workers from other engineering firms in the country to the established munition works. Though in regard to its intended object this scheme was a fiasco, it had the effect, not foreseen by its originators, of helping to break down the War Office policy of dealing exclusively with the traditional sources of supply. For when these independent firms were approached as to transfer of their men, many of them protested that they were already doing a certain amount of Government work as sub-contractors, or were supplying materials to firms engaged in sub-contracts; and even those which as yet were doing nothing of this kind raised the strongest objection to handing over their best skilled men to private armament firms, and offered instead to undertake munition production themselves.

The canvass of employers was carried out during the first fortnight of January, 1915, and Sir H. Llewellyn Smith, of the Board of Trade, reviewing its meagre results in a note dated 23rd January, said : —

"I have therefore been led to the conclusion that, if a large amount of labour in addition to what can be obtained from among the unemployed British and Belgian workpeople is required for armament purposes, it is necessary in the first place to ascertain precisely how much additional work can be devolved on other engineering firms by the armament firms, or given to them direct, and to distribute this work judiciously so as to take advantage to the fullest extent of the plant and labour available. . . ."

One useful outcome of the action of the Board of Trade was that the Master-General of Ordnance was persuaded to sanction a proposal that firms should be informed through the Labour Exchanges that they might make requests for contracts for Army supplies, subject to having been inspected and found to be capable of undertaking the task in question. In the course of the first eighteen months of the War about 11,000 firms were thus inspected through the Labour Exchanges. This led to a scheme by the Board of Trade for a survey of engineering firms, a project which, however, broke down when the Engineering Employers' Federation, which was to have taken an active part in carrying through the survey, took objection to the absence of any specific information as to the types of contract which the War Office might be prepared to offer. The Home Office also arranged to carry out a census of machinery, which was conducted in March by the factory inspectors, and its results communicated to the War Office. No substantial progress, however, was made with the utilisation of the full engineering resources of the nation.

2. THE SHELL SHORTAGE GROWS

A memorandum issued by Lord Kitchener to the G.H.Q. of the Expeditionary Force on 9th January, 1915, states the ammunition position at that date with a frankness which must have had a discouraging effect upon the Commander-in-Chief and his army in France: —

"It is impossible at the present time to maintain a sufficient supply of gun ammunition on the scale which you consider necessary for offensive operations. Every effort is being made in all parts of the world to obtain an unlimited supply of ammunition, but, as you are well aware, the result is still far from being sufficient to maintain the large number of guns which you now have under your command adequately supplied with ammunition for offensive operations. You have pointed out that offensive operations under the new conditions created by this war require a vast expenditure of artillery ammunition, which may for even ten or twenty days necessitate the supply of 50 or 100 rounds per gun per day being available, and unless a reserve can be accumulated to meet an expenditure of this sort it is unwise in embarking on extensive offensive operations against the enemy's trenches. It is, of course, almost impossible to calculate with any accuracy how long offensive operations once undertaken may last before the object is attained, but it is evident that the breaking-off of such operations before accomplishment owing to the want of artillery ammunition, and not on account of a successful termination or a convenient pause in the operations being reached might lead to a serious reverse being sustained by our forces."

Neither this memorandum nor the purport of it was communicated to the Cabinet.* It was not merely a question at that time of supplying a sufficiency of shells for an offensive, but enough to reply to the German bombardment of our trenches. There were no offensive operations undertaken until the following March and then only on a limited scale. The evidence pouring in from the front proved that the shell supply was pitifully unequal to making even a show of defence by artillery. Throughout January and February the burden of telegrams from G.H.Q. to the Master-General of Ordnance is continually: "Stock of shell very low;" "Amount received much below proportion;" "Request that further supplies may be expedited as much as possible." On 21st January, General von Donop wrote to the Chief of the General Staff in France: "It seems quite hopeless for me to give you any dates for delivery of guns or ammunition."

Such information as I was able to obtain, despite the reticence of the military authorities, about the situation increased my already acute uneasiness. I therefore circulated a memorandum to the Cabinet, four days later, on 22nd February, 1915, submitting some Considerations on the Conduct of the War, from which I quote the following: —

"The first and the greatest difficulty is equipment. The number of men we could put in the field is seriously limited by the output of guns and rifles. In this respect we have a great advantage. We are at a disadvantage as compared with the Germans in one material respect, but we are at a great advantage in other respects. As to the disadvantage, the Germans and Austrians between them had, even at the commencement of the War, much larger supplies of war material and more extensive factories for the turning out of supplies than the Allied countries possessed, and they have undoubtedly since made much better use of their manufacturing resources for the purpose of increasing that output. Germany is the best organised country in the world, and her organisation has told.

Those are the disadvantages. What about the advantages? The

---

* The first week of the battle of the Somme we had 3½ times as many guns in France as on 1st January, 1915, and the expenditure of shells during that week by the artillery taking part in the battle was 237 per gun per day.

manufacturing resources at the disposal of the Allies are
enormously greater than those which Germany and Austria can
command.   In this computation Russia barely counts, but the
manufacturing resources of France and Great Britain between
them are at least equal to those of Germany and Austria, and the
seas being free to them they can more easily obtain material. But
apart from that they have practically the whole of America, which
is the greatest manufacturing country in the world, and Japan to
draw upon.

I believe that France has strained her resources to the utmost,
and she can hardly do much more. She has now abolished the sale
of absinthe, and that will have an appreciable effect upon the
productivity of her workmen. She is, therefore, doing all she can
to contribute. I do not believe Great Britain has ever yet done
anything like what she could do in the matter of increasing her
war equipment. Great things have been accomplished in the last
few months, but I sincerely believe that we could double our
effective energies if we organised our factories thoroughly. All
the engineering works of the country ought to be turned on to the
production of war material. The population ought to be prepared
to suffer all sorts of deprivations and even hardships whilst this
process is going on. As to America, I feel confident from what I
have heard that we have tapped only a small percentage of this
great available reserve of supply.

Special attention should be given to the laying down of
machinery which is essential to the turning out of rifles and
cannon. I hear it takes months to complete these machines, but
even if they are only ready in September we shall need them all.*
My first suggestion, therefore, would be that full powers should
be taken, if we do not already possess them, as I think we do, to
mobilise the whole of our manufacturing strength for the purpose
of turning out, at the earliest possible moment, war material. I
have always thought that our complete command over the railways
equips us with the necessary powers without resorting to legislation. But legislation which would enable us to commandeer all
the works in the United Kingdom, and, if necessary, to deal with
labour   difficulties   and   shortcomings,   would   undoubtedly
strengthen our hands. We might even take full powers to close
public-houses altogether in areas where armaments were being
manufactured. As to our railway powers, I made the suggestion
some time ago to the War Office that they should be used. I am
not sure of the extent to which that has been done.''

* Without the necessary machines and gauges manufacture could not start. These
additional machines were not ordered by the War Office and by the armament firms in
any appreciable quantities for another six months. It was done then after the big gun
programme which had followed the Boulogne Gun Conference. It was one of the first
steps taken by the Ministry of Munitions.

At this time the Ordnance Department had manœuvred the political meddlers with munitions out of action. The Cabinet Committee on Munitions had ceased to exist. Its last meeting was held on 1st January, 1915. The Board of Trade was supposed by the rest of the Cabinet to be functioning entirely in the direction of organising our engineering skill. As a matter of fact it was then conforming to the War Office policy and trying vainly to carry out its scheme for transferring skilled workers from factories and workshops not engaged in war work to the traditional armament firms. The War Office seemed to be carefully shutting its eyes to the magnitude of the task confronting it, and our army in the field was watching with dismay the approach of the summer campaign, conscious that its supplies were quite inadequate, and that the outlook for any increase was of the blackest.

At a Conference held at 10, Downing Street on Friday, 5th March, 1915, at which the Prime Minister, Lord Kitchener, myself, General von Donop, Mr. M'Kenna, Lord Crewe, Sir George Gibb and Sir George Askwith were present—a conference of which some account appears in a letter to Mr. Balfour, which I reproduce a little farther on—I urged again that there should be a fuller utilisation of existing engineering firms, and in particular I drew attention to the need for expediting the supply of rifles, which was still so inadequate that many of our troops in training had no rifles to drill with. Both Lord Kitchener and General von Donop seemed quite satisfied with the prospects about rifles, of which they hoped we should have about two million by the beginning of 1916. When I pointed out that the House of Commons had already voted 3,000,000 men, Kitchener was taken aback, and declared that they had not yet begun to calculate the military equipment—guns, ammunition, etc.—for such a force.

The conference decided that an investigation should be set on foot to find out what machinery was lying idle which could produce war material, and that Lord Kitchener should be asked to calculate what munitions would be required for an army of 3,000,000.

3.   CORRESPONDENCE WITH MR. BALFOUR

With the disappearance in January of the Cabinet Committee on Munitions there had ceased to be any effective instrument either for prodding along the War Office officials in regard to this vital issue, or for carrying out the tasks they were leaving undone.

Some time before the conference on March 5th, I had established contact with Mr. Balfour, who was a member of the War Council and of the Committee of Imperial Defence. Mr. Asquith had retained him on these bodies in order to secure his experience and advice in the national interest. From time to time I had poured into his ears my misgivings as to the whole position, and I had especially impressed upon him the delays in providing our troops with adequate support owing to the refusal of the War Office to make full use of our manufacturing resources. I had an implicit belief in his patriotism and a great admiration for his high intellectual gifts. Moreover, he had some war experience. He knew his Generals well. He had not forgotten the incompetent complacencies of the Boer War. He had suffered from them at that time. Their blunders had helped to discredit his administration. On returning from the Conference I received the following letter from him: —

" 4, Carlton Gardens,
Pall Mall, S.W.1.
March 5th, 1915.

My dear Chancellor of the Exchequer,

I know you won't take it amiss my dictating this letter, for my own handwriting is rather a trial to my correspondents. I most earnestly trust that you are not letting slide the matter about which we talked the day before yesterday. Putting labour troubles altogether on one side, the position seems to me to be most unsatisfactory, and unless you will take in hand the organisation of the engineering resources of the country in the interests of military equipment, I do not see how any improvement is to be expected. I am afraid it really *is* the fact that the Contracts Department of the War Office deliberately rejected the opportunity of getting the rifle-making plant which was offered to them some time ago. They supposed, poor things, that they had already had enough! !

I find it very difficult to understand how we have enough even for our own needs, putting aside the needs of our Allies. Apart from what we can purchase abroad, I gather that our output at the present moment is quite insufficient for our own needs. We make about 45,000 *new* rifles a month, and we enlist 60,000 a month; and large numbers of our existing levies are unarmed.

Lord K. seems, however, more preoccupied about the shell question than about the rifle question.

Everybody seems to admit that there would be no difficulty in making the *metallic* framework of the shell to any extent we may desire. It is the *fuses* which present all the difficulty. Now will anybody tell me that with proper organisation it is materially impossible greatly to increase the output of fuses? It may be so, but I do not feel at all inclined to accept it on the authority of the Ordnance people at the War Office. They are admirable people, and are doing splendid work, but their training cannot have been of the kind which would enable them successfully to exploit the manufacturing resources of the country.

In this connection I cannot help feeling surprised at the attitude which the Russian Foreign Office are now taking up. They are not only indifferent to the augmentation of the Allied Forces by the adhesion of fresh States to the Entente; they appear positively

to dislike it. This would be perfectly intelligible if they themselves possessed an overwhelming strength in well-equipped armies.
But if they are as ill-provided as in our moments of pessimism we
suppose, their confidence is truly amazing.

Personally, I should rather like to see the Greeks sent off to
occupy Smyrna and the adjacent country. This might bring in
the Italians, and it would be an additional reason for not employing the Greeks in Gallipoli. I do not quite understand why the
Admiralty ever expressed a strong desire for their assistance; and
their plan of landing a large force on the Peninsula and fighting
the Turks inch by inch seems to me altogether absurd. With the
only road over which supplies can reach the Turks partly destroyed
and effectively enfiladed by ships of war, we can well afford (it
seems to me) to leave the garrison at Gallipoli to stew in its own
juice—provided always the ships of war are able unassisted
successively to reduce the forts, which the Admiralty assures us is
the case.*

I did not mean, however, to trouble you with all this; my object
in writing was merely to beg you to do what is possible to bring
in outside manufacturers to the assistance of the War Office.

Yours sincerely,   ARTHUR JAMES BALFOUR."

Before I received the letter I had written Mr. Balfour as follows: —

"March 6th, 1915.
Dear Mr. Balfour,

Yesterday we had an informal meeting to discuss the labour
difficulties on the Clyde and on the Tyne. The Prime Minister
and Lord Kitchener were there; M'Kenna, Sir George Gibb and
Sir George Askwith were also present, but the Admiralty were not
represented. After disposing of the issue raised by the Clyde
strike we proceeded to discuss the important question of munitions
of war.

Von Donop assured us as far as rifles were concerned that the
position was satisfactory. He is confident that he will be able to
supply the men now in course of training with rifles of sorts by
the end of September. This equipment will include resighted
rifles; it also includes 130,000 to 140,000 rifles which von Donop
said were not worth resighting but were good enough to kill
Germans with in this country.

If recruiting goes on at the rate at which it is proceeding now
we shall be able to equip the whole of our new forces with rifles
by about the beginning of February next year. All this is accepting von Donop's optimistic estimate of the output. Now they are

---

* I did not accept Mr. Balfour's views as to the possibility of forcing the Straits
for navigation without occupying Gallipoli. Had we deputed this task to the Greek
Army early on in the war, all our subsequent difficulties would have been averted.

being turned out at the rate of 30,000 or 40,000 a month, and von Donop is entitled to say that they are well ahead of contract time. Gradually he hopes to expedite the rate of output until in September it becomes 100,000 a month, and in December 155,000 a month. HE CANNOT QUICKEN THE PACE NOW BECAUSE IT TAKES NINE MONTHS TO CONSTRUCT THE NECESSARY PLANT AND MACHINERY FOR THE PURPOSE OF TURNING OUT A RIFLE. Had this been done in August of last year we should have had our rifles ready for the new armies by June instead of September—the difference being a vital one, for the present figures mean that we cannot send all our new forces into the field until the summer is past. They are much better than I hoped, but there is no provision made in them for supplying a single rifle to our Allies, and that is the most serious feature in the outlook. The Russians, as you know, are deplorably short of rifles; they are better off for shells.*

Once more we decided yesterday to take the step in industrial organisation which we resolved upon in October and which until recently we were all under the impression had actually been taken. The War Office admit that they were deplorably short of shells, of rifle ammunition and of fuses; they also admit that they can do nothing this year in this country to supply the deficiencies of our Allies. That is almost a disastrous admission as far as the prospects of the War for the next twelve months are concerned. Nothing can remedy this state of things except the placing at the head of this new Executive of an energetic, fearless man who will not be cajoled and bamboozled by von Donop nor bullied by anyone else.

I sincerely wish you had been present. These views have to be pressed on the War Office, and as the mere fact that it should be necessary to do so at the end of eight months' war is in itself a reflection upon War Office organisation, it is quite an unpleasant function to undertake, and I am sorry to say I had very little support. It is essential that your influence and position should be behind this pressure. There will be an adjourned meeting for Kitchener to produce further figures. I hope it will be held early in the week and that it will be possible for you to attend. THE FATE OF THE WAR DEPENDS UPON STRONG ACTION BEING TAKEN IMMEDIATELY TO ORGANISE OUR ENGINEERING RESERVES FOR THE PURPOSE OF INCREASING THE OUTPUT NOT MERELY FOR OURSELVES BUT FOR OUR ALLIES. During yesterday's discussion it was assumed that we could do nothing in this country to aid Russia, and that it was quite as much as we could do between now and the end of the year to equip our new forces.

Yours sincerely,
D. LL. G."

* The War Office had withheld from the Cabinet all information as to the serious shell shortage on the Eastern Front.

4. D.O.R.A. AND MUNITIONS

Four days after the conference above described I laid before the House of Commons, on 9th March, 1915, a Bill to amend and extend the provisions of the Defence of the Realm Act.

This was the third edition of D.O.R.A., and was designed to give very greatly increased powers to the Authorities to secure munition production.

The first "Defence of the Realm Act" had been carried on 8th August, 1914, and gave general powers to His Majesty's Government to make regulations for the conduct of affairs under war conditions; the second, passed on 28th August, 1914, extended these powers and included powers of control over armament factories and their workers.

This third D.O.R.A. extended the power of control so as to enable the Government to take over and use any factory or workshop whatever, to control its processes and output, to remove its plant elsewhere if necessary, to commandeer empty premises for the housing of workmen engaged on war work, and to annul any contracts which stood in the way of firms carrying out the production of war material.

The possession of the powers conferred on the Government by this new measure undoubtedly strengthened its hands in subsequent negotiations with firms and workers. Had those powers been resolutely and intelligently applied, without loss of time, they might have gone far to solve some if the most serious difficulties with which we were at the time confronted. An attempt was indeed made by the Board of Trade to apply the power of taking over armament works as a means of checking the excessive profits these were making —profits which had led to grave discontent among the workers, who felt with some reason that the appeals made to them to put forth their utmost efforts were in fact appeals to increase the wealth of war profiteers. But the negotiations over this proposal broke down, and later on this matter was dealt with by me by means of provisions with regard to Excess Profits incorporated in the Munitions Act.

In the course of the discussions on the Bill, Mr. Bonar Law made some very helpful observations which are relevant to the story. He began by saying: —

"... I wish to say at once that the powers which are now demanded are probably the most drastic that have ever been put to any House of Commons. They enable the Government to go to any factory and tell them what they are to make and what they are not to make, or to go to any factory and tell them that their machinery is not being employed to the best advantage, and that we are going to take it away and use it for another purpose."

The Chancellor of the Exchequer: " For war material."

Mr. Bonar Law proceeded to say that the mere fact that the

Government were asking for such drastic powers and rushing the Bill through gave him ground for anxiety, and he continued: —

". . . I have said, speaking in this House last Monday, that I had some doubt whether in one respect the Government were doing everything they could to end this war. I expressed that doubt. I had no knowledge, and I have none now; but I did express the doubt whether we had shortness of ammunition or of other munitions of war, and I said I believed that if that was so after seven months of war, in a country like this, which is the greatest manufacturing country in the world, and where there is immense power of adapting one form of manufacture to another— that if there is that shortage, I do not think the industrial resources of the country have been used to the greatest advantage. I cannot understand why, if this Bill is necessary to-day, the necessity of it could not have been foreseen in August or September, and why it should not have been introduced then."

This quotation shows that the uneasiness as to the failure of the War Office to make the best use of our manufacturing capacity was spreading. It was in the course of this discussion that I said that " the Government were on the look-out for a good, strong business man with some ' push and go ' in him who would be able to put the thing through." The phrase caught on and the public anxiously awaited the advent of the " man of push and go." There were several experiments made by Lord Kitchener in the way of satisfying the demand.

The Bill was passed without any division or challenge. The Ordnance Department could not complain that they were not equipped with the fullest powers to make the best use of the manufacturing capacity of this country. There were no symptoms, however, of any eagerness on their part to exploit these new powers by setting works outside the Armament ring to the manufacture of war material. I therefore urged the Prime Minister to summon another Council meeting to discuss the position once more. At this meeting it was decided to appoint a special Committee to deal with the questions I raised. On 22nd March the Committee met and drew up the outlines of a plan, as the result of which the Prime Minister wrote me the following letter: —

" 10, Downing Street,
Whitehall, S.W.

22nd March, 1915.

My dear Chancellor of the Exchequer,
    In reference to the discussions of this afternoon, and the conclusions to which we came, I wish to submit to you one or two supplementary observations.

(1) I think, on reflection, that the scheme as a whole is on right lines.

(2) It is essential to its working that Kitchener should be brought in.

(3) As regards the composition of the proposed Committee, I am disposed to think that (on the political side) in addition to yourself and A.J.B. you should have a working financier, such as Montagu.

(4) That given your two (more or less capable) business men, say Grant and Arthur Pease (as to both of whom I hope you will make further enquiries), you ought to have—in what Balfour calls a session—*two* representatives of the Admiralty and War Office. The Admiralty men might be Black and perhaps Hopwood. The War Office, von Donop and Sir Charles Harris (the latter a man of really high quality). You might tell me what you think of these suggestions at or after the Cabinet.

Yours always,
(Signed) H. H. A."

But on the 25th March, Lord Kitchener wrote to him, requiring that the Committee should be subject to a variety of strict limitations; it must not interfere in any way with any of the regular armament firms, nor must it place any contracts with any firms who were already doing any contracting or sub-contracting for the War Office; nor make any use of labour from any firms which might in future be registered at the War Office as possible sources of supply of war material. It was, in short, to be a quite powerless body, which would act as an adviser to the War Office—all pertinent and serviceable advice being rejected in advance, as a condition precedent to the acceptance of the Committee.

Mr. Balfour, to whom this letter was shown, wrote me:—

". . . I cannot help suspecting that K. has only an imperfect grasp of the problem with which he has been faced for seven months.

I do not believe you will get 'forrader' by correspondence. The only thing is to talk it over with K. directly, although I know how difficult it is to make this operation a success. . . ."

But no discussion was successful in inducing the Secretary of State for War to agree that this Committee should have really effective executive powers. Its constitution was in the main that of an advisory body. The conversations which led to this lame conclusion occupied three weeks. In the course of these discussions a very trenchant memorandum was put in by the late Mr. Edwin Montagu, a man of exceptional insight and grasp of realities. This memorandum is worth reading as a contemporaneous statement of the difficulties experienced in dealing with the War Office:—

" The Prime Minister.

The Chancellor of the Exchequer, Mr. Balfour and I are going to see von Donop and Booth this afternoon, but I want to put once again, in a nutshell, the position as I see it.

You can have alternatively in contemplation two Committees or kinds of Committee. On the one hand you may leave Lord Kitchener directly responsible for the supply of munitions of war, working through the agency of the various men he collects for the purpose. You can have all the contracts, all the opportunities for resource, initiative energy and large view concentrated through von Donop and an overworked Secretary of State who admits again and again that he is incompetent by reason of his lack of knowledge of English conditions. If you do this, Lord Kitchener will welcome a Committee to tell him when he is wrong. Neither he nor his subordinates will be under any necessity to accept the advice of the Committee, the Committee will have no responsibility and will, I do not hesitate to say, suffer the same fate as your Cabinet Committee of last September. You can appoint such a Committee but I am quite certain it will not lead to the production of any new munitions of war and you will not find the Chancellor of the Exchequer or Mr. Balfour or anybody who does not wish to waste his time serving on such a Committee.

It is not for me to suggest any explanation of the War Office's . . . continued, bigoted, prejudiced reluctance to buy rifles or to increase the munitions of war, but that the solution of the suggestion above is most unsatisfactory can be supported by the evidence that : —

(1) Lord Kitchener, as he says, knows nothing about the problem.

(2) Lord Kitchener is overworked.

(3) Lord Kitchener admits that it would have been better to take the advice (and he did not take it) of the Committee in September.

(4) Lord Kitchener views with complete complacency figures which *mean nothing* unless labour is obtained, looks with complete satisfaction at machinery provided at Government expense which is idle because there is no labour, and works quite happily to a maximum of 350,000 shells a month, a maximum not yet by any means in sight. If you assume that an Army Corps wants 100 guns and each gun wants 17 shells per day, that shows a requirement of 1,700 shells per day per Army Corps, or 51,000 shells per Army Corps per month, which means that 350,000 will supply shell for seven Army Corps and we are talking of an Army of one million men.

On the other hand you can have a Committee which will be responsible and take the blame for any shortage of munitions of war from this time forward, which will try to infuse new life into von Donop, Lord Kitchener having failed, which will be responsible directly, under whatever scheme of devolution it may work, for all Army contracts for munitions of war in the future. There need be no necessity for strict terms of reference, for Lord Kitchener can rest secure that the members of the Committee have no motive but to increase the supply of munitions of war. All that it requires is an assurance that the War Office will not continue to bonnet it, to hoodwink it and to neglect its advice and to conduct its own business independently of the Committee. The Committee wants not only existence but power. It wants the surrender by Kitchener of this part of his activities and he will be represented on it by Baker, von Donop and Booth. This Committee Kitchener will not have. That he will not have it is evidenced by his continued objections and his repeated attempts to forestall its appointment. In a private letter to you I am sure you will forgive me in describing as impertinent to you his treatment of the suggestions you made for the working of the Committee, for he accepted them when you sent them across after they had been approved by the Chancellor of the Exchequer and then inserted words in putting them into his own document which made them quite useless for the purpose you and the Chancellor of the Exchequer had in mind. You stipulated that the Committee should concur in all new contracts; he made you stipulate that the Committee should concur in all new contracts which the Committee placed. This is making a meaningless farce out of a practical suggestion.

Therefore it really seems to me that there is a difference of principle which cannot be bridged except by you. The responsibility is now yours. George's view or Kitchener's must prevail. If you take the first alternative above, very well then, the project fails and Kitchener stews the British Army in his own juice. If you take the second alternative, Kitchener is relieved of responsibility, which falls on George and Balfour (and as an accidental result George negotiates in his own way with the men working on munitions of war). I submit most respectfully that the situation is serious, that delay does not improve it, that if you think the situation is as satisfactory as it can be, if Kitchener has his way, then I say no more. If you think that the situation demands that George's suggestion should be carried out, then you must impose your will on Kitchener, for I am certain that there can be no accommodation of this vital difference of principle except by the surrender of one or the other to your wishes."

In the event the Prime Minister seems to have decided on a compromise which turned out to be quite unworkable. The first meeting of the Committee was held on 12th April, 1915, three weeks after the War Council had decided to appoint it as a matter of extreme urgency.   There were in all five further meetings between that date and 13th May.   With the reconstruction of the Government and the formation of the Ministry of Munitions at the end of May, its functions were taken over by that new Department.

Five days before its first meeting Lord Kitchener had constituted at the War Office an " Armaments Output Committee " with the help of Mr. George M. Booth, of the Booth firm of engineers.   It was he who became known as the " man of push and go," with the ostensible function of securing labour for the established armament firms, which had been subsidised considerably to extend their works, and were finding difficulty in staffing the extensions.

This Armaments Output Committee became informally, though not technically, subordinate to the Munitions of War Committee, and from the outset Mr. Booth consulted with me as to the steps he was proposing to take to organise labour in different areas for munition production.

With the work of the Munitions of War Committee it is hardly necessary to deal here in much detail.   It was given, by the Prime Minister, terms of reference that nominally empowered it to take all steps necessary for the purpose of ensuring the promptest and most efficient application of all the available productive resources of the country to the manufacture and supply of munitions of war for the Navy and Army.   Actually it was doomed to futility, first by the extreme reluctance of the War Office to supply it with information which was essential to the proper discharge of its duties, and ultimately by the blank refusal of the War Office to relinquish to it the task of organising munition production.   The first difficulty is referred to by Mr. Balfour in a note he sent to the Committee.

" The War Office have a natural objection to stating the number of men they propose to put in the field on any particular date, and probably the Committee would be reluctant to press them upon such points of policy.   This reticence, however, makes it extremely difficult to draw up trustworthy statistical estimates of the amount of munitions of war that will be required at different dates."

But it was historically of importance because its setting-up marked the clear recognition by the Government that the War Office and Admiralty could not be expected to carry out in addition to their other duties a task so vast as the supply of munitions in war-time had become; and thus it proved a stepping-stone to the creation of a Ministry of Munitions.

The original members of the Committee were myself, as its chairman, supported by Mr. Balfour, Mr. Edwin Montagu,

E

Mr. George Booth, and Mr. Arthur Henderson, together with General von Donop and Mr. Harold Baker from the War Office, and Sir Frederick Black and Admiral Tudor from the Admiralty. Sir H. Llewellyn Smith from the Board of Trade was co-opted at the first meeting, and Sir Percy Girouard on 26th April.

Among the tasks which this Committee undertook was the carrying out by means of a deputation to France of a further and more detailed survey of the way in which the French were organising their munition production, and the adoption of a scheme prepared for its consideration by Sir Percy Girouard, for the regional organisation of munition firms.

It is significant that at the last meeting held by the Munitions of War Committee, on 13th May, the first business considered was a memorandum prepared by Mr. Balfour in which he pointed out that there were not enough field-guns to supply the divisions then being sent out, and that even for the guns they had, there would be only half the necessary ammunition in June and less than half in July.

5. THE GREAT SHELL SCANDAL

But although the munition shortage with which we were faced in the spring of 1915 covered all or most branches of war material, the most pressing need in the field was for shells for our artillery.

On 31st December, 1914, Sir John French had informed the War Office, on the basis of his experience during the first five months of war, what his requirements in the way of shells would be in order to maintain the regular defence of the front and the exceptional expenditure necessitated by special attacks. For the principal artillery of his forces—the 18-pounders, the 4.5-inch howitzers and the 4.7-inch field-guns—he laid down his requirements as: —

50 rounds per gun per day for the 18-pdrs.
40   „   „   „   4.5-in.
25   „   „   „   4.7-in.

The number of rounds per gun per day actually supplied to him for these weapons, month by month, were: —

	Month	18-pdr.	4.5-in.	4.7-in.
1914	Nov.	9.9	6.8	10.8
	Dec.	6.0	4.6	7.6
1915	Jan.	4.9	4.2	7.6
	Feb.	5.3	6.5	5.3
	Mar.	8.6	6.5	5.3
	Apr.	10.6	8.2	4.2
	May	11.0	6.1	4.3

These figures require no comment from me. They speak for themselves. The consequences of this deficiency were tragic for the troops who had to hold the line during these months. Throughout those months our men were being battered by the Germans without any effective means of retaliation. Retaliation meant protection. The Germans would have hesitated to open fire on our trenches had they known we could return shell for shell. But they knew too well that they could rain explosives on our poor fellows with practical impunity. And when we attacked, our advance was not supported by adequate artillery preparation or counter-battery work, and our men were held up by unbroken wire and there slaughtered by machine-guns. This calamity was due to the utter inadequacy of the preliminary bombardment. It was not the fault of our artillery; their guns were not heavy enough and their shell supply for heavy and light guns was not only painfully inadequate but inappropriate to the task, for it was mostly shrapnel.

On 21st December, 1914, I stated in the House of Commons: "What we stint in material, we squander in life; that is the one great lesson of munitions." The truth of that statement was brought home to us in the following months, when our men were left without any means of replying effectively to the German fire.

I have already shown how Sir John French constantly called for more munitions at the end of 1914. He continued to send urgent messages for greater support. When the battle of Neuve-Chapelle had been in progress three days, Sir John French had to wire Lord Kitchener on the 13th March, 1915: —

"Cessation of the forward movement is necessitated to-day by the fatigue of the troops, and above all by the want of ammunition. If we are to obtain results of value, we must have all possible support in men and ammunition from home."

On the 16th March he wired: —

"The supply has fallen short, especially in 18-pounder and 4.5-inch, of what I was led to expect and I am, therefore, compelled to abandon further offensive operations until sufficient reserves are accumulated."

And in a reinforcing telegram of the same date he added: —

"The delay is really most deplorable. Now is the time to strike. Can nothing be done to expedite action operations now?"

Sir John French followed up these telegrams by a letter to the War Secretary, dated 18th March, in which he declared that the results of the Army Council's efforts to supply him with ammunition had been "consistently disappointing."

"If the supply of ammunition cannot be maintained on a considerably increased scale it follows that the offensive efforts of the Army must be spasmodic and separated by considerable intervals of time. They cannot therefore lead to decisive results. . . .

Up to the present time the mud and the shortage of artillery munition have been the most potent factors in restricting us to the defensive. But the weather and the state of the ground have no longer to be reckoned with as limiting the scope of our operations. . . .

. . . I desire to state with all the weight of my authority as Commander-in-Chief of the British Army in France, that the object of His Majesty's Government cannot be attained unless the supply of artillery ammunition can be increased sufficiently to enable the Army to engage in sustained offensive operations, and I further desire to impress on them the very serious nature of the effort that it is necessary to make to achieve this end."

The War Office reply to this letter complained that the artillery had used, in the first 16 days of March, 200 to 220 rounds per gun —about 13 rounds per gun per day! This included the shells fired at the battle of Neuve-Chapelle. For this operation shells had been saved up for weeks. The War Office asked that "*in view of the effects achieved, which appear to have been to reduce the defence to a dazed and demoralised condition* [my italics] the utmost economy will be made in the expenditure of ammunition," and begged that less ammunition of the heavier natures should be expended.

There was an explanation for Lord Kitchener's abnormal frugality in the matter of shells, apart from the natural bent of his mind. The one campaign that had brought him renown and rank—in fact made him "Lord K. of K."—was waged on the basis of a tender for the total cost of the operation, which he submitted to that most austere of all Chancellors, Sir Michael Hicks Beach. The latter refused to give his sanction to operations against the Mahdi without having a most careful estimate of the cost, and the expenses were consequently cut down to the lowest figure. Lord Kitchener undertook to keep within this estimate and succeeded in doing so. The formidable Chancellor had won for himself a reputation by fighting every proposal, from whatever quarter it came, which would involve any additional expenditure. He looked at every project entirely from that angle. Sometimes this provoked a combination of all the spending Departments against the Treasury. There is a story told of those days which illustrates the internal conflicts in the Cabinet which were aroused by this attitude of mind. A Conservative Minister was asked after a Cabinet meeting whether anything important had been decided that day. He replied: "Nothing, except that we gave Hicks Beach the usual 19 to 1." Lord Kitchener, knowing the Chancellor's reputation, very astutely played upon it by contracting with him to run the expedition on the cheap.

It is a curious illustration of the way in which Lord Kitchener's mind worked about these matters, that just after this battle of Neuve-Chapelle, Kitchener stalked into the Cabinet with his most military stride, and with that ominous cast in his eye exaggerated and emphasised—a sure sign of surging anger—and as soon as he sat down he exclaimed in husky tones charged with suppressed emotion: " Oh, it is terrible—terrible! "

" Were the casualties very heavy?" we inquired, anxiously. " I'm not thinking for the moment about the casualties," replied Kitchener, " but for all the shells that were wasted! " He had just been given the actual figures of the artillery ammunition fired in the course of the battle.

Sir John French's retort to the War Office complaint (quoted above) about his rate of ammunition expenditure, was that he had said nothing about the German defence being " dazed and demoralised " and that such impression as had been made on them was due to the high-explosive shells from our heavier artillery. He added: " There is no evidence in my possession to show that the preliminary bombardment of Neuve-Chapelle was unnecessarily severe. In fact, at two places it was inadequate, and very heavy losses resulted. . . . Our losses and the amount of ground gained are the best indication as to whether the expenditure of artillery ammunition was on an unnecessarily extravagant scale."

(The total ground gained by us was equal to about one square mile in area; and our casualties were 12,892—i.e., 583 officers and 12,309 other ranks.)

Speaking in the House of Lords on 15th March, 1915, on the Second Reading of the Defence of the Realm (Amendment) Bill, to which I have already referred, Lord Kitchener so far departed from his habitual reticence as to state:—

> " The work of supplying and equipping new Armies depends largely on our ability to obtain the war material required. . . . Notwithstanding these efforts to meet our requirements, we have unfortunately found that the output is not only not equal to our necessities but does not fulfil our expectations, for a very large number of our orders have not been completed by the dates on which they were promised.
>
> The progress in equipping our new Armies and also in supplying the necessary war material for our forces in the field has been seriously hampered by the failure to obtain sufficient labour and by delays in the production of the necessary plant. . . ."

This open admission by Lord Kitchener of the serious nature of the munitions situation created some uneasiness in the public mind, and considerably helped the negotiations in which I was engaged during the next few days with representatives of the Trade Unions, to arrange for the prevention of strikes and lock-outs in establishments engaged on war work, and for the dilution of labour by the introduction of unskilled workers—negotiations which resulted in the "Treasury Agreement" on this matter, of which I give an account later on.

For the next few weeks there was a comparative lull in the reports about munition shortage. No very big operations were undertaken on the British Front in France, and possibly the fact that we were at the time engaged in negotiations with Italy, with a view to her intervention in the War on our side, made the military authorities chary of allowing any fresh details of our munition difficulties to leak out.

The illusion that things were going well in this respect was heightened by a letter which Lord Kitchener wrote to Mr. Asquith on 14th April, in the following terms:—

"War Office,
April 14, 1915.

My dear Prime Minister,
    I have had a talk with French. He told me I could let you know that with the present supply of ammunition he will have as much as his troops will be able to use on the next forward movement."

On the strength of this assurance, the Prime Minister delivered on 20th April his famous Newcastle speech, in which he declared that there was no truth in the statement that our Army or that of our Allies were being crippled or hampered by our failure to supply the necessary ammunition; and that it was neither true nor fair to suggest that there had been anything in the nature of a general slackness in the armaments industry on the part of either employers or employed.

On the following day I had to take part in a debate on munitions in the House of Commons, and in the course of my speech I gave full credit to the War Office for their actual achievements, and stressed the magnitude of the task with which they had been confronted. The telegrams from the front complaining of the shell shortage were not communicated to the Cabinet. I have no knowledge as to whether the Prime Minister saw them. Lord Kitchener had given me his assurances as to the present adequacy of the Army's equipment, and on the strength of such information as was given me by the War Office I put up the best defence I could for the shortage. I was anxious to conciliate the War Office and carry it along with us in the efforts we were making to increase the munitions supply. I knew this could not be done without persuading those who were in supreme control to depart from traditional ideas and practices, and I was at that time doing my best to convince them. I

therefore dwelt in my speech in the House rather on their achievements than on their shortcomings. I pointed to the fact that whereas
we had only promised the French six divisions we had already put
six times as many in the field. "That was the problem which
confronted the War Office, and which they had to face. I do not
say that they could not have done more, but I want the House of
Commons to know what has actually been done by the War Office."

I passed on to make a brief reference to some of the difficulties we
were experiencing: drink, short time, trade union restrictions; and
to the efforts which were being made by the Munitions of War
Committee and the Armaments Output Committee to cope with
these matters.

I ended on a note of optimism, based on my confidence that there
was nothing in the problem confronting us which our nation was
incapable of meeting and overcoming. But I was in fact far from
optimistic about the progress we were making at the time, though
to have given public expression to my views would at that moment
probably have done more harm than good, in view of the diplomatic
situation in reference to Italy.

The Opposition drew attention to the discrepancy between what
Mr. Asquith had said at Newcastle on the previous day and
Lord Kitchener's statement five weeks previously in the House of
Lords, about the output of ammunition being equal neither to our
expectations nor to our necessities. They put in a plea for more
information as to the situation and for better co-ordination of effort
in the production of ammunition, with which latter recommendation
I expressed myself in my speech as in full agreement.

It must, I think, be accepted that Lord Kitchener had somehow
misunderstood what French said to him about the adequacy of the
shell supply in France. Certainly the statement, expanded
emphatically as it was by Mr. Asquith at Newcastle, received a
prompt and dramatic refutation only two days later, when the
Germans opened a fresh offensive at Ypres, with the new and added
horror of the first gas attack; for our army found itself deplorably
deficient in artillery ammunition with which to extricate the
doomed infantry from the death-cloud that was annihilating them.

The introduction of gas gave fresh emphasis to the lesson that the
technical side of this war was supremely important. It was a method
of fighting which we were not ready to employ; we were, therefore,
not prepared to meet such an attack. A feeling of anger and horror
ran through the whole nation. The main criticism we had to face
was the fact that no preparations whatever had been made to protect
our men against this deadly weapon, although we had received
through French sources more than one warning—on 30th March and
15th April—that the Germans were reported to be preparing this
new method of attack, and on 17th April, five days before they

Published on April 21st, 1915.   Reproduced by courtesy of " Punch."

" DELIVERING THE GOODS."

themselves used it, the Germans published the false charge that the British had been using shells and bombs with asphyxiating gas. That was obviously designed as a defence in advance for the use they were proposing to make of this cruel weapon of war. I may add that the French, though warned before ourselves, were equally unprepared.

Rough-and-ready methods of protecting troops against the chlorine fumes were improvised by the officers at the front, and at home Lord Kitchener took a deep personal interest in the providing of appliances for anti-gas defence, which were promptly put in hand by the War Office; but the episode added to the growing public anxiety as to our unpreparedness to cope with a foe that had at his disposal the resources of science directed by a skilled and highly organised industrialism, and who was resolved to make the most ruthless use of all his advantages.

The serious breach which had been made by this weapon in our front induced the Army Commanders to attempt a counter-attack at Festubert on 9th May, in an effort to relieve the pressure on the troops at Ypres. In his book "1914" Sir John French wrote of this battle : —

> "After all our demands, less than 8 per cent. of our shells were high explosive, and we had only sufficient supply for about 40 minutes of artillery preparation for this attack. On the tower of a ruined church I spent several hours in close observation of the operations. Nothing since the battle of the Aisne had ever impressed me so deeply with the terrible shortage of artillery and ammunition as did the events of that day. As I watched the Aubers Bridge, I clearly saw the great inequality of the artillery duels, and, as attack after attack failed, I could see that the absence of sufficient artillery support was doubling and trebling our losses in men."

Our losses at this battle were very heavy—gains there were none.

Three days after this battle started I received an unexpected visit from two gentlemen—one being Sir John French's secretary, Brinsley Fitzgerald, and the other one of his A.D.C.'s, Captain F. Guest. They had been sent over by the Commander-in-Chief to lay before Mr. Balfour, Mr. Bonar Law, and myself certain facts and documents referring to the shortage of ammunition. They had with them copies of correspondence and a memorandum by Sir John French, emphasising the need for high-explosive shell and containing a demand for a monthly supply of gun ammunition to be furnished within the next three months. The Commander-in-Chief was tired of remonstrances to the War Office which produced nothing but counter-remonstrances, so he decided to appeal over their heads to leading politicians and Press men. This was the first communication on the shell question that I had received from the Commander-in-Chief.

Sir John has since stated that the reason why he selected me to be a recipient of his complaint was because I had always shown a special interest in the subject. As part of his campaign to expose what he considered a dangerous situation, he also furnished information and gave his views to the Military Correspondent of *The Times,* and on 14th May there appeared a report from him in that paper, under the headlines: "NEED FOR SHELLS: BRITISH ATTACKS CHECKED: LIMITED SUPPLY THE CAUSE."

As this report is practically an epitome of the information communicated to me by Sir John French's emissaries, I quote the following passages: —

"The results of our attacks on Sunday last in the districts of Fromelles and Richeburg were disappointing. We found the enemy much more strongly posted than we expected. We had not sufficient high explosive to level his parapets to the ground after the French practice, and when our infantry gallantly stormed the trenches, as they did in both attacks, they found a garrison undismayed, many entanglements still intact, and Maxims on all sides ready to pour in streams of bullets. We could not maintain ourselves in the trenches won, and our reserves were not thrown in because the conditions for success in an assault were not present.

The attacks were well planned and valiantly conducted. The infantry did splendidly, but the conditions were too hard. *The want of an unlimited supply of high explosive was a fatal bar to our success. . . .*

The value of the German troops in the attack has greatly deteriorated, and we can deal easily with them in the open. But until we are thoroughly equipped for this trench warfare, we attack under grave disadvantages. . . .

To break this hard crust we need more high explosives, more heavy howitzers, and more men. This special form of warfare has no precedent in history.

It is certain that we can smash the German crust if we have the means. So the means we must have, and as quickly as possible."

This article created very considerable public anxiety and consternation. It was the first time the public had ever been so plainly told from the army front how serious was the munition shortage; and I may add that the visit of Sir John French's representatives similarly gave me my first clear and authoritative information as to the full gravity of the position. As I have said, the Cabinet had not been shown the Commander-in-Chief's frequent telegrams on the subject, and we had been compelled to form our opinions on the basis of general statements, rumours, and a common-sense interpretation of the facts known to us. Although I had taken an active interest in increasing the output of munitions and had assisted the War Office by every means at my disposal to achieve this aim, all vital telegrams from the front on the subject of the shell shortage had been withheld from me, even when I was Chairman of the Committee appointed by the Prime Minister to consider the munition question.

Now, however, it was clear that after eight months we were still fatally short of munitions for the kind of war in which we were entangled. An even graver trouble was that as far as I could see, there was no prospect of our getting an adequate supply with the present methods of organisation. The unavailing sacrifice of the lives of our men would continue, the War would be prolonged, and ultimate victory would be jeopardised, unless someone took the matter in hand.

So strongly did I feel on the subject that I addressed the following letter to Mr. Asquith: —

" May 19th, 1915.

My dear Prime Minister,

Certain facts have been brought to my notice on the question of munitions which I have felt bound to call your attention to. I write to you inasmuch as my appointment as Chairman of the Munitions Committee came direct from you.

In order properly to discharge our functions as a Committee it was essential that all information as to the character of the explosive most urgently needed and the present supply available should be afforded to us. I am now informed, on what appears to be reliable information: —

(1) That in order to attack highly developed trenches protected by barbed-wire entanglements, shrapnel is useless, and high-explosive shells indispensable;

(2) That those who are responsible for conducting operations at the front have for months impressed this fact upon the War Office, and asked in the first instance that 25 per cent. of the shells sent to France should be high explosive, and that afterwards this percentage was increased to 50 per cent.;

(3) That notwithstanding these urgent representations, the percentage of high-explosive shell provided for the 18-pounders has never exceeded 8 per cent.; that when the great combined attack to break through the German lines was made by the French and British armies last Sunday week, the French prepared the attack with an overwhelming bombardment of high explosive which utterly demolished the German trenches and barbed-wire entanglements, thus enabling the French to penetrate the German lines for four miles without any excessive loss of life. In spite of the fact that the French spent their high-explosive shells lavishly, they have still in reserve hundreds of thousands of shells of the same kind for the purpose of

continuing their operations. On the other hand, our armies had less than 45,000 high-explosive shells in all. Of these about 18,000 were 18-pounders. They therefore had to rely on shrapnel, so that when our troops advanced to the attack the German fortifications were barely pockmarked. The Germans rose in their trenches and mocked at our advancing troops, and then calmly mowed them down in thousands. The Germans themselves have barely lost 200 men.

I am also told that the attack on Saturday last had to be made by night—a risky operation—because of the deficiencies in high-explosive shell, and that after the battle there were not more than 2,000 high-explosive shells left for all our guns.

(4) That a full report on ammunition was sent to the War Office weeks ago from Headquarters in France, and that later on another report on guns was sent. Neither of these reports has ever been shown to the Munitions Committee, and I gather they have not been seen by you.

If these facts are approximately correct, I hesitate to think what action the public would insist on if they were known. But it is quite clear that the proceedings of a Munitions Committee from which vital information of this character is withheld must be a farce. I cannot, therefore, continue to preside over it under such conditions. *It is now eight months since I ventured to call the attention of the Cabinet to the importance of mobilising all our engineering resources for the production of munitions and equipments of war.* In October of last year I brought a full report from France showing how the French Ministry for War had coped with the difficulty. The Cabinet at that date decided that the same course should be pursued here, and a Cabinet Committee was set up for that purpose. We met at the War Office, and it was there agreed, with the Secretary of State in the chair, that steps of that kind should be taken in this country. *I regret to say after some inquiry that action on those lines has not been taken even to this hour except at Leeds.*

A Cabinet Committee cannot have executive power; it can only advise and recommend. It is for the department to act. They have not done so, and all the horrible loss of life which has occurred in consequence of the lack of high-explosive shell is the result.

Private firms cannot turn out shrapnel because of the complicated character of the shell; but the testimony is unanimous that the high explosive is a simple shell and that any engineering concern could easily produce it. That has been the experience of France.

Ever sincerely,

D. Lloyd George."

This letter played its part—an important one—in the course of events which led to the reconstruction of the Government by the formation of the first Coalition—a matter with which I deal in more detail elsewhere in this narrative.

Lord Northcliffe (who at that time owned *The Times* as well as the *Daily Mail*) was personally responsible for the publication by *The Times* of the dispatch from its Military Correspondent, Colonel Repington.   Lord Northcliffe had for some time been receiving an unending stream of letters and statements from men at the front about the shell shortage, but all efforts to give publicity to these complaints had been diligently blacked out of his proofs by the Censor.   He was not content with the news that the Ministry was to be reconstructed.   He attributed the blame for the shell shortage to Lord Kitchener, and he resolved to drive him out of office if he possibly could.   On hearing that he would be retained in the reconstructed Ministry, he came out on 21st May with an article in the *Daily Mail* with a headline that ran: " THE SHELLS SCANDAL: LORD KITCHENER'S TRAGIC BLUNDER."

The *Daily Mail* and *The Times* were solemnly burned on the Stock Exchange that afternoon.   But the campaign for more shells went on.   On 25th May *The Times* published a letter from Bishop Furse, at that time Bishop of Pretoria, now Bishop of St. Albans, who had just returned from a visit to the Front.   The following extracts from his letter give some picture of the situation which the Bishop had found: —

" . . . When battalion after battalion of infantry—and, as was recently the case in the Ypres salient, regiment after regiment of cavalry, too—have to sit in trenches day after day, night after night, being pounded by high explosives from enemy guns, with no guns behind them capable of keeping down the enemy's fire, then the conclusion they draw is obvious—namely, that the nation has failed to provide sufficient guns or ammunition to meet those of the enemy.

When, night after night and day after day, the men in the trenches know that for every one hand grenade or rifle grenade or trench mortar bomb which they throw at the enemy they will get back in answer anything from five to ten, then the conclusion they draw is also obvious—namely, that the nation does not somehow realise the situation, or, if it does, has not made it its business to supply what is necessary. . . . They know that it is little short of murder for a nation to ask men, however full of the right spirit, to face an enemy amply equipped with big guns and the right kind of ammunition, unless they are at least equipped with equally effective munitions of war.

There can only be one impression left on the minds of men

in such a case, and that is that somehow or other the nation does not know the truth, does not understand, and is not backing them, for, knowing the old country as they do, they have no doubt that if Germany can produce these things, we can, if we will. . . ."

An officer home from the front stated in the *Northwich Chronicle* of 22nd May, 1915: —

" . . . People at home do not appear to realise how critical the position is out here. . . . The Germans have still unlimited supplies of munitions. . . . You can rub it in about our need for men and munitions of war. I am sorry to say that in the ten days' battle about Ypres our men suffered heavily owing to lack of ammunition. The Germans poured shells into our lines. . . . For our men it was a terrible time, while the Germans shelled us heavily and we, owing to shortage of ammunition, could not reply effectively. It is up to everybody at home to realise what such a situation means, and for people to understand that successful war cannot be waged without enormous supplies being available on the spot."

The two foregoing extracts represent the point of view of an onlooker and of a man in the trenches. I will quote, as the view of the man behind the guns an extract from a striking letter written to me at the time by Captain H. FitzHerbert Wright, M.P. for Leominster, who was serving as an artillery officer on the Western Front. The address on his letter was " Belgium, 29/5/15." He said: —

" . . . . I rejoined the 4th North Midland Brigade (Howitzer) on the outbreak of the War and have been serving out here for nearly 13 weeks as a Captain and Officer Commanding the Ammunition Column. . . . As O.C. Amm. Col., all the shells fired by my brigade pass through my hands. We have been attached to two divisions—the 4th and the 46th, both in the 2nd Army. When we first got into the firing line in the first week of March we were allowed 20 rounds per gun per day: 80 *rounds per day per battery.* We have been in action throughout. Our allowance is now two rounds per gun per day, *or eight rounds per battery per day.* It isn't that our fellows have made bad practice, or that there are not any targets suitable for our 50-pound lyddite shells. General Smith-Dorrien has publicly and privately given us the highest praise for the accuracy and effectiveness of our fire, and our fellows are made much of by all the infantry over whom they have fired; and, as to targets, we daily see the German trenches, and works growing and growing, simply asking to be pounded. I have to-day returned from having a week with our 1st Battery, spent mainly in an observation station, and I speak of what I have seen. The battery commanders in our Brigade, the Q.F. brigades, the R.H.A. and the Heavy are now not allowed to fire except by order of the General even one round.

The R.H.A. adjutant told me he had to send 1,500 rounds down to the 1st Army for the recent fighting down South, and he had now an empty park and column; one of the officers of the Heavies told me his park and column are at this moment empty (4.7-inch shells) and he may not fire even in the event of an attack without express orders. My batteries in 12 weeks have averaged a little over 60 rounds per battery a week. Naturally, I don't know the reason, but I suspect, and we all suspect, that there are no shells for us. Anyhow, here we are inviting attack, seeing the enemy firing daily 20 or 30 rounds into our lines to our one into theirs. We don't know or care who is to blame; we only know that we are being starved to death for want of shells, and our infantry fated daily to a more and more terrible task if an attack either by the Germans or ourselves takes place in our zone. I know nothing of other zones except by hearsay. We want to be fed; soldiers do not live by bread alone. . . .

Nor is that all; we are outclassed in guns, number and quality; we are outranged; I am not now speaking of our Brigade, but generally. So far as our Brigade is concerned, our guns were pretty old in South Africa, and are, therefore, getting into years now. The 5-inch Howitzer never should have come out here. I raised this matter last September through Talbot and tried to get the 4.5-inch Howitzer, the Regular gun, but got the answer direct from W.O. that it was impossible as there were none, and the output of guns hadn't yet overtaken the wastage. However, we are doing our best and, having had good positions well concealed, at short ranges have, as I already quoted, done well. If we got into the open or had to shoot at anything over 3,500 yards we should be off the map in five minutes. We fire one round a minute, and the shell takes 20 seconds to go the distance. A q.f. at from 10 to 15 rounds a minute would find us easy victims.

Nor is that all: outclassed in guns; little or no ammunition; that sums up the Artillery part of the show, except to say that much of the shells we have are shrapnel—that does not apply to my Brigade, which has only lyddite—which is less useful than rain, against the German trenches.

Now for the infantry—and more magnificent infantry will never be seen. In our division there are two machine-guns per battalion. The Germans have 16; our Regulars have six or eight; in our Division we have two trench mortars on a front of not less than three miles; the Germans have them at frequent intervals all along; our hand grenades are in many cases " hand "-made and truly " hand " grenades; a few are thrown and the Germans promptly answer with 50-pound bombs. We call that showing our superiority. I suppose of courage—certainly not of equipment. Our lights are ridiculous beside the German lights . . . we do not use gas. Personally, I hope we shan't have to, though if it is true that our air reconnaissance reports that what were supposed to be light railways coming up their lines are in reality 18-inch pipes conjectured to be used for gas on a large scale, it is probable we shall never have the chance, even if we want to.

Now are these facts anything for England, the richest country in the world or nearly, anything to be proud of? Are they not a matter rather for sackcloth and ashes?

If we get ammunition we can hold on, though the poor infantry will go on getting cut to pieces. If we get plenty of ammunition we can go ahead. I suppose you know that the Artists, now a training corps for officers, rejoices in the name of the Suicides Club—magnificent, cheery fellows? Where is the responsibility for that name being more than justified by the casualty lists?

Never mind where is the responsibility; get the mess cleared up. You have the pluck and go of ten. More power to you!

I hope I haven't by any fault of diction or over-emphasis led you to think I am exaggerating. I am but dotting the 'i's' and crossing the 't's' of the Bishop's letter. He and I are old friends since the Eton days. . . ."

I have in my possession a bundle of letters, blue-pencilled by the censor or stamped by him "NOT TO BE PUBLISHED" which were sent to me by Northcliffe about this time to show me the sorts of reports he was receiving from France, but was not allowed to print. The circumstances in which these came to me from him are described as follows by Tom Clarke in his interesting book, "My Northcliffe Diary": —

"May 25, 1915: Several stories from officers at the front supporting Northcliffe's allegation *re* shell shortage having been refused publication by the censors at the Press Bureau, the Chief has given instructions that we must not submit them to the Censor. When it was pointed out that we might be trapped on a technical point, he said, 'I have been threatened so much in the past few weeks that I do not mind now. Send all these censored proofs to Lloyd George and Curzon. They know the truth, and it will let them see how the Press Bureau is keeping it back.'"

Here are a few specimens culled from this collection of appeals and complaints: —

"We had some artillery officers to mess the other evening, and they were very worried. They had had orders from General Headquarters to fire only a certain number of shells a day and their requests for supplies were always avoided by some excuse. . . ."

" . . . We have just to sit tight in the trenches while the German high explosives batter them to bits, and the main part of our casualties in the 16-hour bombardment which I described in the last letter were from this cause. . . . Out of our company of from 150 to 200 men only 13 came out of the trenches after the last attack."

" . . . It makes your heart break to see those men going forward and then held up—one after another, fighting and struggling, until, wearied out, they collapse like a wet cloth. And why? Because there is not an adequate supply of high explosives to blow the wire to bits, and let our men go at the enemy."

" . . . I have often heard the wish expressed that a representative of the manufacturing population at home might be present in one of our front trenches to witness the eagerness and anxiety of officers and men as they watch the enemy's trench being bombarded preparatory to an assault. There is not one who does not realise that on the intensity and volume of that fire his life and all his chances of success depend. On these occasions shrapnel gives no confidence to those who have had a little experience; they know that it has as much effect as one would expect from a handful of gravel on a German machine-gun emplacement, and they know that over some 200 yards it is only machine-guns that can stop them. When the first line has been destroyed by them (i.e., by German machine-guns) many of us have seen the second immediately throw themselves over our parapet to certain and conscious destruction.

Actually to witness this heroic perseverance and self-sacrifice of a fighting body which in quality and war experience cannot soon —if ever—be replaced, and to know that it is all due to the tardy organisation of the war machinery at home raises thoughts that cannot be expressed ' in print.' "

Although statements of this nature were banned by the Censor from the columns of the Press, the facts they set out were becoming common knowledge in every newspaper office, and in countless homes throughout the land. That knowledge doubtless played an important part in making the country ripe for the change of Government which was announced on 19th May, when Mr. Asquith, having invited his fellow-ministers of the Liberal Government to resign their offices, reconstructed his Ministry as a Coalition Government, including the leaders of the Conservative Party.

CHAPTER VII

THE POLITICS OF THE WAR

No nation engaged in a struggle with a redoubtable foe can afford to dissipate its energies and distract its executive by party controversy. The last days of July, 1914, found the traditional British parties confronting each other in the fiercest political conflict waged since the suppression of the last Jacobite rebellion. We were faced with the prospect of an internecine struggle which would have rent the nation into warring factions such as these islands have not witnessed since the great Civil Wars. The threatened uprising of Ulster against the dominion of an Irish Parliament was not a bluff. The Orange North would have fought before it submitted. The Curragh incident, the gun-running in Ulster, followed by the arming of the South (which was the beginning of the bloodshed of the six years that followed) all pointed towards the possibilities of bloody strife once more on a political battlefield. Political and religious issues had not so long ago been referred in these islands to the arbitrament of the sword. It is never safe to say that such things will not happen again. "The thing that hath been, it is that which shall be, and that which is done, is that which shall be done, and there is no new thing under the sun." This saying, uttered over 2,000 years ago, is being verified in every generation, and it is never quite wise to assume that it has exhausted its application to any branch of human thought or activity. The thinker and the striker have always worked in a close partnership—more or less willing, and less rather than more understanding. Unionists who attended Ulster meetings in England tell me that they never saw such depths of fierce indignation as that aroused by the threat of force to subject the Protestants of the North to the rule of the Catholic South. On the other hand, I myself never witnessed such an outburst of ferocious anger as that which was aroused in the House of Commons when the late Mr. John Ward and Mr. J. H. Thomas denounced the attempt of certain Army officials to override the constitution by threatening to disobey orders and refusing to carry out laws of which they disapproved. The North had armed, the South was arming. What would have happened?

There was no surety that if bloodshed ensued its flow could have been confined to Ireland. There are towns on this side of the

Channel where it would have been difficult to keep the peace amongst the votaries of warring creeds if their fellow-religionists in Ireland on either side were being slain. Wisdom might have intervened. But it might not. Mankind was only too ready for the shedding of blood, as we were to discover in a few days.

Then there came real war, like a mighty rushing wind, the struggle not of sects and factions, but of nations and continents, and the incipient fires of civil war were swept into the great conflagration. All the same the spreading flame of national dissension in Britain encouraged the warmongers of Germany and Austria to plunge. England was supposed to be temporarily out of the reckoning. Without her tenacious aid, France and Russia would soon collapse. The Ulster trouble was an undoubted factor in precipitating the Great War. How little the German rulers knew the temper of the British people! At the sound of the trumpet they all fell into line and wheeled against the common danger. There was not a perceptible break or gap in their ranks. This coming together of all creeds and sections to face a national peril was immediately reflected in the House of Commons. Its mood quickly changed. A few days before the outbreak of war the Prime Minister had been howled down by Unionist members excited beyond the bounds of Parliamentary decorum. A little later and the same members were cheering to the rafters the moving eloquence with which he called the nation to wage war with all its strength against the invaders of Belgium. In the course of a single day angry political passions were silenced and were followed by the just wrath which is too deep to be easily lashed into the frothing fury that so often churns the shallow waters of party recrimination. During the autumn and winter of 1914 and the early spring of 1915 this temper continued in the political world. Party politics and party bitterness disappeared. In fact, the Liberal Government received more unanimous and cordial support from Unionists confronting them than from the Liberal and Labour benches behind.

The reasons for this attitude are interesting and significant, and account to a large extent, if closely examined, for the political developments of the next six years. Previous wars in which this country had been engaged by no means closed down the hostilities of parties. They rather stoked political and personal antagonisms into fiercer enmity. Some of these wars actually became the dividing line of parties. The change which took place in 1914 cannot be explained by the supposition that we are more patriotic than our ancestors. The Conservative Party had in recent years become increasingly Germanophobe. Rivalry between the two Empires for supremacy on the seas and in the marts of the world accounted largely for the remarkable swing round in the Conservative attitude towards Germany. The Conservatives were far from desiring war anywhere. But when war with Germany came, there could be no doubt as to its popularity with Conservatives, Press and rank and file. It was something many of their most ardent spirits had hoped for. Others feared it was inevitable that we should be forced sooner or later to try conclusions with a Power that seemed to be preparing to destroy us. So when it came with a Liberal Government in power it was an auspicious combination of events of which they had not dreamed. There was a note of exhilaration in their support of the War. On the other hand, the Liberals felt the obligation of honour involved in the Belgian Treaty, and they promptly if unhappily followed a course prescribed by the greatest of their leaders in 1870 when he protected Belgium from invasion during the Franco-Prussian War. So the Conservatives entered the War with enthusiasm and the Liberals with reluctant conviction. Conservatives in particular were well pleased by Mr. Asquith's choice of Lord Kitchener as War Director inside his Cabinet. Lord Kitchener had no Party associations; but if he had any leanings they were towards Conservatism. Even those leanings were inherited prejudices rather than convictions. The latter he had neither the time nor the inclination to acquire during his busy life on duties for his country in environments far removed from our Party conflicts. At any rate his appointment to the War Office was a guarantee of the Government's intention to prosecute the War vigorously, and that Party considerations should not enter into its conduct. His selection for what was practically a War Dictatorship gave satisfaction and confidence to the nation generally and to the Conservative Party in particular. It undoubtedly had the effect of restraining criticism, for doubts cast on the War direction implied censure of Lord Kitchener. For the first few months of the War his influence was paramount. His very picture on the walls counted more than all the appeals of all the political leaders of all parties.

The Liberal Government commanded a working majority in the House of Commons. It is true it was dependent for that majority on a Coalition of groups—the Liberal, Nationalist, and Labour groups. The country has been governed by Coalitions for the greater part of the last half-century. In the 1914 Parliament the Conservatives, in fact, constituted the largest party in the House, but they could not attract the support of any other section. It followed that the Liberal Government could not be dismissed except by dissolution, and that was unthinkable in the agony of the Great War. It would have been an unspeakable crime to divide the nation when even united it could barely be saved from defeat, so formidable was the foe we had challenged. The Conservatives were led by men of high character and capacity whose patriotism was above suspicion—Mr. Bonar Law, Mr. Balfour, Lord Lansdowne, Sir Edward Carson, and Lord Curzon. Such men were much too high minded to desire electoral victory bought at such a cost to their country. Liberals will admit that their actions throughout the War were dictated by the highest motives of patriotism and that during that period they were willing to sink all Party dealing and rivalries and maintain their opponents in full possession of power so long as that power was wielded in the achievement of victory for their country's banner.

The men of the Army and Navy who at the bidding of their country were undergoing hardships and facing death on the seas from Scapa Flow to Coromandel, and in strange lands from Nieuport to Nineveh, were of many different political faiths, and there were multitudes whose faith had not yet been cast in any party mould. Men of political parties and unions left their badges at home and joined the new fraternity of sacrifice, and others whose opinions were unformed and who were still unattached entered the same comradeship. They expected—and they had a right to expect—that their jeopardy should not be increased by the irrelevant bickerings at home of those men who could afford to indulge in untimely animosities with complete immunity to themselves. Diversion and dissipation of thought and energy in attack or defence in time-honoured Party quarrels which had no bearing on the issues of the War (and which could not be dealt with during the War) would have weakened a front which had no superfluous strength to spare and intensified dangers already almost too appalling for human nature to bear. That is why France with her face all wrinkled with Party lines, displayed the *union sacrée* to the eyes of the world, and Britain, also riven with Party schisms, presented the spectacle of a united front.

There was an undoubted advantage from the point of view of national unity in having a Liberal rather than a Tory Government in power when war was declared. There was a further advantage in having a Government at the head of affairs which had the support of Labour. This secured the adhesion of the great Labour organisations whose action and sympathetic aid was essential to its vigorous prosecution. Had Labour been hostile the War could not have been carried on effectively. Had Labour been lukewarm victory would have been secured with increased and increasing difficulty. The most prominent and influential leaders of trade unionism worked for victory throughout the War. Without their help it could not have been achieved. But beyond and above all these considerations, as a factor in the attainment of national unity, was the circumstance that the War had been declared by a party which by tradition and training regarded war with the deepest aversion, and has more especially since the days of Gladstone, Cobden and Bright, regarded itself as specially charged with the promotion of the cause of peace.

The spring of 1915 witnessed a growing change in the attitude of Parliament. Questions multiplied, debates became more prolonged, the atmosphere became more critical, the note more challenging. Mr. M'Kenna's administration of the Home Office provoked much dissatisfaction, and not merely on the Unionist benches. His policy towards residents of enemy extraction in this country was thought to be too protective, too indifferent to the dangers which might arise from espionage. The country was all camp and arsenal, and valuable information for the enemy was visible everywhere without speering or spying. Mr. M'Kenna's rigid and fretful answers, though always technically complete, were provocative. Whilst administering the letter of his trust, he showed too clearly that he had no sympathy with its spirit. And the nation was uneasy. Its sons were falling, and information was undoubtedly getting through from the shores of Britain which helped the enemy in the slaughter. Subsequent events proved that intelligence of great value to the enemy percolated to Germany through the agency of persons living unmolested in England under Mr. M'Kenna's indulgent regime. War is a ruthless business and those who wage it cannot afford to be too discriminating. The nation was right in thinking that this was not the time to risk the national security on glib pedantries. The anxiety of the people found expression in both Houses of Parliament, and the challenge, at first friendly, quickly became more insistent and ended on a note of undisguised anger.

Then came the rumours that our gallant troops were being inadequately provided with ammunition. Men were falling fast under the continuous bombardment of an enemy well equipped with the most formidable guns lavishly provided with an overwhelming supply of high explosives. Casualties were multiplying at an alarming rate. Though the figures were withheld from the public by a prudent War Office there was, as I have already shown, a growing feeling that our losses were great. With that in the mind of the nation, information leaked through as to the helplessness of our troops under the hammering of the Teutonic Thor. The facts were too poignant not to provoke a cry from those who knew them. The article in *The Times* would have forced Parliament to take sharp cognisance of the lamentable deficiency had not Mr. Asquith anticipated its intervention by a dramatic move.

CHAPTER VIII

THE POLITICAL CRISIS IN MAY, 1915

POLITICAL crises never come out of the blue. Clouds gather in the sky, sometimes from one quarter, sometimes from many. Suddenly one of those clouds is black with menace, approaches with surprising speed, hangs right overhead, and breaks into angry flashes.

The political crisis of May, 1915, was no exception to this meteorological rule. It was due to a combination of factors which had been at work for some time. The final addition of one extra cause for discontent at the existing conditions provoked the storm which swept away the Liberal Government, which had weathered many tempests. It is not correct to ascribe the change in government solely, or mainly, to the shortage of shell for our armies. The general dissatisfaction with the conduct of the War, of which there were many symptoms, and of which the culmination was reached in the second half of May, was not only due to the realisation of the munitions situation. Other contributing factors were the failure of the offensive in France, as to which expectations had been unduly raised; and disappointment over the result of the Dardanelles, with a growing feeling that the expedition was either misconceived or muddled. The disagreement between the First Lord of the Admiralty and the First Sea Lord deepened this feeling.

Underlying the various specific grounds for anxiety in different directions was a sense of revolt against the attitude of the Government and what was regarded as its leisurely and take-for-granted attitude in dealing with vitally serious matters, matters of life and death to the whole of the Allies and the British Empire, and to hundreds of thousands of gallant young men who had offered their lives to their country. The War was not being treated either with sufficient seriousness or adequate energy. So far back as the beginning of this year I had urged that more constant attention should be paid to the higher conduct of the War. *And for five and a half weeks, from the 6th April to the 14th May, the War Council had not been convened,* and the machinery set up by the Government for exercising a general supervision over the conduct of the War had not been afforded an opportunity to exercise the functions for which it had been created and for which it was responsible.

There was a genuine conviction on the part of many who had no desire to provoke a Ministerial crisis that if an improvement were not soon effected we should lose the War. This opinion was held very strongly by many members of the Opposition, who had so far loyally supported the Government, but were becoming increasingly restive. In fact, it was obvious that unless prompt action were taken to convince the country that a fresh urge was being put into the direction of affairs there would be a most dangerous division in the nation, and that this division might develop on party lines. Nothing could have been more fatal to that national unity which was essential to victory in so deadly a struggle.

On 14th May the War Council sat again for the first time after a long period of coma. Its meeting was purely formal, and only one or two members were summoned. On that day there appeared in the Press the violent outburst on the shell situation to which I have already referred in a previous section, and next day occurred the incident which actually brought matters to a head. This was the resignation from the Admiralty of Lord Fisher over our Dardanelles policy. In view of the controversy which arose later on as to the interference of the political with the naval chiefs in the matter of strategy, it is interesting to note that this particular crisis arose partly from the complete subservience of Ministers to our chief military adviser in the conduct of the War on land, and partly from the overriding of our principal naval adviser by a combination of generals and statesmen in the conduct of the War at sea. It had long been known that Lord Fisher was opposed to the attempt to force the Dardanelles by the Navy alone, but his resignation, which deprived the country of the services of its most distinguished naval expert, was the match which, applied to the discontent generated everywhere, blew up the complacency of statesmen. With it went the Government under which the War began.

I heard of Lord Fisher's contemplated resignation quite accidentally. On the morning of Saturday, 15th May, as I was passing through the entrance lobby of No. 10, Downing Street, I met Lord Fisher, and was struck by a dour change in his attitude. A combative grimness had taken the place of his usually genial greeting; the lower lip of his set mouth was thrust forward, and the droop at the corner was more marked than usual. His curiously Oriental features were more than ever those of a graven image in an Eastern temple, with a sinister frown.

" I have resigned! " was his greeting, and on my inquiring the reason he replied, " I can stand it no longer." He then informed me that he was on his way to see the Prime Minister, having made up his mind to take no further part in the Dardanelles " foolishness," and was off to Scotland that night.

I tried to persuade him to postpone his departure until the

Monday, which would give him an opportunity of placing his case before a War Council, but he declined to wait another hour. I told him that so far as the Council was concerned he had never expressed any dissent from the policy or the plans for the expedition; that though I was a member of the War Council and had been opposed to that venture from the start I had not heard one word of protest from him; and that it was only right that we should be given an opportunity of hearing his objections, weighing his advice, and taking the appropriate action. His answer was that Mr. Churchill was his Chief, and that by the traditions of the service he was not entitled to differ from him in public. On being reminded by me that the Council was a Council of War, and that he was bound as a member of that Council to speak his mind freely to all his colleagues around the table, he stated that he had at the outset made an emphatic protest against the whole expedition to the Prime Minister privately, and had left to him the responsibility of communicating or withholding that knowledge. Here he was referring to a conversation he and Mr. Churchill had with Mr. Asquith before the War Council meeting on the 28th January. This protest had never been passed on to the Council.

Failing to shake him in his purpose, I sent a message to Mr. Asquith. He was at Mr. Geoffrey Howard's wedding. (He had a queer liking for weddings and funerals and rarely missed one which he might be expected to attend.) I conveyed to him that I thought it was important he should see Lord Fisher at once. But the Prime Minister's powers of persuasion and authority were equally unavailing with the First Sea Lord, who subsequently visited Mr. M'Kenna, his former Chief at the Admiralty. Mr. M'Kenna was also an opponent of the Dardanelles expedition. At this period Mr. Winston Churchill was Mr. M'Kenna's pet aversion, for Mr. Churchill had supplanted him at the Admiralty. He was, therefore, not in a mood to extricate his supplanter from his troubles. Whatever happened at this interview, the impulsive old sailor left for Scotland that night, his departure producing an inevitable crisis, for political circles in London were seething with disquieting rumours, and there was a general feeling that things were being muddled badly and that the War was therefore not going well for us. The next I heard of the matter was when I saw Mr. M'Kenna that afternoon. Lord Fisher had reported to him the conversation he had with me. Mr. M'Kenna said that the "old boy" was quite obdurate and was not open to persuasion.

The following Monday morning Mr. Bonar Law, who had for years been a personal friend of mine and on terms of greater cordiality with me than is usual between political adversaries who are taking a strenuous part in party conflicts, came to see me at the Treasury.

Informing me that he had received a communication which seemed to him authentic indicating that Lord Fisher had resigned, he asked me point-blank if that were the case. He alluded to an unsigned letter received by him which had obviously been written by the First Sea Lord. Lord Fisher's characters and style were so dashing and on so bold a scale that no one could fail to know at a glance who had written a letter of his. The signature was superfluous.

On being told by me that his information was correct Mr. Bonar Law emphasised the grave nature of the political question raised, especially as he was convinced that the Government were misinformed about the shell situation. His party had supported the Government consistently throughout the months of the War, without seeking party advantage, but there was a growing discontent amongst Conservatives at this attitude of unqualified support, especially over the treatment of alien enemies, the deficiency of shells, and the failure of the Dardanelles expedition. Matters indeed, had come to such a pitch that it would be impossible for him to restrain his followers, and yet it was essential to avoid any division in the nation in face of the enemy. He was specially emphatic as to the impossibility of allowing Mr. Churchill to remain at the Admiralty if Lord Fisher persisted in his resignation. On this point he made it clear that the Opposition meant at all hazards to force a Parliamentary challenge. After some discussion we agreed that the only certain way to preserve a united front was to arrange for more complete co-operation between parties in the direction of the War. I asked him if he would wait a few minutes while I went to No. 10 to see the Prime Minister. I went alone to see Mr. Asquith and put the circumstances quite plainly before him. The Prime Minister at once recognised that in order to avert a serious Parliamentary conflict, which would certainly lower the prestige of the Government, if it did not actually bring about its defeat, it was necessary to reconstruct the Cabinet and admit into it some of the leaders of the Unionist Party.

This decision took an incredibly short time. I left Mr. Asquith and returned to Mr. Bonar Law and invited him to accompany me to the Cabinet Room to talk things over with the Prime Minister. In less than a quarter of an hour we realised that the Liberal Government was at an end and that for it would be substituted a Coalition Government. It was decided that Mr. Bonar Law should write a letter to the Prime Minister explaining the position in order to enable the latter to sound his leading colleagues.

Later in the day I received the following letter from Mr. Bonar Law. The enclosure fairly represented the attitude he adopted in the morning conversations, first with me and then with the Prime Minister.

" Lansdowne House,
Berkeley Square, W.
17th May, 1915.

Dear Lloyd George,

I enclose copy of the letter.

You will see we have altered it to the extent that we do not definitely offer Coalition but the substance is the same.

Yours sincerely,

A. BONAR LAW."

" Lansdowne House,
17th May, 1915.

Dear Mr. Asquith,

Lord Lansdowne and I have learnt with dismay that Lord Fisher has resigned, and we have come to the conclusion that we cannot allow the House to adjourn until this fact has been made known and discussed.

We think that the time has come when we ought to have a clear statement from you as to the policy which the Government intend to pursue. In our opinion things cannot go on as they are, and some change in the constitution of the Government seems to us inevitable if it is to retain a sufficient measure of public confidence to conduct the War to a successful conclusion.

The situation in Italy makes it particularly undesirable to have anything in the nature of a controversial discussion in the House of Commons at present, and if you are prepared to take the necessary steps to secure the object which I have indicated, and if Lord Fisher's resignation is in the meantime postponed, we shall be ready to keep silence now. Otherwise I must to-day ask you whether Lord Fisher has resigned, and press for a day to discuss the situation arising out of his resignation.

Yours, etc.,

A. BONAR LAW."

The story of the formation of the new Ministry has been told from different angles by many writers great and petty. The actual appointments were a subject of something which in business might be termed haggling between the parties. The worst controversy came over Lord Haldane and Mr. M'Kenna. The Conservatives had taken a fierce dislike to both on quite unreasonable grounds, and were bent on leaving them out. They were both personal friends of the Prime Minister—his friendship with Lord Haldane being of very long standing. What was the offence of these special objects of Conservative animosity? Lord Haldane was the originator and organiser of the Expeditionary Force, which had served the Allies so promptly and so effectively. It was a fine piece of organisation. He was the creator of the General Staff, which might have saved us

many a tragic error had it not been practically dismantled by Lord
Kitchener.   The Officers' Training Corps, which equipped the new
armies with a splendid team of young lieutenants, was also his idea.
But in one of those philosophic dissertations which gave him and his
friends equal pleasure he had referred to Germany as his " spiritual
home."   That was an *ex post facto* crime for which he must be
banished from the sight of all patriotic men.   There was also a rooted
conviction in the Unionist mind that Lord Haldane, after his visit to
Berlin, had failed to warn the Cabinet as to the German preparations
for war which he must have observed.   All these criticisms were in
my judgment fundamentally unjust, and inflicted a deep wrong on
a man whose patriotic energy had rendered greater service to the
nation in the reorganisation of the Army than any War Secretary
since the days of Cardwell.   However, temper was bitter and uncon-
scionable on this subject, and Mr. Asquith and Sir Edward Grey
sacrificed friendship to expediency.

Mr. M'Kenna's crime, as I have already explained, was that in his
administration at the Home Office he had been too tender to aliens.
And in days when a rush-light at a farm building on the coast became
a signal to the enemy the Home Office indulgence to alien enemies
dwelling within our gates was considered to be treason.   So he also
must go.   Mr. Asquith saved him and sacrificed Haldane.   Lord
Haldane was not qualified to fight a personal battle for himself.   Mr.
M'Kenna was.   So Lord Haldane was driven in disgrace into the
wilderness and Mr. M'Kenna was promoted to the second place in
the Government.

Meanwhile, on the same day the subject of munitions was debated
in the House of Commons, where, as a member put it, the one word
impressed on the hearts of most members would be " Shells."
Arguments were put forward for the formation of a Coalition
Cabinet, and the Government were pressed to have a debate on the
whole subject of munitions.   This was refused by Mr. Asquith.   The
next day, in the House of Lords, Lord Kitchener admitted the delay
in producing the material which it had been foreseen would be
required, and attributed it to the unprecedented and almost
unlimited calls on the manufacturing resources of the country.   On
the 19th, the Prime Minister announced to the House that steps were
in contemplation which would involve the " reconstruction of the
Government on a broader personal and political basis."   In other
words, he had been persuaded by the general discontent with the
conduct of the War shown on all sides to form the first Coalition
Government.   On the same day I again wrote to Mr. Asquith who
had been responsible for my appointment as Chairman of the
Cabinet Munitions Committee, a letter on the subject of munitions,
which has already been recorded in an earlier section of this
narrative.   I was anxious that the munitions situation should be

recognised as an essential part of the problems which the new Coalition would have to face at the outset of its existence. I did not think it was in the national interest that it should be submerged in controversies about the Dardanelles or the treatment of aliens.

As the whole political situation was in the melting pot, I decided to postpone for a few days a tour I had contemplated making round some of the centres of munition production in order to address the workers. On the 21st some of the Ministers and the leaders of the Opposition met in conclave at Downing Street in what was really the first joint meeting of the new combination. The main subject of our deliberations for that meeting and for almost all the rest of the week was the composition of the new Government. It was only settled at a late hour on the 25th. The task was a difficult one, for it entailed much consideration of the balancing of parties, as well as of personal claims inside the parties.

Mr. Asquith honoured me with his particular confidence during these discussions. The appointments took up valuable time, but at last they were concluded. The most notable change was the taking of Mr. Winston Churchill out of the Admiralty and placing him in charge of the Duchy of Lancaster, a post generally reserved either for beginners in the Cabinet or for distinguished politicians who had reached the first stages of unmistakable decrepitude. It was a cruel and unjust degradation. The Dardanelles failure was due not so much to Mr. Churchill's precipitancy as to Lord Kitchener's and Mr. Asquith's procrastination. Mr. Churchill's part in that unfortunate enterprise had been worked out by him with the most meticulous care to the last particular, and nothing had been overlooked or neglected as far as the naval operations were concerned. The fatal delays and mishandlings had all been in the other branch of the Service. It is true that the conception of a one-sided Naval operation without simultaneous military action was due to Mr. Churchill's impetuosity, but both the Prime Minister and Lord Kitchener were equally convinced that it was the right course to pursue. When I learned the office finally offered to Mr. Churchill, it came to me as an unpleasant surprise. I reckoned it would have been impossible to keep him at the Admiralty, in view of the dispute which had precipitated the crisis. The Unionists would not, and could not in the circumstances, have assented to his retention in that office. But it was quite unnecessary in order to propitiate them to fling him from the masthead, whence he had been directing the fire, down to the lower deck to polish the brass. In the first sorting out and allotment of offices in which I had taken part, it had been arranged that he should be placed in the Colonial Office, where his energies would have been helpfully employed in organising our resources in the Empire beyond the seas; and I cannot to this hour explain the change of plans which suddenly occurred. The brutality

10. Downing Street.
Whitehall. S.W

Tu. 25 May 1915

My dear Lloyd George,

I cannot let this
troubled & tumultuous chapter
in our lives bring close without
trying to let you know
what an incalculable help
& support I have found in
you all through. I shall
never forget your
devotion, your unselfishness,
your powers of resource, what

Facsimile of a letter written on the 25th of

140

is (after all) the test of all things — freedom — self-forgetfulness.

These are the rare things that make the drudgery and squalor of politics, with its constant revelation of the large part played by petty & personal ambitions, endurable, and give to its dullness a lightning streak of nobility

I thank you with all my heart

Always your affecte

H. H. Asquith

May, 1915, by Mr. Asquith to Mr. Lloyd George.

141

of the fall stunned Mr. Churchill, and for a year or two of the War his fine brain was of no avail in helping in its prosecution.

Apart from the appointment of individuals, one of the most important decisions reached, and one which concerned me most particularly was that taken to form a separate department under a Minister of Cabinet rank, to undertake the difficult and complicated work of mobilising the national resources for the production of munitions, and so to relieve the executive military authorities from a duty which had grown far too heavy to be carried out by them. Since I had consistently taken a great interest in the subject, had shown by every means in my power the importance I attached to it, and had been the head of the Cabinet Committee dealing with it, the Prime Minister invited me to take charge of the new Ministry of Munitions.

On 26th May, 1915, the names of the first Coalition Cabinet were published, and the following announcement appeared in the Press:

" The Prime Minister has decided that a new department shall be created, to be called the Ministry of Munitions, charged with organising the supply of munitions of war. Mr. Lloyd George has undertaken the formation and temporary direction of this department, and during his tenure of office as Minister of Munitions will vacate the office of Chancellor of the Exchequer."

The change in the Government had taken place; the Coalition was formed, and the War Council reorganised under the title of the Dardanelles Committee, which more accurately described its scope. Owing to the general upheaval occasioned by the political change, the newly formed Committee did not actually meet until the 7th June, or three weeks after the last session of the body it superseded. In fact, at this stage, when both in the east and west there were urgent questions awaiting decision, those especially charged with the control of our war policy met only once during a period of nearly nine weeks. So fully occupied was I in organising the new Ministry of Munitions, that for a time I was personally unable to pay as much attention as I had done to the general conduct of the War, and did not, during June, attend any of the sittings of the new Committee.

CHAPTER IX

THE MINISTRY OF MUNITIONS:
ESTABLISHMENT AND LABOUR PROBLEMS

1. MY APPOINTMENT

IT was on Whit-Monday, 1915, that I finally left the Treasury to take up my duty as Minister of Munitions. It was a serious decision for me to make. As Chancellor of the Exchequer I had been holding the highest and most responsible office under the Prime Minister— the post which ranked next to his in Parliamentary importance, and in that position had been initiating and carrying through schemes of social amelioration which were very congenial to my disposition and upbringing. I was exchanging all that for the terrible task of manufacturing engines for human mutilation and slaughter.

Whatever I had done directly or indirectly to hasten or assist in the creation of this department, which I regarded as most urgently necessary, the last thing I desired was to have to assume control of it. I had no wish to give up the Chancellorship of the Exchequer for something of an unknown nature. I cannot say that I undertook the functions of my new office with any feelings of exhilarate confidence. I was taking in hand the organisation of a business that was quite new to me. The only insight given me into its workings had revealed a state of utter confusion and chaos. I was leaving a well-established and well-organised department, staffed by some of the picked men of the Civil Service, and directed in all its ramifications by well-defined rules and traditions which worked with perfect smoothness. I was taking in hand a department with no staff, no regulations, no traditions. All new departments are viewed with a certain measure of suspicion by the older establishments. But the department which mattered most to the success of the new Ministry regarded it not only with distrust but with profound dislike, veiled behind a mask of contempt. Its very existence was a statutory expression of a national verdict of failure delivered by the High Court of Parliament against the War Office. It was cut out of the living body of the War Office, and that hurt. There is no historical testimony as to Adam's sensations after the rib had been torn out of his side. But he must have felt sore and resentful. In his case, however, the knowledge that by the operation he had secured a helpmate more than reconciled him to the excision.   The War Office was surly, suspicious, and hostile, and no help the new Ministry tendered or gave softened the animosity of the War Lords towards it.   Although Lord Kitchener personally treated me with every courtesy, his entourage were unsympathetic to the new venture, and later on he was stimulated by the hostility of his own and other departments to acquiesce in the erection of barriers in my way.   This antagonism was one of the difficulties I foresaw and certainly endured.

Politically it was for me a wilderness of risks with no oasis in sight. There were numerous possibilities of serious conflict with organised labour over trade union regulations, hours of labour, wages, restrictions on modility, and, most serious of all, over what I called dilution, i.e. the mixing of the skilled labour with unskilled.   Here you touched one of the most sensitive nerves of trade unionism.   The question of drink had to be tackled, foreboding quarrels with a powerful trade in England and Wales, Scotland and Ireland.   No wonder my old uncle and foster-father, Richard Lloyd, whose advice I was wont to listen to above all others, wrote to me and counselled me not to leave the Treasury.   Yet in spite of all this, I felt as I reviewed all the circumstances of the national situation, and realised beyond a shadow of doubt the supreme and vital importance of a proper supply of munitions for our success in the war, and remembered the insistence with which I had urged this upon the Government, that I was in honour bound to accept if the Prime Minister thought I was the man best fitted for this post.   I made my decision; and I never had cause to regret it.   As I look back to-day upon the problems which were then presented to me, the extraordinary difficulties that surrounded the work which I took in hand, my own inexperience in that kind of work, the chaos and tangle with which I was confronted, I feel that in many ways the creation of the Ministry of Munitions was the most formidable task I ever undertook.

I was heartened to face the overwhelming responsibility of this step by a letter which I received at the time from Mr. Asquith.   It ran as follows : —

“ 10, Downing Street, S.W.
25th May, 1915.

My dear Lloyd George,

I cannot let this troubled and tumultuous chapter in our history pass without letting you know what incalculable help and support I have found in you all through.   I shall never forget your devotion, your unselfishness, your powers of resource, and what is (after all) the best of things, your self-forgetfulness.

These are the rare things which make the squalor and drudgery of politics, with its constant revelations of the large part played by petty and personal motives, endurable, and give to this drabness the lightning streak of nobility.

I thank you with all my heart,

Always yours affectionately,

H. H. ASQUITH."

This letter from the man who had been my colleague for ten years, and to whom I had been principal Parliamentary lieutenant for seven years, gave me great delight. The black squad of envy had not yet succeeded in poisoning the wells of confidence between captain and second officer.

I received further encouragement from many quarters from friends near and far who wished me well and realised the terrific responsibility of my new venture. Amongst the letters which came to me was one which I specially prized for its understanding and sincerity from a great American statesman whose vision and superb courage I had always admired—Theodore Roosevelt.

" Oyster Bay,

Long Island, N.Y.

1st June, 1915.

My dear Lloyd George,

In a sense it is not my affair, but as one of your admirers and sympathisers I wish to congratulate you upon the action that has been taken in getting a Coalition Cabinet, and especially upon your part therein. More than all I wish to congratulate you upon what you have done in connection with this War. When the War is over, you will again take up the work of dealing with the Labour question, with Irish Home Rule, with many other matters. But the prime business at present for you to do is to save your country; and I admire the single-hearted manner with which you have devoted yourself to this great duty. I am sorry Redmond could not see his way to take office also, but, of course, there may have been reasons of which I know nothing that made it inadvisable for him to do so.

Give my regards to Edward Grey,

Faithfully yours,

THEODORE ROOSEVELT."

The contiguity of these three famous names—Roosevelt, Asquith and Grey—reminds me how, shortly before the War, I met the former at a luncheon party given by Sir Edward Grey to Mr. Roosevelt when Mr. Asquith and I were the only other guests. Mr. Roosevelt was not the type of man who would attract Mr. Asquith. His vehemence repelled the unexcitable Englishman. Asquith was a man of refractory prejudices which he never concealed. This gave a certain arrogance to his manner when dealing with men he did not care for. It was obvious during the table talk that Mr. Asquith had an instinctive dislike, which was not far removed from contempt, for the dynamic American. The Prime Minister made no allowance for the real greatness of the man. He was irritated by his mannerisms. Roosevelt flung out commonplaces with the same forceful and portentous emphasis as he uttered truths which showed penetration and breadth of judgment. The more stale the platitude the greater the emphasis. This kind of conversation always annoyed the British Premier and gave a note of supercilious derision to his mien and voice. Roosevelt felt it and gradually his torrential flow of sense and sentiment dried up. The meal was hardly a success.

The Royal Warrant formally appointing me Minister of Munitions was not actually issued until 9th June, the day on which the Ministry of Munitions Act became law. But without waiting for this I had begun immediately to set about the organisation of the new department.

The quarters allotted to the Ministry were at No. 6, Whitehall Gardens—a pleasant, old-fashioned house, just off Whitehall, not at all designed for office purposes. It had been vacated a short time before by that well-known art dealer, Mr. Lockett Agnew. It was more suitable for the residence of a man of artistic proclivities than for the head office of a manufacturer.

I went there with my two secretaries, and found that before I could even start to build up a new Ministry it was necessary to provide at least the bare requirements of an office. My first encounter with red tape was characteristic of the action of this departmental bindweed.

The sole articles of furniture in the office of the new department were two tables and a chair. My secretaries gave urgent orders for an adequate supply of furniture, but before this had been delivered, a squad from the Office of Works appeared on the scene to take away the little we had, on the ground that it did not belong to the new department and therefore must be removed. They were ultimately prevailed upon to be merciful, and until the new equipment arrived, I was allowed one table to write upon and one chair to sit at the said table.

This is Colonel House's description of his visit to me at this time:

" This was, I believe, George's first day as Minister of Munitions in his new Whitehall quarters. There was no furniture in the room except a table and one chair. He insisted upon me taking the chair, which I declined to do, declaring that a seat on the table was more suitable for me than for a Cabinet official.

He spoke again and again of ' military red tape,' which he declared he would cut out as speedily as possible. He was full of energy and enthusiasm, and I feel certain something will soon happen in his department. He reminds me more of the virile, aggressive type of American politician than any member of the Cabinet. . . . He has something dynamic within him which his colleagues have not and which is badly needed in this great hour. . . ."

Red tape, then, was worsted in its first round—the only casualties being a temporary general inconvenience. I retained my table and chair against all rules and orders until a reasonable consignment of suitable furniture was allocated to me. I was soon to find that this was not a serious attack but a reconnaissance to investigate and to rattle. Later on red tape resorted to all the devices in its well-stocked armoury to delay, impede and thwart. A more formidable and unexpected antagonist next appeared in the person of human vanity. My room was an old Adam drawing-room, where every panel glittered with long pier-glasses. They no doubt would be an essential accessory to a hairdresser's or haberdasher's trade, but I found them fatal to the transaction of business in armaments. When callers came in I noticed that their eyes wandered from my direction, and that their minds soon followed the rambling gaze. I realised the cause of this distraction. The glistening mirrors reflected the face and figure of my interviewers from every angle. This was too much for the most hard-faced business man. I do not pretend to be above the ordinary human weakness in this respect, but a day's contemplation of a countenance full of anxiety and dubiety more than satisfied my own appetite. I ordered the glasses to be covered over. Difficulty number two was thus blotted out.

I sat in my bare room to survey my problem. What was it? On the one hand I had to envisage all the wide range of activity covered by the supply of munitions—the innumerable requirements of the Army in the field, and the multiplicity of different materials, processes, and co-ordinations necessary to produce those goods; and on the other I had to inform myself as to the available resources of material, machinery and labour, here and abroad, for supplying those requirements. I had to ascertain the existing state and organisation of production of munitions under War Office direction. The whole field had to be plotted out and suitable men selected to take charge of each section of it.

First came the creation of a staff. The Ministry of Munitions was from first to last a business-man organisation. Its most distinctive feature was the appointment I made of successful business men to the chief executive posts. On 14th June, 1915, I announced in the House of Commons my intention of utilising, as far as possible, the " business brains of the community . . . some of them at my elbow in London, to advise, to counsel, to guide, to inform, to instruct, and to direct," others " in the localities, to organise for us, to undertake the business in each particular locality on our behalf." The first position in every department was entrusted by me to one of these distinguished captains of industry, to whom I gave authority and personal support that enabled them to break through much of the routine and aloofness which characterised the normal administration of Government contracts. I had no office staff except my two able Private Secretaries, Mr. J. T. Davies (now Sir John T. Davies) and Miss F. L. Stevenson, both of whom accompanied me from the Treasury. Miss Stevenson was the first woman secretary appointed by a Minister. The precedent, I see, has since been followed by most Ministers and heads of departments. Later on Mr. (now Sir) William Sutherland volunteered to assist when the correspondence and the interviews overwhelmed my small staff. He was an experienced Civil Servant, and a man of outstanding abilities. During the troublous times which were in store for me his shrewdness and vision served to help me to avoid many a hidden political trap. The Labour Department of the Board of Trade offered to assist in supervising and directing my arrangements with Labour. For this I was profoundly grateful. The Ordnance Department had little to spare me in the way of staff. For this also I was equally grateful. The War Office placed Sir Percy Girouard at my disposal. Of him I shall have something to say later on. But the men who were to organise and drive the production of guns, rifles, machine-guns, shell, and trench mortars were still to be found. What kind should I look for? I received hundreds of letters from " push-and-goes " and their admiring friends. I had a large number of genuine offers from Company Directors, who offered to place at my service the temporary assistance of managers in whose capacity they had acquired confidence. I had first of all to decide in my own mind the type of man I needed for the highest posts. Sir Eric Geddes told me that when he came to visit me at my new department it seemed to him that I was pulling names out of a hat and distributing them to the different jobs that waited to be done; but I am afraid the task of putting suitable men to departments could not be carried out quite so simply as that.

I knew that upon my success or failure in attracting the right sort of man and placing him in the right sort of place depended the efficiency of the new department and its chances of achieving its purpose. It was not sufficient to peruse testimonials or letters of recommendation—not even honest ones—testifying to the efficiency shown by men in the perfectly organised branches where they had served, and which they were prepared temporarily to quit in order to serve the State. Here each man would be called upon to build up a business of which he knew nothing, and do it better than experts who had been trained and spent their professional lives in that line of activity. The most difficult task was to choose wisely between two types of successful business men. The failures were easily spotted and eliminated. The knowledgeable men who knew all about the subject, but did not possess the essential gift of translating their knowledge into effective action, constituted the most dangerous trap, but it was discernible by judicious inquiry as to antecedents, and could then be evaded. But those who have made a success in their business careers can be divided into two classes. There is the careful and cautious man who has a complete mastery of all the details of his trade and attends to them steadily and assiduously. By this means he gradually builds up a business, or if he has acquired control of an already established concern keeps it going and slowly extends it. He does not command those gifts of intuition, rapid decision, and force which enable an improviser to create and hustle along a gigantic new enterprise, and certainly not with material of which he has no previous experience. He is useful in a secondary position, but as an initiator he would be a disappointment if not a disaster. The great improvisers who constitute the second class are rare men anywhere, but in an emergency their value to a country is beyond price, and these were the men I needed for first place. In any great crisis, time is a determining factor, and these men save the days, weeks and months which make the difference between victory and defeat. In selecting the leading hustlers I had to bear all these considerations in mind.

I cannot claim that my first choices were always the best. They were, I think, the best available at the time. I found that some were admirable workers provided they were under the control and direction of others, but not equal to the responsibility of a supreme position. It was then that I realised thoroughly for the first time that men ought to be marked like army lorries with their carrying capacity: " Not to carry more than three tons." The three-tonners are perfect so long as you do not overload them with burdens for which they are not constructed by Providence. I have seen that happen in Law and Politics. The barrister who acquired a great practice as a junior and failed completely when he took silk; the politician who showed great promise as an Under-Secretary and achieved nothing when promoted to the headship of a department. As I went along I discovered that one or two first-rate men were better suited for duties inside the department other than those for which I had originally chosen them.

During the War the neglect of this maxim was a fruitful source of our disasters; the excellent Brigadier who was promoted to a corps and the successful Corps Commander who was given an army, neither of them being equal to the higher responsibility cast upon them. In the Navy also there are many such illustrations of dashing captains who were lifted above their capabilities. However, with all able misfits, I shifted them about and found substitutes. But in the quality of the men themselves I was never disappointed, for when they found the post that suited them best they proved themselves to be first rate. Men who did not seem to fit into the functions originally designated for them became quite indispensable in equally responsible positions where they were finally placed. And some of them were promoted from tasks where they were rendering conspicuous service to other more important positions where their compelling powers were more urgently needed.

No more remarkable collection of men was ever gathered together under the same roof. Between them they had touched the industrial life of the country and of the Empire at every point. To use a current phrase " All the means of production, distribution, and exchange " were aggregately at their command.

One of the first to tender his services was Sir Eric Geddes. He came from the North-Eastern Railway, and he had the make of one of their powerful locomotives. That is the impression he gave me when one morning he rolled into my room. He struck me immediately as a man of exceptional force and capacity. I knew that he was a find, and I was grateful to Lord Knaresborough, the chairman of the company, for offering to release him during the period of the War. He turned out to be one of the most remarkable men which the State called to its aid in this anxious hour for Britain and her Empire. He will appear again and again in my story of the War.

There was also Sir Ernest Moir, who had constructed some of our finest docks and harbours, a man of exceptional ability and tact. Sir Frederick T. Hopkinson, a man of similar experience, came to our aid. There was Sir Hubert Llewellyn Smith. When I first met him at the Board of Trade in 1906 I considered him to be the most resourceful and suggestive mind in the whole of our Civil Service at that time—and withal a man whose long service at the Board of Trade had brought him intelligently into direct contact with every branch of commerce and industry throughout the world. There was Sir John Hunter, who had directed the construction of our largest and most famous bridge. There were Sir Hardman Lever and Sir John Mann, two of the ablest accountants in this country. There were expert financiers like Sir Alexander Roger, who turned out to be an energetic and efficient organiser. The iron and steel industry lent us of the very best. The armament firms placed at our disposal not only Sir Percy Girouard, but Sir Glyn West, who had a much longer practical experience of the actual processes of gun making. We also had Sir Charles Ellis, whose suave and attractive personality served us so well in the handling of this collection of men of clashing temperaments. There was James Stevenson (afterwards Lord Stevenson), whose experience in organising throughout the country business dealings in a famous brand of Scotch whisky was voluntarily transferred to the business of organising in the provinces the activities of an even more potent spirit—that of patriotism. With Sir Hubert Llewellyn Smith there was Mr. Beveridge (now Sir William Beveridge), a man who was credited with an unrivalled knowledge of labour problems. In the organisation of the welfare branch of our new factories we had the valuable direction of Mr. Seebohm Rowntree, who is not only a highly successful man of business, but a student of social conditions of world-wide fame. Coal gave us the dynamic personality of Sir L. W. Llewellyn. The railways lent us not only Sir Eric Geddes, but Sir Henry Fowler and Sir Ralph Wedgwood. There was Sir Arthur Duckham, one of the ablest engineers in the land—a man of unusual capacity and attainments. The publishing world gave us Sir Edward Iliffe, who carried out with remarkable success the vital task of organising machine tool production. Shipping was represented by Sir George Booth, a member of the well-known firm of Booth Brothers. Though known, as I have said, as the man of " push-and-go," he was neither, but he had other invaluable qualities. He was rather a conciliator than a compeller. I found his tact and geniality invaluable in a Ministry of energetic talents. And through the portals of the Board of Trade there wafted into this Ministry of solid and material industrialism a breeze from the foothills of Parnassus in the person of Mr. Umberto Wolff. The statistician of the Ministry of Munitions is now one of the most eminent economists in the world —Sir Walter Layton. The Parliamentary Under-Secretary, Dr. Addison, was a man with a high order of intellectual capacity, full of ideas, resourcefulness and courage. My military secretary, whom I designed as liaison officer with the War Office, was Sir Ivor Philipps, an experienced soldier and a good business man. The Explosives Department gave me that eminent judge, Lord Fletcher Moulton. He was one of the subtlest brains in England. As usually happens his subtlety caused distrust and misunderstanding amongst blunter minds. He was not only one of the greatest lawyers of his day, he was also a man of distinguished scientific attainments. When he placed his great gifts at the disposal of the War Office for the solution of the new problems created by the unprecedented demand for explosives, he rendered service of incalculable value to the country. Of such were the personal components of this strange Ministry. If not a Ministry of all the talents it was undoubtedly a Ministry of all the industries—war and peace, production, transport, law, medicine, science, the Civil Service, politics, and poetry—and all at their best. It was a wonderful array of talent. It was a formidable battery of dynamic energy. But I saw that unless firmly controlled and carefully watched there would be constant explosions which would make the whole machine unworkable. At first I placed Sir Percy Girouard in charge as chief engineer of the concern. He was an out-and-out Kitchener man. He had worked with and for him in Egypt. When the War broke out and Lord Kitchener took charge, Sir Percy was taken out of Armstrong's and put in charge of part of the munition organisation at the War Office. He was delivered over to me with the munitions problem.

Sir Percy Girouard had a great reputation, honourably won by distinguished engineering achievements in our Colonial Empire. He was a man of great natural gifts and accomplishments, and he was credited with possessing a resourcefulness which approximated to the genius of purposeful action. In addition to that he was a man of considerable charm, with a pleasant sense of humour fortified by much interesting and entertaining reminiscence. I discovered that he had a gift of persuasive speech which was invaluable at the meetings we held in London and in the provinces to stimulate co-operation. Although he was primarily a railway man and his success had been achieved in that sphere, his association with Armstrong's had furnished him with experience in the manufacture of every kind of munition of war. But I soon discovered that he suffered from the same drawback as his old chief, Lord Kitchener. They had both spent their exceptional physical reserves in hard work under climatic conditions which are not congenial to men born and bred in a temperate clime. His stock of vitality had been burnt out in great tasks driven through under tropical suns—the vivid spirit was still there and the habits and movements of an old energy were also visible, but these took the form of an unsettling restlessness rather than that of a steady activity. He dashed about from the War Office to the Ministry and back from the Ministry to the War Office, where he spent most of his time, to and from one department after another attending to no detail of any kind in any of them. When he came to see me he was always in such a hurry that he never sat down. He rushed into my room like a man who was chased by a problem and could not stay too long lest it caught him up.

He had one curious mannerism. I observed that when I pressed him with inconvenient questions of detail as to the progress made, he seemed to hide behind his eyeglass, and I could get no farther. From him I learnt less than nothing of what the various departments of the Ministry were doing, for such information as he acquired he gleaned from the War Office, and it was, therefore, misleading. All this feverish bustle gave the impression of a propelling eagerness to urge everybody along, but I soon discovered that it was the symptom of a spent nervous system. Reluctantly I felt he had no longer the steady nerve and the calm industry which are essential in the chief organiser of a new department where there were so many men quite new to the tasks entrusted to their charge, and I felt that a man of a totally different calibre would be more useful. So we parted company.

His place was not filled. I soon realised that all the hustling that was necessary would have to be done by myself, with the aid of the energetic departmental chiefs whom I had chosen.

Describing these appointments in a speech in the House of Commons on 29th July, 1915, when I was reporting progress on the arrangements of the new Ministry, I said: —

"We have had practically to create a new staff. That is a very difficult undertaking if you have to do it immediately, because, obviously, everything depends upon the staff and the men you select. And under ordinary conditions you would take a very long time to choose your instruments. You cannot do that when you are engaged in emergency work. Fortunately we have had placed at our disposal the services of very considerable men in the business world—men of wide experience, men, some of them, who are in charge of very considerable undertakings. They have placed their services voluntarily at the disposal of the Minister of Munitions, and are rendering excellent services each in his own department. I think I can say that there are at least 90 men of first-class business experience who have placed their services voluntarily at the disposal of the Ministry of Munitions, the vast majority of them without any remuneration at all. [Cheers.] Some of them were managers of very great concerns, and the firms with which they were connected are in most, if not in all, cases paying them salaries which the State could not afford to pay. These men are exceedingly helpful; in fact, without their help it would have been quite impossible to have improvised a great department on the scale on which this department necessarily had to be organised and arranged."

After going as thoroughly into the actual munition position as the time and information at my disposal would permit, there were visible a few outstanding and dominant facts: —

(1) The War Office had not made any thorough survey of its needs on the assumption that the British Army was to develop into a gigantic force of at least 70 divisions, that its task would necessitate breaking through formidable double and often multiple lines of entrenchments, defended by masses of artillery, heavy as well as light, and thousands of machine-guns, and that this operation would be a prolonged one. It had not, for instance, come to any final decision as to the number and calibre of the guns which would be required for this purpose. The quantity and type of the guns ordered were both obviously inadequate to the undertaking in front of it. Nor had it calculated the number of machine-guns required for so great a force.

(2) Until the number and especially the size of the guns had been decided no one could be expected to compute the numbers and sizes of the shells required.

(3) There had been no computation made of the number of machine-guns required for an army fighting under modern conditions.

(4) There had been no survey of the capacity of this country or America to produce the number of guns, shells, machine-guns, and rifles needed. It was found later on, when the programme was settled, that we did not possess in Britain and could not purchase in the States the necessary machine tools to execute the agreed programme. We had to make a start with manufacture of those tools before we began on the extra guns, etc.

(5) The War Office had instituted no inquiry into our capacity for filling shells with explosives. Investigation by the new Ministry revealed the facts (a) that our capacity in this respect was not more than one-tenth of the need; and (b) that even if we had the necessary filling appliances, we possessed only a small proportion of the explosive hitherto used. We therefore had to encourage experiments to be made in order to find other equally effective explosives, and to provide a different set of appliances to suit the result of these experiments.

It horrifies me to imagine what would have happened if this state of things had been allowed to go on for a few more months without any perception of its existence, and therefore without any attempt at amendment. What if all Ministers had retained complete confidence in the military direction of the War? The sensitiveness of the War Office to any suggestion that established methods were not the best and the repression of civilian inquisitiveness as to these methods or their results might have postponed discovery of this fatal neglect until it was too late to set them right. Even with all the strenuous endeavour put by some of the ablest business and scientific heads in the country into survey, investigation, consultation and construction, with a view to ascertain needs, defects and remedies, and then to drive through to production, we were only just able to fulfil the requirements of the Army for the summer campaign of 1916. It is such an incredible story of lack of forethought and intelligent inquiry that it is necessary to give more detailed and documented information on these vital points. That I propose to do later on in the course of my narrative. The tale has its lessons for every form of bureaucratic enterprise. It also contains its warning to those who heedlessly lead nations towards war. They should understand something of the risk they incur and the precarious character of the gamble into which they are plunging.

The work which fell upon me was by no means wholly of a kind which could be done sitting at a desk. One very urgent problem was to secure the hearty co-operation of employers in converting their factories and workshops to the production of arms. Another was equally vital: the securing of the good will of the workers and their agreement to the further speeding-up of production and the dilution of labour which it would involve. Labour, I knew, would be one of my chief difficulties. So during the first week of June I made a tour of the districts which were the centres of the engineering industry, in order to harness local enthusiasm to munition production in the service of the new Ministry.

At Manchester, Liverpool, Birmingham, Cardiff and Bristol, I met representatives of the chief engineering firms and of the trade unions affected, and urged them to organise local committees to assist in producing munitions of war and to arrange the allocation of contracts between them in such a way as to ensure the maximum output from the engineering works of the district. I stressed the importance of local responsibility and of systematic decentralisation as a means of saving time and red tape, and I appealed to both business men and trade unionists to work together with one will.

I will quote a passage from a speech I delivered at Manchester in order to show the nature of the appeal I made to employers and workers alike: —

" I have only held this office for a few days, it is true. I had some insight before then into the position of things, but what I have seen has convinced me from overwhelming testimony that the nation has not yet concentrated one half of its industrial strength on the problem of carrying this great conflict through successfully. It is a war of munitions. We are fighting against the best-organised community in the world; the best-organised whether for war or peace, and we have been employing too much the haphazard, leisurely, go-as-you-please methods, which, believe me, would not have enabled us to maintain our place as a nation, even in peace, very much longer. The nation now needs all the machinery that is capable of being used for turning out munitions or equipment, all the skill that is available for that purpose, all the industry, all the labour, and all the strength, power, and resource of everyone to the utmost, everything that would help us to overcome our difficulty and supply our shortages. We want to mobilise in such a way as to produce in the shortest space of time the greatest quantity of the best and most efficient war material. That means victory; it means a great saving of national strength and resources, for it shortens the War; it means an enormous saving of life. . . ."

I pointed out why the Government had taken powers under the Defence of the Realm Act to control the workshops of the country, and to insist that Government work—the work of the country—must take precedence over all civil work. I then discussed the relations of the Government with labour. Two things were essential to the efficiency of the new organisation for munitions of war—to increase the mobility of labour and to secure greater subordination in labour to the direction and control of the State. The State must be able to say where and under what conditions it required a man's services. "When the house is on fire, questions of procedure and precedence, of etiquette and time and division of labour must disappear." I added:—

> "... I can only say this, that to introduce compulsion as an important element in organising the nation's resources of skilled industry and trade does not necessarily mean conscription in the ordinary sense of the term. Conscription means raising by compulsory methods armies to fight Britain's battles abroad. Even that is a question not of principle but of necessity. If the necessity arose I am certain no man of any party would protest. But pray do not talk about it as if it were anti-democratic. We won and saved our liberties in this land on more than one occasion by compulsory service. France saved the liberty she had won in the great Revolution from the fangs of tyrannical military empires purely by compulsory service. The great Republic of the West won its independence, saved its national existence, by compulsory service. And two of the greatest countries of Europe to-day, France and Italy, are defending their national existence and liberties by means of compulsory service. It has been the greatest weapon in the hands of democracy many a time for the winning and preservation of freedom. . . ."

I appealed to the workmen to give up, for the period of the War, the unwritten rules by which output was limited, and I gave an undertaking that piece rates should not be reduced. In the same way I urged suspension of trade union rules forbidding dilution in order that unskilled men and women might be brought in to make up for the shortage of skilled men. I pointed out that the refusal of unenlisted labour to submit to discipline contrasted strangely with the position of the voluntary army at the front:—

> "The enlisted workman cannot choose his locality of action. He cannot say, 'I am quite prepared to fight at Neuve-Chapelle, but I won't fight at Festubert, and I am not going near the place they call "Wipers."' He cannot say, 'I have been in the trenches eight hours and a half, and my trades union won't allow me to work more than eight hours.'"

With special reference to what I expected from Lancashire, I added in my Manchester speech:—

> "Lancashire's private works, when they are fully engaged, and after you have mobilised them, can turn out a quarter of a million of high-explosive shells a month. A gentleman near me tells me

that you can turn out a lot more. Well, the more the merrier; but we want you to start from that and then work up in the direction of a million."

I quote a Press report of this meeting, because it gives a fair idea of the spirit which commanded all classes to whom I appealed:—

" Manchester, Thursday (June 3).

Lord Derby and the Lancashire men gave a hearty reception to Mr. Lloyd George's speech. . . . Separate munition committees were appointed for three divisions of Lancashire, embracing the whole county. . . . A satisfactory preliminary discussion took place as to the best means of mapping out the work. Mr. Lloyd George had said that he aimed at an output of a quarter of a million shells per month from Lancashire alone, and the reply was a promise of a million a month within a short time.

All this is excellent, but the bitter tragedy is that the organisation was not accomplished six months ago. Manchester masters tell me that, in the past, they have asked the War Office again and again for a statement of what was wanted, only to be put off with a polite acknowledgement or a reference to the Labour Bureau."

On the following day I spoke in similar terms at Liverpool. I repeated my reassurance to the workers about the temporary nature of the relaxations of ordinary rules and practices which they were being asked to accept.

A resolution was carried, pledging those present to do all they could to increase the output of munitions. This resolution was seconded in a significant speech delivered by one of the workmen's representatives. It is worth quoting:—

" Mr. Clarke, a representative of the Amalgamated Society of Engineers, seconded the resolution. He said: 'We have learned now that things are not going so well at the front as we thought they were. Certain newspapers have hidden the truth from us, and have presented too rosy a picture. It was only yesterday when they heard Mr. Lloyd George's speech* that the workmen realised the terrible urgency of the matter. Now that we know, I am sure that there will be no difficulty.' "

Press comment on this speech stated:—

" The general feeling in representative trade union circles in London with regard to Mr. Lloyd George's speech is one of unanimous agreement. One prominent trade unionist said: 'We are delighted with the definiteness of the speech, and only wish it had been given eight months ago. We have been annoyed at the

* My speech at Manchester.

campaign in favour of conscription, because we knew there were hundreds of thousands of men for whom no equipment could be immediately obtained. . . ."

While I was thus engaged in stimulating the organisation of the country for munition production, the Ministry of Munitions Bill was carried through Parliament. This measure set up the new Ministry and gave it its powers. They were laid down as follows in Clause 2 (1) of the Act. I quote that section as it is a good example of the comprehensiveness and elasticity required in legislation for coping with an emergency.

"The Minister of Munitions shall have such administrative powers and duties in relation to the supply of munitions for the present War as may be conferred on him by his Majesty in Council, and his Majesty may also, if he considers it expedient that, in connection with the supply of munitions, any powers or duties of a Government Department or authority, whether conferred by statute or otherwise, should be transferred to, or exercised or performed concurrently by, the Minister of Munitions, by Order in Council make the necessary provision for the purpose, and any Order made in pursuance of this section may include any supplemental provisions which appear necessary for the purpose of giving full effect to the Order."

In other words, the job of the new Ministry—the responsibilities hitherto held by the War Office or Admiralty which it was to take over and the new tasks it was to undertake, were not defined by Act of Parliament, but left to be fixed by Orders in Council, which, without the waste of valuable time involved in Parliamentary procedure, could adopt the power to the need as it arose.

At the outset it was broadly laid down that the new department should be guided by the "general requirements and specific requisitions" of the Army Council. This might have been taken to mean—and indeed, the Army Council did its best to impose such an interpretation—that the Ministry was no more than a Supply Department unable to exercise any initiative and only empowered to act on programmes and orders transmitted to it from the military authorities. Fortunately, however, the Order in Council defining my functions was more explicit. It set out that my duty was: —

"to ensure such supply of munitions for the Present War as may be required by the Army Council or the Admiralty, *or may otherwise be found necessary.*"

This final saving clause which I have italicised, gave me authority, of which I made full and industrious use, to acquaint myself directly with the needs present and future of the Army and make plans to meet them. Had I been limited by the shortsighted vision of the Army Council we should have continued to be in arrears with supplies to the end of the War.

On this matter I am tempted to quote an extract from the official history of the Ministry of Munitions. This book was written years after I had left the Ministry. I had no responsibility for its preparation, and as a matter of fact was not consulted as to any part of its contents. Referring to the interpretation I placed upon my functions at the Ministry, it says: —

" This wide view of his position and responsibilities is reflected throughout his career as Minister of Munitions, and his vision of the character and probable length of the conflict that lay ahead not only had a profound effect on the munitions programmes actually adopted in his period, but enabled the Ministry to meet much larger programmes later on. He laid the foundations of the Ministry's productive capacity on a scale so vast that it was almost sufficient—as far as guns, gun ammunition, rifles, machine-guns, and trench warfare supplies were concerned—to carry the country to the end of the War. The great developments undertaken under his successors were principally directed to meet new demands for aircraft, for chemical warfare, and for increased quantities of steel for shipbuilding, motor transport, tanks and railways."

A good deal of play has been made in some quarters with the fact that the new factories organised by the Ministry of Munitions, and the fresh orders for shells which it issued, only began to bear fruit on a large scale by the spring of 1916, and that until that time the bulk of the supplies reaching our armies in the field were in respect of orders given by the War Office before the new Ministry was created.

I have not the slightest desire to claim any unmerited approbation for the Ministry of Munitions, or to rob the War Office of the smallest of its true titles of praise. But in loyalty to the many splendid colleagues who co-operated with me for munitions production, and to the magnificent work they performed, I am bound to point out that this suggestion is ill-founded.

It is true that, partly under pressure from the Cabinet Committee on Munitions, and the Munitions of War Committee, appointed in the spring of 1915, to the activities of both of which I have already referred, the War Office had by the beginning of June, 1915, placed extensive orders at home and abroad for shells. But it was one thing to order, and quite another to ensure delivery. By the 29th May, 1915, out of 5,797,274 shell bodies ordered by the War Office for delivery by or before that date, only 1,968,252 had actually been delivered—this after ten months of war. A more important consideration is the fact that of the shells actually manufactured a comparatively large number were not fitted with fuses and filled with explosive. They were just a collection of harmless steel mugs. The steps taken by the Ministry to reorganise the munitions industry throughout the country and to speed up production during these first seven months of its existence were successful in bringing up the total of deliveries on War Office orders from the two millions at which it stood on 1st June to 14 millions by the end of December, 1915, and for the first time adequate measures were taken to complete these with fuse and explosive.

The failure of the War Office orders to materialise was largely due to its stubborn and stupid adherence to the policy of dealing only with the recognised armament firms, and leaving these firms themselves to organise—or leave unorganised—the rest of the engineering industry in the country. The Ordnance Department could have exercised complete control over the manufacturing resources of the country; powers for that purpose had indeed been thrust upon them by the Defence of the Realm Act which I brought in on 9th March, 1915, but no great use had been made of them. The Ordnance Department was still convinced that it was too risky to entrust the manufacture of munitions to inexperienced firms, and that the only safe course was to give the order to the well-established armament manufacturers, leaving it to them to peddle out the simplest components. As far as American orders were concerned, a departure from this principle was enforced by the Cabinet Committee, although control was impossible and supervision difficult over production in the States. At home, where both supervision and control were practicable, War Office stubbornness was invincible. One of the attributes of small minds is that they resent a change in their accustomed methods merely because it implies a censure on their past record.

So far as the yield of War Office orders was concerned, the difference between the deliveries from August, 1914, to June, 1915, and those from June, 1915, to April, 1916, was due largely to the fact that during the latter period the Ministry of Munitions had taken on the direct organisation of the outside firms and of the labour for munition production, and after August, 1915, had also taken charge of the Government ordnance factories, including the Royal Laboratory at Woolwich, which at that time was still responsible for nearly the whole of the shell filling and completion, and was doing the job by tedious and antiquated pre-War methods. M. Albert Thomas, the French Munition Minister, who visited Woolwich at this date, called it " *une vieille boîte.*"

As I have already indicated, the lack of foresight on the part of the War Office was further shown by its failure to set up a programme authority to study the necessities, possibilities and probabilities of the future—as distinct from the mere tabulation of quantities due on contracts placed. It is necessary that I should develop the full effect of this oversight.

When certain munitions or components had to be manufactured, the Ordnance Department never undertook a careful survey of the reserves of manufacturing capacity available in this country for that purpose and how that capacity could be best utilised for the provision of an adequate supply. Had they done so they would have discovered that in order to exploit these reserves to their full capacity it was necessary to secure certain machine tools, gauges and gadgets, the manufacture of which would occupy several months. The fact that this had not been seen to at the very beginning of the War had not merely wasted the period of ten months which had already elapsed, but the delays involved a further wait of several anxious and fateful months before the process of manufacturing guns, rifles, machine guns and even shells on an adequate scale could be even commenced. A third and in some respects a more disastrous failure was their complete neglect to investigate the explosives problem. They had taken no steps to enlarge their capacity for filling shells even to the limit of the orders which they themselves had already given for shell bodies. In fact, they had not even considered the question of whether there was a sufficient supply available of the explosive material with which these shells were charged to meet even the requirements of their own limited programmes. As I shall point out later on, the War Office had been already warned by Lord Moulton that the available supplies would not be forthcoming in sufficient quantities and that the nature of the explosive would therefore have to be changed. Had this deplorable blunder not been remedied in time, the British Army could not have been equipped in 1916 with a third of the material needful for the operations.

The Ordnance Department administered a prescribed system, and it was passive, if not hostile, where new expedients were concerned. This passivity was shown in the matter of Lord Moulton's request for executive powers in regard to the high explosives in December, 1914; in the proposed extension of his sphere to propellants in the spring of 1915; in the delay in the adoption of newer forms of high explosives, and in the reluctance to approve the Stokes gun. Perhaps the most striking illustration of the limited horizon of the War Office authorities can be found in their refusal (backed, it may be observed, by the Secretary of State) to admit the necessity for the guns which in August, 1915, I ordered in excess of War Office demand. This is an incident with which I deal more fully elsewhere.

Most of the special steps that were taken after the formation of the Ministry of Munitions to stimulate production could equally well have been taken in 1914. It was to those special steps that the greatly accelerated yield on account of outstanding War Office orders in the latter part of 1915, as well as the immense augmentation of output in 1916 on direct orders of the Ministry, was mainly due.

In the month of July the Ministry of Munitions took over from the War Office responsibility for the administration of outstanding contracts. Its work therefore had a dual character. It had, on the one hand, to speed up these existing contracts, consulting closely and co-operating actively with the existing armament firms in order to relieve their difficulties in regard to materials and labour, while on the other hand it was at the same time opening up fresh sources of supply, both by organising outside firms for munition production, and by establishing new Government factories, and securing equipment, labour and materials for their use.

It requires some effort to envisage the wide range of our task. Few people would at the outset imagine how much is covered by the phrase: " Munitions of war," or dream of the colossal ramifications of the industries concerned in their production.

The making of a gun or shell-case, for instance, involves the metal trades, blast-furnaces, steel works, iron and steel foundries, forges, stamps, drops and dies, rolling-mills, drawn rod and wire works—and behind them, the colliery and the iron-ore quarry.

It requires factories, and these in turn require machinery, covered electrical plant, factory equipment and machine tools; engines, pumps, turbines, road and rail transport; boiler-making and constructional engineering work.

The explosives for filling and propelling the shell from the gun involve the output of chemical works, dye works, gas works, and a great deal of very careful laboratory experiment, investigation and testing.

Small arms and ammunition, and all the miscellaneous stores used in trench warfare, involve numerous components all requiring ferrous and non-ferrous metals in manufactured forms, woodwork, textile products, optical glass, vulcanite.

Shells loomed so large in the public eye at the time when the Ministry was formed, that there is a danger of the fact being overlooked that the department became responsible for the production and supply, not only of ammunition and guns, of rifles and machine-guns, but also of mechanical transport, trench warfare stores, optical munitions and glassware, metals and materials, tanks, bombs, poison gas, railway material, machine tools, timber, electrical power, agricultural machinery, mineral oils and building materials.

In place of the War Office method of contracting with a few experienced firms for supplies of finished articles—a method which had worked satisfactorily in peace-time, but had proved quite inadequate to this war—the Ministry of Munitions had to concern itself directly with the production of every raw material and intermediate stage of manufacture of each component in its munitions supplies;

and this in regard to a range and variety of armaments hitherto undreamed of.

2. CENTRAL AND AREA ORGANISATION

When the Ministry of Munitions Act was laid before Parliament at the beginning of June, 1915, the existing bodies for the providing of munitions were three in number, viz.: —

(a) The Munitions Supply Organisation under the War Office, presided over by the Master-General of Ordnance, run almost exclusively by Army Officers, with the addition of one important civilian intruder in the person of Lord Moulton, who had been given a position as chairman of the Committee of High Explosives supply;

(b) The Armaments Output Committee, which Lord Kitchener had set up with Sir Percy Girouard and Mr. G. M. Booth at its head, originally to take up the problem of labour supply, though it had actually made an extremely useful but limited start on the question of area organisation;

(c) The Munitions of War Committee—now virtually defunct, as its Chairman had become Minister of Munitions (designate).

In the course of the month of June most of the supply functions for which General von Donop's department had been responsible were transferred to the Ministry, which also amalgamated with itself the work of the Armaments Output Committee; so that by 1st July, in place of the three bodies I have mentioned, there was now the one Ministry in charge of output and supply. Woolwich Arsenal remained under the Ordnance Department until August, 1915, and responsibility for design and invention until the end of the year.

Four departments were at first set up; Sir Percy Girouard undertook munitions supply; Lord Moulton explosives supply; Brigadier-General L. C. Jackson the Engineers' Munitions Department, and Mr. Beveridge took charge of the Secretariat and the organisation of labour.

Supporting them was an array of the experienced business men I have mentioned. I will not detail the whole of this original organisation, but illustrate its structure along one branch. Sir Percy Girouard, the Director-General of Munitions Supply, had immediately under him nine men, each in charge of a particular job or group of jobs. One of these, Mr. Eric Geddes, held the position of a Deputy Director-General of Munitions Supply. He was set to supervise a group of sub-departments, each in charge of an experienced man; Mr. Moir was responsible to Geddes for machine-guns; Mr. Hopkinson for small arms ammunition; Mr. Brown for rifles; Major Symon for guns and equipment, ammunition wagons and optical munitions; and Mr. D. Bain for horse-drawn transport vehicles. As the War progressed, several of these sub-departments grew in importance, and required the undivided attention of a Deputy Director-General. Before I left the Ministry, munitions supply was one of three supply departments (the others being explosives supply and trench warfare supply), and was divided into ten main sub-departments, half of which were again sub-divided into four or five sections; and these various departments, sub-departments and sections were being run by experienced business men on business lines.

It was in such fashion that we modelled our headquarters. In the same spirit we approached the organisation of the country into areas for munition production.

I have already mentioned how the Armaments Output Committee, acting under the direction of the Munitions of War Committee and with my active support, had in April and May made a beginning with this task of area organisation.

In a number of areas district committees were set up to co-ordinate munition production, and they undertook the establishment of national shell factories in their centres. The first of such schemes was the one adopted at Leeds, which received Government sanction on 13th May, on the recommendation of the Munitions of War Committee. A description of this Leeds experiment was published in leaflet form, entitled *National Munitions Factories: Working Model*, with a view to stimulating similar movements in other districts.

The tour which I undertook during the first week of June had as one of its objects the encouragement of this system. At all meetings I urged that no time should be lost in setting up committees, and recommended that as far as possible districts should co-ordinate their efforts so as to form one organisation rather than several.

Very widespread zeal and activity was aroused by this appeal, and the effect was greatly to accelerate local organisation in the districts I had visited. This spirit of energetic devotion to the task of making good the munition shortage became general during June. Deputations from local committees called daily at the new Ministry. Many of these I saw and did my best to stimulate, direct, and assist. A copious correspondence poured in from business men offering their services and asking for information in regard to requirements, specifications, contracts, labour. Business men were encouraged to offer their services and they responded to the more sympathetic treatment accorded to them. It was imperative that anything in the nature of delay and confusion at this stage should be avoided, and I quickly saw that the branch in the Ministry dealing with local matters would have to be strengthened.

Early in June Mr. Stevenson, who had joined Mr. Booth's " District Department " almost immediately after the formation of the new Ministry and had taken up work in connection with the organisation of local committees, was asked by me to submit a scheme of area organisation.

I give the outline of the plan adopted for area organisation as it may be of value to those who will be called upon to organise the national energy for other tasks.

The scheme adopted was generally described by me in a speech in the House of Commons on 23rd June as follows: —

" No staff, however able, could adequately cope from the centre with the gigantic and novel character of the operations which must be put through during the next few weeks if the country is to be saved. We have, therefore, decided to organise the country in districts. I am relying very considerably upon the decentralisation which I have outlined. There is no time to organise a Central Department which would be sufficiently strong and which would be sufficiently well equipped to make the most of the resources of each district. . . . There is only one way of organising the resources of the country efficiently within the time at our disposal. That is that each district should undertake to do the work for itself, and that we should place at their disposal everything that a Government can in the way of expert advice and in the way of material, because we have ourselves offered to supply the material wherever it is required. Anything in the way of expert advice, specifications, samples, inspection and material— that we can supply; but we must rely upon the great business men of each locality to do the organisation in those districts for themselves; and they are doing it."

Here is Stevenson's description of his methods: —

" The first thing I did was to call for a map. I might as well have called for the moon. But, nothing daunted, I went out and bought one, for the price of which the Government still owe me. I divided the map into ten areas, the limits of which (with a few exceptions) followed county boundaries, and proceeded on the ordinary commercial lines of decentralisation. This scheme was approved by Mr. Lloyd George, and an Area Office was established in each (viz. Newcastle, Manchester, Leeds, Birmingham, Cardiff, Bristol, London, Edinburgh, Glasgow, Dublin, and Belfast) with the object of relieving the pressure at headquarters, securing local information and disposing of sectional difficulties. Curiously enough, one county was left out—Hereford—with the remark: ' We will leave that to the Board of Agriculture!' But in that neglected county the greatest shell filling factory in the Kingdom was later built. . . ."

Within the main Areas nearly fifty Boards of Management were appointed. The procedure was somewhat as follows: The Boards of Management would undertake orders for specified quantities, say of shell, to be delivered within specified dates at a specified price. These orders were distributed amongst various engineering firms in the district or entrusted to National Factories managed by the Board, and the Boards were responsible to the Government for the shells manufactured.

The Area Offices exercised a general supervision over the local Boards of Management within their areas, and were each provided with an Organising Secretary, a Superintending Engineer, and a Labour Officer. The Secretary combined with secretarial duties the work of Establishment Officer and of sub-accountant for the district; was responsible for dealing with applications for petrol by firms engaged on munition work and a variety of other tasks. The Engineer was charged to develop the resources of the Area as fully as possible along the lines laid down from time to time by the Minister of Munitions, to ascertain details of and report on available machinery, to inspect National Shell Factories, advise on the capabilities of firms, and report on the progress of contracts. The Labour Officer had, of course, to supervise the supply and distribution of labour; and the great expansion of the work in connection with dilution, and the investigation of general conditions of labour led later on, in November, 1916, to the splitting-up of this work between two independent officers, dealing respectively with dilution and investigation.

It would be a mistake to suppose that all this harnessing of local energy and creation of district organisation went through easily and smoothly. Particularly in the early stages it required constant attention and very careful handling to ensure that the machinery worked.

Frictions and hitches had constantly to be overcome, and an agreed method of working settled. I had constantly to settle local and general questions—some important, many trivial—which delayed action. On 26th August, 1915, I issued a memorandum entitled: " Decisions for the Guidance of Boards of Management," which summarised the conclusions I had come to with them on the basis of our conferences, and this served thenceforward as their charter.

Summarising briefly some of the results obtained by these Boards of Management in the recruiting of hitherto inexperienced firms for munition production, I may say that in the course of the War they secured an output of 65 million empty shell, and over 606 million components; nearly 10 million trench warfare articles and over four million items in connection with aeronautical supplies. Nor was this great work done regardless of cost to the State, for it is estimated that the National Factories managed by these Boards saved the country £1¾ million based on the standard prices hitherto charged by contractors for the various articles produced.

There are many things which were done in the War that experience has taught should be done differently another time—

though Heaven forbid there should be another time! But the ultimate opinion of everybody acquainted with the Area Organisation and the Boards of Management, as war-time organisations, is that exactly the same policy should be again adopted, were it ever to become necessary once more to harness the outside resources of the country to armaments supply.

Such was the machine we constructed. My next concern was to devise methods which would ensure that every department got ahead with its job at full speed, and that breakdown or failure in any quarter should be promptly remedied instead of being allowed to drift on unnoticed till disaster occurred.

The Ministry had set things moving in the country as a result of my tour of some of the industrial districts and of the communications with industrial leaders, employers and workmen throughout the country. I had gathered a very able staff of first-class men at headquarters to do the work. It remained now to drive the machine at full speed as soon as it was put together.

So I proceeded to institute a system under which, as each department of the Ministry was organised—guns, explosives, shells, machine-guns, bombs, factory construction, labour supply, and so on—its head should make a weekly report of the progress of the branch to Mr. W. T. Layton (now Sir Walter Layton), who had been appointed Director of Statistics, and that he should collect these reports and furnish me with a weekly summary. As soon as each branch definitely got into working order and was in a position to start production it was asked to submit a statement showing its anticipated output week by week. The weekly reports of results actually achieved were constantly checked against the figures of anticipation, and we were thus able to see just how far each single section was keeping abreast of its task.

The weekly budget prepared by Mr. Layton, showing the promises and performances of each department, would be handed over to me at the week-end, and I would take it down with me to my cottage at Walton Heath; for whenever I could, I would escape from London on Saturday. There I would take this weekly budget, and go carefully through it, scribbling notes to be subsequently dictated and sent to the departmental heads on points which struck me in regard to the progress of the work. A few specimens taken at random will serve to illustrate these minutings: —

DR. ADDISON.

Weekly Report. Trench Warfare.

The discrepancy between promise and deliveries is discouraging. What steps have been taken to speed it up?

Bomb deliveries are also disappointing.

D. LL. G.
30/9/15.

SIR FREDERICK BLACK.

Notes on Weekly Report for Week Ending Sept. 18th.

The contrast between shells promised and shells delivered is most discouraging, and the discrepancy is bad enough for contractors; but when you come to the national shell factories it is grotesque. Is there no means of improving the situation? Whose duty is it to call for explanations from individual contractors and from Boards of Management, and whose duty is it to keep them both up to the mark?

I am afraid that the department dealing with this phase of our work is considerably overtaxed. The men in charge are exceptionally able men, but they have too much to do.

Filling Factories.

Having regard to the urgent importance of increasing our filling capacity, this report is not as encouraging as I would wish it to be. The interviews at the conferences we have had the last two or three days will improve matters, but I hope special attention will be directed to this all-important branch. Both in the matter of national projectile factories and filling factories I urge that the great builders should be called into conference and invited to assist us by placing at our disposal men who can speed up erection of these buildings. Please see that this is done.   D. LL. G.

30/9/15.

GENERAL DU CANE.

I understand that the lag in the delivery of six-inch Howitzer shell is partly attributable to the delay in delivery of certain cartridges for N.T.C. charges. Could this be hurried up?

D. LL. G.

14/3/16.

GENERAL DU CANE.

As there has been a good deal of trouble about ineffective fuses and gaines, I am very anxious there should be no further failures. You spoke very highly of the latest designs, but I should like to feel that the test has been of such a character that nothing is left to chance. So much depends upon these latest designs; if they fail, the ammunition at a very critical time would not achieve the necessary results. I should be very glad if you would, therefore, take the necessary steps for proving on a considerable scale the efficiency of the new designs.   D. LL. G.

10/5/16.

In addition to firing this bombardment of notes and queries at the departmental heads of the Ministry, I was, of course, in constant personal touch with them through the week, providing them as far as possible with stimulation, correction and counsel. I was at the office from 9 a.m. until 8 p.m. and often later, and available for consultation with the officials of the Ministry when any difficulty arose.

Very early in the working of the Ministry I began the system of calling a weekly meeting of the heads of departments, at which I could discuss verbally with them the features in their weekly reports, and any matters arising in my minutes to them which required further consultation.

It was a great advantage and saving of time to have them all together for these meetings. For when one of them was asked why his output was failing to keep up to the level estimated for it he might give the explanation that he had not been supplied with some raw material, semi-manufactured product, or other component which was essential for the output of his particular section. In such a case, as the officer responsible for the supply of that missing component would also be present, the matter could be thrashed out without delay and a great deal of time and paper saved which would otherwise have been used in following a conventional routine of noting one man's complaint, sending it to another for comments, and thereafter having a docket flying about like a shuttlecock from department to department, while excuses instead of output were being multiplied.

My aim throughout was to tone up this staff to a pitch of high endeavour by every appeal that moves men to do their best—by praise; by emulation; by fear of exposure to criticism; and, above all, by the urge of a genuine spirit of patriotism. I think all those who were familiar with the working of the Ministry will agree that this aim was very successfully realised.

These meetings also stimulated healthy competition. No departmental head cared to have attention drawn to deficiencies in adapting performance to promise at meetings attended by his colleagues. There was no time to consider susceptibilities. The nation was in grave jeopardy and time counted. We had already lost months, we could not now afford to lose even a day.

The work of the whole Ministry was very closely interlocked. Failure to keep abreast of shell-filling might be the result of a failure to supply fuses or high explosives. This might proceed from a labour shortage in a particular district. In the weekly conference the trouble could be tracked down immediately to its root, and the responsible officer charged to rectify it. Meantime some arrangement might be improvised to get temporarily round the difficulty.

One immense advantage of these meetings was that in course of time they built up a very strong team-spirit among the men I had gathered round me. They were a diverse crowd—each an experienced leader accustomed to run his own business and to give orders rather than to receive them. It was essential for the success of the Ministry that they should learn to curb their independence, and to co-operate with each other. They began the process at these weekly meetings, even if at first it was occasionally in the role of mutual accusers. By degrees they grew to be really friendly, and with one or two possible exceptions they ended by becoming a close-knit band of fellow-workers, with a healthy *esprit de corps*.

My efforts to stimulate progress could not, of course, be confined to the staff of the Ministry. I had to be in continuous touch with industry all over the country. Frequently I would send for the manufacturers in some particular line—guns, rifles, machine tools— to consult with them about their output and stir them up to greater activity. I travelled round the country, visiting works and speaking to the workers, smoothing over labour difficulties, composing quarrels, urging increased output. The honour of the nation at home was pledged to our men at the front, that they should be furnished as fully and as speedily as was humanly possible with the weapons and defences that they needed in their struggle; and I held myself responsible that no effort should be spared and no reasonable expedient neglected to secure the fulfilment of that pledge.

I have been a pretty hard worker all my life, from boyhood right up to the present day. But I have never worked harder than during the period when I was carrying through the organisation of our munition supplies—not even during my Premiership, strenuous and arduous as those years were.

I generally worked an hour or two before breakfast, perusing essential papers and annotating them. It was my custom to invite to breakfast people who wished to see me, or whom I wished to see on munition business; sometimes important and influential American visitors wanted to discuss matters of moment with me, not necessarily connected with the Ministry of Munitions, and breakfast was a convenient opportunity for meeting them.

But my day would have started much earlier than this. As I have already mentioned, I would from the moment of waking have been at work upon papers and reports which I had taken overnight to my bedside.

By nine o'clock I was at work in my office at the Ministry of Munitions. The pressure of the task made it inevitable that many ancient traditions should be broken. After dealing with any important letter or documents which had come to hand, there would be some matter which I had already decided to tackle that morning— maybe guns or shell-filling or rifles—and there would be departmental heads to see and their problems to settle; arrangements to make about division of raw material, perhaps, between rival claimants for its use, and so on. Often, too, there would be Cabinet Meetings to attend in the morning, although for the first few weeks of my tenure of the Ministry, imperative business prevented my attending. I was told that at one meeting Mr. Balfour asked: "What has become of the Minister of Munitions? I have not seen him for some time."

Lunch would probably be used, like breakfast, as an opportunity to meet someone with whom I had urgent munition business to discuss. In the afternoon the House of Commons claimed me, though as soon as I had replied to the numerous questions affecting my department which were habitually on the Paper, I would escape, if the nature of the succeeding business made it possible, to get on with my job.

Constant difficulties arose with the War Office, which necessitated consultations with Lord Kitchener, and frequently with the Prime Minister. These were often lengthy matters. The War Office was at that period a perpetual source of obstruction.

Labour difficulties involved me in frequent visits to industrial centres, and consultation with deputations of workers or shop stewards. Especially in the earlier days, before the control of profits had become general, there was a bad spirit stirring among the men, and syndicalist agitators caused a good deal of trouble. In this respect the Glasgow district gave us the most trouble, although there was considerable agitation of an obstructive character in the Newcastle, Sheffield, and other areas.

I need not refer to the various public meetings I had to address from time to time round the country, in order to rouse the nation to the vital issues confronting us, and keep up enthusiasm for munition output. My recollection of those days is one of an unceasing drive. Although I was urging on the Ministry and all my staff there as hard as I could, I think I can claim that I asked from none of them an effort greater than I was myself making.

3. THE PROBLEM OF LABOUR

Looking back to-day upon the problem which from the outset of the War confronted the nation in regard to the arming and equipping of our troops, it seems a little curious that at the beginning of the hostilities there was in some quarters expectation and fear of acute unemployment. Within the first week, the Cabinet Committee on the Prevention and Relief of Distress, of which the President of the Local Government Board, Mr. (now Sir) Herbert Samuel, was chairman, invited the Mayors and Provosts throughout the country to form local committees to provide against unemployment. Local authorities were urged to expedite public works and to frame schemes which might be put in hand if serious distress should arise. Acting on this impulse, employers and workers in the engineering industry held a meeting on 19th August, 1914, "to discuss ways and means whereby the unemployment contingent upon the national distress may be minimised." The Director of Army contracts issued in the same month from the War Office a circular entitled: " Memorandum as to minimising of unemployment during the War," in which he recommended the abandonment of overtime work as a means of spreading the available employment among as many hands as possible.

By mid-September, however, the Board of Trade discovered that the feared unemployment was not materialising; by November there was an unsatisfied demand for 6,000 armament workers, and the shortage of labour grew as the need for munitions increased until the deficiency of workers became one of our greatest problems.

The Cabinet Committee on munitions, the appointment of which in October, 1914, I have already described, was not called together from 23rd October until 23rd December; and at this latter meeting the supply of labour was found to have become a matter of acute difficulty.

There were three main causes operating to accentuate the labour difficulty. The first was the fact that enlistment had been particularly heavy in the big industrial districts, especially those associated with engineering. Between 4th August and 4th November, 1914, the enlistment per 10,000 of the population had been only 80 in the East of England and 88 in the South-West, while it was 150 in Yorkshire, Durham and Northumberland, 196 in Warwickshire and Midland Counties and 237 in Southern Scotland, in all of which areas the population was mainly industrial. The same high percentage of recruitment obtained also in South Wales and other industrial centres. By October, 1914, 12.2 per cent. of the male workers in the engineering trades had enlisted—a proportion which rose by July, 1915, to 19.5 per cent. In far too many cases it was the most energetic and competent skilled workers who rushed to the colours and the less efficient who were left behind.

The second cause was the fact that as labour grew less plentiful and the demands on it increased, workers found themselves in a stronger bargaining position than they had ever experienced. Employers were unwilling to quarrel with and dismiss a worker whom they would find hard to replace, and there was a growing competition to secure the services of the skilled artisan. If dismissed from one post he could get another job immediately, often at higher pay. This led to a tendency among some workers to bad timekeeping, slackness at their work and in certain cases to excessive drinking. The number against whom such charges would be brought was no doubt a relatively small percentage of the whole body of workers. None the less, the failure of a few men in a factory to keep their own process up to time had often the effect of holding back all the other workers engaged on the job. As a result, we were getting nothing like the full possible output even from the staff of workers which the nation still retained in its factories.

A third cause of the shortage of labour for munition production was the fact that the War Office policy was, as I have said, to deal only with a limited number of firms. In consequence, most of the engineering shops in the country were doing little or no work for munition production, but were carrying on with private contracts, on the principle of " business as usual." This meant that a considerable proportion of the engineering labour in the country was not being mobilised for munition production.

For solving the labour problem, therefore, it was obvious that the steps needed were : —

(a) To check the enlistment of skilled men; if possible to recover from the Army those who had already joined up; and ultimately to dilute the available supply by bringing in as much additional unskilled labour as could be safely utilised in the processes of manufacture.

(b) To induce workers to keep better time and abstain from slacking at their work and continually changing their employer.

(c) To ensure a more rigid control of drinking facilities in munition areas.

(d) To train and employ women for the class of work for which they were suitable.

(e) To bring the needed munition work and the available labour in the kingdom together, either by transferring all workers to the established armament firms, or by spreading our production among all the shops in the kingdom.

Prior to the setting up of the Ministry of Munitions, the handling of the labour problem was primarily the duty of the Board of Trade, working in consultation with the War Office. The Board of Trade gave a great deal of time and effort to this task and worked out various schemes for dealing with it. A number of causes, however, combined to hinder these schemes from having the desired effect.

At the Committee of Imperial Defence on the 27th of January, 1915, Lord Kitchener expressed fears that any attempt to conserve to British manufacturers their pivotal men might directly or indirectly prejudice recruiting more than seemed likely at first sight. He objected to any system which entailed the rejection of any willing recruit. In consequence of Lord Kitchener's attitude, the only conclusion reached by the Committee was a recommendation that when a valuable man in industry was recruited the firm should fill his place with some man or woman ineligible for the Army.

In the course of January, 1915, arrangements were made whereby valuable skilled men serving with the colours could be released and sent back to the munition firms from which they had gone out. But no considerable numbers were actually released under this system until the late summer. A War Office scheme for " badging " was brought into existence in March, 1915, but during the first seven or eight months of the War, when enthusiasm for enlistment had been at its height, the most vital industries suffered losses which no subsequent efforts could altogether repair. When once a man had joined the colours no power could make him return to civil work against his will, and the influence of all his military superiors, from the General Officer to the youngest corporal, was exerted to keep him in the Army if he looked like becoming a useful soldier.

Broadly, therefore, it may be said that the activity of the recruiting officer in denuding the country of its best skilled workers was subject to no effective check during the first year of the War. Every outside influence was against the retention of the artisan at home—especially the patriotism of the worker, who often could not be persuaded that his work was necessary to the equipment of the Army. Moreover, during the period of voluntary recruitment the man who remained at his home post was liable to be taunted as a coward and insulted in the streets with white feathers.

Arising out of the discussion in the Cabinet Committee on munitions on 23rd December, 1914, various efforts were made to bring about the expansion and dilution of the available labour. Belgian workmen were taken on as fully as possible, and a certain number of women were brought into armament work. The first systematic attempt to enrol women for replacement of male labour was made by the Board of Trade on 16th March, 1915. In two-and-a-half months, to 4th June, 1915, some 78,946 women were enrolled on the Special War Register for women for work connected with munitions, but only 1,816 of these were actually given jobs.

The subsequent history of women's work in the production of munitions is one of the brightest chapters in the story. I give elsewhere some account of their efficiency and of their fine devotion and courage in connection with shell-filling. It was one of the many curious revolutions effected by the War that the lead in organising women and girls for national service was taken by the very people who, prior to the War had been, in the cause of women's suffrage, the thorniest opponents of the Government. Mrs. Pankhurst and her daughter Christobel, Miss Annie Kenney, Mrs. Drummond and other prominent suffragettes were prime movers in this new crusade.

On 18th July, 1915, they headed a great Women's War Pageant, in which thousands of women demonstrators marched for miles along London streets through rain and mud, escorting a deputation that waited on me, as Minister of Munitions, to express their welcome of the National Register and to offer their services to help the country. While voicing the demand of the women to be permitted to take part in war work, Mrs. Pankhurst also put in a plea for wage conditions which would safeguard their standard of living and prevent them from being sweated or exploited by manufacturers.   In reply I gave a guarantee that they should have a fair minimum wage for time work and should receive for piece work the same rates as were paid to men.   These conditions, sedulously enforced by the Ministry throughout the duration of the War, had a permanent effect upon the status of women workers in this country.   For although the emergency work upon which they were engaged was only temporary, and the regulations in which the agreement was embodied applied only to women engaging on what previously had been regarded as men's work, yet a standard was set up which could not easily be set aside afterwards; and it may confidently be claimed that the low and variable wages which were paid to women in the metal trades before the War are gone never to return.

In the War Office establishments, and the metal and chemical industries, which by mid-1916 were engaged in munition production to the extent of at least 75 per cent. of their total output, the women and girls employed rose from 82,589 in July, 1914, to 340,844 by July, 1916.   By November, 1918, the grand total of women employed on work directly or indirectly to Government order was 1,587,300. These figures give some indication of the immense growth of the effort made by women on behalf of their country during the War.

The difficulties which had to be overcome to secure the admission of women workers on this scale into branches of industry which had previously been a male preserve were, of course, immense.   But I will not further digress here to deal with them, as they were a part of the general problem of dilution of labour which I discuss in the following pages.

During the opening months of 1915 the Board of Trade made a series of efforts to draw supplies of labour to the established armament firms from other engineering concerns.   This was in accordance with the War Office policy of giving its contracts only to the recognised munition firms, and was based on the assumption that outside firms were doing only civilian work.   The results achieved were very meagre, partly because it transpired that many of these firms were devoting a part at least of their energy to sub-contracts for munition production, partly because they resented most intensely the proposal to filch away from them their best workmen and demanded as an alternative that they should themselves be given War Office contracts to execute.   A further difficulty was that the workmen themselves were unwilling to leave their homes and take up work in some distant part of the country for a strange concern. It soon became clear that the transference of labour from commercial to Government work could only be achieved by compulsory measures.

In one respect, indeed, many outside firms intimated that they would welcome compulsion.   They were tied up by contracts they had entered into for civilian commercial work, and although they

o

were anxious to assist the Government they could not break these contracts without incurring penalties. If, however, the Government would either give them statutory release from their obligations, or would take over their works under the system of Government control laid down in the Defence of the Realm Act, this difficulty would be surmounted.

On legal advice being taken, it was found that the existing powers were not adequate for this matter, and the outcome was the new Defence of the Realm Act which I laid before the House of Commons on 9th March. That measure authorised the Government " to require any work in any factory or workshop to be done in accordance with the directions of the Admiralty or Army Council given with the object of making the factory or workshop, or the plant or labour therein, as useful as possible for the production of war material." And it further provided that " where the fulfilment by any person of any contract is interfered with by the necessity on the part of himself or any other person of complying with any requirement, regulation or restriction of the Admiralty or the Army Council that necessity is a good defence to any action or proceeding taken against that person in respect of the non-fulfilment of the contract in so far as it is due to that interference."

Owing, however, to the persistence of the War Office in clinging affectionately to its traditional policy of dealing only with the established munition firms, comparatively little use was made of these powers prior to the establishment of the Ministry of Munitions.

Quite the most difficult problem in regard to labour was that of securing their wholehearted co-operation in the urgent task of munition production—by sticking in the same workshop, keeping good time, working steadily and avoiding strikes; and in particular by consenting to those relaxations of their trade union rules which would make possible an extensive dilution of skilled by unskilled workers, and a considerable use of overtime in cases of emergency.

When the first drafts for the new D.O.R.A. were under consideration, as submitted on 26th February, it was at first proposed to insert clauses which would have made illegal under penalty any strike or lock-out in any firm engaged on the construction of war material, and which would have provided compulsory arbitration in the case of all disputes. I decided, however, to see what could be done to achieve the same end by a voluntary agreement with the trade unions.

Accordingly, on 17th March, 1915, a representative meeting of trade unionists was summoned " to consult with the Chancellor of the Exchequer and the President of the Board of Trade on certain matters of importance to labour arising out of the recent decision of the Government, embodied in the Defence of the Realm

(Amendment) Act, to take further steps to organise the resources of the country to meet naval and military requirements."

The Conference was held in the gloomy board room of the Treasury, with the gilt throne of Queen Anne at one end of the room. There was a tradition that once upon a time it had been occupied by kings and queens who came to discuss their finances with the Lords of the Treasury. The last sovereign who sat upon it was the first Hanoverian George. Since he understood no English and the Lords of the Treasury understood no German our sovereigns ceased to go through the formality of attending these meetings at the Treasury to arrange their finance, and the once glistening and plushed throne has now a sad look of tarnished and torn neglect. The room was so crowded with the representatives of workers in many trades that some of them had to lean against this rickety throne of the last of the Stuarts. I had invited Mr. Balfour to be present. He had addressed many an assembly largely composed of workmen, but this was his first experience of sitting down to confer with them on a basis of equality. So far he had only talked to them; now he was talked to by them. The expression on his face was one of quizzical and embarrassed wonder.

He was surprised to find the workmen's representatives talked so well. They put their points clearly and succinctly, wasting neither time nor words. On the other hand, there was just a note of aggressiveness in manner and tone to which he was not quite accustomed from such quarters. For the moment it almost quelled him, and he was silent throughout. He did not quite recover his ease even after they left. He liked new experiences, but not of this sort. This was a portent which had for the first time appeared in the quarter of the sky where he had shone for a generation, and it came uncomfortably near. His ideas of Government were inherited from the days when Queen Anne sat on that throne. They were only changed to the extent that the fact of her being the last occupant constituted a triumph for the subject and thus modified the Constitution in a popular direction. But this scene was fundamentally different. He saw those stalwart artisans leaning against and sitting on the steps of the throne of the dead queen, and on equal terms negotiating conditions with the Government of the day upon a question vitally affecting the conduct of a great war. Queen Anne was indeed dead. I had watched his mood for years from an opposing bench. In looking at him now I felt that his detached and enquiring mind was bewildered by this sudden revelation of a new power and that he must take time to assimilate the experience.

The Conference met on 17th-19th March, 1915.

Opening the proceedings, I said that those present were being invited to consider the need for a larger output of munitions, and the steps which the Government proposed to take to organise industry to that end. Every belligerent country had found the expenditure of war material exceeded all anticipation. I referred to the very drastic powers which the Government had now assumed to control or take over any works in the country which were either turning out munitions of war or were capable of being adapted for that purpose, and told them that this was the matter on which I wanted to consult with them.

The "taking-over" of these works would not mean that their present owners and managers would be turned out adrift, and some admiral or general put in charge. The works would be run as formerly, except that they would be entirely turned over to munition production, and, of course, under such control there would have to be a limitation of private profits.

But if the Board of Trade were going in this manner to interfere with the rights and interests of the capital, the owner and managements of these concerns, it was only just that they should similarly ask the workers to consent to such limitations as might be found vitally necessary in the national interest of their ordinary privileges. In particular, I wanted to ensure that certain trade union regulations which might be more than justified in peace-time should be modified in such a way as to avoid hampering the nation's munition supplies in the existing emergency, and particularly that if any disputes arose, either about such relaxation of normal trade union rules, or about hours or rates of pay, the matter should be settled by peaceful arbitration, and pending a settlement the workers should carry on with their job. The Government did not say that workmen ought never to complain, or to ask for an increase in wages. "Our point is that during the time the questions at issue are being adjudicated upon, the work shall go on. . . . We want to get some kind of understanding with you about that before we undertake the control of these works."

I then laid before the representatives of the trade unions a series of propositions which had the object of providing that there should be no stoppage of work for Government purposes by strike or lock-out, pending a settlement of any disputes that might arise between employers and workpeople, and that all such disputes should be referred to arbitration; and that for the duration of the War, all trade union restrictions tending to limit output or the employment of semi-skilled or female labour should be suspended.

The workers' representatives were then left together to prepare their own draft of the undertaking they were prepared to give on these points. This draft was discussed and amended, and finally on 19th March a memorandum was presented by Mr. Arthur Henderson which had been accepted with only two dissensions. It was accordingly signed on behalf of the Government by myself and by

Mr. Runciman, and on behalf of the workmen's representatives by Mr. Henderson and Mr. Mosses. I undertook to provide enough copies for every union to send one to each of its members.

This document was known as the "Treasury Agreement." It occupied an important place throughout the War in the negotiations with labour, because it set out clearly, in terms which the trade union leaders recognised to be fair and just, the conditions under which munition labour was thereafter progressively organised. It stipulated for the admission of unskilled and semi-skilled workers to dilute the existing body of skilled labour, provided that they were paid the same wages as had customarily been paid for the work; it furnished a scheme of arbitration to take the place of strikes; and it laid down that the private profits of the manufacturers were to be subject to limitation.

In the following week an agreement on similar lines was specially negotiated by me with the Amalgamated Society of Engineers, whose representatives, though present at the previous conference, had attended without power to sign.

These two agreements, though important because of the solutions they reached, failed to become immediately operative. There was one difficulty remaining. The workers, quite naturally, declined to confirm the suggested proposals limiting their own freedom until the Government implemented its undertaking to restrict private profit. Mr. Runciman was at the time busily engaged in negotiation with the heads of the armament firms in an effort to arrive at an agreed basis of limitation of profits, but in the end these negotiations came to nothing. The matter was ultimately dealt with by the Munitions of War Act in June, 1915, which provided that the establishments engaged in munitions work could be brought under the control of the Ministry, that their profits should be limited, and that in such controlled establishments trade union rules restricting output should be suspended.

This question of controlling private profits was in fact vital to the whole issue of labour supply. It was useless to ask the workers on the plea of a grave emergency to put their whole effort into manufacture and to stop striking or agitating for higher wages or to accept modifications of rules and restrictions designed for their protection, which they had won from employers through years of struggle, when they saw those same employers busily amassing colossal fortunes out of the emergency. In a "Memorandum on Labour for Armaments," by Sir H. Llewellyn Smith, dated 9th June, 1915, this situation is expressed as follows: —

> "The difficulty, as it has been expressed, both by workmen's representatives at the two Treasury Conferences and by employers themselves (as in the shipbuilding employers' deputation received

to-day) is that the workmen, though engaged on armament work, still feel themselves to be working essentially for private employers, with whom they have only a ' cash nexus,' and that in the present circumstances a ' cash nexus ' is quite inadequate to secure control. . . .

So long as contractors' profits are not brought under control, the workmen feel that any sacrifice they may make of their rules and restrictions will directly increase the profits of private persons, and their unwillingness to make the sacrifice is made almost insuperable by this suspicion."

It is true that during this period there had been a steady tendency for wages to rise, and that in addition, on account of the regular full work available in this country, combined with overtime, the workers were earning considerably more than they had previously done. But on the other hand, prices of food and other necessities had also been rising at a pace which in some cases almost outstripped any advance in wages. Strikes were in consequence occurring with ever-increasing frequency. Mr. I. H. Mitchell, of the Industrial Commissioners Department, when reviewing the tendencies of the last six months in June, 1915, wrote : —

" I am quite satisfied that the labour difficulty has been largely caused by the men being of opinion that, while they were being called upon to be patriotic and refrain from using the strong economic position they occupied, employers, merchants and traders were being allowed perfect freedom to exploit to the fullest the Nation's needs. This view was frankly submitted to me by the leaders of the Clyde engineers' strike in February last. As soon as Labour realised that nothing was being done to curtail and prevent this exploitation by employers, it let loose the pent-up desire to make the most they could in the general scramble. This has grown until now many unions are openly exploiting the needs of the Nation. If the work is Government work, it is the signal for a demand for more money. Trade union leaders who, from August last year until February this year, loyally held their members back from making demands, are now with them in the rush to make the most of the opportunity."

I may sum up as follows the labour situation as it presented itself when the Ministry of Munitions was formed in June, 1915 : —

Recruiting had taken away from industry a considerable number of its most essential workers and was still being pushed forward without any limitation other than that resulting from the belated badging of key men in the more important armament firms. Arrangements had been made by Lord Kitchener to permit the release from the colours of skilled workers badly needed by firms engaged on war work, but of a quarter of a million men employed in the metal trades who had joined the forces, only about 5,000 had actually been brought back.

The principle of dilution of skilled labour, though adopted in the Treasury agreement, had not yet been confirmed by the trade unions and put into force.

Profits of the firms engaged in war work were still unlimited, and were attaining unprecedented dimensions. Industrial unrest, stimulated by this spectacle, was growing rapidly. Whereas the number of disputes involving stoppage of work known to the Board of Trade at the beginning of 1915 was 10, 47 fresh disputes arose in February, 74 in March, 44 in April, and 63 in May. As regards labour this was the general situation with which the Ministry of Munitions was at the outset of its existence called upon to deal.

My first step for coping with this situation was to lay before Parliament, on 23rd June, 1915, the Munitions of War Bill. This was a measure designed to implement by Statute the various proposals which had already been discussed with the employers and workers in the munition industry. It dealt with the settlement of labour differences, the prohibition of lock-outs and strikes, the controlling of establishments engaged in production of munitions and the limitation of their profits, the control of munition workers and the issue to them of badges; and it also provided for voluntary enrolment of a body of munition workers to be at the disposal of the Ministry and work where the need for their services was the greatest. Introducing this Bill, I reminded the House of the tremendous task which production of munitions for modern war had turned out to be, and outlined the steps I was taking to organise the available national resources for this end. I mentioned some of the difficulties, such as the question of supply of raw material. I hinted that the Government might find it necessary to take complete control of the metal market. It might have to deal firmly with people who attempted to hold up necessary supplies in order to exploit higher prices. It might have to take steps to prevent a coal shortage. Existing machinery was often idle because there were no skilled men to use it. Many such men had enlisted in the Army, and must be found and brought back from the firing line to the workshop. The holding up of work through the slackness of a minority had to be remedied, and the restriction of output because of yard regulations, written and unwritten, must be avoided. The question of compulsory service in the production of munitions of war, I said, had been the subject of a very frank discussion between the leaders of the trade unions and myself, and I was bound to point out that if there were an inadequate supply of labour for the purpose of turning out the munitions of war which were necessary for the safety of the country, compulsion would be inevitable. The trade union leaders put forward as an alternative the proposal that the

Government should give them an opportunity of securing the men required. They said: " Give us seven days, and if in seven days we cannot get the men, we will admit that our case is considerably weakened." To this I had agreed. But even if the required workers were forthcoming voluntarily, I explained that it would still be necessary to take powers in the Bill to enforce contracts with them and to secure discipline in the workshops. Here again an agreed solution had been reached for the setting up of a Munitions Court.

I then came to the very important provisions in the Bill with regard to limitations of profits from munition work: —

> " The trade unions insisted, and I think properly insisted, on their share of the bargain. They said, workmen are quite willing to work for the State, to put their whole strength and to suspend their trade union regulations, as long as they know that the work is of advantage to the country. But the objection in their minds always is that they are suspending trade union regulations important to them in order to increase the profits of individual employers. That they will not assent to, and they say, as a condition of all the other provisions to which they have given their assent, there must be a clause in the Bill which will limit the profits of those establishments which are working for the State, and that the provisions which I have enumerated only apply to establishments where the profits are limited. That is why we propose to set up controlled establishments, so that where the State assumes control of a workshop all the conditions which I have referred to shall apply to that workshop. That means the workshops where the munitions of war are being supplied at the present moment. It means practically that the State assumes control of the profits of these establishments, that whatever suspension of regulations takes place it will be entirely for the benefit of the State and not of the individual employer, and upon those conditions the trade union leaders are prepared to accept those suggestions which I have already made."

The Munitions of War Bill quickly passed through its Parliamentary stages and received the Royal Assent on 2nd July. No time was lost in bringing to the solution of the labour problem the aid which its powers afforded.

I made a systematic effort to get back skilled men serving with the Colours to resume their work in the munition firms. On 9th June I sent a circular letter to engineering and shipbuilding firms to get lists of the skilled men in their employ who had enlisted, and telegrams were sent by the Adjutant-General to certain Commanding Officers to ascertain what skilled men were in their units. But Lord Kitchener stipulated that, for the time being, only those men should be released who were not yet overseas or in units ready to be sent out.

The recovery of skilled mechanics from the ranks, however, under this strict limitation was not very successful. From July to the end of October, 1915, the total number thus brought back, either under the " bulk scheme " for release of those known to be skilled mechanics, or the individual release of men specially asked for by their own firms, barely exceeded 5,000. The flower of the skilled mechanics who had joined the Army was either already abroad or in the " barred " units at home. Speaking on 20th December, 1915, in the House of Commons, I said : —

> " We are trying to get men from the Colours. . . . It is like getting through barbed-wire entanglements without heavy guns. There are entrenchments behind entrenchments. You have not merely the Army, the Corps, the Division, the Brigade, the Battalion, and the Company, but the Platoon, and even the Squad— everybody fighting to prevent men from coming away. I am not surprised. I am not blaming them. Skilled men at any trade are skilled men at every trade. Your intelligent skilled man is a good man in the trenches, and nobody wants to lose him. Therefore, every corporal fights against parting with a good, intelligent, skilled workman. As my honourable friend points out, the men themselves feel that they are running away from danger in order to go back to comfort and high wages and emoluments, and they don't like it. It is a very creditable story. . . ."

By August I had discovered that the bulk of the men we wanted were in the " barred " units, and I wrote to Lord Kitchener making a very urgent plea for the release of at least the most valuable of these.

Throughout August and September, 1915, a correspondence was in progress between the Ministry and the War Office, and eventually arrangements were made in September for a census of skilled munition workers in all units not yet sent out of the country, and of those offering themselves some forty thousand were passed by investigators as suitable. By the end of October steps were being taken to allocate these men to munitions works.

Great as were the difficulties of carrying out the schemes for return of skilled workers from the Colours, the difficulties in the way of introducing dilution of labour were far greater, though the ultimate results of this policy were more fruitful.

The fundamental opposition to dilution came from the craft unions. Through long years they had built up as a protection against the dangers of cut wages, unemployment, and blackleg labour an elaborate system of rules and customs which were designed to control the rate of output and narrow the doorway into the industry. The rules were highly artificial in many cases; men appertaining to certain crafts alone were permitted to touch certain work, even though it might be of a kind which any handy man could do with little or no special training; and a man doing one job might not carry out the simplest task ancillary to it which ought by these rules to be allocated to another class of craftsman, but must stand by and wait till the other type of craftsman was called in, and executed that limited operation. Experience of a restricted market for their labour had made the unions develop every means of restricting its supply, and they were afraid, not without reason, that if the door were thrown open they would after the War suffer from a congested labour market, and that if sharp demarcations between the crafts were once broken down they would be difficult to re-establish. It was not a fear of falling wages during the War which troubled them. I had guaranteed that this would not occur. It was rather a dread of losing the tradition of mystery and technical difficulty which they had built up to protect their craft, and the apprehension of an overcrowded supply of workmen in their particular trade, leading to unemployment, lower wage rates, and a reduced standard of craftsmanship and of living in years to come. The patriotic appeal of our national necessity made difficult headway against these quite natural and—as the event proved in some cases—justifiable fears. Clemenceau once said that there was no difficulty in inducing Frenchmen to give their lives for their country, but they would not give their money. This is not to be wondered at when we remember that in actual fact the fires of patriotism are too often quenched when they come up against the cool waters of " business." Trade unionists flocked to the standard of their country when volunteers were called for to face death, but I was told that men at the front, daily confronted with death and needing shells to protect and defend themselves, wrote home to their fellow trade unionists entreating them not to surrender any of the privileges of their craft, although strict adhesion to these privileges was impeding the supply of the munitions they so sadly needed. The war-time profiteers were not infrequently brothers or fathers of those who suffered and died at the front, and with altered circumstances might have shown equal self-sacrifice. But unhappily for sentiment, when you come to business matters you discover that business is business, and admits of no divided loyalties. Our statesmen more recently have rediscovered this truism at Ottawa.

It was perhaps unfortunate that the first branch of the engineering industry where it was found necessary to raise the issue of dilution was the machine tool trade, since this was regarded as the very special preserve of the skilled worker, and was one the output of which, unlike that of shells or machine-guns, would continue its importance after the War. When we attempted to increase munitions manufacture in this country we found that our first need was machine tools, which did not as yet exist in quantities sufficient even to permit the carrying out of the orders already placed by the

War Office, far less the greatly augmented production at which the Ministry aimed.   At a conference I summoned of machine tool makers on 15th July, an agreement with the trade unions was reached for a programme of night shifts and labour dilution.   But when the officers of the Ministry tried to carry through this arrangement they came up against bitter opposition from shop stewards and local trade union committees.   At Woolwich Arsenal the local committee resolved: " That we refuse to entertain the proposal to allow the introduction of semi-skilled men on work now done by fully qualified mechanics, as it is not proved there is the shortage claimed."   And at the works of Messrs. J. Lang and Sons, Johnstone, the workers' committee declared: " That no woman shall be put to work a lathe, and if this is done the men will know how to protect their rights."   This was in August, 1915, and I had to weigh carefully the alternatives of taking drastic action or trying conciliation. Had stern action proved successful without rousing wide antagonism, it would greatly have expedited the process of dilution.   If it had failed against a massed opposition on the part of the skilled workers —for it would obviously have been impossible to punish them all— the campaign for dilution might have been permanently lost.   As yet the Ministry was in its early stages, and a realisation of the immense and urgent need for greater munition output had not fully captured the minds and imaginations of the whole body of workers.   I decided to try persuasion first.

On 9th September, 1915, I visited the Trades Union Congress at Bristol, and addressed it on the subject. I told them how German trade unions had organised and expanded their services for munition production. The War, I declared, had become a conflict between the mechanics of Germany and Austria and the mechanics of Great Britain and France. But as yet this country was not doing its best in the struggle. Only 15 per cent. of the machinery which could be used for turning out rifles, cannon and shells (in all of which there was a shortage) was working night shifts.   The problem, I pointed out, was largely one of labour.   If every skilled man were working his utmost there would still not be nearly enough.   The issue of dilution was not one of turning off a skilled man to make room for an unskilled, but one of concentrating the skilled men on the work which only they could do.   At present highly skilled workmen with years of training were doing work which could as easily be done by those who had only a few weeks' or a few days' training, and we could not equip our armies unless organised labour was prepared to assist by suspending during the War all restriction which made it difficult to use skilled labour in the best way by employing unskilled under skilled direction wherever possible.

I then proceeded to explain the bargain which had been made with the trade union leaders at the Treasury Conference. " Has the State kept the bargain? [A voice: 'No.'] I am going to tell you. Profits, restrictions of profits. Does anybody say we have not kept the bargain? [A voice: 'Nobody knows!'] Nobody knows? We have declared 715 establishments producing munitions of war to be 'controlled establishments'; we have put them under control of the State . . . and do not forget this, we have not asked any trade union to suspend any regulations except in an establishment where we control the profits. What have we done about controlling the profits? We have controlled them by an Act of Parliament. . . . We are restricting them on the basis of what they earned before the War. . . . They are only going to get the standard which is based upon the profit made before the War, with any allowance which is made by us in respect of increased capital which they have put in. What do we do with the balance? We put it into the Treasury to carry on the War. [Cheers.] It is the first time it has ever been done in the history of any country. You have practically taken over the whole of the engineering works of this country and controlled them by the State. I have seen resolutions passed from time to time at Trade Union Congresses [laughter] about nationalising the industries of this country. We have done it. [Cheers and laughter.] . . ."

I told the Congress about the undertaking, embodied in an Act of Parliament, that conditions would be restored at the end of the War, and, further, I gave them a guarantee that piece rates should nowhere be cut down in munition works as a result of any increase in output; and that unskilled men and women should be paid the same rate as had been given to skilled men for the jobs transferred to them. Having dealt with the way in which the Government was keeping its side of the bargain, I indulged in some plain speaking on the failure of the trade unionists to do their share. I referred to the refusal of men to admit semi-skilled workers, the squabbles between coppersmiths and plumbers as to the dividing line between their jobs, and the penalising of men who worked faster than the average " A complaint came to me from Woolwich that there was a deliberate attempt to keep down the output. The Labour Advisory Committee investigated it, and a trade unionist defended the men in this particular case. The significance of his testimony was this —and I am quoting now from the report of the investigators: 'The trade unionist witness regretted having to acknowledge that the workmen in several departments restricted output in order to maintain the prices obtained before the War, and this was continued up to the present time.' Well, that is not carrying out the bargain. [A voice: 'It is not playing the game.'] I agree."

It is fair that I should record the fact that a crowded assembly of trade union delegates listened to this plain speaking not only without resentment but with a swelling appreciation. A week later there was held a conference of trade union executives to discuss dilution, and a series of resolutions favourable to the plan was adopted. Following on this expression of approval, I set up a Central Munitions Labour Supply Committee, containing representatives of the Ministry, of the Employers and the Employed, presided over by Mr. Arthur Henderson, which proceeded to co-operate with the Ministry in organising labour dilution and dealing with the multitudinous problems of wage rates and local conditions of employment, transfer of labour, etc., which arose in this connection.

By the end of 1915 labour troubles were interfering seriously in some areas with the output of munitions. I suspected that in some cases the failure of a firm to deliver up to schedule was due to a certain degree of slackness and inefficiency on the part of the management, but in a great many cases it was traceable to the activities of men inside the works who deliberately fostered discontent. The trouble did not come from the trade unions or their officials. They honourably adhered to their agreement with the State. But an agitation known as the " shop steward " movement arose in the greatest of the munition works. These " stewards " were chosen by the workers in a given factory or workshop to present grievances to the management. They felt they must justify their existence by searching out wrongs which had escaped the notice of the local trade union secretary. It gradually became a formidable element of disturbance in the largest munition areas. Glasgow was one of the worst districts, and the agitation amongst the workers seriously interfered with the output, especially with the delivery of big guns. I decided to visit the works to see for myself what the position was, and put before the men and their leaders the exact facts with regard to the military position, and the peril in which their fellow-workmen at the front were placed by the absence of adequate artillery of the heavier kinds to enable them to contend with their foes on equal terms.

Accompanied by Mr. Arthur Henderson I arrived at Glasgow on Christmas Eve, and we both went to Beardmore's works, where the delivery of heavy artillery was being seriously retarded by labour difficulties. At my request, the shop stewards were brought together and I then told them why I had come and made my appeal for their assistance in stimulating greater activity in production. A man who seemed to be their leader stepped to the front and started haranguing me on the servitude of labour in private establishments. He was a strong man, with a fine open face, the natural pleasantness of which was overlaid by a theatrical frown which he had succeeded in implanting upon a kindly countenance. He struck an attitude, and in a loud, challenging voice he said, " I am as much a slave of Sir William Beardmore as if I had the letter ' B ' branded on my brow," his hand passing across the wrinkled forehead. This was my first acquaintance with Mr. David Kirkwood. I discovered that he was fundamentally a reasonable man to deal with. He promised that if Mr. Henderson put our case before a free assembly of workers, he would do his best to secure a fair hearing.

There was another spokesman who seemed to me to be a natural savage. He came right up to me with threatening mien and locked fists, talking in an ill-tempered and angry voice. I must say the rest of his comrades were not too pleased with his attitude. Later on I met Mr. Gallagher, a Communist, whose manners were quite perfect, and whose tones were soft, but he left no doubt in my mind that his was the most sinister influence.

The following morning (that is Christmas morning) we addressed a great gathering of workmen at the St. Andrew's Hall. Mr. Henderson took the chair; four-fifths of the workmen were anxious to hear all that was being said, but a minority were determined to disturb the proceedings and deprive us of a hearing. They were specially annoyed with Mr. Henderson, and he had by far the worst time. On the whole I was heard quite well, with a few surmountable interruptions. Mr. Kirkwood played the game and got up in the middle of the most turbulent elements, and put in a plea for a fair hearing. The visit, for a time at least, had a quieting effect and a quickening influence upon production. Some weeks later we had further trouble, and then strong action had to be taken in the way of deportation of some of the leaders, and the prosecution of others.

We were as yet, however, far from having reached full victory; there were still some entrenched obstructions and restrictions to break through. Even the greatest convulsion fails to tear out of the soil a well-grounded suspicion.

In this case its roots were so deep that they resisted the shattering bombardment of a year of horror. Throughout the autumn of 1915 discussion and disagreements continued as to the application of the principle of dilution, and in December I brought forward the Munitions of War (Amendment) Bill in order to give statutory force to the various points on which agreement had been reached. Even at this stage the Amalgamated Society of Engineers was still holding out, and when the Bill had reached its Committee stage, they sent a deputation to wait on Mr. Asquith and myself, armed with a resolution declaring that a series of amendments which they proposed—

" . . . are essential as an element of justice in the administration of the Munitions of War Act, 1915, and should be incorporated in the Amended Act if we are to maintain our influence with our members in securing the high standard of production required. Further, that a Committee representative of the conference be instructed to wait upon the Prime Minister and the Minister of Munitions and intimate the decision of this conference *as the basis of our continued co-operation.*"

The veiled threat in the last line of this resolution naturally stirred Mr. Asquith to anger. When challenged the deputation protested that they had not meant it in that way, and that all they wanted was to secure that the various provisions of the protection of wage levels and conditions of employment which had been set out in two circulars issued by the Ministry (Circulars L.2 and L.3) as conditions under which dilution was to be carried out should be given the force of statute. To my challenge whether they could cite a single instance in which an unskilled man, introduced into a controlled establishment, had been refused these rates, Mr. Brownlie, the engineers' secretary, had to admit they could not, and Mr. Asquith and I pointed out to them that some of their people had persistently tried to block dilution, and were at present making objections with little real substance as an excuse for their attitude. I would be willing to meet them in regard to incorporating the provisions of the two circulars in the Bill, if they on their side would guarantee that henceforward they would really co-operate in the dilution scheme, and not merely fall back upon some new demand as a pretext for doing nothing.

The deputation accepted this offer, and signed a document pledging the Conference and membership of the Society to accept the scheme of dilution and co-operating actively therein if the Government incorporated in the Bill the rates of pay and conditions of labour in controlled establishments set out in the Ministry's two circulars.

The Bill was re-committed and amended in accordance with this agreement, and thereafter dilution made rapid headway.

4. THE ROYAL ENCOURAGEMENT OF MUNITION WORKERS

The story of the steps taken to organise labour for the munition factories, and to induce them to put forward their best efforts and submit to control and the suspension of cherished trade union regulations and practices, would not be complete without a tribute to the vitally important help rendered by the late King George V. to the nation by heartening and encouraging the munition workers and those who were creating the district organisations.

It would be hard to over-estimate the value of the national service rendered by the Sovereign's visits to munitions areas and the personal relations he established with the workers there. I have shown in my narrative how dangerous a gulf had threatened to open between the outlook of the men in the trenches and that of the men at home in the workshops. While those who joined the Army felt they were serving King and Country, and put on with khaki a spirit of loyal comradeship and unquestioning service, those who remained in the familiar civilian environment of the workshop found it hard to escape from the old traditional atmosphere of jealous care for their rights as against their employers, the fear of exploitation, the readiness to " down tools " at any threat of encroachment upon their hard-won privileges. It was no easy task to persuade them that they too were in the service of the State for the defence of the nation; and to this end nothing could have been happier than the spontaneous resolve of the King to go about among them, to shake them by the hand, talk with them, and make a direct appeal to their patriotism and citizenship.

In the spring of 1915, when labour troubles were beginning to make themselves felt, King George began this practice of visiting the places where munitions were being produced. On 17th March he went to Woolwich Arsenal, and inspected the royal gun and carriage factories there, and the royal laboratory where explosives were made and tested. At the end of April he similarly visited the other royal factories, the small arms factory at Enfield and the gunpowder factory at Waltham Abbey. He followed up this visit by sending a special royal message to the workers at these factories, expressing his keen interest in their work, and his conviction that all engaged in the workshops would do their utmost, individually and collectively, to support their comrades at the front. On 12th May the King paid a two days' visit to Portsmouth, and went through the dockyards there, and again sent them a message on his return expressing " appreciation of the part which, by their devotion to duty, they are taking in maintaining the strength and efficiency of the Fleet."

Hardly had he got back to Buckingham Palace before he was off again on a week's tour of the shipyards and armament factories of the north. He spent May 17th and 18th on the Clyde, touring round from early morning to visit shipbuilding yards. At one of the largest, that of the Fairfield Shipbuilding and Engineering Co., the workmen presented him with a resolution expressing their loyalty and determination to press forward as efficiently and rapidly as possible with the Government work on which they were engaged. Replying, he said this resolution " will be universally welcomed, and will strengthen the confidence of the Nation in ultimate victory. It will indeed be a happy outcome if my visit to the Clyde has in any way conduced to this expression of patriotic resolve on the part of the men of one of the most important shipyards in this renowned industrial centre."

From the Clyde the King went to the Tyne, where he also spent two days, and spoke personally with a number of foremen and workers in the armament works and shipyards. He met the members of the North-East Coast Armaments Committee, and encouraged them in their task. He thanked the workmen in a speech for what had been done, but urged that more was still required. He voiced the hope " that all restrictive rules and regulations would be removed, and that all would work to one common end and purpose." This was a courageous gesture on the King's part to help forward the solution of the very difficult problem of suspending the trade union restrictions, which at that time were seriously hampering output. He followed it up a fortnight later by sending a message to the Armaments Committee urging " workers to do all they can." King George concluded this tour by visiting Barrow-in-Furness on 21st May. Whilst there he received a message from the Wallsend workers declaring their resolve to get ahead with the Government work, and replied expressing his appreciation. On 10th June he sent a message to the Barrow workers, appreciating " their assurances of loyalty and of resolution to do their utmost to assist in bringing to a victorious conclusion the great war which has now been raging for ten months."

The formation of the Ministry of Munitions called forth the King's keen any sympathetic interest. I have the most grateful recollections of the good will he showed to me in my anxious task, and of his readiness to give that personal help and encouragement which was so valuable a means of maintaining and improving the spirit of the munition workers. On 22nd July he started off and toured the munition areas of the Midlands. At Coventry he went round the works, and spoke personally to the foremen in all the shops. The members of the Coventry Armaments Output Committee were presented to him. Then he went on to Birmingham, where he spent the next day. So much interested did he show himself to be in the process of munition manufacture that it was difficult for the members of his suite to draw him away and enable him to keep to his time-table. Here again he insisted on having the members of the Munitions Committee and of the District Board of Management presented to him, and spoke warmly to them of the " zeal and cheerfulness " he had noted amongst the workers. This he followed up ten days later with a special message of encouragement.

Towards the end of September the King made another munitions tour, this time in Yorkshire, where he spent three days at Leeds and Sheffield. He moved among the munition workers, chatting freely with them. He picked out one worker at Sheffield, whom he recognised as having served with him when he was a midshipman in H.M.S. *Bacchante*. He watched another making shells, and remarked to him: " I am glad you realise the importance of the work in hand. Without an adequate supply of shells we cannot expect to win."

Words like these, uttered " man to man " by the Head of State to the artisan, naturally ran like wildfire through the works. It was this directness of personal contact, free from pomp or any trace of arrogance and aloofness, which made the King's visits to the munition areas such a valuable aid in the task of rousing the workers' enthusiasm and breaking through their reluctance to accept new methods and regulations. It was a real service to the men fighting our battles at the front who were in such peril of being overwhelmed by the superior equipment of the enemy.

The stimulation of the munition workers was of course only one among the myriad tasks imposed upon the Sovereign by the War— tasks to which he applied himself with indefatigable zeal, after a fashion which established him more firmly than ever in the affection of his people. His was the only throne in all the combatant countries which did not rock throughout all those critical years. Most of them, indeed, were overthrown. As one who was privileged to hold high and responsible office under the Crown all through the War I had special opportunities of witnessing how thoroughly the King discharged his duty to the country. Nowhere was the part he played more fruitful and valuable than in the encouragement of our munition workers.

5.   THE DRINK TROUBLE

One of the most serious obstacles encountered in the way of increasing the output of munitions was the heavy drinking in certain areas. France had dealt drastically with the problem by prohibiting absinthe: Russia by forbidding vodka. The question of drinking facilities has always been a dangerous topic for Governments to tackle, and the War Government, being naturally anxious to avoid controversial subjects, shrank from tackling it for many precious months. We consequently lost substantially in production. It is difficult for us to-day to realise how seriously excessive drinking contributed to diminish the output. Britain to-day is a much more sober country than it has ever been in my memory. There is still a good deal of heavy drinking, drunkenness still occurs, and the national health suffers from it, but the sight of a drunken man or woman reeling down the street has grown a rare spectacle, and the consumption of alcohol has fallen off very heavily. The discipline and restriction compelled by the exigencies of the War is largely responsible for this salutary change. This must ever be counted as one of the good things occasionally garnered from things evil. The memory of pre-war conditions is growing fainter, and it is becoming quite hard to remind oneself of the very different state of affairs which too often prevailed then. Cases of drunkenness appearing before the courts were three times as numerous in pre-war years as they are now. The quantity of spirits (alcoholic content) drunk in 1913 was two and a half times what it is to-day.

That may give the rising generation, growing up to the new and better tradition of to-day, some idea how commonplace and widespread insobriety must have been in some areas of this country up to the Great War. During the first five months of the War it became a serious element in the struggle to avert defeat. On the home front alcoholic indulgence shared with professional rigidity the dishonour of being our most dangerous foe. It is one of the themes of my book to tell how both of them were beaten off, though not without heavy casualties. The first effect of the War was rather to increase the habit of excessive drinking, and, indeed, to raise it into a real menace to the nation. It is easy to understand that this would be so. The sudden onset of unaccustomed danger drove many who were out of the danger zone to the vicarious philosophy of " Let us eat and drink —especially drink—for to-morrow our comrades may die!"

The disorganisation of social habit through the War, the reckless excitement that thrilled the air, the feeling that the tables of the law had once more been smashed amid the thunders of a grimmer Sinai, led some of both sexes to excesses in all directions, and as war work increased the earnings of multitudes, those who drank, drank deeply, for they could afford the indulgence as they never did before. The evil was not confined to men—it spread to women. My attention was specially directed to this problem through the reports that excessive drinking among the workers in the firms engaged on armament production was gravely hindering the output of munitions. The reports of eye-witnesses were very grave and alarming, especially when taken in conjunction with the fact—of which I was already aware—that deliveries of munitions of war were in arrears, and that there were persistent rumours of serious shortage in France.

Liquor consumption had certainly gone up rapidly. Drunkenness was greatly on the increase, particularly in the industrial areas which we relied on for munitions. A considerable percentage of the workers failed to turn up on a Monday morning, and when they appeared on Tuesday they were much the worse for their week-end debauch. Some of them took to extending their leisure at both ends of the week. One bank holiday a great number of men failed to turn up for a whole week. No wonder output was unsatisfactory. I passed on such reports as I received to the War Office and Admiralty. They replied that they were only too painfully aware of the facts and that their official reports showed an even worse state of affairs than anything revealed in mine. I decided that the time demanded that this peril to our armies ought to be instantly and firmly tackled, and on 28th February, 1915, I began to stir up public opinion on the subject of this increasing and menacing evil, with a view to making strong action possible. Speaking at Bangor on that day I said: —

" I hear of workmen in armament works who refuse to work a full week's work for the nation's need. What is the reason? They are a minority. The vast majority belong to a class we can depend upon. The others are a minority. But, you must remember, a small minority of workmen can throw a whole works out of gear. What is the reason? Sometimes it is one thing, sometimes it is another, but let us be perfectly candid. It is mostly the lure of the drink. They refuse to work full time, and when they return their strength and efficiency are impaired by the way in which they have spent their leisure. Drink is doing more damage in the War than all the German submarines put together. . . . We have got great powers to deal with drink, and we mean to use them. We shall use them in a spirit of moderation, we shall use them discreetly, we shall use them wisely, but we shall use them quite fearlessly, and I have no doubt that, as the country's needs demand it, the country will support our action, and will allow no indulgence of that kind to interfere with its prospects in this terrible war which has been thrust upon us."

A month later, on 29th March, 1915, I received a deputation from the Shipbuilding Employers' Federation, who were unanimous in urging that the sale of excisable liquors should be totally prohibited during the period of the War. In particular, they asked for the closing of public-houses and clubs in the areas where war munitions were being produced. They pointed out that in spite of Sunday labour and all overtime the total period worked on the average in almost all shipyards was below the normal number of hours per week, and though work was in progress night and day for seven days a week, less productiveness was being secured from the men than before the War. The deputation was of the opinion that this was principally due to drink. The figures of weekly takings in public houses near the yards were convincing evidence of the increased sale of liquor. Allowing for the enhanced price of intoxicants and for the greater number of men now employed in shipbuilding, the takings had in one case under observation risen 20 per cent., in another 40 per cent.

The damage done by the drink habit was sufficiently illustrated by the case of a battleship coming in for immediate repairs and having those repairs delayed a whole day by the absence of the riveters through drink and conviviality. This case, they said, was one of hundreds. Nor was this the only reason in favour of prohibition as against curtailment. As long as public-houses were open there would be found men to break the rules of the yard and come late to work in order to secure drink beforehand. And the indisposition to work after the consumption of excessive alcohol was too obvious to need elaboration. They urged total prohibition during the War. It was certainly not a teetotal deputation. Neither in figure nor physiognomy did they give any indication of having spent their leisure hours in the service of the Band of Hope. When prohibition came in in America this incident explained to me why the majority of employers were stout prohibitionists. It also explained the rumours that they drew a definite line between national prohibition and personal abstinence.

The evidence was not to be lightly disregarded. Replying to the deputation, I said : —

"Success in the War is now purely a question of munitions. I say that, not on my own authority, but on the authority of our great General, Sir John French. He has made it quite clear what his conviction is on the subject. I think I can venture to say that that is also the conviction of the Secretary of State for War, and it is the conviction of all those who know anything about the military problem—that in order to enable us to win, all we require is an increase, and an enormous increase, in the shells, rifles, and all the other munitions and equipment which are necessary to carry through a great war. You have proved to us to-day quite clearly that the excessive drinking in the works connected with these operations is interfering seriously with that output. I can only promise you this at the present moment, that the words you have addressed to my colleagues and myself will be taken into the most careful consideration. . . . I had the privilege of an audience with his Majesty this morning, and I am permitted by him to say that he is very deeply concerned on this question—very deeply concerned—and the concern which is felt by him is, I am certain, shared by all his subjects in this country."

His Majesty had indeed shown the most anxious interest in the problem of drink, and had talked over with me the various possible methods of combating it. Reports had been coming in to him from many quarters as to the damaging effect of drink on production. He was himself prepared to go to any length of personal self-sacrifice for this end, and on 30th March, the day after I had received this deputation, he sent me, through his secretary, Lord Stamfordham, a remarkable letter, which, after saying that "nothing but the most vigorous measures will successfully cope with the grave situation now existing in our armament factories," proceeded : —

"We have before us the statements, not merely of the employers, but of the Admiralty and War Office officials responsible for the supply of munitions of war, for the transport of troops, their food, and ammunition. From this evidence it is without doubt largely due to drink that we are unable to secure the output of war material indispensable to meet the requirements of our Army in the field, and that there has been such serious delay in the conveyance of the necessary reinforcements and supplies to aid our gallant troops at the front.

The continuance of such a state of things must inevitably result in the prolongation of the horrors and burdens of this terrible war.

I am to add that if it be deemed advisable, the King will be prepared to set the example by giving up all alcoholic liquor himself, and issuing orders against its consumption in the Royal Household, so that no difference shall be made, so far as his Majesty is concerned, between the treatment of rich and poor in this question."

This royal gesture became known as " The King's Pledge," which the nation at large was urged to adopt in conformity with the King's example.   There was sound wisdom in the scheme, for the workers habitually complained, and with all-too-good reason, that while their employers and the members of the so-called upper classes were eternally lecturing and rebuking them for drinking, they were themselves freely and often excessively enjoying the alcohol which they sought to deny to their employees.   " The King's Pledge," and the fact that a number of distinguished persons and prominent men in every branch of industry followed his Majesty in subscribing to it, very greatly strengthened the hands of the Government in the measures which it subsequently took to limit and control the supplies of intoxicants.   Lord Kitchener was amongst those who gave practical support to the King's initiative and adhered to it to the end.   It was always a subject of general debate at Ministerial and Military tables whether total abstinence had increased or diminished the vision and efficiency of the Secretary of State for War, or whether it had left it *in statu quo*, and there were three distinct views on this point, each emphatically held and controverted.

Unfortunately, despite its considerably moral value, the King's example was not adopted widely enough to make any deep impression on the problem itself.   The House of Commons flatly declined to pass any such self-denying ordinance for its own observance, and this attitude on the part of the nation's legislators helped to prevent " The King's Pledge " from becoming the starting-point which King George and his advisers had hoped it might prove for a big voluntary movement of national sobriety.   It remained, therefore, to reinforce this initial impulse by statutory powers.

I was at this time giving very serious consideration to the idea of dealing with the drink traffic by buying out on behalf of the State all the private interests, and thus enabling the Government to obtain a perfectly free hand to carry through whatever measures were felt to be in the national interest, unhindered by the immensely powerful influence which the trade has always been able to exert on politics in this country.   To this end I caused an investigation to be made by Sir William Plender as to the probable total value of the interests it would be necessary to acquire.   On 30th March, he furnished me with a preliminary memorandum which showed that the market value of the shares in Breweries was approximately £68,786,000, while the value of the property owned by Breweries in Great Britain, including all tied houses, together with the value of all free public-houses and other on-licences would be £225,000,000 to £250,000,000.

It will be observed that this rough estimate did not include the value of distilleries.

I then secured the appointment of a "Liquor Trade Finance Committee" to advise the Government on the financial arrangements that would have to be made if it should be decided by the State to purchase the properties of the Breweries in England and Wales, to control the branches of the Retail Liquor Trade not so purchased, and to prohibit temporarily the retail trade in spirits, while permitting the continuance of the sale of beer below a certain alcoholic strength. The Committee reported on 15th April, 1915, submitting a series of recommendations as to the extent and manner of effecting the State acquisition of liquor interests, should such a step be decided on. This Committee estimated the total cost of transfer to the State of the properties of Breweries and the interests of the licensees of free houses in England and Wales at £250 million, excluding allowances in respect of certain off-licences for compensation to the holders of grocers' licences, compensation to officials and employees, and any other expenditure involved in the carrying through of such acquisition.

To politicians bred in pre-war traditions of national expenditure, the sum involved in this purchase seemed prodigious. It was held by some that in view of the heavy burdens we were already bearing to finance our war effort, it would be folly to choose this moment to incur this further heavy outlay. The sum required was barely one-fortieth of the ultimate cost of the War. In return the nation would have secured an asset which, on the basis of present profits would have given a return of 8 per cent.

The real statesmanship of the temperance cause was on my side. But a powerful section of temperance advocates were up in arms against the abhorrent suggestion that the State should sully its soul by becoming the manufacturer and distributor of alcoholic poison. They had no objection to share by taxation in the profits made by selling this poison to their fellow citizens. But the conscience of a devotee is an eccentric thing and argument never converts but only exasperates a true believer. The resistance of this section grew. On the practical side I was faced with the difficulty that the interests which would have to be dealt with by way of purchase or compensation were so numerous and varied in character that the negotiations threatened to take many months. I secured the adhesion of some of the leading brewers to my scheme. I did not despair of securing the adhesion of the rest. The Conservative leaders were consulted as to their attitude and they intimated that they would offer no opposition to the deal if the Government came to the conclusion that it was essential as a war measure. But a number of influential local optionists brought such pressure to bear on the Prime Minister that he feared serious trouble inside the Party, and in view of the urgency of the problem of reducing excessive drinking in the interests of munition output I decided for the time being to proceed with a more limited reform.

During the course of the negotiations I received from Mr. Edwin Montagu the following contribution to the discussions in a letter which he wrote me. As it puts the case against restriction forcibly and wittily, I think it worth reproducing: —

" (1) I believe and believe firmly that almost without exception, except in the cases of apoplexy, a shot in the stomach, or a congested liver, a man with a moderate amount of alcohol is a better citizen, a better man, a more vigorous individual, than he would be without it. Medical evidence shows that alcohol is a poison; like so many other poisons in moderation, it is beneficial, and total abstinence seems to me to be morally as great a weakness as insobriety.

(2) I cannot find myself in agreement with you that there is any evidence that drink has hampered us in this War on any substantial scale which calls for heroic remedies. Evil exists— there is broken time, there is disinclination to work; it is true that, even with Sunday labour and overtime, the average hours worked are less per week in many important trades than before the War. I believe this to be largely to due to overtime itself. If a man is called upon to work substantially longer one day than he is accustomed to work, the next day he is disinclined to work, and if he is a free agent may refuse to work. Our party anyhow, believes that trade unions are good institutions. They fixed the working day and its length probably empirically because experience showed them that, let us say, eight hours was the maximum which a member of their union could work regularly to produce the full economical output of which he was capable. They insisted that overtime should be treated as overtime because they found that it was economically bad, and it seems to me that the War has proved that insistence upon overtime leads to irregular work and a smaller output, and it should be avoided as much as possible.

(3) It is true that receipts from the sale of drink are large, but this is due mainly to your own taxation, which has increased the price of beer, and to the increase in the price of raw material and of labour, which has increased the price of whisky.

(4) It is true that employers and officials alike attribute everything that is wrong not to drunkenness, but to drink; but you must remember that although the Tory habit of mind is to be found on

both sides of the House of Commons you are now for the first time coming into contact with the Tory mind, naked and unashamed, in bulk, and I cannot help feeling alarmed that you regard it as honest, as unprejudiced as the habit of mind to which you are accustomed. I regard it as being a worse habit of mind. It is a habit of mind which treats the working man as a machine with no vested interest in his habits and with no right to humane consideration. Just as if an engine can do 500 revolutions a minute it can do 30,000 in an hour and 300,000 in 10 hours, so they think a man who can drill 6 holes in an hour ought to drill 60 in 10 hours and 600 in 100 hours. Anything wrong with their system they are accustomed to put down to the unpatriotism, to the want of a sense of duty, the gross habits of these animals whom they regard as their inferiors. When you say to me that it is not only the evidence of the employers but also the evidence of the War Office and the Admiralty I am more emphatic in regarding the source of information as tainted. Likely it was these gentlemen, who would like to work on paper according to theory, dismissing from their minds all human factors, found the British working man an intolerable nuisance. They would like to regulate him in all his actions, to measure his food like sailors on a ship or prisoners in a gaol, to dictate to him what time he went to bed and what time he arose, where he should live and even what he should think, to drill and perhaps to flog him to approximate him to the ideal nigger working for an average mine-owner in a Rand mine.

(5) It is said that holidays would not be so attractive to the labourers if the public-houses were closed. But you are not going to close the public-houses; you are, I think, driven by a belief that you cannot with fairness deny a stimulant to a man in the Black Squad who works under horrible climatic conditions in the open air and you are going to allow him to have light beer. He will go to the public-house to get his light beer just as he goes now to get his strong beer. His holidays will be just as attractive, and if your object is to make it unattractive you will have to close picture palaces and deprive him of all opportunity for amusement.

(6) Every one of the deputation which waited on you the other day drinks moderately—they told you so—but they would be insulted if you told them that they were unfitted for work because of this habit, and I really believe that you run grave danger by insulting or being understood to insult the people of this country of all classes by interfering with their liberty. The agricultural labourer, the honest, self-controlled artisan, the small tradesman, inspired by patriotic motives and doing his duty, may feel that those who are running the War do not trust them, and you may impair the fighting enthusiasm of your country. I hear rumours from all sources, from the Opposition, from the Labour Party, from

total abstainers and excessive drinkers, from political 'wire-pullers' that you will be met with opposition. But you will, of course, succeed in overcoming all this and I would only urge in conclusion two important things: —

(1) You must consult Labour so that you may find your difficulties lessened by their acquiescence. You may have to persuade employers to give them something else whilst you are doing this.

(2) You ought, I think, to consult some financial expert on the finance. You will, of course, not be misled by the desire of the brewers and the distillers to get out of the trade which is continually having to fight hostility on the part of the community.

But I think the Governor of the Bank would be able to give us information as to the best way of carrying out your project. If you issue £200,000,000 of 4 per cent. stock you must, I fear, create a disastrous effect upon our credit. The Irish Land Stock is an example of the effects of a particular stock in a particular interest. I do not see how you can expect your brewer friends to hold your stock; they will run to the market and unload it, and when it approximates to a price of 50, it will bring down with it the price of all other Government stock, not to the same level, but down, and I would urge that at once you ought to get the Stock Exchange Committee to fix a minimum price for it in order to make it unsaleable, at any rate, for the present.

You will notice that I make two suggestions at the end, after letting myself go in the earlier part of what I have written. I am now going to assume that I am wrong in all my objections, and that you are going full steam ahead."

This pungent letter will give an idea of the division inside the Government on the drink issue. With regard to Mr. Montagu's suggestion that diminished production was due to fatigue arising from long hours, the figures I give later on as to the average hours actually worked in the yards and factories at that time supply a complete answer.

Having decided for the time being to abandon the attempt to purchase the whole of the liquor trade, I prepared a measure to secure its more effective control—a measure which further enabled the experiment to be made of State purchase and management of the liquor traffic on a small scale in particular areas. With this programme in view I laid before the House of Commons on 29th April a further instalment of D.O.R.A.—the Defence of the Realm (Amendment) (No. 3) Bill—designed to deal with the evil of drink in those munition-making areas where it was proving especially disastrous to the nation, and at the same time I outlined other plans for a nation-wide limitation of the peril.

In commending this Bill to the House I drew attention to the very alarming evidence which had come to hand of the effects of excessive drinking. A selection of this was published a couple of days later as a Government White Paper. This gave statistics of time lost in the shipyards and engineering shops of the Clyde and Tyne, and reports by officers of the Admiralty and the Home Office.

The reports were almost unanimous in making the same assertions as to lost time and energy due to alcohol. Statistics compiled from 15 firms in the Clyde district, for example, showed that of the iron-workers, 27.6 per cent. were working more than 53 hours per week, 39.4 per cent. between 40 and 53 hours, while 33 per cent. were working less than 40 hours per week. It was a minority that slacked, but a minority large and important enough to be disastrous to our national output.

The measure I proposed was to the effect that any area of import-ance for the production and transport of war materials might be placed under special control as regards the sale and supply of alcohol. The areas were to be defined by Orders in Council, and regulations applied to them which might empower the Government to close down the private liquor industry in the area, and become itself the sole supplier of intoxicants; to acquire, either temporarily or perman-ently, all licensed premises and businesses; to open, without licence, places of refreshment in which liquor could be sold; and generally to control the licensing and sale of intoxicants within the area. The Bill was duly carried, and a Central Control Board was set up to deal with Liquor Traffic. This Board issued on 12th June a set of regulations by which it took power, in any area placed under its control, to close any licensed premises or clubs, to regulate their hours of opening, to prohibit the sale or supply of any specified class of intoxicant, to impose conditions and restrictions upon licensed premises or take them under its supervision and to regulate the amount of liquor that could be brought into an area or transported within it. It further took power to prohibit in an area all sale of liquor except by the Board of Control, to prohibit treating, etc.

In July a series of Orders in Council was issued, defining the chief munition areas in the country and placing them under the Board of Liquor Control. During the following months the Board began to make effective use of its powers, issuing the " No Treating " Order in October, 1915, and drastically restricting the hours of sale of intoxicants. For the London area the hours of opening were in November narrowed down to what had previously been the " Sunday " hours.

It will be noted that I avoided total prohibition, despite the earnestness with which this policy was urged on me, in all good faith, by many who had not previously been associated with the "blue ribbon" movement. I realised clearly enough, what has since then been demonstrated in the United States, that it is futile to legislate far in advance of popular opinion or the public conscience. Restriction and limitation the nation would accept, and a considerable degree of reform could be achieved under State control, where the element of private profit and exploitation was eliminated. I confined my objective to this practical programme.

Even this reasonable scheme encountered very bitter opposition, and in my further proposals for a general discouragement of drinking I was at first compelled to swallow an almost complete defeat. In my speech on the 29th April I had said that I intended in my Budget to impose a graded surtax on the heavier beers, to quadruple the tax on wines, to double the taxes on spirits, and to raise the maximum permissible dilution of spirits from 25 per cent. to 36 per cent. under proof. These proposals roused considerable opposition both in and out of the House of Commons. The Irish Party was particularly angry in view of the big brewing and distilling interests in that country. One by one I was compelled to abandon, for the time being, these proposed taxes, and could only retain one insignificant but quite useful little restriction in the shape of a prohibition on the sale of spirits less than three years old, the object being to prohibit the newer and more fiery spirit. Even round this a fierce controversy arose between the rival distilling interests—the " Pot versus Patent " fight —for manufacturers of pot-still whisky made a practice of keeping their product several years to mature, whereas the output of the patent still was marketed straight away.

But although I lost this opening round I succeeded in subsequent years in carrying through the policy of high taxation of alcoholic beverages, dilution of spirits and encouragement of lighter beers. In this campaign I was able to utilise the aid of the Food Controller, under whose care the supplies of grain required for brewing and distilling had been placed. Not only was the total amount brewed and distilled restricted, but the release of such grain as was allowed was made conditional upon a proportion of the beer being of a light character, and the spirits being considerably diluted. The nation sang music-hall ditties bewailing " Lloyd George's Be-e-e-er," but the statistics of insobriety showed a rapid decline. The compulsory dilution of spirits and the elimination of the heavier beers had an especially beneficial effect, for they reduced the quantity of alcohol content of the beverages imbibed by a high percentage. The weekly average of convictions for drunkenness in England and Wales, which in 1913 were 3,482, had by the first part of 1917 fallen to 929.

The following are the figures for the total consumption of absolute alcohol in Great Britain during the War years: —

    1914....................89 million gallons
    1915....................81   ,,   ,,
    1916....................73   ,,   ,,
    1917....................45   ,,   ,,
    1918....................37   ,,   ,,

These figures represent the amount of alcohol estimated to have been consumed in all forms of alcoholic beverages—spirits, wines and beers—and the rapid decline in the last two years is only partly due to the fact that millions of men had left our shores. It is mainly attributable to the effectiveness of the drink restriction policy which was instituted and enforced.

While by means of progressive measures of taxation, dilution and limitation of the intoxicating beverages in the country, we were able to reduce very considerably the effective supplies of them obtained by the people, and especially the quantity of proof spirit and alcohol consumed, we were pressing forward in the industrial areas devoted to munition production the limitation of hours and drinking facilities. But I was by no means satisfied to adopt a purely negative policy. The Liquor Control Board had been given powers to take over the whole business of liquor supply within an area, and in four of the areas it experimentally adopted these powers, the first area so treated being that of Gretna Green—from which was developed the Carlisle experiment in State management of the liquor trade, an experiment which is still with us, and on which I will forbear comment beyond the unchallengeable statement that in the opinion of many highly competent observers it has more than justified the faith of those who authorised the venture, and has demonstrated that State management is capable of giving an orderly and adequate provision of alcoholic refreshment under conditions which promote sobriety and social amenity. The positive policy of the Control Board was shown in another very important direction—that of finding a satisfactory substitute in the scheduled areas for the drinking-dens whose opportunity of catering for the leisure of the workers was being curtailed. This led it to the appointment of a Canteens Committee. In its first report, dated 12th October, 1915, the Control Board stated: —

". . . The Board incline to the view that excessive drinking may often be traced to the want of adequate facilities for food, refreshment, and recreation, particularly in conjunction with long hours and overtime. The improvement of public-houses and the provision of canteens may therefore do much to render less necessary the imposition of purely restrictive measures. . . ."

The Board pointed out that drink was often resorted to when food was inadequate or improper; and that it was important

"to supply for large numbers of persons at specified times a suitable dietary . . . at a reasonable cost.

In endeavouring to meet this requirement, the Board have proceeded on two collateral lines of action: —

(a) The increase of facilities for obtaining suitable meals at public-houses, and

(b) The establishment wherever necessary of industrial canteens inside or within easy access of the works, supplying both substantial meals and light refreshment at reasonable prices."

A number of voluntary organisations rendered great help in the promotion of these canteens, such as the Y.M.C.A. and Y.W.C.A., Lady Lawrence's Munition Makers' Canteen Committee, the Salvation Army, and the Church Army. As to the actual provision of canteen premises and equipment, however, there was a question whether the Board or the employers should finance this; and it seemed much more desirable that the employers should undertake this responsibility, as it ensured their interest and gave a better prospect of permanence to the canteens. Accordingly, I secured Treasury sanction for an arrangement whereby the cost of building and equipping canteens might be charged by controlled establishments against their current profits under Part III of the Munitions of War Act, 1915, on condition that such buildings were maintained thereafter permanently as canteens, save by permission of the Ministry or of the Government Department which should inherit its duties.

This concession operated from November, 1915, until November, 1918, during which period 867 schemes of canteens at controlled establishments were approved, the total cost of them which was recommended for writing off gross profits being £1,909,135. About 1 million workpeople were employed in the establishments to which these canteens were attached.

The habit of regular and wholesome meals which these canteens encouraged, combined with the limitation and dilution of alcoholic beverages, helped to establish the post-war tradition of moderation in drinking and an improved standard of healthy living with which we are now familiar.

The progress which was made amply warranted me in stating to a temperance deputation which waited on me in 1917 to urge total prohibition, that by confining our objectives to practical and attainable limits we had been able in the last year or two to achieve a far bigger advance toward national sobriety than had hitherto been effected in a far longer period by all persuasive and legislative efforts in combination.

6. WELFARE CONDITIONS IN THE WORKSHOPS

One of the most welcome features of my post as Minister of Munitions was the opportunity it placed within my reach of doing something to better the social and industrial conditions in the manufacturing establishments which came under my direct or indirect control. Legislation reflected the growing desire in industry among both workers and employers for better standards in the workshops. In matters of this kind the law cannot move very far in advance of public opinion, save at the risk of becoming a dead letter. Various measures were sanctioned to a greater or less extent by the demands of workers, the successful experiment of enlightened employers, the zeal of practical reformers, and the growth of a progressive public opinion.

They represented, of course, only the minimum demand enforceable by law upon industry. Their incidence was limited and partial, and they did not go very far to ensure the highest attainable measure of amenity, health or comfort for the worker. Some employers were doing good pioneer work in the voluntary creation of improved conditions for their staffs, but they were in those days the exception rather than the rule.

The establishment of the Ministry of Munitions and the new industrial development which it organised gave an impulse to important changes in the general situation.

In the first place, the State as represented by the Ministry became a large-scale direct employer of industrial labour, and on an even larger scale an indirect employer of labour in the establishments engaged in munition work which were brought under its control. It was thus in a position to exercise persuasion, pressure, and, if necessary, compulsion, upon employers throughout the country to adopt higher standards for ensuring the welfare of their workers during the hours of employment.

In the second place, the withdrawal of a large part of the male population from industry into our fighting forces brought about the introduction of female labour on a scale never previously contemplated, and into industrial occupations which had formerly been staffed exclusively by men. There had, of course, before the War been a considerable body of female labour employed in certain types of factory—particularly in textiles—but it now invaded unusual fields of the heavy industries, the shell-filling factories, and even shipbuilding. In most of these establishments rough and unseemly conditions prevailed and had hitherto been put up with by the men workers, but it was recognised as impossible to ask women to submit to them.

A singularly favourable opportunity thus presented itself for introducing into industry a great forward movement for improving the general conditions of the welfare of the workers—an opportunity of which as Minister of Munitions I proceeded forthwith to take full advantage.

One of the first tasks of the Ministry of Munitions was the creation of national filling and explosive factories; and from August, 1915, a woman staff inspector of the Ministry was at work visiting these as fast as they were opened up and keeping in touch with the Boards of Management regarding the very important and varied questions of the welfare of women in this often dangerous work. Her duties included advice and help in the selection of woman supervisors, in the training of the special types of labour required, and in the provision of doctors and nurses for its care. In September, 1915, I appointed a Health of Munition Workers Committee to advise on questions concerning " industrial fatigue, hours of labour. and other matters affecting the personal health and physical efficiency " of the munition worker. It was a strong Committee representing the concentrated experience of the Home Office, of employers, labour, and medical experts. The Chairman was Sir George Newman and the members included Sir Thomas Barlow, Dr. Leonard E. Hill, three leading officers of the Home Office factory department, Sir W. M. Fletcher, Secretary of the Medical Research Committee, Mr. Clynes, Professor Boycott, Mr. Samuel Osborne, and Mrs. H. J. Tennant. It rendered invaluable service throughout the War by recommendations which supplied us with a practical programme for welfare work, and became a forerunner of the Industrial Fatigue Research Committee which has since the War carried out such important investigations into the conditions of industrial efficiency. Throughout the autumn of 1915 the supply departments of the Ministry of Munitions, working in consultation with this Committee, were organising measures to promote the welfare of munition workers in the national factories. In December, 1915, I took the further step of appointing Mr. B. Seebohm Rowntree Director of the Welfare Section of the Ministry, which I invited him to organise. Mr. Rowntree is well known, not only as a great employer of labour, but as one of the foremost and most successful pioneers in the development of improved conditions in his works. I should like to pay tribute here to the skill, energy, sympathy, and address with which he organised this new department. The work he did helped to transform the conditions for munition labour during the War, and has left a permanent mark upon conditions in our industries.

It was a difficult problem which confronted the new Welfare Section. In a large number of the existing factories conditions were very rough and primitive, and there was no tradition of care for the health or comfort of the employee beyond the minimum that was already compulsory under the Factory Acts. The pressure of work had, of course, been greatly intensified by the necessities of the War. Hours were long, and premises often crowded. New factories and extensions of existing factories were being rapidly run up, and these temporary erections were often occupied and buzzing with activity before any thought had been given to the provision of accessories in the shape of lavatories, cloak-rooms, mess-rooms, or canteens. And, in addition, they were being increasingly staffed by women and girls, for whose supervision no appropriate arrangements had been made.

The Health of Munition Workers Committee, in a memorandum issued in January, 1916, urged the need for attention to this side of the problem of production:—

" If the present long hours, the lack of healthful and sympathetic oversight, the inability to obtain good wholesome food, and the great difficulties of travelling are allowed to continue, it will be impracticable to secure or maintain for an extended period the high maximum output of which women are undoubtedly capable."

Under the Munitions of War (Amendment) Act of January, 1916, I had taken powers to control not only the wages but the conditions of employment of women workers on munitions, and also of semi-skilled and unskilled men and boys taking the work of skilled men in controlled firms. The Welfare Section of the Ministry, however, while holding these powers in reserve, adopted the deliberate policy of educating rather than compelling the firms engaged on munition work to put in hand arrangements for the welfare of their employees. Mr. Rowntree held that this was the only way of ensuring that the improved conditions so created would continue permanently after the War.

In the first instance the Welfare Section naturally devoted its principal effort to securing proper conditions for the women workers. At the outset they were often worse off than the existing male staffs, for no special accommodation or provision had in most cases been furnished for them, and they had no person of their own sex in authority to whom to appeal. In April, 1916, I ruled that women supervisors should be appointed in all national factories where women or young persons were employed, and that they should be approved by the Welfare Section. Their introduction into these national factories served as a precedent for their introduction into controlled establishments. In the same month a start was made by the Section with the development of welfare supervision for boys.

The welfare arrangements which were initiated included the provision of staffs and proper accommodation. The staffs comprised supervisors and assistant supervisors of welfare, and in the larger works, matrons, nurses, lady doctors, cloak-room attendants, etc.

The provision of welfare accommodation included such matters

H

as washing facilities, sanitary conveniences, cloak-rooms, canteens, seats in work-rooms, supplies of overalls and caps, and recreation facilities.   It was necessary to persuade some employers that one broken basin and a jug of cold water was insufficient washing provision for a staff of 300 workers; that workers engaged in hot, heavy and exhausting work should be able to have convenient access to clean drinking water and not to be reduced to running the risk of typhoid by drinking water intended only for manufacturing purposes; that the efficiency of workers would be increased if they were not required to work all day in clothes drenched in the morning on the way to the factory, and if they could take their meals in comfort in a messroom, or—better still—get cheap and wholesome food in the canteen, instead of gobbling scrappy meals beside their machines.

The policy of persuasion was, however, justified by its results. The demand for welfare supervisors grew to such an extent that special training courses were arranged by the department—a function later on taken over by the London School of Economics and by most of the provincial universities.   Over 1,000 supervisors of varying grades were working in munition factories at the date of the Armistice.   Allowing for the fact that their appointment had been made compulsory in T.N.T. factories and practically compulsory in national factories, probably some 700 had been appointed voluntarily by heads of firms or boards of management.

The welfare policy of the department ensured the standard of physical comfort for nearly 350,000 workers in the national factories and Government establishments, much above the minimum required under the Factory and Workshop Acts, and it stimulated a similar provision of canteens, rest rooms, ambulance rooms, and other material comforts, to a greater or less degree in a large proportion of the other controlled establishments, in which at least 400,000 women munition workers were employed.   This increased comfort was extended in some measure at least among a million and a quarter men and nearly a quarter of a million boys similarly employed by controlled firms and in national factories.

The department built, or promoted the building of, 11,738 flats and houses for munition workers.   It provided hostels for more than 23,500 workers and secured further accommodation in a large number of other cases, together with lodgings and billets in private houses for munition workers.   It provided directly for canteens and mess-rooms in the great majority of the 150 national and Government factories, while the Central Liquor Control Board approved on behalf of the Department the canteens of some 740 controlled establishments.

Its work in promoting intelligent care for the health and comfort of employees, the convenience of their hours, the hygienic conditions of their work, is perhaps less susceptible to statistical statement, but was at least as important in the permanent impression it made on our national industrial conditions.

As early as 1917-18 the " Factory Inspectors' Annual Report " bore witness to the effect of the welfare movement stimulated by the Ministry of Munitions in permeating the standards of non-munition trades, such as: —

" Cotton and woollen and worsted textiles, in laundries, in potteries, in biscuit factories . . . where conditions, with honourable individual exceptions, have long been stationary, but here too . . . the new movement has begun to take effect. . . . In these and many other developments moving towards social welfare in non-munition factories in 1917, there is really less sudden a growth than it is apt to be considered. Enlightened workers have been asking for these things, and enlightened manufacturers have been demonstrating for many years that these improving conditions are both rightly demanded and practicable. Now common sense awakened sees that the pace must be greatly quickened. . . . It is not only in controlled and national factories that material advance has been made. The whole spirit of management has quickly changed in many factories and industries where no new welfare order runs, and where State control of profits has not entered."

Legislative provision for the extension of the welfare movement was in full operation when the work of the department ceased. The principles established by the Ministry through persuasion were being gradually followed up by the Home Office with definite legislation. As early as August, 1916, the Police, Factories, etc., Miscellaneous Provision Acts gave definite powers of enforcing welfare provision. The Trade Boards Act of 1918 authorised trade boards " to make representations " to Government departments with regard to working conditions in their trade, while in the organised industries an increasing number of Joint Industrial Councils were beginning to consider questions of hours, conditions, and training. The prospect of legislative provision for a 48-hour week for all factory workers had appeared on the horizon.

In the light of these and other subsequent developments, there seems to have been a certain note of prophecy in a speech made by me as Minister of Munitions in February, 1916, when I remarked: —

" It is a strange irony, but no small compensation, that the making of weapons of destruction should afford the occasion to humanise industry. Yet such is the case. Old prejudices have vanished, new ideas are abroad; employers and workers, the public and the State, are favourable to new methods. This opportunity must not be allowed to slip. It may well be that, when the tumult of war is a distant echo, and the making of munitions a nightmare of the past, the effort now being made to soften asperities, to secure the welfare of the workers, and to build a bridge of sympathy and understanding between employer and employed, will have left behind results of permanent and enduring value to the workers, to the nation and to mankind at large."

CHAPTER X

THE STRATEGY OF THE WAR

EASTERN v. WESTERN FRONTS

IN the foregoing pages I have told something of the way in which the Ministry of Munitions was inaugurated, and of the human side of the problems with which it was faced. Before proceeding further to describe its practical achievements in the sphere of munition production, I must turn back to give some account of the battlefields for which these supplies were required, and the strategy they were designed to support.

For if it had involved tedious and incessant effort to break down the barriers of routine and military inertia which hampered the equipment of our forces, the parallel task of ensuring that our resources of man-power and munitions should be used in the most effective manner was still harder, and in fact was never carried out satisfactorily until the closing period of the War. I will now give a brief sketch of this problem, and of the efforts made to secure what I conceived at the time to be a wise solution.

There was during the early months of the War practically no effective War Council in the country keeping the position in constant review by directing and co-ordinating our efforts. There was a sense of leisureliness, if not of casualness, in our exertions.

After the great battles of the Marne and Ypres the War seemed to be settling down to normality. It was becoming accepted as if it were an ordinary part of the daily existence of nations. The people everywhere were adapting themselves to war conditions. The population of Whitehall, high and low, were no exception. That may account for the fact that there was a " no great hurry " atmosphere about our movements. The Germans had failed to capture Paris. It is true their armies were clamped firmly in Belgium and some of the richest departments of France, but they were kept within the limits of these autumnal conquests and could get no farther. The safety of the Channel ports had been assured by the battle of Ypres. There was some fighting in Poland and the Russian steam-roller had been pushed back by the Germans, but it had made up for that by rolling forward in Galicia. The Central Powers had been checked. We could now take our time to enrol and equip. That was the official temper—I am not sure that it did not represent the national attitude towards the end of 1914.

The fact that we were lavishing life and treasure away every day the War was prolonged; that Russia had revealed a dangerous weakness in the matter of equipment of her great armies, and that another campaign might therefore lead to her collapse and leave all the fighting to France and ourselves; that the position of Serbia was precarious and that the Central Powers might any day sweep her out of the way and open the road to the East; that unless we stirred ourselves up immediately we might not be able to put a well-equipped army in the field until the third year of the War: all these possibilities never seemed to come into the reckoning to disturb the general equanimity.

As far as the people at large were concerned, this composure was attributable to their unshaken confidence in our military chiefs and naval captains. What I had already seen of the official military attitude towards the equipment of our armies and their failure to grasp the new conditions of war as they had developed in France, convinced me that there was no justification for this remarkable complacency.

This induced me to write the following letter to the Prime Minister: —

" 11, Downing Street, W.

31st December, 1914.

My dear Prime Minister,

I am uneasy about the prospects of the War unless the Government take some decisive measures to grip the situation. I can see no signs anywhere that our military leaders and guides are considering any plans for extricating us from our present unsatisfactory position. Had I not been a witness of their deplorable lack of prevision I should not have thought it possible that men so responsibly placed could have so little forethought. You remember the guns and ammunition incident. When I raised the question in the Cabinet, the War Office had only ordered 600 guns in all. These were to be delivered before next September. The immense manufacturing resources of the country had not been organised for cannon, rifles, or ammunition, and America was not even explored. As a result of the activities and suggestions of the Cabinet Committee, 4,000 guns are now promised before that date. Ammunition has also been provided for those guns. Rifles not yet satisfactory. . . .

No real effort has been made until this week to ascertain the Russian position. Now K. has invited a Russian officer to come over to confer with a view to helping Russia with ammunition. Two months ago I pressed it on the War Office. Had it been done then we could have helped Russia, whilst Archangel was still open, and saved her from the peril of exhausted caissons.

Could we not have a series of meetings of the War Committee of the C.I.D. at an early date? Occasional meetings at intervals of a week or a fortnight will end in nothing.

Forgive me for intruding on your well-earned rest, but I feel that a continuation of the present deadlock is full of danger.

Sincerely yours,

D. LLOYD GEORGE."

This letter led to the calling of a War Committee at an early date to review the position. In order to form an opinion on the discussions and decisions of this Committee it is necessary to recall the military position at that date.

When the campaign of 1914 on all fronts came to an end owing to weather conditions, the Supreme Command, political, military and naval in the belligerent countries, had time to review the position and to decide upon their future course of action. Every army found its first plans baffled and broken by the fighting that had taken place. Not one of the elaborate schemes so carefully prepared and perfected for years by experts and lying in their bureaux ready to put into resistless operation on " the day "—for they all had their eagerly expected " day "—survived the actual clash of battle. Something went wrong with them all.

There was the long-prepared and pigeon-holed German plan for crushing France in a few weeks by an outflanking march of overwhelming forces through Belgium, followed by an immediate turning to the east with the victorious troops to roll up the armies of Russia. It had been worked out to the last detail. Nothing had been overlooked except the extent and effect of Britain's military intervention, and also perhaps the equally important fact that the execution of the plan would be in the hands of different men from those who originated it. That scheme had now failed utterly and its fragments were scattered along the banks of the Marne and the Yser. The pigeon-hole at Berlin was empty. The thwarting of the invincible plan had not been anticipated. A new plan must therefore be worked out.

The French plan of attacking with the first and second armies south of Metz, and with the fourth and fifth north of it never had a chance of success. It was based on an assumption that never materialised. The British idea of holding the Germans on the Belgian Front whilst the French dealt with them lower down was based on the same complete miscalculation of the German strategy as that which misled the French generals. This was merely conforming to the French strategy. Had Sir John French's idea of the occupation of Antwerp been adopted there would have been a different situation to deal with.

The Austrian dream of an easy march from Belgrade to Nish had a rude awakening, for the Serbian peasants inflicted two disastrous defeats on their jaunty invaders. The Russians had some successes against Austria. Against Germany, if they ever had a plan, it never came off. The invasion of East Prussia was little more than a chivalrous improvisation to save France from the blunders of her generals. It came to a bad end at Tannenberg.

The great struggles of 1914, therefore, had shattered every military dream and wrecked every military hope on both sides. The military leaders were bereft of any clear idea how ultimate victory could be attained. Every army had its failures. Every army had its successes. At the end of the 1914 campaign they all rejoiced in the victories and forgot the defeats. That was the general state of mind in and behind the lines. But no one had any clear notion what to attempt next. New plans must therefore be thought of for the 1915 campaign.

I was bold enough to form an opinion as to the general situation and rash enough to express it. As I have been severely criticised in certain professional quarters for my impertinent activities in this direction, I feel bound to state the considerations that led me to challenge the policy or lack of policy which in the event was responsible for prolonging the War, added enormously to its sacrifices in human life, increased its burdens and brought the cause of the Allies to the very brink of irretrievable disaster.

Why should a civilian who had made no study of the science of war have concerned himself at all with strategical questions? Why not leave that phase of the war problem to men who had devoted their lives to such a study? My answer to those who charge me with meddling in a business of which I knew nothing except what I had learnt by a reading of past wars, and conversations with soldiers whom I had met here and in France, is that as events developed it became increasingly evident to the rawest amateur mind that the military were fumbling badly with their job. The Allied strategy in France had been a sanguinary mistake which nearly brought us to irretrievable defeat. When it failed the High Commands had no rational alternative to propose. The Allied generals were completely baffled by the decision of the Germans to dig in. They could think of nothing better than the sacrifice of millions of men in a hopeless effort to break through. Even then they had not worked out what mechanical aid was necessary to carry out such an operation, nor had they given any real systematic thought to the methods of providing their armies with the requisite machinery for putting into effect their hazy and crazy plans.

How crazy were their ideas at this stage can be ascertained by reading the painful story of a succession of foolish offensives which for years were to mow down the flower of British and French youth by the million in vain efforts to rush machine guns, skilfully concealed and effectively protected.

The primary responsibility for success or failure rested with Governments, and they could not shuffle off any part of that responsibility by pleading that they had placed their trust in experts who were obviously unequal to their task.

By the end of the year over a million young men had volunteered and had been duly enrolled either in the Kitchener armies or in the Territorials, and thousands were still streaming in. Amongst them were the pick of the youth of the country in physique, brain and character. In every sphere of life all that was best amongst the young men of the land joined the Army. It cannot be said as yet that they had donned the King's uniform, for in the best-equipped of all countries for the manufacture of men's apparel, the War Office had not yet succeeded in procuring the necessary supply of uniforms for all their recruits. But it was already evident that the human material which was everywhere being trained into soldiers was of a higher quality than anything to which drill sergeants had hitherto been accustomed. The Universities were drained of all the physically fit—so were all the professions. Artisans, miners, labourers—all contributed of their choicest.

In some quarters the prejudice against leaving home to join the Army still lingered. Recruiting agencies had still in some areas a difficulty in overcoming the tradition about the youth who for some unsatisfactory reason "ran away to become a soldier." And it took some time and much appeal to break it down. I had taken my part in these recruiting appeals especially amongst Nonconformists, who had always been inclined to hold aloof from the Army, and also amongst my Welsh fellow-countrymen of all creeds. For these reasons, apart altogether from my responsibility as a Member of the Cabinet that declared war, I felt a special obligation to see that the men who volunteered to face death for their country's honour, should be equipped with the best their country could provide them with in order to fight its battles, and that the most effective use should be made of their valour in the battlefield. The events of the last few months had shaken any confidence I ever had in the wisdom of military leadership and I was full of apprehension lest the flower of Britain's youth should be mown down through professional rigidity, narrowness and lack of vision.

I had no pretence to any knowledge of strategy, but there were certain obvious facts which were apparent even to the uninitiated in the mysteries of war.

The first was that if the resources of the belligerents on both sides were assessed—in men, material and money—the Allied Powers possessed an overwhelming advantage over their foes provided their resources were effectively utilised and wisely directed.

This Allied superiority was, however, completely neutralised by the fact that two out of the three Great Powers (Britain and Russia) that constituted the Alliance against Germany and Austria were inferior in equipment to their foes. As far as heavy artillery went France was also inferior. Equipment was therefore the most urgent problem for the Allies. Unless they exerted themselves to the utmost to make up their deficiencies in this respect, victory was unattainable. Two out of the three (Britain and France) had great manufacturing capacity, and America with its infinite resources was also at their call for that purpose. The third, Russia, was very deficient in manufacturing capacity and had no credit for purchase abroad, but had an inexhaustible reserve of the best human material. As to equipment, therefore, the problem was first to utilise all our available resources at home and across the seas to increase the numbers and power of our machinery of war and to do so without loss of time, and secondly to pool the output fairly and distribute it where it could be most effectively used for the Allied cause.

The second and outstanding fact was that Germans had largely neutralised the Allied superiority in man-power on the Western Front not only by better equipment but by constructing the most extensive and formidable line of entrenchments ever known in the history of war.

There was no way of outflanking the German lines in France and Flanders, and any attempt to force them by frontal attacks would involve losses so colossal that no sane man would contemplate such a sacrifice of human life as a possibility, if there were any other means available of breaking through on a more vulnerable front. At any rate the Allies had not the necessary gun-power to make any effort to break through on the west a feasible operation, and it would take years to equip them with an artillery numerous and heavy enough for such an attempt.

The third was that, whilst the Central Powers had an entire front of 600 miles on the west which presented no great physical difficulties for them in the way of entrenchment in length or in the character of the soil, on the Eastern and South-Eastern Fronts they had a line of thousands of miles to defend, much of it swamp which was too soft in summer and too hard in winter for any entrenching tools to handle. Moreover, their man-power would not suffice to garrison effectively so extensive a fortress.

The fourth was that on that front, Germans and Austrians were confronted with a foe who could turn out millions of brave men traditionally fearless and skilful in war, who only needed efficient equipment to make their numbers and their valour irresistible.

On the South-Eastern and Southern sections of that Front the

Central Powers had to defend their positions with an army drawn from a population, three-fifths of which belonged to races hostile to the governing races in the two Empires and entirely sympathetic to the Allied population on their frontiers. The Slavs, Roumanians, and Italians who constituted the majority of the people ruled by Franz Joseph had been straining for freedom from the dominion of a privileged racial caste, and their prospect of gaining it would be accelerated by the defeat of the German regime, whilst it might be indefinitely postponed by a Teutonic victory.

Out of a total population of over 50 millions in Austria-Hungary, only 12 millions were Germans and 10 millions Magyars. Almost 30 millions belonged to populations which were kith and kin to the nations with which Austria was either at war, or was about to wage war. Even the Magyars were not too eager to follow the rash lead of Vienna. It was known that Count Tisza, the ablest and calmest of all the Hungarian statesmen, was rootedly opposed to the mad plunge into war with the Serbian Slavs. What made Austria specially vulnerable was that the provinces contiguous to her actual or contingent foes were populated by the races who by blood were nearly related to the enemies of the Empire. This proved to be a source of weakness to the Austrian armies during the whole course of the War, and a danger against which they found it impossible to guard. Whenever the Russians gained an appreciable advantage in their attacks, Slavonic regiments surrendered with ease and even with ill-concealed satisfaction, to the onslaught of ill-equipped Russian armies. One Czech regiment marched through into pre-destined captivity in Russia with the band playing.

It was also quite obvious to anyone who surveyed the possibilities of the Balkans with some knowledge of the disposition and quality of its peoples, that if the Allied Powers had taken strong and timely action they could have organised out of the warlike races that inhabit this turbulent peninsula from the Danube down to the Chersonese and thence southward to the Peloponnesus, a formidable confederation with an army of trained men already tempered in the fires of war. The Serbians had at that time an available force of 300,000 men. The Roumanians could put at least half a million men in the field. The number of fighting men available in Roumania was placed by the War Office at 900,000. The Greeks had 400,000 trained men. The Bulgarians owed a deep debt of gratitude to Russia for the part she had played in their liberation, and their memories of Gladstone's fiery crusade on their behalf against Turkish oppression turned their hearts towards Britain. If attached to the Allied side they could have placed another 400,000 men at the disposal of the Alliance. All the contingents were of the doughtiest fighting material with recent war experience. The organisation of such a confederacy would have involved loans which in the aggregate would not have amounted to one week's cost of the War to the British and French taxpayer. There would also have been some difficulty in the way of a preliminary arrangement of the spoils. But this was by no means an insuperable obstacle to agreement. There was plenty of honest loot awaiting the plunderers without transgressing any principle of racial liberty or self-determination. The Slavonic provinces of Southern Austria would have satisfied Serbia. Roumania would have been only too pleased at the prospect of annexing Transylvania with its three millions of men of their own blood. The Bulgarians could have been brought in by the prospect of the re-annexation of Adrianople and a port on the Aegean; and the Greeks had an eye on the littoral of Asia Minor, where their own people had built up prosperous towns and brought the valleys into fruitful cultivation. It would have been necessary to take in hand immediately the equipment of the various armies that composed the confederation. That would have been a gradual process. At first an addition of light artillery and ammunition, with a few machine guns, would have sufficed in these mountain fastnesses. The presence of 100,000 British troops, or a composite army of British and French, equal to half the forces subsequently sent to the Dardanelles or one-third of the numbers sacrificed in the spring and summer of 1915 in vain attacks on infrangible German redoubts in France and Flanders, would have given that moral strength to the Balkan Armies imparted by the physical presence of the banners and soldiers of the great Western Powers. Such a contingent would have had an incalculable effect in welding, inspiring, sustaining and restraining all the other elements in this formidable combination.

The Central Powers were much better equipped in the matter of heavy artillery than were the Allies. A break through in France demanded superiority in guns of the heaviest calibre and an overwhelming supply of ammunition. The Allies could not hope to achieve supremacy in this respect for two years. The question of inferior equipment in the heavier calibres did not present so formidable a difficulty in a great operation on the Eastern and South-Eastern Fronts as it did in the west. The Eastern Front not being so well fortified, the Allies could then, with lighter guns and less ammunition, make more effective use of their superiority in numbers. The Russians repeatedly demonstrated this fact in their attacks on the Austrians. They only failed to exploit their victories because of the shortage of gun ammunition for their field artillery and of the lack of rifles. These deficiencies could have been supplied by their western allies, had they consented to forego their unpractical and costly offensives.

Apart from the heterogeneity of the Austrian Armies their organisation, training, munitionment and direction were not comparable to that of their great military neighbour. For these reasons Austria was often a source of weakness, and constantly a source of anxiety, to the German Supreme Headquarters, and more than once they had to detach troops which they could ill dispense from their own special tasks and their own frontiers, in order either to save Austria from collapse or to clear some impending menace from her frontiers. This weakness, which was so painfully apparent to the German Staff, was completely overlooked by both the French and British military direction. The French and British commands were therefore implored by statesmen and soldiers of position and experience in both countries not to commit their armies to repeated and wasteful attacks delivered against an impregnable front defended by an invincible armament, whilst completely neglecting a vulnerable front which could have been penetrated with a third of the troops wasted so prodigally in the ghastly carnage of the western battlefield.

Before coming to these conclusions I had made a careful study of the main facts of the military position with such information as was available to me. I never missed an opportunity of seeking the opinions of such military experts as were accessible to a civilian minister on every aspect of the situation.

It is a mistake to assume that a competent opinion can only be formed by general officers who have taken no part in the actual fighting, and who have never had any personal acquaintance with the physical conditions under which modern warfare is conducted. Men who have passed months of vigilance, anxiety and horror in the fighting line have also their contribution to make to the facts upon which strategy must be based. It is a curious reflection on the methods of promotion in the British Army during the Great War that scarcely one of these men ever reached the topmost ranks—except amongst the Dominion troops. I saw many of these fighting officers right through the War and learned much from them.

As to equipment, I have already given an idea of the efforts I made up to the end of 1914 to quicken manufacture at home and in America. I had also drawn attention to the pressing need for helping Russia. As to the general strategy of the War, at the end of December, 1914, I wrote the following memorandum, which I circulated to the War Council.

2, Whitehall Gardens, S.W.
January 1, 1915.

SUGGESTIONS AS TO THE MILITARY POSITION

Now that the new armies are in course of training and will, with the Territorials, be ready by the end of March to the extent of at least half a million men, I suggest that it is time the Government should take counsel with the military experts as to the use which shall be made of this magnificent force. It is a force of a totally different character from any which has hitherto left these shores. It has been drawn almost exclusively from the better class of artisan, the upper and the lower middle classes. In intelligence, education and character it is vastly superior to any army ever raised in this country, and as it has been drawn not from the ranks of those who have generally cut themselves off from home ties and about whose fate there is therefore not the same anxiety at home, the people of this country will take an intimate personal interest in its fate of a kind which they have never displayed before in our military expeditions. So that if this superb army is thrown away upon futile enterprises such as those we have witnessed during the last few weeks, the country will be uncontrollably indignant at the lack of prevision and intelligence shown in our plans. I may add that operations such as those we have witnessed during the past few months will inevitably destroy the *morale* of the best troops. Good soldiers will face any dangers and endure any hardships which promise ultimate progress, but this intermittent flinging themselves against impregnable positions breaks the stoutest hearts in the end.

There are therefore three or four considerations I wish to urge on the military situation.

1. STALEMATE ON THE WESTERN FRONT

I cannot pretend to have any military knowledge, but the little I saw and gathered in France as to the military position, coupled with such reading on the subjects as I have been able to indulge in, convinced me that any attempt to force the carefully prepared German lines in the west would end in failure and in appalling loss of life, and I then expressed this view to my colleagues. General Foch told me that there would be no more retreats on the French side, and I could well appreciate his confidence after I had driven past trench behind trench from Paris all the way to the Aisne. The French generals are confident that even if the whole of the German Army now occupied in Poland were thrown on the Western Front, the French and British troops would still be able to hold their own. The same observation, of course, must apply to the German military position. We were told the other day that the Germans had, during the last few months, prepared a series of trenches of the same kind on their side right up to the Rhine. After three or four months of the most tenacious fighting, involving very heavy losses, the French have not at any one point on the line gained a couple of miles. Would the throwing of an additional half-million men on this front make any real difference? To force the line you would require at least three to one; our reinforcements would not guarantee two to one, or anything approaching such a predominance. Is it not therefore better that we should recognise the impossibility of this particular task, and try and think out some way by which the distinct numerical advantage which the Allies will have attained a few months hence can be rendered effective?

2.   EXTENSION, AND CONSEQUENT ATTENUATION, OF ENEMY'S FRONT

Another consideration which ought to weigh with us is the importance of attenuating the enemy's line by forcing him largely to extend it. The Germans now defend a front of 600 miles. No wastage in sight will so reduce their forces to such numbers as would make any part of this line untenable. The French returns of wounded prove that 79 per cent. of the wounded return to the line: 54 per cent. of the French wounded have already returned; 25 per cent. are convalescent and will soon be back. It is a fundamental mistake always committed by the press to exaggerate the enemy's losses; the slight and curable character of most wounds is always overlooked. But if the length of the German line is doubled, even at the present rate of attrition, it might become at an early date so thin as to be easily penetrable.

3.   FORCING THE ENEMY TO FIGHT ON UNFAVOURABLE GROUND

The enemy is now fighting in country which is admirably adapted to his present entrenching tactics. He would be at a disadvantage if he were forced to fight in the open.

4.   NECESSITY OF WINNING A DEFINITE VICTORY SOMEWHERE

There is another consideration which is political as well as military, but which nevertheless cannot be overlooked in an exhausting war like this, where we have to secure continuous exertion and sacrifice on the part of our people, and where we have also to think of hesitating neutrals with large armies who are still in doubt as to their action. There is a real danger that the people of Great Britain and of France will sooner or later get tired of long casualty lists explained by monotonous and rather banal telegrams from head-quarters about " heavy cannonades," " making a little progress " at certain points, " recovering trenches," the loss of which has never been reported, etc., with the net result that we have not advanced a yard after weeks of heavy fighting. Britishers have ceased to be taken in by reports which exaggerate slight successes and suppress reverses; neutral states have never been deceived by these reports. The public will soon realise that the Germans are now in effective occupation of a larger proportion of Allied territory than they were in possession of at the date of the Battle of the Aisne. This is true of Belgium, of France, and of Poland. These occupied territories contain some of the richest coalfields and industrial centres in Europe, and the most sanguinary attacks have not succeeded in moving the Germans (on an average) a single yard out of these territories. A clear definite victory which has visibly materialised in guns and prisoners captured, in unmistakable retreats of the enemy's armies, and in large sections of enemy territory occupied, will alone satisfy the public that tangible results are being achieved by the great sacrifices they are making, and decide neutrals that it is at last safe for them to throw in their lot with us.

5.   AN ALTERNATIVE SUGGESTION

Inasmuch as these objects cannot be accomplished by attacks on the Western Front, some alternative ought to be sought. I venture to make one or two suggestions. I have heard of a proposal that there should be an attack in the direction of Denmark upon the north coast of Germany. This proposal is associated with the name of Lord Fisher. For the moment I cannot venture to express any opinion upon it, as I should like to know more about the military and naval possibilities of such an enterprise. It strikes me as being very hazardous, and by no means certain to fulfil the purpose which its originators have in view. Schleswig-Holstein, with its narrow neck, could be easily defended by a comparatively small German force, strongly entrenched against a hostile army seeking to advance into Prussian territory, and there is no room for flanking operations. But at the present moment I would rather not criticise this plan. My purpose is rather to put forward another alternative, and I think more promising scheme for consideration by the Prime Minister and his advisers. It would involve *two independent operations* which would have the common purpose of bringing Germany down by the process of knocking the props under her, and the further purpose of so compelling her to attenuate her line of defence as to make it more easily penetrable. I will explain these two propositions in a little more detail.

6.   THE FIRST OPERATION

I suggest that our new forces should be employed in an attack upon Austria, in conjunction with the Serbians, the Roumanians and the Greeks. The assistance of the two latter countries would be assured if they knew that a great English force would be there to support them. Roumania could put 300,000 men in the field, whilst retaining a sufficient force to keep the Bulgarians in check. As this move might decide the Bulgarians to remain honestly neutral, the Roumanians could spare another 200,000. The Greeks and Montenegrins have an army of 200,000 available. How many men could we spare? By the beginning of April we shall have in this country 700,000 men who will have undergone a six months' training. Of these 400,000 would be Territorials, 200,000 of whom will have been in camp continuously for eight months. We shall have in France a force of 300,000 men, provided we do not waste it

on barbed wire.   The French can easily defend their lines against
the troops which Germany can spare from defending Silesia after
the Austrian armies have been withdrawn to defend their southern
frontier.   We should require 200,000 experienced troops to stiffen
the new armies.   We should thus have a force of 1,000,000 available.
Four hundred thousand men might be left here as reserve to throw
into France in case of need if the French were hard pressed before
the southern diversion against Austria had developed.   Some of
them might be sent to Boulogne so as to be at hand in case of
emergency.   Subsequently this force could be used to reinforce the
new Expeditionary Force from time to time.   This would leave
600,000 available for the Austrian expedition.   Gradually this force
could be increased as the new armies were equipped.

This would mean an army of between 1,400,000 and 1,600,000
men to attack Austria on her most vulnerable frontier.   Here the
population is almost entirely friendly, consisting as it does of
Slavonic races who hate both the Germans and the Magyars.   We
could send our troops up either through Salonika or, I believe, by
landing them on the Dalmatian coast.   We could seize islands there
which might make an admirable base for supplies not far removed
from the railway through Bosnia into Austria.   This operation
would force the Austrians to detach a considerable army from the
defence of Cracow, and thus leave Silesia undefended.   The
Austrians could not withdraw the whole of their army to face this
new attack, because in that case the Russians could pour through
the Carpathians and capture either Vienna or Budapest.   The front
which would be developed would be much too lengthy for the
Austrian forces to entrench and hold.   The Germans would be
compelled either to send large forces to support their Austrian allies
or to abandon them.   In the first case Germans would have to hold
an enormous length of extended front, in the aggregate 1,200 miles,
and the Allies would, for the first time, enjoy the full advantage
of the superior numbers which by that time they can put into the
field.*   On the other hand, if the Germans decline to quit their own
frontiers, and leave the Austrians to their fate, that empire would be
rapidly disposed of as a military entity, and about 2,500,000 men
(including Russians), engaged in the task of attacking it would be
free to assail the Germans.

7.   TWO INCIDENTAL ADVANTAGES OF THIS COURSE

1. Something which could be called a victory would be thus
within our reach, and the public would be satisfied to support with
all their resources the conduct of the War for a much longer period
without grumbling or stint.

* The Germans would also render themselves liable to a dangerous attack in the
rear from the immense forces which by that date Russia will have placed in the field.

2. Italy would not only be encouraged by this formidable demonstration, she would be forced to come in in her own interest, because the operations would be conducted largely along the coast which she is looking forward to annexing to her kingdom, as the population is predominantly Italian. She must view with very great jealousy any occupation of this territory by Serbian troops, and Italian public opinion would not countenance any proposal on the part of the Italian Ministry to come to the aid of Austria if we made it clear that the whole of this littoral would become Italian territory if Italy helped to conquer it.

8.   THE SECOND OPERATION

This involves an attack upon Turkey. There are four conditions which an attack on Turkey ought, in my judgment, to fulfil: —

1. That it should not involve the absorption of such a large force as to weaken our offensive in the main field of operations;

2. That we should operate at a distance which would not be far from the sea, so as not to waste too many of our troops in maintaining long lines of communication and so as also to have the support of the Fleet in any eventualities;

3. That it should have the effect of forcing Turkey to fight at a long distance from her base of supplies and in country which would be disadvantageous to her;

4. That it should give us the chance of winning a dramatic victory, which would encourage our people at home, whilst it would be a corresponding discouragement to our enemies.

Perhaps I ought to add a fifth: it would be a great advantage from this point of view if it were in territory which appeals to the imagination of the people as a whole.

What operations would meet these conditions? It is supposed that the Turks are gathering together a great army for the invasion of Egypt. The sections show that they have collected something like 80,000 troops in Syria, and that they are slowly moving them along towards the Egyptian frontier. I would let them entangle themselves in this venture, and whilst they were engaged in attacking our forces on the Suez Canal, I would suggest that a force of 100,000 should be landed in Syria to cut them off. They could not maintain themselves in that country very long once their railway communications were cut. They would therefore be forced either to fight or to surrender. The distance from Constantinople to Syria would not permit them to bring up reinforcements in time to produce any impression upon the situation. A force of 80,000 Turks would be wiped out and the whole of Syria would fall into our hands. The pressure upon Russia in the Caucasus would be relieved; the Turkish Army in Europe could not effectively attack our lines of communication as they would be bound to take steps to redeem the situation in Syria, and, if possible, recover the country.

Unless we are prepared for some project of this character I frankly despair of our achieving any success in this War. I can see nothing but an eternal stalemate on any other lines. The process of economic exhaustion alone will not bring us a triumphant peace as long as Germany is in possession of these rich allied territories. No country has ever given in under such pressure, apart from defeat in the field. Burke was always indulging in prophecies of victory as a result of France's exhaustion. The war with France went on for twenty years after he indulged in his futile predictions. Germany and Austria between them have 3,000,000 young men quite as well trained as the men of the Kitchener Armies, ready to take the place of the men now in the trenches when these fall. At that rate the process of exhaustion will take at least ten years. In soil, in minerals, in scientific equipment, Germany is a country of enormous resources. In the number of men who have a scientific training it is infinitely the richest country in the world. That must not be left out of account when we talk about the process of exhaustion. No doubt they will suffer a good deal from lack of copper. We must not depend too much on this. German industries dependent on copper will suffer, but one way or another copper will be found for ammunition. Copper in small quantities will get in through neutral countries; neutrals cannot resist the prices offered by Germany for their copper supplies. Moreover, they have some copper mines in Germany. Some of them were working at a profit at the date of the War. There must be many more lower grade copper mines which would not have paid under ordinary conditions, just like the copper mines of North Wales, but which would become immediately profitable when the price of copper is doubled or trebled. Moreover, they have inexhaustible supplies of coal and iron, and as long as they have the Hungarian plains they can frugally feed themselves. There is an enthusiasm and a spirit, according to every testimony, which cannot be worn down by a two or three years' siege of German armies entrenched in enemy territory. The German spirit will not be broken by the bombardment of Dixmude or Roulers.

We cannot allow things to drift. We ought to look well ahead and discuss every possible project for bringing the War to a successful conclusion. Supply and ammunition difficulties, severe economic pressure, financial embarrassments, even privation and distress—nations will face them cheerfully as long as their armies in the field are in unbeaten possession of their enemies' land. But once defeat which is unmistakable comes their way, moderate economic troubles make a deep impression on their judgment. Such defeats are not to be compassed along our present lines of attack, and we ought to seek others.

If a decision were come to in favour of some such plan of campaign as I have outlined, it will take weeks to make the necessary preparations for it. I cannot recollect that in our discussions at the C.I.D. such an operation was ever contemplated. The ground therefore has not been surveyed. It would take some time to collect the necessary intelligence as to the country, so as to decide where to land the Army and what shall be the line of attack. Transport would have to be carefully and secretly gathered. Large forces might have to be accumulated in the Mediterranean, ostensibly for Egypt. It might be desirable to send an advance force through Salonika, to assist Serbia. Military arrangements would have to be made with Roumania, Serbia, Greece and, perhaps, Italy. All this must take time. Expeditions decided upon and organised with insufficient care and preparation generally end disastrously. And as similar considerations will probably apply to any alternative campaign, I urge the importance of our taking counsel and pressing to a decision without delay.

                                                        D. LL. G.

When I wrote this memorandum I had five months' experience of what war under modern conditions meant. After four and a half years of the closest acquaintance with its problems I stand by the main thesis of this document.

Both the rival armies had attempted to break through the defences of their opponents in the west and had failed after the most sanguinary battles. The Germans recognised the impracticability of attempting to force the western barrier and decided to go for the east. By strengthening their entrenchments in the west they reckoned on being able to hold the Allied forces with two men to the combined French and British three. When in 1916 they changed their strategy and attacked the strongly fortified French positions at Verdun, their effort failed and they wasted irrecoverable time and opportunity. On the Allied side there was considerable division of opinion on the issue of the " way round " by the eastern flank.

The controversy that arose on this subject has been represented as a struggle between the amateur and the professional soldier—between the ignorant politician and the trained warrior. This is a wanton and rather silly misrepresentation of the origin of that conflict of ideas which divided those who were responsible for war direction in the Allied countries from 1915 up to the end. There were highly placed politicians on both sides of the controversy. But there were also military men of outstanding ability who took different sides. I had a conversation with Lord Kitchener on my memorandum. His attitude towards it was certainly not that of the professional who resents the intrusion of amateurs. Quite the contrary. He expressed a considerable measure of agreement with my general theme. He was emphatic about the impossibility of penetrating the German lines on the Western Front, and driving the German Armies out of France and Flanders, without incurring sacrifices which he rightly considered prohibitive if another way could be found of defeating the Central Powers involving the payment of a smaller toll in human life.

The day after I circulated my memorandum, Lord Kitchener, in one of his periodic flashes of insight, wrote this remarkable letter to Sir John French to the headquarters in France:—[*]

" January 2nd, 1915.

There does not appear to be much sign of the contemplated push through on the part of the French Army. Probably they find themselves up against the same problem all along the line as you do in your part, viz. trenches that render attack only a waste of men for a few yards gained of quite worthless ground. The feeling is gaining ground that, although it is essential to defend the lines we hold, troops over and above what are necessary for that service could be better employed elsewhere.

I suppose we must now recognise that the French Army cannot make a sufficient break through the German lines of defence to cause a complete change of the situation and bring about the retreat of the German forces from Northern Belgium. If that is so, then the German lines in France may be looked upon as a fortress that cannot be carried by assault, and also cannot be completely invested—with the result that the lines can only be held by an investing force, while operations proceed elsewhere.

The question of *where* anything effective can be accomplished opens a large field, and requires a good deal of study. What are the views of your staff? Russia is hard pressed in the Caucasus, and can only just hold her own in Poland. Fresh forces are necessary to change the deadlock; Italy and Roumania seem the most likely providers; therefore some action that would help to bring these out seems attractive, though full of difficulties."

At that moment Kitchener was definitely opposed to the Western Front superstition and had turned his mind to the " way round."

In coming to this conclusion I do not suggest that Lord Kitchener had been influenced by the arguments submitted to him in my memorandum the day before he wrote this letter, but in giving expression to views he had no doubt already formed as to the unwisdom of wasting his new armies on impossible frontal attacks in France and as to the desirability of forcing the issue on some other front, he was sustained by the fact that he discovered he had political support inside the Cabinet for his ideas. At the same time Mr. Winston Churchill's mind was moving in the same direction. Lord

[*] Sir George Arthur's " Life of Lord Kitchener," Vol. II, p. 35.

Kitchener, Mr. Churchill and I arrived at similar conclusions independently of each other.

A few days later Sir John French, when brought over from France to attend a Committee that was examining the strategical position, expressed his opinion that " complete success against the Germans in the western theatre of war, though possible, was not probable. If we found it impossible to break through, he agreed that it would be desirable to seek new spheres of activity in Austria, for example."

It is a rather significant coincidence that a proposal almost identical with mine was submitted on 1st January, 1915, by General Gallieni to M. Briand and to the French Premier, M. Viviani. Gallieni was a man of tried genius, and was recognised as being one of the most resourceful of the Allied Generals. M. Poincaré in his " Memoirs " refers sympathetically to the Gallieni plan and he goes on to say that General Franchet d'Esperey, one of the soundest and most successful of the French Generals, had already suggested it to him when he saw him at his Army Headquarters at the French Front. General Gallieni's views on the subject are recorded by his secretaries in their highly interesting book " Gallieni Parle. . ."

" The participation of France in the War in the East, the intervention of one of our armies in the Balkan theatre, is perhaps the question which interested him most deeply from the time he became Minister! He saw in it consequences such as no one then anticipated.

From 1914 on a French Expedition to the Balkans could and should be for us the happy solution; in fact the only one which would permit a prompt ending of the War in victory. ONE CANNOT BREAK THROUGH ON THE WESTERN FRONT, he complained. The German offensive on the Yser, made under excellent conditions and which nevertheless failed, proves that to us. Therefore we must find another way. Towards the East! Take Constantinople. How? We need a harbour, quays, in order to disembark troops, and a railway, in order to transport them. Therefore Salonika. Therefore through Salonika march on Constantinople. From there go up the Danube with the Balkans people who will have joined us. AND THAT WOULD HAVE SOLVED THE IMPORTANT QUESTION OF CORN: The Roumanians, even the Russians whose ports we would have opened up, would not be obliged to sell at a miserable price to Germany and so supply her.

Such was my plan. I had been to see Briand. He, Briand, went to consult Joffre, who said: ' That is a personal ambition of Gallieni who wants to get a command. I won't give a man. Why search elsewhere and far off for what I shall get here in March [1915]. I feel sure I shall break through and drive the Germans back home.'

We had spoken about this plan with the English who agreed. The matter had been studied very closely here and with the Allies. It was in view of Joffre's opposition that the English decided—an idea from their Navy—to take Constantinople from the sea; to force the Dardanelles. And the French followed them."

I have been informed on unimpeachable authority that General Castelnau was also of the same opinion.

A contemporary historian, who had obviously drawn his inspiration from the War Office, rather contemptuously refers to the Salonika idea as " Mr. Lloyd George's fancy." The fact that some of the ablest statesmen and soldiers in France had conceived the same " fancy " reconciles me to this flippant and ill-informed comment.

I have quoted sufficient military authority of unchallenged distinction to make it clear that my idea of an attack on the Central Powers through the Balkans was not the wild phantasy of an inexpert civilian mind, wandering recklessly into regions which he was not qualified to explore.

When these great soldiers expressed a doubt as to the feasibility of battering a way through the barriers erected by the Germans in the west, they did not mean it could never be done at any time and at any cost. They meant that it could not be achieved without an expenditure of time, treasure and life which no normal person would be prepared to contemplate. The " Westerners " never visualised a massacre of millions of the best young men of France and Britain. At first they deluded themselves with the assurance of speedy victory. Later on, the Western Front became the shrine of Moloch, demanding and justifying such sacrifice as even its most infatuated priest would not have dreamt of offering had he known in 1915 what this worship meant.

The policy of western holocausts was only tolerated by British, French and Italian public opinion owing to an elaborate system of concealing repulses and suppressing casualties.

We did not " break through " until the autumn of 1918, although we made several attempts in 1915, 1916 and 1917, all ending in terrible slaughter. In every case the losses we actually sustained were appreciably greater than those we inflicted, although officially they were less. Until the Germans had been weakened by poor and scanty food, and were confronted with the overwhelming Allied reinforcements pouring in from America, our offensives on the Western Front invariably failed to accomplish the object we sought to attain. Even then we had not succeeded in driving them out of France and Belgium at the date of the Armistice, and they only gave up their resistance when the Turks and Bulgarians had been broken in the south-east and Austria had consequently decided to relinquish the fight. The French and ourselves lost over 5,000,000 men in killed and wounded in attack after attack upon the scientific frontiers erected by the Germans in the west. Sir Willian Robertson, in one of the several memoranda he submitted to the Cabinet for its enlightenment on the true principles of sound strategy, once stated that "Every fool knows that you cannot be too strong at the decisive point." This is an observation none the less sensible because it is a platitude. But every wise man also knows that the decisive point is the one at which you have the best chance of beating your enemy with the least risk and at the lowest cost, and that only "every fool" would deliberately choose to fight him at the point which presents the greatest difficulty in overcoming him, and offers him the best opportunity for beating off your attacks and inflicting the heaviest losses on your troops. "Every fool" would also know that the attack at the decisive point must be made at the decisive moment. In 1915 the moment had certainly not arrived which made the Western Front the decisive point. The poor fools to whose judgment Sir William Robertson referred in his memorandum know now what the strategy of attacking the foe at his strongest point has cost the world. But unfortunately they could not foresee it then—except for a few "meddlers," military and amateur.

There was, at least, some excuse for French reluctance to detach their troops from their own country. As M. Clemenceau almost daily reminded the French public: "The Germans are at Noyon"—that is, they were within 40 miles of the cherished capital, which at one moment they had within their clutch, had they but closed their fingers before withdrawing their hands. Some of the fairest provinces of France were in German occupation: and only a leader who commanded the unchallenged confidence of his countrymen could possess the influence necessary under those conditions to induce them to acquiesce in the withdrawal of French men and French guns from the defence of the *patrie,* and ship them hundreds of miles away to the east to fight alongside and on behalf of races, and to liberate provinces, in which they had no particular interest.

But the British military direction had no such excuse. Wellington was not sent to Spain because Castlereagh preferred Spaniards to Prussians, but because some one in authority had the sense to perceive that the Spanish Peninsula was the flank where British troops could direct the most dangerous blow against the might of their great foe. Sherman in the famous march through Georgia acted upon the same principle.

It was these considerations that prompted Lord Kitchener, Mr. Winston Churchill and myself simultaneously, but without previous consultation, to come to the conclusion that the greatest help that Britain with her command of the sea could afford to the Allies, was to organise, equip and strengthen an attack upon the weakest point of the great fortress in which the Central Powers were entrenched.

CHAPTER XI

THE WAR COUNCIL AND THE BALKANS

DURING the first two months of the War there was no established War Council. There were sporadic and irregular consultations from time to time between the Secretary of State for War and the First Lord, between each of them individually and the Prime Minister and, now and again, between the two War Lords and the Prime Minister sitting together. The Foreign Secretary was occasionally brought in. I was not summoned to these conferences except when there were matters to be decided that directly affected finance. At the end of November the Prime Minister decided to establish a War Council and early in January he assembled it to examine the various proposals put forward by Mr. Winston Churchill, Sir Maurice Hankey, and myself. Mr. Churchill urged with all the inexorable force and pertinacity, together with the mastery of detail which he always commands when he is really interested in a subject, the merits of his Dardanelles scheme. I gave my reasons for preferring a landing at Salonika. The plan of forcing the Dardanelles by naval action had been examined more than once in the past by naval authorities when the possibility of bringing pressure to bear upon the Turkish rulers at Constantinople had been contemplated. Each time it had been condemned as being too risky an operation without the occupation not merely of Gallipoli but of the Asiatic shores as well. Every time the project was explored the dangers were foreseen which were actually experienced when it was tried later on by the Allies. The difficulty was obvious—that of forcing by marine action a passage through narrow straits commanded on both sides by defensible heights. It was always apprehended that even if the Narrows could be forced in spite of mines and fortifications, they might be closed against the return of the Fleet as long as either of the two shores remained in the hands of the enemy. When the Greeks offered to join the Allies earlier on in the War they were prepared to send an adequate contingent to occupy the Gallipoli Peninsula. Had they done so the whole story of the Dardanelles would have been different. The story of the whole War would also have differed fundamentally from that which was told by the event. But for some inscrutable reason Sir Edward Grey rejected Greek overtures of help. His tiresome hesitancies helped us into the War, but they hindered us when we were well in it. A more virile and understanding treatment of the Balkan situation would have brought Greece and also Bulgaria into the War. Italy could also have been brought in sooner.

If Lord Kitchener had had at his disposal an adequate force to subdue the Gallipoli garrison, and also to occupy the Asiatic side of the Straits and to hold their own there against the attacks of the Turkish Army on the mainland, then there was a great deal to be said for the Dardanelles plan. But he stoutly insisted that he could not spare more than a Brigade at that time. That, I was convinced at the time, was an underestimate of the reserves of men at his disposal, and I know it now. It was due primarily to apprehension that the Russian Army might collapse, enabling Germany to concentrate great forces on the Western Front. In addition, Lord Kitchener was from time to time afflicted by incomprehensible fear of denuding this country of regular troops and thus leaving it open to all the peril of an impossible invasion from an enemy that dare not sail his ships in any part of the German ocean, except for a few hours' dash half-way across and back at full speed.

There was another factor which played a great part in Lord Kitchener's estimate of our available military strength at this stage of the War. He had the old regular general's contempt for the quality of our Territorial Army. He had always in his mind the volunteers of his younger days—imperfectly organised, deficient in equipment, with inadequate fire practice and hardly drilled at all. The Volunteer Force was the bedraggled starveling of the War Office, eking out its meagre finances by local concerts, entertainments and subscriptions. I recall its financial straits. The lawyer to whom I was articled was the local captain in his little town. Such training for war as I ever acquired was given me by a sergeant-major in that company of Volunteers to which I belonged. He drilled the men, played the cornet in the band, and sold tickets for the concerts. When Kitchener returned to England to take over the direction of the War and found a great force of 270,000 men called the Territorial Army, he thought of it in the terms of the Volunteers who were the joke of the Regulars—a few hundred thousand young men officered by middle-aged professional men who were allowed to put on uniform and play at soldiers. He did not realise the revolution which had been effected in this force by Haldane's genius. On the first occasion when I had any lengthy and intimate conversation with Kitchener on the War one evening after the declaration, he spent nearly the whole of the time in deriding the Territorial Army. He was full of jest and merriment at its expense. This miscalculation had quite an important effect upon the course of the War during the first few months. There are competent soldiers who maintain that Lord Kitchener could easily have thrown at least ten more divisions of excellent troops into the battle line during the decisive days of the Battle of Ypres had he placed greater trust in the Territorials that were available. And there is no doubt that if he had known their full value he could by the spring of 1915 have sent several divisions to Salonika. They were excellent material and by that time they had received six months of constant training in camps. The Balkan Expeditionary Force need not have been made up exclusively of Territorials. Some of the Territorial divisions might have been sent to France to relieve Regular divisions who were garrisoning sloppy trenches, and these highly trained soldiers could have been spared for the Balkans as a stiffening for the Expeditionary Force. The weather was not propitious for fighting in Flanders. There was also a substantial force of Australians and New Zealanders mustered in Egypt. These might have been sent to Salonika. We all know now what first-class fighters they were.

But unless one takes the Territorials and Dominion troops into account, even if there had been a division or two of Regulars available and these had been doubled by the accession of an equivalent French contingent, Lord Kitchener was clearly not in a position at that time to send a sufficient number of troops for the double operation of driving the Turks out of Gallipoli and of holding Chanak against the main Turkish Army. On the other hand, the occupation of Salonika was not a big military operation. The Greeks would have offered no real protest against the landing and there was no enemy within striking reach to prevent it. The first two or three months of the year would have been occupied in improving the railway communications—a very necessary operation. Parts of the line could have been doubled. Locomotives, carriages and wagons for the conveyance of troops and material could have been landed, sidings could have been erected and roads could have been improved.* By the time the winter snows had melted in the Balkans and the river floods from the Danube to the Vardar had subsided, Lord Kitchener could have accumulated a considerable force on the spot, and with the aid of the French troops which by that time could have been spared, the Salonika Army would have been so formidable that the Bulgarians would have hesitated to intervene on the side of our foes. The Official War History is emphatically of that opinion.† Long before Germany disentangled herself from

---

* The Official Military History of the Military Operations in Macedonia discussing the suitability of Salonika for a landing says: " The carrying-power of the railways was low, but, according to the estimate of the British General Staff, it could have been greatly increased under British, or French control—it was indeed considered that the six trains a day in each direction on the Belgrade line could have been at least doubled if an understanding had been reached with Greece at an early stage. The road communication with and in New Serbia was very much worse than that of the railways, but that again could have been bettered. . . ."

† Page 48, Military Operations: Macedonia.

her great drive in Russia, the combined Allied forces in that area drawn from Serbia, Britain and France with a probable accession of over half a million men from Greece and Roumania would have been so powerful that it would have been a hopeless enterprise for Austria, even with German assistance, to launch an attack in so difficult a terrain.   The bastion of the Balkans would have been behind us as an impregnable fortress, and not in front of us, impenetrable and unscaleable when defended by resolute troops as we found it to be from 1916 to 1918.

Even the equipment at our disposal at that date would have been sufficient to enable us to defend such a position against any enemy.

Shrapnel, of which we had a fair supply, would have been effective against troops advancing in the open across slopes visible from the high ground which the Allied forces would have occupied. We could then at our leisure have perfected the equipment and organisation of our Balkan allies, and when all was ready launched an attack on Austria in combination with Russia and Italy. Italy came in on the Allied side in May and would have come in sooner had there been resolute action on an effective scale in the Balkans.

We had several discussions at the War Committee on the various and rival proposals that were put forward. These lasted several days. Sir John French was brought over from France to take part in one of the discussions. His opinions, which I have already quoted, were favourable to an attack on the south-eastern flank.

I presented the case for a Salonika landing to the War Council, but I was at a disadvantage in converting my colleagues. Mr. Winston Churchill had been in constant touch with Lord Kitchener, and when the former has a scheme agitating his powerful mind, as everyone who is acquainted with his method knows quite well, he is indefatigable in pressing it upon the acceptance of everyone who matters in the decision. On the other hand, I saw Lord Kitchener only on very rare occasions. At that date the War Lords were very exclusive and kept very much to themselves. They were both naturally very busy and had no time to spare for civilian amateurs.

The First Lord of the Admiralty had another advantage in urging his proposal, and that was decisive. He was prepared to act without waiting for an immediate dispatch of troops. His proposal was a purely naval operation in its initial stages. Troops would only be called for after the Narrows had been forced, and therefore after all the forts had been demolished. Even then their role was to be a modest one. Lord Kitchener knew that the completion of such a task by the Navy would take some time. Meanwhile, there would be no call for troops or ammunition from the Army. On the other hand, the Salonika plan did involve the immediate landing of a certain number of troops, with guns, ammunition, stores, sea and land transport. This idea of a purely naval operation was a welcome relief to an embarrassed Secretary of State who was always being pressed to send more troops and munitions to every theatre. His worries in this quarter would be shouldered for two or three months by the Admirals. So Lord Kitchener swung round to the Dardanelles plan, and that settled it. Every Minister at that Council, including the Prime Minister, Sir Edward Grey, Mr. Balfour and Lord Crewe, followed Lord Kitchener's lead as to the Dardanelles attack. I stood alone in expressing a different and doubting view. Lord Fisher was dumb. I was not aware at the time that he and other Admirals were opposed to the venture as a purely naval operation unsupported by troops.

The Dardanelles scheme was, therefore, resolved upon and preparations were immediately made to carry it through. Mr. Churchill threw into the execution of his scheme all his impulse and ardent energy. I pressed at a later meeting of the Committee that some action should be taken to make the Salonika expedition more practicable in the event of the attack on the Dardanelles failing. Accordingly, after the Dardanelles decision had been taken I secured the unanimous consent of the Committee to a proposal that Lord Kitchener should take steps immediately to improve the transport arrangements from Salonika to Nish by doubling the line where feasible, and by increasing the number of locomotives, sidings, carriage wagons, and other transport facilities on the Salonika railway. Lord Kitchener undertook to take the matter in hand. But nothing was done to carry out the order of the War Committee, and no further notice was taken of it. When we were compelled to send an expeditionary force at the end of the year to prevent the victorious Central Powers and Bulgaria from marching through to the Mediterranean, not a single additional rail had been placed, not an additional siding had been constructed, not an additional wagon had been landed. Not a road had been widened or mended. Not even a survey had been made of the transport facilities available on rail or road and the means by which they could be improved. The result was that when Serbia was attacked in the autumn by the Central Powers the General Staff gave it as one of their reasons against sending an expeditionary force at that date to the aid of the hard-pressed Serbians, that there were no means of transporting such a force up the line. Even at the end of 1916, when General Joffre had been thoroughly converted to the importance of Salonika, and the Allies had been in occupation of that part for twelve months, the number of troops that could be dispatched and effectively used in that area was limited by the fact that up to that date no steps had been taken to improve the transport accommodation. A force adequate to the need could not be sent there for that reason.

As soon as the Cabinet Committee had come to a final decision that the attack on the Dardanelles was to proceed, I ceased to challenge the wisdom of the enterprise, feeling that it was better to press forward energetically with one or other of these outflanking operations than to abandon all idea of taking action in that direction.   I continued to urge the dispatch of troops to Gallipoli in time and sufficient numbers, and especially with an adequate equipment of guns and ammunition.   Whilst discussions and preparations were proceeding, reports came in from the Balkans that emphasised the peril of delay.   A very striking letter from Mr. George Trevelyan. the eminent historian, written to Mr. (Now Sir Francis) Acland, was passed on to me amongst other members of the Cabinet, including the Foreign Secretary.   He was at the time travelling in the Balkans with Mr. Seton Watson, the great authority on Balkan politics, and his letter is a very calm and informative view of the position and the attitude of the various Balkan States at that time.

> " Sofia,
> January 15th, 1915.
>
> Dear Francis Acland,
>   We* came here from Nish yesterday and are going on to Bucharest to-morrow.   We had a long conversation with Sir Henry Bax Ironside, who is as much impressed as Mr. Des Graz by the danger Serbia will be in if a big Austrian army with German corps to stiffen it comes to the attack.   As everything we have seen and heard in Serbia leads us to suppose that Serbia cannot resist such an attack successfully if unaided, we have to-day telegraphed to Grey urging that every diplomatic and military effort should be made to save Serbia and prevent the annihilation of our influence in the Near East which will certainly result from a disaster to Serbia.
>   I wrote to you in much the same sense from Nish—you may even get this letter and that one together—urging that British troops should be sent from Egypt or anywhere else, if the Germans come against Serbia or a fresh and overwhelming number of Austrians. The moral effect would be very great on a mercurial people like the Serbians, just as the moral effect of the arrival of the ammunition was very great in December.   On the Austrians also the moral effect would be great—they were much disconcerted in December by a false report that the Russians had joined the Serbians at the time of the Serbian *retour* offensive—because ten Russian N.C.O.'s were seen.   Even the presence of our Blue-jackets at Belgrade has done the Austrians intellectual damage.
>   We did not wire from Nish, not because Mr. Des Graz† was opposed to this view, but I talked the matter over with him and he was most deeply impressed with the danger of Serbia and the

---

* Mr. Seton Watson and himself.
† The British representative in Serbia.

need for military help if the expected invasion in force took place, especially with German aid. I deferred wiring till I came here, because I wanted to know whether there was any danger of Bulgaria marching against Greece, if Greece came up the Vardar valley to help Serbia. Bax Ironside is confident there is no longer such a danger, that Bulgaria has now decided on neutrality at least unless and until Serbia is crushed and the whole Entente game lost in these parts. If this is so we could use the Vardar valley to convey British troops to aid Serbia and Greece herself ought to march. Watson points out that British troops might also or alternatively be sent via Antivari or Dalmatia—but there we trench on military questions where I am out of my depth. The *principle* is that we must save Serbia or lose the whole Near East with results on the whole War imaginable by you.

We have not yet been to Bucharest and may not be much wiser when we have been. But though all have hopes, none we have yet seen, Serbian or English, has any confidence that Roumania will march till after the battle is lost and won. Other measures must, therefore, be taken to save Serbia if she is attacked in force, besides efforts to bring Roumania in.

You may wonder why we have wired and written so little about the Macedonian question. I have told you what the general Serbian attitude is about it—I did so in my last letter. But as we don't know what Prince Trubetskoi has been and is doing about it, we don't know enough to proffer advice or to judge whether any special treatment of the Macedonian question now can help to save Serbia *now*—for the crisis of the invasion, if it comes, may be on her any week. In general, however, we can say from numerous conversations with Serbians from the Crown Prince downwards that the more Yugo-Slavia and Adriatic expansion are dwelt upon, the more Serbians will be willing to concede to Macedonia. And that Serbia will only concede at the friendly dictation of the Great Powers her Allies.

It should be borne in mind that the Serbians are a mercurial people, though they have such stout stuff in them. They may begin retiring, even in disorder and despair, and then if something is done, or something turns up to put fresh heart in them, they may do wonders.

Diplomatically everything seems uncertain and fluctuating from hour to hour with regard to the action or inaction of Roumania and Bulgaria—perhaps of Greece. It is no very wild guess to suppose that the ultimate choice of Roumania and Bulgaria respectively or jointly, will depend on the result of the coming attempt to conquer Serbia if such attempt is made. Of course, the Roumanians ought to help to save her during that invasion, and they *may*, and every effort should be made to make Roumania do so. But other plans should be prepared to save Serbia, on the assumption that Roumania will not march till she sees who is the victor, for that is the only safe assumption. We do not wish to give the impression that Serbia is at the last gasp. Her spirit is splendid and her Army, if halved by losses, is in good estate. But if, as at present expected, Germany and Austria can mobilise against her numbers that are beyond her power to resist, the result of the whole War may be affected by an abnormal effort to help her.

GEORGE TREVELYAN."

We were to discover too soon how accurate were Mr. Trevelyan's and Mr. Seton Watson's prognostications about Bulgaria and Serbia. We had other communications which confirmed the impression given by Mr. Trevelyan's letter. The Balkans were a frightful mix-up, and it was clear that they might be consolidated on the side that took the boldest action in that quarter ere it was too late.

At the end of January a report was received from our Minister at Sofia referring to a message from the Russian Foreign Minister, which expressed great apprehension as to the possible attitude of Bulgaria. The Minister thought these fears well founded, that there was a growing feeling at Sofia that Russia was not succeeding in her military operations, and that when the weather improved sufficiently to enable the Germans to advance, Warsaw would fall into their hands. That was the opinion of the Bulgarian generals, and the Minister warned us that unless Bulgaria was persuaded we were on the winning side no territorial bribe would bring her into the Alliance. They were not as much concerned about territorial extensions as with the drift of the War, which they were watching with anxious eyes before deciding which side to join. I called Lord Kitchener's attention to this telegram, and the following correspondence ensued:—

" January 29th, 1915.

Dear Lord Kitchener,
You will I am sure have seen Telegram Number 14 in last night's sections from Sofia. It is so obviously the German interest to crush Serbia in order to detach Bulgaria from the Triple Entente and to free a way to Constantinople that it is risky to doubt the accuracy of the telegram. The French delayed assistance to Antwerp until it was too late. This time the responsibility is ours and we shall not be held blameless if a catastrophe occurs.

Ever sincerely,

D. LLOYD GEORGE."

" War Office,
Whitehall.
29th January, 1915.

My dear Lloyd George,
    I think we all see the danger. The difficulty is that our forces are tied up in France and that the situation requires a fighting force in Serbia. To go there with a small force such as a Brigade would be useless unless followed by others, as we should be laughed at as soon as it was discovered that we were only an Army *pour rire.* We might force Greece in as a belligerent, but very few Greek troops would reach Serbia while Bulgaria maintained the attitude she has adopted.
    I cannot help thinking Bulgaria wishes to see Serbia perish and with that object stops all assistance being given her by Roumania and Greece. See enclosed which please return.

Yours very truly,

KITCHENER."

As to Lord Kitchener's plea that he could only spare a Brigade for the occupation of Salonika, he had at home at that time a fine division of regular troops not yet sent to any front. This would have provided the necessary nucleus and stiffening for the 14 Territorial divisions available at that date at home. Two or three divisions of these gallant Territorial troops he soon after sent to Flanders and found fit enough to take their place in the first-line trenches to defend the British position against Germany's best soldiers. There were also 39,000 Australians and New Zealanders in Egypt. They were all equal, to say the least, to anything the Bulgarians or Austrians could have brought against them. On the Western Front the French and ourselves already considerably outnumbered the Germans, and, although we lacked the heavy artillery necessary for attack, we had shown ourselves, even when we were much weaker, strong enough to resist a German attack. Had we sent a few of these available divisions the French could and would also have sent an equal number of troops. Their pride would not have permitted them to go unrepresented in equal strength in so important a theatre. On that point they always displayed a certain useful touchiness, if not jealousy. If the French and ourselves had, in consequence of this expedition to the East, been compelled to economise our men on the Western Front, the foolish offensives which cost the Allies over 100,00 men during the first four months of 1915 would have been avoided. There were plenty of men for rash and ill-considered ventures on the Western Front, but only a Brigade could be spared for an enterprise which, as events proved before the end of the year, was essential to save the Allied cause from a great disaster.
    As the enclosure of Lord Kitchener's letter was concerned with

the attitude of Roumania, which was also represented as waiting and watching, but not yet willing to take the risk of joining the Allies, I replied to Lord Kitchener: —

> " Treasury Chambers,
> Whitehall, S.W.
> January 29th, 1915.
>
> Dear Lord Kitchener,
>   I return the Sofia despatch. Thanks.
>   I am fairly confident you will not get these Balkan States to decide until they see Khaki!
>
> Ever sincerely,
> D. LLOYD GEORGE."

At a meeting of the War Council on January 28th Lord Kitchener had one more of those flashes which now and again cast their rays deep into the gloom of the stormy problems which were raging around us. He said " that he was impressed by the advantages which Germany derived from her central position. This enabled the enemy to co-ordinate their efforts. The Allies, on the other hand, were all acting independently. In his opinion there should be some central authority where all the Allies were represented and full information was available. Attacks should be arranged to take place simultaneously. This would cause appeals for assistance to be made to the German Great General Staff from all parts of the War simultaneously. These attacks might be continued for ten days or so, after which there would be a period of rest. During these offensive operations he would suspend all communication between the Allied countries and Germany."

I was entirely in favour of Lord Kitchener's suggestion, and I said that I was going to Paris shortly to meet the Finance Ministers of the Allies. Possibly an opportunity might occur to make the suggestion informally and to get one or other of the Allies to put forward a more formal proposal. Mr. Balfour agreed. The conclusion arrived at was that I was to avail myself of any favourable opportunity which might present itself in Paris to start the idea of a central body to provide the Allies with facilities for consultation, with a view to greater co-ordination of effort.

Somewhere about the end of January and the beginning of February the French Secretary for War, M. Millerand, had visited London to discuss the position. He was a sturdy and aggressive exponent of the views of the French Commander-in-Chief. He held a brief for General Joffre and fought his case with all the tenacity and forensic skill of a tenacious advocate. General Joffre did not want to part with a single battalion from his French command. He was convinced that he could break through the German lines that year. Later on this confidence received a horrible interpretation in a succession of sanguinary and futile offensives which culminated in that climax of stubborn folly—the Champagne attack, which was repelled with a loss of 200,000 men. However, all the decisions of the War Cabinet were unfolded to him, including the preparations that were to be made for a landing at Salonika when troops were available. When I visited Paris I found that M. Millerand had never repeated these conversations to his colleagues.

I visited France in company with the Governor of the Bank of England (the late Lord Cunliffe) and we met M. Ribot, the French Finance Minister, and M. Bark, the Russian Foreign Minister, to discuss the terms on which advances should be made to Russia with a view to enabling that country to make necessary purchases in America. As suggested, I took occasion to discuss the whole military position with the leading members of the French Cabinet.

Nothing came of the discussions at the time, the French military authorities being obsessed by the notion that their Great Headquarters had, and ought to have, the supreme control of the land war. The naval direction they were prepared to leave to us. But their view was that as far as the Continent was concerned we had neither the forces nor the experience that entitled us to equality of authority in the strategy of the War. Joffre was at that time the unchallenged dictator as far as the War direction was concerned.

I also visited Sir John French's Headquarters and there met Sir William Robertson for the first time. He had hitherto taken no part in the fighting, either directly or indirectly. For the first part of the War he was Quartermaster-General, and as such was reported to have organised supplies in the confusion of the hurried retreat from Mons, to the general satisfaction of the Army. He was then promoted from stores to strategy, and was now chief of Sir John French's staff. So far he had not been responsible for planning any of the battles. Later on he was the Commander-in-Chief's principal adviser in deciding the strategy and planning the tactics of Neuve-Chapelle and Loos. He was an impressive personality, with that slowness of speech and positiveness of statement which gives confidence to the uninitiated in the mysteries of a profession. He also possessed a blunt humour which pleased the Army, especially when it was expressed in ranker language and when exercised at the expense of someone other than the person who repeated the scornful witticisms.

On my return there was a further discussion on the Serbian intentions. I greatly regretted our delays in taking action in the Balkans. I pointed out that the War Council had approved this Serbian project in principle some weeks ago. When I was in Paris I had discussed it with members of the French Government, with the result that they had brought it to the attention of their Cabinet

Meeting, and the French Government had now expressed approval in principle.

I thought it certain that if we made it clear that we intended to send a division the French would do the same. They were very anxious to co-operate in any military enterprise in the Near East.

I subsequently embodied in a letter to Sir Edward Grey the result of my conversations in Paris and at the British Headquarters: —

" February 7th, 1915.

My dear Grey,

During my visit to Paris I had several opportunities of discussing with Ministers the question of.the Balkans. When I first mentioned it to the Minister of Finance I found that Millerand had never repeated to his colleagues that the suggestion of an expeditionary force to Salonika had been made to him when he was in England. I found subsequently, in conversations with the Prime Minister, Delcassé, and with Briand, that they had also been kept in the dark as to the conversations which took place in England between Millerand and British Ministers. They were astonished, and not a little annoyed, that the matter had not been reported to them. I found that their attitude was much more friendly to the idea than was that of Millerand. Briand, who is much the ablest man in the Ministry, was strongly for it—in fact, he told me that he had been for some time urging some diversion of this kind upon General Joffre. I met Briand at Sir Francis Bertie's and the three of us had a prolonged talk on the position. Briand told us that the Cabinet had considered the suggestion on Thursday: that Millerand stood absolutely alone in his opposition to it, Delcassé hesitating a little, not knowing what the attitude of Russia would be towards it: the rest of the Cabinet being perfectly unanimously in favour of the principle of an expeditionary force of two divisions being sent to Salonika at the earliest practicable moment, preparations to be made at once, and the troops to be sent as soon as Generals Joffre and French could be persuaded to spare them. The French wished for an expeditionary force in which the French Army should be represented. They therefore suggested that one British and one French division should be sent. The President of the Republic was present at the Council; he also approved of this course.

It is now a question of persuading Joffre. Briand was of opinion, and so was the President, that if a joint note were addressed to Roumania and Greece, asking them whether they would be prepared to declare war immediately if an expeditionary force of two divisions were sent to Salonika, and if they replied in the affirmative, then no doubt General Joffre would gladly spare the necessary force. Briand said it was too preposterous to imagine that if 40,000 men from the west brought in 800,000 from the east, thus withdrawing German pressure on the west, any General could possibly object to such a plan.

Briand told Bertie and myself that he would propose at yesterday's meeting of the French Cabinet that a joint note should be sent in those terms to Roumania and to Greece. Bark, the Russian Finance Minister, who was present, strongly supported the proposal and thought Russia would gladly send a small force to occupy Serbian Macedonia, so as to make an attack by Bulgaria impossible. Isvolsky, whom Bark consulted on the subject, was also emphatically of the same opinion.

The French are very anxious to be represented in the expeditionary force. Briand thinks it desirable from the point of view of a final settlement that France and England should establish a right to a voice in the settlement of the Balkans by having a force there. He does not want Russia to feel that she alone is the arbiter of the fate of the Balkan peoples.

I found the President, Briand and the Prime Minister very sceptical as to what Russia would or could do in the immediate future. They were very doubtful as to whether Russia was in a position, owing to her lack of rifles and ammunition, to bring in anything like an overwhelming force on the eastern frontier for some months; in fact, they were very inclined to take our War Office view as to the effective number of the Russian troops in the coming spring and summer.

I have no idea what Delcassé's view is after yesterday's Cabinet Council, but I hope you will bear in mind in discussing the question with him that with the exception of Millerand he was the only man amongst the French Ministers who expressed any doubt at all as to the feasibility of this plan. Briand is in favour of an operation on a much larger scale, *and he told me that he had had the idea examined by experts in the War Office, and that they reported favourably on the proposal, provided troops could be spared by General Joffre and Lord Kitchener.*

Bertie was present and heard the whole of the conversation, and he may have reported to you its purport separately. When he and I first saw the President he examined all the objections, but I could see that even then he was quite friendly to the idea and at the Council on the following day, as I have already pointed out, he spoke in favour of its adoption.

Yesterday I saw Sir John French and General Robertson, the new Chief of Staff. Every soldier I have met since the beginning of the War has placed Robertson in the forefront as the most conspicuous success amongst our generals, and he made a deep impression on the Governor of the Bank, Montagu, and myself yesterday. He is a shrewd, clear-headed, strong man. No general except Kitchener made quite the same impression on my mind as Robertson did yesterday. French introduced the idea of an expedition, and at first he was hostile, not in principle, but on the ground that he could not spare the troops. *However, he called Robertson in, and when I explained to him exactly what the proposal was, he had no hesitation in saying that it was ' good strategy.' He maintained that view throughout the discussion.* This influenced French's attitude very considerably. I told him we were very anxious to carry his judgment along with ours in any scheme which affected the military operations for which he was responsible. Ultimately he agreed that if the Roumanians and the Greeks promised to march on our undertaking to send an expeditionary force to Salonika, he would spare at least a Division for the purpose. He is willing, and, I think, anxious, to come over to discuss the project with the War Council. He suggested that he should be invited, and I hope that the Prime Minister and Kitchener can see their way to asking him to attend an early meeting of the War Council.

Robertson would have gone further than French: he would send not merely one but two Divisions at once if Greece came in, and even on the offchance of forcing a decision in the Balkans. He thinks it will compel Bulgaria to at least neutrality. If Briand is as successful in the mission which he promised to undertake to General Joffre, then there is no reason why the expeditionary force should not start within a week or ten days at the outside.

I am sure you will agree that there is every reason why the joint note should be sent without delay. It is quite clear from the telegrams which have appeared in the sections during the last few days that anything in the nature of an arrangement between the Balkan States is impossible. I think the attitude of the Serbian Prime Minister as revealed in our telegrams from Nish is unalter-able. I doubt whether it would be possible for him to give up a substantial part of his territory in advance until he actually gets something in return. It would produce such a feeling of dis-couragement in his army as to paralyse their efforts. They have done so brilliantly that it would be a misfortune if this were to happen.

There are several ominous telegrams which indicate clearly that Bulgaria is hardening into opposition to the Triple Entente. There is the telegram about the success of their borrowing mission to Berlin. The Germans are not such fools as to advance money without receiving some assurance as to Bulgaria's action in certain contingencies. There are the telegrams from Dedeagatch about the laying of mines. Those mines can only be used against the Entente Powers. There are the rumours about bands being organised to attack the railways: and there are one or two others, all pointing in the same direction. Then the Roumanian news is for the moment discouraging—the trouble they have taken to explain away the loan raised in England, amongst other items of news. I am afraid that they have a better appreciation of the Russian position than we have, and that they are losing confidence in the Russian strength. *Unless, therefore, we mean to allow the great possibilities of the Balkans to slip out of our hands, we ought not to dilly-dally any longer. If we fail to take timely action here, our condemnation will be a terrible one.* As I read the sections I feel that even days count now. My experience yesterday shows that the generals, if properly taken in hand, can be persuaded. No general likes to have his troops taken away to another sphere of action. His mind is naturally concentrated on the trenches in front of him, unless he is a very big man indeed, and a man, moreover, who has the responsibility, not merely for the success of the operations under his immediate control: and neither Joffre nor French are quite in this position.

I should like to see you to-morrow to give you a fuller account of my interviews, but I thought it well to send you a summarised report before you see Delcassé.

Yours sincerely,

D. LLOYD GEORGE."

In the conversations which I had subsequently with the Prime Minister and the Foreign Secretary, I strongly urged that a conference should immediately be summoned either at Salonika or one of the Greek islands which the Foreign Ministers of France, Russia, Serbia, Greece and Roumania should be invited to attend, in order to deliberate on the whole of the position in the Balkans, and endeavour to establish the basis of an understanding for effective co-operation between all these States against the Central Powers. I was strongly of opinion that the Bulgarian Government should also be asked to send a representative to this conference. Sir Edward Grey objected to such a gathering on the ground that it would be quite impossible for him to leave the Foreign Office at so critical a moment for the length of time it would take to attend a meeting at such a distance. I pointed out that proceeding by way of Brindisi it would take him less than a week to get there, and that he need not be absent for a longer period than a fortnight or three weeks in all. There would be no difficulty in getting M. Sazonoff there as far as travelling was concerned, for Petrograd to Salonika would be a matter of three or four days' journey at the outside. The Foreign Secretary was, however, so unwilling to entertain this proposal that it fell through.

Had this suggestion been adopted a Balkan Confederation on the

Allied side could have been negotiated. It would have been necessary to give our plenipotentiary full powers not only to arrange geographical terms, but also to dispense liberal financial aid. The Balkan kingdoms—never rich—had been impoverished by a succession of wars with Turkey and amongst themselves. Loans from Britain and France would have encouraged them to take the risks of war. It was not a question of bribery but of sheer necessity, if they were to equip themselves adequately to encounter the hazards of alliance. The Germans realised that. They therefore did not trust their interests to the ordinary diplomatic representation, but sent to Sofia a special emissary of high standing and great ability. He knew the importance of giving financial help to Bulgaria and accordingly promised a handsome advance. It was not the decisive factor in her choice, but it was one of the inducements. Grey might not have been the best man to manipulate and persuade the fractious elements that had to be brought together. In fact, he was not. But he might have found a suitable colleague or a substitute. The Czar Ferdinand was not at that date as pro-German as was generally assumed. On the contrary he was definitely anti-Kaiser. He was a man who possessed an inordinate pride of pedigree. He was a Bourbon. And Wilhelm in one of his fits of boyish recklessness had offended his vanity when they were visiting at the same Schloss. He had been tempted to greet the self-important Bulgarian Emperor rather rudely as he was leaning over a parapet in deep contemplation of the view. The Bourbon blood never forgave the insult. Ferdinand would have been personally better pleased to co-operate with the Czar of Russia and the Kings of England and Italy. But as the issue of the War was very much in doubt he waited for some clear indication of the way things were going on the battlefield. By September the chances of Bulgarian expansion seemed more likely to be realised by throwing in his lot with the Central Powers than by joining the Allies, so he declared finally, but after considerable hesitation, for the former. A meeting with him in the spring would have produced different results. We were then about to attack the Dardanelles. By September our attacks had been beaten off. It is true that in the early spring Russia was not doing too well, but her position was by no means irretrievable. By the autumn her armies had been driven helter-skelter out of Poland and beyond. Ferdinand then came to the conclusion that the Bulgarian opportunity was with the victorious Germans. We missed our chance of organising a confederation that would have decided the War by 1916, and all through lack of enterprise and gumption.

If special diplomatic methods were not to be tried in the Balkans I begged the War Council to send more troops to that theatre so as to secure a favourable military decision there.

On 19th February the War Council met and the discussion is very illuminating because of the light it throws upon the views taken at the time of the prospects of the War.

"LORD KITCHENER said that the War Committee ought to consider very seriously before advising the removal of the XXIXth Division to the East. The situation in Russia had greatly deteriorated during the last week or two. The Russians had lost very heavily in men and, what was more serious, they had lost very heavily in rifles, of which they were short. If the Germans could inflict a sufficiently decisive defeat on the Russians they would be in a position to bring back great masses of troops very rapidly to France, and there would be a great demand for reinforcements in the western theatre of war.

MR. LLOYD GEORGE agreed that the position was very serious. Russia might receive a knock-out blow. Had we to admit that we were impotent in view of such a contingency? *In his opinion the Germans would not send their forces west, but would endeavour to smash Serbia and settle the Balkan question. The view appeared now to prevail that Germany would aim at the conquest of the north-east corner of Serbia with a view to establishing through communication and direct access to Bulgaria and thence to Constantinople.* (My italics.)

THE PRIME MINISTER agreed, but considered that the most effective way would be to strike a big blow at the Dardanelles.

LORD KITCHENER agreed with the Prime Minister. If the fact of not sending the XXIXth Division would in any way jeopardise the success of the attack on the Dardanelles he would dispatch it. *He doubted whether the Germans would attack Serbia as suggested by Mr. Lloyd George.*

MR. LLOYD GEORGE suggested that we ought to send more than three divisions. It was worth while to take some risks in order to achieve a decisive operation which might win the War. From the discussion he gathered that the maximum force available for operations in the East was as follows: —

The Australian and New Zealanders (including mounted troops)	39,000
The XXIXth Division	19,000
Naval Division	10,000
Marines	4,000
French Division	15,000
Russians	10,000
Total	97,000

LORD KITCHENER said he had every intention of supporting the Dardanelles operation, but considered two divisions on the spot to be sufficient at first.   There was no object in sending out troops from here which he might require.

SIR EDWARD GREY asked if we were safe in the West.

MR. LLOYD GEORGE said he had spoken on this subject with a great many officers who had been at the Front.   There was a general agreement that our army could not carry out a successful attack without a very heavy loss of life, and the same was true of the French Army.   No doubt it was also true of the Germans; for the Germans to attack, therefore, would be the best thing that could happen.   It was just as costly for them to try and break us as for us to try and break them. . . ."

On 24th February there was a further discussion which constitutes a very useful addendum to the report of the last meeting.

". . . MR. LLOYD GEORGE agreed that a force ought to be sent to the Levant, which could, if necessary, be used after the Navy had cleared the Dardanelles to occupy the Gallipoli Peninsula or Constantinople.   He wished to know, however, whether in the event of a naval attack failing (and it was something of an experiment) it was proposed that the Army should be used to undertake an operation in which the Navy had failed.

MR. CHURCHILL said that this was not the intention.   He could however, conceive a case where the Navy had almost succeeded, but where a military force would just make the difference between failure and success.

MR. LLOYD GEORGE hoped that the Army would not be required or expected to pull the chestnuts out of the fire for the Navy.   If we failed at the Dardanelles we ought to be ready immediately to try something else.   In his opinion we were committed by this operation to some action in the Near East, but not necessarily to a siege of the Dardanelles."

CHAPTER XII

ALLIED PROCRASTINATION

SUCH meagre and cautious reports as were vouchsafed to Cabinet Ministers as to the progress of the War did not enlighten us as to what was really happening on or behind the battlefields. There was an impression left on our minds that the military authorities thought it better we should not be told too much. Secrecy was essential to success. The Prime Minister and Mr. Churchill knew a good deal more about the situation than we did. But they were not fully apprised of the facts. Casualties were scrupulously withheld. In fact, there was no considered statement submitted to the War Council on the military position, showing the relative strength of the Allies and of the Central Powers in men or machinery. I often doubt whether anyone inside the War Office had taken the trouble to make a careful survey. We therefore knew nothing of the numbers on the various fronts, either our own or those of our Allies or our foes; what reserves were available; what was the equipment in guns, machine-guns, rifles or ammunition on both sides; or when our new armies would be ready. Lord Kitchener told us he had no troops to send to the Dardanelles. We had to accept it on his authority for he never condescended to details. We had to decide every issue without being informed as to the most relevant facts. Those of us who were members of the so-called Council of War were not much better off in that respect than other Ministers who had to be satisfied with a perfunctory statement from Lord Kitchener at the beginning of a Cabinet sitting. We had to forage here and there on our own initiative for information essential to our utility as war councillors. Sometimes we scrounged an important fact, more often we picked a snub.

I was a diligent seeker after truth. In spite of travestied and medicated reports I was convinced we were not doing well. I was equally convinced we were not doing our best. We had decided to launch a serious adventure in the Dardanelles. We had also resolved to prepare the ground for an alternative in Salonika if the Dardanelles failed. I saw clearly that we were tackling neither of these plans with the whole of our available military strength. We just dawdled and put off. In the Dardanelles both Lord Kitchener and the Prime Minister were hopeful that the Navy would do the trick, in which case very few troops would be needed. If the Navy failed altogether then no soldiers would be required for that enterprise. Elsewhere there was nothing in particular happening in France. Germany had abandoned any idea of attempting a further advance in the west. We were building up an army to turn her out altogether. We were raising great new armies but not taking adequate steps to equip them. We were very dependent for ultimate success on Russia. But we knew nothing about her plans, and very little about the resources in men or munitions with which these plans had to be carried out. All we knew about Russia was that she was being beaten, that she was short of rifles and getting shorter because she was losing more in retreat than she gained in manufacture. But we were not at pains to ascertain the truth. There was no co-ordination of effort. There was no connected plan of action. There was no sense of the importance of time. We were still much too leisurely and casual for a matter of life and death. It was not an absence of fussing but a lack of clear vision and resolute drive. I began to realise that it was not composure but confusion. In spite of official reticence, disquieting scraps of news and rumours percolated through. They made me uneasy as to the course of events, still uneasier as to the way events were directed on the Allied side.

On the 22nd February I circulated to my colleagues the following memorandum: —

" I am anxious to put before my colleagues a few considerations on the general situation. It must be acknowledged to be one of the utmost gravity, and one which, if it is not taken in hand at once firmly and boldly, may end in irretrievable disaster for the cause of the Allies and for the future of the British Empire. This may very well appear to some of my colleagues to be the language of morbid pessimism, but I hope, before they come to that conclusion, they will do me the honour of perusing the reasons set forth here which have led me to this conclusion.

The Press and the Country have up to the present treated the progress of the War as one of almost unbroken success. Their method is a simple one. Every trivial military incident which turns to our advantage is magnified and elaborated in headlines which occupy half a column and descriptions which take a page. On the other hand, grave misfortunes such as those which have befallen the armies of our Russian Allies in the course of the last few days are relegated to a few lines of type, whilst they are explained away in a column of leaded matter. I am afraid that many who have a more intimate acquaintance with the facts are pursuing the same mental process. They concentrate their gaze upon those incidents and aspects of the military situation which suit their hopes, whilst they deliberately shut their eyes to the developments which might conduce to the awakening of their fears. The only pathway to ultimate success is paved by reality. Unless we look facts, however unpleasant, in the face, we shall never grapple with them.

What are the salient facts of the situation? Not a yard of German territory is now in the occupation of the Allies. Practically the whole of Belgium is in German occupation. Some of the richest departments of France and Russia are now firmly held by the enemy. The Germans are now in possession of larger tracts of allied territory than they have ever held before. A still more serious fact: whilst they maintain possession of the country occupied by them in the west with comparative ease, they have at last established a complete military predominance in the east. It is true that they drove the Russians out of East Prussia some months ago, and the Russians came back afterwards; but as Lord Kitchener pointed out, there is a serious difference between what happened then and what is occurring now. Then the Russians were in a position to bring up considerable reserves to overpower the enemy, and the German reserves were not ready to take the field. Now the position is entirely reversed. Large German reserves have taken the field. The remarkable report circulated by Lord Kitchener from the pen of a Dutch officer points out that after sending huge reinforcements to East Prussia and North Poland to overwhelm the Russians, they have still numbers behind them they could throw in, but which have not been sent to the frontiers because there is no room for them.

That is the German position now. What about the Russian position?"

I then proceeded to examine in detail the seriousness of the Russian position in reference to rifles and the present situation and the future prospects of the Allies and the Central Powers in respect of man-power. I dwelt on the fact that it was useless to reckon the enormous reserves of men available in Russia without taking into account the possibility of arming them. And I drew the inference that unless and until we took steps to equip the Russians, the Central Powers had more fighting men than the Allies at their disposal. I then proceeded: —

"Having regard to the superior equipment of the German-Austrian forces and to the fact that when we come to attack them they will be found to have entrenched their positions in allied soil, it is idle to hope for victory unless we secure a great numerical superiority over these forces. Where can we hope to find it? Russia cannot now, according to the War Office report, put and maintain 2,000,000 of fully armed and equipped men on all her assailed frontiers. Even if she could, that leaves us with a

deficiency of 2,000,000. It will be observed that in the figures
which I have given I have credited Great Britain with 2,000,000.
When can she put 2,000,000 into the field? When can she put
1,000,000 into the fighting line? Is it quite certain that by the
time 1,000,000 are ready Germany will not have added at least
another 1,000,000 to her reserves?

I am sorry to draw so menacing a picture, but I should, indeed,
be happy if I thought the appearance of the landscape did not
justify the gloomy colours with which I have attempted to paint
it. The Dutch report circulated by Lord Kitchener gives still
more alarming figures. If these be even approximately accurate
we could not hope to bring the War to a successful termination
for years to come. But even with my more moderate figures, the
problem is the most serious with which British statesmen have
ever been faced.

The first thing to do is to find out exactly where we stand. Who
can present a reliable estimate of the military resources of the
Allies? We ought to have a conference between the military
authorities of the three countries, at which a candid exposure of
the position of each country is made and some military convention
agreed to as to our future action. General Paget is a good soldier,
but his qualities are not altogether fitted for a detailed investigation into questions of equipment. We know approximately, at any
rate, how France is situated. We have not the slightest notion of
what the position of Russia is. I strongly urged as far back as
October that we should take drastic measures to ascertain
accurately the Russian position as to equipment and munitions.
We are entitled not merely to ask but to demand frankness from
our Russian Allies. Russia is not in this war to help France and
Belgium and ourselves. France came in to assist Russia when she
was menaced; Belgium came in on account of France; we came in
to protect Belgium; so that indirectly we are in because Russia
was attacked. Germany was not merely at peace with us but was
extremely anxious to maintain the peace not merely with us, but
with France as well. She engaged in this war to try conclusions
with Russia before Russia was prepared to attack her. We are
helping Russia with men, with material, with money. France and
ourselves have already advanced £50,000,000 or £60,000,000 of
money to Russia and we have promised another £100,000,000.
We are, therefore, justified in demanding candour from Russia.
Germany knows all about the Russian forces, their numbers,
disposition and equipment. All we want is that our great ally
should supply us with information which her enemies already
possess.

What next? Every effort must be made to increase the number
of men whom we can put into the field and to shorten the period

in which they could be put into the fighting lines. How is that
to be done? If France could put 3,000,000 of men under arms
and Germany 5,000,000, then the whole of the Allied countries
ought to be able, on the basis of population, sooner or later to
count on 20,000,000. That may be an impossibility, but it is an
indication of the enormous reserves of men fit to bear arms that
the Allies have to draw upon. The problem resolves itself into
one of: —

1. The training and equipping of these men in the shortest
space of time.
2. The maintaining of the *status quo* without any appreciable aggravation until the Allied countries are prepared to throw
overwhelming forces into the battlefield.
How are these two objects to be attained?"

Here followed a passage on the urgent need for developing our
potential resources for munition production which I have already
quoted on page 100 in telling the story of the fight for munitions.
After dealing with the issue of materials, I proceeded as follows: —

" Now with regard to the raising of men. France has probably
brought every available man she can spare into line. That is far
from being the case with either the British Empire or with Russia.
Great Britain, on the French basis, ought to have 3,500,000 now
under arms, instead of 2,000,000. The Dominions and the
Colonies ought to have, on the same basis, 1,200,000 men instead of
100,000. I believe we could with a special effort raise our
3,500,000, or, if that be found inconsistent with the turning out of
the necessary equipment, we could certainly raise 3,000,000. I
still think it is unnecessary to obtain compulsory powers. The
young men of this country will enlist in our armies if it is brought
home to them that their services are needed. I ventured to suggest
some time ago that the best method of doing so would be by
determining the quota each county and town ought to contribute
in proportion to its population, and leaving it to local pressure
and local patriotism to do the rest. If we officially announce that
a particular county is expected to contribute, say, 10,000 men;
that up to the present 6,000 have been enrolled in that county,
and that 4,000 more ought to enlist in order to make up the quota,
local pride will fill up the ranks for us.
Some means ought also to be taken to induce our self-governing
colonies to take upon themselves a larger share of responsibility in
the matter of levies. They are under the impression now that
they are doing all that is expected of them. The peril ought to
be brought home to them. The optimistic telegrams which we
publish have deluded them into the belief that all is going well,

and that all they need do is to send a few thousand to the Mother Country as a token of their sympathy and esteem for her. When they realise that she is in real peril, I do not doubt their response.

Russia, on the French basis,* ought to have 12,000,000 men under arms. That is probably more than she could equip for some years, but having regard to her primary responsibility as far as the Allies are concerned for the struggle, the numbers of her men ought to bear some relation to her enormous resources in vigorous manhood.

All this must necessarily take time. We have hitherto proceeded as if the War could not possibly last beyond next autumn. We should now take exactly the other line—assume that it will last not merely through the year, but conceivably through next year as well. Capital, therefore, ought to be spent on laying down machinery which will enormously expedite the output of rifles, cannon and all other machinery and munitions of war towards the latter end of the year and the beginning of the next. If it turns out that my estimate errs on the side of pessimism the worst that happens will be that we shall have spent a considerable amount of money, we shall have caused a considerable amount of inconvenience to the population. But all that is nothing compared with the disaster of having to face another year of war with inadequate preparation. This the public will never forgive after the warning we have received, nor ought they to be expected to forgive.

But what is to be done in the meantime? It looks as if during the best part of the present year the Allies must content themselves to be in a position of military inferiority to Germany. During this period the best we can hope for is that we shall be able to hold our own. Can we even accomplish this without summoning some fresh forces to our aid? Having regard to the overwhelming forces at the disposal of Germany there is at least an element of doubt. There are only two directions in which we can turn for any prospect of assistance—the Balkan States and Italy. The Balkans we might conceivably have brought in some months ago, but the Allies have been unfortunate in this quarter. We have only succeeded in bringing in the Turks against us without engaging any other Balkan Power on our behalf. Is it too late to do anything now? Lord Kitchener pointed out the other day at the Council that the Germans had taken risks by attacking the Russians with their full forces before they were quite ready, in order to be prepared to meet the attack of our reinforcements in April. With the one exception of our initial action against Turkey, where our promptitude was unmistakable, our risks have all been in the contrary direction; we have generally taken them too late. The

* Of the proportion of recruits to population.

momentous step we have taken in attempting to force the Dardanelles must have a decisive effect one way or the other on the Balkans. Are we prepared for either or for any event?

If this great movement succeeds—then, if we are prepared to take immediate advantage of it—its influence may be decisive as far as the Balkan States are concerned. This means that if we have a large force ready, not merely to occupy Gallipoli, but to take any other military action which may be necessary in order to establish our supremacy in that quarter, Roumania, Greece, and, I think, very probably, Bulgaria will declare for us. If, on the other hand, we have no force on the spot adequate to cope with the Turkish Army, it may be that most of the effect of such a brilliant *coup* might be lost. To bring Bulgaria, Roumania and Greece in with Serbia means throwing an aggregate army of 1,500,000 on to the Austrian flank. This will not only relieve the pressure on Russia, but indirectly on France. It will tend to equalise things, and thus give time to re-equip the Russian Army.

Now let us take the other contingency—the failure of the Dardanelles effort. Unless it is at once countered, such a failure will be disastrous in the Balkans, and might very well be disastrous throughout the East. The Bulgarian general pointed out that not merely Bulgaria but Roumania and Italy have a good deal to gain in the way of territory by throwing in their lot with Germany. There is only one guarantee against a catastrophe being precipitated in that quarter as a result of a repulse in the Dardanelles. There must be a strong British force there available to support our friends. Is it quite out of the question that we should anticipate our April preparations by three or four weeks and thus follow the German example of taking risks so as to arrive in time?

The sending of a large expeditionary force undoubtedly involves large preparations—ships, transports to carry troops and their equipment to Salonika or Lemnos, also preparations for transporting them up country; and the Committee of Imperial Defence decided some weeks ago that these preparations should be immediately undertaken, so that if an expedition was at any time determined upon, no delay need ensue owing to lack of sea or land transport. I understand that the Admiralty have done all that was entrusted to them in this respect; I know nothing of the steps taken by the War Office respecting the railways and the roads.

My final suggestion is that a special diplomatic mission, based on our readiness to dispatch and maintain a large expeditionary force in the Balkans, should immediately be sent to Greece and Roumania to negotiate a military convention. Germany has not depended upon her ordinary diplomatic representatives where the situation presented any greater possibilities friendly or hostile to her welfare. She has sent von der Goltz to Constantinople, Sofia, and Bucharest; von Buelow to Italy; Dernberg to America. She has not yet depended upon her X——s in critical situations. No doubt they are very good men in their way, but the mere fact that they have remained so long in inferior diplomatic berths proves that, in the opinion of the Foreign Office, their qualities are not of the first order.

D. Ll. G.

P.S.—Since writing the above I have read a remarkable report from General Paget, which confirms in essentials the view I have repeatedly expressed as to the Balkan situation. I was privileged to see this document through the courtesy of the Prime Minister. I respectfully suggest that every member of the War Council should have an opportunity of perusing reports which bear so intimately on decisions they are asked to come to. To consult them without trusting them with the only information which makes their judgment worth having is worse than futile.

D. Ll. G.

February 22, 1915."

On receipt of this memorandum Lord Fisher sent me a letter which is worth reproducing as a characteristic comment from a very remarkable man.

" Admiralty.

Dear Mr. Lloyd George,

I am in complete accord with your phenomenal paper! Yesterday I had to write these following words to a most influential personage: —

' Rashness in War is Prudence, and Prudence in War is Criminal.

The Dardanelles futile without soldiers!'

23/2/15.   Yours, FISHER."

Lord Kitchener had sent General Paget to the Balkans to report on the position there. That report confirmed all the information I had previously gathered as to the prospects and probabilities in that quarter. According to him, the Serbian Army, after a series of brilliant victories against overwhelming Austrian forces, had succeeded in clearing their country of all enemy troops, and were now in a strong position behind their Danubian frontier. They had neither the numbers nor the transport and equipment which would enable them to take the offensive, but the very able generals which they were fortunate enough to possess were satisfied that if Roumania could be persuaded to join the Entente and advance against the Austrians with a force of 300,000 men, the Serbian Army would conform and take up the offensive. The Report urged that one or two Divisions of British, French or Russians troops should co-operate with the Serbian Army and that the presence of British troops would most certainly tend to induce Bulgaria to maintain neutrality, if indeed she would not seize the opportunity of attacking the Turks. Such action on our part, or even the definite proposal of such action, would in his opinion cause Roumania to enter into the War, at such a time when her aid would be most invaluable. During the passage of the Russian Army across the Carpathians, the Roumanian Army of even 200,000 men operating against the southern flank of the already somewhat demoralised Austrian Army, would assist the Russians to an almost invaluable extent. Roumania was hesitating, but her action would be most prompt if British troops were to co-operate in a campaign on the Danube. There were no fortifications of modern standard between Belgrade and Vienna. That was the substance of the Paget report. It was a soldier's opinion confirming that which had already been formed by other soldiers as well as civilians.

Eighteen months later Roumania came in with an army of four or five hundred thousand men, but by that time Russia was beaten and broken. Her armies had been driven hundreds of miles nearer Petrograd. They could no longer hold their own when attacked, even in their own country. The Balkans were in the hands of the Central Powers; communication between the west and Roumania was completely cut off; we could afford no aid in either men or material, and fighting alone she fell without rendering any service to the Allies by her sacrifice. The poor aid Russia was able to give to the last remnant of her beaten army could not avail, and the very effort to afford that aid finally exhausted the Russian strength.

Two or three days after my memorandum was circulated, Lord Kitchener circulated a reply to it. The document recalled the curious mixture of sagacity and opacity which constituted the make-up of this extraordinary man: —

" REMARKS BY THE SECRETARY OF STATE FOR WAR ON THE CHANCELLOR OF THE EXCHEQUER'S MEMORANDUM ON THE CONDUCT OF THE WAR.

I would like to make the following observations on the Chancellor of the Exchequer's very interesting paper on the state of the War.

I will not now refer to the figures quoted by the Chancellor, as the seriousness of our position can be realised and considered quite apart from the question of the numbers of the combatants on either side. The Chancellor rightly points out that the Russian Colossus, as some people described our Russian ally, has not produced that effect on the progress of the War which those who took an optimistic view anticipated. Nevertheless, in my opinion

Russia has done remarkably well, and, according to my view of the situation, she will be found to have saved us six months out of the three years which, as my colleagues will remember, I estimated, in the House of Lords, might be the duration of the War. We must remember that at the outset our chief requirement was time, and though the Germans have strained every effort they have not succeeded in giving a knock-out blow at any time during the seven months of hostilities. It is true that they occupy a large expanse of territory outside their country, but the War is not on that account more likely to end in their favour.

If we are victorious the end of the War must come through one of the two following causes: (1) by a decisive victory, or a succession of decisive victories, of the Allies, which may take place just as well outside German territory as within it; or (2) by attrition, for when Germany is no longer able to support her armies in sufficient strength in the field she must sue for peace. I think it would be interesting to obtain, and I am arranging with Lord Moulton to furnish, a mathematical calculation of approximate dates when attrition might force our enemies to sue for peace. *As far as I can judge now, I think that about the beginning of 1917 this state of affairs may be reached.* [My italics.]

I leave out of calculation the possibility of the starving of Germany and Austria, where 105 millions of civilian population have to be fed.

With regard to the Chancellor of the Exchequer's practical suggestions, I am glad to think that there are more factories available for the output of war material in this country, but the real crux of the situation is, in my opinion, the organisation of the skilled labour required to work the machinery, and, if the Chancellor of the Exchequer could help us in this and in the many labour difficulties with which we are confronted, I have little doubt that in time an increased number of men, up to a total of 3,000,000, may be recruited and trained fit to take the field.

In the efforts we are now making to raise, arm and equip 2,000,000 men we are faced with grave difficulties, not the least of which is that, constantly, our manufacturers find themselves unable, owing to shortage of skilled labour, to keep their promises of delivery of arms, ammunition, etc. This shortage could be very much lessened by the employment of unskilled together with skilled labour on the same machines, but trade union rules do not admit of this. One of the first essentials, therefore, is to secure the requisite modifications of those rules.

A committee is sitting, on which Sir George Gibb represents the War Office, for the purpose of organising labour. I understand that they have been more or less successful in some of their efforts to induce trade unions to agree to modify the restrictive regulations which they now impose on labour; but if the Chancellor of the Exchequer could use his great powers to persuade the trade unions to deal with this matter at once, he would be doing a great deal to help us in preparing an army of the dimensions he regards as necessary. I quite agree with him that the closing of public houses in areas occupied by our labouring classes would have a very good effect, but such a measure would no doubt have to be carried out with care, as the men might resent any interference with their present habits. I would suggest, in this connection, that by keeping the public-houses closed up to 11 a.m. it would be possible to get the men into the works before they had had an opportunity of obtaining intoxicants.

We are making a great effort to increase our armies in the theatre of the War up to 2,000,000 men, including those required to maintain the force in the field. We are just beginning to see the results that have been achieved, and the difficulties that we have to face in the creation of these new armies. Until we can actually put into the field a considerable number of our new forces I doubt whether it would be advisable to attempt further increases, except as regards the placing of orders for the necessary armament. Our present output will, of course, be continuous, and will not cease when any specific quantities of articles are delivered: every effort is continually being made to increase production, but the great difficulty I foresee is that to which I have referred, viz. the labour question.

When our new armies are prepared to take the field, it will be undoubtedly a matter of vital importance that they should be employed in the most effective manner, so as to secure decisive results, and that they should not be scattered on subsidiary enterprises.

Much depends upon the success of the Navy in forcing the Dardanelles, but we have not sufficient men available at present to attack the Turkish troops on the Gallipoli Peninsula. As the situation develops in the Near East, we shall be better able to judge how our troops could be best employed when ready.   K.

February 25, 1915."

This document is the first in which our Generals committed themselves to the idea of a " War of Attrition." Their avowed aim was to " break through " and drive the Germans back across the Rhine, a routed and broken mob, chased by cavalry.

It is no part of my task to describe military operations and I shall therefore not attempt even to summarise the story of the Dardanelles Campaign with its incomprehensible blunders and its tragic failure. The poignant tale has been told by a master hand in Mr. Winston

Churchill's volumes of the " World Crisis." A small force of a few thousands landed in time would easily have overwhelmed the wretched garrison to whom the defence of Gallipoli had been entrusted by the careless Turks. When we sent an army numbering tens of thousands to attack in April, Turkish reinforcements had arrived which were strong enough to prevent us from capturing one of our objectives. We were always too late. We ran race after race with the sluggish Turk and each time he invariably won, and arrived first at the winning post. He delayed and procrastinated according to his wont, but we beat him at the dawdling game. He gave us many chances and we never took one.

Whilst that tragedy was visibly developing scene by scene and act after act, I was a helpless spectator who possessed neither the official position nor the personal influence with the War Directors which would enable me effectively to intervene.

During the whole of the summer months the Serbians remained on the defensive, whilst our strength was being muddled away on the Western Front in attack after attack upon German positions defended by much more powerful artillery than any the Allies could command. Hundreds of thousands of British and French troops were killed and wounded, and ammunition was lavished upon fruitless and costly attacks against impregnable fortresses. The Germans soon became convinced that they need feel no anxiety as to these onslaughts. As soon as they saw how feckless our efforts were in the Dardanelles they ceased to worry about that operation and postponed dealing with it until the autumn. They were right. Scores of thousands of the Allied troops fell in belated and therefore fruitless assaults on Achi Baba and the heights above Suvla and in clinging on to the rocky slopes of Anzac. In the east, as well as in the west, the German game of attrition was a great success. So they left the south-eastern flank to the Turk and in the west they left their entrenchments to be defended by numbers which were considerably inferior to those which were arrayed against them, and they turned their attention to the east with a resolve not merely to relieve the pressure upon their sorely tried allies in the Carpathians but to defeat the Russian Army along the whole front, and if possible, to destroy it.

CHAPTER XIII

THE RUSSIAN COLLAPSE

POIGNANT APPEALS FROM THE RUSSIAN SOLDIERS

THE failure of the Allied military chiefs to realise that the event of this war would ultimately be determined by equipment on land, sea and air ought to have been brought home to the most blinkered mind by the Russian defeats in 1915, and by the grave consequences that ensued.

On the Western Front we hailed a recovery of ground on a front of two or three kilometres to a depth of one kilometre as a victory. We had several triumphs of that kind during the year 1915. They were attained at a heavy cost of human life on our own side, and comparatively small losses to the Germans. In the aggregate we succeeded in tearing out of German claws a few square miles of French and Flemish soil. The balance of advantage was every time with the enemy. We captured nothing of any strategic value. We expended over 10,000,000 shells and added hundreds of thousands to the ghastly casualty lists of the War. During the same period on the Eastern Front the Germans drove the Russian armies on a front of 500 miles to a distance ranging from 90 to 300 miles from their original entrenchments. Every shell told. The price they paid in German lives for their vast conquests was not half what we sacrificed in the attainment of trivial results. They captured more great cities and provinces than we did hamlets and shell-harrowed fields.

The great retreat of 1915, in which, with unexampled carnage the Russian armies were driven pell-mell out of Poland and the Baltic provinces up to Riga, was entirely due to Russian inferiority in artillery, rifles and ammunition of all kinds. Amongst my papers there are reports written at that date by British officers who were observers of the actual fighting, and I have had the advantage of perusing some of the dispatches sent from the Russian generals at the front to their Government. They afford poignant and convincing evidence of the fact that the Russian rout was due to lack of material. Even before the end of the campaign of 1914, the Russian Army's resistance threatened to break down altogether through lack of equipment. There were some distressing appeals sent in November and December, 1914, from General Yanushkevitch, the Chief of the Staff of the Grand Duke Nicholas, Commander-in-Chief of the Russian Armies, from the fighting front to General Sukhomlinoff, the Secretary of State for War.

Here are a few specimens couched in language which might well be called hysterical had it not been fully justified by the tragic facts: —

"22/XI-1914.

Yanushkevitch to Sukhomlinoff.

. . . . I should be infinitely obliged to you, on behalf of the Army, if you would consider it possible to hurry up Rudsky [a well-known metallurgical works in the Baltic provinces] for the promptest output of shells. This is a nightmare to me. With the reduction in the number of guns and quantity of cartridges, 50 to 60 per cent. more casualties have started."

He went so far as to suggest that even the appearance of shells without any means of explosion might encourage the troops.

"Would it not be possible in addition to everything else to increase the quantity of shells (fuses are not necessary, but there will be shots). At any rate the spirits of the troops will be kept up. (A drowning man always catches at a straw.) The matter of the provision of rifles has been successfully arranged: up to 50 per cent. has been secured. . . ."

General Sukhomlinoff, in reply sent a telegram which he intended to be reassuring, but which must have had a very depressing effect upon its recipient. He was doing his best to speed up production, and ends up by saying: —

". . . I myself visit the works and urge them, but come upon strikes, shortage of coal, non-delivery of lathes from abroad—and we have none."

Workmen, miners, railwaymen and foreigners were all to blame. The Czarist Ministers were alone blameless. How completely the equipment of the poor Russian soldiers had been neglected is revealed in a fuller message from Yanushkevitch to Sukhomlinoff dated 6th December, 1914: —

"I know that by my wailing I caused you trouble and worry, but what is to be done? You know that my hair stands on end at the thought that, owing to the shortage of cartridges and rifles, we shall have to submit to Wilhelm. . . . *The fewer the cartridges the greater the loss.* If it were possible to throw in 150,000 to 250,000 men at once, it would be possible in 1 to 1½ weeks to hurl back the enemy and secure an advantageous position immediately. . . . That is why I consider it my duty to make a humble appeal to you.   Many of the men are without boots and have frost-bitten feet; they are without short fur coats or sweaters, and are beginning to catch severe colds.   As a result, where officers have been killed off, mass surrenders and captures have started, in some cases on the initiative of ensigns.   They say, ' Why should we perish of hunger and cold, without boots, the artillery is silent, and we are killed like partridges. The Germans are better off. Let us go.'   The Cossacks, who in an attack had recovered 500 that had been captured, were abused by the latter: ' Who asked you, fools; we do not want to hunger and freeze again.'   These occurrences are truly sad—but they are threatening. That is why I am now raising my voice. The English offer to help in executing the orders in their country, in America and Japan.   Be merciful and give us instructions for everything possible to be ordered (horse-shoes, cartridges, rifles).   Nothing will be in excess. The Army will absorb everything like an insatiable monster. Forgive me, for God's sake. Believe me that I am not exaggerating.   I am speaking from my conscience. . . ."

Here was a war that had been foreseen for years past by the Government of the Czar.   For this contingency preparations had been made; at least the French peasants had supplied cash in plenty for such preparations.   How had it been spent?

The Grand Duke Nicholas, who commanded this Army, was a fine soldier, and an honourable man.   He took for granted that his colleagues and comrades at the War Office were of the same pure metal.   His disappointments come out in the telegrams of the Chief of his Staff.   Here is another to the egregious Sukhomlinoff: —

" 10/12/14.

In order not to worry you, I have, by order of the G.D. [Grand Duke], sent an S O S by wire to General Vernander, describing to him the picture in regard to the cartridges.   Both Commanders-in-Chief [at the fronts] have sent such telegrams that my hair stands on end.   Cartridges are disappearing.   In Germany articles have already appeared that ' we are at our last gasp, as we are almost not replying to their firing; that on the evidence of our soldiers [prisoners] our numbers are shrinking without being replaced, and the artillery has been forbidden to shoot.'   The deduction to be made from this is that victory is at hand.   And the reinforcements promised for the 1st December have not as yet come to hand."

General Yanushkevitch to General Sukhomlinoff.

" February, 1915.

. . . 2-3 times a day cartridges are asked for from the fronts, and there are none.   My heart is heavy. . . ."

General Sukhomlinoff to General Yanushkevitch.

> " 24th February, 1915.
> . . . The eighth month of a fierce campaign is making itself felt by an exhaustion of stocks with all armies, and with use of projectiles.
> Positively all possible measures are being taken, and the Grand Duke Serge Mikhailovitch, who is now at the head of this business, can convince himself that the constant orders abroad have not promoted the development of our private industry, and with Government factories one does not get very far, especially when, moreover, the means therefore had to be acquired by sheer force —at the bayonet point and at a risk of losing one's position in the service. . . ."

At that time such information as I was able to secure about the Russian situation, despite the reticence of the military authorities, increased my already acute uneasiness. In February I laid my views before Mr. Asquith in writing as follows:—

> " Treasury Chambers,
> Whitehall, S.W.
> February 18th, 1915.

My dear Prime Minister,
The situation revealed by Lord Kitchener's statement at this morning's Cabinet is a grave one, and I strongly urge that the War Council should take it into consideration at once. After seven months' war we do not even now know approximately the position of the Russians. Sir John French told me that he had been assured by the Russian officers who visited him that Russia would have 3,000,000 of men fully equipped in the field next month, and that they could then sweep back the German and Austrian armies opposed to them. The War Office compute the Russian forces now at 1,200,000. If Sir John French's information be correct the Russian reinforcements available in March would come to 1,800,000. Now we learn that the Russians have no rifles to equip their new men with and that they can only turn out rifles at the rate of 40,000 per month. At that rate they can only bring 500,000 more men into the field by this time next year. The Germans are capturing more than 40,000 Russians with their rifles each month. What is the truth about their equipment? We surely ought to know. Our fate depends upon it.
I ventured in October last to express my doubts as to the Russian equipment, and I suggested then that we should take definite steps to ascertain how they were situated. I thought then it might be possible to arrange a meeting between the three

War Ministers—or responsible representatives. X is a futile person with no authority and but little intelligence. Y, for this kind of work, is no better.

We ought to have a searching and candid survey of the whole military situation with a view to devising the best means of meeting it—otherwise we shall drift into irretrievable disaster.

There has been deplorable lack of co-ordination between East and West, and as long as it lasts the Germans will continue winning. *Mere optimistic bluff is not going to float us through this hurricane.*

Ever sincerely,

D. LLOYD GEORGE."

Nothing was done, however, to improve the position. The same kind of messages as I have already quoted continued to come from Russian generals at the front, and much the same sort of reply came from the self-complacent ministers at Petrograd.

General Yanushkevitch to General Sukhomlinoff.

" March, 1915.

. . . Our strategy is now dead, as we cannot undertake anything, since we are helpless materially. If we could only repel attacks; it is painful that instead of being able to throw in every month 1,440 companies we must be satisfied with 350. . . ."

Yanushkevitch to Sukhomlinoff.

" March, 1915.

. . . You know that during the Russo-Japanese war they fought for about two weeks and vegetated for 2-3 months but now there are divisions that have already been fighting for 85 days. That is no longer fighting, but a titanic struggle to the death. . . . I feel quite heavy at heart. At night I imagine I hear someone's voice: ' You have been sold, you have missed, you have overslept.' "

As usual in Russia when failure was due to an incompetent and corrupt system the blame was attributed to other causes. The Jews always come in handy on occasions when corrupt or incompetent Gentiles make a mess of national affairs.

Yanushkevitch to Sukhomlinoff.

" 27th April, 1915.

. . . In some places they are already blowing up bridges, stores. This is all done for money; probably the Jews are doing it. *There is no one else to do it.*

The question of cartridges and rifles is, I may say, a bloody one."

Yanushkevitch to Sukhomlinoff.

"21st May.

. . . Ivanoff, reckoning 40 shots per day per rifle, and 5,000 rifles to the division, requires five million rifle cartridges per day and 40 parks of light cartridges per month. If one compares this with the colossal expenditure of the French during the last operations in Champagne (100,000 per 24 hours for 10 days, over 50,000 along the whole front daily) one's tongue clings to one's throat. . . .

From all armies the cry goes up: Give cartridges!"

Yanushkevitch to Sukhomlinoff.

"27th May.

. . . Yesterday the Germans dropped on to a section of one of the regiments 3,000 heavy shells. They demolished everything. And we fired barely 100. . . ."

Some hint of the difficulties which beset the Russian arrangements for munition production may be gleaned from the following extracts taken from a report sent us at the time from a British officer who was then in Russia: —

"May 26th, 1915.

It is rumoured that Manikovski is to be nominated as Chief of the Artillery Department . . . and that the Grand Duke Serge is to be asked to take sick leave . . . He [Manikovski] said that the Grand Duke Serge was a man of great ability, but he had never smelt powder, and he loved the Artillery Department and all its ways 'like a man will still love a woman, though he knows all the time that she is a bad lot.' . . . He has worked hard and has all details at his finger-tips, though he is very ill and should be in bed. His fault is that he obstinately underestimates the number of shells required per gun per month, and sees no necessity for an adequate reserve. *He has trusted too much to the promises of Vickers and Creusot, whose failure has upset all calculations. . . .*"

Yanushkevitch wrote on the same date that the Commander-in-Chief "was appointing Lord Kitchener his agent, with 'carte blanche' to procure shells, rifles and ammunition." He added that " it was against the law of Russia to give such powers to a foreign General, but 'since it is a question now whether Russia should be victorious or defeated, we will spit on those laws. . . .'"

A despatch on 30th May, 1915, stated: —

"The powder expert in the French Mission thinks it would be impossible to form new factories, as there is already a want of trained personnel. . . . The Russian Government should be urged to give larger orders for machinery, provided Lord Kitchener really sees his way to providing fuses."

The Russians had a pathetic belief in Lord Kitchener and talked with confidence of shells provided on the guarantee of Lord Kitchener.

Here is a telegram from Yanushkevitch to the Russian War Office: —

"June, 1915.

Orders have been given to Kitchener, as the political situation and the phantom of strikes, etc., do not entitle one to ignore this not very profitable offer from abroad, *but one secured by the guarantee of Kitchener* [to give prompt assistance] . . . The III and VIII Armies have melted away. Three corps from three divisions with 5,000 bayonets each. Staffs of officers are vanishing, and the supplementary units, on receipt of rifles on the fighting days vie with each other in surrendering!"

Yanushkevitch to Sukhomlinoff.

"June, 1915.

. . . A bilious telegram was sent to Ivanoff. The reply was 'in 12 corps there are seven divisions, representing 12,000 bayonets! There are no rifles and 150,000 are without rifles. . . . From hour to hour it is worse. We await the heavenly manna from you. The chief thing is—cannot rifles be purchased? . . .'"

A further despatch of 8th June throws a sinister light on the working of the professional mind when confronted with the consequences of its inefficiency, lack of vision and energy: —

". . . The French Technical Mission regards Smislovski as the real enemy of all progress. They say he has opposed their work in every way in his power because, if they show themselves able to produce shell in Russia, it will be direct proof of inefficiency in the Artillery Department, which people will say might have increased the output months ago. . . ."

The story reads painfully like an echo in a higher key of the lethargy, the lack of vision, the conflict between patriotism and professional vanity which hampered munition supply everywhere.

In July and August we also had reports from British officers at the Russian Front as to what was happening there. They wrote within sound of the German guns: —

> "The First Army was hopelessly weak in heavy artillery. For instance, north of Tysekanov the 1st Turkestan Corps had to fight 42 enemy guns of big calibre with only two. As a result, the 11th Siberian Division was practically destroyed. The German preponderance in heavy artillery seems to have created something of a panic."

It was not that the Russians had not entrenched. They were driven out of territory which for 30 years had been prepared for defence by highly skilled engineers. Great fortresses, which had been devised with ingenuity and constructed with an immense amount of labour, were destroyed in a few hours by the terrible cannon brought up by the German Army. The Russians, with their inferior equipment and serious shell deficiency, were quite unable to reply. Retreat was the only expedient open to them to save their armies from complete destruction. They were short of the machine-guns which would have enabled them to fight rearguard actions to delay the enemy and inflict upon his advancing troops losses which, in course of time, would have exhausted his strength and forced him to pause. In this unequal contest between machinery and men the great losses were almost entirely amongst Russian men, and these are described as "appalling." They had no guns which would stand up for one hour against the massed cannon of their ruthless foe, and when they had a few they were either silenced by the crashing missiles that rained on and around them, or their scant supply of ammunition was soon exhausted.

From another part of the front where the Russians had made considerable progress against the Austrians it was reported that the victorious Russians had been forced to retreat because of the lack of ammunition. Such ammunition as Headquarters could spare was urgently needed to meet the German onslaught. The vanquished Austrians then avenged their retreat in perfect security against the disarmed victors. The report further stated (18th June, 1915): —

> "As we are forced to save shells the enemy can inflict loss unpunished."

Another account states: —

> "All the late advances have been pure murder, as we attacked

against a large quantity of field and heavy artillery without adequate preparation. I think the casualties in the ordinary sense of the word must have been 1½ million."

Here is another extract from another quarter of the 900-mile battlefield, where the Germans were still pursuing their long-range massacre of defenceless Russians: —

"This Army [the Third Russian Army] is now a harmless mob. We are very short of ammunition and guns. All realise the futility of sending men against the enemy; they with their artillery and we with ours."

At this time—ten months after the outbreak of war—Britain was just beginning to set about the task of systematically organising her enormous manufacturing resources to produce suitable weapons and sufficient supplies of ammunition for herself.

Until the Germans arrived with their superior equipment and technique, the Russians had been doing very well against the Austrians. But when Mackensen came with his great guns and his efficiently trained German soldiers, the Russians were quite unable with their inferior equipment to withstand the onslaught. As one British officer said during the retreat in May: "To-day is the eighteenth day of uninterrupted battle and retreat. I fancy they have had very little to eat. This army has been thoroughly spoilt up to now [30th May] by having only Austrians against them. They did not know what real fighting meant . . . The Russians even now are possibly in numerical superiority, but the *morale* of the Third Army has been temporarily shattered." And by June he reported that "the Third Army is reduced to a quarter of its strength, and its *morale* has been crushed owing to losses from artillery fire to which the Russians are unable to reply in consequence of lack of shell and rifle ammunition." The Russian General Staff, in their official apology for the retirement, point out how over-whelming was the German concentration of guns, and proceed "as a natural result all the Russians in the beaten zone who were not killed or wounded were stunned and contused." In this remarkable document there is a paragraph which is reminiscent of something I heard from the lips of an eminent British General as to the stupidity of spoiling troops by teaching them to expect that their enemies should be crushed by a preliminary bombardment before they were called upon to attack them. "It is evident that the enemy infantry which has been pampered and spoilt by such artillery support, and has been accustomed to attack only when the enemy is poisoned and overwhelmed by it, will soon be forced to fight in far more difficult conditions."

A comment written at the time (30th May) upon that observation by Colonel Knox, the shrewdest and best informed of the British officers at the Russian Front, was: "It is a pity that the poor Russian infantry cannot get a little pampering and spoiling of the same kind."

It was not merely an inferiority in guns that contributed to this disaster. There was a shortage of rifles and of rifle ammunition. Of the units which were sent to the front to replace the enormous casualties, only 25 per cent. came with a rifle. And there were no rifles at the front to supply the deficiency. Once more to quote from one of the British observers (18th June): —

"The Russian guns are everywhere outnumbered by the German, and we have, of course, far less shell. The Russian infantry has not only to fight without proper artillery support; many of the units are much below strength, for there are insufficient rifles to arm the drafts, and, to crown them all, there seems to be serious danger of shortage in rifle ammunition."

When the Russians held their own they could pick up and pass on to the unarmed living the rifles of the fallen, and the unexhausted bandoleers of the stricken multitude also provided a reserve of cartridges; but when the retreat began these sources of supply failed, and the shortage became more and more serious.

That was early in June, and the fighting went on until the end of September. By July the Russians had ceased to fight with any hope of victory; strategy was confined to the problem of an extrication which fell short of annihilation. The Russian strategy was reduced to an effort to frustrate the German effort to Sedanise them on a grand scale. Their highest idea of tactics was a skilful retreat.

"August 29, 1915.

The men were tired out from retiring every night and digging trenches in the morning, only to be shelled in the afternoon by an artillery to which they could hardly reply. The casualties were appalling. They were put at one million and a half in this summer drive."

As one Russian officer said: "The munitions shortage is bleeding the Russian Army to death."

At first the Russian generals were sustained by the thought that the Germans had exhausted all their reserves of ammunition in their first overwhelming attack, that they would not be able to continue to bombard on such a formidable scale, and that once they left depots which they had taken weeks to stock and store, the advantages which their superior artillery had given them would disappear.

RUSSIAN RETREATS
IN AUGUST 1915

August 9TH ••••••••
August 11TH ∿∿∿∿∿
August 13TH ╍╍╍╍
August 17TH ▬▬▬▬

In the sequel they were sadly disillusioned, for throughout the summer and into the late autumn, the Germans renewed the attack by the same methods and with a superiority of equipment which became greater and greater through the loss of Russian guns and the depletion of Russian dumps.   Weeks after the date of that characteristic military document about the danger of demoralising storm troops by too much artillery preparation, the " spoilt and pampered " Germans drove the shattered Russian Armies before them across rivers, through marshes, demolishing carefully prepared defences and redoubtable fortresses until the Russian winter which had destroyed Napoleon once more came to the rescue of the hunted defenders of Holy Russia.

In Britain we were apt to compare the immense might of Russia to a steam-roller which moved slowly, but crushed surely as it moved forward.   When the great retreat began we were reminded that a steam-roller always moved backwards as well as forwards.   The French comment upon the steam-roller obsession was that the Russians were more of a threshing machine which gradually absorbed the German strength and ultimately beat it all into straw.   This disastrous campaign proved that the Germans possessed the machine and that the Russians provided the battered sheaves.

Whilst these disturbing reports were coming in from the Russian Front, a well-authenticated rumour reached me that the War Office were annoyed with their tenor and were taking steps to remove the man who had despatched them from Russia.   These tales from the Russian Front were discouraging the soldiers who lined the trenches in Whitehall.   The question of whether they were reliable or not had nothing to do with the case.   The old maxim applied: The greater the truth, the worse the libel.   These reports were depressing and the greater their truth, the deeper the depression which they caused; so the man who was principally responsible for sending them must be taken away from a position where he was bound to see things that were disheartening, and where he evidently felt he was in duty bound to pass them on to his chiefs with a view of procuring amendment.   When I heard this on good authority I immediately went to the Prime Minister and Lord Grey, and asked them to intervene.   There was far too much repression of the real facts on all fronts, and I contended that to dismiss a man because he was letting us know in time what was the actual situation in Russia was an outrage and a peril.   The Prime Minister promptly interposed his authority and this distinguished officer remained at his post.   But the detailed reports of defeats on the Eastern Front and their cause which came into the hands of Cabinet Ministers in 1915 were much toned down when 1916 arrived.   Whether this happened at Petrograd or London I am not in a position to tell.

These resounding disasters laid the foundations of the Russian

Revolution. The true state of affairs might be kept from British Cabinet Ministers, and, with the help of the censor, from the British public, but they could not be concealed for any length of time from the people they most concerned—the people of Russia. When mutilated soldiers returned to their homes and carried the news to the Russian villages of defeat after defeat and of the fact that these defeats were attributable to lack of preparation on the part of their rulers, and told their neighbours of the ghastly casualties which had been inflicted upon their fellow-countrymen in consequence of this neglect, the effect was, first of all, one of consternation, and gradually of smouldering resentment. In one small village, out of 26 young men who had gone to the front, 24 had been destroyed in the murderous campaign. The Russian peasant moved slowly but the town workers expressed their indignation in alarming riots which were only quelled by the rifles of the police. From the Moscow rioters came the cry: "Beasts! Beasts! You have no ammunition to fight the Germans, but you have plenty to shoot down Russians."

Inside the Army the deficiencies in equipment naturally created a sense of growing dissatisfaction and distrust. At first it was directed against the Allies: later on it turned against the Czar and his advisers, and then both Czardom and the Alliance fell together into the same pit of righteous wrath. Here is a report from the Russian Front which came into my hands just as I entered upon my duties as Minister of Munitions:—

"August 29, 1915.

Officers cannot understand why England, with her highly developed industries, is unable to help Russia with munitions. They come to me and ask why we do not send out shell and rifles. When I tried to explain that we have not sufficient for our own requirements, they simply do not believe, and go on to argue that it is in our own interest to help, for they will do the fighting if we will only give them the wherewithal to do it."

CHAPTER XIV

WHY WERE THE RUSSIAN ARMIES ILL EQUIPPED?

THE bitter rebuke of those bewildered Russian officers whose men had been slaughtered for lack of proper munitions is true in substance and in fact, and history will return a true bill against the military directors of France and Britain for their selfish obtuseness in abandoning their Russian comrades in arms to hopeless carnage, when they might so easily have saved them and in so doing have rendered the most effective help to their own countries. They never could be taught to appreciate the fact that a great victory over the Germans in Poland would be a greater service to France and Belgium than a slight advance into the German lines in Champagne, or even than the capture of a molehill in Flanders.

They could unquestionably have saved Russia had they taken the right action and taken it in time. For instance, had the manufacturing resources of our country been mobilised for the production of munitions of war as soon as we decided to fight in August, 1914, and had the military chiefs foreseen in time (as they ought to have realised as soon as the Germans dug themselves into the soil of France after the Marne) that the War would resolve itself into an attack and defence of formidable earthworks, impenetrable except by overwhelming artillery, then the same systematic methods for increasing the output of rifles, machine-guns and guns of heavier calibre with abundant ammunition as were inaugurated by the Ministry of Munitions in 1915, might just as easily have been taken in August or September, 1914—in fact, more easily, for all the pivotal skilled men would have been kept at home. The result of prompt action on an adequate scale would have been that by the end of the year we could have increased our output of the lighter type of shell by hundreds of thousands, and by the summer of 1915 we should have had at our disposal a fine equipment of guns of every calibre—light, medium and heavy, with a full complement of shells. We could have added hundreds of thousands to our stocks of rifles, and what is quite as important, we should have had thousands of machine-guns, which owing to the delays, were not available until late in 1916. In 1915, this great equipment would have exceeded the needs of our armies for defence in the field at that time. The new recruits were not ready to take part in the fighting until September, 1915, and those who were then placed in the battle line were barely one-tenth of the total recruitment up to that date. That fact would have enabled us, without impinging on our own requirements, to double the Russian equipment of medium and heavy guns, and to more than treble their meagre supply of shells. Had we postponed efforts to break through in the west until we were quite ready, the Russian Armies could have been supplied with an equipment which would have enabled them to break up the Austrians, whilst repelling the Germans. We could have furnished them with sufficient rifles for their fighting men, and with hundreds of machine-guns to assist them in defending their fortified posts. Had the French contributed even a moderate quota out of their more considerable supplies of guns and ammunition, the Russian Armies instead of being a mere target for Krupp's great guns, would have become a redoubtable weapon for attack and defence. That would have compelled the Germans to weaken their forces on the Western Front in men and mechanism and thus make their defensive line in France and Flanders more vulnerable.

The way the Allied War direction failed to utilise the gigantic resources of Russia in men is the best proof of the lack of vision and of ordinary business intelligence which nearly lost the War and succeeded in prolonging it for years with increasing havoc, ruin and ghastliness.

Russia had such reserves of vigorous and sturdy youth that four and a half years of devastating war, followed by many more years of ravaging disease and the wholesale massacre of revolution and counter-revolution, seem to have made no appreciable impression upon their inexhaustible numbers. By the end of 1916 over 13,000,000 had been called up, and it was estimated then that there were still left several millions of fit men of military age never yet summoned to the colours. As to the 13,000,000 that joined the army, the first contingent of these millions were highly trained and well officered. Most of the number who were waiting their turn at the gates of the slaughter house had received quite as thorough a training for military service as that which either Britain, France, or America could afford to give to their recruits the last year or two of the War. As one Russian general was reported to have said when the Duma complained of the horrible casualties: " Don't worry yourself. Thank God, of men at all events we have enough." In courage and endurance they had no superior on either side on any battlefield. But their equipment in guns, rifles, machine-guns, ammunition, and transport was the poorest in the field (except later on, when our Salonika Army was deliberately kept on quarter rations of shot and shell), and for that reason they were beaten in action by troops inferior in numbers and sometimes in quality, and slaughtered by the million without the means of defence or retaliation. Their country was a half-primitive peasant land, unskilled in industrial arts and therefore unable to provide her gallant young defenders with adequate weapons. In spite of the infinite natural resources of the country, it had none of the developed or accumulated wealth which commanded the credit that would have enabled it to purchase essential equipment or supplies in the only available neutral market in the world that could furnish it with its needs—the United States of America. When that credit was partially forthcoming it was frittered away by corrupt incompetence. On the other hand France with a population less than a third that of Russia soon came to the end of her man-power, and for filling up the gaps made by war in her armies had to depend upon successive combings from her workshops and farms, upon the patch-ups turned out from the hospitals, and upon the young boys who became of military age during the years of the War. She supplemented these by coloured men from French Colonies in Africa and Asia. Any and every material for soldiering she could lay her hands on was thrown into the fiery furnace. Her divisions at the commencement of the War each numbered 20,000 men. By 1918 many of them had been reduced to less than half this strength, and even at that were kept up with difficulty. But France has some of the finest arsenals in the world for the production of weapons, especially for land warfare, and her engineers in other departments were highly skilled craftsmen. Her resources for turning out every machine and device for waging a mechanical war were capable of an expansion which seemed to be limited only by the demand. France was also a country rich in wealth accumulated by generations of toil and frugality. Her credit thus stood high in the world.

As for Great Britain, when the War broke out she had millions of young men of military age, but not four per cent. of them had received any military training. As soon as war was proclaimed hundred thousand after hundred thousand flocked to the colours. But only gradually were they absorbed, drilled and fashioned into an army. It was the end of the second year of the War before a million of them could be placed in the battle line. By that time France had lost over 2,000,000 and the Russian casualties were 5,000,000. We did not possess the officers, the training sergeants, and all that constitutes a *cadre* capable without loss of valuable time of making out of the best raw material soldiers fit to encounter the finest army in the world. But we were the greatest manufacturing country in Europe. There are no finer craftsmen in the world than those employed in our metal trades of all kinds. Their resourcefulness and adaptability were amply demonstrated as soon as they were put to the test. We were also the richest nation in Europe. Britain was the greatest creditor nation in the world. She had lent £4,000,000,000 to the nations of the earth and in the main the security was good. So British credit in America was good enough to guarantee any order for equipment which that country had any reasonable hope of executing.

Britain and France jointly arranged a substantial credit for Russia in America, but when I entered the Ministry of Munitions I found that the more powerful financial countries had managed to hustle and trample down Russia's best chances of utilising her foreign credits. M. Albert Thomas and I did our best to secure a fair distribution and co-ordination of the Allied orders in America. It was then almost too late.

Had Britain explored her unsuspected resources and then organised them for war as soon as she risked her own greatness and the lives of her own children in the demoniac venture she could, in the late summer of 1915, have equipped 2,000,000 Russians with almost as powerful an armoury of machines and missiles as that with which she sent 1,500,000 Britons into action in the summer and autumn of 1916. With some help from France, which her armies could, as I shall point out later on, easily spare and spare to their own advantage, and with the further aid of the American factories which our credit could purchase, Russia would easily, in the campaign of 1915, have held Germany in check and overthrown the inferior armies of Austria. Instead of which what happened? I have endeavoured to summarise the pitiful story of the disaster that befell a great country and the mutilation and death that came to millions of her brave sons through the incompetency of her rulers and the blind and selfish folly of her friends.

The Russian failure to make the best of the resources at their command, natural and acquired, was not due to any lack of mental quality in the race. They are an exceptionally gifted nation. But they have the leisurely and casual habits of a peasant people. With them time does not count and organisation has no meaning. They wait for the seasons, and for months of the year there is nothing they can do to help fruition but keep warm until the sun comes round to call them to their labours. When their first spell of toil is over they have another period of loitering about, doing little until the fructifying rays have completed their task. The industrialism of the west, which demands incessant, well-directed, wasteless toil, has never entered the lives or fashioned the habits of 90 per cent. of the Russian people. One or two illustrations of the way this ingrained and hereditary tendency of mind affected all their work came to my notice during the War. A Russian officer whom I met at a Conference during the War told me that the real Russian was essentially an unpractical dreamer, and he challenged me to name one who had ever displayed any aptitude for business in trade, finance or politics. I named several. He annotated each name by saying: " He is not a Russian, he is a German," or again, " He is an Armenian." " He is a Georgian." " He is a Scandinavian." " He is a Jew." Then I said: " What about yourself?" He replied: "I am a Greek." That is much too wholesale an indictment of a race that numbers well over a hundred millions and has accomplished great things. But my experience of doing business with them taught me that there was an unwelcome ingredient of truth in this cynicism.

Here is a fair illustration of their strange combination of genius and ineptitude. Their chemists were men of exceptional knowledge, ingenuity and imagination. Early in 1915 the Russian munitionment encountered the same class of difficulty as arrested our activities at one point. There was an inadequate supply of the kind of explosive which had hitherto been used for the purpose of filling their cartridges and shells, and it was essential that another source of supply should be discovered without loss of time. In their case as in ours the matter was referred to chemists for investigation. After weeks spent by these scientists apparently without any practical issue, inquiry was made at the laboratory to ascertain what progress had been made with the solution of the difficulty. It was discovered that the chemists had forgotten all about the urgent task which they had been specifically invited to solve. They had in the course of their experiments got on the track of a new chemical discovery which was infinitely more important to them than the explosive ingredients of a shell, and they were pursuing this trail with an eagerness and an enthusiasm which made them quite oblivious of the fact that their country was engaged in a life and death struggle with a foreign foe, and that they had been called upon to use their scientific skill to save it from an impending catastrophe. Here is another illustration of the same kind of practical defect in the Russian temperament. When the Germans let loose their first gas attack in Russia there were at first the same crude improvisations to protect the troops as we were forced to attempt. These proving ineffective, British and French aid was invoked. We were asked to send immediately a supply of the masks which had been invented for the protection of the Allied troops in the west from these chemical horrors. We instantly sent to Petrograd hundreds of thousands of our latest pattern. Before they were forwarded to the front they were submitted to a preliminary examination by a Russian chemist, who had no hesitation in coming to the conclusion that they were by no means perfect. The consignment was, therefore, detained at Petrograd, whilst Russian professors were devoting their time to devising something better. The perfect mask was never invented. The English masks were ultimately transmitted to their destination, but meanwhile thousands of gallant Russian soldiers had been choked by the agonising fumes.

Had we not known something of the inefficiency of Russia under its autocracy we might have pointed to the great arsenals of Perm and Petrograd and many another finely equipped workshop planted here and there in their vast country. For our neglect we could have put in the plea that we honestly thought Russia was quite able to furnish the needs of her own armies without much outside aid. M. Albert

Thomas told me on his return from a visit to Russia in 1916 that he was filled with envy when he went through the Putiloff works near Petrograd. They were equipped with the most modern machinery. In that respect they surpassed the finest of the French arsenals. But the management was incompetent, indolent and muddled. The incompetence of Russian management, however, was not a new discovery, and it needed no special journey to reveal it to western eyes. At any rate, it was known by 1915, and Britain and France in co-operation ought to have averted its calamitous results to the Allied cause by supplying the equipment which Russian management had failed to provide. When the Teutonic hurricane burst on the doomed armies of the Muscovites in May, 1915, their fine arsenals had succeeded in turning out the first four heavy guns manufactured there since the War began. But not a gun above the calibre of three inches reached Russia from abroad in 1914, and in 1915 Russia had to face the calamities of that year without any adequate help in heavy artillery and ammunition, for lack of which her valiant army was perishing.

CHAPTER XV

WHAT WOULD HAVE HAPPENED HAD THE ALLIES POOLED THEIR RESOURCES

WHILST the Russian armies were being shattered and pounded by the overwhelming artillery of Germany, and were unable to put up any defence owing to the lack of rifles and ammunition, the French were hoarding their shells as if they were golden francs, and were pointing with pride to the enormous accumulation of reserve dumps behind the lines. I recollect a munition conference in Paris where French generals flourished their statistics of accumulated millions with all the pride of possession and of achievement. What about Britain? When Britain began to manufacture in earnest, and turned out her hundreds of guns, great and small, and her hundreds of thousands of shells of all calibres, the British generals treated the production as if we were preparing to enter for some great race or contest where it was essential that the British equipment should be equal to and if achievable better than that which had been provided for any competitor in the field. The military leaders in both these countries never seemed to have grasped what ought to have been their dominant thought—that they were engaged with Russia in a common enterprise where it was vital to the attainment of a common end that they should pool their resources, and each of them be put in the best position to contribute his share to the speedy accomplishment of that aim. The team spirit was conspicuously absent during the first years of the War. Each player was thinking too much of his own scoring and too little of victory for his side. The recognition by the French generals of the towering fact that Russia had an overwhelming superiority in men never had any effective practical outcome, except a constantly expressed demand that Russia should send a large contingent of these men to France to aid the French Army in its defence of French territory, and to save French manhood from an undue share of the sacrifice which such defence involved. Quantities of guns, rifles and ammunition were sent from Britain and France to Russia before her final collapse, but they were dispatched reluctantly; they were quite inadequate to the need, and when they reached the hard-pressed armies of Russia, they came too late to avert the final collapse.

The answer of the French and British generals to every suggestion for the remunitionment of Russia was that they had nothing to spare in 1914, 1915 or 1916, and that when they gave anything away to Russia it was out of their own dire need. That was a complete answer if fatuous and wasteful efforts to crash through the formidable German entrenchments were the best strategy for either of those years. Allied Generalship on the Western Front never gave any weight to the fact that up to the third quarter of 1916, the Germans had a definite superiority in heavy guns in the west as well as the east. I am not sure that they even realised it. They could see their own guns; they could not visualise those of the enemy. And yet their own Intelligence Officers supplied them with abundant evidence of the Allied inferiority in artillery. In 1916 I was shown a French memorandum which gave the comparative strength of the German and French artillery in the greatest battle of the War—the battle of Verdun—three months after it had commenced, when both sides had brought up every gun they could spare in the west.

The following is a translation of this memorandum, in which I have, for the convenience of the reader, rendered the French measurements of calibres into their equivalents in inches: —

SUB-SECRETARIAT OF STATE   9th July, 1916
  for Artillery and Munitions

    CABINET

  Technical Service

COMPARATIVE TABLE OF FRENCH AND GERMAN ARTILLERY IN LINE ON THE VERDUN FRONT

Subdivisions.			On the German side on 26th May, 1916.		On the French side. Average between 21st February and 20th May, 1916.	
			%	Description of calibres.	%	Description of calibres.
Very heavy	..	..	2	16½ in., 15 in., 12 in.	1	A.L.G.P. (very powerful heavy guns*)
Heavy	..	..	35	8.3 in., 5.9 in.	13	6.1 in., 8.7 in., 10.6 in.
Medium	..	..	43	4.1 in.	19	3¾ in., 4.1 in., 4.7 in.
Light	..	..	20	3 in.	67	2.95 in., 3.1 in., 3¼ in.
TOTAL OF PIECES IN THE LINE				2,000		1,600

* 5½ in., 7½ in., 7.9 in., 9½ in., 11 in., 12 in., 14.6 in.

This table shows that the Germans not only possessed a total numerical superiority of guns on the Verdun Front, but that they had approximately 740 heavy and very heavy guns against the French 224—or more than three times their equipment of these powerful weapons. They had more guns and heavier guns than the French in the west, although they were engaged in massing all the artillery they could spare for their campaign in the east against Russia.

The western generals will point to these figures as a proof that they could not send a single gun or shell away from their front to help at any other. What it does demonstrate is the folly of attempting with inferior artillery to attack a highly trained army skilfully entrenched and armed with superior weapons. Anyone who has seen the German entrenchments will realise how formidable an enterprise it was to capture them. The fortresses of Beaumont Hamel, Posières and Thiepval will serve as specimens. They were excavated deep down under the surface. These dug-out fortresses were strengthened by iron girders and concrete so that no shell could hope to penetrate their well-equipped depths. To shell them was like bombarding the Catacombs. On the other hand, the German task in attacking the French lines was equally hopeless. The Allies had considerable numerical superiority on the Western Front. They also could entrench, and they had a sufficient equipment of guns, machine-guns, rifles and grenades to repel every advance by German troops. That was the lesson of Verdun.

On the Russian Front there was not the same need for heavy artillery as on the west. Neither Austrians nor Germans could dig such a tremendous line of triplex entrenchments along so vast a front. It was more of a war of movement. There the *soixante-quinze* would have come by its own, provided there were plenty of ammunition. The millions blazed away in stubborn and stupid offensives in the west would have served. Had there been enough heavy artillery to effect a break in the Austrian lines the lighter and more mobile guns would have done the rest. And a few hundred machine-guns with adequate ammunition would have completely held up the German advance.

To anyone who had the advantage of perusing the despatches from our able military representative on the Eastern Front, or any reliable history of the 1915 campaign, it must be evident that the overwhelming defeats sustained by the Russian Armies were not due to any inferiority in numbers (the Russians outnumbered the Germans along the whole line) or to any lack of courage, endurance or discipline on the part of Russian soldiers whose undaunted valour under dismaying conditions must always remain a marvel. Neither were these disasters attributable to lack of skill on the part of the Russian generals in the field. By common consent their conduct of the retreat was at least competent. The enveloping tactics of the German marshals were thwarted at every turn and the Russian Armies escaped without any wholesale loss of equipment. This was due to a combination of skilful generalship on the part of the leaders and fine fighting qualities in the men they led. It is easy to lead into action a well-equipped army hopeful of victory. It is not so easy to lead broken and discouraged troops out of a succession of fields where they have been stricken and stricken again by a foe whom they know to be much better equipped than they are. Let us give the Grand Duke Nicholas and his generals the credit of having achieved this feat. But why was so gallant an army, so competently led, driven like a herd of cattle across the plains and marshes of Poland? The answer is to be found in the extracts I have given from the reports of impartial British officers, who witnessed this agony of brave men who had been deprived by official stupidity of the means of defending themselves and the country for which they were prepared to die. They were not vanquished by better troops—they never had a chance of measuring their quality as fighting-men with the soldiers who were arrayed against them. They saw millions of German shells hurtling through the air in their direction and bursting into destructive fury amongst them, they heard the deadly rattle of the machine-guns carried forward by the advancing Germans, but they rarely came up against the foe that pelted them at a safe distance with bullet and shell. Their defences were shattered by the monster guns of Germany. The survivors of this bombardment were left among the debris without a shelter to protect them from such a rain of fire and brimstone as has not fallen on mankind since the days of Gomorrah. Had they advanced machine-guns would have mowed them down. Orderly retreat was their only chance of saving themselves and their country. Even in retreat hundreds of thousands were destroyed in the open by the terrible blizzard of shrapnel and high explosive.

Had the Russian artillery been doubled, especially in the medium and heavy calibres; had there been an abundant supply of shell for light as well as heavy; had the Russian posts been defended by an adequate quota of machine-guns, the German troops would have encountered the same resistance on the Eastern Front as they experienced whenever they attacked in the west, and they could not have afforded the cumulative losses inflicted upon them in a series of attacks. On the Austrian Front, where the quality of the enemy troops was distinctly inferior for a variety of reasons which I have already given—reasons which do not in the least reflect on Austrian valour—the impetuous onslaught of the Russians following a sufficient preliminary attack would not only have successfully broken the Austrian lines, but that success could have been exploited and pushed perhaps to the gates of Vienna. The Austrian Armies were a different proposition from the German. The German Armies were homogeneous and bore an equal intensity of hatred against Slav and Gaul. In a struggle between Teuton and Slav three-fifths of the Austrian troops had a deeper detestation of their Teutonic comrades than of their Slavonic foes. The Russians partly for that reason won comparatively easy victories against the Austrians, and they were only unable to take advantage of the victories owing to lack of ammunition. A well-equipped Russian army could have crossed the Carpathians, penetrated through the Hungarian and Austrian plains up to their Slavonic kinsmen in Croatia or Czecho-Slovakia and then imperilled the capital of the Empire. Roumania would, under those conditions, have felt safe in throwing her 500,000 on the Austrian flank, and

Bulgaria would have known it was better to fight on the Allied side or to keep out of it altogether.

It may be said that the Germans would then have come to the rescue of their chief ally. Of course they would. They would have been bound to do so for their own preservation. But they could not have afforded Austria effective assistance without dangerously weakening their own Western Front. They could not have withdrawn any part of their troops from the Polish Front, as that would have placed in jeopardy the roads that led to the heart of Prussia. The battles of Loos, Artois and Champagne, if they had been fought at all, would have been fought under conditions twice as favourable to the French and British Armies as those which turned them into a futile massacre of myriads of brave young men. These gallant fellows were sacrificed on the altar of misguided and antiquated theories which had already been discredited by repeated exposure. The sacrifice was in vain. It did not liberate France and it failed to save Russia. The excuse they put forward, after their failure, for fighting these profligate battles, was that hard-pressed Russia demanded these attacks in order to prevent the Germans from increasing their forces on the Eastern Front. The Germans never arrested their victorious march for a single hour, because hundreds of miles to the west the French and British generals were piling up shell dumps behind the front and making other elaborate preparations to send their infantry to be shot down by German machine-guns in fruitless efforts to break through impregnable German defences. Each time French and British generals were sure of victory. Previous experience ought to have taught them to know better. The best help we could have given Russia would have been to send her artillery a portion of the ammunition we wasted in battles that achieved nothing but the building up still higher of the ghastly pyramid of casualties amongst our own troops.

To sum up: Had we sent to Russia half the shells subsequently wasted in these ill-conceived battles and one-fifth of the guns that fired them, not only would the Russian defeat have been averted, but the Germans would have sustained a repulse by the side of which the capture of a few blood-stained kilometres in France would have seemed a mockery. What more? Austria would have been crumpled up. Only prompt transference to the Austrian Front of several divisions of German infantry and several batteries of German guns from France could have saved the Dual Monarchy from utter collapse. Had Russia been victorious, then Bulgaria would have entered the War on the Allied side. A Balkan Federation—including Serbia, Roumania and Greece, and perhaps Bulgaria—on the south, and an Italian army on the west, with a victorious Russia on the east marching against a routed and divided Austria, might have ended the War in 1915. That may be a sanguine estimate of possibilities. The certainty is that if the Russian equipment had been strengthened Austria would, by the end of the 1915 campaign, have been tottering towards her fall. Germany would have been hard put to it to keep her troublesome ally from collapsing. By the spring of 1916 Britain, Russia, Italy and the Balkan Confederation, all now fully equipped (certainly if we had started manufacturing in time), could have directed a convergent attack on Austria which would have completed her disintegration. An isolated and weakened Germany would then have had to face the full strength of France and Britain and would gladly have made the peace of a foe outmanœuvred and overwhelmed.

Instead of this we left Russia to her fate and we thereby precipitated the Balkan tragedy, which had such an influence on the prolongation of the War.

Surveying the position twelve months after we had entered into the War, I felt that things were going badly for the Allies in the east and in the west. All our attacks in France had turned out to be costly failures, and I had a conviction, shared to a certain extent by Lord Kitchener, that the one in which we were then engaged would turn out to be a sanguinary defeat for the Allied cause. The armies of our greatest Ally were in a position where they hailed a mere escape from complete destruction as a triumph of strategy. The bumper harvest of a conquered Poland was pouring into the depleted granaries of Germany (whose harvest had failed), thus neutralising our blockade. In the East we were making no progress in Mesopotamia, and we were not only held up in Egypt but we lived in daily dread of an invasion of the Delta by the Turkish forces across the Canal. In Gallipoli we had suffered defeat after defeat and there were rumours, which proved to be only too true, that Serbia was soon to be trampled down under the ruthless heel of the advancing legions of the Teuton. My ten weeks at the Ministry of Munitions had driven home to my consciousness the painful truth that most of this could have been avoided, had we organised our resources in time and distributed them wisely. This prompted me to write the following statement in September, 1915, as a preface to a collection of my War appeals published by Messrs. Hodder and Stoughton. I was anxious to rouse public opinion from a complacency created by official reports concocted out of spurious victories. I felt it was the only way to enforce a change. Reading it now, 17 years after it was written, when one is able to peruse the story of 1914-15 and to ruminate upon it in the quiet of one's study, I cannot find any essential inaccuracy or exaggeration in the survey which I then gave of the Allied position.

" After twelve months of war my conviction is stronger than ever that this country could not have kept out of it without imperilling its security and impairing its honour. We could not have looked on cynically with folded arms whilst the country we had given our word to protect was being ravaged and trodden by one of our co-trustees. If British women and children were being brutally destroyed on the high seas by German submarines this nation would have insisted on calling the infanticide Empire to a stern reckoning. Everything that has happened since the declaration of war has demonstrated clearly that a military system so regardless of good faith, of honourable obligations, and of the elementary impulses of humanity, constituted a menace to civilisation of the most sinister character; and despite the cost of suppressing it, the well-being of humanity demands that such a system should be challenged and destroyed. The fact that events have also shown that the might of this military clique has exceeded the gloomiest prognostications provides an additional argument for its destruction. The greater the might the darker the menace.

Nor have the untoward incidents of the War weakened my faith in ultimate victory—always provided that the allied nations put forth the whole of their strength ere it is too late. Anything less must lead to defeat. The Allied countries have an overwhelming preponderance in the raw material that goes to the making and equipment of armies, whether in men, money, or accessible metals and machinery. But this material has to be mobilised and utilised. It would be idle to pretend that the first twelve months of the War have seen this task accomplished satisfactorily. Had the Allies realised in time the full strength of their redoubtable and resourceful foes—nay, what is more, had they realised their own strength and resources, and taken prompt action to organise them, to-day we should have witnessed the triumphant spectacle of their guns pouring out a stream of shot and shell which would have deluged the German trenches with fire and scorched the German legions back across their own frontiers.

What is the actual position? It is thoroughly well known to the Germans, and anyone in any land, belligerent or neutral, who reads intelligently the military news must by now have a comprehension of it. With the resources of Great Britain, France, Russia —yea, of the whole industrial world—at the disposal of the Allies, it is obvious that the Central Powers have still an overwhelming superiority in all the material and equipment of war. The result of this deplorable fact is exactly what might have been foreseen. The iron heel of Germany has sunk deeper than ever into French and Belgian soil. Poland is entirely German. Lithuania is rapidly following. Russian fortresses, deemed impregnable, are falling like sand castles before the resistless tide of Teutonic invasion. When will that tide recede? When will it be stemmed? As soon as the Allies are supplied with abundance of war material.

That is why I am recalling these unpleasant facts, because I wish to stir my countrymen to put forth their strength to amend the situation. To dwell on such events is the most disagreeable task which can fall to the lot of a public man. For all that, the public man who either shirks these facts himself, or does not do his best to force others to face them until they are redressed, is guilty of high treason to the State which he has sworn to serve.

There has been a great awakening in all the Allied countries, and prodigious efforts are being put forth to equip the armies in the field. I know what we are doing, our exertions are undoubtedly immense. But can we do more, either in men or material? Nothing but our best and utmost can pull us through. Are we now straining every nerve to make up for lost time? Are we getting all the men we shall want to put into the fighting line next year to enable us even to hold our own? Does every man who can help, whether by fighting or by providing material, understand clearly that ruin awaits remissness? How many people in this country fully apprehend the full significance of the Russian retreat? For over twelve months Russia has, in spite of deficiencies in equipment, absorbed the energies of half the German and four-fifths of the Austrian forces. Is it realised that Russia has for the time being made her contribution—and what an heroic contribution it is!— to the struggle for European freedom, and that we cannot for many months to come expect the same active help from the Russian Armies that we have hitherto received? Who is to take the Russian place in the fight while those armies are re-equipping? Who is to bear the weight which has hitherto fallen on Russian shoulders? France cannot be expected to sustain much heavier burdens than those which she now bears with a quiet courage that has astonished and moved the world. Italy is putting her strength into the fight. What could she do more? There is only Britain left. Is Britain prepared to fill up the great gap that will be created when Russia has retired to re-arm? Is she fully prepared to cope with all the possibilities of the next few months—in the west, without forgetting the east? Upon the answer which Government, employers, workmen, financiers, young men who can bear arms, women who can work in factories—in fact, the whole people of this great land— give to this question, will depend the liberties of Europe for many a generation.

A shrewd and sagacious observer told me the other day that in his judgment the course pursued by this country during the next three months would decide the fate of the War. If we are not allowed to equip our factories and workshops with adequate labour to supply our armies, because we must not transgress regulations applicable to normal conditions; if practices are maintained which restrict the output of essential war material; if the nation hesitates, when the need is clear, to take the necessary steps to call forth its manhood to defend honour and existence; if vital decisions are postponed until too late; if we neglect to make ready for all probable eventualities; if, in fact, we give ground for the accusation that we are slouching into disaster as if we were walking along the ordinary paths of peace without an enemy in sight; then I can see no hope; but if we sacrifice all we own, and all we like for our native land; if our preparations are characterised by grip, resolution, and a prompt readiness in every sphere, then victory is assured."

CHAPTER XVI

THE FUTILE ALLIED OFFENSIVES ON THE WESTERN FRONT

WHILST the Germans were engaged in these tremendous operations to rout and wreck the great armies of Russia, the military authorities in France, Britain and Italy could think of no more effective means of coming to their aid than to hurl great masses of their troops against impregnable positions in France, Flanders, and the Austrian Alps. No decision on the part of their enemies could have suited the Central Powers better than this course, pursued with an obstinate and senseless determination which sacrificed the flower of the Allied armies in vain efforts to break through defences bristling with cannon and machine-guns, and with two or three equally powerful positions to fall back upon in the event of the first being carried. The Allies at the same time pursued in listless and ineffective fashion, with inadequate troops, inefficiently equipped, and always timed to arrive too late, their efforts to capture Gallipoli. Had they spared in time one-fifth of the soldiers sacrificed in these futile attempts in France to reinforce the Dardanelles Expedition, Gallipoli could have been captured with comparative ease. We encountered defeat after defeat in that quarter, each defeat being a telling blow which resounded throughout the Balkans where Bulgaria and Roumania were watching the turn of events. As the collapse of Russia became more and more complete, as our failure to force the Dardanelles was becoming more and more evident, the fight of our friends in Bulgaria became fainter and feebler, the pro-German party in military circles at Sofia became more buoyant and insistent, the wily Bulgarian Monarch thought he saw more clearly on which side his bread was buttered, and the brave Serbian Army behind the Danube became more and more despondent. They saw now the approaching doom of their isolated country.

The infatuation of a break-through which haunted the western generals like a disease of the mind still prompted them to organise another and, as they thought, overwhelming attack on the German entrenchments. This was timed to take place in September, 1915. After the decision had been taken, a lingering doubt seems to have entered Lord Kitchener's mind as to the wisdom of such a proceeding. According to the " Official History of the War," published under the auspices of the War Office, the British Military Authorities, after the Boulogne Munitions Conference in June, seem to have undertaken for the first time a careful survey of the equipment of the armies on the Western Front—French, British and German—more especially in heavy guns and ammunition. They discovered what they ought to have ascertained and provided against in September, 1914—that the German proportion of heavy artillery was twice that of the Allies and that the German shell production per day was also double that of France and Britain together and that: —

> " Taking these several important factors into consideration, the British Military Authorities arrived at the conclusion that an offensive on the Western Front, if it was to have a reasonable chance of success, would have to be delivered on a continuous front of twenty-five miles, by a force of not less than thirty-six divisions, supported by 1,150 heavy guns and howitzers and the normal complement of field artillery. They maintained that this quantity of guns and the necessary ammunition could not be provided before the spring of 1916, and that until then it was preferable, whatever the general situation, to remain on the active defensive in the western theatre of war."

This sensible conclusion was not conveyed by the generals to their respective Governments in time to influence a decision. I have no recollection that Lord Kitchener ever communicated to the Cabinet or the War Council the resolution now revealed by the Official History.

It was not good for civilians to be told that events had proved them to be right and the military wrong. But Lord Kitchener did at last inform the Cabinet that he was opposed to the autumn offensive which General Joffre contemplated launching in September, and in which the latter was anxious that the British Army should participate by an attack on the German right. Sir John French was fully alive to the drawbacks and dangers of the proposed operation, and I believe that at first Sir Douglas Haig shared his opinion. These risks of the proposed operation were pointed out with great force by members of the Cabinet, including the Prime Minister. Nevertheless, the Cabinet as a whole (there were at least two exceptions) adopted Lord Kitchener's view that we had no option in the matter but to fall in with the plan to which the French Commander-in-Chief so stubbornly and stupidly adhered. In consequence of this weak decision the great autumn offensive was undertaken. The Allied armies were badly beaten with terrible casualties. Our new armies entered into action for the first time and fought with conspicuous valour, and tens of thousands of them fell in the futile carnage of the Loos offensive.

On the eve of this offensive Lord Kitchener was authorised to visit France in order to persuade General Joffre to postpone the attack, but his mission was a failure. He reported that "General Joffre was quite determined both on political and military grounds (the main element in the former being the situation in Russia) to take the offensive without delay and on a considerable scale. Sir John French agreed with the French Commander-in-Chief as to the urgency of the step from the military point of view." Lord Kitchener, though far from sanguine that any substantial military advantage would be achieved, was strongly of opinion that we could not without serious and perhaps fatal injury to the Alliance refuse the co-operation which Joffre expected.

Even after the failure of this last ill-judged offensive of the 1915 campaign had become quite evident to any sane observer, General Joffre persisted for weeks in attack after attack. When he became convinced that further efforts were fruitless except to add to the already appalling casualty list, he intimated to his Government that he had no intention of persevering with his plan that year. Accordingly he said he would be prepared to assist in carrying out the project which had been urged upon him by the ablest members of the French Government for sending a force to Salonika to help Serbia. Before General Joffre was convinced by lacerating facts that his offensive had failed, the losses in the Champagne attack were three times those in the Dardanelles. Millions of shells were also wasted—10,000,000 in all, including French and British. Half of the men who fell in these criminal attacks would either have stormed Gallipoli or, had they been sent to Salonika, would have enabled Serbia to throw the invading army into the Danube. One third of the shells would have averted the Russian retreat.

CHAPTER XVII

THE SERBIAN TRAGEDY

WHILST the billy-goat tactics of western generals in butting away the strength of their armies against unbreakable walls was proceeding in a succession of sickening thuds, what was happening to the Allies on the Eastern and South-Eastern Fronts? I have told the story of how the might of Russia was broken through lack of equipment. What about Serbia? Ominous warnings came from Sofia, Bucharest, Athens and Nish in the summer of 1915 that Austria was gathering a great force in the valleys that pointed towards the Danube. Later on we heard that German troops were arriving in great numbers. It was known that Bulgaria had practically decided to throw in her lot with the Central Powers and join them in the attack on her neighbour.

The sinister effect of the Russian disaster was soon felt in the changed attitude of Bulgaria. About the third week in August, 1915, when what was supposed to be the impregnable fortress of Kovno fell before the German guns and the Russian armies were still being driven daily league after league towards Petrograd, a message reached the British Foreign Office from its representative at Sofia warning us that " the capture of Kovno had made a deep impression on the governing and military circles at the Bulgarian capital and had given rise to anticipation of a crushing disaster to Russian arms." He further warned us " that the elements most favourable to us had, during the last few days, become so impressed with Germany's military strength that they would hesitate to take the course which would expose Bulgaria to a German attack." A few weeks later the crafty Ferdinand, who had been crouching behind a complacent Ministry until he found which belligerent alliance was the highest bidder and the likeliest winner, thought the time had come to throw in his lot openly with Germany and Austria. If the blow fell upon Serbia it was not for lack of timely information as to what fate was being prepared for her by the Central Powers. Late in September there percolated through the news that the Austrians were massing troops in the valleys that ran toward the Danube and that several German divisions had already arrived to reinforce them. There could be no doubt as to the intention and imminence of their movements.

The probability of a German-Austrian attack on Serbia was alluded to in the Press, and was even discussed in the House of Commons about the end of September, 1915. When the matter was raised in Parliament, Sir Edward Grey made a statement to the House in the following terms: —

" If, on the other hand, the Bulgarian mobilisation were to result in Bulgaria assuming an aggressive attitude on the side of our enemies, *we are prepared to give to our friends in the Balkans all the support in our power, in the manner that would be most welcome to them, in concert with our Allies, without reserve and without qualification. We are, of course, in consultation with our Allies on the situation, and I believe the view that I express is theirs also.*"

As Sir Edward Carson subsequently said, after the blow had fallen: —

" That was one of the most important declarations that could be made in this House. I believed it, when I was a party to it, to be the policy of His Majesty's Government, but I believed more. I believed that our military advisers never would have allowed us to make that declaration unless we had actual preparations and plans which were ready when the moment came to enable us to strike and assist our gallant little Ally in the field of battle."

The Grey declaration satisfied an anxious House of Commons. It was hailed with delight throughout Serbia as a promise that her powerful friends in the west would come to her rescue if any evil befell her, and, of course, come in time to save her. The Germans had a better understanding of the value of Allied pledges than either Parliament or the Serbian people. They never faltered or halted in their march. The German military leaders had come to the conclusion that there was nothing to apprehend from an attack which was being carefully engineered on the Western Front. In fact, they welcomed it. They knew their General Joffre, and they felt that whilst his mind was concentrated on his plans in Champagne he had none left for any other theatre of war. The Allied generals were preparing a smoke screen, not to conceal their own designs—those were visible from any aeroplane—but to hide from their own vision those of the Central Powers lest the spectacle should induce the Allied statesmen to divert their forces from the pursuit of the impracticable. The western offensive began on 25th September. In two days it was obvious to any intelligent observer that the French had failed in their main purpose of breaking through the German lines and that the British attack had equally failed at Loos. The

Germans knew it, and continued to pour division after division into the Danubian basin. General Joffre, however, persisted in hurling troops against German entrenchments only to discover after he had captured them what he knew before, that there was an equally formidable position a few hundred yards behind. Still he persevered week after week, making no perceptible indent in this succession of entrenchments. There was nothing new in this. Every soldier in France could have told him in advance what he had rediscovered with the loss of scores of thousands of precious lives. Sir William Robertson, in a memorandum he issued about that time, said: "We know perfectly well there is no insuperable difficulty in breaking through the first-line defence. It has been done several times in this theatre during the summer. It is the second and third lines which give the trouble." These lines were never reached, or at least were not retained. Whilst this was going on, the western generals, heedless of the pitiful appeals of the Serbian people watching the fall of the avalanche towards their home, continued to waste valuable time on a hopeless task in France. Once engaged on it, the French and British generals found it difficult to extricate their armies without further hard struggling. They threw all their reserves into the cruel German trap with its teeth of steel that pierced and crushed flesh and blood with a relentless grip.

On 7th October, the Germans and Austrians crossed the Danube at five different points. A telegram announcing that fact reached here the same day. As I shall point out later on, Lord Kitchener did not see that telegram until the following day, and when a War Council met to discuss the military position on the 8th he was not aware that the armies of the Central Powers had already invaded Serbia. When at last he heard of it and communicated the news to the Cabinet, it was decided that he should go over to France to confer with General Joffre on the new situation which had arisen in the east. They discussed the sending of French and British troops to help the hard-pressed Serbs. On 9th October, General Joffre submitted to Lord Kitchener a memorandum, which is summarised as follows: —

"The reasons for the intervention of the Allies in the Balkans are: —

The necessity to check German projects in the new theatre of operations which they have now commenced, and the moral obligation not to leave our Ally Serbia alone to bear the brunt of our common enemies.

The initiative of the operations in the Balkans belongs to our adversaries and they are capable of keeping a numerical superiority whatever we do. There can, therefore, be no question of our engaging in a general action which would offer no chances of success.

Our rôle should be to prevent the crushing of the Serbs, to ensure their communication with the sea, and eventually to secure a zone of retreat. Also we should thus bar the way to the Germans from access to Salonika.

He considers therefore : —

1.   That the mission of the troops should be to hold Salonika strongly as a base for the French, English and Serbian Armies.

2.   To cover and hold the railway line between Salonika and Uskub in order to ensure our communication with the Serbian Army and the supplies of that army.

3.   To cover the right of the Serbian Army, preventing any attempt of the enemy on Central Serbia.

To attain these objects a force of 150,000 men, which is more than the Bulgarians can put in the field on this side, appears sufficient.

In case events such as, for example, a new distribution of Greek and Roumanian forces, lead the Allies to take a different attitude, and to increase later the amount of their effort, General Joffre states that France, having a limited number of men at her disposal, cannot take part in such an effort, the responsibility for which would fall entirely on the British Government.

General Joffre strongly advocates that the Italian Government should be urged at first to send forces to Salonika and eventually to open the road to Serbia via Durazzo."

This document contains proposals so like those I had repeatedly pressed on the Cabinet that I feel entitled to call attention to the similarity. The only difference is one of date—a fatal divergence.

If the document had been penned three—even two—months earlier and acted upon immediately, the Balkans would not have fallen into German hands and Lord Kitchener's prediction of victory in 1917 would have been realised. It was now too late to avert disaster, and this was obvious to anyone who could see beyond the trenches in front of him. General Joffre was not gifted with such vision.

This report was discussed at a full meeting of what was still known as the Dardanelles Committee on 11th October. The military advice given to that Committee was that no troops should be sent to the Mediterranean, either to the Dardanelles or to Salonika, until the offensive in France had been brought to a conclusion. Both Sir Douglas Haig and General Joffre had stated that their object was " to gain further ground in order to consolidate what we had already won." In their judgment " our position was such that in certain sections we had either to go forward or to go back." Sir William Robertson thought that "to do this would entail a considerable amount of fighting generally in the neighbourhood of Loos." When asked whether, if the result of this contemplated action were favourable, it would lead to any modification of the strategic position, he admitted "it would not, unless General Joffre was also able to supply pressure and make progress in Champagne." We were given to understand that General Joffre had practically come to the conclusion already that the general offensive must be postponed for three months. The great offensive was an admitted failure. All the same, the French Commander-in-Chief declared he could not send any troops away from France until he knew definitely whether the Germans contemplated a counter offensive. Of that he could not be certain for another fortnight. That meant, according to Sir William Robertson, that no troops could be moved, either British or French, from the battle area for another two or three weeks. Whilst this discussion was taking place the Germans and Austrians were advancing in Serbian territory (they had already marched onward for four days) and the Bulgarians on that very day were hurling 300,000 men across the lines of communication between Serbia and Salonika. What strategy! What generals! What statesmen to tolerate either!

The military experts were pressed for information as to the date when they could be in a position to spare troops from France. There was a good deal of desultory and confusing talk on this point as to what ought to be the destination of these troops, assuming they could be spared. Some suggested that they should be dispatched to the Dardanelles to reinforce the army in Gallipoli, to enable it to make another attack on the Turkish positions in that Peninsula. The French were opposed to this plan unless at the same time an army was landed to occupy the Asiatic shore. They were strongly of opinion that the mere capture of Gallipoli, and the forcing of the Narrows would only entice the Allied fleets into a trap, which would be closed as soon as they entered the Marmora. The Allied fleets would there have no means of replenishing their fuel supplies, and would soon be reduced to impotence. They ought to have thought of that before agreeing to the Gallipoli Expedition. Others, notably Mr. Bonar Law and Sir Edward Carson, were for landing the troops at Salonika and pushing along immediately to the help of Serbia. The Chief of the Staff objected that the Salonika railway was not equipped with the necessary means of transport to enable the Allies to carry any considerable body of troops even as far as Uskub. That revealed the fact that although the War Committee had decided in January last to take immediate steps to double the line where feasible, to construct sidings, and to increase the rolling stock, nothing had been done to carry out that order. I supported the view urged so strongly by Mr. Bonar Law and Sir Edward Carson. I supplemented this with a suggestion that we should immediately communicate with the Greeks and the Roumanians, pledging the Allies to send 250,000 troops without delay to Salonika, if they on their part were prepared to join in a combined effort to rescue Serbia. I pointed out that the Roumanians could put 400,000 men in the field, and the Greeks at least 200,000, which with our 250,000 would make an aggregate of 850,000; that with such a force Bulgaria could be neutralised, or if she intervened could be crushed; and that at any rate it would enable the Serbians to hold their own against the attack which was being made upon them. Lord Curzon and others thought it was too late to send any support, and that we had better utilise our troops as reinforcements for the Gallipoli expeditionary force with a view to making a fresh attack on the Turks. Others suggested a landing at Alexandretta, and others that we should dispatch our forces to Egypt without prejudice to their ultimate destination or action, and for this purpose neither Alexandretta nor Salonika, nor the Adriatic side of the Straits would be ruled out. Meanwhile some distinguished general officer should be sent out to the Mediterranean to survey the situation, report upon it, and advise as to the best course to be adopted.

A " too-late " council is necessarily desperate and distracted. The conclusions of this distracted council were an embodiment of its despair. They were as follows: —

" 1. Immediate instructions to be given for the dispatch, *so soon as the present operations are over*, of an adequate substantial force from France to Egypt without prejudice to its ultimate destination, transport for which is to be prepared by the Admiralty.

2. A specially selected general to proceed without delay to the Near East and to consider and report as to which particular sphere, and with what particular objective, we should direct our attention.

3. The General Staff, War Office, to state in what way their views given in their Appreciation of the 9th October would be modified if both Greece and Roumania were to act with the Allies."

These conclusions meant the practical abandonment of Serbia to her doom. The combined armies of Germany, Austria and Bulgaria had no difficulty in sweeping the depleted, outnumbered and ill-equipped army of Serbia out of the way, capturing the Balkans and clearing the road to Constantinople.

In the meantime it was decided to send General Monro to the Mediterranean. On 31st October he recommended the evacuation of the Gallipoli Peninsula. At the first meeting of the new War Committee on 3rd November (to which I shall refer later on) it was decided to send Lord Kitchener to view the situation for himself. Their decision was not dictated solely by military considerations. Lord Kitchener's influence in the Cabinet was not what it had been in the first year of the War. It had waned very rapidly in recent months. In 1914 he was practically military dictator and his decisions upon any questions affecting the War were final. The Members of the Cabinet were frankly intimidated by his presence because of his repute and his enormous influence amongst all classes of the people outside. A word from him was decisive and no one dared to challenge it at a Cabinet meeting. I think I may say I was the first to do so on munitions and on subsidiary questions like the Welsh Division and the appointment of Nonconformist chaplains. But my colleagues regarded my intervention on these questions with a certain amount of uneasiness approaching dismay. Gradually one mistake after another committed by the military, for which he was held responsible as the Supreme War Lord, lowered his prestige and weakened his influence; and there was a very general feeling that his usefulness had been exhausted. This feeling subsequently found practical expression in the appointment of Sir William Robertson, as Chief of the Imperial General Staff, with exceptional powers all carved out of Lord Kitchener's authority. On this occasion there was a mute hope that once Lord Kitchener went to the Mediterranean, and especially if he returned to Egypt, the sphere of his greatest triumphs, he might find it worth while to remain there to direct the great forces accumulated in the western Mediterranean, in Egypt, Gallipoli, and either Salonika or Alexandretta. When the appointment was made, a member of the Cabinet pushed a note to me on which was written: *" Malbrouck s'en va t'en guerre.* But will he return?"

I was much disturbed about the abandonment of Serbia and the gross neglect to take the most obvious precautions to avert it. On 12th October I circulated the following memorandum on the position to my colleagues: —

" The helplessness of four great Powers to save from destruction one little country after another that relied on their protection is one of the most pitiable spectacles of this War.

The appreciation of the existing situation in the Balkans circulated by the General Staff is a distressing document! It might all be compressed into two words: Too late! It might easily have been foreseen that a march through Serbia into Bulgaria would be one of the most obvious and profitable of moves for the German General Staff to contemplate, by connecting up their railway system with Turkey: —

1. They could aim a most direct and effective blow—in fact,

the only direct and effective blow they could possibly aim—at the British Empire.

2. They could have at their disposal a reserve of two or three millions of men of the best fighting quality added to their own reserves, and thus more than redress in their favour the balance in the war of attrition which is now proceeding.

3. They could have a fair chance of destroying a great British force which is holding on by tooth and claw to a rim of the Gallipoli Peninsula.

4. They could strike a ringing blow at our prestige in the East.

5. They could render perfectly nugatory our-sea-power in so far as South-Eastern Europe and a large part of Asia are concerned.

6. By the process of equipping the Turks and ultimately perhaps the Persians and Afghans, they could force us in 1916 to divert large masses of troops from the main theatre of operations in France to defend our own possessions in Egypt and in the Far East.

7. They could, by the same means, divert a large number of Russians to defend their frontiers in the Caucasus and their interests in Persia.

8. All this they could achieve by overcoming the resistance of an ill-equipped army of 300,000 Serbians, a considerable portion of these having their attention engaged by the prospect of a hostile Bulgarian army attacking them from behind. Not a very formidable proposition for the military power that has rolled up the great armies of Russia, whilst, at the same time, holding in check the combined forces of France and Britain! It was therefore obvious even to the civilian mind that it was too tempting a project for the Germans not to seize upon.

There were two reasons why it was clear that they could not postpone putting this project into execution: —

1. The Turkish ammunition was gradually being exhausted, and Turkey could not have sustained a series of attacks such as those we had been making on the Gallipoli Peninsula much longer without having her store of ammunition replenished.

2. The winter was coming on, when Serbian roads and passes would be very difficult to negotiate.

3. This year the Germans have an undoubted superiority over the Allies in: —

(a) Material of war;
(b) Equipped and trained men.

Next year the position will be equalised in both respects. It would not be like the Germans if they did not take full advantage of their temporary superiority.

It is, of course, easy to be wise after the event, but these are considerations which have been repeatedly urged during the past few months at the War Council and Cabinet meetings. I have often braved my colleagues by the frequency with which I have called attention to them. I circulated two papers calling attention to the possibilities in the Near East as far back as December and February last. It perplexes the mere civilian to find any explanation for the neglect of the military authorities to provide against so disastrous a blow to our Empire, when it was so clear to any careful observer that it was impending. It is incredible that the fifth day after the blow had actually fallen finds us without a plan —unless the sending of some general—not yet fixed upon—to the eastern Mediterranean to scout for a scheme of operations can be called a plan. The Cabinet may depend upon it that when it becomes clear to the British public that we have been taken by surprise and that we have not made the slightest preparation to counter the German thrust, confidence will vanish in our capacity to conduct the War, and rightly so.

It may be asked: What would you do now? The question is not who is to blame, but how are we to set it right? I am not at all sure that they are not more or less the same questions. This is a matter which I propose to return to later on, because I think it is essential. We have been let down so often that it is criminal folly on our part to depend any longer for the safety of the Empire on our present military organisation. But dealing merely with the Balkan tangle, I think even now we ought to make one great effort to save Serbia. There are two reasons for doing so. The first is that the abandonment of Serbia to her fate would be fatal to the prestige of Great Britain among the Allies and throughout the world. The hostility of Bulgaria and the neutrality of Greece and Roumania are attributable to the conviction which has permeated all neutral countries that Germany is irresistible and that we are impotent to protect nations which have incurred her wrath. Our complete failure to protect Belgium started this idea. Our inability to give effective support to Russia has confirmed it: and the abandonment of Serbia to her doom will root it deeper than ever in the mind of the world. The effect in the East will be incalculable.

The second reason is that Serbia now provides the only barrier between us and the military reconstruction of a great hostile Moslem Power, which would be a menace to Egypt, Tripoli, Tunis, Algiers and Morocco, and also to our hold on India. Surely the averting of such a catastrophe is worth one great final effort? Is such an effort beyond our compass?

The General Staff reckon that the German and Austrian armies engaged in the operations aggregate 200,000 men; that the Bulgarians number 300,000. We have, therefore, a total force of 500,000 to cope with in the Balkans. It is also, I understand, the reckoning of the General Staff that unless the Germans withdraw troops either from Russia or from France they cannot materially increase the strength of their armies in the Balkans. Serbia has an army of 300,000 men, very brave, very ably led. Their defeat of the Austrians last year demonstrated these two facts. They are fighting in a country they thoroughly understand, and they are fighting with all the ferocity with which a small mountain race always defend their native land. In numbers, therefore, the combined Bulgarian and Teutonic forces only overtop the Serbians alone by 200,000 men. Is it quite out of the question to make up this deficiency when so much depends on it for the Allies? Could not Roumania and Greece be persuaded or pressed to come in even now? Mere appeals to their sense of honour and their treaty obligations will not affect them in the least. They are naturally thinking about the security of their own countries, and they are paralysed by the German power and our impotence. It must be shown to them that we are quite capable of giving them all the necessary military support to protect them and enable them to carry through their undertaking. Why should we not promise them support, provided they come to the aid of Serbia immediately? They have men and equipment quite adequate to the conducting of a three months' campaign. Roumania, Serbia and Greece between them could put nearly a million men into the field, as against the Germano-Bulgarian combination of half a million. We could hold the Turkish forces in Gallipoli so as to prevent Turkey from sending any considerable reinforcements to the aid of the Bulgarians. Turkey has plenty of men available, but until the Germans arrive in Constantinople she has not the necessary munitions to equip fresh armies. If we said to the Greeks and the Roumanians that if they took the field immediately we could place at their disposal straight away 30,000 men who have already landed at Salonika, and that in a month's time we would guarantee that those 30,000 would be 100,000; that in two months' time the 100,000 would become 150,000; and that by the end of the year we could undertake to have at least 250,000 men operating the Balkans; that in addition to that we could help them with ammunition—a promise which France and ourselves could afford to give if we dropped the offensive in the west—their whole attitude would be changed. In addition to this we could undertake, with the aid of Italy, to furnish the Russians with 500,000 rifles, thus enabling Russia to place another three-quarters of a million men in the line. If this were done, Roumania would feel herself secure from any Austro-German attack as the Austro-German armies would have as much as they could possibly do to hold their own against the increased pressure of the Russian armies. Russia might, under those circumstances, even promise definitely to detach 100,000 men to assist the Roumanians against any attack which might be made upon them.

The situation is desperate, and nothing but prompt, courageous, and even daring action can retrieve it. What risks do we run by making this promise?

1. We should have definitely to postpone the offensive in the west. When it has failed now, after the most prolonged and careful preparation, why should it be assumed that it will succeed three months hence? The French and ourselves will not be appreciably better off in the matter of big guns—not until the late spring of next year. We have already lost—French and British—between 500,000 and 600,000 men in the two great attempts made since May last to pierce the German line. To ignore the costly lesson thus given us and to make another effort of the same kind without adequate equipment of heavy guns and ammunition would be wantonly to throw away the lives of the very fine body of men who have volunteered for the new armies.

2. We might fail to redeem our promise to the Roumanians and Greeks. The French have promised 64,000 men when the offensive is over. I am not sure whether those 64,000 include the 15,000 French troops already landed at Salonika. But let us assume that they do. I understand that there are considerable drafts on their way to the Dardanelles. These might be safely diverted to Salonika so long as the Turks on the Gallipoli Peninsula are cut off from the fresh supplies of ammunition they are hoping to get from the Germans. That would bring our forces at Salonika up to about 100,000 men.* We should have to find the remaining 150,000. I understand that on the Western Front the French claim that with our army they have a superiority of very nearly 1,000,000 over the Germans. If even 400,000 men were taken away from the west our superiority would still be overwhelming. The Germans have already demonstrated clearly that a superiority of three to two does not enable the offensive to break through a well-entrenched line. Why, then, should it be supposed that when the Germans are in inferior numbers they could break through our lines? Are the French soldiers and ours so inferior in quality to the German *Landsturm*?

If the Germans brought half a million from the east they would still be in a slight minority in the west. With the increased

* French 64,000
British withdrawn from Gallipoli plus drafts, about...........................35,000
99,000

pressure the Russians could bring to bear by means of reinforcements we had enabled them to equip and put into the field, the Germans, so far from being in a position to withdraw troops from the east, might have to draw heavily on their reserves in order to hold their own on that frontier.

3. The risk that we could not furnish the 500,000 rifles for Russia. Why not? Our American rifles will be coming in shortly, and we could, for the sake of a great effort to save a desperate situation, spare 150,000 rifles to equip 200,000 Russians who are ready in every other respect for the field. The temporary risks we might have to face by parting with the rifles are not comparable with those we run if nothing effective is done to save the situation in the Balkans. The Italians must be financed to part with their 300,000 Vitalis, and the French would surely spare 50,000 rifles to help the Allied cause out of the worst plight it has yet been in.

I earnestly press that the offer should be definitely made to Russia and Greece without loss of time. If Greece shows any reluctance to come in, the appeal to her might take the form of a demand that she should redeem her treaty obligations to Serbia. We are in this War to enforce international treaties, and a demand of that kind could not be interpreted as the bullying of a small nationality when we are actually engaged in a war with the greatest military power in the world on the same ground. Greece is always at the mercy of a great Sea Power. Germany cannot protect her against us, and I have information from reliable Greek sources that this line would have much greater effect upon the King of Greece than an appeal to his honour to redeem his bond to Serbia.

The notion that we are satisfying the needs of this critical situation by making another attack on the Gallipoli Peninsula is, to my mind, an insane one. We have failed repeatedly when the Turks were short of ammunition. Are we now to succeed when they are reinforced with German heavy guns and abundance of ammunition? It is by no means improbable that the Turks, thus re-equipped, might drive us into the sea before reinforcements ever reached our army on that Peninsula. This probability is indicated in clear terms in Colonel Hankey's report. If we neglect his warning our responsibility will be great. But even assuming we can hold our own, an attack on positions which have been proved to be impregnable against gallant assaults would end in the loss of another 50,000 or 60,000 men with nothing achieved. It is quite clear to anyone who reads the document prepared by the General Staff that this was no part of their original plan. It has simply been spatch-cocked into their document by strong Dardanellian influences. It has been done so badly that the simplest of us can see it. The recommendations of the General

L

Staff were that it would confine ourselves to the offensive in France. We are now not merely to send out a general to trawl the eastern Mediterranean for a new policy, but before he reports we are to send 150,000 men away from France—from the only objective which the General Staff are prepared to stake their reputation upon recommending!

D. Ll. G.

October 12th, 1915."

To this Sir Edward Grey replied: —

" FOREIGN OFFICE,
October 13th, 1915.

My dear Lloyd George,

Your memorandum has come to me since the telegrams to Bucharest and Athens were sent last night, and for the moment I suppose they settle one point in your memorandum.

I am no judge of the military consideration involved, but as Kitchener agrees and you desire it and the Prime Minister authorises it I sent the telegrams at once. From the political point of view I am as strongly in favour of the line now taken as you can be, and I am glad to be able to say anything diplomatically which is backed by action or the prospects of action.

What I do feel to be useless is constant diplomatic effort based neither on military nor naval success, without the prospect of such success, and without any offer of action. These last telegrams are not open to that criticism.

For the rest I wish to avoid drift in our strategy, and if I differ from the conclusions of your paper at all it is that I think our strategic decisions should be based on naval and military opinion founded upon good staff work. I urged strongly and I understood you also to urge the same thing, and I hope the staff work now being done under Murray will be encouraged and continued. I do not like to discard its conclusions. But I agree that the opinion expressed by the Staff about the Gallipoli Peninsula is more provisional and tentative than final.

It is, however, vital to come to a decision quickly either to attempt to force the Dardanelles or to evacuate—so it seems to me, and I would accept either decision rather than none.

I was not sure whether your memorandum was addressed specially to me or not; it deals mainly with military strategy on which I am qualified to be guided rather than to guide.

Yours sincerely,
E. GREY."

The irony of his sentence about " military and naval opinion based on good staff work " is withering. But the greatest irony of all, after what had happened, was that he meant every word of it. The way he had been betrayed by the Military to give in the House of Commons pledges to Serbia they had no hope of redeeming did not seem to diminish his childish faith in their advice.

Considerable delays ensued in sending troops to the Mediterranean. On 19th October M. Millerand, the French Secretary of State for War, came over to discuss the position. He was accompanied by General Joffre. I find amongst my papers the following note made by a secretary of what took place at the discussions: —

"Ll.G. saw Millerand to-day, who says that Ll.G. was right after all and that an expedition in the Balkans should have been undertaken last spring. He is now concerned that the Dardanelles operations are a failure, and though he fears it is too late to render very effective assistance in the Balkans, yet he is in favour of France and Britain sending troops there. He and Ll.G. together drew up a plan upon which France and England are to act for a campaign in the Balkans."

Our plan suggested that: —

"The prevention of the German effort to get through to Constantinople should be regarded as the primary objective of the joint expeditionary force. If, by the time the new force can arrive at the eastern Mediterranean, Serbia is still blocking the way, the French and British forces should proceed to Salonika to help the Serbians to keep the railway free to Uskub.

If by the date of the arrival of the troops the Germans have forced their way through to Constantinople, the two Governments to decide their course then on the advice of their Generals. . . . The two Governments have agreed to go on sending to the help of Serbia sufficient contingents to constitute a force of 150,000 men.

Should the present situation become greatly altered owing to unforeseen circumstances arising, both Governments would then take steps in common as to the new directions to give to their troops."

Greece was pressed to send troops to assist in saving Russia, but the appeal to her came too late, because by that time the armies of the Central Powers and of Bulgaria had overwhelmed Serbian resistance, and the Greeks put in the plea that they were afraid of standing up against the victors when there were no Allied troops within sight to assist them. They had the fate of Serbia before their eyes. Serbia had been abandoned by the Allies in defiance of the solemn pledges of timely support. The Greeks were naturally apprehensive of a repetition of the same desertion in their own case. The sweeping victories of the Central Powers on the Eastern Front naturally impressed all the South-Eastern States more than the capture by the Allies of a few kilometres in France. Russia had collapsed; Serbia had been overrun; the Dardanelles expedition had been a complete failure, and even in the west the Allies had not succeeded in breaking through, and the Germans, victorious on every front, were advancing southwards with seven-league boots. They were already in the defiles of the Balkans, soon they would be on their Southern slopes. At that time there was nothing between them and the Greek frontier. Greece with her small army would be easily devoured by this terrible monster.

Sir Edward Carson, disgusted with what he conceived to be the deception practised upon Serbia, had resigned. Mr. Bonar Law and I shared his opinion about the whole transaction, but on the whole decided that we could not withdraw from the Ministry at this critical juncture. I am not sure that we were right.

There was a general feeling that there was a disastrous lack of grip in the direction of the War, and that the Cabinet ought to take upon itself a more direct responsibility in controlling its conduct. Suggestions were put forward for the setting-up of a War Committee which would exercise a more constant supervision over the direction of the War. I was amongst those who made representations to the Prime Minister upon this point. On the 29th October I received from him the following memorandum: —

" CONDUCT OF THE WAR

The proposal, as I understand it, is that there should be a small Committee of the Cabinet, not less than three or more than five in number, to deal executively with the conduct of the War.

It is understood that the Committee will from time to time call to their aid, for the purposes both of discussion and decision, other members of the Cabinet, either because their departments are concerned in the particular matter which is being dealt with or for other special reasons.

The Cabinet to remain as it is in numbers and composition.

The plenum of the Cabinet to be constantly informed of the decisions and actions of the Committee, and in all questions which involve a change or new departure in policy to be consulted before decisive action is taken.

Parliament to be informed that this method of procedure has been adopted, and to be told the names of the members of the Committee.

October 28, 1915.   H. H. A."

On 31st October I replied: —

> " 11, Downing Street,
> Whitehall, S.W.
> October 31, 1915.

My dear Prime Minister,

I am sorry to trouble you when you must be worried with the anxieties of the situation, but I feel I must put to you my view of the position before you come to a final decision.   The appointment of a small Committee with fairly full powers will undoubtedly be a great improvement on the sort of Duma which has been sitting on war problems up to the present.   But unless there is a complete change in the War Office the new Council will be just as impotent as the Cabinet and old Council have proved themselves to be.   Our war Administration have committed every blunder that the enemy could wish them to be guilty of.   It was quite clear, even to the civilian mind, soon after the War began that this War would ultimately be decided by superiority in quality and quantity of material, and by the wearing down of the enemy in numbers. The Allies had the advantage in both respects, and the War Office have by an incredible lack of foresight and energy thrown away both these advantages.

As to material, whilst the Germans were spending the whole of the late autumn and winter of 1914 in increasing their guns, rifles and ammunition for the summer campaign, our War Office did nothing substantial till the end of 1914 and in the spring of 1915.   Then they did it under pressure from outside, and even then they were satisfied with giving orders whilst taking no steps to see that they were or even could be executed.   The result has been that the campaign of 1915 has been lost to us.   We could not help Russia in ammunition because we have not even now an adequate equipment, more especially in rifles and heavy guns and trench appliances, for ourselves.   The full story of the neglect of the War Office in this respect has not yet been told.   It is worse than I expected it would be when I first took up the work of the Ministry of Munitions—how they ordered shell without taking measures to see that there were fuses and primers, cartridge cases, gaines and the necessary arrangements for filling, so that huge stocks of empty shells were piled up at Woolwich with no means of completing them which was in the least commensurate with the demand.

As to attrition, by prompt action in the Balkans we could have added a million and a half to our reserves of men, most of it excellent fighting material.   Roumania, Greece, and, I think, Bulgaria, could have been brought in, not by words, but by prompt and strong action.   On the other hand, we could have cut off the enemy from the magnificent reservoir of men in the Turkish Empire who are only awaiting equipment to become one of the most formidable fighting machines in the world. *In July the Intelligence Department of the War Office warned Kitchener that the Germans were likely to break through to Constantinople. We were constantly warned that Bulgaria was becoming more and more hostile.* One or two Cabinet Ministers, including myself, urged that steps should be taken to prepare for this probable German move. Nothing was done; even when information came in that the Germans and Austrians were accumulating forces in the valleys of Hungary and in the Bukovina, no plan of action was thought out. *Kitchener never knew that they had crossed the Danube 20 hours after the news reached the War Office that they had effected a crossing at five points.* A fortnight after the crossing his only plan was to send a general to the Mediterranean to report on the situation. Days after the road to Constantinople had been cleared through Bulgaria and weeks after the actual commencement of the struggle upon which the fate of our rule in Egypt may depend, we are forced by the French to take some action. You will recollect that the Committee of Imperial Defence as far back as February last decided that all the necessary preparations should be made for rendering a landing at Salonika effective whenever the Cabinet decided to take that course. Kitchener never took the slightest notice of that decision, and not even a mule had been bought for transport when the German blow fell on Serbia.

The public may have delusions now about Kitchener, but the moment these facts are told in the House of Commons I have very little doubt what will be thought and said by all sections.

If I thought the appointment of a small Committee would put an end to all these amazing series of blunders, I should be satisfied. But I have gone on for months always thinking that every mistake must surely be the last, and finding myself constantly surprised by the capacity of our great War Lords for blundering. I wrote you in December last calling your attention to the stupidity of the War Office, and telling you that, in my judgement, unless we showed greater grip as a Government in the management of the War, it must end in inevitable disaster. I have protested at each stage, sometimes in writing, sometimes by intervention in the Cabinet and at the War Council. I did so long before the North-cliffe Press began its campaign. At best the chances are against the next few weeks bringing much cheer—they might bring ruin to Serbia and for us retreat in the Balkans and disaster in Gallipoli. The nation would endure this and a good deal more if they knew everything was being done that human effort and foresight could compass to ensure final victory; but their confidence has been rudely shaken by what they can see of our unpreparedness in the

Balkans. The friendly Press are showing marked symptoms of mutiny. The steadfast loyalty of our own party to your leadership has so far saved the Government, but you will forgive me for saying that I doubt whether that would save us if a catastrophe befell Serbia or our forces in the Dardanelles and all the facts on the conduct of the War were dragged out as they would be. Every mistake and omission would then be brought out with accumulative force. The row in the Commons will come last. Press and public will be moved before the party politician, but in the end he will follow public opinion, and we must have a good answer when the time comes. There is only one answer that can satisfy the public, and that is that you have already made an end of the futile regime that tumbled along from one fatuity to another. I am quite willing to face the inevitable tumult when it comes if this answer can be given, but I have very reluctantly come to the conclusion that I can no longer be responsible for the present war direction, and at the Cabinet to-morrow I propose with your permission to raise the real issue.

Ever sincerely,

D. LLOYD GEORGE."

The allusion in my letter to the fact that Lord Kitchener never knew the Germans had crossed the Danube for 20 hours after the news had reached the War Office is explained in the following note made after the Committee meeting by one of my secretaries: —

"At a Cabinet last week, before the German advance into Serbia had begun, but when news of it was being expected at every moment, Ll. G. asked K. in the Cabinet whether there was any news of the Germans having crossed the Danube. K. said that up to the time when he came to the Cabinet he had received no news. Ll. G. suggested that the news might have come in since and said he would get the P. M.'s secretary to telephone to the War Office and ask if any news had been received, as he considered it most important to know when the Germans had begun to cross the Danube. The following is the reply which Ll. G. received and which he read out to the Cabinet. A telegram had been received in the War Office the day before. K. did not express the least surprise that he had not seen the telegram. Here is a copy of it: —

' Late *yesterday* afternoon enemy xd. Danube with one batt. at   . Aust. troops xd. the Slava in 5 difft. places between Sabac and Belgrade. They are so far not in large force. Fight is continuing.'

> 10. Downing Street,
> Whitehall. S.W.
>
> K does not read the telegrams — & we dont see them — it is intolerable
>
> E. C

Facsimile of a note passed by Lord Carson (then Sir Edward Carson) to Mr. Lloyd George, during a Cabinet Meeting, in September, 1915.

Immediately this telegram was read to the Cabinet, Sir Edward Carson passed Ll. G. the following note : —

' K. does not read the telegrams—and we don't see them—it is intolerable.

E. C. "

On 4th November I received the following letter from Mr. Asquith : —

10, Downing Street,
Whitehall, S.W.
3rd Nov. 1915.

" Secret.

My dear Lloyd George,

What I wanted you to know before to-morrow's Cabinet was that, in view of the conflicting opinions now to hand of Monro and the other generals in regard to the future of the Dardanelles, I arranged to-day that K. should proceed without delay (to-morrow, Thursday night) to Alexandria, and after visiting Gallipoli and Salonika, and conferring with all our military and diplomatic experts in that quarter of the world, advise us as to our strategy in the eastern theatre.

In the meantime I propose to take over the War Office, and I am confident that in the course of the next month I can put things there on a better footing, and in particular come to a complete understanding with you on all the important problems which are connected with the design, fabrication and supply of munitions.

We avoid by this method of procedure the immediate super-session of K. as War Minister, while attaining the same result. And I suppose even B. L. [Bonar Law] would hardly object to such a plan.

Yours very sincerely,
H. H. A.

P.S.—This is for yourself alone; I have not said anything to any of our colleagues. But I regard it as of the first moment that in this matter you and I should act together."

The Germans invaded Serbia on October 7th. The Cabinet decided on 11th October that a general should be sent to the Mediterranean to examine the position there and decide what action should be taken. As already mentioned, General Monro was chosen. Appointed on 15th October, he started on his voyage of discovery for methods of helping Serbia on 22nd October and arrived at Mudros on 28th October. On 31st October he recommended that our troops should be withdrawn from the Gallipoli Peninsula and transported to Egypt for re-equipment. In the meantime, a certain number of British and French troops had landed at Salonika, the first contingent reaching that port on 3rd October. Two divisions only were dis-embarked by 7th October, the day on which the offensive against

L*

Serbia was launched by the forces of the Central Powers. Had we dropped the fatal offensive in France as soon as it became clear that it could not succeed in its main purpose, and sent immediately to the Mediterranean a number equal to those who fell in futile attacks after that date, the bastion of the Balkans would have been held by us with the help of what was left of the Serbian Army; and neither Germans, Austrians, nor Bulgarians possessed the necessary strength to force those defiles against such a garrison.

The growing feeling of anxiety, developing into criticism of the military direction, is reflected in a letter which I received at this time from the late Lord Charles Beresford. At that time, he was still a figure of some distinction and he had attracted to himself a good deal of popular esteem. He always possessed a certain flair which revealed itself even in his most histrionic performances and in his most exuberant and extravagant utterances.

> " 1, Great Cumberland Place,
>   London, W.
>
> Dear Mr. Lloyd George,   16th October, 1915.
>   Please excuse dictation.
> I hope I shall be able to see you in the House some day next week, as I do not think it would be wise or politic to meet you except at a private house or in the House of Commons; there are many people who jump to conclusions, and such people would at once think that there was an intrigue afoot.
>
> We are, in my opinion, drifting to certain destruction. We have no policy, no objective, and nothing has been thought out ahead. It is imperative that we leave the Gallipoli Peninsula. Suvla Bay and Anzac must be evacuated shortly owing to their being under water. It is too late now to land an army in Asia Minor; the country will soon be a marsh. We shall have to lose a rearguard in the evacuation, but that would be better than losing 140,000 men there now, plus another 140,000 or 200,000 necessary for reinforcements, owing to casualties and the ravages of disease which has now set in. We cannot get through the Dardanelles, and we are wasting life and destroying prestige by remaining in the Gallipoli Peninsula. I believe the Fleet could secure the retreat, even to a portion of the rearguard.
>
> In every way fronts are changed, new military situations created, and new objectives undertaken. We have now taken a new objective and formed a new front at Salonika—an excellent reason for withdrawing from an impossible position in Gallipoli.
>
> We want about 200,000 men of the Allies landed at Salonika. It would be fatal to send them in driblets. If the Serbians are crushed the Germans will get to Constantinople. They will open up the whole of Asia for supplies. Roumania and Greece will out

of fear probably throw in their lot with Germany.   There is a spark in Islam now which would under these circumstances be fanned into a violent flame, more particularly if we remain in the Gallipoli Peninsula.   Looking ahead, we should probably have to denude our Allies in France of a large portion of our army in order to fight for the defence of our Empire in the East and Egypt. Surely some dispatch should be sent or method taken to show the Greeks that they must come out on one side or the other.

There will be a tremendous reaction in the country when the people know the truth, and I am afraid that the whole of the Cabinet will go down.   Democracy are not reasonable when they are excited.   If the people bring about the downfall of the Cabinet what have we got to put in its place?   We should have a reign of chaos during the greatest crisis the Empire has ever faced.

One of the great dangers consists in having Lord Kitchener in the Cabinet.   The people believe in him, but they do not know he is wasting his time talking on political subjects.   I have been to him several times and pointed out that he ought to leave the Cabinet on the plea that he cannot devote his time to it.   His business is to take an envelope, write on it what men he wants, and what munitions he wants, and present that to the Cabinet. The question of how they are to be got has nothing whatever to do with him.   It is a political question of tremendous difficulty which must be argued out by the Cabinet.   Lord Kitchener's difficulty would be well illustrated if there was a debate in the Cabinet on conscription or voluntary service.   Which side would he take?

In war, quick decisions and prompt actions are wanted.   Neither are possible without a definite policy, and a clear objective for the military and naval forces, upon which depends the success or failure of the policy.   The Government have no policy, and the military have no objective.   It does not require that a man should be in the Cabinet to see the danger that exists to our Empire through this lamentable state of affairs.   We are wasting days and weeks, when every hour, indeed, every minute, is of vital importance to us in the near future.

In my opinion, our policy should be: —

1. Evacuate the Dardanelles;
2. Send 200,000 (an allied force) men to Salonika with plenty of guns;
3. Get across the railway between Belgrade and Constantinople by some means between Nish and Sofia.

I know the country and the difficulties attending such a proposition, but risks and difficulties must be met in war provided a substantial result is possible of attainment.   Risks such as we are undertaking in Gallipoli have no excuse whatever. It was a risk courting defeat, and is certain to affect our prestige in the Balkans, with the Allies, and worse than all, with our great Eastern Empire.

Yours very sincerely,

CHARLES BERESFORD.

The Rt. Hon. D. Lloyd George, M.P."

This letter reflects the rising and spreading sense of dubiety amongst men who were watching the course of events with some accumulated knowledge and experience. As yet the general public were still trustful if a little mystified. Their faith in Kitchener and their invincible belief in British luck had not yet been shaken.

One culminating illustration at this period of our military leaders' capacity for blundering remains to be recorded. Upon the return of Lord Kitchener, at the end of November, 1915, from his expedition to the Balkans, the antipathy of the British General Staff to any operations in that theatre crystallised into a definite recommendation that the Salonika expedition should be recalled. Rumour had it that Kitchener had somehow been talked over by the plausible and adroit King Constantine of Greece into favouring this step. The General Staff advised that we should withdraw from both the Dardanelles and Salonika and concentrate our forces on the defence of Egypt.

The French Government had vision enough to be furious at this suggestion. It urged very wisely that such an action would be naturally regarded throughout the East as a token of weakness and irresolution, and would mean the utter loss of the Balkans. Not only would it spell the final abandonment of the last shattered remnants of the army of our ally, Serbia: it would also drive both Roumania and Greece into the arms of Germany, adding something like another million men to their forces in that war theatre, imperilling the southern flank of the Russians, and turning the whole Balkan coast, including the harbours of Greece, into enemy bases for submarine activity in the Mediterranean. On Friday, 3rd December, 1915, the French sent an angry telegram, challenging the shilly-shallying attitude of the British Government—the proposal to leave Salonika and the lack of firmness we were showing in our handling of Greece. They complained bitterly that we had gone back on our decision at the Paris Council which had taken place a week previously, and that Lord Kitchener had evidently made arrangements with the King of Greece which were quite outside the intentions of the French. They requested that representatives of the British Government should meet them the following day at Calais to discuss the position.

As yet the British Cabinet had not reached a definite decision upon the issue. It had been postponed from one meeting to another.

Upon receipt of the French Government's telegram, the Prime Minister went to Calais, taking Lord Kitchener and Mr. Balfour with him. He did not invite me to join the party, doubtless because my strong opposition to any abandonment of the Balkans was well known, and I did not even hear of the telegram from France till the Saturday morning when our representatives had already departed for Calais.

On their return we were informed that they had succeeded in talking the French round to their point of view and that the evacuation of Salonika had been agreed upon. But the telegrams on Monday from Paris were far from supporting this interpretation of the proceedings, and showed that the French were still very dissatisfied, and that no satisfactory arrangement had really been arrived at on the Saturday.

While everything was in this state of chaos, a telegram came to say that M. Albert Thomas was on his way over to have a talk with me on the subject of the Calais Conference, and to explain to me the real opinion of the French. Meanwhile at the War Council that morning (6th December, 1915) the matter was discussed. Mr. Bonar Law was the only one present who agreed with my view of the matter, all the rest being for immediate evacuation. Lord Kitchener read a telegram from Greece which said that the Germans demanded the evacuation of the Balkans by the Allied troops, and were willing to allow the Greeks to cover the re-embarkation. I am recorded as having said " It is a good thing that the Germans and the British have found something to agree upon at last. Surely this must be the beginning of peace! "

Shortly afterwards M. Albert Thomas arrived, and explained to me the reason for his visit. I learned that when the French deputation to the Calais conference returned to Paris and admitted that they had agreed to the evacuation of the Balkans, the rest of the French Cabinet expressed the greatest dissatisfaction with this conclusion. The deputation insisted that they had been told that this was the view taken unanimously by the British Government, and that in those circumstances they had felt bound to acquiesce: whereupon M. Thomas interposed that he knew it was not the view of the whole British Cabinet, as I had told him when he was last in London that I was entirely opposed to evacuating the Balkans and was very much in favour of engaging in a Balkan campaign this year or next. The French Cabinet ultimately refused to accept the decision arrived at on the previous day at Calais. Thereupon, M. Thomas offered to come over to London and see me in an effort to obtain a reconsideration of their decision by the British Government.

Naturally I promised him all the help and backing I could furnish. He attended more than one prolonged meeting of our leaders at which he set forth very passionately the desire of the French to remain at Salonika. Perhaps the best help I afforded him was an arrangement I made for him to lunch at 10, Downing Street with the Prime Minister. I am not sure that the favourable personal impression he made on his host and hostess was not more helpful to his cause than all his eloquence in Council. However that may be, the final outcome of these discussions was that Lord Kitchener was sent over to Paris to consult with the French Cabinet, with full powers to make any arrangements on behalf of our Government. He did not much like the idea of going. "The French are not very keen on me at present for some reason," he said. However, he went, and the upshot was an agreement for the Allies to remain at Salonika and fortify it in preparation for an effective campaign in 1916. So narrowly was averted an act of incredible folly. But the effective campaign was not waged in 1916. The French and British military chiefs took care that the Salonika expedition should not be equipped with the guns and ammunition which would justify offensive operations. And in order further to deprive General Sarrail of all temptation to attack they deprived him of all the means of transport essential to an advance.

Speaking on 20th December, 1915, in the House of Commons, having in mind the fatal tardiness which had brought so much disaster to the Allied cause in the Dardanelles, the Balkans, Russia and Mesopotamia, I used the following words: —

". . . Too late in moving here, too late in arriving there, too late in coming to this decision, too late in starting with enterprises, too late in preparing! In this war the footsteps of the Allied forces have been dogged by the mocking spectre of 'too late,' and unless we quicken our movements damnation will fall on the sacred cause for which so much gallant blood has flowed. . . ."

That summed up my considered opinion at the time on the muddled campaign of 1915. That is my judgment to-day after a careful perusal of all the documents and histories written on the subject from every point of view.

CHAPTER XVIII

THE BALKANS AND THE SOMME

THE whole strategic possibilities of the War for the Allies was changed by the Serbian collapse. The opportunities offered for a formidable movement against the eastern flank of the Central Powers had been, if not entirely lost, at least made more difficult and doubtful. The constant allurement to amateur and other strategists of such a chance to divert troops from the Western charnel-house was shut down. The general staffs of France and Britain had not won *the* War, but they had won *their* war. The Dardanelles had been evacuated; the Balkans had been transferred from Allied to enemy hands; the road to the Danube, to Constantinople and the Black Sea had been finally blocked; Serbia had been wiped out; Russia was tottering to her fall; Roumania was isolated. What consummate strategy! The Germans had not been beaten, but the politicians had been thwarted. The Brass Hats were triumphant. They sang their chortling *Te Deums* from Chantilly to Whitehall. The East with its opportunities, which were also temptations, was no more. Hail to the blood-red sun of the West!

It is true that forces which numerically appeared to be very powerful were sent to Salonika; and there was every appearance of a formidable army of British, French, Serbians and Greeks, numbering in the aggregate hundreds of thousands, being assembled in that theatre. It was for all offensive purposes reduced to stagnation and impotence by an equipment so· inadequate as to render this conglomerate army quite incapable of making any effective attack upon the enemy. The General Staffs were determined that all temptation to action must be removed from generals performing in that theatre. There were two possible uses to which the Salonika Expeditionary Force could be put. One was that it should be sufficiently strong to hold up the Bulgarians and a certain number of Austrian and German and Turkish troops, and to prevent them from being thrown on to other points where their accession might have been harmful and perhaps decisive. This plan would also have had the effect of preventing the surly and suspicious King of Greece, who was only too sympathetic to the Germans, from throwing in his lot with them under the pretext that he could not resist the invasion of such a powerful force. As it was, he handed over Kavalla and a Greek Division to the enemy as an offering to propitiate an idol he feared as well as adored. He might have given them the whole of the Greek Army had we not been there. If that was to be the sole purpose of the occupation of Salonika, the force was much too large, and a smaller army well entrenched at Salonika, supported with an adequate quota of guns, would have answered equally well. It could easily have been reinforced by sea had there been an attack; there was no object in accumulating large forces there and providing them with powerful offensive armaments.

The second alternative was that we should have an army at Salonika which could either have attacked the Turks on the right flank, cut their communications with Germany, and possibly captured their capital; or, on the other hand, stormed the defiles of the Balkans, broken through and defeated the Bulgarian Army, re-established relations with Roumania, and through Roumania with Russia; in fact, recreated the chance which had been lost through the fatal strategy of the early autumn of 1915. The fine achievement of the Serbian Army under General Misitsch later on, when it fought its way through to Monastir, proves that this was not outside the region of attainment by an army which was even moderately equipped with artillery and ammunition.

The military chiefs pursued neither of these policies. As I shall point out later on, the Salonika Army was left practically without any guns or ammunition which would have enabled it to bombard its way through the crudest defences in such a difficult terrain. It was camped on the malarial plains of the Struma and the Vardar for two years without being given the means of fighting its way to healthier ground. The British Staff were in favour of the first course and would have reduced the force to dimensions sufficient for the discharge of this rôle. The French Staff hesitated between the two. The argument between them went on for months. The French Commander-in-Chief, once an obdurate Westerner, now feigned conversion to some of the tenets of the Eastern faith. Here undoubtedly the reasons were political and personal. The influence of General Joffre in France had considerably diminished, owing to his failure to put the defences of Verdun in order for a whole month after he had been warned that an attack was impending. The autocratic authority which he once exerted, and which up to that date was quite sufficient to intimidate Governments and to compel them against their judgment to conform to his stubborn will, had faded almost to vanishing point, since the German guns at Verdun had laid bare his limitations. The leading statesmen of France, including the President and the President of the Council, believed in attacking the enemy on the south-eastern flank. In this they were supported by—in fact they were acting on the suggestion of—the most gifted soldier in the French Army, General Gallieni.

General Joffre, therefore, in order to placate the men who for the first time had become his masters, deferred to their wishes about reinforcing the Salonika Front. It was his offering on the altar of the offended gods. The Moloch of the Western Front had been temporarily satiated. Some sacrifice might now be spared for the idols of the Élysée. General Joffre's influence had been strong enough to resist their plan when it would have been useful and perhaps decisive; but his authority was too weak to offer any effective opposition when the plan had ceased to have anything like the same value. This is one of the comic interludes which are woven into every tragedy.

Joffre came over to London on 9th June, 1916, to persuade the British Cabinet to join the French in strengthening the forces at Salonika. At that time the great offensive on the Somme had been agreed to by both Staffs and both Governments. I was one of the members of the Cabinet who accepted Lord Kitchener's view as to the futility of launching this attack. Lord Kitchener reluctantly withdrew his objections and the rest of us were overruled. The preparations were now far advanced. It was part of General Joffre's case that the offensive was essential in order to relieve the pressure on the French at Verdun. For the same reason we had been asked to take over a considerable sector of the Western Front hitherto occupied by French troops. The French needed every battalion they could spare for the defence of Verdun. It is one of the incomprehensible episodes of the War that the French Commander-in-Chief, the ruthless advocate of the " all for the west " policy, should at such a juncture come over to Britain to beg us to join the French in sending a considerable contingent of French and British soldiers to Salonika in order to launch a stage attack which must fail for lack of guns and ammunition.

At the Conference which was held in Downing Street, General Joffre presented his case with great force and eloquence. As to whether he was a good soldier or not, let others judge. Although I may not be competent to express an opinion I still hold one, and hold it strongly. As to his gifts as an orator, I feel that as an old Parliamentarian I am quite equal to forming a judgment, and quite entitled to state it. He was one of the most forceful and dramatic speakers I heard at any conference which I ever attended. But although on this occasion he spoke with all the outward visible manifestations of earnestness and sincerity, in voice, gesture, language, and facial expression, it was difficult to believe that he was convinced even by his own eloquence. He was urging an attack with forces devoid of the armament necessary to achieve their purpose, and he made no suggestion that the equipment should be strengthened up to the point of effectiveness. It was one of the most cynical performances I have ever listened to. Having regard to the inevitable loss of brave lives which would have been entailed in such a futile enterprise, it would have been wicked had it not been that he was relying upon our turning his proposal down. I realised that he did not mean business and that an offensive at Salonika unsupported by the necessary guns and ammunition must fail; I also knew that such a failure must discourage any future attempt under more favourable conditions.

Here is an official summary, taken down at the time, of the part I took in the discussion: —

" Mr. Lloyd George said that he had always been in favour of an advance from Salonika, but that unless there was a fair chance of success he considered it fatal; and because the facts before him were not convincing that it would be successful, he, as a supporter of the principle of an advance, was doubtful. We had had a bad experience at the Dardanelles, where we lost about 200,000 men as well as prestige. Unless there was a reasonable chance of success he was entirely opposed to it. The facts given by our General Staff had not been seriously controverted by General Joffre to-day. To attack a good army, in strong positions, with only twenty-four French and six British heavy howitzers was very dangerous. General Joffre said that we should be keeping the enemy busy and quoted the Russians. But the Russians were occupying the attentions of the Austrians, the Bulgarians were not helping anyone. If there was a fair chance of breaking right through and threatening the enemy's flank, the Roumanians might come in on our side. But General Joffre does not say there is this chance; he did not contemplate breaking through the Bulgarian lines—he was only thinking of comparatively trifling victories. To attempt the operation with inadequate strength was to discredit it. Sir Douglas Haig has in front of him very serious operations undertaken merely to relieve the pressure on France. This consideration had appeared conclusive to the War Committee, otherwise they were opposed to the offensive at the present time, considered purely as a military operation. The Ministry of Munitions were sending heavy guns to France, but nothing like what Sir Douglas Haig wanted, and therefore Sir Douglas Haig would prefer to undertake his operations later, when he was sure of a full supply of these guns. The test was whether General Joffre in these circumstances would like to see, say, fifty howitzers diverted from France to Salonika. Mr. Lloyd George said that he was as firm a believer in an eventual offensive from Salonika as M. Briand himself, and urged that we should not begin any advance from Salonika until we were quite ready, as an unsuccessful offensive would prejudice any further offensive on this flank. No Government after the failure would try it a second time. This indeed was the main reason for his opposition. The Allies were not yet equipped to defeat the Bulgarians—to say nothing of the possibility of Turkish opposition in addition."

So, much to the secret satisfaction of General Joffre, we turned our backs on Salonika and our faces once more to the Somme. It ranks with Verdun as one of the two bloodiest battles ever fought on this earth up to that date. The casualties on both sides were well over a million. It was not responsible for the failure of the German effort to capture Verdun. It was only an element in slackening up a German offensive which had already slowed down and was by now a practical and almost an acknowledged failure. The French Commander-in-Chief said in May that the Germans had already been beaten at Verdun. Had the battle continued to rage around the remaining forts which held up the German Army we could have helped to reinforce the hard-pressed French Army either by sending troops to the battle area or by taking over another sector of the French Front. The Somme campaign certainly did not save Russia. That great country was being rapidly driven by the German guns towards the maelstrom of anarchy. You could even then hear the roar of the waters. That is, we might have heard it had it not been for the thunders of the Somme. This deafened our ears and obscured our vision so that we could not perceive the approaching catastrophe in Russia and therefore did not take measures to avert it. One-third of the Somme guns and ammunition transferred in time to the banks of another river, the Dnieper, would have won a great victory for Russia and deferred the Revolution until after the War.

It is claimed that the battle of the Somme destroyed the old German Army by killing off its best officers and men. It killed off far more of our best and of the French best. The battle of the Somme was fought by the volunteer armies raised in 1914 and 1915. These contained the choicest and best of our young manhood. The officers were drawn mainly from our public schools and universities. Over 400,000 of our men fell in this bullheaded fight and the slaughter amongst our young officers was appalling. The " Official History of the War," writing of the first attack, says: —

> " For this disastrous loss of the finest manhood of the United Kingdom and Ireland there was only a small gain of ground to show. . . ."

Summing up the effect on the British Army of the whole battle it says: —

> " Munitions and the technique of their use improved, but never again was the spirit or the quality of the officers and men so high, nor the general state of the training, leading and, above all, discipline of the new British Armies in France so good. The losses sustained were not only heavy but irreplaceable."

Had it not been for the inexplicable stupidity of the Germans in provoking a quarrel with America and bringing that mighty people into the War against them just as they had succeeded in eliminating another powerful foe—Russia—the Somme would not have saved us from an inextricable stalemate. I was not surprised to read in the British " Official History of the War " that M. Poincaré is reported to have said that the greatest of all French soldiers, General Foch, was opposed to the Somme offensive. When the results came to be summed up they reminded me of an observation made by Mr. Balfour when the project of this great offensive first came from the French Staff. He said: " The French are short of men; yet they want to do something which would reduce their numbers still more." At that time he was in favour of telling the French that we thought they were going to make a mistake.

Whilst the French generals and our own were reporting victory after victory against the German Army on the Western Front; whilst our Intelligence Departments at the front were assuring their Chiefs, and through them, their Governments at home, that five-sixths of the German divisions had been hammered to pulp and that the remaining divisions would soon be reduced to the same state, the German General Staff were detaching several divisions from the battle area in France and sending them to the Carpathians to join the Austrians and Bulgarians in an attack on Roumania. No one on the Allied side seemed to have anticipated this move—at least, no one made any plans to counter it, if and when it came. The whole mind of the western strategists was concentrated on one or other of the hamlets along the Somme. They exaggerated the effect of every slight advance, and worked themselves into a belief that the Germans were so pulverised by these attacks that they had not the men, the guns, nor the spirit to fight anywhere much longer. They were only waiting, with hand cupped to ear, for the crack which would signify the final break of the German barrier, and they were massing cavalry immediately behind the French and British battle line in order to complete the rout of the tattered remains of the German Army. This is no exaggeration of their illusions. I saw them at this moment of exaltation.

When the battle of the Somme was being fought, I traversed the front from Verdun to Ypres. With M. Albert Thomas I visited General Haig at his Headquarters, and with him I drove to General Cavan's Headquarters to meet General Joffre. The latter and M. Thomas were anxious to secure a number of six-inch howitzers for the French Front. We had followed the advice given by the young French artillery officer at the Boulogne Conference (described in the next chapter) and manufactured these howitzers on a great scale, with a view to concentrating a plunging fire to demolish the enemy trenches. The French had gone in more for the long-range gun, and they were short of howitzers.

When we reached General Cavan's quarters there was a heavy bombardment going on from our eight-inch howitzers assembled in the valley below, known to the soldiers as the Happy Valley. The roar of the guns beneath and the shrill " keen " of the shells overhead were deafening. We could hardly carry on a conversation. We found the noises were worse inside Lord Cavan's quarters than outside. After we had arranged the matter of the howitzers we got on to a general talk about the offensive. Both Generals—Joffre and Haig—were elated with the successes already achieved. On my way to this rendezvous I had driven through squadrons of cavalry clattering proudly to the front. When I asked what they were for, Sir Douglas Haig explained that they were brought up as near the front line as possible, so as to be ready to charge through the gap which was to be made by the Guards in the coming attack. The cavalry were to exploit the anticipated success and finish the German rout.

The Guards could be seen marching in a long column through the valley on their way to the front line preparatory to the attack. Raymond Asquith was amongst them. Before I reached Ypres I heard that the attack had failed and that the brilliant son of the British Prime Minister was amongst the fallen. When I ventured to express to Generals Joffre and Haig my doubts as to whether cavalry could ever operate successfully on a front bristling for miles behind the enemy line with barbed wire and machine-guns, both Generals fell ecstatically on me, and Joffre in particular explained that he expected the French cavalry to ride through the broken German lines on his front the following morning. You could hear the distant racket of the massed guns of France which were at that moment tearing a breach for the French horsemen. Just then a Press photographer, of whose presence we were all unaware, snapped us.

The conversation gave me an idea of the exaltation produced in brave men by a battle. They were quite incapable of looking beyond and around or even through the struggle just in front of them. That would have been all right had the Allied Governments been advised on the whole field of the War by independent advisers, who were superior or equal in capacity and will power to these resolute soldiers, whose vision was clouded by the smoke of the battle in which they were engaged. But neither the French nor ourselves had military counsellors at the side of Ministers comparable in ability and force to Joffre, Foch and Haig. General Gallieni had been a sick man for years and therefore did not possess sufficient vitality to enforce the advice which his genius counselled. Of Sir William Robertson I shall have something to say later on. A mistaken loyalty to Sir Douglas Haig fettered his common sense. The result was that the break through was postponed from victory to victory. We suffered enormous losses. Some of them were irreplaceable—in the case of officers and in the picked men who had joined the Kitchener armies in the first moments of enthusiasm. The Germans flaunted our wild onslaught on the Somme and advertised its failure by their

Roumanian campaign. They marched to the Danube to celebrate and exploit their victorious repulse of the Allied Armies on the Western stream. Mackensen crossed the great river from the Bulgarian side and marched on Bucharest. Falkenhayn's army had already fallen like an avalanche from the Carpathian heights and overwhelmed the ill-equipped Roumanian Armies on the plains. Roumania, with its oil and wheat, fell into German hands, and thus months and years were added to the War.

Before the attack on Roumania came, I was disturbed by news from the Balkans, which indicated a movement on the part of Bulgaria against her Trans-Danubian neighbour. We had also received a disquieting memorandum from Colonel Thomson (afterwards Lord Thomson), our military attaché at Bucharest, as to the equipment of the Roumanian Army. In guns and ammunition it was quite unequal to the armament which the forces of the Central Powers could easily spare for the attack. I spoke to one of the military staff at the War Office on the subject, but he tried to comfort me by assuring me that apart from the fact that the Germans had no troops or guns to spare from the Somme, where he said their losses in men and material were gigantic, it was getting too late for German action in Roumania, as snow would already have fallen on the Carpathians, and the passes were impervious to artillery. Moreover, he did not think much of Colonel Thomson or his report. I was not completely reassured, and a day or two later I sent in to the Chief of the Imperial General Staff the following note : —

> "D.M.O.
>
> I have just seen the telegram announcing the declaration of war by Bulgaria against Roumania. This is an additional ground for the anxiety which I expressed to you on Saturday as to the possibilities in the immediate future in the Balkans. I then expressed some apprehension that Hindenburg, who has strong Eastern proclivities and has always been opposed to the concentration of Germanic forces in the west, would direct his attention to the crushing of Roumania, and that we ought to be thinking out every practicable plan for giving effective support to Roumania in the event of her being heavily attacked. We cannot afford another Serbian tragedy. We were warned early in 1915 that the Germans meant, in confederation with the Bulgars, to wipe Serbia out. In spite of that fact, when the attack came we had not even purchased a single mule to aid the Serbians through Salonika. The result was that when our troops landed there, owing to lack of equipment and appropriate transport, they could not go inland and Serbia was crushed.
>
> I hope that we shall not allow the same catastrophe to befall Roumania through lack of timely forethought.

There are four disquieting facts in the situation: —

1. Hindenburg's well-known Eastern inclinations.

2. The declaration of war by Bulgaria against Roumania. I cannot believe Ferdinand would have taken this risk where it was quite unnecessary unless he had received substantial guarantees of German assistance in the attack on Roumania.

3. The slackening of the German attack on Verdun. Hindenburg will certainly give up this foolish attack at the earliest possible opportunity. The abandonment of this operation will release hundreds of heavy guns and hundreds of thousands of good troops. If in addition to this he were prepared gradually to give ground on the Somme, making us pay for it as he retires, he could transfer several more divisions from the West to the East. He could give up four or five times as much ground as we have won during the past two months without surrendering any vital positions.*

4. I can hardly think that the equipment of the Roumanian Army would enable it long to resist an attack from an Austro-Germanic-Bulgarian force, armed with hundreds of heavy guns and supplied with enormous quantities of heavy shell. The Roumanians are very scantily supplied with heavy guns and I doubt whether their supplies of ammunition are sufficient to enable them to get through a continuous fight lasting over several weeks.

I therefore once more urge that the General Staff should carefully consider what action we could take in conjunction with France and Italy immediately to relieve the pressure on Roumania if a formidable attack developed against her. There may be nothing in my fears, but no harm could be done by being prepared for all contingencies.

D. LLOYD GEORGE.

4/9/16."

The Russians made a gallant effort to help the outnumbered and out-gunned Roumanian Army. But by Christmas the greater part of Roumania was in the hands of the enemy. The Roumanian King was forced to an abject peace, and a country which had been a menace and a peril to the Central Powers became to them a fruitful source of much-needed supplies of oil and corn. Roumania and Serbia were both *hors de combat*; Greece had been neutralised, with the pro-German elements in its Government right on top. Three

---

* I am entitled to point out that five months later the Germans actually adopted this plan and by doing so completely upset the strategy of the Nivelle offensive.

countries which between them could have thrown more than a million excellent soldiers into action on the side of the Allies had been eliminated from the calculations. The effort to save Roumania had finally exhausted the great strength of Russia. The Allied generals, in contemplating the results of their strategy, found refuge in grotesque computations of German losses on the Somme. They were placed at a million on the British Front alone. We were left to imagine what havoc the French had wrought with their guns. Our great offensive had failed in the avowed objective of a break through and we took refuge in statistics. Sir Douglas Haig had not achieved his strategic aim, but a distinguished academician more than made up for the failure by a great statistical triumph he achieved in one of the back rooms of the War Office. The learned professor was acting under the direction and on information supplied by the " Intelligence " Department of the War Office. Surely its officials never displayed greater intelligence than when they played up to the urgent need of the army chiefs for some symbol of victory. As a matter of fact we lost on our front 50 per cent. more men than the Germans did. The French casualties were not as heavy as ours but they also were heavier than the German losses.

Thus ended the third campaign of the Great War.

CHAPTER XIX

MINISTRY OF MUNITIONS: PRACTICAL ACHIEVEMENTS

DURING a considerable part of the time occupied by the events described in the foregoing pages, my own departmental work was the development of our munition production. I have already told how, upon my appointment at the beginning of June, 1915, as Minister of Munitions, I proceeded to organise this new Department of State. I must now give some account of the work we were able to carry out during the thirteen months that I was responsible for its direction, until my translation to the War Office in July, 1916.

I shall not, of course, attempt to write a detailed history of the immense range of activities covered by the Ministry; but shall confine my notice to a few only of the developments of outstanding importance which took place during that period. They will serve as samples to illustrate the infinite variety of problems we were faced with, and the measure of success with which we achieved their solution.

1. GUN CONFERENCE AT BOULOGNE

When I undertook the official task of manufacturing munitions for the British Army, the War Office view of my duty was that my sole business was to comply with the demands which came from their Ordnance Department. Once I fulfilled these requisitions my statutory responsibility was, according to their interpretation, at an end. In a letter dated 5th June, 1915, from the War Office, detailing the relations between that Department and the Ministry of Munitions, it was laid down that "the duties of the new Department with regard to the supply of each kind of munitions will begin when the requirements of the War Office have been made known to it, as regards the kind, quantity, and quality of such munitions, and they will end when the delivery of such munitions has been made to the War Office."

I took a different and a much wider view of my responsibility. The rigid and hardened mentality of the War Office refused to bend or give to any facts that were not stale with age, and chronicled in accepted military histories. They rejected all experience which they had not been taught during the training they received in the days of their remote youth. I had been driven by their stubborn attitude to the conclusion that if we waited until our Whitehall generals woke up to the realities it might be too late then to save the situation. For months the Commander-in-Chief in the field had called their attention to the difference between this war and any other war which had ever been waged before by the British or any other army, because of the unexpected substitution of siege warfare for the anticipated war of movement. This altered the munitions problem so far as cannon were concerned in at least three respects: (1) It called for much bigger calibre guns and mortars than any hitherto sent to the field; (2) It necessitated a quite unprecedented expenditure of shell; and (3) shrapnel which was invaluable against masses of men moving in the open field or in searching out inadequate cover, became useless when the opposing troops were sheltering in a deep trench; and therefore the need of the Army was for high explosive of the heaviest calibre to tear up wire and to crash into trenches and parapets. I had learned from the correspondence placed at my disposal by Sir John French that he had repeatedly urged this point of view upon Lord Kitchener. I therefore came to the conclusion that I had to take the risk of a personal initiative, not merely in methods adopted for executing orders which came from the War Office but in determining for myself what the needs of the Army were and in organising my programme accordingly.

Not having the training of a soldier, and having no personal knowledge of these matters beyond what I had acquired during the past few months by contact with French generals and British officers —and these talks were not adequate to enable me to formulate a detailed and reliable programme for guns, machine-guns, and rifles —I decided to take immediate steps to consult with men of authority, and especially with men who had personal experience of the practical exigencies of the situation in the battlefield. It was useless to rely upon the Ordnance Department of the War Office. I was convinced that with them shrapnel was not a necessity of war but had become a point of honour. They felt that they could not desert it without a reflection upon their own prevision and patriotism. I decided, therefore, to go behind them to men who had first-hand knowledge of the actualities and requirements of the present War. This decision was reflected in the following note which I find amongst my papers:

" That a conference be arranged at the earliest moment between the French Military Authorities and M.M. (Minister of Munitions) on the one hand and the British Military Authorities and M.M. on the other with a view to arriving at a common basis for computing the number and calibres of guns and the quantity and natures of ammunition necessary to ensure the success of the next great offensive operation on the Western Front."

This turned out to be a momentous decision, for in the sequel it undoubtedly revolutionised the whole of our ideas as to the scale and character of the requirements of our Army. The conference was fixed for 19th June, 1915, at Boulogne. Before this conference I was confronted with a gun programme which even those who then framed it afterwards admitted was quite unequal to the needs of the military situation. I decided to test its sufficiency by drawing upon the best experience available from the battle front. I made arrangements with M. Albert Thomas, who was organising munitions in France, for the attendance of representatives of the French artillery. I asked him to bring along not merely the official adviser of his Ministry on these matters, but also, if possible, someone from the front who had actual experience of the effect of both the French and German artillery, with a view to ascertaining what kind of guns it would be most useful to manufacture, and in what proportions. Boulogne was crowded up to the attics and the only accommodation available for the conference was a frowsy room at a second-rate hotel (later in the War the whole hotel was completely demolished down to the cellars by a bomb). I had communicated with Sir John French and asked him to send his very best artillery expert to the conference. When I arrived at Boulogne I was met by General Du Cane, who had been sent as the Commander-in-Chief's representative. As I discovered at the time, and even more completely later on, he was a man of great intelligence, and what was even more important to me under these conditions, he was more accessible to the influence of fresh facts and new ideas than most men high up in his profession with whom I had business dealings. The French were not present at the first conference, but I had a full discussion with General Du Cane and handed to him the following note for consideration: —

"Given an army of 1,000,000 men, what equipment would you require in guns of all natures—number of shells before you commenced a serious and sustained attack with a view to breaking through the German lines?"

This gives an idea of my views before the conference began.

Later on in the course of the proceedings this further question was posed: —

"What weekly output of ammunitions should we aim at developing month by month in order to supply an army in France of 18 army corps of 54 divisions, so as to allow it to develop its full power of offence?"

The following day we had two meetings, and there were present, in addition to the British delegates, M. Albert Thomas, General Gossot, of the French War Office, and a young French officer of the French Headquarters Staff of the name of Colonel Walch.

Before we came to the discussion of the guns there were some very important questions of co-ordination between the various Governments to be cleared up. The situation that had arisen abroad was illustrated in the lack of touch between the Allies on vital matters. Each of the Allied countries was running its own war on and behind the various fronts. I found that on munitions supply it was imperative that there should be much more intimate contact between the respective Governments. At the beginning of the year the Allies were still competing in the American market and putting up prices against each other. The Russians and ourselves were competing for T.N.T. whilst all the Allies were doing the same for other explosives and other materials. In one case the British Government withdrew from purchasing when it was discovered that it was being played off against the Russians. The price of picric acid was forced up by the demands of the French, and the whole metal and machinery market was deranged owing to the activity of certain people acting for Russia. Even amongst the Allies themselves there was no efficient system of controlling purchases and no co-ordination. France, for example, could not obtain export licences for coke from this country; and whilst demanding shell steel from us suddenly stopped the export of ferro-silicon.

We then proceeded to consider the question of artillery. For hours we discussed the whole problem of the kind of guns which the experience of the War had proved to be most useful, especially since the War had resolved itself into a question of attacking and defending earthen fortresses. I soon discovered that the ideas of the French general were just as antiquated as our own. He had the same superstitious belief in the efficacy of the wonderful light French gun, the *soixante-quinze*, for all purposes as our own generals had in the all-round potency of shrapnel. I had to contend not with a profession but with a priesthood, devoted to its own chosen idol. General Gossot had not much, if any, experience at the front in this war and his ideas were purely historic. On the other hand, Colonel Walch had been a kind of artillery liaison officer, and in that capacity he had seen the French and German artillery in action from Switzerland up to the British lines, and he had observed with scientific care and accuracy the results produced by the different kinds of guns and shells. He was a young man not only of great intelligence but of reckless courage, for he threw over his commanding officer with some approach to contempt for his ignorance. That demands more fearlessness for an army officer than crossing no-man's-land in the face of a machine-gun. I found afterwards that he was an Alsatian Huguenot, and he was certainly imbued with a full measure of the spirit of Protestant revolt against authority. The conference soon resolved itself into a dialogue between Colonel Walch and myself, neither Thomas, the French General nor General Du Cane taking much part. It was hardly a dialogue; it was rather a cross-examination on my part with a view to extracting from Colonel Walch all the information which he undoubtedly possessed, and obtaining from him his definite opinion as to the kind of gun it would be most useful for us to manufacture for the service of our army, having regard to the kind of warfare to which we were now committed.

The hotel was situated opposite the English Episcopal Church. A few yards lower down was the Scottish Presbyterian Church. After this talk had been going on for hours, I heard through the open windows a distant sound of hymns being sung in these churches and soon after saw the congregations pouring out from the two churches, carrying prayer and hymn books in their hands. It suddenly occurred to me that this was Sunday morning and that I had been discussing earnestly with these officers the problem which was repeatedly referred to by Colonel Walch as a question " which was the best gun for destroying material " and " which was the best gun for killing men." And this on a day consecrated to the worship of the Prince of Peace. The thought made me shudder. I pulled myself together only by reflecting that this was a war that had been forced upon us by the arrogance of brute force crushing down the weak, and that I had been driven by the relentless hand of Fate to choose between giving my individual assent to the shedding of blood and assenting to a surrender of international right and liberty in Europe.

By this time both General Du Cane and I had a very clear idea as to the lines upon which our gun programme ought to proceed. I had the best evidence afterwards that, although he had taken no part in the proceedings, he had listened with great intentness and had not missed a word of the clear and emphatic statements of the young French artillerist.

By that time we had both come to the definite conclusion that our ideas as to the manufacture of artillery would have to be considerably enlarged, and that we should have to develop our gun construction on a very much larger scale than anything that had been hitherto contemplated, both as regards quantity and calibre. On leaving the hotel for the boat, General Du Cane expressed his satisfaction with what he regarded as the most fruitful Council of War he had ever attended, and then he said to me: " What I am about to say to you now will make you think much less of me." I asked him what it was and he replied: " After this conference I have completely changed my mind as to the requirements of the Army." I told him that his admission made me think far more highly of him and that it was creditable both to his intelligence and integrity. He promised that after consultation with the Commander-in-Chief he would prepare a revised estimate of the needs of the Army.

At that date the War had been going on for ten months. Guns and shells had been a subject of vexatious and fretful correspondence between the soldiers at the front and the War Office, and yet this was the first conference that had taken place on that subject between the artillerists with actual battle experience on the French and British Fronts.

As a result of this conference, Sir John French sent to the War Office on 25th June, 1915, a revised estimate of his requirements of heavy guns. The War Office forwarded this letter to the Ministry of Munitions on 30th June, for observations, accompanied by a table showing the additional heavy guns which equipment on this scale would involve for a force of 70 divisions. After an exchange of correspondence, the Ministry submitted a programme of its expected monthly gun deliveries up to the following spring, and towards the end of July drew up a revised programme showing a faster rate of delivery of heavy guns.

I was not, however, satisfied with these programmes. In view of the information I had gathered at Boulogne, I was convinced that for the success of our operations, an overwhelming mass of guns of the heaviest calibres was essential—an opinion confirmed by the success of our advance at Hooge, after a thorough preliminary bombardment with heavy guns, in early August. After careful enquiry as to possible sources of supply in this country and abroad, I decided to put in hand a very greatly increased programme, which would provide guns on a scale ranging for some types up to 25 per cent. above the War Office allowance, and this not for 70 but for 100 divisions.

I felt that to break through the formidable entrenchments of the Germans would involve a battering by artillery far heavier than the War Office yet realised, and that there should also be a margin available to provide for contingencies. If the guns were not all required for the various fronts of the British Army, the surplus would be available to supply the urgent needs of the Russians, who were at that moment suffering severely from the superior artillery of Germany and Austria.

Sir H. Llewellyn Smith, on behalf of the Ministry of Munitions, sent to the War Office a statement showing my new programme, and explained in his covering letter: —

"I am therefore directed to state that orders have already been placed which will not only cover the additional numbers suggested in your letter of 8th September, but will also provide a very considerable margin for possible future needs. The Minister has been influenced in providing such a margin by the important consideration that the ordering of these large quantities will make it worth while to have new machinery on a larger scale installed, both at home and abroad, which will hasten the dates at which considerable deliveries can take place in 1916. A larger number of heavy guns will by this plan be delivered during the critical first months of 1916 than would otherwise have been possible. . . ."

It might have been imagined that the War Office would be delighted to learn that its desires were thus being more than fulfilled. On the contrary, it was furious at the presumption shown by the Ministry in daring to increase or anticipate the programme laid down for it. The preliminary warning of a storm came in the shape of a letter from the War Office, dated 1st October, 1915, which stated that on learning that " the purchase of a large number of heavy howitzers over and above any demand made by the War Office was contemplated by your Ministry," Lord Kitchener had consulted with Sir John French to find out how many he wanted, and obtained his confirmation that the schedule submitted by him in June represented his requirements. The Army Council, therefore, had no wish for my extra guns, and suggested that the orders for them should be transferred to Russia's account.

I directed an impenitent answer to be sent to the War Office. The letter pointed out that the large orders were necessary to secure early delivery of even the War Office figure of requirements, while early delivery of the extra guns might well prove to have a decisive effect on the campaign. The letter continued: —

" Should the Secretary of State differ from the above views, the Minister of Munitions is prepared at any time to discuss the matter with him, or if he should prefer, he might bring it before the attention of the Cabinet. The Minister is not, in any case, prepared to cancel the orders he has placed for the provision of heavy howitzers, unless the Government as a whole will take the responsibility of deciding that the proposed provision is excessive."

If in fact there proved to be a surplus, I said that it would still be possible to pass this on to the Allies. But I made no offer to adopt the suggestion that some of the guns should be manufactured to Russian patterns, as such an alteration of the orders I had placed would have upset the existing arrangements and caused considerable delay in gun production. This called forth the wrath of Lord Kitchener, who expressed his disapproval of the action of the Ministry of Munitions in a memorandum, entitled: " Supply of Heavy Guns to the Army," which he circulated to the Cabinet. In this memorandum he called on the Cabinet to judge between him and me. He recounted the history of the dispute, and pointed out that the additional programme which I had put in hand entailed a provision of the following heavy guns over and above the requirements of the War Office: —

60-pdr.		120 guns, equivalent to 15 divisions
6-in. howitzer		220 ,, ,, ,, 27 ,,
8-in. ,,	⎱	
9.2-in. ,,	⎰	259 ,, ,, ,, 49 ,,
12-in. ,,	⎱	
15-in. ,,	⎰	40 ,, ,, ,, 45 ,,

639

After describing the latest exchange of correspondence with the Ministry on the matter he declared: —

" The point I wish to emphasise is that, if these extra guns are ordered for the War Office, the War Office will not be able to provide the personnel for the batteries required to place them in the field, for, even if the men were forthcoming, it would be quite impossible to find the artillery officers necessary for this service."

He urged, therefore, that these guns should be allotted to Russia, and should be manufactured to Russian calibres and patterns.

Thereupon the matter was thrashed out in the Cabinet. But I gave way neither on the issue of reducing my orders nor on that of making the guns to the Russian pattern, for if surplus guns should be available for the Russians it would be possible to furnish them with ammunition as well. I had for some time been urging that arrangements should be made to equip the Russians; but to change these orders to Russian calibres and patterns would have involved delays and complications in production. The Cabinet appointed a Committee under the chairmanship of Lord Crewe to deal with the matter. It sat once, at the Ministry of Munitions, and examined General von Donop, who repeated his objections to the enlarged programme. I did not state my case in reply. Here is an extract from Sir William Sutherland's notes, taken at the meeting: —

". . . I was somewhat mystified as to what was the official finding of the meeting; the various speeches being severely critical as described, and Mr. Lloyd George, beyond outlining the position generally, not making the spirited and continuous fight so often showed by him in similar circumstances.

'I suppose, sir,' said J. T. Davies when the meeting was over, 'that means the end of your programme.'

'No,' said Mr. Lloyd George, 'it means the end of the Committee,' and straightaway started his orders for the prodigious work."

In fact the Committee adjourned without coming to any decision, and never met again. The subject was dropped—but not the programme. I pushed that through. Before I ceased to be Minister of Munitions, it turned out that even more guns were needed by our Army than the large number I had ordered. When they were furnished by the machinery and facilities the Ministry of Munitions had ordered for the enlargement of production, no difficulty was experienced in finding the necessary complement of officers and men for the batteries. I may here anticipate the course of events so far as to point out that when the Ministry of Munitions finally produced this " unhouselled and unannealed " surplusage of guns, the War Office resolutely refused to part with them to help Russia, on the ground that they were all needed by our own troops in France, and a good many more. It was with difficulty that I persuaded the Staff to dispense with a few of the lighter guns for Russia.

But at first there was a good deal of gibing and sniping about what was called my mad production of heavy guns, and I had evidence that the War Office meant to neutralise my extravagance by refusing to train artillerists to man this wasteful surplus. I decided to take the matter up with the Prime Minister, and if necessary with the War Committee, and in order to check the facts upon which I intended to base my case, I wrote on 15th November, 1915, to General Sir Ivor Philipps, who had been Military Secretary to the Ministry at the time the order was given, to ask him for his recollection of my instructions. He was at that time preparing to leave for France with the Division he commanded. His reply was as follows: —

> " Headquarters,
> 38th (Welsh) Division,
> Avington Park Camp,
> Winchester.

My dear Minister,

When the Big Gun Programme was under discussion you repeatedly urged on your staff that your main object in increasing the order for guns was to ensure the maximum possible delivery at the earliest possible date. This you specially impressed on us, both verbally and in writing. The necessity for impressing early deliveries by giving larger orders to contractors was passed on by me to the departments concerned, and we did our utmost to see that your very clear orders on the subject were carried out.

In many conversations with me you stated that your main objects in placing the Big Gun orders were: —

1. To ensure earliest possible deliveries by giving large orders to firms to encourage them to increase their power of output.

2. To provide guns for 100 divisions, should necessity arise hereafter to put that number in the Field.

M

3. To provide a surplus of very heavy guns to meet the latest views of advanced French artillery experts, that the teachings of the War tended to show that in future more and more heavy guns would be required to secure victory.

4. That if these guns were in excess of our own requirements, they would be invaluable as a reserve to assist our Allies.

It must be remembered that you laboured under great difficulties. You got no assistance from the War Office.

After your Conference at Boulogne with M. Thomas and the French artillery experts, as a result of the information you then collected the War Office at once put forward an increased and entirely revised programme.

No suggestion of this increased programme had been mentioned by the War Office while the ordering of guns was in their hands. When, however, the responsibility was on your shoulders, the demands of the War Office were at once increased.

I do not think you need fear that you have ordered too many guns or shells. What you have to consider in the War Council is, whether you are preparing to man the guns or even half of them when delivered. I fear that the War Council is neglecting this point. You will remember that I prepared a note on the subject when at the Ministry. You have done your share of the work of providing guns and shells; the country will one day appreciate your great work in this respect.

Yours sincerely,

IVOR PHILIPPS."

I have quoted this letter in full because it gives in compact form, and from the pen of a distinguished Army officer, a summary alike of my attitude to this issue and of the War Office reluctance to admit the need for the guns I was providing. In contrast to their attitude then, I may add that a year later, Sir William Robertson, writing in November, 1916, said:—

" We must have a much greater amount of heavy artillery than we now possess, and be able to turn out an almost unlimited amount of ammunition."

At the same time Sir Douglas Haig wrote:—

" An ample supply of munitions is also an essential. The enormous quantities required have been furnished this year with unfailing regularity. But the great reserves required in readiness for next year can only be accumulated by reducing expenditure to an absolute minimum during the winter, and then only provided the output can be maintained at the full rates estimated."

The " Official History of the War " makes it clear that even the "extravagant" programme, for which I took responsibility, was insufficient for the purpose of bombarding the elaborate entrenchments constructed on the Somme plateau by the Germans. The official historian points out that we had a shortage of guns, more especially in the heavier calibres. These were the very calibres where I had exceeded the amended requisition of the War Office and thus drawn on myself Lord Kitchener's censure.

By November, 1916, a whole series of increased demands for big guns had been made by the War Office, and the Ministry of Munitions had been compelled to expand considerably the programme which I had been pressed so hard to curtail. Fortunately I had acquired machinery which was equal to the manufacture of this expanded requisition.

2. NATIONAL FACTORIES

To increase the supply of shells was our most immediate aim, for it was the shell shortage which had chiefly impressed the popular imagination and brought about the crisis which gave birth to the Ministry. But along with shells I had undertaken the responsibility for all the rest of the wide range of military supplies—guns, rifles, machine-guns, bombs, trench-warfare equipment, military transport, and optical instruments. Soon after the formation of the Ministry, tanks were handed over by the Admiralty. Control of the output of the finished article led inevitably to control of the preliminary stages of manufacture, back to the raw materials involved.

The consequence was that the scope of control exercised by the Ministry widened steadily and ineluctably until before the end of the War it covered practically the whole industrial life of the nation. The form of control became increasingly stringent with the progressive shortage of materials, until by the end of the War no one could start a new business or enlarge an old one except for war purposes. Everyone was liable to have buildings, plant or machinery requisitioned for more urgent work. None of the industrial metals and few raw materials could be used by anyone without Government licence. The nation concentrated all its great strength and skill on victory.

The materials which the Ministry of Munitions brought under its control included nearly a hundred main categories, and extended not only to more obvious articles such as iron, steel, copper, chemicals, and machine tools, but to bricks, flax-seed, glass-ware, waste paper and yarn. Ultimately the Ministry assumed responsibility for all visible supplies of such materials, controlled all private importation and the distribution of materials to non-munition as well as to munition trades, thereby virtually bringing all the industries using materials which entered into production of munitions under the control of the department.

. It was not an arbitrary bureaucracy; for the Ministry acted throughout in very close co-operation with the particular trade or industry controlled. Frequently, important members of the trade had official posts and executive authority in the Ministry; while in these and other cases an Advisory Committee representing the trade was constituted as a consultative body to advise the department or section of the Ministry concerned. Where a trade had already a representative association, we discussed matters with it; and if no such body already existed, we sought to promote its formation. By contributing to, or bearing the whole cost of, needed extensions and adaptations of factories on the one hand, and by arrangements for limitation of profits and the operation of the Excess Profits Duty on the other, our national industry was welded into a great public undertaking for the winning of the War.

Even after utilising every workshop and factory capable of turning out munitions, we found that the output would be inadequate unless we supplemented our resources by the setting up of emergency buildings. This was more particularly the case when we came to the larger calibre shells and facilities for shell-filling. I therefore took steps to press forward as soon as the Ministry of Munitions was set up the policy which I had already been promoting as Chairman of the Munitions of War Committee, or organising special national factories for the definite purpose of supplementing our existing resources for munition production; particularly for making shells and explosives, for shell-filling and completing ammunition.

The first few months of the Ministry's existence saw the establishment of an imposing group of these national factories. By the end of December, 1915, when the Ministry had been in existence only seven months, there were, in addition to the Royal Factories at Woolwich, Waltham Abbey, Enfield Lock and Farnborough—which had been transferred from the War Office in the course of the autumn —and certain factories for explosives, no less than 73 new national factories. Of these, 36 were national shell factories for turning out the lighter natures of shell; 13 were national projectile factories, mainly concerned with heavier shell; 13 were national filling factories. There were eight new factories for making explosives, a new factory for filling trench mortar bombs, and two gauge factories which I took over to ensure an adequate supply of gauges for the new concerns which were springing up everywhere to produce munitions. Progress had been hampered in every direction by the inadequate supply of gauges.

As time went on, this array of national factories was steadily increased, both in number and in the variety of the products for the manufacture of which they were erected or adapted. By the end of the War they numbered in all 218; and covered not only every kind of munition, from cannon and aeroplanes to small-arms ammunition, but saw-mills, factories for boxes, tools, optical instruments and ball-bearings, and establishments for sorting and storing salvage.

The total of 218 included the four Royal Factories which were in existence before the War, the wood alcohol factory at Coleford set up by the Woods and Forests Department in 1913, and three or four explosives factories initiated by the War Office or by Lord Moulton's Committee on High Explosives between November, 1914, and May, 1915. Two of the national shell factories had already been begun under the Munitions of War Committee before the Ministry of Munitions was set up. Over nine-tenths of the remaining two hundred odd factories were constructed under the auspices of the Ministry, or with the aid of Government advances, leaving less than a score of establishments which were already engaged on production of necessary supplies such as gauges, ball-bearings, cotton waste or acetone, before they were taken over and nationalised.

The total covers only concerns engaged in manufacture or repair. It excludes the large classes of inspection and storage depots, mines, quarries, and other similar undertakings which were controlled by the Ministry. It excludes also the State-owned plant within the works of contractors, even where operated by servants of the department. And, of course, it does not touch the vast array of private firms which, frequently with the aid of substantial Government subsidies, were busily engaged upon munition manufacture. The great nucleus of national factories stood at the heart of the munitions industry as a colossal supplement to the Royal Ordnance Factories and a guarantee, within the hand of the Government, that the supplies for our armies could be expanded to meet the rapidly increasing demands from the front.

The first group of these factories which I was responsible for setting up was the group of national shell factories. The pioneer of these was the factory at Leeds, started by the Local Munitions Committee in May, 1915. The Leeds engineering firms had been urged to arrange a scheme of co-operation for production of munitions, and like practical men, they went to Woolwich in April to study the processes involved. Thereupon they came to the conclusion that the best way for them to work was to take or erect premises where, with their joint assistance, tools, workmen, supervision and inspection could all be assembled and the work carried out on a non-profit basis by a committee of management.

By 7th May, a draft scheme had secured general approval, and the next day the formal sanction of the Government was given and the work was put in hand forthwith. On 31st May, a national shell factory was approved for Keighley, and when at the beginning of June, I made my tour, as Minister of Munitions-elect, of the industrial districts, I was able to point to the Leeds effort as an example which could be widely applied. The idea was eagerly taken up, and as a result seventeen of these factories had been approved by me before the end of June, and ten more were added before the end of September.

These national shell factories were co-operative undertakings run by Boards of Management approved by the Ministry and provided by the local Munitions Committees. They represented in the main engineering talent which had not hitherto been engaged in any shell production, and at first they were chiefly concerned with the manufacture of the lighter types of shell. As time went on they were able to extend their range to include some of the heavier natures, and before the end of the War three factories at Leeds which had begun as shell factories were transferred to the ordnance factory class.

The national shell factories harnessed the ability of the engineering industry outside the existing armament firms. I was also concerned to make fuller use of the experience inside these firms, particularly for the production of heavy shell. In July, 1915, the actual output of this shell was far below the promises which had been made, and the demands of the army in the field for large high-explosive shell were rapidly growing. I was arranging a big increase in the programme of heavy artillery, and I had to ensure an adequate supply of ammunition for these additional guns, as well as for those already in the field.

Accordingly, on 13th July, 1915, I held a conference with the representatives of nine leading armament firms to see what steps must be taken to ensure the completion not only of existing programmes, but of the new and much bigger programmes which would be required.

The method hitherto adopted by the War Office of relying upon the existing works, extended with the aid of the grants from the Exchequer which I had authorised in the previous autumn, had proved definitely inadequate. But the armament firms strongly disliked the idea of my proceeding to found new and independent national factories for the production of heavy shell. So we reached a compromise. The armament firms would themselves build and manage new factories, additional to their existing works, the Government providing all the capital, both for the building and the running. The new factories would be Government property and the armament firms would provide managers to run them as Government agents, and under the control of the Ministry. The firms setting up and managing these works for the Ministry would get a percentage commission on the output. I must add that Messrs. Cammell Laird refused to take any commission for erection or management of the factory they set up in Nottingham. These factories were known as national projectile factories, as distinct from the national shell factories which I have already described. Seven national projectile factories were started in the following month,

August, 1915, and four in September; and by the end of 1915 the number had risen to thirteen.   Before the War ended there were fifteen, and, in addition, five of the national shell factories were transferred to the department of the Ministry managing the projectile factories, on account of the nature of the work they were carrying out.

Some indication of the speed with which these national factories got into their stride, and of the service they were able to render, can be gathered from the following figures.   Output from the national shell factories started, in the case of the first-established among them, in the summer of 1915, and from the earlier national projectile factories in the autumn of that year.   In these closing months of 1915 their combined output was 200,400 empty shell, nearly all of the lighter natures.   In 1916, their total output was 6,712,300, more than half of which was medium and heavy shell.

In just over three years, from mid-1915 to the close of hostilities in 1918, the combined total output of empty shell from the national shell and national projectile factories was 40,143,300.

Further, the cost of shell produced by these factories was decidedly lower than that of supplies from outside firms—so much so that in the case of the national projectile factories it amply compensated for the loss of value incurred through the difference between the original cost of their erection and equipment and the sums ultimately realised by them on disposal, while the lower costs achieved by the national shell factories not only made a large direct saving in expenditure on supplies, but enabled the charges of outside firms to be checked and reduced.

Like the national shell factories, the national projectile factories were used as time went on for a variety of other purposes in addition to shell production.   In 1917, seven of them were busy on gun repair, one on making gun parts, and another on making guns.   Yet another, Cathcart, turned over to aeroplane work from May, 1917.   Grenade mortars, aero-engines, and shells for the Italians were among the supplies turned out by these factories; and before the end of the War five of them had become classified as ordnance factories, and were mainly occupied in making and repairing cannon.

3.   FILLING THE SHELLS

The two groups of factory I have described, the shell and the projectile factories, ensured a provision of empty shell, but it was also necessary to provide explosives to fill and propel them, and works to carry out the filling and completion of rounds of ammunition.   The story of the arrangements made for shell filling by the War Office is a sardonic comment on the attack directed against civilians for their presumptuous interference with the professional soldier in the discharge of his duties.

The need to secure outside sources of supply for high explosives had been realised early in the War by the War Office, for the excellent reason that the manufacture of high explosives had never been undertaken by the ordnance factories. There was practically no trade capacity for the manufacture of military tri-nitro-toluene, commonly known as T.N.T., a coal extract which eventually became an important ingredient in the bursting charge of high-explosive shell, and the stocks of the commercial explosive which were available needed treatment to bring them up to service standards.

The Defence of the Realm (Consolidation) Act, 1914, became law on 27th November, 1914. Under it the Government had power to take over factories engaged in the production of warlike stores, and the very next day the War Office descended on the Rainham Chemical Works, on the Thames opposite Woolwich, and commandeered them for the purification of crude T.N.T. At this time, however, the available supply was only about 10 or 12 tons a week, provided by a single firm.

The Board of Trade, when approached by the War Office, recommended that a distinguished civilian, Lord Moulton, should be entrusted with the organisation of an adequate supply of explosives. He was the ablest scientific lawyer of his generation. He was appointed Chairman of a Committee of High Explosives. He insisted that a new State factory must be set up for T.N.T. production, and made an arrangement with a firm of acid manufacturers, Messrs. Chance and Hunt, in December, 1914, whereby they set to work in January, 1915, to erect at Oldbury a factory for the Explosives Supply Branch of the War Office. This was the first national factory for manufacturing T.N.T.

Lord Moulton further entered into an arrangement with the Admiralty to set up a big factory at Queen's Ferry for production of gun-cotton. But the site could not be secured until May, 1915, and at the end of that month the Admiralty backed out of the arrangement. The new factory thus fell to the Ministry of Munitions, and was developed for the production of not only gun-cotton, but T.N.T. On becoming Minister of Munitions I found that there had been no survey of the prospective demand for explosives in view of orders already given, and that the provision then made for the production of explosives was quite inadequate to supply prospective requirements. In July, 1915, four more national explosives factories were established by the Ministry, including the huge factory at Gretna for the production of cordite. The construction of this factory had been recommended in May by the Munitions of War Committee, of which I was chairman, and was authorised by me as Minister of Munitions in the following month. It was also based on plans and proposals prepared, at the request of the Committee, by Lord Moulton.

The assistance rendered to the nation by Lord Moulton in this matter of explosives has never been sufficiently recognised.

By the end of the War there were no fewer than 32 H.M. explosives factories among the national factories controlled by the Ministry. We had been compelled to build these factories ourselves, because for some explosives, such as T.N.T., there was before the War an entire lack of industrial capacity, while for others like cordite there appeared to be no prospect of a large-scale demand after the War which would induce existing manufacturers to extend their works. In consequence of these arrangements in the case of explosives, the bulk of our home-produced war supplies came from these new national factories.

At the outbreak of the War, State production was limited to the Royal Gunpowder Factory at Waltham Abbey, which made about 75 short tons (i.e., 150,000 lb.) of cordite and gunpowder a week. By 1917, the national explosives factories were producing over ten times this quantity of cordite weekly, and of explosives of all kinds more than 2,000 tons a week. In the course of the War, the grand total of their output of explosives was over $317\frac{1}{2}$ thousand tons: being 236,251 tons of high explosive (mainly T.N.T.) and 81,341 tons of propellants (mainly cordite). The need for these factories is illustrated by figures given by Lord Moulton in a paper dated 13th April, 1915, which he prepared for the Munitions of War Committee. He showed that the total estimated amounts of high explosives required by the Navy and Army in the months of February and March, 1915, were 4,505,600 lb. The actual supplies obtained and used were 1,038,802 lb., or considerably less than a quarter of the requirements.

Like the national shell and projectile factories, these explosives factories proved of great value, apart from the essential importance of their output, in furnishing data for simplification of process and reduction of cost in the production of supplies by other firms. The system of cost and efficiency returns which was established in them gave rise to a general competition in economy, not only between different national factories, but between these and the trade manufacturers. They provided a very economical source of supply as compared with either American sources or British contractors, and enabled very considerable reductions to be made in 1917 in the contract price for explosives.

But our troubles over explosives were not confined to the difficulties and delays of construction and equipment of our factories in war-time, when there was so much competition for labour and material. The most formidable obstruction I had to overcome came from the tardiness with which the War Office adapted itself to new conditions and fresh demands. It led to an emergency so critical that it very nearly wrecked the whole of our shell programme. This choice specimen of military rigidity in high quarters is best told in the words of Lord Moulton himself. Soon after I was nominated Minister of Munitions I received from him a letter, which apart from the fact that it is a startling exposure of military bureaucracy, is an interesting account of the kind and quantity of explosives fired in the War: —

> " Ministry of Munitions of War,
> Explosives Department,
> Institution of Mechanical Engineers,
> Storey's Gate,
> Westminster, S.W.
> 16th June, 1915.

Dear Mr. Lloyd George,

There is a matter of the greatest importance as to which I must request your advice and help in your position as Minister of Munitions.

From the time that I was first consulted on the question of the provision of high explosives I recognised that the lavish expenditure of these explosives which is characteristic of the present War made it absolutely impossible to proceed on the lines which up to that time had regulated our naval and military services. The adoption of T.N.T. as our principal high explosive was but two or three months old when the War began, and I doubt whether there was at that time a production of 20 *tons per week* of this explosive in the whole of Great Britain, while the production of lyddite must almost have ceased by reason of the belief that it would be substantially superseded by T.N.T. Would-be suppliers were told by War Office officials that it would not be used. Of neither of these explosives was there any Government manufacture or even any industrial manufacture except such as I have mentioned. *When I add that in little more than two days the Germans fired off over 800 tons of such explosives* * you will see how absolutely impossible it was to rely on the sources of supply which then existed. . . .

The only hope of obtaining an adequate supply of explosive lies in the proper production and utilisation of T.N.T.

This produce has the property of animating explosives, of which it forms only a small part, the remainder being principally nitrate of ammonia, a substance which can be obtained in practically unlimited quantities. Schneiderite, which is at the moment the favourite explosive of the French, is of this type. Only one-tenth of it is T.N.T. . . .

So soon as I had realised the position I put it before the naval and military authorities, and pointed out that it was absolutely

* My italics.   D. Ll. G.

necessary to widen the list of high explosives and not to be content with using T.N.T. or lyddite alone. I fear it produced little impression at the time. But two or three months after I had done so, the Research Department at Woolwich demonstrated that by mixing T.N.T. with nitrate of ammonia they produced an explosive which was much more powerful than T.N.T. and equally safe. They showed that this could be done to an extent of one to four without lessening its explosive force and that it could be done to an extent of nearly half and half without even interfering with the existing convenient method of filling shells by melting the T.N.T. and pouring it into the shells. Some two months ago the use of this mixture was approved and directions were given that it should be applied to the whole of the land service for six-inch shells downwards and experiments were directed to be made with regard to the larger shells. . . .

To my great regret I find that those who have charge of the loading of shells have for the last two months completely disregarded the direction and now say that they do not propose to use the mixture for another month. I know of no reason except that they say that they have not got their warming cupboards for the nitrate of ammonia and it will take them some time to get them fitted up. I have no hesitation in saying that such a matter is quite trivial in comparison with the importance of so vital an improvement in our explosive supply at a critical period like this, and that to overcome such a difficulty should not have required more than a few days. . . .

I am certain that the possibility of an adequate supply of high explosives for the needs of the Services depends on the cordial acceptance of the means of economising the T.N.T. such as I have indicated, by artillerists and more especially by those in charge of the loading of shells. *It is hopeless for me to struggle to meet the extraordinary demands created by the War if there is on their part a disregard of or a reluctance to accept the necessary modifications of our artillery methods, which good sense and an appreciation of the magnitude of the problem before us dictate.*

You will excuse my speaking thus frankly, but I am satisfied that I have not said a word that I cannot support, and it is only by your coming to my help as Minister of Munitions that I can hope to obtain immediate and implicit acceptance of these all-important conditions of the supply to the Services.

Yours sincerely
MOULTON."

I realised that unless I could persuade the War Office to accept some considerable modification in the character of the explosive used

* My italics. D. Ll. G.

for filling, it was no use pressing forward the manufacture of shells, for we should not possess a sufficient quantity of the necessary ingredients to complete them. But here I was up against the inveterate rivalry between soldier and sailor. The Admiralty would not forgo their full quota of T.N.T. Why should the War Office be satisfied with a shell which was less perfect than that which the Admiralty insisted upon. This was not a question of factory supplies, but of departmental prestige. However, after a protracted struggle involving a loss of valuable time in the output of complete shell, a certain relaxation was achieved of the maximum requirements of the War Office. This enabled me to get along for a few weeks. But there was not enough T.N.T. to supply all the requirements of the shell programme, even in the reduced proportions which the War Office was prepared to allow. The delay was holding up the orders for machinery for the new filling factories, even the building of these factories. The character of the machine depended on whether the filling should be liquid or dry, and that again depended on the proportions of T.N.T. and ammonium nitrate, and the lay-out of the building depended on the kind of machinery which would be installed. The fight went on, and the consequent delays became more serious until the whole responsibility for design was wrenched from the War Office. We were turning out stacks of empty shell, but owing to these delays in deciding the mixture for the filling, the supply of complete shell was lagging seriously behind.

Two men in particular helped me to overcome this barrier erected by professional suspicion and procrastination. One was Sir Eric Geddes, of whom I have already spoken, the other was Colonel Arthur Lee (now Lord Lee of Fareham). When Sir Ivor Philipps was appointed to the command of the Welsh Division in October, 1915, I invited Colonel Arthur Lee to become his successor. By training he was an artillery officer and thus possessed first-hand knowledge of some of our difficulties. I had known him for years as a Member of the House of Commons He was an able critic of the policies in which I was concerned as a Minister. I recognised his efficiency and intelligence as an opponent. He had taken a leading part in the agitation for eight dreadnoughts in 1908, and I am not sure he was not the inventor of the very telling phrase " We want eight and will not wait." I had on more than one occasion crossed swords with him in debate. He was a skilful swordsman, who gave few openings because he had the gift of both mastering his case thoroughly and presenting it forcibly. Early in the year 1915, on his temporary leave from France, he had brought me some startling information as to the failure of our artillery to make any impression on the barbed-wire entanglements of the enemy. He was a man of untiring industry, great resource, and practical capacity. Although an officer in the Army and proud of his profession, he was one of the few whose judgment was not paralysed by an opinion expressed by a senior in rank. I found that in every crisis he had a cool head, a clear eye, and a stout heart. During the many ensuing years of almost crushing responsibility through which I was destined to pass I found his understanding, his loyalty, and his courage of immeasurable support. As soon as he joined me at the Ministry of Munitions he spent his first few days in scouting around to see what was—and what was not—going on. With unerring judgment he fastened on the shell-filling snag. He it was who also perceived that Eric Geddes was the best man in the Ministry to undertake the task of reorganising that essential part of our business.

Among the interesting developments to which the chemical side of warfare gave rise I must mention the story of acetone. Here again we nearly came to grief for lack of timely forethought. This chemical, which was an essential element in the process of manufacturing cordite, for cartridges great and small, was commonly produced by destructive distillation of wood.

Before the War there was a small factory in the Forest of Dean set up by the Office of Woods and Forests to utilise waste cordwood. In May, 1915, this Office set up two fresh factories at Bideford and Dundee, which were transferred together with the Coleford factory, to the Ministry in October. Messrs. Kynoch's also set up a factory in the New Forest, which was nationalised in 1917. But this country is not one of the great timber-growing lands, and it takes a great deal of wood to produce a ton of acetone, so in practice we were dependent for the great bulk of our supply on imports from America.

But by the spring of 1915 the position in the American acetone market had become extremely delicate. British cordite firms were competing with each other and with the agents for the Allies. Prices were being forced up. American contractors were selling their output twice over and defaulting on their contracts. They even went to the length of insisting upon an advance in price upon their existing contracts with the British Government, and in the case of their default it proved impossible to recover damages from them.

Prompt steps were taken over here to eliminate the competition between British cordite makers for American acetone. But when this had been done and arrangements had been made for the purchase of all overseas supplies immediately available, I was confronted by a much more serious crisis. In the survey we made of all the various prospective requirements, it soon became clear that the supplies of wood alcohol for the manufacture of acetone would prove quite insufficient to meet the increasing demands, particularly in 1916. The matter was urgent, for without the acetone there would be no cordite for our cartridges, for either rifles or big guns.

As Chairman of the Munitions of War Committee I took this matter greatly to heart. While I was casting about for some solution of the difficulty, I ran against the late C. P. Scott, Editor of the *Manchester Guardian.* He was a friend in whose wisdom I had implicit faith. I told him of my problem and that I was on the look-out for a resourceful chemist who would help me to solve it. He said: "There is a very remarkable professor of chemistry in the University of Manchester willing to place his services at the disposal of the State. I must tell you, however, that he was born somewhere near the Vistula, and I am not sure on which side. His name is Weizmann." Scott could guarantee that whatever the country of origin, Weizmann was thoroughly devoted to the cause of the Allies, that the one thing he really cared about was Zionism, and that he was convinced that in the victory of the Allies alone was there any hope for his people. I knew Mr. Scott to be one of the shrewdest judges of men I had ever met. The world renown of his great paper had been built up on the soundness of his judgment—of men as well as of affairs. But I also trusted his patriotism implicitly. Pacifist as he was he believed in the essential justice of our intervention in this War. I took his word about Professor Weizmann and invited him to London to see me. I took to him at once. He is now a man of international fame. He was then quite unknown to the general public, but as soon as I met him I realised that he was a very remarkable personality. His brow gave assurance of a fine intellect and his open countenance gave confidence in his complete sincerity. I told him that we were in a chemical dilemma and asked him to assist us. I explained the shortage in wood alcohol and what it meant in munitionment. Could he help? Dr. Weizmann said he did not know, but he would try. He could produce acetone by a fermentation process on a laboratory scale, but it would require some time before he could guarantee successful production on a manufacturing scale.

"How long can you give me?" he asked. I said: "I cannot give you very long. It is pressing." Weizmann replied: "I will go at it night and day."

In a few weeks' time he came to me and said: "The problem is solved." After a prolonged study of the micro-flora existing on maize and other cereals, also of those occurring in the soil, he had succeeded in isolating an organism capable of transforming the starch of cereals, particularly that of maize, into a mixture of acetone butyl alcohol. The generations of these organisms die very quickly, and in quite a short time, working night and day as he had promised, he had secured a culture which would enable us to get our acetone from maize.

Now maize contains about two-thirds its weight of starch, and our sources of supply were very wide; so that this discovery enabled us to produce very considerable quantities of the vital chemical. To-day this discovery is the centre of an important industry.

In King's Lynn there was an oil-cake factory which had been converted in 1912 to make acetone from the starch content of potatoes. It had come into the field with promises of supply, but the quality of its output was not satisfactory, and financially the company was unsteady. So in March, 1916, it was nationalised, and by June it was making acetone from maize by the Weizmann process with highly successful and valuable results. The shipping shortage in 1917 which forced us to restrict all unnecessary imports, introduced yet another experiment. In the autumn of that year, horse-chestnuts were plentiful, and a national collection of them was organised for the purpose of using their starch content as a substitute for maize. The King's Lynn factory carried out the manufacture, and though at first the poor quality of the material hampered output, these difficulties were overcome, and the Weizmann process was turning out acetone from horse-chestnuts by the time the factory closed in 1918.

When our difficulties were solved through Dr. Weizmann's genius, I said to him: " You have rendered great service to the State, and I should like to ask the Prime Minister to recommend you to His Majesty for some honour." He said: " There is nothing I want for myself." " But is there nothing we can do as a recognition of your valuable assistance to the country?" I asked. He replied: " Yes, I would like you to do something for my people." He then explained his aspirations as to the repatriation of the Jews to the sacred land they had made famous. That was the fount and origin of the famous declaration about the National Home for Jews in Palestine.

As soon as I became Prime Minister I talked the whole matter over with Mr. Balfour, who was then Foreign Secretary. As a scientist he was immensely interested when I told him of Dr. Weizmann's achievement. We were anxious at that time to enlist Jewish support in neutral countries, notably in America. Dr. Weizmann was brought into direct contact with the Foreign Secretary. This was the beginning of an association, the outcome of which, after long examination, was the famous Balfour Declaration which became the charter of the Zionist movement. So that Dr. Weizmann with his discovery not only helped us to win the War, but made a permanent mark upon the map of the world.

Dr. Weizmann is still the same busy, devoted, self-forgetful enthusiast. When I saw him recently he had just returned from a collecting trip abroad for the Zionist cause, in which he raised £70,000. He has collected something like fifteen or sixteen million pounds sterling for the rebuilding of Zion. It is the only reward he seeks, and his name will rank with that of Nehemiah in the fascinating and inspiring story of the children of Israel.

I have paused to tell of Professor Weizmann and his work, because it illustrates the multiplicity of different personalities and interests which were blended into the munition effort of this country. It is, too, a page of world history, the opening sentences of which were written in the Ministry of Munitions.

The story of our successful efforts to produce explosives brings me to the tale of our national filling factories. They really represented the most worrying aspect of the shell problem, for even more serious than the failure of the War Office arrangements for making shells, was their neglect to realise practically that ere shells were fired they must first of all be filled and fused.

At the outbreak of the War, practically the whole of the gun ammunition used by both Army and Navy was filled or assembled at Woolwich. There were five firms in the country which could fill shells. One of them had filled lyddite in the South African War. The other four had done some shell filling for foreign countries. But throughout the opening months of the war Woolwich was and remained substantially the only place where shell was filled.

In May and June, 1915, the national shell factories had started. In July I arranged, at the conference of armament firms of which I have already told, for the erection of national projectile factories. But the provision for shell filling in the country was at that time quite inadequate to deal with the growing supplies of empty shell coming from these factories, from the trade, and from American and Canadian orders. Woolwich was getting choked with stacks of empty shell, while our Army was without ammunition. It was therefore essential to my task that Woolwich should be under the control of the Ministry. Without it I could only manufacture shell carcases. At first the War Office refused to surrender the famous Ordnance Factory to the Ministry. They were supported in this refusal by the Admiralty. It soon became evident that I could not provide complete shells unless the means of filling these were transferred to my control. We were short of shells for the great battle which was being fought in France in September. We had a large stock of empties, but we were short of the completed article. The only practical result of Loos was to transfer Woolwich to the Ministry of Munitions. It was the first War Office institution of whose working I had any experience.

Soon after I entered its mysterious portals I came up against a ghostly potentate known as "The Extract." What was "The Extract"? I received account of it in a carefully prepared report that was presented to me as soon as I took over Woolwich.

In order to understand the procedure which governs the productive power of Woolwich and similarly of Enfield and Waltham Abbey with slight modifications, one must realise that the mainspring of the whole fabric, from a procedure point of view, is this document— " The Extract." " The Extract " is a term with an historical origin, which I need not enter into here, save to say that it was an extract from the proceedings of a Board of Ordnance which met at the Tower, and that this " Extract " was passed from official to official of equal rank who were not in a position to give orders to each other. An " Extract," however, is merely an order to do certain work. This phantom of " The Extract" was backed up by a frightening array of capital letters: M.G.O., D.D.O.S., S.O.S., D.E.O.S., I.R.E.S., C.S.O.F., etc., with a host of other alphabetical combinations glowering in the background. They were entrenched in well-worn professional traditions behind entanglements of red tape, and all ready from Alpha and Omega to die in their ditch rather than surrender the fortress held by them and their official forefathers to the barbarians who threatened their empire from the dark forest of politics.

When I took over Woolwich I soon found why, in the words of Monsieur Albert Thomas, it was " *une vieille boîte.*" It was due to the working of " The Extract " by the Capital Letters. They jostled each other, they were in each other's way, hindering but never hustling, and only acting together when there was any resistance to be offered to the political Hun. They were an alphabetical nightmare. My first duty was not exactly to lay these ghosts, but to put them in their proper places; to see that each of them pushed his own trolley without running into anybody else's. I saw why we had been delayed in divers ways. The men or Ministry that ordered " The Extract " controlled the output, and until Woolwich was transferred to the Ministry of Munitions and at least a few capital letters were on my side, I could not really get along with shell filling and components.

The first step taken by me in the reorganisation of Woolwich was the promotion of Sir Frederick Donaldson, the head of the Arsenal, to an important post I created for him outside Woolwich. He was a man of high intelligence and great knowledge of the technique of his job. To this he added undoubted charm. But years of routine in tranquil days when time did not count, when shells were manufactured to fire at safe targets, when all that mattered was that you should keep the Admiralty and the War Office Sections at Woolwich from interfering with each other, and, above all, ensure that the last penny provided by the estimates should be judiciously expended within the financial year, disqualified him for an emergency where hours were precious to the safety of the State, and improvisations had to supersede routine and regulation. I appointed in his place Mr. Vincent Raven, of the London and North-Eastern Railway, and his quickening influence was soon felt throughout the

Arsenal and resulted in an increased production of completed shell.

Woolwich, with the best management, could not provide anything like the facilities for shell filling demanded by the number of shells already ordered or about to be manufactured. I decided, therefore, to extend the range of national factories by setting up a number of national filling factories. Two were arranged for in July—one at Aintree and one at Coventry. Four more were begun in August, six more in September. Before the end of the War there were eighteen national filling factories engaged in filling shell. Some of them were directly controlled by the Ministry; some by agents, like the national projectile factories; some by Local Boards of Management, like the shell factories, the members serving without fee or reward.

The chief technical difficulties in connection with the carrying through of successful filling operations were not those of skilled labour. The actual filling was a simple process, and the great bulk of the labour in the filling factories was that of unskilled women workers. Such labour difficulties as arose were associated rather with the danger of the work, such as the scare of T.N.T. poisoning which towards the end of 1916 temporarily depleted the staffs; the difficulty of getting workers to observe the regulations for minimising risk of explosions; the repellent character of some of the precautions which had to be adopted, such as the wearing of respirators when handling fulminate of mercury compounds, or the smearing of the face with special grease if engaged with work on tetryl.

The courage of the girls and women engaged in these factories has never been sufficiently recognised. They had to work under conditions of very real danger to life and limb, and what some of them probably dreaded still more, of grotesque disfigurement—for one of the perils which was associated with the shell-filling factories was toxic jaundice resulting from T.N.T. poisoning. This ailment turned their faces a bright and repulsive yellow. The poor girls for this reason were nicknamed by their associates outside as " canaries." They were quite proud of this designation, for they had earned it in the path of duty.

Plutarch relates that at the battle of Pharsalus, Julius Cæsar told his legionaries to thrust their spears at the faces of Pompey's cavalry —patrician exquisites of Rome; and that these young gallants, who would have been brave enough in facing bodily wounds and death, were so terrified of facial disfigurement that they turned in horror and galloped away, holding their hands before their eyes. For girls and women, whose natural instinct it was to prize their looks and complexion, the blotching ugliness of T.N.T. poisoning was a peril which tested their courage perhaps even more than the risk of explosion. In 1916 there were 181 cases of this toxic jaundice, of which 52 ended fatally, and in 1917 there were 189 cases with 44 deaths. But in the course of that year the methods of preventing it were being rigidly perfected, and by 1918 the figures were brought down to 34 cases, of which 10 ended fatally. Despite the number so stricken, and the scare which found expression in the Press, there was no labour shortage at the filling factories.

Another fine story of courage comes from the factory at Hayes, where girls and women were employed to fill gaines. A gaine, it should be explained, is a tube filled with explosive, attached under the nose-cap of a high-explosive shell, and sticking down into the T.N.T. filling. Its purpose is to ensure that the detonation of the fuse in the nose-cap shall effectively detonate the contents of the shell.

In 1915 the frequency of prematures and blinds led to the discovery that a large stock of gaines sent from America had a left-hand instead of a right-hand screw, and tended to come unscrewed in the shell as it rotated in flight. To prevent this, the screwed-in gaines had to be stabbed in two places with cold chisel and hammer to break the thread so that they could not unscrew.

Women workers in the factory at Hayes undertook a large part of this work—risky work, for if a trace of the fulminate were ignited by the blow, the gaine would explode and disembowel them. One morning news came that there had been a terrible explosion at Hayes, in which several women had been killed. My representative went down to visit the scene. Work was being done in a number of little huts, separated off from each other. One of them was badly shattered. At its entrance Lord Lee ran against a busy little woman, about five feet high, white-faced but resolute. " Is this where the explosion took place?" he asked. " Yes," she answered. She was in charge of the hut, and when he entered it he saw bloodstains on the floor, and the survivors carrying on at full speed, with hammer and cold chisel, stabbing gaines.

Lord Lee spoke with the little forewoman. She had at one time been a lady's maid. Now she was doing her bit for the country in the munition factory, and when the explosion had occurred that morning she had calmed and steadied her girls and headed them back to their grim and dangerous task. All she would say was: " I am not going to run away, especially when I think of those poor boys in France who are facing more dangers than we are here."

Before long a safety device was produced to guard workers against the dangers of explosion when stabbing gaines; and later on the introduction of an improved pattern made such stabbing unnecessary. But till that time the girls and women carried on their risky work in the pluckiest fashion, and if one of them was blown to horrible destruction the others would keep up their spirits by singing at their work—singing songs with words of their own composition, which had little perhaps of literary grace, but plenty of crude vigour and unfaltering courage.

That was the kind of spirit shown by our women munition workers. Granted efficient direction, there was nothing it could not accomplish.

The experiences I have narrated in regard to our dealings with Woolwich Arsenal, and the facts set out in Lord Moulton's letter, give some slight hint of the official obstacles which continually interfered with our progress. It has to be borne in mind that we were not carrying on a smooth-running concern, but building from the ground up a vast new range of industries for the production of articles—many of them never before manufactured in this country. We had to find out how to make the best use of whatever materials were available, and this meant that it was impossible to rest content with standard specifications for ingredients, and standard processes of manufacture, however ideal these might be for the leisurely and limited munition production of peace-time.

At the beginning of the War, for example, lyddite was our only high explosive for shell filling. That was all very well when a few tons would satisfy our needs for months, but not when we wanted to fire off hundreds of tons a day; for besides being expensive, lyddite was a substance for the manufacture of which imported materials were needed. Hence the adoption of T.N.T. But again, T.N.T was costly and limited in amount, and as the demand for high-explosive shells grew it became obvious that the supply of pure T.N.T would be nothing like adequate. Hence the development of the amatol mixtures of T.N.T. and ammonium nitrate. But the approved method of filling a shell with T.N.T. was to melt the explosive and pour it in through the opening at the nose where the fuse would eventually be screwed on. When ammonium nitrate was mixed with the hot melted T.N.T.—like sand mixed into treacle—the mixture poured more and more stiffly, and with more than 40 per cent. of the nitrate it would not pour at all. So some way had to be found of mixing the two ingredients dry, and filling shells with the powder, if the maximum economy in the use of T.N.T. was to be observed.

For solving this problem fertile and original minds were needed. Britain is rich in such, and one of my most interesting tasks at the Ministry of Munitions was to get hold of men of real inventive and administrative ability and harness their capacities to the service of our immense task. Often they were men with a holy terror of red tape and official formalities, who would not readily submit to dictation, but if given their head would do work of the very greatest value. They had to be chosen with discrimination so as to separate the men of practical, if somewhat intractable, genius from the mere inventing cranks.

To help us with the problem of shell filling, I had the good fortune to secure the services of Lord Chetwynd, who was recommended to me by Mr. Ellis as the best man to help us in our difficulty. He had, as far as I remember, no practical experience in dealing with explosives, but he had a tremendous store of resource and ingenuity. I was, however, warned that he was very sensitive to any attempt to control him by a bridle of red tape.

We told him he was wanted to build and run a factory that would fill a thousand tons a week of high explosive into shells. He stipulated for and got a very free hand, without control by the departmental managers of the Ministry, and a contract valid till after the cessation of hostilities.

Thus equipped, he went straight ahead in glorious independence. He found a site at Chilwell, near Nottingham, and designed and built his own factory there. While it was being erected he went over to France in October, 1915, as one of a deputation I sent to study the French methods of shell-filling, and satisfied himself that the French practice of filling powdered explosives, by pressing it in through the nose of the shell, could be adapted for amatol. This was important, for to make our supplies of T.N.T. go as far as possible it was desirable to use it with 80 per cent. of ammonium nitrate, which involved filling dry, as such mixture could not be poured. At Woolwich they had designed a process for filling with this 80 : 20 amatol by compressing the powder into cakes and insetting these in the shell. But that meant either having a detachable bottom for the shell or a detachable tapered end, and both these devices proved in practice not only an additional complication and delay, but unsatisfactory and a cause of premature explosion.

Lord Chetwynd went back to Chilwell and determined to fill 80 : 20 powder by pressing through the nose. He hastily designed and ran up a small experimental plant to show it could be done, and when there was a talk of abandoning the 80 : 20 amatol on account of the unsatisfactory results achieved by the Woolwich shells, he challenged a test of those filled by him by pressing through the nose—a test from which they emerged triumphantly. His initiative in this matter was of incalculable benefit to the country, and made possible an immense increase in both the speed and the volume of shell-filling. The Chilwell factory was an amazing place, where powerful explosives were milled and mixed like so much flour. Lord Chetwynd designed his own plant and processes, aiming always at speed, simplicity, and the fullest use of machinery on mass-production lines. He passed his raw material through machines originally used for coal crushing, stone pulverising, sugar-drying, paint-making, sugar-sifting. The T.N.T. he ground between the porcelain rollers of a flour mill. A bread-making plant did the mixing. He bought up a derelict works that had been producing lace-making machinery and used them to manufacture the appliances he designed for filling shells. People objected that it must be highly dangerous to treat high explosives so unceremoniously. Lord Chetwynd's retort was to move to a house at the end of his press-houses. " If anyone is to be blown up, I'll be the first! " he remarked: and his action greatly encouraged his workers. A Zeppelin hunted up and down the Trent all through a January night in 1916 trying to locate and bomb the factory, but without success. A rumour spread next day in true war-time fashion that Lord Chetwynd had caught three German spies trying to signal the Zeppelin with lights, and had shot them out of hand. He was prompt to turn it to account, so he set a policeman as sentry all day over an empty room, and at night made a labourer dig three graves on the hillside. Into these he put stones and filled them in, with a black post at the head of each. That turned the rumour into unquestioned history, and discouraged would-be spies and the unwanted curious from prying round the place.

I have given these notes about Chilwell because they will convey some idea of the difficulties with which we were faced in our task of producing filled shell; and some idea, too, of the men who came to our aid. Besides, Chilwell was the largest of our national filling factories, and was our principal source of supply for the heavier natures of filled shell. Of the high-explosive shell filled during the War in the national factories, of sizes from 60-pounder to 15-inch, over 50 per cent. were filled at Chilwell, which turned out $19\frac{1}{4}$ million of these heavy shells, in addition to a considerable number of lighter shells, aerial bombs, etc.

Chilwell started shell-filling in January, 1916. Some of the national filling factories had begun filling of components—gaines, fuses, etc.—even before this. I had placed Geddes in charge of the whole filling section at the end of 1915, and such were his energy and resource that by the middle of 1916 the new filling factories had got into their stride and were furnishing the Army with complete ammunition on a scale which made possible the terrific bombardments of the Somme offensive.

4. MACHINE-GUNS

During 1914 and the first half of 1915, responsibility for the design and supply of machine-guns rested with the Master-General of Ordnance at the War Office. How completely the military direction failed to appreciate the important part this arm would play in the War is shown by the fact that between August, 1914, and June, 1915, four contracts only were placed by them with Messrs. Vickers for a total of 1,792 machine-guns. This would work out at two machine-guns per battalion, with none left for training at home as provision for machine-gun companies and no margin for losses or breakages.* The first order was dated 11th August, 1914, and was for 192 guns. The second, on 10th September, was for 100. The third, dated 19th September, was for 1,000, and the fourth, a few days later, for another 500. A provision in the third contract laid it down that the rate of delivery should be 50 guns per week. Only 10 to 12 had been the rate specified under the first order. The whole 1,792 guns were to be delivered by June, 1915. In fact, however, only 1,022 had been received by that date.

At the outbreak of the War the allotment of machine-guns to each battalion was only two. This was the equipment of our first Expeditionary Force. An explanation of the failure of the military authorities to realise the importance of this weapon is to be sought in the fact that as one distinguished officer wrote: " The machine-gun was regarded by British authorities as a weapon of opportunity rather than an essential munition of war."

It took our generals many months of terrible loss to realise the worth of the machine-gun. They were converted by representations from officers who had witnessed its deadly effect in action. The farther they were from the fighting line the less impressed were military commanders with the power and peril of the machine-gun. Brigadier-General Baker-Carr, the founder of the Machine-Gun Training Corps, has given in his recent book† a piquant account of the difficulties he experienced in establishing his training school and in convincing the higher command of the importance of the machine-gun. As it bears upon the attitude of the War Office in reference to the manufacture of this devastating weapon, I may be permitted to quote one or two passages.

This is the attitude before the War: —

" At that time, the sole mention of machine-guns was confined to a dozen lines in the ' Infantry Training Manual.' Nobody in authority concerned himself with this weapon of enormous potential importance, and battalion commanders before the War frankly and cordially disliked it.

' What shall I do with the machine-guns to-day, sir?' would be a question frequently asked by the officer in charge on a field day.

' Take the damned things to a flank and hide 'em!' was the usual reply."

In 1915 he was urging an increase in the number of machine-guns: —

" The fighting line, at any rate, had awakened to the realisation of the automatic weapon and many commanders were showing

* In 1918 our equipment of machine-guns was 36 Lewis guns per infantry battalion and 64 Vickers guns per machine-gun battalion. Deficiencies were replaced immediately from reserves at home.
† " From Chauffeur to Brigadier."

themselves eager to learn anything they could, which would help to strengthen their front without increasing the number of men.

Already I was urging the advisability of doubling the number of machine-guns per battalion, i.e. raising it from two to four. I had put forward the suggestion very tentatively to G.H.Q. and had been promptly told to mind my own business. The commanders of larger units, such as armies and army corps, did not at that time appreciate the vast saving of man-power that could be effected by the substitution of machinery for brawn, and it was only when we got within the danger zone that the proposals drew forth a cordial response."

He states that after having met with very little encouragement he set up his machine-gun school behind the lines.

" Not one single member of the Staff of G.H.Q. ever took the trouble to pay a visit to the School during the six months that it was quartered in the Artillery Barracks, a quarter of a mile distant from the General Staff Office."

He talks about the enormous fire power of the German machine-gun and the faith of the German Army in its potency both in attack and defence, and he adds: —

"Although this fact was flagrantly and terribly patent to the soldier in the front line, who was called upon to face the enemy machine-guns, the High Command was unable to realise the crucial importance of it, even after the Battle of the Somme, and it was only in the following year, during the ghastly and bloody fiasco known as the Third Battle of Ypres, that the full truth was forced upon them."

At last, after great pressure from the fighting line, sanction was given to increase the number of machine-guns per battalion from two to four. This was in the summer of 1915. He then says: —

" Within twenty-four hours of hearing the news I put forward a proposal to double this amended establishment. G.H.Q. was horrified.

' Look here, Baker,' I was told indignantly. ' We've given you two extra guns per battalion. You ought to be satisfied.'

Vainly I pointed out that the additional guns were not a personal present to me, but a badly needed increase in the arrangement of the fighting troops. But it was useless to argue."

It is an incredible story for anyone who had no actual experience of the fanatical hostility displayed by the Higher Commands to any new ideas.

Despite the meagre output for our own Army, plant was laid

down in this country in October, 1914, to provide 50 guns a week for the French Government, subject to the proviso that the output for the British Forces should not thereby be delayed. When the Ministry of Munitions was established, it was discovered that negotiations were actually taking place for the payment of £50 premium upon each gun delivered in excess of an average of 50 per week up to the end of December, 1915.

The Vickers gun had been adopted to replace the Maxim, which was obsolescent at the outbreak of the War. Maxims already in service were retained; but the total output of these guns from the Royal Small Arms Factory, Enfield, during the first two or three years of the War amounted to only 666 guns, and production of them ceased entirely in March, 1917, in accordance with the policy, already settled before the War, of abandoning this weapon for land service.

The growing importance of machine-guns became more and more manifest as reports came in from battle after battle describing the appalling casualties inflicted upon our men by this deadly little mechanism. The Germans were the only nation which had realised before the War the potentialities of the machine-gun, and they were arming their troops with 16 per battalion.

But this estimate of the value of the machine-gun was not shared in the War Office. The echo of its devastating racket had not yet penetrated that tranquil sanctuary of the God of War.

The manufacture of machine-guns raised the very important issue of priority as between rifles and machine-guns, of both of which there was a serious and immediate shortage; for the manufacture of both these weapons called for the same raw materials, the same machinery, and the same class of workmen. Geddes, whom I had placed in charge of the output of both machine-guns and rifles, found it impossible to get from the War Office any satisfactory estimate either of the numbers of each that would be required, or of the relative priority to be given to their production. Eventually he went, with Sir Percy Girouard, his immediate superior, to lay the matter before the Secretary for War himself, so as to obtain a ruling for the guidance of manufacture during the next nine months. The report of that interview is perhaps best told in Geddes' own words:—

"I told Kitchener that rifles and machine-guns were the same as shillings and pounds: that nine rifles were equal to a Lewis automatic gun and 13 rifles to a Vickers machine-gun in the productive effort required for their manufacture. I wanted to know the proportions of each wanted for nine months ahead so that I could make my plans. His reply was, 'Do you think I am God Almighty that I can tell you what is wanted nine months ahead?' I replied, 'No, sir! And I do not think that I am either. But we have to work it out between us and try to get it right.' Then he gave me the old War Office answer. 'I want as much of both as you can produce.'

My patience was wearing thin, and I think I spoke fairly definitely. I told him of the weeks I had spent trying to get these very elementary facts out of his subordinates. Eventually he said that the proportion was to be two machine-guns per battalion as a minimum, four as a maximum, and anything above four was a luxury. That was the opinion of the Secretary of State, who was looked upon generally as our greatest soldier, on 26th July, 1915.

I sat down in the War Office and wrote this down. So elated was I at my success in having at last got something upon which I could work that I spelt 'luxury' wrong. I asked Kitchener to sign it. He always had a reluctance to sign documents and said that he gave orders and expected them to be obeyed. I replied that doubtless that was the military way, but I had been brought up to accept a signature as an authority for money I spent, and unless he would sign it, the document was no good to me. He walked out of the room. Girouard caught him in the doorway and said, 'Geddes is like that: he won't act unless you sign a paper.' So Kitchener came back and initialled the document."

Elated at his success in getting this documentary statement from the War Secretary, Geddes brought it to me. As Minister of Munitions I was officially expected only to fulfil the requirements of the War Office, and was not authorised to go beyond them. But I had made inquiries of my own amongst the fighting soldiers who had been in action and they were all in agreement as to the need for more and more machine-guns, so that, when I read this miserable estimate, I was so indignant that I would have torn it up if Geddes had not rescued it from me. He always treasured it.

According to Geddes I said to him: "Take Kitchener's maximum (four per battalion); square it; multiply that result by two; and when you are in sight of that, double it again for good luck."

This calculation gave 32 machine-guns per battalion with another 32 for a margin. That of course meant not that each battalion should take 64 machine-guns into action, but that manufacture should be on that scale to provide for all contingencies. As a matter of fact, in November, 1915, the War Office raised their establishment requirements to 16 machine-guns per battalion, and this was progressively raised by suggestive stages until before the end of the War the total number of these guns issued to the fighting forces and kept in reserve for contingencies exceeded a figure equivalent to an average of 64 per battalion. These included the guns issued to the Machine-Gun Corps and the Air Force, and we had also an ample margin for losses, which were very heavy. The numbers we

Memo of meeting with Lord
Kitchener on machine
guns.

___

Essential 2 per Battalion

If possible run to 4 per Battalion
and above it may be counted
as a luxury

26/6/15   K

Facsimile of a memorandum, drafted by Sir Eric Geddes and initialled by Lord Kitchener, dealing with the supply of machine-guns to the Armies.

had in France at the date of the Armistice were the equivalent of over 80 per battalion. In addition there was ample supply in England to replace inevitable losses and breakages.

As a matter of history, what with the demands from our own forces and the assistance we gave to our Allies, I do not think we ever had too many machine-guns up to the end of the War. On the contrary, the proved utility of this weapon was so great that on 23rd February, 1918, I find the programme we authorised for that year was an output of 138,349 further machine-guns, and another 192,000 in 1919; this, in comparison with a total stock of 1,330 of this arm, old or new, in the hands of our troops in 1st June, 1915.

Nor do I think that the Army ever had cause to regret that the supply proposed by Lord Kitchener in July, 1915, was increased sixteenfold. Photographs taken of dead Highlanders lying in swathes in front of a single German machine-gun on the battlefield of Loos, which I saw some weeks later, taken by Colonel Arthur Lee and brought to me, finally disposed of any qualms I may have had at having taken upon myself the responsibility for overriding military opinion.

The realisation of this expanded programme naturally involved very careful planning on the part of the Ministry. A long view was needed for machine-gun contracts, and as Geddes pointed out at the time, to create a new output of this class of weapon one must formulate a definite concrete plan 9 to 12 months in advance.

The Ministry began by placing a contract with Messrs. Vickers on 19th July, 1915, for 12,000 Vickers machine-guns. Financial assistance was given to enable the firm to extend their plant at Erith and Crayford. The productive capacity of these factories ultimately reached 5,000 machine-guns a month.

We also turned our attention to the Lewis gun. This weapon had been rejected for land service by the military authorities in 1912, on the ground that it was undesirable to multiply types of arms. At the outbreak of the War, they were still emphatic in their preference for the Vickers rather than the Lewis gun. The latter was a much lighter weapon than the Vickers gun, and could therefore be moved about by the soldiers with greater ease. It was indispensable for an advance and for aeroplanes.

But during August, 1914, 45 Lewis guns had been ordered for the Air Service, and in the first week of September contracts were placed for 200 more for general service to be delivered at the rate of 25 per week. The orders were subsequently increased by the War Office, but no effective steps were taken to increase facilities for manufacture and to expedite delivery, so that despite increased requisitions during the nine weeks ended 12th June, deliveries to the War Office averaged only 36 per week.

When the Ministry assumed control I had the position investigated, and found that any effective increase in output was dependent upon the placing of larger orders, which would justify the Birmingham Small Arms Company and the manufacturers in making a considerable extension of their plant. It also depended on arrangements being made to increase the output of the necessary machine tools and gauges for manufacture. Hitherto the War Office and the Admiralty between them had given contracts for under 2,000 Lewis guns—just enough to keep the firm from accepting foreign orders. So an order was placed with them for 10,000 machine-guns to be delivered before the end of May, 1916, and while this contract was running I negotiated a further agreement with them whereby the output was to be extended to 750 guns weekly, with a running contract for this number for the duration of the War. In May, 1917, arrangements were made for this to be increased to 1,800 a week.

In February, 1915, plant and skilled workmen had been brought over to Coventry from France for the manufacture of Hotchkiss guns, and a factory started, from which the Admiralty ordered 1,000 of these machine-guns. The anticipated output of the factory was 25 to 50 guns a week.

On 13th August, 1915, I decided to sanction a scheme for doubling the output of this factory, although the British military authorities did not then accept this type of gun for service use. Accordingly, in September, 1915, the Ministry placed an order for 3,000 machine-guns, and by the beginning of June, 1916, the factory had delivered 1,013. Its output rose to 690 guns a month by the end of October, 1916. The ultimate importance of this weapon, especially for the armament of the tanks, is of course familiar history.

It would be a mistake to suppose that these immense expansions of the supply of machine-guns were carried through with a reckless disregard for expense. Output was of course the chief concern, since the lives of our soldiers were in the balance. But cost was carefully studied. For example, the orders placed by the War Office with Messrs. Vickers in August and September, 1914, ranged from £167 to £162 per gun. The price fixed by the Ministry of Munitions in July, 1915, was £125 per gun. In 1916, it was reduced to £100. In 1918 it was still further brought down to £74.

Our progress in the task of supplying our forces with machine-guns may be summarised as follows:—

At the outbreak of the War, if we ignore the obsolescent Maxim, of which a few were still being turned out at the Royal Small Arms Factory at Enfield (which produced just over 80 of them during the first 18 months of the War), the only supply of machine-guns was the 10 to 12 a week which were the maximum that Vickers could then turn out.

By the end of May, 1915, the total machine-guns delivered to the War Office since August, 1914, were 1,039—775 Vickers and 264

Lewis; and the total number in service, including Maxims, was 1,330. Guns so far ordered numbered 2,305.

How the output of machine-guns rose thereafter is shown by the following little table: —

Year.						Total output.
1914	...	...	...	...	...	287
1915	...	...	...	...	...	6,102
1916	...	...	...	...	...	33,507
1917	...	...	...	...	...	79,746
1918	...	...	...	...	...	120,864
					Total	240,506

Out of this total of 240,506 machine-guns which were manufactured in this country during the War we supplied 26,900 to our Allies, or twenty times as many as our whole stock at the time the Ministry of Munitions was formed.

5. MACHINE-GUN CORPS

It was my duty as Minister of Munitions to furnish the machine-guns required by the Army—and, as I have related, I went at one time considerably in advance of their official requirements in the direction of an intelligent anticipation of the numbers of guns they would presently find it necessary to apply for.

Officially, it was perhaps hardly a part of my duty to ensure that the best use was being made of the large supply of machine-guns, but obviously this was a matter in which I could not fail to be keenly interested. In October, some three months after the question of the number of guns to be provided had been settled by me and when their production was getting into its stride, the project of forming a special Machine-Gun Corps received the Royal Assent.* This was a plan which I strongly supported. I had been informed of the very effective methods employed by the enemy to get the best results from this weapon—methods involving the use of special machine-gun companies, not permanently attached or allotted to any battalion or division.

But I was greatly alarmed to hear, shortly afterwards, that although this Machine-Gun Corps had been authorised, little was being done to make it a reality, and hardly any men were being brought into training for it, out of the millions of men that had been recruited. Orders had, in fact, been issued that no man should be recruited for it or transferred to it from other units. By this date my capacity for amazement at professional repugnance to new ideas or formations had reached saturation point. The estimated deliveries of machine-guns would by March, 1916, reach a cumulative total of more than

* Royal Warrant. Army Order No. 416 of 22nd October, 1915.

10,000, and by midsummer of over 20,000. No doubt there were many other demands for men being made upon the War Office, but the machine-gun was obviously such a formidable factor in defence and attack that only some curious form of unbelief and opposition could be responsible for this, to my mind, otherwise inexplicable and unintelligent failure to train men especially to make the best use of it. I determined, therefore, at the risk of once again interfering in something which was not departmentally my concern, to ascertain the exact position.

In the War Committee of 13th November, 1915, I took up this matter. I laid before the Committee a memorandum setting out the estimated deliveries of machine-guns, and urging adequate preparation for the effective use of this weapon. The memorandum continued : —

"I believe that one machine-gun, with its detachment of ten men, is at a very low estimate equivalent in destructive power to fifty riflemen, especially on the defensive. If that is a correct basis of comparison we could make up for our shortage in men and obtain equivalent fighting value by training 200 machine-gunners instead of 1,000 riflemen. In other words, with 50,000 machine-gunners we could do the work of 250,000 infantry. We could also save in rifles, in which, so far as I can see, the Allies are never going to obtain the numerical superiority over the Germans necessary for a decisive victory.

It seems also, that if our machine-guns are employed on a large scale, on a comprehensive plan, they will, in conjunction with barbed wire and fortification, give us the strategic power *so far enjoyed by the Germans alone* of taking large numbers of troops away from one front, where no offensive is in contemplation, and transferring them to a quarter where active operations are intended.

This is what the Germans have done on the Western Front, to release men for the thrust against Russia, and what they are doing on their Eastern Front, to set free men for attacking Serbia, and for action on the Western Front. This power to replace men, which amounts to strategic elasticity, applies especially, I think, to our present intentions on the Western Front."

General Sir Archibald Murray, who was then acting as Chief of the Imperial General Staff, under Lord Kitchener (at the time away in the Mediterranean), was present at the War Committee, and supported my view. He said that the General Staff had actually started a machine-gun school at Grantham, intended to train a corps of men in machine-gun handling and tactics; but the Adjutant-General would not supply them with any men. They wished to train 10,000 men at a time, taking in a fresh supply every two months, but so far had only had 3,000 men.   He confirmed my estimate that one machine-gun was equal to fifty rifles, and contradicted Mr. M'Kenna's suggestion that mobility was lost with machine-guns.

As a result of my pressure, the War Council decided to ask the Army Council to provide for 10,000 men to be put continuously under instruction.   Actually some considerable delay occurred before this instruction was carried out, but eventually a number of men were drafted from various units to the Corps Training Centre, and even they were not especially picked men like the German machine-gunners, whom Sir Douglas Haig has described as a *corps d'élite*. None the less, they added immensely to the efficiency of our army. Four years later, in November, 1918, the strength of this new branch of the Army which had been initiated under such difficulties amounted to 6,427 officers and 123,835 other ranks.

When one recalls the devastating use made by the Germans of their picked machine-gunners both in attack and defence, and how they saved their own infantry by that process, one is astounded at the tardiness with which our military leaders came to any realisation of the power of the most lethal weapon of the War.

6.   DESIGN AND INVENTION

In this War the engineer and the chemist dominated the battle-field.   When war broke out the Central Powers were much better prepared than the Allies on the mechanical and chemical side in this respect.   The great howitzers of the Germans played a decisive part in the opening conflicts of the War.   Even in 1916 the French artillery was inferior in this type of weapon.   We had practically nothing that counted in trench warfare until late in 1915.   The Teutonic heavy guns (German and Austrian) smashed the concrete fortifications of Liège, compelling in a few hours the surrender of defences which we reckoned would hold out for days if not weeks. The Germans who captured Antwerp were in numbers but a third of the garrison, and in quality they were the second best of the German troops.   Big guns did the work for them.   The German 5.9 shell with its terrifying explosion stopped the French advance, and hurled their armies back towards Paris.   Whilst the German engineers in their workshops gave their comrades superior weapons for attack, their field engineers constructed for them the best defences.   Deep and skilfully constructed entrenchments protected by wire and defended with machine-guns, *Minenwerfer*, and grenades defied the repeated efforts of the Allies to push the German invaders back out of France and Belgium.   Their use of poison gas broke the French and British fronts at Ypres in 1915, and helped to scatter the Russians in Poland.

On their Eastern Front the Germans could defeat and hurl back Russian armies thrice as strong numerically, but destitute of the guns, shells, mortars and gases which the Central Powers possessed. Human valour is no shield against high explosives or machine-gun bullets. As deadlock gripped the battle front it became increasingly clear that if Allied strategy declined to seek a back-door, the only hope of gaining a decisive victory was to produce some new contrivance or improvement in our weapons which might turn the balance. And even a back-door, if barred, needs smashing in.

It soon became evident to clear eyes and gradually to the most obtuse vision that the War would be fought and ultimately decided in the workshop and the laboratory.

Unhappily, at the outbreak of the War and all through its opening months we were definitely behindhand in the field of munition design. Our artillery had not been tested in a great war. Our little stage manœuvres taught us nothing as to what real war would be like. Our heavy artillery was a joke to our foes. We had no trench mortars or grenades. We had vested our confidence so much in shrapnel that we had not worked out a safe high-explosive shell. When we started manufacturing high-explosive shells we had not thought out the problem of how we were to produce a sufficient quantity of explosive for so stupendous a demand, nor had we invented a competent fuse to explode such shells as we were able to fill. Our only modern big gun was the solitary experimental 9.2 inch, which was sent out to the front in September, 1914, and which was nicknamed " Mother " by the troops. Our machine-guns were few in number, and many of them obsolescent in design. The War Office had refused to consider the Lewis gun for land service. We had no trench mortars and no reliable hand grenades. The enemy had both.

Research and design for munitions of war were under the control of the Master-General of Ordnance. During the opening months of the War, he held that, as it would soon be over, it would be foolish to divert to the lengthy and tedious process of working out and approving designs for new weapons the energy which could be better used for producing existing standard types. Thus, when early on in the War a request came from the Front that specimens of captured German *Minenwerfer* should be examined with a view to providing the Army with trench-mortars, the proposal was postponed on the ground that other demands on the capacity of the Ordnance Factory and armament firms were more immediate.

But as the War progressed the military authorities were compelled to face ever multiplying problems of new designs and types of munition which were required by the army in the field. They had also to arrange for the immense growth of output of all supplies, new or old, and this threw a great deal of extra work on the drawing-office at Woolwich. It was inevitable that it should become thoroughly congested and hopelessly in arrears. The Admiralty,

N

which also relied on Woolwich for the same class of work, became so impatient that in May, 1915, it established its own drawing-office at headquarters, and gradually developed it to include simple designing.

Britain is very rich in scientific and inventive ability, and in November, 1914, the General War Committee of the Royal Society was appointed to " organise assistance to the Government in conducting or suggesting scientific investigation in relation to the War, the Committee to have power to add to their number and to appoint Sub-Committees not necessarily restricted to Fellows of the Society." By this step the Government mobilised the most distinguished body of scientists in the world to assist the nation. The Admiralty made considerable use of this body, and referred to it such inventions and suggestions sent in as seemed to hold out some promise of being useful. But the procedure of the War Department remained practically unaltered. Apart from some slight co-operation with the Chemical Sub-Committee which had been set up by the Royal Society, little use was made by the War Committee of the Society for military purposes.

When the Ministry of Munitions was first set up, the Army Council retained responsibility for the kind and quality of the stores we were to supply. The fixing of designs and specifications and the tests to be applied, the research and experimental work in connection with munitions, were still under the War Office, and though the Ministry of Munitions was responsible for providing guns, ammunition, rifles, and other munitions, it was entirely dependent upon the War Office authorities for decision and investigation in respect of the patterns, ingredients, and specifications of these stores.

I soon discovered that the separation of design and manufacture was a serious mistake and led to blunders and delays. It was not improved by the reactionary attitude of the War Office. Our soldiers in the battle line were more progressive. Sir John French set up, early in June, 1915, an Experimental Committee at G.H.Q. to deal with inventions and the application of modern science to the needs of war. At home there was a popular demand for a similar organisation to serve the needs of both the Army and the Navy, and on 22nd June, 1915, Mr. Balfour, who was then First Lord of the Admiralty, definitely formulated a scheme for this purpose. The War Office held aloof, and in July the Admiralty set up an Admiralty Board of Inventions and Research to serve the needs of the Senior Service alone. A similar organisation was shortly afterwards established by me for the Ministry of Munitions.

A very short experience convinced me that the unnatural divorce of design and production was quite unworkable. In particular, I felt it important that the Ministry of Munitions should be able to examine new suggestions and inventions of possible value—a view confirmed by the history of the Stokes gun—and I proceeded to press for the transfer to the Ministry of the authority at least to deal with such new ideas and designs.

The history of the Stokes gun affords an illustration of the impracticability of the dual system. The Army were clamouring for a mortar that would enable them to reply to the bombing appliances with which the Germans harried our trenches. As early as January, 1915, Mr. Wilfred Stokes, an East of England manufacturer of agricultural machinery, had submitted to the War Office a design for a trench mortar of extreme simplicity—a plain steel tube, into which a bomb could be dropped with a cartridge fitted to its base, which would explode on hitting a striker at the base of the tube, and propel the bomb into the enemy trench. You could fire the gun as rapidly as you could drop bombs into it.

The War Office did not approve the type of fuse fitted to the bomb, and turned down the invention. It was brought forward again in March, and again rejected.

Hearing favourable reports of this gun, I arranged to see it for myself, and on 30th June I witnessed it in action in a demonstration at Wormwood Scrubs. I was accompanied by Major-General Ivor Philipps, the Military Secretary to the new Ministry. Both of us were very impressed with its performance. It struck me as having great possibilities.

Officially I was limited at this time in the Ministry to the manufacture of those stores which the War Office approved. It was impossible to pretend that it had passed the design for the Stokes gun—on the contrary, it had twice rejected it.

Happily I had received just before this a donation of £20,000 from one of the Indian Maharajahs, to be expended by me on whatever war purpose seemed to me most useful for the Empire. On the strength of this fund, and in spite of my knowledge that the War Office was opposed to using the Stokes gun, I gave instructions for 1,000 of them to be made forthwith, together with 100,000 bombs— these last not to be completed till a satisfactory fuse had been prepared for them. Meantime I set about reopening the issue with the War Office.

By the second week of August they had been brought to the point of carrying out a further test of the mortar at Shoeburyness. By this time a fuse had been fitted to the bombs, similar to that used on the Mills hand grenade. The Ordnance Board now reported that the gun was better than a 3.7-in. trench mortar which the War Office had been manufacturing, and it was formally approved on 28th August. This was just as well, for already on 22nd August General Headquarters in France had telegraphed the War Office for as many Stokes mortars as could possibly be supplied by 1st

September, and had sent over an officer to consult with the Trench Warfare Department about the smoke bombs it was desired to use in them for a smoke screen in the coming Battle of Loos. Thirty were hastily improvised and sent out.

During the remainder of the War, the Stokes gun became and remained the trench mortar in highest favour and most constant demand. Out of 19,000 trench mortars and trench howitzers issued during the War to our troops, 11,500 were Stokes guns. Throughout 1917 and 1918 the 3-in. Stokes gun was the only form of light trench mortar manufactured, as by this time it had clearly proved its superiority to all rival patterns. And this was the weapon which the Ordnance Department of the War Office had done its best to fling aside as worthless.

Naturally after this experience I was more than ever anxious to bring the supervision of new inventions and improvements in design under the control of a progressively-minded body, which would not suffer from an ingrained habit of rejecting every fresh idea on principle. The fact that we were at that time being held up by the delay in settling the ingredients of shell filling and the design of fresh fuses and gaines made me still more desirous of having complete control in those vital matters. The Admiralty, as I have said, was showing itself far more alert in this respect than the War Office, and in face of the failure of the Ordnance Department to do anything in the matter, was even studying new ideas for land warfare. On the plea that they would be of value to the Royal Naval Air Service, Mr. Churchill had as early as January, 1915, begun investigations into the possibilities of armoured cars, and had set up in February the Admiralty Landships Committee, which carried out work of immense value for the evolution of the tank.

I was, naturally, being deluged at the Ministry of Munitions with letters and calls from people who had some new invention or improvement to propose. The great majority of these ideas were, of course, useless, and many of them came from cranks and lunatics. But it was clear, as in the case of Mr. Stokes, that some of them might prove of value, and it was also evident from the result of the Admiralty researches into land warfare and the rejection of Lord Moulton's recommendations about explosives, that the War Office was failing to carry out the work urgently required in this field. Early in June I arranged with Mr. Balfour to take over all the work of the Admiralty in reference to expedients and inventions for land warfare. This meant, amongst other things, that the manufacture of tanks was handed over to the Ministry.

In reply to a request I made to him, Lord Kitchener sent a message through Sir Reginald Brade that he was agreeable to my taking over the inventions work relating to munitions, for the supply of which my Department was responsible.

Accordingly, on 13th July a meeting was held at which a new Department of the Ministry was set up for dealing with inventions having relation to Munitions of War.

To carry out the duties of this Department I appointed Mr. Ernest Moir. This development was described by me as follows, in the course of a speech which I made in the House of Commons on 28th July on the work of the Ministry:

" I should like to say one word as to what we are doing with regard to inventions. It is essential for the conduct of the War that the fullest use should be made of the best brains of inventors and scientific men. Perhaps hitherto there has been a want of co-ordination among the various methods of dealing with the projects of inventors. So far as naval inventions are concerned, the First Lord of the Admiralty has set up an Inventions Board under the distinguished presidency of Lord Fisher.

I have just concluded arrangements to constitute an Inventions Branch of the Ministry of Munitions, and I hope it will do for inventions for land warfare what Lord Fisher's Committee will do for sea warfare.

The War Office is handing over the whole question of inventions to us, and careful arrangements have been made to secure that the new branch shall keep in close touch with Lord Fisher's Board to avoid duplication and overlapping, and also with the War Office experts and Army authorities who must have the ultimate voice in deciding whether any particular invention is of service in actual warfare.

I have appointed Mr. E. W. Moir, a distinguished engineer who has already given valuable assistance to my department on a voluntary basis, to take charge of the new branch, and he will not only have an expert staff, but also a panel of scientific consultants on technical and scientific points. It ought to be clearly understood that only a very small minority of inventors' projects are of practical value [laughter]. Many projects fail from technical defects, and many others, though technically perfect, are unsuited to the practical conditions of warfare.

The new branch will have justified its existence if one project in a hundred, or even in one thousand, turns out to be of practical utility in the present emergency.

We have got a good many which we are experimenting upon very hopefully."

Despite the optimism of that speech, it turned out that the setting up of this Inventions Department was only the beginning of our troubles. Although their political heads had given consent to the transfer, the officials of the War Office were most reluctant to part with any vestige of their authority, and a duel began between them and my own officials.

By the beginning of September very little progress had been made. I accordingly saw Lord Kitchener and secured his consent to an arrangement whereby Colonel Hickman, of the War Office, and Mr. Moir should keep in touch with each other so that new ideas and suggestions received by the War Office should be passed along to the Ministry.

But despite this friendly effort to come to a satisfactory arrangement, and the accommodating spirit displayed by the Secretary for War, the trouble with the War Office went on unabated. At the end of September the Ordnance Board set up rival bodies analogous to the Advisory Panel of the Ministry of Munitions. On 16th October I received a letter from Moir which I will transcribe, as it gives a vivid picture of the campaign of obstruction which was at that time being waged by the War Office against the Ministry on this and other issues.

"MINISTRY OF MUNITIONS.
Princes Street,
Westminster, S.W.
16th October, 1915.

The Rt. Hon. David Lloyd George, M.P.,
6, Whitehall Gardens, S.W.

Dear Mr. Lloyd George,

Having been asked by General von Donop to call on him on Thursday the General informed me that he saw some difficulty in transferring to the Inventions Branch of the Ministry of Munitions the powers granted to the Secretary of State for War by Clause 30, Sub-Section 12, of the Patents Act, 1907. This Sub-Section provides that the submission of an invention to the War Office or the Admiralty shall not act as publication, and on the 2nd October application was made through Sir Herbert Llewellyn Smith for a transfer of that provision to the Ministry of Munitions.

General von Donop's point was that in sending on from the War Office to the Munitions Inventions Department such inventions as the War Office thought were of no use (for these are admittedly the only suggestions that they are sending us at the present time) they might be running some risk of complaint by the inventor should such ideas leak out through their submission to our Panel of Experts. In such cases the War Office might be blamed. My answer to this was that up to the present as they had only sent to this Department things that, according to their lights, were of no use, I naturally had not insulted our Panel by putting these before them, and had dealt with them myself.

Incidentally, I went on to say that I hoped there would soon be some arrangement made by which this Department would not only see the worthless but also the possible ideas that were useful from the War Office point of view.

I also enlarged on the fact that this Department could get no military assistance, and that the assistance which we already had in the shape of Colonel Goold-Adams and Colonel Heffernan was going to be withdrawn from our Panel for, so far as I could ascertain, no sufficient reason. These two experts on artillery, I told General von Donop, were of immense value to us, and far from wanting to reduce the military members of the Panel we wanted to increase them. The reason for suggesting their removal, General von Donop said, was because the balance of the Ordnance Board was overworked and consequently Colonel Goold-Adams and Colonel Heffernan must return to Woolwich. I asked him if he could get someone to take these two gentlemen's places temporarily on the Ordnance Board. *He said that if they did not return he would have them removed from the Board and would not allow them to return even after the War.*

During the course of conversation I pointed out that although this Department had been informed that we could not be given any military assistance the War Office had been able to get together an Inventions Board numbering 14, and including seven Generals, three Colonels, and three Majors. I also told him that my view of the matter was that our Inventions Department had probably relieved the War Office of a good deal of work.

The whole matter seems to me to be a further indication, if any were necessary, of the spirit of objection to civil assistance by the military authorities, and I think that a good deal of the resistance comes from the gentleman with whom I had the interview.

I have not seen Colonel Goold-Adams, but Colonel Heffernan, with some trepidation, admitted to me recently, that he enjoyed his work with us very much, and that he did not want to give it up. He would be quite willing to carry it on on Saturdays or Sundays if he could not do so in any other way. Unfortunately an engagement of this sort would be a very difficult one to carry out except so far as concerns the attending of experiments or visiting work which is going on.

Both Colonel Goold-Adams and Colonel Heffernan are highly intelligent men, and I consider that they should not be removed from your department either in connection with inventions or anything else. The other six members who are left behind on the Ordnance Board should, I imagine, under stress of war conditions, either be reinforced or could probably find it possible to do the work among themselves.

Of course, we can get on without anybody, but there is, I think, an obvious effort to defeat the objects that you have set yourself out to attain, at least in some of their departments, on the part of the military Authorities.

Yours faithfully,

E. MOIR."

The two officers mentioned in this letter were members of the Inventions section of the Ordnance Board, who had been seconded for work with the Ministry's Inventions Board as a means of keeping liaison with the military authorities. This was part of the arrangement I had come to with Lord Kitchener at the time when it was agreed that inventions should be transferred to the Ministry of Munitions for research and investigation.

A fortnight later Mr. Moir wrote me with the news that Colonel Goold-Adams had been recalled by the War Office. He enclosed the Colonel's letter, which was in the following terms: —

" Ordnance Board Office,

Royal Arsenal,

Woolwich.

29th October, 1915.

Dear Mr. Moir,

. . . I regret to say that I have been officially informed to-day that I am to sever my connection with the Ministry of Munitions, and no reason is given.

I am more than sorry to have to do so, but it cannot be helped.

When you have had an opportunity I hope you will express my regret to Mr. Lloyd George.

Sincerely yours,

H. GOOLD-ADAMS.

P.S.—I need hardly say that if my services or advice are wanted officially at any future date I shall only be too glad to be of assistance.

H. G. A."

The whole position was unsatisfactory. Had the Design Department of the War Office been not only efficient and energetic, with an appreciation of the value of time in war, and had it also worked harmoniously and with good will with the new Manufacturing Department, then no serious mishaps or delays would have ensued. But that was not the case. The process of manufacture in every direction was being held up by mistakes here and procrastination there.

It must be remembered that up to this stage, the Ministry of Munitions had merely been accorded power to make researches and investigations with regard to new inventions and improvements. It had no control over the design of either new or old patterns of munitions. That was still in the hands of the War Office, which retained its Inventions Board with overriding authority over the Ministry's researches.

Moreover, in connection with the expansion of manufacture there constantly arose questions of the possibility of modifying or adapting specifications to suit the exigencies of production; and in these questions the Ministry, which was responsible for production, was powerless until a lengthy process of consultation with the War Office and experimentation by these officials produced ultimate sanction. Such questions arose daily, for the practical experience of war was making matchwood of old theories and traditional patterns of munitions. The standard fuses proved unreliable and caused prematures and " duds," the guns and gun-carriages were seen to be capable of improvement, and the new forms of warfare which developed were calling constantly for new types of weapons, or modifications of existing types. The difficulties with regard to the composition of shell explosive and the ingredients of cordite were causing grave anxiety and delay, and the fuses were thoroughly unsatisfactory. The Ministry, responsible for meeting all these changing demands, was unable to move because of the division of authority with the Ordnance Board. While the Board had been responsible for design and production, it had been able to co-ordinate the two, if it so willed, without delay. Obviously, it was desirable, since the Ministry had taken over production, that it should also have the responsibility for design. This divided authority, with the consequent delays on the part of the War Office in coming to vital decisions on fuses and explosives, seriously impeded the work of production of completed shells. Shell cases multiplied at a great rate, but the same pace could not be kept in the matter of the completion until the design of the fuses and the ingredients of the explosives were finally settled.

As I have pointed out, the position with regard to explosives was critical and threatened us with a disastrous shortage of shells for the front. The delays of the War Office in coming to a decision were seriously impeding production. A letter written by General Du Cane on 22nd October, 1915, to Colonel Arthur Lee, who had just taken over Sir Ivor Philipps's position as Military Secretary to the Ministry of Munitions, revealed other directions in which the handling of design by the War Office was proving a source of danger as well as of delay. General Du Cane presided over the Experiments Committee at G.H.Q. in France. The gaines which detonated the shells were so ill-designed that they caused premature explosions which burst our guns at an alarming rate. The total number of our guns at that date was not high.

N*

Here is an extract from General Du Cane's letter: —

". . . I feel pretty confident that you will never get your show running smoothly until you get full responsibility for pattern and experiments. I am pretty sure that you will find that the system by which the War Office and Ordnance Board retain the responsibility for these matters is your great stumbling-block. The M.G.O.'s people seem to me to be mentally exhausted and the Ordnance Board and Experimental Department at Shoebury to be hopelessly congested.

K.'s great argument for keeping control was that he must be responsible for the safety of the troops, because being voluntary soldiers they would all run away or desert if we burst guns like the French. He has failed hopelessly as regards safety, and the result of his control now is to prevent the causes of the trouble being definitely ascertained.

At present our H.E. for 13 and 18 pounders is so unreliable that we cannot use it in large quantities. We have lost 36 guns since the 21st September for an average of one accident to something between 4,000 and 5,000 rounds. That is worse than the French ever were.

During the recent operations the French accidents were one to 120,000 rounds. We have a long way to go yet. I suggested to L.G. that he shall ask the French for 200,000 of their fuses so that we could use them while we are getting our own right. . . .

The loss of 36 guns in a month by prematures represents the highest percentage of bursts ever suffered by any artillery on either side in this war."

Accordingly in mid-November I wrote the following letter to the Prime Minister: —

" 6, Whitehall Gardens,
Whitehall, S.W.

My dear P.M.,
I hope it will now be possible to come to a decision as to the future of the Ordnance Board.

Important munitions are being held up or retarded, and I am receiving serious complaints from the Department as to the position of matters. The present situation is an impossible one. M. Thomas has complete control of design as well as manufacture, but I am helpless.

Yours sincerely,
D. LLOYD GEORGE."

Mr. Asquith was at that time temporarily acting as Secretary for War, in the absence of Lord Kitchener, who had gone to the Mediterranean, and he supported my attitude. Strong protests were raised by the officials at the War Office.   General von Donop foresaw a general relaxation of strictness of design which would endanger the safety of the Army.   Sir Charles Harris, the Assistant Financial Secretary, protested against the breach with precedent and the over-throwing of the remarkable instrument of efficiency existing in the Ordnance Board.   Manufacturing questions were, according to him, a part only, and that not the most important part, of the Board's work. "To make a civilian department responsible for the design of munitions as well as for their supply would be to head straight back to the inefficiency that had been experienced in the Egyptian campaign of 1880.   The Ordnance Board ought to be strengthened, not abolished."

But in November, 1915, people were more impressed with the hindrances to action before their eyes than with what a Treasury clerk witnessed in 1880, and despite these protests the Prime Minister decided to transfer design of munitions to the Ministry, and to abandon the Ordnance Board control.   This decision was embodied in the following memorandum noted by Sir Reginald Brade: —

" The transfer to the Ministry of Munitions of the responsibility for designs, patterns, and specifications for testing of arms and ammunition, and for the examination of inventions bearing on such munitions, leaves to the War Office the following functions only in regard to munitions of war, viz.: —

1.   The duty of fixing the requirements of the Army both as regards the general nature and amount of the munitions required, together with the duty of allocating all such material.

2.   The duty of receipt, custody and actual distribution of all such supplies.

· These functions fall to the General Staff and the Quartermaster-General's department respectively.   This is the system in force with the Army in the field, and, in altered conditions, should be followed in the War Office during the War.

As regards the staffs hitherto employed in this work, such officers and others as are necessary for the performance of the limited functions remaining to the War Office should be retained; the balance being placed at the disposal of the Ministry of Munitions. The exact details must be worked out in conference between repre-sentatives of the two offices.

The above was dictated to me by the Prime Minister with instructions to notify it as his decision arrived at after consideration of the relative positions of the War Office and the Ministry of Munitions in which each stands now that the transfer of duties . . . has been approved."

Following this decision, on 29th November, 1915, the new duties in regard to design were formally undertaken by the Ministry, and the control of experimental and research bodies, such as the Research Department, Woolwich, was also transferred from the War Office. The Department of Munitions Design, formed within the Ministry, was placed under the control of General Du Cane. The Ordnance Board was dissolved on 4th December, 1915, and reconstituted as the Ordnance Committee and advisory body to both the Ministry of Munitions and the Admiralty.

I quote an extract from a letter I wrote at this date, 30th November, 1915: —

" Lord Kitchener comes home to-day. They have not been able to keep him away. However, in his absence the Prime Minister has handed over the Ordnance Board to me. I have been fighting for this for months, but the War Office have dodged me, and by keeping the Ordnance Board have been able to limit very considerably the energies of all this department. Moreover, when anything *was* accomplished it was only after hard fighting and much unpleasantness."

One last fight remained. Whatever else the War Office failed to do, they at least lived up to the old tradition of the British Army of never knowing when they were beaten. Not only inventions, but design and inspection had now, in set terms, been transferred to the Ministry of Munitions. " Very well," said the War Office in effect, " go ahead, and design and inspect your munitions. But before we issue them to the Army, *we* reserve the right to submit them to our own tests and inspection, and to send out only those designs of which we also approve."

Accordingly the War Office refused to transfer their testing and experimental staff at the school of musketry at Hythe, maintained the department of the Director of Artillery at the War Office as an overriding authority superior to the Ministry of Munitions, and generally set themselves to nullify wherever possible the change which had been decided on.

General Du Cane, fresh from the battle zone, found himself pitchforked into this internecine conflict. On 14th December he submitted the following memorandum upon the position: —

" RELATIONS WITH THE WAR OFFICE.

When the Prime Minister and Mr. Lloyd George first discussed with me the formation of a Military Department in the Ministry, to be responsible for the design of munitions, I pointed out to them that this proposal would depend for success on two conditions being fulfilled, viz.: —

1.   The necessary officers being placed at the disposal of the Ministry.

2.   The removal of possible causes of friction that might result from the maintenance of a rival technical department in the War Office.

The first of these conditions has been fulfilled, but the second has not.

Before I was appointed to my present position I had an interview with the Prime Minister at the War Office, at which he said that he fully recognised the difficulties that must result from my having personal relations with the M.G.O. and the officers of the D. of A.'s directorate in the circumstances that must result from the contemplated measure of reorganisation, and instructions were issued by him that the General Staff would deal with the ' requirements and allocation,' and the Q.M.G. with ' distribution.'

These instructions have not been carried out, and the D. of A.'s directorate still exists at the War Office and deals with these subjects.   It is true that arrangements have been made for references from the Ministry on the subject of ' requirements,' to be sent to the Director of Staff Duties, but this officer refers them again to the D. of A. and merely passes on his replies.

The difficult situation that it was hoped to avert, therefore, actually exists.   There is still a rival technical department at the War Office, tenacious of its position.   The officers of this department feel deep resentment at being deprived of their most important functions, and while they are the officers who should be in the closest possible touch with my department, working harmoniously with my officers, the relations are so strained that they result in their avoiding one another as much as possible.   The bad effects of this situation are already beginning to be felt, and if it is allowed to continue it will inevitably result in acute friction and loss of efficiency.

I submit that it is essential that effect should be given at once to the Prime Minister's decision, that a proper channel of communication should be established with the War Office, and that cordial and harmonious relations should be established without any further delay.   If this cannot be brought about, I must confess my inability to look forward to the task before me with confidence.

J. P. Du Cane, D.G.M.D., M.G.

14/12/15."

This was plain speaking, and not by a civilian, but by a highly placed staff officer of acknowledged ability and of long military experience.   But the War Office still fought on, and on 5th January, 1916, a letter was received at the Ministry, in the following terms:—

" War Office, London,
January 5th, 1916.

Sir,

With reference to your letter No. D.G.M.D./General/8, dated the 13th December, 1915, I am commanded by the Army Council to inform you that they observe that it is proposed in the letter under reply that the final approval to new designs, or amendments to existing designs, should be given by the Director-General Munitions Design. The Army Council, however, consider it most desirable that the approval should not be given until they have expressed their concurrence as to its suitability for adoption as meeting the requirements of the Service. I am to add that the Army Council are strongly of opinion, confirmed by experience, that in most cases before final approval is given to inventions or designs, practical trials on conditions formulated by the Army Council, carried out by troops under the orders and observation of responsible military commanders selected by the Council, are essential. Any special conditions which the Ministry of Munitions desired would be added to those formulated by the Army Council.

In accordance with the views expressed above, the Council desire to retain at their own disposal an experimental staff at Hythe, but they will be glad to arrange for the Director-General Munitions Design to obtain from this staff and that of the Machine-Gun School any assistance that he may desire, and, so far as is possible, they will endeavour to meet the wishes of the Ministry of Munitions as regards the transfer, or loan to that Department, of individual officers now serving at Hythe.

I am, etc.,

R. H. BRADE."

I do not need to point out that this letter was, in effect, a flat refusal on the part of the Army Council to acquiesce in and carry out loyally the decisions already made as to the transfer of design and inspection to the Ministry. I had no option but to bring the matter before the Cabinet War Committee—somewhat, I think, to the Prime Minister's bewilderment, for he had assumed that this was all settled and done with. It was thrashed out in two meetings, on 26th January and 3rd February, 1916, and a formula ultimately agreed which laid it down that: —

" (a) The responsibility for designs, patterns, and specifications and for testing arms and ammunition rests with the Ministry of Munitions.

(b) The Army Council is responsible for the general nature and amount of the weapons and equipment required, but there shall be no court of appeal set up in the War Office from the decisions of the Ministry of Munitions under (a).

(c) When it is necessary that new weapons, stores, or articles of equipment should undergo practical trials by troops, either at home or in the field, the co-operation of the Army Council should be sought by the Ministry.

(d) The Army Council should be represented on Advisory Committees or bodies under the Ministry of Munitions to the extent that the Army Council think desirable."

By this time the War Office had shot their last bolt, and the decisions embodied in the above clauses formed the basis upon which the work of munition design was carried forward thereafter by the Ministry with ever-increasing smoothness and efficiency. But after what an expenditure of time, mental concentration and energy! Meanwhile we had to put up with unsatisfactory gaines and fuses which often caused more trouble to our troops than to the enemy. In February, 1916, a decision was arrived at which ought to have been reached in June, 1915. It naturally took the new department some time to perfect their designs. Manufacturers proceeded with the mechanisms already settled and sanctioned, and when the great battle was fought later on in the year we suffered in the quality of our shells from the delay.

7. TANKS

British in conception, design and manufacture, the Tank was the one outstanding and dramatic innovation brought forth by the War in the sphere of mechanical aids to warfare. It was the ultimate British reply to the machine-guns and heavily fortified trench systems of the German Army, and there is no doubt whatever that it played a very important part in helping the Allies to victory. It might have played a still greater part if it had been developed more promptly through a livelier display of sympathy and encouragement on the part of the War Office, and if its use in the field had been more intelligently exploited. Even in spite of blunders in these respects, the Tank saved an immense number of British lives, and gave invaluable stimulus to the morale of our troops, while spreading terror and alarm among those of the enemy.

I am not concerned here to enter upon the controversial question of the origin of the Tank. The idea of a mechanically propelled, travelling fortress was one which had occurred to a number of inventive minds, even before the War. My own connection with its development only started after I had entered on my duties as Minister of Munitions. In that office, and subsequently as Secretary of State for War and as Prime Minister, I had a good deal to do with the later stages in the evolution and manufacture of this new weapon. The first tentative experiments, mainly carried out by the Air Department of the Admiralty, and backed by the foresight and enthusiasm of Mr. Winston Churchill had already been undertaken when I came on the scene.

My first encounter with the early attempts to produce a self-propelled machine, capable of crossing trenches and forcing its way through entanglements, was when on 30th June, 1915, I was invited with Mr. Winston Churchill to witness an exhibition by R.N.A.S. officers at Wormwood Scrubs of experiments with a wire-cutter affixed to a caterpillar tractor. This was not a tank, nor indeed anything like it; but it was one of the early experimental models, tested and later abandoned in the search for a device which would accomplish what the Tank ultimately achieved.

I was surprised to find that these experiments were being conducted by naval men, mostly temporary officers and ratings of the armoured car division of the Royal Naval Air Force. On enquiry I found that the Admiralty had till then been, and still were responsible for the experimental work of developing this machine for land warfare, and were carrying out their work with funds voted for the Navy and with naval personnel! This was sufficiently astonishing. But my astonishment was succeeded by admiration of Mr. Churchill's enterprise when I discovered that he alone of those in authority before whom the idea of a mobile armoured shelter was placed, had had the vision to appreciate its potential value, and the pluck to back, practically and financially, the experiments for its development.

Later I discovered that the project for a machine-gun destroyer, propelled on the caterpillar principle, had in fact been put forward in October, 1914, by a soldier, Colonel Swinton, who realised how deadly the German machine-guns were proving to our infantry, and laid his idea before the Secretary to the Committee of Imperial Defence, Colonel Hankey, who quickly appreciated its value and importance. Colonel Swinton had followed this up at the beginning of January, 1915, by pressing the matter personally on the War Office. Colonel Hankey had put forward the suggestion, along with other new ideas, in a memorandum dated 28th December, 1914, to the Committee of Imperial Defence. Mr. Churchill wrote to the Prime Minister on 5th January, 1915, supporting the proposal, and fortunately he also proceeded to initiate independent measures for investigation and experiment financed from the Navy vote. "Fortunately," because though the War Office set up a Committee to investigate Colonel Swinton's suggestion, it dropped the project after a few experiments and decided to take no further action. As Mr. Churchill, when Secretary of State for War, said four-and-a-half years later in his evidence before the Royal Commission on Awards to Inventors, with reference to the part played by the War Office:

"Certain investigations and experiments were made, but the matter came to a dead end. . . . I formed the opinion that no real progress was being made and that the military authorities were quite unconvinced either of the practicability of making such engines or of their value when made."

After seeing the experiments at Wormwood Scrubs, I arranged with Mr. Balfour, the new First Lord of the Admiralty that the Ministry of Munitions should undertake responsibility for the manufacture of tanks, while the Admiralty Committee continued experiments. Major Albert Stern, as Chairman of the Ministry's Tank Committee, threw great energy into their production.

The first-fruits of this arrangement appeared when, at the beginning of February, 1916, I went with other Ministers, including Lord Kitchener and various naval and military officers and some representatives from G.H.Q., France, to witness the official trial of the first machine—later known as the "Mother" Tank—at Hatfield Park. The experiment was a complete success, the tank achieving even more than it was asked to accomplish. And I can recall the feeling of delighted amazement with which I saw for the first time the ungainly monster, bearing the inscription "H.M.S. Centipede" on its breast, plough through thick entanglements, wallow through deep mud, and heave its huge bulk over parapets and across trenches. At last, I thought, we have the answer to the German machine-guns and wire. Mr. Balfour's delight was as great as my own, and it was only with difficulty that some of us persuaded him to disembark from H.M. Landship, whilst she crossed the last test, a trench several feet wide.

Sir William Robertson was also very favourably impressed, but Lord Kitchener scoffed as the huge, clumsy creature lumbered and tumbled about, though always moving forward, and expressed the opinion that it would be very quickly knocked out by artillery. He certainly gave me the impression at the time that he thought little of the invention; but a different light is shed upon his attitude by a letter I have quite recently received from General Sir Robert Whigham, who in 1916 was a member of the Army Council, and accompanied Lord Kitchener to the Hatfield trial. He writes: —

". . . Lord Kitchener was so much impressed that he remarked to Sir William Robertson that it was far too valuable a weapon for so much publicity. He then left the trial ground before the trials were concluded, with the deliberate intention of creating the impression that he did not think there was anything to be gained from them. Sir William Robertson followed him straight away, taking me with him, to my great disappointment as I was just going to have a ride in the tank! During the drive back to London, Sir William explained to me the reason of Lord Kitchener's and his.

own early departure, and impressed on me the necessity for maintaining absolute secrecy about the tank, explaining that Lord Kitchener was rather disturbed at so many people being present at the trials as he feared they would get talked about and the Germans would get to hear of them. It is a matter of history that after these trials fifty tanks were ordered and that Lord Kitchener went to his death before they were ready for the field. I do know, however, that he had great expectations of them, for he used to send for me pretty frequently while he was S. of S. and I was D.C.I.G.S., and he referred to them more than once in the course of conversation. His one fear was that the Germans would get to hear of them before they were ready."

Out of fairness to Lord Kitchener's memory I insert this letter here.

If this is the correct interpretation of Lord Kitchener's view, I can only express regret that he did not see fit to inform me of it at the time, in view of the fact that I was responsible as Minister of Munitions for the manufacture of these weapons.

The mention of this tank test recalls to my mind an incident which amused us all at the time, on the occasion of another similar test which took place on Lord Iveagh's estate. The elephantine monstrosity crashed through shrubberies, smashing young trees and bushes into the earth, and leaving behind it a wide trail of destruction. I went to inspect this mashed and mutilated track, and there in the middle of it I found a partridge's nest full of eggs—and incredible to relate, not a single egg had been broken!

The work of production and supply naturally fell to the Ministry of Munitions, and on 12th February, 1916, only a few days after the trials at Hatfield, the War Office formally placed an order for 100 tanks. Soon after manufacture had started, the number of tanks asked for was increased to 150, and work was pressed on at full speed, since the necessity was urgent; but production presented special difficulties, because the type was entirely new and parts had still to be improvised. Shortly after the commencement of the Somme battle, the military authorities decided to make use of a number of the machines as soon as they could be produced, to help on our renewed offensive before the winter months, and in August, 1916, upwards of 50 were shipped over to France. On 15th September, just seven months after the signature of the " charter " authorising their construction, some 49 of these were thrown into the battle.

Not the least remarkable thing about the introduction of these new weapons is the fact that although thousands of persons of all grades necessarily knew all about them, the secret of the tanks was so well kept that their first appearance came as a real surprise to the enemy. The very name " Tank " reflects the fact that during construction they were camouflaged even in name by being described as tanks and water carriers.   Hence the tests at Hatfield were described on the programme as a " Tank Trial."

But the decision of the army chiefs to launch the first handful of these machines on a comparatively local operation in September, 1916, instead of waiting until a much larger number were available to carry out a great drive, has always appeared to me to have been a foolish blunder.   It was contrary to the views of those who had first realised the need for such a weapon, had conceived it, fought for its adoption, designed it, produced it, and carried out the training of those who were to man it in the field.   We made the same error as the Germans committed in April, 1915, when by their initial use of poison gas on a small sector alone, they gave away the secret of a new and deadly form of attack, which, had it been used for the first time on a grand scale, might have produced results of a decisive character.

Mr. Montagu, who succeeded me as Minister of Munitions, supported the " tankers " in their earnest endeavours to keep the tanks from being thrown into action until several hundred had been manufactured and manned by trained crews.   I saw the Prime Minister, and begged him to intervene authoritatively.   He did not disagree, but referred me to Sir William Robertson.   I urged the C.I.G.S. to exert his influence with the Commander-in-Chief.   He answered in his most laconic style, " Haig wants them."   So the great secret was sold for the battered ruin of a little hamlet on the Somme, which was not worth capturing.

In spite, however, of this decision of the Commander-in-Chief in the field, and of the remarkable moral effect produced by the tanks when they went into action, an atmosphere of doubt and prejudice lingered for some time at the War Office.   On 26th September, 1916, the Army Council asked for an additional 1,000 tanks; but after the orders for these machines, and for the vast number of component parts required had been placed, and the complicated machinery for the production of this mass of materials had been set in action, I discovered that the demand had without my knowledge been cancelled by the Army Council.   I at once countermanded this cancellation, and took steps to ensure that production should continue.

I retained my belief in the tanks, and my interest in their development and use, throughout the War.   Even when I ceased to be directly concerned in their production or employment, the subject not infrequently came under my notice as Chairman of the War Cabinet to which questions were referred, owing to the disagreement of some of those responsible for the origin of the tanks with the methods and tactics employed in their use.   Questions of delay in production and supply, sometimes due to lack of continuity in the policy of G.H.Q., sometimes due to difficulties of manufacture, also came up.   Indeed, there were moments when I regretted that in the case of the tanks I

Comparison of Shell Filling.

Nature.	Week Ending Sept 25th 1915.	Week Ending Jany 8th 1916	Week Ending July 15th 1916
H.E.			
18 Pr.	—	18,492	264,207
13 Pr	—	2,000	7,144
4.5"	20,989	36,985	180,411
4.7"	626	7,284	8,538
4.7" Chemical	—	—	3,512
5"	—	3,770	3,071
60 Pr.	3,153	7,912	30,288
6"	5,451	5,025	39,181
8"	1,585	4,019	30,469
9.2" How?	1,227	529	23,322
9.2" Gun.	—	638	544
12"	80	283	2,491
15"	—	—	218
Forward	33,111	86,937	593,396

	Total Rounds	Total Round 4.7" & Above	
Week ending Sept 25th 1915	119,901	15,426	
Week ending Jany 8th 1916	281,613	37,477	
Week ending July 15th 1916	1,179,021	168,881	
%age increase July 1916 over Sept 1915	883	995	

Facsimile of table supplied by Sir Eric Geddes to
in Shell Production during the first year of the

386

Weeks Ending Sept. 25th 1915, Jan.y 8th 1916 and July 15th 1916.

Nature.	Week Ending Sept 25th 1915	Week Ending Jan.y 8th 1916	Week Ending July 15th 1916.
Brought Forward.	33.111	86.937	593.396
Shrapnel.			
18 Pr. Home.	50.964	125.084	338554
18 Pr. Abroad.	—	43,300	153,362
15 Pr.	6,924	—	—
13 Pr.	14,740	1420	20,252
4.5"	10.858	11,803	—
4.5" Incendiary	—	—	.790
10 Pr.	—	4,297	—
2.75"	—	499	1,971
4.7"	—	—	5.900
5"	442	127	131
60 Pr.	2,862	7890	20.861
.6"	—	—	355
Anti Aircraft Special	—	256	43,449
Home	119,901	238,313	1,025.659
Total Abroad		43,300	153,362

Tons of H.E.	Tons of Propellant		
123	110		
239	217		
1,651	1,111		
1,242	910		

Mr. Lloyd George, showing the remarkable increase
Ministry of Munitions, September, 1915, to July, 1916.

had not taken the same course as I had adopted in regard to heavy artillery and machine-guns, and organised at the outset for a larger supply than the War Office demanded.

I do not consider that the tanks were correctly used until the Battle of Cambrai in November, 1917. This action, though indecisive, if not sterile of result—through no fault of the new arm—will, I think, go down to history as one of the epoch-making events of the War, marking the beginning of a new era in mechanical warfare. Nevertheless, even after the remarkable success of the machines, there was a slowness to realise and a reluctance to admit their potentialities, alike as savers of life and as begetters of victory. But by the summer of 1918 their value was definitely established. Joint arrangements were made by the British, French and Americans for their production on a great scale, and the plans for the continuation of operations during 1919 contemplated their employment, as well as that of cross-country tractors, in immense numbers. In fact, had the advance of the Allies in 1919 taken place, it would have been a devastating march of hordes of mechanical caterpillars.

8. SUMMARY OF ACHIEVEMENTS OF THE MINISTRY

I will not weary my readers by further details of the complex problems which the Ministry of Munitions had to tackle. Some indication of their variety may be gleaned from the fact that the preparation of a single product such as a complete round of 18-pounder high-explosive shell involved the manufacture and assembly of 78 accurately gauged components—15 for the cartridge, 11 for the shell, and 52 for the fuse, gaine, etc. And the main types of shell ran to some twenty-six different sizes and kinds.

By September, 1915, three months after I had taken over the Ministry of Munitions, we were producing 120,000 filled shells of all kinds weekly, as against the 70,000 a week when I took over the job of munitions. In January, 1916, the figure had risen to 238,000 per week; and in mid-July, just after I had left the Ministry of Munitions to go to the War Office, the total weekly output of filled shell rose to 1,025,659.* These figures exclude our purchases from abroad. In commemoration of the passing of the million mark, Sir Eric Geddes supplied me with a table, signed by himself showing this remarkable progress, which I reproduce.

To show the progress which was achieved by the methods we instituted in the Ministry of Munitions, I also give the following table which sets out the total supplies of filled shell which were forthcoming from all sources during the ten months from 1st August, 1914, to 30th June, 1915, and in the twelve months July, 1915, to June, 1916: —

* These figures do not represent the full scale and weight of the increase. The most valuable results were in the increased production of heavy shell.

Total output of filled shell or complete rounds: —

				Aug. 1914, to June, 1915.	July, 1915, to June, 1916.
Light	...	...	...	1,877,300	14,748,800
Medium	...	...	...	389,000	3,895,800
Heavy	...	...	...	26,500	566,500
Very Heavy	...	...	...	14,000	288,300
Total	...	...	...	2,306,800	19,499,400

On 6th July, 1916, the day on which I left the Ministry of Munitions to become Secretary of State for War, I was furnished with a report signed by Sir Walter Layton, which stated that: —

"A year's output at the rate prevalent in 1914-15 can now be obtained in the following periods: —

Shell.	18-pdr. Ammunition	...	...	Three weeks
	Field Howitzer ditto	...	...	Two weeks
	Medium Gun and			
	Howitzer ditto	...	...	Eleven days
	Heavy Howitzer ditto	...	...	Four days

The present weekly output in the first three classes is practically equivalent to the whole stock in existence before the War. There was no stock of heavy howitzer ammunition before the War.

A statement could be made on similar lines for other munitions."

I have already shown how, when I took over the Ministry of Munitions in June, 1915, the allowance of shells per battery was eight rounds per day (two rounds per gun). Contrast this with the following extract from the diary of an Artillery Officer (taken from the Royal Artillery Commemoration Book): —

"August 18th, 1916.

The men are very tired, and the layers are nearly exhausted, although we have changed them as often as possible.

My guns have already fired nearly 1,000 rounds each and are almost too hot to touch. . . . At three in the morning I got a telephone message to say that the remainder of the programme was cancelled, and that I was to drop back to my normal 400 rounds a day."

The same officer, under date 1st August, 1916, writes: —

"There are 15 batteries altogether. . . . on a piece of ground four hundred yards long by two hundred wide."

Similar progress can be recorded with respect to artillery. At the outbreak of the War the total number of guns available was 1,902, of which 1,573 were light, and 329 were ranked as heavies at that date (i.e., 4.7-inch guns and upwards). In the following ten months to 30th June, 1915, there were manufactured 1,105 fresh guns, 1,011 light and 94 heavy. Between 1st July, 1915, and 30th June, 1916, the number of guns manufactured was 5,006—4,112 light and 894 heavy. The number of guns of 6-inch calibre and upwards was multiplied nearly fivefold.

I have given elsewhere the figures for the notable growth in our machine-gun supply in this period. Of grenades our output during the year July, 1915—June, 1916, was 27,000,000 as compared with 68,000 produced from August, 1914, to June, 1915. We similarly produced 4,279 trench mortars as compared with the War Office 312.

The effect of this artillery can perhaps best be understood by the evidence of some German records which I will quote. The history of the 27th (Württemberg) Division, one of the best divisions which fought at the Somme, states: —

" . . . A culminating point was reached which was never again approached. What we experienced surpassed all previous conception. The enemy's fire never ceased for an hour. It fell night and day on the front line and tore fearful gaps in the ranks of the defenders. It fell on the approaches to the front line, and made all movement towards the front hell. It fell on the rearward trenches and the battery positions and smashed men and material in a manner never seen before or since. It repeatedly reached even the resting battalions behind the front, and occasioned there terrible losses. *Our artillery was powerless against it.* . . . In the Somme fighting of 1916 there was a spirit of heroism which was never again found in the division, however conspicuous its fighting power remained until the end of the War."

The history continues that the men of 1918 had not the " temper, the steadfastness and the spirit of sacrifice of their predecessors. . . ."

Captain von Hentig, of the General Staff of the Guards Reserve Division, writes: —

" The Somme was the muddy grave of the German field army, and of the faith in the infallibility of the German leadership, dug by British Industry and its shells. . . ."

Captain Hierl, an acute critic of the War, says of the Somme: —

" The immense material superiority of the enemy did not fail to have its psychological effect on the German combatants. The enemy commanders may put this down to the credit side of their account as the profit of their attrition procedure. . . . The great enemy superiority in war apparatus and men was thus made to pull its weight, whilst the superiority of the German leadership and training did not get its proper return. . . ."

This evidence from the other side of the battle front demonstrates beyond challenge the importance of the success achieved by the Ministry of Munitions in equipping our forces for battle.

The figures I have given for the increase of output in 1915-16 represent only the first-fruits of the hard work put into the organisation of the Ministry of Munitions. But its greatest claim to recognition is due to the fact that it was organised with a view to expansion if the necessity arose. The business was planned from the commencement not to furnish adequate supplies for one final battle in 1916, but on the assumption that the War might last for years, that there might be a succession of prolonged fights on a great scale and that the demand for munitions of every kind would probably increase and not diminish. That is why up to the end of the War manufacture kept pace with the growing need for more guns, more trench mortars, more machine-guns, more rifles, more ammunition, more explosives, more tanks, and more lorries.

When we organised our factories and ordered our machinery it was on the basis of a demand far beyond that which was contemplated by the Military Staffs in 1915. I was then accused of megalomania because I took this view of the undertaking which was entrusted to me. But in 1916, 1917, and 1918, the generals were very pleased that the swollen-headed plans of 1915 had all materialised and that the stocks in hand were ready to answer to every call made upon them by the soldiers at the front.

It was a much criticised Ministry. When we had hardly begun to pull things together, and to restore order out of chaos, all the confusion was attributed to the new Ministry. "The house that is building is never like the house that is built" and we were blamed for all the untidiness, for the mortar and material scattered about, for the girder skeleton, the unfilled framework, and the unfinished state of the structure.

When I first went to the Ministry of Munitions there was no organisation—when I left it there was no better organised Department in Whitehall, and I should like any of its critics to name one of the old-established Departments which was superior to it in all-round efficiency. The organisation of a big business from the foundation is not an easy task when all the circumstances are favourable. It is none the easier when the ground is cumbered with ill-designed, badly-constructed and ramshackle buildings thrown about at random. It is specially difficult if the old directors from whom this part of the business has been wrenched, and who are thoroughly unfriendly to the new management, still retain an over-riding jurisdiction in vital details.

That we should have succeeded in spite of these difficulties was a triumph for the capable men who threw the whole of their energies into the performance of their arduous duties. Without their ceaseless toil, and their great resourcefulness, achievement would have been quite unattainable in the time and under the conditions.

My view of the functions of the head of such a concern was that its success would depend upon his having a clear idea in his own mind as to the objectives which he should strive to attain, and a definite plan as to the best way of reaching them. After that success would depend upon his gift of choosing the right persons to direct every branch of the business, upon his power of drawing the best service out of them by encouragement, stimulation and support; upon the exercise of such a close and constant supervision over every detail (without getting lost in a jungle of details) as would enable him to discover where things were going wrong, and upon his taking the right steps to remedy deficiencies when he found them, and taking them in time.

I claim for my competent staff and for myself, that when at a critical moment in our history this crucial task devolved upon us, we did not fail our country.

CHAPTER XX

ALLIED   RELATIONS   WITH   AMERICA

DURING the first part of the War, I was not departmentally concerned with our diplomatic relations with the Neutral Powers.   I had, how-ever, a very definite interest in the attitude adopted by the United States of America towards the Allies, inasmuch as that great country represented the one important outside source of supply for munitions of war—a matter with which, as I have already related, I very early concerned myself.   As a member of the first Cabinet Committee on Munitions Supply, I was already in October, 1914, promoting arrangements for large orders of munitions from the States, and as Chairman of the Munitions of War Committee, and later as Minister of Munitions, I was responsible for a steadily growing stream of supplies from across the Atlantic, which swelled by degrees to con-siderable dimensions, up to the point when we perfected arrange-ments for manufacture at home.

During this period, therefore, I had a very special incentive to watch the course of our relations with America.   The maintenance of a good understanding with her was not only a necessary condition if our munition supplies were to continue uninterrupted, but a factor of vital importance in ensuring a just and satisfactory settlement of the struggle, whenever the hour of peace should strike.

When a war is in progress, neutral countries are often placed in an embarrassing position.   Themselves at peace with all the world, they naturally seek to maintain their normal commercial relations with both the belligerent parties.   In addition, they endeavour if possible to improve the shining hour by doing an increased and more profitable business, by supplying the additional demands created by the war at the inflated prices made possible by war's restriction of supplies.   But while they thus earn greater profits, they are subject to greater hazards and less consideration.   Nations fighting for their lives cannot always pause to observe punctilios.   Their every action is an act of war, and their attitude to neutrals is governed, not by the conventions of peace, but by the exigencies of a deadly strife.

The country which is determined at all costs to remain neutral must therefore be prepared to pocket its pride and put up with repeated irritations and infringements of its interests by the belliger-ents on both sides; compensating itself for these annoyances by the enhanced profits of its war-time trade. Should the difficulties of neutrality prove too great, it is left with the choice either of treating the violation of its rights by one of the belligerent parties as a *casus belli*, or of taking sides, not on the strength of war-time incidents, but rather on its view of the rights and wrongs of the principal conflict. Such, briefly stated, was the problem which confronted the United States of America during the course of the World War. Prior to Armageddon, the firm tradition of the States was to hold utterly aloof from all concern with the tangled relations of the Old World—a tradition enshrined in its doctrine of America for Americans, and let Europe keep its greedy hand off our Continent. In turn, America would leave the rest of the world to Europe alone. Up to the date of the Great War Americans maintained with ostentatious stiffness this traditional attitude. They sought to return to it with a snap when they let go their end of the Treaty of Versailles. Gradually in Europe, Asia and Polynesia alike American statesmen have been driven out of this position by inexorable facts.

It is true that Colonel House, President Wilson's *alter ego*, was keenly interested in international affairs, and visited Europe in the summer of 1914 in the rôle of disinterested and benevolent adviser, to urge a better understanding between everybody and everybody else. It is to his credit and that of Mr. Theodore Roosevelt that they both understood that the theoretical aloofness of America no longer had any basis in realities, and that she would be intimately affected by any European upheaval, whether she professed to ignore it or not. The affable Colonel's visit to Europe was, through no fault of his own, fruitless. Wisdom expressed in gentle tones could not be heard above the roar of the nearing cataract. He found hearty sympathy for his ideas in England, a trumpeting militarism in Germany and political chaos in France. The mass of the American public was as remote in its thoughts and interests from these things as though they were happenings on another planet.

During the opening stages of the war, opinion in the United States was quite as overwhelmingly in favour of maintaining firm neutrality towards the European struggle as opinion was in Britain three days before the declaration of war. With regard to the merits of the respective belligerents, the predominant opinion in America was supposed by this country and France to be pro-Ally, though there was a strong pro-German section among the large German-American population of the Middle West, and a chronic hostility to England amongst the Irish. The intellectuals were believed to be pro-Ally. A careful sounding of opinion among American Universities and Colleges carried out by Sir Gilbert Parker, the distinguished Canadian novelist, in October, 1914, showed an overwhelming sympathy for the Allies. But despite this general tendency, it would be true to say that on the whole, opinion in the States was neither pro-Ally nor pro-German, but simply and solely pro-American. In war, sympathy is a long way off support. President Wilson was universally acclaimed when in mid-August he made a speech calling on the citizens of the United States to observe strict neutrality in act and speech, and at that date even Mr. Theodore Roosevelt rejoiced that his country was geographically able to keep out of the fight. An analysis of the American Press made by Sir Gilbert Parker, at the end of September, 1914, showed that while far more of the leading papers were friendly to the Allies than to Germany, the majority were definitely neutral, and viewed the merits on both sides with a detached impartiality.

Belgium was thousands of miles away from Illinois. German destroyers and submarines at Ostend were not within a few steam hours of New York. German guns at Calais could not block the principal highway to America's powerful ports. German Zeppelins could not bomb Washington and kill women and children in their homes. These things were very remote. We cannot impute this indifference to callousness. An earthquake in Japan with a loss of tens of thousands of lives does not occupy as many columns of a British newspaper as does a railway accident near Carlisle with the loss of a score of lives.

Apart from this, the moral issues were not so free from ambiguity to the American conscience. Many people in this country were unreasonably astonished at this attitude on the part of America. Filled with anger at Germany's wanton aggression in Belgium, and with fear of the threatening monster of Prussian militarism, they could not understand how the great Democracy of the New World should hesitate for an instant about the merits of the issue upon which we had drawn our sword, or should fail to ally itself with us in defence of liberty and justice.

But to the onlookers in America, the issue was not so simple. On 22nd August, 1914, Colonel House wrote to President Wilson: —

" The saddest feature of the situation to me is that there is no good outcome to look forward to. If the Allies win, it means largely the domination of Russia on the Continent of Europe; and if Germany wins, it means the unspeakable tyranny of militarism for generations to come."

Britain and France never quite realised the handicap to their propaganda in neutral countries which was involved in their alliance with the Czarist regime. America shuddered at the idea of any close association with the Government of Russia—brutal, tyrannical and corrupt, in fact, rotten to the core—and that went far to neutralise the horror felt at the Belgian tragedy. America also had a large and politically important Irish-American population, trained to hatred of England as to a religion. Let us be fair. Britain had for centuries given cruel cause for this rooted animosity, and we had not yet repaired the wrong we had burnt into the sensitive and retentive Irish soul. Add to this the fact that Americans were by long tradition accustomed to think of Britain as the despotic monarchy from whose greedy clutch the States had wrested themselves free in the heroic struggles of the War of Independence. There were other considerations which compelled neutrality. The German population in America were a highly respected, diligent, and peaceable element of the community, with characteristics that furnished little evidence in support of the legend of Prussian ferocity. Moreover, they commanded millions of useful votes, which might determine the issue of crucial elections. In these circumstances it will be clear that the general sympathy of America with the Allied cause was bound to be considerably qualified and non-committal. Americans might strongly desire to see the Allies victorious, but not strongly enough to be prepared to endure with patience losses or inconvenience to themselves, or risks to their respective political parties, as the price of Allied victory.

In short, America was not bound by treaty commitments to enter the War on either side. While the predominant opinion (whenever an opinion was formed) was that, on balance, the Allies were in the right, that verdict was too qualified to impose an obligation of honour to march with them to and through the gates of Hell. Failing such obligation, the issue of neutrality or participation in the War became one purely of relative expediency for America. It was her interest to maintain her trade, her prestige, the security of her citizens, and to keep her young men out of the shambles. She would only be forced to fight if fighting was better calculated than neutrality to defend these interests.

It so fell out that while American intellectual sympathies were in the main with the Allies, American commercial interests were open to more frequent and obvious interference by them. Germany's chief power was on land, Britain's on the sea. Germany's invasion of Belgium, her devastation of France, might rouse disinterested wrath in America. But it did not touch American pockets. On the other hand, Britain's firm measures to prevent contraband of war from reaching Germany, and her wide and constantly widening interpretation of contraband, caused serious inconvenience to American shipping and direct interference with American business. Time and time again, the friction created by this interference generated between the two countries a perilous heat which seemed to be within an ace of producing a rupture of diplomatic relations. Once or twice the language of protest bordered on the minatory. These protests undoubtedly introduced a certain element of timidity into our blockade, and Germany profited by the relaxation. Later on, Lord Robert Cecil tightened up our clutch.

To be weighed against these annoyances was the fact that Britain was far and away the wealthiest of the belligerents and was able to place in the United States—and pay cash for—orders for colossal war supplies for herself and her Allies. If we were interfering with America's potential trade with our enemies, at least we were providing her with a magnificent market in Britain, France, and Russia, which stimulated her industries to an unprecedented level of activity and profitableness. This fact had its influence in holding back the hand of the American Government whenever, excited to intense irritation by some new incident of the Blockade, it contemplated retaliatory measures.

Throughout 1914 and 1915, until the prospect of the Presidential election of 1916 began to loom high above the horizon and import a new complication of the issues, the story of the relations between America and the belligerents is that of a country driven backwards and forwards between the two sides by an alternation of incidents, any one of which might easily have tipped the scales for war, had it not been counterpoised by new troubles on the other side; and had it not also been for the stubborn determination of President Wilson to keep his country out of the fight if he possibly could.

The opening weeks of the War found American opinion, as I have said, strongly on the Allied side. We never quite knew where President Wilson's real sympathies lay. We felt that, in the tremendous struggle which was constantly before his eyes, he would have been more than human had his heart not been engaged on one side or the other, whatever his hand might do or his tongue might speak. But his deportment was so studiously unpleasant to both sides that they each suspected him of being antipathetic to their own side. We only knew for a fact that the President was severe in his judgment of Allied actions, and we did not realise that this was due to the fear lest his private sympathies should pervert the strict impartiality of attitude which he was imposing on himself.

Very shortly, the use which Britain made of her sea-power to prevent supplies reaching the Central Powers, even through neutral countries, provoked an outcry in America, particularly from the powerful Copper Trust. Copper was a vital necessity for munitions, and we did our best to stop any supplies of it from reaching Germany. Had Germany been confined to the use of her own ports, this would have been quite a simple matter. But she was bordered by neutral States—Holland, Scandinavia, and at first Italy—and consignments, ostensibly destined for these countries, were really being sent for her benefit. And the United States were very large producers of copper.

On 5th October 1914, Sir Cecil Spring-Rice, our Ambassador in Washington, wrote : —

" The copper interests here are very powerful. . . . We shall have to find some means of crippling Krupp without ruining the mining states here, who possess the ear of the Secretary of State and have a commanding influence in the Senate."

On 3rd November he wrote: —

" We have command of the seas and this is a reason why we are likely to fall foul of all the neutrals. The American conscience is on our side, but the American pocket is being touched. Copper and oil are dear to the American heart and the export is a matter of great importance. We are stopping the export and the consequence is a howl which is increasing in volume. We should probably do the same. But the howl may become very furious soon. . . ."

Early in November, 1914, in accordance with a plan prepared by Mr. Leverton Harris, an agent was sent to New York from this country to attempt to solve this problem by buying up as much as possible of the American stock of copper on condition that the producers should undertake to sell only to purchasers approved by us. But this business proposition was not successful, for pro-German influences were exerted to defeat it. We then proceeded, at Gibraltar and elsewhere, to hold up all copper consignments to neutral countries until we were satisfied as to the bona fides of the consignees. The Governments of the neutral countries in Europe came to the aid of their manufacturers by prohibiting the export of copper, which simplified our release of cargoes to meet their bona fide requirements. We then told the American copper producers that if they continued to sell copper to Germany, we should buy none from them ourselves, but should hold up all their European consignments. Two of the largest American refining companies promptly entered into an agreement with us, and before long most of the others were glad to come into line. One of the last to come in was the great Guggenheim group. Its hand was forced by an announcement made, in reply to a question in Parliament, that the firms whose consignments were safeguarded by agreements with us were welcome to announce the fact, so that orders might be placed with them. Thereupon Guggenheim cabled their representative in London to sign an agreement with the Admiralty.

By the beginning of March, 1915, we had secured control of 95 per cent. of the exportable copper of the United States, and the powerful influence of the Copper Trust was no longer a menace to good relations between us and the States.

Fortunately for the Allies, American annoyance at any action on our part which hampered their trade would ere long be counterbalanced by anger at some more exasperating deed by the Germans.

If in the autumn of 1914 we were holding up neutral vessels and requiring certificates of ultimate destination before we would release their cargoes, the Germans were sowing mines all round the narrow seas, which sank neutral shipping without warning, and were brutally bombarding the unprotected watering places of Scarborough and Whitby. In January, 1915, the Germans took the further step of bombing with Zeppelins the towns of King's Lynn and Yarmouth, and at the end of that month their submarines began a form of attack which was in the end to bring the United States into the War, by sinking unarmed merchant vessels in the open sea.

While these acts increased the moral condemnation of Germany by American opinion, it remained the case that our actions regarding contraband were a more frequent irritation. From a well-informed source we learnt in January, 1915, that the United States was growing less interested in the War as a main item of news: "The air-raid has been commented on in the strongest terms in every paper I have seen, but these things no longer excite surprise. I think I told you that I had seen signs of the public being bored with the War. The proof came last week when the earthquake was reported and the War went to the second or third page." And from another source we were told: "There is a lack of proportion in the information we have concerning the British Navy. We scarcely ever hear of it except when some British ship is blown up by a German torpedo, or when a British ship holds up an American cargo. You can readily see the dangerous psychological effect of this. . . . 'War news' no longer sells. But 'interference with American trade' does sell. It sells, and it has a certain unfortunate effect upon what I call the 'headline mind.'"

As to the general sentiment in the Middle West, we were told: "The German Army wins admiration for its efficiency and courageous performance, but sympathy with its purposes or ideals was lost the day it stepped into Belgium. The War is deplored as unnecessary and preventable, and no one desires anything more than a speedy and conclusive peace. But it must be conclusive. Peace without definite victory would satisfy no one. 'This thing has got started,' they say, 'so let's have it finished once for all.' Meanwhile everyone out here is very busy with his own affairs."

Towards the end of January, 1915, an adroit attempt was made to embroil us with America. The *Dacia*, a German merchantman, laid up in America since July, 1914, was bought by a German-American, registered as an American vessel and sent with a cargo of cotton for Bremen, via Rotterdam. We made it known that we refused to recognise the transfer of flag, and Germans waited hopefully for us to seize the American ship and thus produce a storm in the States. The *Dacia* was duly seized, but by the French Navy, and the plot miscarried. The French cause was popular in the

o

States, and hitherto they had played a minor part in the capture of contraband. President Wilson could of course protest to France, and did so without avail. But his protest did not mark a culmination —perhaps critical—of a series of protests, as it would have done had Britain been the culprit.

Germany thereupon proceeded to announce a submarine blockade of Britain, and declared she would sink every merchant vessel in the seas surrounding these islands after 18th February, 1915, and would not guarantee safety to passengers or crews, even of neutral shipping, since British vessels might be hoisting neutral flags in these dangerous waters, and her submarines would therefore ignore the nationality of flags. This called forth a very strong note from President Wilson, to which Germany only replied that if he would stop all export of munitions to the Allies, and take steps to ensure supplies of raw materials and food to Germany, they would reconsider their attitude.

Britain replied to the submarine campaign by an Order in Council virtually blockading Germany. We did not actually use the technical term " Blockade," as what we announced was not merely or mainly a close investment of German ports, but a cutting off of supplies for Germany by detaining all vessels carrying goods of presumed enemy destination, ownership, or origin. This was of course a novel though obvious variation of the principle of blockade, made necessary by modern progress in transport, which turned every neutral harbour on the Continent into a potential German port. Naturally the flutter of notes backwards and forwards across the Atlantic grew denser and intenser.

During these months, Colonel House was visiting the belligerent countries of Europe as the President's emissary to take soundings as to the possible terms of peace. His presence and the understanding he achieved of the practical realities of the situation, doubtless helped to ease friction between us and America. But his peace efforts were doomed to frustration. At that stage of the War, he found in Britain a readiness to consider a peace based on restoration and indemnity for Belgium, but Germany refused to promise restoration, and would not hear of indemnity.

On 7th May, 1915, while Colonel House was in London, news came of the sinking of the *Lusitania*. That put a sharp end to all possibility of promoting peace talk between England and Germany. The question of the moment became rather whether the United States themselves could any longer maintain their neutrality. The Colonel himself held that they could not and should not hold back any longer. He wrote on 9th May to President Wilson: —

". . . Our intervention will save, rather than increase, the loss of life.

America has come to the parting of the ways, when she must

decide whether she stands for civilised or uncivilised warfare. We can no longer remain neutral spectators. Our action in this crisis will determine the part we will play when peace is made, and how far we may influence a settlement for the lasting good of humanity. We are being weighed in the balance, and our position amongst the nations is being assessed by mankind."*

President Wilson sent a strong note to Germany; but it was a protest, not an ultimatum. The Austrian Ambassador at Washington sounded Bryan, the Secretary of State, and got the assurance that America did not mean to fight. He promptly advised Berlin, which was encouraged to be unaccommodating to Wilson. The click of the President's typewriter had no deadlier rattle behind it. House, meantime, was trying to arrange that Germany would abandon her submarine warfare if England ceased to stop food supplies for Germany. Sir Edward Grey was prepared to consider this.† But he never consulted the Cabinet as to this proposal. Had he done so they would have turned it down emphatically. Whether he consulted the Prime Minister before expressing his readiness to enter into an arrangement on this basis I am not prepared to say. Germany, however, stiffened by the reassurance that America would in no circumstances fight, refused the proposal, and said that she had plenty of food. What she wanted was raw materials. Naturally there could be no thought of letting these in for her munition manufacturers, and the proposal fell through. Had Germany accepted Colonel House's suggestion, the whole course of the War might have been changed. There certainly would have been no starving population in Germany in 1918. That means there would have been no revolution in November, 1918, and the War would have been prolonged for another year. But apart from that, Germany might not have declared that indiscriminate sinking of all ships which brought America into the War. Once more German military arrogance had blundered and by doing so had saved us from one of our worst blunders.

In connection with our blockade policy I should like to pay tribute here to the services rendered by Lord Robert Cecil in pressing forward the firm maintenance and full development of our activities in this field. When he became Under-Secretary of State for Foreign Affairs on 31st May, 1915, the Reprisals Order was already in force. Nevertheless, there was hesitation in high places about maintaining its provisions, as exemplified by Sir Edward Grey's readiness to consider abandoning an essential part of it on Colonel House's suggestion. Such hesitation was not shared by Lord Robert Cecil. In Council and in public he urged its strict observance. His advice

* " Intimate Papers " of Colonel House. Volume I, page 434.
† ibid., page 443.

was consistently in favour of bold measures. His activities in the Foreign Office were directed to the same end. Ultimately, in February, 1916, it was decided to appoint a Minister of Blockade, with Cabinet rank, to co-ordinate the work of all the various Committees and Departments dealing with this matter in its various aspects. Lord Robert Cecil was the obvious choice for this post, and he agreed to undertake it—without salary—in addition to his work as Under-Secretary to the Foreign Office. He was appointed on 23rd February, 1916, and it was largely due to him that the great national and international organisation of the blockade weapon was tightened so that it became one of the decisive factors in our ultimate victory.

Notes continued to pass between the United States and Germany throughout 1915 about the *Lusitania*. That a thousand non-combatant passengers—men, women, and children—including over a hundred American citizens, should have been thus massacred in cold blood was a severe strain on the President's pacifism. He stood it, although Germany repeatedly refused his request that she should at least disavow the action of her submarine commander. Gerard, the American Ambassador in Berlin, wrote to Colonel House on 1st June that: " It is the German hope to keep the *Lusitania* matter ' jollied along ' until the American people get excited about baseball or a new scandal and forget." President Wilson put the best face he could upon the matter by making a speech in which he suggested that the American people were " too proud to fight." He shrank from taking the action urged upon him by his principal adviser. Mr. Theodore Roosevelt launched a characteristic attack on the President's inaction: —

> " Unless we act with immediate decision and vigour we shall have failed in the duty demanded by humanity at large, and demanded even more clearly by the self-respect of the American Republic. . . .
>
> For many months our Government has preserved between right and wrong a neutrality which would have excited the emulous admiration of Pontius Pilate, the arch-typical neutral of all time . . ."*

The situation was complicated by the fact that while notes were passing about the *Lusitania,* another liner, the *Arabic*, was also torpedoed and sunk. Colonel House now wanted the President to proceed to war without further notes, and for a time the situation was exceedingly strained. But the German Government promised to instruct their submarine commanders not to sink further liners without warning, and after very strong pressure even went so far

* " Fear God and Take Your Own Part," page 353.

as to proffer a tentative disavowal of the action of the submarine commander who sank the *Arabic*. This belated action just—only just—enabled the "will to peace" of the President to survive the Presidential election.

The situation was not eased by information coming to light just at this time, through an indiscretion of the Austrian Ambassador, that the Austrian Embassy, aided by Von Papen, the German military attaché, was planning to cripple American munition plants, so as to interfere with supplies for the Allies. Von Papen and Boy-Ed, the German attachés, and Dumba, the Austrian Ambassador, were sent home, but President Wilson still kept his temper. The Presidential election was drawing nigh, and Wilson was determined to stand for re-election as the man who kept America out of the War.

Probably there was no very powerful desire among the American people at this stage to join in the fight. On 17th September, 1916, Spring-Rice wrote: "The majority want to make money and not to make war." In November he reported that anti-German feeling was growing stronger, together with the view that a victory of the Central Powers would be an immense calamity to the States. But in practice this sympathy showed itself rather in a greater eagerness to do business with the Allies than to make war on Germany. At the beginning of October we raised a loan on the American market to finance purchases of supplies. The loan was for 500,000,000 dollars, secured on the joint credit of France and Britain, in the form of 5 per cent. five-year bonds. In two days it was over-subscribed by about 200,000,000 dollars. As a proof of good will to the Allied cause, this was very gratifying. But Sir Cecil Spring-Rice, writing on 7th October, 1916, of the success of the loan, declared again: "It cannot be too often repeated that the American people are determined to hold aloof if they possibly can, and that the Government cannot take any action of which the great mass of the people do not approve."

Such, in brief outline, was the course and temper of American neutrality prior to the winter of 1916, when the re-elected President made his public bid for peace, to which I shall have later on to refer.

But even in the course of these first two years of War, President Wilson was continually on the alert for an opportunity to intervene and shorten or end the conflict. One effort in particular which he made, in the winter and early spring of 1915-16, was of special interest. As I was called into the discussion that followed, it is an essential part of my War Memoirs.

CHAPTER XXI

PRESIDENT WILSON'S PEACE MOVES

SEVERAL tentative movements were made in neutral countries for mediation during the first few weeks of the War, but they came to nothing. Whether President Wilson could have succeeded in arresting the mad plunge of Europe into war, had he intervened authoritatively and in time, will always remain a matter of conjecture. He made no effort. The suddenness with which the negotiations flared up and exploded the powder magazine probably took him by surprise. In that respect he was not alone.

When the War broke out, President Wilson made a well-intentioned but quite ineffectual gesture. He wrote on August 5th, 1914, to each of the belligerent monarchs a letter in the following terms: —

" Sir,

As official head of one of the Powers signatory to the Hague Convention, I feel it to be my privilege and my duty under Article 3 of the Convention to say to your Majesty in a spirit of most earnest friendship, that I should welcome an opportunity to act in the interest of European peace, either now or at any time that might be thought more suitable as an occasion to serve your Majesty and all concerned in a way that would afford me lasting cause for gratitude and happiness.

WOODROW WILSON."

While that letter was crossing the Atlantic, the Austrians were pressing down on their coveted prey, Serbia; French troops were singing as they swept over the frontier into the lost provinces of Alsace and Lorraine; the German General Staff was at last putting into effect its darling plan, minutely elaborated for years past, of an advance through Belgium that would encircle and destroy the army of France, and bring decisive victory in six weeks. To attempt to hold back the momentum of these vast forces with an offer of mediation was at that stage as futile as to think of arresting the descending blade of the guillotine with an appeal for mercy. Where Sir Edward Grey's proposal for a conference, made before war was declared, was scarcely heard (it certainly was not heeded) in the confusion, the polite and formal plea of a comparatively un-weaponed America for pause and reflection, coming as it did when armies were on foreign soil, could serve only to place on record her goodwill to all parties alike.

The replies were not hurried, and when they came they were universally discouraging. Having started, however reluctantly, the combatant nations all meant to fight it out to the bitter end. Germany was on the whole winning, so her rulers were in no mood for peace. France was pulling herself together after an inglorious beginning. Britain had barely started, but her stubborn spirit had caught a fire which could not easily be put out. Austria, in the act of inflicting what she thought would be an easy castigation on Serbia, had the whip wrenched out of her hand by the gallant army of the Serbs, and her flesh stung with the shame of a scourging inflicted upon her by the people she had despised. She was in a mood to revenge the humiliation by overwhelming force. The Russian tradition had always been to make a clumsy start. The defeat of Tannenberg did not, therefore, dismay this loose-limbed but stout-hearted giant. No one wanted peace. Every nation engaged in the struggle resented the idea of stopping the fight once it had begun. There were far fewer pacifists amongst them on 1st January, 1915, than on 1st August, 1914. There was a deep instinct in the minds of men that this conflict had been coming for a long time, and once it had begun it was better to get it over and done with. The voice of the mediator was, therefore, not heard in any land, and his rôle was everywhere an unpopular one. President Wilson's time for intervention had already passed, and it could not be resumed until the nations were beginning to feel the strain.

The message sent in November, 1914, by Mr. Thomas Nelson Page, the American Ambassador in Rome, to Mr. J. W. Bryan is remarkable, not only for its picture of the belligerent frame of mind but also for the prophetic vision of post-War troubles: —

> " American Embassy, Rome,
> November 19, 1914.
>
> [received December 7.]
> . . . I am conscious here of a strong undercurrent of conviction that when one side or the other in the present war prevails, America will become the next object of attack, either on the part of Germany or of Japan, as the case may be. It seems to be considered that the War will not end until one or the other party is absolutely discouraged and that no tenders of friendly offices will avail before that crisis. Also there is frequent expression of the thought that even should the War be ended in its present status, it would only be a truce until the belligerents, more especially

Germany, had recuperated sufficiently to attack again with better success, and that permanency of peace will depend on a condition in which absolute disarmament can be insisted upon. . . .

THOMAS NELSON PAGE."

At the close of 1915 there was some peace talk whispered about. The losses on all sides had been beyond anything the students of war had ever contemplated. The advantage was still with the Central Powers, but it was becoming increasingly clear to them that they could not cash their gains without incurring further sacrifices even more appalling than those which they had already sustained. The great new army of the British Empire, well drilled and fully equipped, would come into action in its full strength for the first time in the impending campaign of 1916. Neutral spectators had, therefore, some hope that the hour was propitious for taking definite steps towards mediation.

President Wilson was anxious for peace. Apart from the fact that his humane instincts were horrified by the slaughter and barbarity of the War on land and sea, his embarrassments as a neutral were increasing and intensifying each successive month. As I have already related, the British were searching his ships and the Germans were threatening to sink them. The British blockade was interfering daily with American commerce. That roused angry resentment in the American breast. On the other hand, the German counter-measures were an outrage on humanity. The reverberations of the War in the American Electorate were complicating American politics, and the Presidential election was not so far off. There was a powerful German vote which resented the tolerance extended by the Administration to the manufacture of munitions of war for the Allies. There was a still more powerful Irish vote which hated Britain. Apart from these groups, American sentiment was on the whole on the side of the Allies. The wanton trampling down of Belgium by the German legions was largely responsible for the creation of that opinion. War against the Allies was impossible. No Government could have carried the American public into such a war. Intervention on the other side would also mean a divided nation. The poor President was, therefore, harassed and perplexed by a terrible dilemma. What would suit him best would be the part of peacemaker. It fitted in with his temperament as well as with his political difficulties. He therefore sent Colonel House from the ark as a dove of peace to spy out the waters of the deluge in Europe and to report to his chief whether there was a sign of subsidence and any peak visible on which the harbinger of peace could plant her feet.

In this capacity Colonel House visited France, Germany, and Britain with a view to taking soundings about the possibility of bringing the War to an end, and as to the response which would be accorded to any proposal made by President Wilson in that direction. He flew from capital to capital. In Germany he found no prospect of any readiness to consider a peace which would conform to the President's ideals, let alone to the aims of the Allies. The furthest he got with von Bethmann-Hollweg was that Germany might consent to relinquish her conquests of Belgium and French territory in return for a sufficient indemnity. In his highly interesting "Intimate Papers" he gives a graphic account of the American Ambassador's interview with the German Emperor: —

"The Kaiser talked of peace and how it should be made and by whom, declaring that ' I and my cousins, George and Nicholas, will make peace when the time comes.' Gerard says to hear him talk one would think that the German, English, and Russian peoples were so many pawns upon a chess-board. He made it clear that mere democracies like France and the United States could never take part in such a conference. His whole attitude was that war was a royal sport, to be indulged in by hereditary monarchs and concluded at their will. . . ."*

Colonel House reached Paris with an intensified conviction that the German Government would not agree to peace terms which even the most moderate of Allied statesmen could accept. Thereafter he developed the line that any American intervention must take the form of a threat to Germany, followed if necessary by open hostilities, with a view to shortening the War; and, moreover, that such intervention was necessary not only to shorten the duration of the conflict, but to ensure that the peace ultimately made should be one of justice embodying the ideals of the President, rather than one of victorious allies carving up their defeated foe.

To this end, Colonel House urged both in Paris and in London that at a suitable moment the Allies should accept an offer from the President to call a conference of all the belligerents to discuss terms on which the War might be ended; it being understood that if terms acceptable to Wilson were agreed to by the Allies but rejected by Germany, the United States should come in on the side of the Allies to compel Germany's agreement.

It is difficult to come to any clear conclusion as to the reception accorded to the House mission in Paris. He himself clearly formed a favourable impression of the attitude of M. Briand, who was then Prime Minister of France, towards his pacific efforts. But M. Briand was one of those pleasant men who take a long time to understand, and after a prolonged acquaintance you were never quite sure that you knew him sufficiently well even then. He was an enigma even to his closest friends, and no one ever knew what his innermost

* "Intimate Papers," Vol. II, page 139.

thoughts were on any subject. However, by disposition he was a conciliator. He had a greater personal delight in reconciliation than in strife. But although inscrutable where his own individual opinions were concerned, there could be no doubt as to his sensitiveness to parliamentary opinion. And any suspicion of leanings towards pacifism was a crime in Paris. M. Clemenceau was a typical representative of the general attitude of the governing classes in the French metropolis. As for the French peasantry, they had resigned themselves to the leadership of Paris, and they were prepared to go through right to the end if those who were in supreme charge of the interests of their country felt it was necessary for the honour and safety of France to fight on. M. Briand could hardly have dragged France into a Peace Conference at that date unless he had had the most complete assurance that the terms offered would be favourable to France and would contain a guarantee for her future safety. Any rumour of a disposition on his part to countenance such a parley would have ensured his immediate downfall. British Ministers, therefore, felt that Colonel House's sanguine disposition had misled him into taking too hopeful a view of the co-operation of France in an endeavour to initiate *pourparlers* with an enemy whose arms, taking the terrain of the War as a whole, were triumphant in the East and the West.

In Britain, the British Cabinet was divided between two points of view. It was not so much that there were some Members of the Cabinet in favour of peace and others opposed, as that the majority were still convinced of the certainty of ultimate victory, while a formidable minority entertained doubts of the possibility of success if the War were prolonged beyond this year. The leading members of this defeatist junta were the Chancellor of the Exchequer and the President of the Board of Trade. Their pessimism had deepened Sir Edward Grey's natural gloom. Mr. Runciman was anxious as to the effect of the submarine campaign upon our sea transport. In his opinion our shipping capacity had already been strained to the utmost by the demands made upon it for the feeding of our population and of our armies, and the carriage of essential raw material for ourselves and our Allies. A few more thousands of our tonnage sunk by the German swordfish that swarmed around the approaches to our harbours, and we could not carry on. Mr. M'Kenna had also serious misgivings as to the financial position. He doubted whether it would be possible much longer for us to raise the funds necessary to enable us to finance essential purchases for ourselves and the Allies in countries across the sea, at the rate we were then expending our reserves on the War. He circulated to the Cabinet in September, 1915, two dismal papers from Sir John Bradbury and Mr. J. M. Keynes respectively. Sir John Bradbury was an exceptionally able man, with exceptionally orthodox ideas about finance and the gold standard. He ends an elaborate and discouraging review of the financial possibilities as follows: —

" It seems clear . . . that unless there is either an early and very large reduction of civil and military consumption, an increase of production by the withdrawal of a part of our forces in the field and their return to civil employment or a drastic curtailment of credits to Allies, further borrowing here will only be possible at the price of such an inflation of credit in relation to available commodities as will finally upset the balance of exchange and seriously impair our power to purchase either munitions or food-stuffs in America."

Mr. Keynes was more alarming and much more jargonish in his formidable paper. With the help of what he hints is an over-sanguine estimate of our borrowing possibilities in America we would get through to the end of the financial year, i.e., the 31st of March, 1916, provided our liabilities were not increased by fresh orders (he does not specifically mention our orders at the Ministry of Munitions for machine tools and rifles), but after that, the Deluge —unless peace intervenes. As to our existing commitments: —

". . . We ought to be able to do this without producing a catastrophe in the current financial year [i.e. up to 31st March, 1916], *provided peace puts us in a position to cancel the inflationism immediately afterwards. Otherwise the expenditure of the succeeding months will rapidly render our difficulties insupportable. This leads us to the meaning of ' inflationism ' and the consequences of depending upon it."*

Then comes a professional exposition on the character and inevitability of " the catastrophe," and he concludes: —

" The alternatives presented to us are, therefore, alternatives of degree. If by flinging out our resources lavishly we could be sure of finishing the War early next spring, I estimate that they might be about equal to our needs. If, on the other hand, it would be over-sanguine to anticipate this, it must be considered whether it is more desirable to average our expenditure, or alternatively, to be lavish until about next January, to appreciate the prospects in front of us somewhat suddenly at about that date, and then, having regard to the near future, to curtail rigorously, and tell our Allies that for the future they must look to themselves.

It is certain that our present scale of expenditure is only possible as a violent temporary spurt to be followed by a strong reaction; that the limitations of our resources are in sight; and that, in the case of any expenditure, we must consider not only as heretofore, whether it would be useful, but also whether we can afford it."

Mr. Winston Churchill in one of his amusing outbursts, once said that this country was governed by the 31st March. Put the British Empire at one end of the scale and the 31st March at the other, and the latter would win every time. That was Mr. M'Kenna's view.

Chancellor and President of the Board of Trade more than hinted at the possibility of starvation for our sea-fed island. Mr. M'Kenna's nerve was shaken by these vaticinations of his chief adviser, Mr. J. M. Keynes. The latter was much too mercurial and impulsive a counsellor for a great emergency. He dashed at conclusions with acrobatic ease. It made things no better that he rushed into opposite conclusions with the same agility. He is an entertaining economist whose bright but shallow dissertations on finance and political economy, when not taken seriously, always provide a source of innocent merriment to his readers. But the Chancellor of the Exchequer, not being specially gifted with a sense of humour, sought not amusement but guidance in this rather whimsical edition of Walter Bagehot, and thus he was led astray at a critical moment. Mr. Keynes was for the first time lifted by the Chancellor of the Exchequer into the rocking-chair of a pundit, and it was thought that his very signature appended to a financial document would carry weight. It seems rather absurd when now not even his friends—least of all his friends—have any longer the slightest faith in his judgments on finance.

Luckily Mr. Bonar Law and I knew well what value to attach to any counsel which came from the source of the Chancellor's inspiration and, therefore, we both treated the fantastic prediction of British bankruptcy " in the spring " with the measure of respect which was due to the volatile soothsayer who was responsible for this presage of misfortune. I was still less impressed by these prophecies of evil because I knew it was part of the campaign which the Treasury were waging against my great gun programme. They had succeeded in scaring Lord Kitchener. I knew more about the resources of credit of this country. Mr. Bonar Law urged that American (North and South) securities held in this country should be mobilised and sold or pledged to pay for purchases overseas. This practical suggestion was subsequently adopted and all went well.

When the hour of indicated doom struck and we still bought greater quantities than ever of food, raw material and munitions from abroad and were paying for them and our credit was still high, the date of impending collapse was postponed until the autumn. The fall of the year and the fall of the British Empire would arrive on the scene arm in arm. In his forecasts Mr. Keynes made the same mistake which had brought the late Mr. Baxter's prophecies into disrepute. He had been too definite in the dates for the end of the world. Some of these had already passed. When the fateful days arrived without any indication of the heavens above us being rolled together as a scroll, a fresh date further on was chosen. You may do that kind of thing once and perhaps twice, but repeated failures discredit the prophet. The Cabinet as a whole were not, therefore, at this time unduly depressed by Mr. M'Kenna's pictures of approaching famine, because they had ceased to believe in the impish Baxter who at the Chancellor's invitation had wandered into the Treasury.

After Colonel House had put his views before Sir Edward Grey and the Prime Minister, the latter decided that it would be desirable that other Ministers should be brought into consultation. It was therefore arranged that on 14th February, 1916, Mr. Asquith, Sir Edward Grey, Mr. Balfour and myself should be invited to meet Colonel House at dinner at Lord Reading's house. He there placed before us his ideas as to the summoning by President Wilson of a conference of all the belligerents to discuss peace terms. Colonel House has given some account of this important talk in his "Intimate Papers," but that account is by no means complete, and unless the whole purport of the conversations is given the public cannot judge the reasons for the failure of this peace move. He states in his book that at the Reading dinner the terms of an acceptable peace were outlined by me, who, "somewhat to his surprise and apparently also of Sir Edward Grey" was ready to agree to intervention by the President. As the sequel was determined by these terms, I propose to set out exactly what my proposal was. I was opposed to the summoning of a conference without some preliminary understanding with the President as to the minimum terms which the Allies were to insist upon with his sanction and support. A conference without such an agreement would have been productive of the most serious consequences to the *morale* of the Allied Countries, in the event of its failure. Having regard to the unpropitious military situation such a fiasco was quite within the realms of probability. In my opinion, therefore, it was undesirable to take such a risk unless we were practically assured beforehand that if Germany proved intractable on these terms the U.S.A. would throw in her lot with us.

These terms were acceptable to the Prime Minister, Sir Edward Grey, Mr. Balfour, Lord Reading, and also to Colonel House. The latter, who knew President Wilson's mind better than any living man, was convinced that the terms would also meet the President's view of the justice of the case. It is interesting to recall these terms in order to show the conditions of peace which would have satisfied the British leaders of that date. They included the restoration of the independence of Belgium and Serbia, and the surrender of Alsace and Lorraine to France, provided that the loss of territory thus incurred by Germany would be compensated by concessions to her in other places outside Europe. There were to be adjustments of the frontiers between Italy and Austria so as to liberate Italian communities still under the Austrian yoke. Russia was to be given an outlet to the sea. There were also to be guarantees against any future recurrence of such a catastrophe as this World War.

Colonel House promised to cable to President Wilson a full report of the proceedings and to obtain his assent to the conclusions arrived at before the British Government notified their acceptance of President Wilson's proposal. Sir Edward Grey insisted that before any final decision was taken the Allies should be consulted.

Why was this conference never summoned? Who was responsible? Had it come off either Germany would have accepted the terms as soon as she realised that President Wilson was committed to their enforcement, or, in the event of their rejection, America would have come into the War in the spring of 1916, instead of 12 months later. The world would have been saved a whole year of ruin, havoc and devastation. What a difference it would have made! Was the fiasco due to Sir Edward Grey's reluctance to press the idea upon our French Allies, or was it attributable to the insertion by President Wilson of one fatal word in the gentleman's agreement suggested by Colonel House? The document as cabled by Colonel House definitely committed the President to war (subject of course to the assent of Congress) in the event of rejection by Germany of a conference into which he was prepared to enter with a pledge to the Allies of support for minimum terms. The President in his reply inserted the word " Probably " in front of the undertaking. Sir Edward Grey's view was that this completely changed the character of the proposal, and, therefore, he did not think it worth while to communicate the purport of the negotiations to the Allies. As far as I can recollect he made no effort with President Wilson through Colonel House or any other intermediary to restore the position as it was left by the Reading dinner conversations. The real explanation probably is that President Wilson was afraid of public opinion in the U.S.A. and Sir Edward Grey was frightened of our Allies. The world was once more sacrificed to the timidity of statesmanship. This great and at one time promising plan thus fell through. The bloody campaigns of 1916 were fought without any decision. Hundreds of thousands of brave young men fell on the scarred heights of Verdun, on the muddy plateau above the Somme, in the foothills of the Istrian and Tyrolese Alps, in the forests and swamps of Russia, on the slopes of the Carpathians, and in the torrid regions of Mesopotamia and Central Africa. Every military staff in all the armies at every stage of the sanguinary road was convinced that victory was awaiting their strategy just round the next corner. Politicians must not be allowed to snatch triumph out of their grasp just as it was all but within reach. Peace discussions were therefore postponed until the deafening sound of the great guns abated.

Looking back on this period in the light of the information which came later to hand, it is clear that if Colonel House's plan had been acted upon, the most that could have been hoped from such a conference as President Wilson could then have assembled would have been the earlier entry of the United States into the struggle, and the shortening of the War which that event would have brought about. Nothing is more certain than that Germany in 1916 would have insisted on terms which would have been entirely incompatible with those that the President's Vicar-General in the outside world, Colonel House, had agreed upon with us. A secret dispatch from Washington in the spring of 1917 advised us that when Bernstorff handed to the State Department of the U.S.A. the note informing them of Germany's intention to embark upon unrestricted submarine warfare, he made simultaneously a confidential communication to Colonel House, putting in writing Germany's peace terms. These were: —

1. The practical occupation of Belgium;
2. The straightening out of their French frontier in order to include the French iron fields;
3. Indemnity from France;
4. Full compensation for all commercial losses.

It will be seen that these terms were not only entirely at variance with those which had been suggested by America, but were obviously utterly inacceptable to the Allies. They were in fact terms which assumed Germany to be victorious, and no peace could possibly have been based on them.

Whether the declaration of these terms by Germany at a conference would have brought President Wilson into the War on the Allied side in 1916 is perhaps slightly less certain. The President was at that time resolutely pacifist, and it is possible that Colonel House credited him with a greater readiness to participate in the struggle than he would actually have shown when it came to the test. While he could not have accepted the German terms, he might at that stage have contented himself with trying to balance them against the proposals of the Allies, and urge the *via media* of an inacceptable and inconclusive peace. Count Bernstorff noted in the course of a report on 6th September, 1916, that: " Wilson regards it as in the interest of America that neither of the combatants should gain a decisive victory." President Wilson fought his election in the late autumn on his policy of keeping America out of the War. On this he won.

In this connection I am tempted to quote an interesting letter which Theodore Roosevelt wrote after the American Presidential Election in November, 1916, to Lord Lee of Fareham. At that time Roosevelt was an energetic supporter of the Allied cause, and Lee had suggested that he should visit England and lecture on the issues

of the War. Writing to decline the invitation, he hints—what was
in fact the case—that his uncompromising support of the Allied
cause had lost him the sympathy of both the political parties in the
States to such an extent that no one, least of all Wilson, would dare
to associate himself with a policy publicly advocated by him. His
letter was in the following terms: —

" Sagamore Hill,
November 10th, 1916.

Dear Arthur,
    I have carefully considered your letter (no letter from Grey has
come). My dear fellow, I hate not to do anything you ask. But
my judgment is most strongly and unqualifiedly that it would be
a grave error for me to do so in this case. I have consulted
Whitridge and Bacon, both of whom are at this moment more
interested in the success of the Allies than in any internal
American questions, and they agree with me—Whitridge feeling
at least as strongly as I do in the matter. Wilson has probably
been elected, and if Hughes were elected it would only slightly
alter the case so far as this particular proposal is concerned. For
a number of months to come the American public would positively
resent any conduct on my part which would be construed as
indicating my presuming to give advice about, or an expression of,
American opinion. Wilson would certainly endeavour to do
exactly the opposite to what he thought I had indicated; even
Hughes, if elected, would resent any seeming desire of the British
and French to consult me; and my coming over would give every
greedy sensation-monger in the Yellow Press, and even in the Pale
Saffron Press, the cue to advertise the fact, with statements and
inferences grotesquely false but very mischievous. Moreover, those
whom I spoke to on your side of the War could not but feel that
my words carry weight, and to this extent I cannot be guilty of
deception towards them, for my words carry no weight, and it
would be unwise to pay any heed to what I said as representing the
American people. At the moment I am as completely out of
sympathy with the American people as I would have been out of
sympathy with the English people in 1910 or the French people in
1904. The Wilson " policies " are those of the Democrats, who
have just polled a bare plurality of the popular vote. Mr. Wilson
would like to antagonise every proposition I make. The Repub-
licans by an overwhelming majority nominated Hughes precisely
because he did *not* represent my views; they thought it wise to
dodge the issues I thought it vital to raise. No other man of
national importance (for Root really exerted not the slightest
weight in the campaign and only spoke once to a half-empty hall)
took the stand I took—which I took in every speech. I was the

only man who raised my voice about Wilson's iniquity in suffering the German submarines to do as they did on our coast.

If I went abroad I could give you no advice of even the slightest worth. I would diminish my already almost imperceptible influence here at home. I would expose myself to bitter malefications—no matter how much one condemns one's own country, one cannot stand condemnation of it by promiscuous outsiders (*you* may say *anything* and I will say ditto to it). I would like to visit the front at the head of an American division of 12 regiments like my Rough Riders—but not otherwise.

Always yours,

THEODORE ROOSEVELT.

P.S.—The amiable Bryce steadily exerts what influence he has here on behalf of the Pacifist crowd, who are really the tepid enemies of the Allies."

This rather bitter and disillusioned letter shows the doubts and uncertainties with which the strongest American leader of his time viewed the prospect of his country taking a really bold and decided course in its dealings with the combatant nations of Europe. Later on, history was to afford another proof that the bold course is the best one.

CHAPTER XXII

THE IRISH REBELLION

THE long-drawn-out and wearisome tragedy of the relations between Great Britain and Ireland played an important part in the World War. There can be little doubt that the expectation on the Continent that Britain had for the moment sunk so deep in the quagmires of the Irish bog as to be unable to extricate her feet in time to march eastward, was one of the considerations which encouraged Germany to guarantee Austria unconditional support in her Serbian adventure. The continued unrest in Ireland, and the political differences between statesmen here as to the proper method of dealing with them, imported an undercurrent of divided counsel and party feeling into our deliberations about our principal task. And ultimately, the rebellion of Easter, 1916, quickly though it was suppressed, interposed a deplorable distraction and left an aftermath of bitterness and danger which hampered us throughout the remainder of the War and for years afterwards.

Nor can it be forgotten that the Irish situation formed an abiding ground of antagonism to Great Britain amongst the large and politically powerful Irish-American section in the United States. Had there been no Irish grievance, it is by no means improbable that America would have come much earlier into the War, and by so much shortened its duration.

I do not propose to enter on a discussion of the Irish question. But in considering the events of 1916, and the part I was called on to play in bringing about some alleviation of the trouble, it is important to bear in mind the background against which those events were set.

In the early summer of 1914, in view of the fact that the Liberal Government had succeeded after a three years' fight in carrying through a measure of Home Rule, the Protestant North had reached a state of incipient rebellion, and was arming and drilling for resistance to the decision of the Imperial Parliament. The Catholic South had begun to copy these tactics, and raise National Volunteers to match the Ulster Volunteers of the North. There was a gun-running at Larne to supply Ulster with guns from Germany; and then one at Howth to supply Southern Ireland. The paradox of the situation was that Ulster's rebellion was acclaimed by a powerful

416

section of British opinion as loyalty, while Southern Ireland's preparations to defend the decision of the Imperial Parliament were
denounced as sedition.

At the outbreak of the Great War, the Home Rule Act was suspended in order to allay the threatened rebellion of Ulster, backed
by the Unionist party in Great Britain, and to procure a measure of
unity, in face of the common danger. For the moment this action
achieved its purpose, but it may be doubted whether in the long
run it proved profitable. For Southern Ireland, seeing its hopes
dashed at the moment when they were about to be realised, at first
sulked in resentment and soon became a mass of seething disaffection;
and, after an interlude of strife and suffering of a deplorable
character, it had to be pacified by concessions far more extensive
than would have satisfied it in 1914.

The irritation of Southern Ireland was exacerbated by a number
of needless follies. When the World War broke out, its spokesman,
Mr. Redmond. pledged its full support to Britain in the conflict, and
heartily encouraged the efforts to recruit its young men for the army.
But with extraordinary tactlessness, old officers were let loose on
Munster, Connaught and Leinster to lure men to the colours to the
strains of " God Save the King." Both the tune and the tone were
anathema in those parts, and roused every instinct of sedition. I
relate further on, in my sketch of Lord Kitchener, how he approved
the embroidery of the Red Hand of Ulster on the banner of the
northern division, but banned the South Irish Harp on the southern.
The slap in the face which this curious procedure administered to
Southern Ireland stamped out every spark of kindling enthusiasm
there, and caused a serious set-back to recruiting.

Throughout 1915 and early 1916, seditious movements grew in
strength. The Irish Volunteers. a body openly formed to enforce
the Sinn Fein policy of complete independence for Ireland, drilled
publicly and rapidly recruited their numbers. Funds came to them
from America. with leaflets designed to increase disaffection. In
Dublin especially the note of rebellion was everywhere to be heard.
Full information of these developments was supplied to the Irish
Secretary, Mr. Augustine Birrell, but he, wisely or unwisely, refused
to sanction any drastic action to suppress the movement. He was
content to hope and pray that matters would not come to a head till
the War was over—after which the coming into force of the postponed
Home Rule Act would solve the difficulty.

Admittedly the problem was an awkward one for statesmanship.
How could action be taken against the Irish Volunteers unless corresponding action were also taken against the Ulster Volunteers, who
were also armed to resist the Government and to oppose an Act now
on the Statute Book? How could we defend the rights of Belgium
and in the same breath coerce Ireland for arming to secure for herself

a measure of independence which the majority of the House of
Commons had admitted to be just? How could we resort to coercion
in Ireland—unless events made it inevitable—and maintain with
America the friendly relations which were essential to our success
in the War? There seemed plenty of excellent reasons for doing
nothing. There always are. So nothing was done.

In April, 1916, the inevitable happened. Encouraged by Germany
and the Irish-Americans, the Sinn Fein leaders in Dublin decided
to bring matters to a head by an open rebellion. A ship was to come
over from Germany to Ireland, bringing the Irish revolutionary
leader, Sir Roger Casement, and an outbreak was timed to take
effect on Easter Day, 23rd April, two days following his arrival.

Sir Roger Casement failed to turn up in Ireland on the 21st, and
on the following day the news appeared that he and the ship which
bore him had been captured by the British. Notices were sent out
by the Irish Volunteer headquarters to postpone the Sunday arrangements. But on Easter Monday, 24th April, a rising occurred in
Dublin and some parts of the country.

The provincial disturbances were small and easily suppressed.
The Dublin outbreak was far more serious, and for a time the Irish
capital was held by the forces of revolt. Troops were hastily
summoned, martial law proclaimed, and in a couple of days the rising
had been quelled, not without bloodshed. Several of the rebellious
leaders were tried by court martial and shot.

Obviously matters could not be allowed to rest there, and after
going into the matter carefully, Mr. Asquith went over to Dublin
to examine the situation on the spot. Martial law was still in force,
and the three principal officers of the Crown—the Lord Lieutenant,
Lord Wimborne, the Chief Secretary for Ireland, Mr. Birrell, and his
Under-Secretary, Sir Matthew Nathan—had all resigned their posts.

On his return, Mr. Asquith approached me with the suggestion
that I should take up the task of trying to negotiate a settlement with
the Irish revolutionary leaders. My sympathy with their cause
was known. On the other hand, I had been recently very much
detached from the Irish developments, as I had been fully immersed
in my task of equipping our armies with munitions, specially in view
of the coming campaign on the Somme.

The request came at an awkward moment. For some time I had
been urging on our leaders a measure of closer co-ordination with our
Russian Ally, and had at last got them to agree to a practical step in
this direction. Lord Kitchener was to proceed to Russia via
Archangel to consult with the military authorities there about closer
co-operation in the field, and it had been arranged that I should go
with him to find out for myself the truth about the appalling shortage
of equipment of which we had heard, and see in what way the
Ministry of Munitions could best help to remedy it. These were

10 Downing Street.
Whitehall S.W.

Secret   22 May 16

My dear Lloyd George,

I hope you may
see your way to take
up Ireland: at any
rate for a short time.
It is a unique opportu-
nity, and there is
no one else who could
do so much to
bring about a permanent
solution

Yrs very sincerely.

H. H. Asquith

Facsimile of the letter written by Mr. Asquith which induced Mr. Lloyd
George to abandon his proposed visit to Russia with Lord Kitchener.

matters in which I was for the moment far more closely interested than I was in the pitiable and rather squalid tragedy which had overtaken our lack of policy in Ireland.

But my plans were upset by Mr. Asquith's proposal. It was conveyed to me in a letter which I reproduce in facsimile, the terms of which were as follows: —

> " 10, Downing Street,
> Whitehall, S.W.
>
> SECRET.   22nd May, 1916.
>
> My dear Lloyd George,
>
> I hope you may see your way to take up Ireland; at any rate for a short time. It is a *unique* opportunity and there is no one else who could do so much to bring about a permanent solution.
>
> Yours very sincerely,
> H. H. ASQUITH."

For me at least this letter has a peculiar interest, for it saved my life! Much against my own inclination, I decided that I could not refuse Mr. Asquith's request, so I had to tell Lord Kitchener that I could not accompany him on his voyage, and I asked him to do his best to find out for me the munition position there and the way in which he thought the British Munitions Ministry could render any help in the equipment of the Russian Armies. Even while Mr. Asquith was penning his letter, an obscure German vessel was steaming across the North Sea towards the cold northern waters around the Orkneys, bearing a mine which it was presently to loose at a venture off the Scottish coast in the hope of sinking some vessel from the Grand Fleet cruising around these wind-swept Scottish islands. A fortnight later that mine struck the *Hampshire* with the renowned and almost legendary figure of our British Minister of War aboard. But for this letter, I should have been with him and shared his fate. This escape, at least, I owe to Ireland.

On 25th May, Mr. Asquith announced in the House of Commons that I had undertaken to devote my time and energies to seeking a solution of the Irish situation, and he explained that my decision was the outcome of the unanimous request of all my colleagues in the Government. I had already begun to consult with the political leaders of both the Irish Nationalist and the Ulster Unionist parties. The negotiations were conducted at the Ministry of Munitions. The Nationalists were represented by Mr. John Redmond, Mr. John Dillon, Mr. T. P. O'Connor and Mr. Devlin. Ulster was represented by Sir Edward Carson and Mr. James Craig.

Redmond was not only a great orator but possessed elements of statesmanship of a high order. The fact that he was given no chance to apply his qualities in the rebuilding of his native land is one of the myriad tragedies of Irish history. Devlin had all the charm, wit and eloquence of Irishmen at their best. To these graces and powers he added fundamental shrewdness and sagacity. Of Carson—one of the most remarkable products of Irish soil—I speak later on. Craig (afterwards Lord Craigavon, the Irish Premier) possessed all the gifts of an American political boss of the nineteenth century. T. P. O'Connor had a much wider experience of the world than his colleagues and that made him more tolerant and accommodating as a negotiator. Redmond, O'Connor, Devlin, Carson and Craig displayed a genuine anxiety to reach a settlement. Dillon was difficult. He had the temperament and mental equipment of the fanatic. He always found it hard to accommodate his ideas to the tyranny of facts. In private he was genial, pleasant and gentle of speech. In public he was a scold. In negotiation he was inclined to be truculent and unyielding. His stubbornness over comparatively trivial details helped to wreck the Buckingham Palace negotiations just before the War. When he ultimately gave assent to the terms reached in these negotiations he did so with a mental reservation, and his rigid and niggling interpretation of the arrangement arrived at proved to be fatal later on, for it made it impossible for Redmond and Devlin to meet Unionist misgiving by even the slightest appearance of concession.

After a discussion I laid before them a series of proposals. These proposals were: —

1. To bring the Home Rule Act into immediate operation;

2. To introduce at once an Amending Bill, as a strictly War Emergency Act to cover only the period of the War and a short specified interval after it;

3. During that period the Irish members to remain at Westminster in their full numbers;

4. During this war emergency six Ulster counties to be left as at present under the Imperial Government;

5. Immediately after the War an Imperial Conference of representatives from all the Dominions of the Empire to be held to consider the future government of the Empire, including the question of the Government of Ireland;

6. Immediately after this Conference, and during the interval provided for by the War Emergency Act, the permanent settlement of all the great outstanding problems, such as the permanent position of the exempted counties, the question of finance, and other problems, which cannot be dealt with during the War, would be proceeded with.

The above is an abbreviated summary of my proposals, which in their full form extended to fourteen clauses. Sir Edward Carson and Mr. Redmond promptly went over to Ireland to consult with their respective followers about the scheme. Despite the fact that it contained proposals most unpalatable to each of the disputing factions in Ireland, both sides agreed to accept it, and to do their best to work it loyally.

I wish the story could end there. But it cannot. The plan which held out such promise for a settlement of the ancient grievance of Ireland, and which was accepted by both parties in Ireland itself, was thereafter deliberately smashed by extremists on both sides. My first warning of this opposition came in the shape of a memorandum sent to me on 11th June, 1916, by a prominent Unionist member of the Cabinet—the day before my scheme was accepted without opposition by the Ulster Unionist Council, and a week before it was also unanimously approved by a gathering of Nationalists at Belfast. The memorandum was as follows: —

" Information reaches me from both England and Ireland, North and South, that there is no disposition to come to a settlement, that the line taken by the leading Unionists, as the result of their interviews in London, is that the Unionist Party in Ireland are being driven by the Prime Minister and Minister of Munitions into accepting a situation which they know to be morally wrong and wrong politically, that the Nationalist Party are sullen and hostile and have no intention of abandoning their policy and programme whatever may be the decision of their leaders.

At the same time I hear the gravest accounts of the condition of Ireland. If one half of what I have heard is true it seems to me to be quite clear that this is not the moment to embark upon any political experiment. The situation is very different from what I believed it to be when we first discussed this question, far graver and more serious, and unless I am wholly misinformed I don't think it would be possible for me to give my assent to any agreement including the adoption of Home Rule, the more so as I have excellent authority for the opinion I hold very strongly that, whatever may be said or written, the U.S.A. will not interfere with the supply of munitions or other supplies."

This unexpected communication by one of my own Cabinet colleagues, who had been a party to the decision authorising me to carry out the negotiations, and who had talked over with me my scheme before I finally submitted it to the leaders of Irish opinion, was characteristic of the type of bitter partisan hostility which the prospect of a settlement of the Irish trouble called forth from extremists who would rather see no settlement at all than one which did not fully conform with their ideas. On 23rd June—the very day on which final approval of the proposals was recorded by a representative Conference of the Ulster Nationalists—a manifesto denouncing it was issued by five Unionist Peers—Lords Balfour of

Burleigh, Cromer, Halsbury, Midleton and Salisbury. Two days later Lord Selborne, the President of the Board of Agriculture, resigned from the Cabinet as a protest against the scheme.

Lord Lansdowne, the veteran Tory leader, fired the next shot. On 28th June I received the following note from Mr. Asquith: —

> " 10, Downing Street,
> Whitehall, S.W.
> 28th June, 1916.
>
> My dear Lloyd George,
> Please look at enclosed which has just come from Lansdowne.
> Yours,
> H. H. A."

The enclosure was the following letter: —

> " Lansdowne House,
> Berkeley Square, W.
> 28th June, 1916.
>
> My dear Asquith,
> You will, I am sure, have noted that my consent to the postponement of further discussion as to the Irish settlement was given with considerable reluctance and not without misgivings. I agreed, not because I was convinced that further inquiry was likely to produce satisfactory results, but because it seemed to me that, having regard to the extreme gravity of the situation, no suggestion which gave us breathing time ought to be put aside.
> The discussion towards the close was hurried, and I am not sure that we were *ad diem* as to the scope of the enquiry. I may, therefore, perhaps be allowed to make my own views clear.
> What we want to know is, not merely whether under a Nationalist Government, Sir John Maxwell, with his 40,000 men, will be able to put down another Sinn Fein rebellion, or whether our military and naval resources would be sufficient to prevent a German-Irish landing. The question seems rather to be whether, with a Nationalist executive, it would be possible to deal effectively and promptly with domestic disorder, e.g., with sporadic but organised disturbances, occurring simultaneously all over the country. Could we deal with them as effectively and as promptly as we could if they were to occur now?
> Another point which it seems to me requires to be cleared up is this. Do Messrs. Redmond and Devlin understand that, if a Nationalist Government is set up, we shall still make use of the Defence of the Realm Acts, and that their suggestion that under the new dispensation the ordinary law will suffice cannot be entertained?
> And do they understand that Mr. Devlin's promise of an

immediate amnesty for the persons who are now imprisoned owing to the part which they took in the recent rebellion is not one which can be entertained?

I understand that you advised the S.W. Unionists yesterday to formulate their demands as to the safeguards which they considered indispensable.

Would it be possible to press them to put in a statement of their requirements, and, if we find that they are reasonable, could the Nationalist leaders be required to accept them as one of the conditions of settlement?

Believe me, yours sincerely,

LANSDOWNE."

On 10th July Mr. Asquith made a statement in the House of Commons in which he set out the main features of the agreement which had been reached. The following night Lord Lansdowne spoke in the House of Lords about the proposals, in terms which Mr. Redmond characterised as "a gross insult to Ireland . . . a declaration of war on the Irish people, and the announcement of a policy of coercion."

On 17th July a meeting was held at the Carlton Club of Conservative members of both houses of the Imperial Parliament, at which an "Imperial Unionist Association" was formed to "watch negotiations as to the Irish question between the Government and the Nationalist Party." This Association proceeded to adopt a resolution calling for stern measures of repression in Ireland, and opposing any idea of immediate Home Rule. In conformity with the wishes of their followers, the Unionist members of the Coalition Cabinet insisted on serious modifications in the terms which had been agreed between me and the Irish leaders, when a Bill was being drafted to carry them into law.

This situation was exposed by Mr. Redmond on 24th July, when he raised the question on a motion for adjournment of the House of Commons. Sir Edward Carson, placated by the proposed exclusion of the six counties from the scheme, urged strongly that a settlement should be made with the South. But the other Conservative members of the Cabinet were obdurate, and mangled the terms which I had originally put forward until Mr. Redmond was no longer willing to accept them.

The matter was concluded by Mr. Asquith's announcement in the House of Commons on 31st July that Mr. H. E. Duke, the member of Parliament for Exeter, was to be appointed Chief Secretary for Ireland. With this step we reverted to the old and unsatisfactory system of control, of which the Royal Commission on the Rebellion of Ireland had already stated in its report, issued on 26th June and published on 3rd July, 1916, that: —

" If the Irish system of government be regarded as a whole, it is anomalous in quiet times, and almost unworkable in times of crisis."

The revival of that " anomalous " and " almost unworkable " system led to the persistent growth of further disaffection, culminating in the chaos of the immediate post-war years, and the ultimate settlement of the problem on lines which involved far bigger concessions to Southern Ireland than would have been made in the scheme I had proposed. The last word has not yet been spoken in this unhappy feud that Britain has inherited from a foreign foe, who, having conquered England first, then proceeded to annex Ireland.

CHAPTER XXIII

THE COMING OF CONSCRIPTION

APART from the proposals I had placed before the Liberal and Conservative leaders in 1910 for a National Militia, no statesman had ever contemplated that the military contribution of this country to a European war should exceed the limits of our normal regular army. Our ideas were embodied in the Expeditionary Force created by Mr. Haldane. After the declaration of war an appeal was made for 100,000 men. Their main use was intended to be as units for filling gaps in the ranks. It was only when the numbers who volunteered reached a figure which was beyond the highest hopes of enthusiasts that the Cabinet and Parliament widened their view of the part we were destined to play on the battlefields of Armageddon.

We had always visualised Britain playing her traditional rôle in Continental wars. Our Navy would keep the seas for the Allies. Our wealth would help them to finance their foreign purchases. Our Army would play a subordinate part in the struggle.

But why was not Conscription adopted from the moment the Cabinet decided to raise an army on the Continental scale? Obviously it would have provided the most effective method for organising the man-power of this country.

To the British people the idea was unfamiliar, and we move slowly in these islands. Bred on a soil for centuries inviolate, we were accustomed to send abroad only small, professional armies, the ranks of which, in so far as they were British, could be filled by the recruiting sergeant on a voluntary basis, with the allurement of uniform and the King's shilling. Our national defence had been the fleet, which requires far fewer men than does an army, and for whose needs in the darkest moments of the Napoleonic struggle, the Press-gang—long since passed into the limbo of forgotten evils—had troubled only the sea-port towns and their vicinity.

Not only were we unused to the idea of universal and compulsory national service for war; we also had a strong traditional objection to the creation of large armed forces, as potential instruments of tyranny and an infringement of personal liberty; and, moreover, among wide sections of the nation there was a tendency to look down on the common soldier's vocation.

Besides, in the early days, few conceived that the War would be a long-drawn-out affair. It was surmised that no nation could sustain war on the modern scale for more than a short time. Pacifist and militarist writers agreed about that. " Over by Christmas " was the popular slogan, which was used to excuse the corresponding cry, " Business as usual."

For these reasons it was thought by all those who had the supreme responsibility of interpreting public opinion that it would have been impossible at the outset of the War to carry through a scheme for the mobilisation of the whole country, such as was adopted in France. And to add to these negative arguments against such a procedure, there was the positive fact that recruits during the first months were pouring in, on a voluntary basis, far more rapidly than the military authorities could handle them. In the first three months of the War, 900,000 new recruits were enlisted, at an average of 300,000 a month, in addition to the reservists recalled to the Colours and the Territorials already enlisted. The army authorities had neither barracks in which to house these men, uniforms in which to clothe them, nor weapons with which to drill and train them. Far from needing to adopt special measures to secure men for the forces, we were driven to raise and stiffen the physical standard for recruits, in order to check this unmanageable spate.

As time passed, however, a series of developments occurred to modify the situation.

The military authorities, for their part, improvised by the time the first rush of recruits was over, a technique for handling supplies of men on this unprecedented scale. The stream itself dwindled by the end of the year to an average of 30,000 a week.

Already before the close of 1914, it was becoming clear that the unregulated process of voluntary recruiting had swept into the Army large numbers of men who were vitally necessary in the workshops, for the production of munitions of war and in other civilian avocations essential even in war. Many of them, from their skill, intelligence, and experience, were pivotal men and irreplaceable. Efforts were made to get some of them back, but the salvage operations were not very successful. The obvious lesson was that if the War were not to be bungled and lost, our resources of man-power must be more intelligently applied.

The War had not ended by Christmas. On the contrary, it was settling down into a long-drawn-out struggle, which would demand from us not only a far bigger military force on the Continent and elsewhere than had at first been expected, but would require a continuous stream of fresh men to replace casualties and keep the armies up to strength.

As the magnitude of the struggle, and its life-and-death importance for us, was borne in upon the nation, the popular antipathy to military service died away, and was replaced by a healthy impatience at the spectacle of sturdy young men " skrimshanking " at home while fathers of families were in the trenches.

These developments weakened the case for persistence in the voluntary system, and helped to prepare men's minds for its abandonment when eventually it proved incapable of furnishing the Army with an adequate supply of fresh recruits.

Not the least of the difficulties which had to be overcome before conscription was eventually adopted, was the hostility engendered by its advocates.   These were associated before the War in the popular mind with extreme Jingoism, and in consequence opposition to any suggestion of national military service had become an article of faith with some Liberals and Socialists.   An agitation for conscription was begun early in the struggle from the same quarters, which kept alive the feud and gave it the semblance of a party issue.   It would have been far easier for the Government to introduce national service at an early date, if the matter had not taken on such a violently controversial colour, so that its adoption looked like a Chauvinist triumph.

My own attitude to this question has never been based on considerations of political orthodoxy.   Long before the War I had formed the opinion that there was much to be said in favour of some system of national training, and of universal liability to military service for national defence.   I have told how I advanced this suggestion when talking with the German Ambassador years before the War, and how the matter was also discussed as a practical proposition with the leaders of the Conservative Party by the Liberal Government in 1910.

Looking backward, there is no doubt at all that we should have been able to organise the nation for war far more effectively in 1914, and bring the conflict to a successful issue far more quickly and economically, if at the very outset we had mobilised the whole nation —its man-power, money, materials and brains—on a war footing and bent all our resources to the task of victory on rational and systematic lines.   Towards the end, something approaching this condition was in fact reached, but there had intervened a long and deplorably extravagant prelude of waste and hesitation.   But a majority of the Cabinet opposed conscription not only as inexpedient, but because at that time they were strongly antagonistic to it on principle, and there was no pressure from the Conservative opposition to apply conscription.

A decision having been reached, with something like national unity, to rely as long as possible upon the voluntary principle, every effort was made to stimulate its successful working.   At first, recruiting meetings, posters, literature, and other forms of popular appeal were employed.   The recruiting crusade was well organised.   The services of expert propagandists, political agents, advertising agents, and public speakers, lay and clerical, were requisitioned, and their combined work in agitation and enlistment was a triumphant success. By degrees, other more systematic approaches to the manhood of the nation were improvised, and only after these repeated promptings and combings proved unavailing to maintain our supply of recruits did we turn of necessity to compulsory service.

The first of these systematic steps was the " Householders' Return," organised early in November, 1914, by the Parliamentary Recruiting Committee. This was a return of men eligible and willing to serve, and was secured by means of forms sent to every householder in the Kingdom, with a covering letter signed by Messrs. Asquith, Bonar Law, and Arthur Henderson, the leaders of the three political parties, appealing to every eligible man to hold himself ready to enlist in the forces of the Crown.

This scheme, reinforced by the appeals of poster and public meeting, helped to maintain the steady flow of recruits well into 1915. At the beginning of the year, on 8th January, 1915, when conscription was being debated in the House of Lords, the official attitude of the Government at that time was stated by Lord Crewe in the following phrase: "We do not regard the possibility of compulsion as being within the landscape, as we now see it." More than three months later, on 20th April, I myself stated in reply to a question in the House of Commons that: "The Government are not of opinion that there is any ground for thinking that the War would be more successfully prosecuted by means of conscription." Both of these statements as to the Government's attitude were determined by the fact that as yet the voluntary system was continuing to yield as adequate a flow of recruits as could be absorbed by our training and equipping facilities at that date.

That the attitude of some of us on this issue was purely realist, and not doctrinaire, is illustrated by a weighty pronouncement which Lord Haldane made in the course of the debate on 8th January, 1915. to which I have already referred. After declaring that hitherto the voluntary system was proving adequate, and showed no signs of breaking down, he added: —

". . . By the Common Law of this country it is the duty of every subject of the Realm to assist the Sovereign in repelling the invasion of its shores and in defence of the Realm. That is a duty which rests on no Statute, but is inherent in the Constitution of the country. It has been laid down . . . that any subject at a time of emergency may be asked to give himself and his property for the defence of the nation. Therefore compulsory service is not foreign to the Constitution of this country. Given a great national emergency I think it is your duty to resort to it. I can conceive a state of things in which we might resort to it. . . . At a time of national necessity every other consideration must yield to national interest, and we should bar nothing in the way of principle if it should become necessary."

This statement was of importance, not only for its value as a summary of the Common Law position with regard to compulsory national service, but as showing that Lord Haldane himself and others like-minded in the Cabinet were approaching the issue purely on the basis of practical expediency, and held no theoretic objection or prejudice against its adoption. I may also refer here to the statement made by me at Manchester on 3rd June, which I have already quoted in my account of the Ministry of Munitions, where I emphasised that there was nothing anti-democratic in conscription; on the contrary, every great democracy had resorted to it in times of national danger as a fit and proper democratic weapon for self-defence; and if necessity arose we ought without hesitation to apply the same weapon ourselves in this present conflict.

As a matter of fact, I had become painfully aware, long before I actually became principally responsible for creating a Ministry of Munitions, that the haphazard results of the voluntary system in a national emergency of this magnitude were leading to deplorable waste and mismanagement of our available man-power. I was eager to press forward some scheme for a more systematic co-ordination of these resources, and one of the first acts of the new Cabinet formed by Mr. Asquith at the end of May, 1915, when he established the first Coalition Government, was to instruct Mr. Walter Long to draft a Bill for the setting up of a National Register. The aim of this Register was twofold. By providing a complete record of the number and distribution of men at different age levels throughout the country it would enable us to calculate our available resources of men for military service, and also inform us what supplies of men were available for production of munitions.

Some time was lost in discussion of the points raised, but ultimately on 5th July the National Registration Bill was laid before Parliament and carried by a large majority. Opposition to it, based mainly on the presumption that it was a preliminary to conscription, came from a small group of Liberal and Labour Members, and, of course, from Messrs. MacDonald and Snowden, who throughout the War persistently opposed every effort to secure recruits for the national defence. Indeed, three months earlier, the Independent Labour Party, of which Mr. Ramsay MacDonald was the leading light, had carried in their Norwich Conference a resolution censuring the official Labour Party for its work on behalf of recruiting.

The returns obtained by the National Register showed that there were about five million men of military age in Great Britain who were not already serving with the Forces. Of these, there were, of course, a considerable number physically unfit for military service, and, further, a number in " barred" occupations who were held non-recruitable because indispensable to the maintenance of national industry and in particular of munitions. It was estimated that Great Britain contained a residue of 1,700,000 to 1,800,000 fit men available as recruits not yet serving with the Forces. This figure was proved later on to be an under-estimate of our reserves of man-power.

While this register was being compiled, a Cabinet Committee on our national resources in men and money had carried out in August, 1915, an investigation into the situation, and in a Report dated 2nd September, 1915, it pointed out that voluntary recruiting was not enabling us to make a military effort comparable to the resources of the country. Lord Kitchener was aiming at an army of 70 divisions in all theatres by the latter part of 1916. The Committee held that " a 100-division army would bear a truer relation both to our dangers and to the exertions of our Allies." After making all allowance for our naval, financial, and industrial contributions, " it cannot be claimed that an army of 70 divisions represents our true proportionate contribution of men to the Allied line of battle."

Taking the 70-division scheme, however, as the standard to be reached, the Committee showed that present methods would be insufficient. In addition to the Regular reserves and Territorial forces mobilised at the beginning of the War, the fresh recruits accepted and passed into the Army in 13 months totalled 1,888,000. " The recruiting records for the last six months, show an average yield of 20,000 a week, resulting in an effective yield to our military forces of probably 19,000 men." Lord Kitchener was asking for at least 30,000 a week, a figure which a month later he raised to 35,000. " Even the yield of 20,000 a week can only be maintained by repeated canvassing of individuals and by every form of social, and in some cases of economic, pressure upon all classes of men (except munition workers) from 17 to 45, whether married or single, whether usefully employed or not, and whether or not they can be spared from their trade or district."

The Committee reported the evidence it had received in statements to it by the President of the Board of Trade, the Chancellor of the Exchequer, Lord Kitchener, and myself. From its record of my own evidence I cull the following extracts: —

> Asked by the Committee what form of compulsion the Minister of Munitions considered necessary, " Mr. Lloyd George said he would take the same powers exactly as were taken in France. He would make everybody between certain ages liable to serve in the Army at home or abroad, and only during the duration of the War. With this general and basic authority ' you could work the rest all right.' "

And in my concluding remarks I am reported as saying: —

" You will not get through without some measure of military compulsion or compulsion for military service. The longer you delay the nearer you will be to disaster. I am certain you cannot get through without it. I do not believe, for instance, that you can keep your armies at the front without it, unless you are going deliberately to cut their numbers down to a figure which will be inadequate, and which is known to be inadequate in advance. The number of men you should put at the front does not depend on us in the least. It is going to depend on the Germans and what the Germans are going to do during the next three months in Russia. If they succeed in putting the Russians out of action during 1916 as a great offensive force, for us simply to keep 70 divisions at the front is suicide.* Not only that, it is murder, because to send a number of men who are obviously inadequate is just murdering our own countrymen without attaining any purpose at all. . . ."

The President of the Board of Trade, Mr. Runciman, argued to the Committee that on the basis of the statistics he had at his disposal there would, after leaving a sufficient number of men in industry, be less than half the number available for the Army which Lord Kitchener considered indispensable to maintain his 70 divisions, and not more than half of these could be secured by voluntary recruiting. The Committee felt that this argument " would appear to lead directly, if unconsciously, to compulsory military service " (of which Mr. Runciman was a leading opponent). But they did not agree with his sweeping exclusion by whole classes of large numbers of potential recruits from his calculations.

The statement of the Chancellor of the Exchequer, Mr. M'Kenna, was to the effect that Britain could not afford to carry on her financial aid to her Allies and at the same time maintain an army of 70 divisions in the field. One or other of the two tasks we might compass, but not both. The Committee found his arguments ingenious but unconvincing, and reminded the Cabinet that " whereas a few months ago the possibility of raising a substantial loan in the United States was scouted altogether, and whereas a few weeks ago we were assured that £20,000,000 was the utmost limit, the Chancellor of the Exchequer now hopes to borrow £100,000,000 sterling from this quarter during the present year, and to repeat the operation in a subsequent year."

Lord Kitchener told the Committee that " it would be his duty to ask Parliament before the end of the year for a Bill giving him compulsory powers." He added, however, that he regretted the

* In 1918 we had 89 divisions including Dominion, etc., troops.

raising of the question of compulsory service at the present time, because he had intended to choose his own time for rushing it on the country as a non-party measure of military emergency, whereas it was now being revived as a party issue. Before deciding on his scheme for compulsion he wanted to see the results of the National Registration.

The Committee concluded in their report dated 2nd September, 1915, that " the men are available for the 70-divisions army, but the number cannot be obtained on a voluntary basis." They posed as questions for the Cabinet: —

> "First: Whether the 70-divisions scheme is to be cut down to the limits which can be supplied by voluntary enlistment, or whether it is to be carried out by compulsory measures.
>
> Secondly: Assuming that the 70-divisions scheme is to be carried out and that compulsion is to be used, whether a decision should be taken now or some time later in the year."

At this time the Cabinet was broadly divided into three sections on the question of conscription. There was the group of those who had come to regard a measure of compulsory national service as vitally necessary for the successful prosecution of the War, and in consequence were anxious to bring it in with the smallest possible delay. At the other extreme stood those who through principle or prejudice were as strongly opposed to it, and prepared to fight it to the last ditch. Between them were some, who were not opposed in principle, and admitted that we might have to resort to compulsion, but were loath to admit the need for so radical a change of system until it was proved to be unavoidable, and only then if they were sure it would command general approval by the mass of the people. They anticipated that any attempt to carry and enforce compulsory universal service would excite such opposition as to make the proposal unworkable.

On 8th October, 1915, Lord Kitchener laid before the Cabinet a memorandum on " Recruiting for the Army," which began with the ominous statement: —

> "The voluntary system, as at present administered, fails to produce the number of recruits required to maintain the armies in the field."

He proposed that a scheme of conscription by ballot should be introduced, based on the returns of the National Register. Each district should be expected to furnish a quota of recruits in accordance with the numbers of men available within the area, as shown by the Register. If voluntary recruiting failed to produce the full quota, the balance would be obtained by a ballot of the eligible men not yet enlisted.

This scheme was, however, severely criticised as clumsy and unworkable, and it was not further proceeded with. It was recognised that if the voluntary system could not be continued the alternative must be a national measure of compulsory service.

The opponents of this argued in the Cabinet and outside that conscription was impracticable because the volunteers already enlisted would be unwilling to serve alongside pressed men, and while a separation of conscript and volunteer armies was unworkable, their mingling would be disastrous. Lord Curzon took the trouble to have extensive enquiries made from officers and men of all ranks in France on this question, and the quite unanimous verdict returned was that these fears were without foundation. The army in the field felt strongly that those at home who would not come out otherwise should be fetched, and while it was suggested that the conscripts might at first have to put up with a certain measure of chaff and ragging, this would soon pass, and the difference in their conditions of enlistment be forgotten.

Actually, of course, this was what took place when conscription was put into force. Here again it turned out that those who raised imaginary objections to a firm policy were flinching at shadows. Our bane throughout those early periods of the War was the incurable tendency of a number of people in high places to argue that measures vitally necessary for the success of our effort could not, for some reason or other, be taken. Thus we were told that the outside firms could not learn to make munitions; that the finances of the country could not stand the strain of our total effort; that the men needed for our Army could not be spared from industry; that gunners could not be trained to operate our programme of big guns; that the country would not stand conscription; that volunteers would not fight beside pressed men; and so on. Every one of these arguments was falsified by the event. Unhappily, each one of these objections served for a greater or less time to hold up and paralyse the efforts we should have been making to win the War. The advice of these prophets of the impossible cost us months and years of prolonged warfare, and hundreds and thousands of British lives.

In deference to the objections of the anti-conscriptionists, and to the hesitations of the middle group of the Cabinet, one final effort was made, in the form of the Derby Scheme, to galvanise the voluntary system into renewed vigour. It was generally recognised, both in the Cabinet and in the country, that if this failed, conscription would be inevitable.

The Derby Scheme owes its name to the fact that Lord Derby, although for many years a strong supporter of the introduction of Universal Military Service, consented to become Director of Recruiting and to carry through a last canvass of the country's man-power, in order to give the voluntary system the utmost opportunity of furnishing the men needed for the Army. He was appointed on 5th October, 1915, and the post carried, at his request, no pay and no military rank.

The authorship of the plan which he set himself to administer has not hitherto been made public.

The main feature of the Derby Scheme was a personal canvass of every man in the Kingdom between the ages of 18 and 41, working on the basis of the National Register. Each man was asked to attest —to pledge himself to join up when called for—subject to the undertaking that all attested men would be divided into two classes, the single and the married, and each of these into 23 groups according to age; that the military authorities would call the men up by class and group as wanted for the Army, beginning with the younger single men, and would call up none of the married men till all the single men had been summoned to the colours.

The married men were encouraged to put down their names in the light of an assurance that not only would they be left at home till the single men had all been called in, but that if the single men did not attest in adequate numbers the married men would not be bound by their attestation pledge. This was stated by Mr. Asquith in a speech he delivered in the House of Commons on 2nd November, 1915:—

" I am told by Lord Derby that there is some doubt among the married men who are now being asked to enlist as to whether they may not be called upon to serve, having enlisted, while younger and unmarried men are holding back and not doing their duty. Let them disabuse themselves of that notion at once. So far as I am concerned, I would certainly say that the obligation of the married men to enlist is an obligation which ought not to be enforced, and ought not to be held binding on them unless and until we can obtain, I hope by voluntary effort, but if it were needed, and as a last resort by other means, as I have stated, the unmarried men."

This position was rendered still more definite and explicit by correspondence between Lord Derby and Mr. Asquith, which confirmed the pledge that no attested married men should be called up unless and until the unmarried men had been recruited voluntarily or conscripted by Act of Parliament.

Every possible effort was made to ensure the full success of the Derby Scheme. His Majesty the King wrote a special appeal: " To My People," supporting the scheme, which was issued on 23rd October. The instructions to the local Recruiting Committees as to carrying out the canvass were jointly considered, approved and signed by Lord Derby, by the Chairman of the Parliamentary

Recruiting Committee, and by Mr. Arthur Henderson, Chairman of the Labour Recruiting Committee. The closing day for the canvass, originally fixed as November 30th, was extended to December 15th.

The result was rather what might have been anticipated. Married men attested in considerable numbers, secure in the assurance that they would not be expected to fulfil their promise unless and until all the single men had been called up. The single men attested much less generally. Out of 2,179,231 single men of military age not enlisted before 23rd October, 1915, the number presenting themselves under the Derby Scheme, and enlisted, attested or medically rejected, was 1,150,000, leaving 1,029,231, or nearly half the total, outside the scheme. Of those who put down their names, so many were either the medically unfit or " starred " men—men employed in jobs from which it was held that in the national interest they could not be spared for the Army—that Lord Derby estimated the net number of single men he would actually get for the Army through his scheme would be only 343,386 out of the total of 2,179,231 in the country.

In face of these figures, it was obviously impossible to pretend that Mr. Asquith's pledge to the married men had been fulfilled. Over a million single men had refused to attest, and the policy of recruiting them compulsorily was the inevitable sequel. As regards popular support for such a policy, all the attested married men were naturally insistent on it. They protested that it would be a breach of the promise made to them to summon them to the colours while so many unmarried men were left at home.

Accordingly, on 5th January, 1916, after much heated discussion in the Cabinet, the first definite measure of conscription was introduced, when Mr. Asquith laid before Parliament a Military Service Bill to compel the attestation of all unmarried men, and widowers without children or dependents, between the ages of 18 and 41. Defending the Bill against the objections of anti-conscriptionists inside and outside the Government, he urged that it was necessary in redemption of the pledge he had given to Lord Derby—a pledge which he certainly considered to be within the limits and upon the general line of policy which had been agreed upon by the Cabinet. He was himself of the opinion that no case had been made out for general compulsion, and he thought the Bill would be sincerely supported by those who either on principle or—as in his case—on the ground of expediency were opposed to compulsion.

This line of argument failed to convince some of his opponents. Sir John Simon resigned from the Government rather than support conscription in any form, and rallied about three dozen other Liberal members into an opposition to attack the measure.

Sir John Simon, speaking on 5th January, 1916, in the debate on the Military Service Bill, declared that his opposition to any measure of conscription was one of fundamental principle, and he added that there were other members of the Government who had not resigned whose views on the matter were indistinguishable from his own. The reference was, of course, recognised as applying to Mr. M'Kenna and Mr. Runciman, who had both opposed the measure strongly in the Cabinet. They did not, however, carry their principles to the point of resigning. When it came to the direct issue they based their objection, not on the fundamental principle with which Sir John Simon credited them, but on the argument that we could not spare from our national industries as many men as would be taken into the Army through conscription, nor afford to keep them under arms when we had got them. During the days immediately prior to the introduction of the measure it was thought that they also might resign if they could not get the Bill so modified as to limit and reduce the numbers liable to be called up under it.

Mr. Redmond and his Irish Nationalists opposed the Bill on its first introduction, but when they knew definitely that Ireland would be excluded from its scope they withdrew their opposition. The reason for the exclusion of Ireland was that the Bill was intended to implement the pledge given in connection with the Derby Scheme, and this scheme had not been worked in Ireland.

Mr. Arthur Henderson and the Labour Party were placed in a rather difficult position by a resolution of the Trades Unions at their Bristol Conference on 5th January condemning the Government's proposals. Mr. Asquith was, however, able to give Mr. Henderson official assurance that nothing in the nature of industrial conscription was contained in or implied by the Bill, and in consequence Mr. Henderson spoke and voted in support of the Second Reading. A minority of the Labour Party, led by Messrs. Ramsay MacDonald, Snowden, and Thomas, opposed the measure.

Carried through all its stages by overwhelming majorities, the Bill became law on 27th January, 1916. At midnight on 1st March all single men who had not already joined up were automatically reckoned as enlisted in His Majesty's forces for the period of the War. The single men attested under the Derby scheme had already been all called up, and a first call was now made on the attested married men, of whom the groups aged 19 to 27 were summoned to the colours.

So ended the first round. But the issue could not rest there. Forces were at work which, with a march as inevitable as destiny, pressed the nation forward into a complete system of compulsory service.

With the advance of the spring of 1916 there came a call from the military authorities for more recruits. This meant summoning the older groups of attested married men. But at the rumour of this a violent agitation broke out.   These fathers of families declared that before they were called for, a much closer comb-out ought to be made of the single men, very many of whom were still at home, exempted from military service because they were in starred occupations. Further, it was insisted that the younger unattested married men ought to be called up before their elders were sent to the trenches. And the older men, with serious responsibilities for children, for houses, for businesses, ought to have some arrangement made to relieve them of their financial difficulties—leases, mortgages, and so on—before they were taken for the Army.

Fierce and long were the debates in the Cabinet on this issue. The calling up of the older classes of married men was postponed while the new phase of the problem was being studied.   Mr. Asquith promised that on 18th April he would make a statement about recruiting, but on that day he had to announce a postponement because of Cabinet disagreements; and he followed this on the 19th by announcing a further postponement, as disagreement in the Cabinet was so serious as to threaten the break-up of the Government. He adjourned the House of Commons till 25th April, on which date a secret session of the House was held to thrash out the problem.

The existing shortage of men for the Army was proving itself serious, and the methods so far available for securing new recruits were proving insufficient.   A month previously, on 21st March, 1916, the Chief of the Imperial General Staff, Sir William Robertson, had submitted a memorandum in which he stated that: —

". . . As regards personnel we are not now in an appreciably better position for making that ' maximum effort ' . . . than we were when I raised the question nearly three months ago.   At the present time the infantry serving abroad is 78,000 below its establishment; the 13 Territorial Divisions at home are also deficient of 50,000 men. . . .   Of the 193,891 men called up under the Military Service Act no fewer than 57,416 have failed to appear. . . ."

A note by the Army Council on 15th April, 1916, showed that the estimated deficit would on 30th June be 179,000 men, and that while as yet there were only 52 divisions abroad instead of the intended 62, there was a deficit of 66,000 men in their establishment.

At the Secret Session of Parliament on 25th April the situation was passed under review, and the Prime Minister put forward the Government proposals to deal with it.   These were officially announced afterwards to include the extension of service of time-expired men, transfer of recruits from territorial to regular units, prompt enlistment of men whose exemption certificates had expired, and recruitment of all youths as they reached the age of 18.   Further efforts were also proposed to enlist unattested married men, and if in a month's time 50,000 of these were not forthcoming and 15,000 a week thereafter, then compulsion would be resorted to.

A second secret session was held on 26th April, and on the following day Mr. Walter Long introduced a Bill embodying the Government's proposals; but it was so adversely criticised that Mr. Asquith withdrew it. There was by now a quite general impatience with any further paltering or half-measures, which Mr. Asquith, with his usual good sense, clearly recognised. On 2nd May he announced that the Government would bring in a measure to impose general and immediate compulsory military service. This was introduced on the following day, and on 25th May it received the Royal Assent. The opposition to it was of quite a trivial nature. Sir John Simon's band of non-co-operators had sunk to 27, and Mr. Ramsay MacDonald's Labour group to 10.

I was in charge of the measure on its second reading in the House of Commons, and speaking on that occasion I challenged the appeal to principle made by its opponents, in the following passage: —

" I have waited for this great overriding principle and I have not heard it yet. Is this Bill inconsistent with the principles of either Liberalism or democracy? Is it inconsistent with the principles of democracy that the State should demand the services and help of every man to defend its life when it is at stake? There is not and never has been a country yet faced with a great military peril that has ever saved itself without resort to compulsion. Never. It is true of autocracies, it is even more true of democracies. Where is the principle? I have a personal interest in finding out, because I have been told that I am a traitor to Liberal principles because I supported conscription; therefore I am personally interested in seeking it out. I cannot find it. Every great democracy which has been challenged, which has had its liberties menaced, has defended itself by resort to compulsion, from Greece downwards. Washington won independence for America by compulsory measures; America defended its independence in 1812 by compulsory measures. Lincoln was not merely a great democrat, but his career was in itself the greatest triumph that democracy has ever achieved in the sphere of government. He proclaimed the principle of ' Government of the People, by the People, for the People,' and he kept it alive by conscription. In the French Revolution the French people defended their newly obtained liberties against every effort of the autocracies of Europe by compulsion and by conscriptionary levies. France is defending her country to-day by conscription. In Italy the Italian democracy are seeking to redeem their enthralled brethren by compulsion. In Serbia the Serbian peasants defended their mountains by compulsory measures, and they are going to win them back by the same means. When honourable members say that conscription is contrary to the principles of liberty and true democracy, they are talking in defiance of the whole teaching of history and of common sense."

I also remarked that in the face of the national emergency which made this measure imperative, I would submit to be driven out of my party, and out of public life altogether, rather than refuse it my support.

I had in fact been pressing the need for compulsory military service on the Government for a considerable time, and the importance of the part I had played in finally carrying it through was attested by two letters which I received at the time from Sir William Robertson. The first of these was of some length, and in it Robertson was good enough to comment in warm terms on my " great courage and patriotism," and wound up with the assertion that " but for you it would not have been done." The second was shorter, and I transcribe it in full: —

" War Office.
2/5/1916.

Dear Mr. Lloyd George,
    The Bill introduced to-day should more than compensate you for the rubbishy Press attacks of the last week or two. The great thing is to get the Bill, and for it the Empire's thanks are due to you—alone.

Yours very truly,
Wm. Robertson."

These expressions of appreciation are perhaps the more important, because Sir William Robertson was not always in as cordial sympathy with my ideas. But if my zeal for this cause won me some approval in quarters not uniformly favourable to me, it added a fresh edge to the bitterness of those who held that my determination to fight the War through without hesitation or reserve, was a most improper and, indeed, unholy attitude. The distrust and hostility of this section of Liberal opinion was thenceforward confirmed and ineradicable. Speaking at Conway on 6th May, 1916, in advocacy of the Military Service Bill, I found myself compelled to reply to a series of attacks which had been directed against me by a prominent Liberal journalist who was at that time in close touch with some of my colleagues, for " abandoning Liberalism," " throwing such fervour into the prosecution of the War," and " having differences of opinion with my chief." To the first charge, the fact that a vast majority of Liberals in the House of Commons had supported the Conscription Bill sufficiently gave the lie. To the second charge I pleaded guilty on the ground that while I hated war I held, once we had decided to wage war, that we must wage it effectively. " That is why I have had no sympathy with those who seem to think that because war is hateful, you ought to fight it with a sort of savour of regret in your actions. Doubting hand never yet struck firm blow."

Of my relations with Mr. Asquith I declared : —

" I have worked with him for ten years; I have served under him for eight. If we had not worked harmoniously—and we have —let me tell you here at once it would have been my fault and not his. I have never worked with anyone who could be more considerate, and I disdain the things they have said. But we have had our differences. Good Heavens! What use would I have been if I had not differed? I should have been no use at all. He has shown me great kindness during the years I have worked with him. I should have ill requited them if I had not told my opinions freely, frankly, independently, whether they agree with his or not.

Freedom of speech is essential in everything, but there is one place where it is vital and that is in the Council Chamber. The councillor who professes to agree with everything that falls from his leader has betrayed him."

Looking backward after the event, no one can now doubt that the adoption of conscription was vitally necessary for carrying the War through to victory. Without it we should have been overwhelmed when Russia, Roumania and Serbia had all cracked and the French Army was threatening mutiny.

The effect on our Allies was heartening. Lord Esher in a memorandum dated 4th May, 1916, reported an interview he had just had with M. Briand, and stated : —

" M. Briand spoke with enthusiasm and deep content of yesterday's proceedings in the English Parliament. He is certain that it will have far-reaching results in Germany, and will accentuate the uneasiness, growing fast among the Central Powers, as to the ultimate issue of the War. . . . The adoption of compulsory service in England will, he thinks, have a lowering effect on German mentality and *morale*.

The effect in France will be even greater.

In spite of all that England has done, which is well known to the French Government, there are many people in France in whose minds doubts still linger as to the determination of England to go through with the War to the bitter end. To these people the adoption by the English Parliament of a procedure so foreign to the traditions and habits of the English people will be a ' *coup de massue.*' The whole French nation, he says, will now recognise that England means to make every necessary sacrifice, and any doubts that existed will be at once dispelled."

While recognising the necessity for the introduction of compulsory service, I have always emphasised and paid tribute to the magnificence of the voluntary effort which the manhood of the country put forward in 1914 and 1915. In my speech at Conway on 6th May, to which I have already referred, I said: —

" The achievement of the nation in raising by voluntary methods those huge armies is something of which we may very well be proud. It is almost unparalleled in the history of war, and nothing which has happened since in the way of compulsory measures can ever detract from the pride we possess in the fact that we are the first nation in the history of the world that has raised over three millions of men for any great military enterprise purely by voluntary means. Young men from every quarter of this country flocked to the standard of international right as to a great crusade. It was a glorious achievement, and well may Britain be proud of it!"

According to a memorandum of the Committee of Imperial Defence, dated 17th April, 1916, the number of men who had by that date actually gone into service with the forces, naval and military, including those already serving at the outbreak of war, was 3,769,659, to which there should be added those in attested groups of married men not yet called up, and single men attested but retained in starred occupations, to a total of 697,000, making a grand total of 4,667,000 men as our full volunteer force, exclusive of contingents from the Dominions and India, which would bring the sum to well over 5,000,000.

On the day when the Military Service Bill received the Royal Assent, the King issued a " message to his people," in the following terms: —

" Buckingham Palace,
25th May, 1916.

To enable our country to organise more effectively its military resources in the present great struggle for the cause of civilisation, I have, acting on the advice of my Ministers, deemed it necessary to enrol every able-bodied man between the ages of eighteen and forty-one.

I desire to take this opportunity of expressing to my people my recognition and appreciation of the splendid patriotism and self-sacrifice which they have displayed in raising by voluntary enlistment since the commencement of the War, no less than 5,041,000 men, an effort far surpassing that of any other nation in similar circumstances recorded in history, and one which will be a lasting source of pride to future generations. I am confident that the magnificent spirit which has hitherto sustained my people through the trials of this terrible war will inspire them to endure the additional sacrifice now imposed upon them, and that it will, with God's help, lead us and our Allies to a victory which shall achieve the liberation of Europe.

GEORGE R.I."

CHAPTER XXIV

DISINTEGRATION OF THE LIBERAL PARTY

THE fissures which showed themselves in the ranks of Liberalism during the debate on conscription were not of sudden growth. They had been steadily forming and widening during the previous twelve months. At the first challenge in 1914 a gust of patriotic fervour had swept the party forward in united resolve, and there were very few who felt compelled by their principles to join with Lord Morley, Mr. Trevelyan, and Mr. Burns in withdrawing from the Government and deciding to hold aloof from the conflict. The leaders of the National Liberal Federation issued on 8th August a circular announcing the indefinite suspension of party propaganda and calling on Liberals to sink political differences and give themselves to the service of the country; and the *Liberal Magazine* declared, " In the great war in which we are engaged, at whatever cost we must win."

But as the War went on the men brought up on the peace-loving precepts of Cobden and Bright and Gladstone disliked it more and more. They had no doubt or hesitation as to the justice or inevitability of our part in it. But they gradually became depressed at the sight of the dread machinery which thrust itself upon them everywhere in the highways and byways, and at the evidence of the accumulating horror which spread desolation throughout the land. The larger and more sagacious half of the party treated the War as a disagreeable necessity forced upon us in the defence of liberty, and to be brought to an end all the sooner by a vigorous organisation of all our available resources into a great national effort. But the real political sectary in his heart argued thus: " War is a hideous thing. You must show your aversion by waging it half-heartedly. Wield the sword with your left hand, and let your right nurse its strength until the blessed day arrives when it will be needed once more for swinging the sword of the Lord and of Gideon in the eternal fight for the principles to which we are attached." The men who threw the whole of their strength and spirit into waging war effectively were disliked and distrusted more and more by the sectarians. Every cannon and shell turned out by these men weighed them down deeper into perdition. Hence the heavier the guns they turned out the deeper their damnation. The men who won their admiration and trust were those leaders who proved the sincerity of their shudder

444

by waging war nervelessly. The more ineffective they became the greater was the trust which was placed in the integrity of their leadership by these high-minded followers. Even under the accommodating Premiership of Mr. Asquith there were ominous growls and occasional outbursts of impatience from the straitest of his supporters. They resented conscription, which had consequently to be carried in two steps. There is no greater mistake than to try to leap an abyss in two jumps.

The Opposition Lobbies, it is true, were not overcrowded with malcontents. Real Parliamentary opinion can rarely be gathered from a perusal of divisions lists. There were sinister grumblings in the corridors and tea-rooms. The activities of the Ministry of Munitions in turning out guns, rifles, shot, and shell on an unprecedented scale provoked irritation and even resentment amongst certain Liberals in Press, Parliament and Club. The personal attitude of old political friends towards me changed and chilled after I became Minister of Munitions. It found petulant expression in speeches and articles, and I felt myself shunned and even spurned by men who once had greeted me with cordiality and enthusiasm. I was treated as one tainted with the leprosy of war. I had a sense of political isolation more complete than I had ever experienced during the whole of my lifetime. My old friends were turning their backs on me. The Conservatives had not yet forgotten the part I had played in the bitter controversies of the last few years, and the Liberals were resentful and sulky.

This attitude hurt me deeply, but it did not slow down by one pulsation my resolve to work energetically and to the limit of my power at the terrible task to which I had been called. I had assented to the declaration of war with tenacious reluctance, but once I was persuaded of its inevitable justice I threw myself with all my energy into the task of helping my country to vindicate the right. I was encouraged during these difficult times by a message which I received, early in 1916, from Theodore Roosevelt through a friend of his, Colonel Arthur Lee (now Lord Lee of Fareham), who acted as my military liaison officer at the Ministry of Munitions. Roosevelt's letter ran as follows: —

" Dear Arthur,
    Your letter was most interesting and I am more pleased than I can say that you are so hard at work and in so congenial and useful a way. Give my heartiest regards to Lloyd George. Do tell him I admire him immensely. I have always fundamentally agreed with his social program, but I wish it supplemented by Lord Roberts's external program. Nevertheless, my agreement with him in program is small compared with the fact that I so greatly admire the character he is now showing in this great crisis. It is often true

that the only way to render great services is by willingness on the part of the statesman to lose his future, or, at any rate, his present position in political life, just exactly as the soldier may have to pay with his physical life in order to render service in battle.   In a very small and unimportant way I have done this myself during the last eighteen months.   I have paid no heed, and shall not pay the slightest heed, to the effect upon my own fortunes, of anything that I say.   What I am trying to do is to make this country go right, and I don't give a damn as what my countrymen think of me in the present or the future, provided only I can make them wake up to the sense of their duty.   In an infinitely greater emergency, Lloyd George seems to me to be following the same line of conduct in trying to serve Great Britain at present.

Don't make any mistake about me.   I don't believe there is any chance of my being nominated, because, as I wrote Lodge the other day, it would be utter folly to nominate me, unless the country was in heroic mood.   If they put ' Safety First ' ahead of honour and duty, then they don't want me, and they need not expect that I will pussy-foot in any shape or way on the great issues that I regard as vital, and to which I regard all others as subordinate.

I hope you have by this time seen a copy of my book.   Read the first chapter and the conclusion.   Perhaps Lloyd George might be interested in looking at two or three sentences that you may care to show him. . . ."

As long as the party was united there was no organised secession. Sir John Simon's feeble efforts to lead a " cave " on conscription were a ridiculous failure.   He is a very able man, but he commands neither the boldness, the breadth, nor the inspiration that are essential to great leadership.   But apart from these issues there was inside the Cabinet a definite group which sought to drive a wedge between the Prime Minister and myself.   As long as I was at the Exchequer I saw Mr. Asquith almost every morning before the Cabinet and discussed with him matters of urgency.   Interviews were easily arranged when I worked at the Treasury Buildings, which had a door opening into 10, Downing Street.

On my way to the Treasury from 11, Downing Street I passed through the Prime Minister's residence.   We invariably got on well and pleasantly together when we met.   But when I went to the Ministry of Munitions I had to be there by nine o'clock and I found it difficult to leave until late in the evening.   I thus saw much less of Mr. Asquith.   In fact I saw very little of him alone for months.   That was the opportunity of the mischief-makers and they took full advantage of it.   When I left the Exchequer and Mr. M'Kenna took my place it was understood that his appointment was to be provisional.   I was to return to my post at the Treasury as soon as I had set munitions going. This arrangement was a mistake and did much harm. The very possibility of its ever materialising made of Mr. M'Kenna a bitter enemy and poisoned his personal relations towards me. Ever afterwards they remained septic. This condition made business transactions in which I was engaged as Minister—all involving finance—very difficult. I ought to have assured him from the outset that I had no intention of ever claiming the redemption of the Prime Minister's pledge. Mr. M'Kenna possessed many of the gifts that make a good administrator in times that do not call specially for imagination, breadth of vision, or human insight. He knew the details of his job as Chancellor, he was a competent arithmetician, a ready reckoner (Mr. Balfour once said he was " an adroit account-ant "), he was, in fact, a master of finance in blinkers. His chief defect, as I have already pointed out, was that he was apt to divide his more conspicuous colleagues into those he liked and those he viewed with distrust, suspicion, and jealousy. This peculiarity made him a source of weakness and distraction in a team. His was the most active personal element in the disintegration of the Asquith Coali-tion. A lady with a gift of satirical analysis of character once said to me that he was like one of those shilling paint-boxes given to children. The blocks were hard and angular, the colours were all very definite and crude. He possessed none of those delicate tints which you find on an artist's palette.

From June, 1915, to June, 1916, I was so immersed in the hurry-ing on of munitions for our hard-pressed Army that I had very little time to watch the political situation or to keep in touch with politicians in or out of the House of Commons, and I did not quite realise how far hostile intrigues had gone. When, later on at the end of 1916, the definite split came in the party and most of the Liberal members of the Cabinet declined further responsibility for the con-duct of the War except under conditions of personal leadership which were inacceptable to the nation, all restraint disappeared and no likely opportunity was missed for criticising and occasionally embarrassing the Government of the day. The attacks were gener-ally left to guerillas, but the sympathy and encouragement of leaders to these snipings were not wanting and were barely concealed. On two or three conspicuous occasions which appeared to be propitious, leaders and all joined in the assault, horse, foot and artillery. The official organisation set to work energetically in the country to spread suspicions and undermine confidence in the War Cabinet which was prosecuting the War with such excessive zeal. Multitudes of true Liberals did their best to save Liberalism from the eternal reproach of presenting this factiousness as the only contribution which their party was able to make to the security of the nation at a time of unparalleled danger in its history. For this they were persecuted, and for this they have never been forgiven by those whose futility in a grave emergency has doomed Liberalism to a generation of querulous impotence.

What would have happened had the party kept together to the end? It is impossible to surmise. There was one man who, if he had survived the War, might have kept the Liberal leaders from separating—the late Mr. Percy Illingworth. Without his powerful help as Chief Whip, Mr. Asquith was unequal to the task of reconciling personal differences and imposing unity. Percy Illingworth was the best type of Englishman—straight, competent, fearless, with a complete subordination of self to duty. He was devoted to Mr. Asquith as his leader—he was proud of him as a Yorkshireman. He was attached to me as a friend. He was loyal to us both, and we both knew and trusted him implicitly. He had a thorough cognisance of the intrigues of little men who plotted incessantly to separate us, and as long as he was there he kept a vigilant eye upon their activities and intimidated them with his Yorkshire bluntness of speech. In January, 1915, he died of typhoid acquired by eating a bad oyster. Had he been alive in 1916 there would have been no split between Mr. Asquith and myself. Of that I am convinced. What trifling incidents often precipitate important events! A rotten mollusc poisoned the whole Liberal Party for years and left it enfeebled. Later on the bite of a monkey in Greece altered the whole course of events in the Levant and had its reactions much further afield.

War has always been fatal to Liberalism. " Peace, Retrenchment, and Reform " have no meaning in war. Moreover, a nation, to make war effectively, must be prepared to surrender individual right and freedom for the time being. If the war is prolonged, that submission becomes a habit. Victory is the triumph of force and not of reason. After every great war there is a period during which belligerent nations incline to divide into two extreme camps—roughly known as revolutionary and reactionary. In that temper Liberalism is at a disadvantage. That is why it is to-day at a discount throughout Europe. Even in America its doctrines assume the form of a dictatorship. The temporary collapse of the Liberal Party in this country was inevitable from the moment it became responsible for the initiation and conduct of a great war. The instinct of the ordinary Liberal in that respect was sound. The War therefore made him uneasy.

1914 was a catastrophe for Liberalism. That was unfortunate, but the issues at stake were too big for treatment in terms of party interests. The challenge to international right and freedom was so tremendous that Liberalism—above all Liberalism—could not shirk it. When millions of men placed their lives at the disposal of their country without giving a thought to the political complexion of the Government or Minister to whose call they were responding or whose decrees they were obeying, it would be but a sorry boast for politicians who face no such danger to claim that they also had forgotten party interests in their country's peril. But there are certain obvious principles which should govern politics in such circumstances. Any combination of parties in a national emergency, if it is to be effective, involves a readiness in all the parties concerned to give and take. The moment it becomes a blind or subterfuge for the attainment of its aims by one party in the combination, then it is a selfish fraud practised on the nation. The two War Coalitions were honestly worked for patriotic ends. I saw Mr. Asquith at the head of two War Governments, one Liberal, the other Coalition, and from a close acquaintance with him during both administrations, I am able to say, and do say unhesitatingly and without qualification that, once war was declared, in neither of his Governments did he give any thought to party advantage. Indeed, so completely did he forget even party principles during his second administration that, in his desire to propitiate old opponents and so ensure unity, he assented to a Protectionist Budget, and even went so far as to pledge the country, by an agreement entered into with its Allies at the famous Paris Conference, to a drastic and far-reaching policy of protection after the War.

Whether general danger to a community comes from flood, fire or war, the instinct that leads to common action rather than to divided counsels is the same. It is evinced primarily by a readiness to co-operate with anyone who is willing and fit to climb the ladder, play the hose, handle the axe, or in any useful way face and fight the fire.

This elementary parable represents my views on the correct position of the party system during a war great enough to demand the undivided attention and whole energy of a nation.

For my own part, throughout the whole War, I never made inquiries as to a helper's political past. And when I knew the party to which he belonged, that fact exercised no influence whatever on my judgment of his qualification. I only wanted to ascertain his fitness for his job.

The two men of whom I saw most during the last two years of the War, when I had supreme direction, were Mr. Bonar Law and Lord Milner, both of whom belonged to the political side opposed to my own. And yet at our numerous conferences and consultations I was never even remotely conscious of their party associations. Why should I have been? When specialists are called into consultation on a case of serious illness, foolish indeed would be the relative and even criminal would be the doctor who thought more of the political views of these experts than of their qualifications to assist in pulling the patient through the crisis. Unhappily for the Liberal Party it included, at that supreme time of trial, many doctors and kinsmen who took another and narrower view of their responsibilities, and who protested stoutly that consultants tainted with political heresy should be excluded from the sick-room. And these bigots have never forgiven those who adopted a different attitude.

CHAPTER XXV

LORD KITCHENER:
A CHARACTER STUDY

To me Lord Kitchener is one of the unsolved mysteries of the War. Was he a great man, or was he a great disappointment? There were many competent observers who knew him well, but took different views of his character—there were many who held conflicting estimates alternatively and simultaneously. But no one who ever saw him regarded him as an ordinary man, for his very appearance had a distinction all its own. What he did well he did with a sway that was peculiar to himself. When he saw his vision was penetrating. Even his failings were not ordinary. He held childish opinions on some matters, but they were not commonplace. When he did silly things, as the wisest men occasionally do, they were extraordinarily silly. His intuitions, his improvisations, his visions—yes, even his stupidities—were all far removed from the average.

A lady with a pernicious gift for stinging epigram described him as " Not a great man, but a great poster." He was, indeed, the greatest " poster " since Boulanger, but he was far more. He was certainly not a Boulanger, for he was conspicuously free from the vice of the *poseur*. After having been in close touch with him and having seen him at work every week and almost every day, for nearly two years, I could not even then quite make up my mind about his qualities. Of this I feel certain, he had flashes of greatness. He was like one of those revolving lighthouses which radiate momentary gleams of revealing light far out into the surrounding gloom and then suddenly relapse into complete darkness. There were no intermediate stages. Now and again he would express an opinion or give utterance to an illuminating phrase that penetrated the fog of war, and then sometimes he would indulge in a garrulousness which displayed the greatest ignorance of the elementary conditions with which he had to deal. He had an ineffable contempt for the Territorials and a puerile fear of the Senussi. I heard him talk of the Territorials as if they were a worthless rabble of make-believes. On the other hand, I heard him talk with woe of the possibility of a million Senussi horsemen sweeping into the Egyptian Delta.

Whether he had always been so, or whether the tropical sun had scorched and parched some of his intelligence, leaving merely oases of verdure and fertility, I cannot judge, for I only met him once previously, some three years before the War. He was then full of admiration for the German Army and pitying contempt for the French Army. " They will walk through them like partridges," was one of his phrases. I discovered that his opinion was not based on military but on political reasons. There is no greater fatuity than a political judgment dressed in a military uniform. What convinced him of the superiority of the German to the French soldier was that the latter had been demoralised by democratic views and concomitant ideas of liberty which were utterly incompatible with true discipline, whereas the former was trained to obey his superiors. He was right and he was wrong. The German system proved superior for the short course, but French democracy was the better in the long run. The autocratic system of the German Empire crashed hopelessly when it had to bear the burden of a great defeat.

Kitchener's rigid point of view and its reactionary arrogance showed itself in other directions. Some of his mental veins had hardened and any pressure on them produced apoplectic results. He vehemently opposed the recognition of Nonconformist denominations not already included in the Army List, and his refusal to appoint chaplains of what he evidently thought were superfluous and eccentric sects provoked the most angry scenes I have ever witnessed at a Cabinet. The Army only recognised three or four denominations. The others, not being on the Army List, had no existence for him. He did not realise that with an army that was being multiplied tenfold and drawing recruits from classes, or types, untapped by the ordinary recruiting sergeant, the variety of religious beliefs held must necessarily be greater. To his mind the religious services provided for the regulars of the old army ought to be good enough for these amateur soldiers. The vital importance of encouraging national co-operation by deferring to all legitimate susceptibilities did not occur to him. This showed the light occulted. When he gave way, however, he did it thoroughly. I well remember how, when he had been overruled by the Cabinet on the question of chaplains he took a piece of paper, started writing, and turning to me said: " Come now, tell me the names of these sects for which you want padres. Is this list right? Primitive Baptists, Calvinistic Wesleyans, Congregational Methodists. . . ?" It was not intended to cast ridicule; he simply had never heard the correct names of these great religious bodies. I gave him the right titles. He wrote them all down carefully. As soon as he returned to the War Office he took steps to invite representatives of all these denominations to attend a Chaplains Committee there. It functioned right through the War without any friction.

A smaller man, according to the wont of small men, would have pretended to signify agreement, and then have placed every obstacle in the path of execution. Lord Kitchener may or may not have been a great man, but he certainly was not a small one, and here his action was one of greatness, for having been overruled he loyally accepted defeat.

His attitude towards the various nationalities that constitute the people of the United Kingdom was more obdurate, and his obstinacy had far-reaching and fatal results. Scotchmen had by tradition established a military title to their nationality, and it was a title Lord Kitchener respected and honoured. But although Welshmen and Irishmen had also their separate national regiments, he declined to encourage their national sentiments when it came to the point of raising separate Welsh and Irish divisions. The case of the Welsh division was one with which I was naturally particularly concerned. In order to encourage recruiting in the Principality, a number of influential Welshmen, with the Earl of Plymouth at their head, decided to form and raise a purely Welsh division. Colonel Owen Thomas took a very active part in this effort. But when the proposal came before Lord Kitchener he promptly vetoed it. The question was thereupon raised by me in the Cabinet, and there was a fierce fight. In the end the cause of the Welsh division was carried. Lord Kitchener came to me afterwards and said: " What was the name of the officer who pressed this scheme forward?" I told him it was Colonel Owen Thomas. "Can you bring him along to me?" asked Kitchener, and I promised to do so. The Colonel was summoned post haste to London, and I took him round to Kitchener, at the War Office. Kitchener bent on him a terrific frown, and Thomas, though a stout-hearted fellow, visibly quailed on seeing that imposing personage with his stern face and his terrifying eyes. Lord Kitchener rumbled forth: " I understand you are a Colonel." Thomas timidly signified assent. " Would you like to become a Brigadier-General?" Thomas could not find his tongue, and I answered promptly for him, " Of course he would!" " Then I will make you a Brigadier-General for this Welsh division. Carry on!" said Kitchener.

In the case of the Welsh division he thus made a handsome surrender. But unhappily for the country, he maintained his dislike for the Irish division. This formation represented poor John Redmond's last effort to bring Ireland effectively into the War. He addressed recruiting meetings throughout Ireland, and his eloquence won thousands of young Irish Nationalists and Catholics to fight under the standard of freedom and justice raised by the British Empire. His brother, William Redmond, one of the best loved members of the House of Commons, took a commission in this new unit, and he subsequently fell fighting under the British flag in France. But Lord Kitchener did his best to damp the ardour of the Redmonds. He refused commissions to educated young Irishmen of the class and type who were being made officers in England, Scotland,

and Wales, for no conceivable reason except that he distrusted and disliked their nationalism. The culminating incident will take an invidiously prominent place in the tragic history of Irish relations with Great Britain. Nationalist ladies, fired with enthusiasm for the new Irish division, for Mr. Redmond and for the cause to which they were devoting themselves, embroidered a silken flag with the Irish harp emblazoned upon it. At the same moment the patriotic ladies of Ulster were embroidering the Red Hand of Ulster on the flag which they designed to present to a division which was being raised in Ulster. In due course the two flags were presented to the respective divisions. One was taken and the other was left. When Lord Kitchener heard of the green flag and its Irish harp he ordered that it should be taken away. But the Ulster flag was allowed to fly gloriously over the heads of the Orange soldiers of the Protestant North. Ireland was deeply hurt. Her pride was cut to the quick, her sense of fair play was outraged, her sympathy with the Holy War against the military dictatorship of Europe was killed, and John Redmond's heart was broken. He ought to have appealed to Parliament, but he probably knew it was too late to avert the evil. From that moment the effort of Irish Nationalism to reconcile England and Ireland by uniting the two peoples in a common effort for the oppressed of another land failed, and Lord Kitchener's sinister order constituted the first word in a new chapter of Irish history.

Like all great men he had a sense of humour. Amongst my papers I came across a pleasant reminder of this fact. A Welsh mariner interned at Ruhleben had sent home a letter in which he had sought successfully to convey without censorship to his relations at home some notion of the severity of the conditions in that camp. The letter was sent on to Kitchener. Here is the letter: —

> " Englisches Lager,
> Barake 11,
> Ruhleben,
> Bei Spandau,
> BERLIN.
>
> Dear Wife and Children,
>
> I have your letter of the 1st, and am pleased to know you are all well. I am afraid we are here for a long time and we dread the winter. I wish I were at home with you.
>
> I am still keeping well and I cannot say any more. My love to you all, and my respects to Cig, Tan, Menin, and Siwgr, whom I have not seen this long time, but hope to see when I get home.
>
> &c., &c.''

A footnote by Lord Kitchener's correspondent explains that: —

" The words as above (Cig, Tan, Menin, Siwgr) are Welsh, and the interpretation of them respectively is: —

Meat
Fire
Butter
Sugar."

A copy was sent on by Lord Kitchener to Sir Edward Grey and myself with this endorsement: —

" Sir Edward Grey.
Mr. Lloyd George.
    The value of the Welsh language in dealing with the cultured Teuton.   K."

When I met him subsequently at the Cabinet he chortled over the incident.

His was a hypnotic personality and the impulse of his magnetism moved multitudes of men to willing action. Was he a great organiser? I cannot tell, even though I saw his greatest tasks. He undoubtedly possessed some of the rarest qualities of the great organiser—the gifts of improvisation, of driver, of leadership. But he had developed two patent defects, a reluctance to delegate and, more serious still, an inability to choose the right men.

Lord Kitchener was one of the first to realise the magnitude of the War. When most men talked of peace before Christmas he predicted a three years' struggle and set out—as far as men were concerned—to prepare for it. He made a call first for half a million and then for a million more. He knew that with the means at his disposal not one half of them would be available for the field for a full year. As a matter of fact the first battle of the first divisions of the " K " army was fought in September, 1915. His views as to the duration of the campaign changed somewhat from time to time, and in the spring of 1915, he predicted that the German reserves would be exhausted by September. But nothing can rob him of the credit for the vision that foresaw in August, 1914, a three years' campaign, and for the energy and wisdom with which he set out at once to prepare for it.

I doubt whether any other man could at that moment have attracted the hundreds of thousands who rallied to the flag at his appeal. And those who were responsible for placing the striking portrait of Lord Kitchener's strong face on the appeals to fight for " King and Country " had a genius for publicity. It was eminently the face of a commander. The resolution of its firm lines, the mixture of calm penetration and determination in the steady eyes, the intelligence of the broad square brow, all gave an impression of irresistible strength that inspired everyone who saw it. And in those stormy days who was there who did not gaze on those granite features with a confidence of the kind that led the nation to heights of sacrifice? Kitchener was cast in nature's mould for a hero.

Another proof of Lord Kitchener's military vision was given in August, 1914, when the intention of the Germans to advance through Belgium was still unknown. General Joffre and his advisers were confident that the real blow would come from the Ardennes and that no serious German forces would advance in the Mons direction. Their view was that the roads in that quarter were not suited for the progress and maintenance of a great army. Lord Kitchener took a different view; and I have a distinct recollection of his expressing his opinion to the Cabinet. The event proved he was right. The French Commander's mistake was very nearly fatal to the Allied cause.

Kitchener had not the mind for directing a great war conducted along lines to which he was completely unaccustomed either by training or experience. He never took to the manufacture of heavy guns for field warfare and he was sceptical of the prodigal expenditure of shells in trench warfare. He did not realise the part which the machine-gun was destined to play in the War.

As the operations developed on lines which were farther and farther removed from his conception of warfare he became less and less effective and his judgment was less and less trusted by his colleagues. It is not too much to say that during the last few months of his stay at the War Office he was a *roi fainéant*. Sir William Robertson was appointed to the position of Chief of the Imperial General Staff, with powers that reduced Lord Kitchener's position to that of a signatory Minister. He held the Seals of Office, but so far as war direction was concerned he had to use them under Sir William Robertson's orders. It was no doubt a humiliating position for a great soldier, because he was in every respect a greater man and a greater soldier than the keeper of his seals. Nevertheless, his hold on the public never diminished, and to the end there was always a small crowd waiting outside the War Office watching to catch a glimpse of him. And when the sad news broke upon London that he had gone down with the *Hampshire* in the cruel waters of the North Atlantic, a pall of dismay descended on the spirit of the people. Men and women spoke of the event in hushed tones of terror. The news of a defeat would not have produced such a sense of irreparable disaster. The tidings of the German advance of March, 1918, did not send such a shudder of despair through Britain as did the news of the tragic end of this remarkable man. I am not capable of analysing Lord Kitchener's attributes or gifts. But he was one of the great personalities of the War who exercised an indubitable effect on its course and thus on the destiny of the whole world. Great Britain and her Allies owe to the memory of Lord Kitchener the undying gratitude and the enduring fame which are the due of great service rendered greatly in a great cause.

CHAPTER XXVI

AT THE MINISTRY FOR WAR

ON the 6th day of June, 1916, I walked across from the Ministry of Munitions to attend a War Council at 10, Downing Street. Before I entered the Cabinet Chamber the Prime Minister's Secretary, Mr. Bonham Carter, beckoned me into his room and jerked out something about the *Hampshire*. Usually quiet and composed, he was obviously labouring under some suppressed emotion which rendered his speech scarcely articulate. At last he was able to convey to me the startling news that the cruiser in which Lord Kitchener had sailed for Russia had struck a mine off the Orkneys and that Lord Kitchener and his staff had all been drowned. When I entered the Cabinet Room I found the Prime Minister, Sir Edward Grey, Mr. Balfour and Sir Maurice Hankey sitting at the table all looking stunned by the tragedy. One realised how deep was the impression made by the personality of this extraordinary man on all who came in contact with him. Sir Maurice Hankey and I quite forgot for the moment that had it not been for the Irish negotiations we also would have shared the same fate.

The passing of Lord Kitchener left an empty place at the War Office. I realised that this post might be offered to me. But I was far from eager to go to the War Office under present conditions. Although the post of Secretary of State for War was a much more exalted one than that of the Minister of Munitions, and during the present hostilities came second in importance only to that of Prime Minister, it had during recent months declined very much in real influence. Lord Kitchener had lost much of his grip, and, as I have related above, the effective direction of War Office matters had been delegated by a special Order in Council to his Chief of Staff. I had no liking for the prospect of finding myself a mere ornamental figurehead in Whitehall. It is a part I would play grudgingly and gracelessly. Had the Secretaryship of State been a live office where the Minister exercised supreme control subject to Prime Minister and Cabinet, I should have welcomed the promotion. It would have afforded the opportunity to pull things together and alter the direction of affairs. I was becoming increasingly dismayed and dissatisfied at the course along which affairs were drifting, and seriously considered whether I could not render more effective help to our country by resigning office altogether, in order that, as an independent critic, not bound by the traditions of Cabinet unity, I might urge in Parliament and in the country a more vigorous and intelligent prosecution of the War.

Among my papers I find the draft of a memorandum which I prepared on 17th June, 1916, for the purpose of laying before Mr. Asquith my views in reply to his offer of the Secretaryship for War. This is what I had set down : —

" I wrote you the other day asking you to let me have an opportunity of placing before you certain serious considerations before you made up your mind finally about the War Office. Let me at once relieve your mind of one possible anxiety. During the eight years I have had the privilege of serving under you I have no doubt given you from time to time a good deal of worry, but it has never been due to any personal claims I have ever pressed upon you. You were good enough to admit that, when the present Coalition Administration was formed. I do not now propose to ask you for any personal consideration or advancement, as you will realise later on. I have made other plans. But that emboldens me to place before you one or two considerations of a very urgent character. . . .

1. If the Allies are to be pulled together and to be induced to co-operate, you must have a Secretary of State for War who, apart from possessing personality, will possess real power and influence. No statesman with any self-respect would consent to occupy office under the humiliating conditions to which poor Kitchener had been reduced during the last few months of his life. Many a time I have seen him wince under the indignity of his position. Unless the Secretary of State has the ultimate· say in patronage he will be treated with supreme contempt in his own department, and by the whole of the Army. Such a man would have no weight in the councils of the Allies, at a time when it is most urgent that his voice should be cast on the side of unity and co-operation.

2. There are many important spheres of activity in the British Army which would be better placed under civilian than under military direction. It is no use referring to what is done in Continental armies. Those armies numbered millions, and the best brains of the nation were attracted by the great prizes which were to be won by service in them. Ours was a small thing. The rewards were necessarily limited in number and scope. Where good brains are to be found in the British Army they ought to be put into tasks which civilians cannot discharge. They are wasted on mere business and contractual jobs. On the other hand, if the brains devoted to that class of work are not

good, the Army suffers very severely and there is extravagance without efficiency. I never can get a soldier to realise this; he has a rooted prejudice against giving what has always been regarded as a military job to a civilian.

3. Soldiers are not very eager to promote brilliant subordinates, who may, if very successful, dim their lustre. They are not consciously influenced by such rivalries, but unconsciously they undoubtedly are. They prefer a safe, second-rate man in a position affording great opportunities, to running the risk of creating formidable rivals by choosing men of exceptional powers. This undoubtedly accounts for one or two appointments in the British Army, and still more for two or three non-appointments. A civilian on the other side would have no sense of rivalries in military promotion and he would insist upon the best man being appointed.

4. No wise civilian would ever dream of embarking upon strategy. A man who did that would be fit for no post in any ministry. He would be a danger. There you must be advised by the expert. But the expert must also have his schemes checked by the common sense of the civilian. That is what happens in the War Committee. Great strategical enterprises ought to be submitted not merely to the Secretary of State, but to the War Committee. The soldiers in this war have not been a conspicuous success. Up to the present there has not been a plan conceived and carried out by them which has not ended in bloody failure.

These are some of the thoughts I wanted to put before you determined your action. As I have already stated, I have no personal interest in the matter. I propose now to take a course which I had determined upon long ago. I have been profoundly dissatisfied for a long time with the progress and conduct of the War. I have expressed my dissatisfaction in writing and orally to you, the War Committee and the Cabinet. Had it not been for the fact that I had undertaken a task the carrying out of which was vital to the success of our Army, I should long ago have joined Carson, with whom I have been in the main in complete sympathy in his criticisms of the conduct of the War. But when there was trouble with labour, when the organisation which I had with the help of others created had not yet borne fruit, I felt as if I were running away from the post of difficulty. But now the Munitions Department has been an undoubted success. Ammunition is pouring in. When I came in we were manufacturing in this country 70,000 shells a week; that is about one-sixth of what we spend now in a single week of ordinary trench warfare activity. The whole ammunition reserve was under 75,000; we produce more than twice that per day now. The guns are coming in by the hundred.   The policy for which I was mainly responsible in respect of heavy guns—a policy, by the way, which I heard described by one of my colleagues as " sheer lunacy," and which has been consistently opposed by him and by others for months— has now been demonstrated by the facts of the War to be the only one that can possibly achieve success.   Our Army in France is now sending in a requisition for hundreds more of heavy guns than had ever been ordered by the War Office.   Had it not been that I had in defiance of all authority high and low made arrangements for the manufacture of these guns, the requisition would be in vain.

I am only pointing out these things in order to show that the Munitions Department ought almost to be able to run itself now.   I therefore feel that my position in the Ministry is an anomalous one, as I am completely out of sympathy with the spirit and the method of the War direction.   I feel we cannot win on these lines.   We are undoubtedly losing the War, and nothing can save us but the nation itself.   The people do not realise how grave the situation is.   I feel they ought to be told. They ought to have a chance of saving themselves, otherwise they have a right to turn round on those who hold these views and say when disaster comes: ' Why did you not tell us in time?' I know you have always taken a more optimistic view of the prospects, but I think you will agree that up to the present my gloomy forebodings have been realised.   I hope to God I am wrong; but if I am not, I should feel I had been guilty of a gross neglect of duty if in order to retain a pleasant office I had chosen to muzzle myself and not warn them in time of the danger impending their country.   This is no newly formed resolution on my part, as the Lord Chief Justice can tell you, for I intimated to him many weeks ago my intention on the subject.   There are things which must be said not merely to our own countrymen, but to the Allies, which cannot be said by one who is still a member of the Cabinet, and yet it is essential to the winning of the War that these warnings should be uttered. I have found it very difficult to refrain from expressing my opinion in conversations, and I am conscious that to do so whilst I am still a member of the Government lays me open to the charge of disloyalty, so that I find myself in the unhappy position of having to choose between disloyalty to my colleagues and the betrayal of my country.

It is with deep regret that from an overwhelming sense of public duty I feel that I must sever my association with you and with some of my other colleagues who have shown me great kind-ness and goodwill, but I am profoundly convinced that I can render better service to my country in a very dark hour by standing outside and telling them what I know.   I believe the Government is rapidly losing the confidence of the nation. It cannot retain it by artificially prolonging the life of Parliament. The nation ought to have an opportunity of choosing its own policy and its own representatives to expound it, and I specially feel that the men in the trenches ought to have an opportunity of choosing the Parliament and the policy on which their lives depend. Here again I am conscious of being out of touch with several of my colleagues and I cannot help seeing that there is an attempt being made to put off a decision on this important question until it is too late to act.

As to Ireland, as far as I am concerned it must be either through or off in the course of the next few days; but I feel that outside the Government I can be more helpful even in the settlement of that question."

That memorandum gives a pretty definite indication of the views I had formed by that time about the situation; and it shows some of the reasons why I was reluctant to take on the position of Secretary of State for War. However, after further talks with Mr. Asquith, with Lord Reading, who was strongly opposed to resignation, with Mr. Bonar Law, and also with Lord Beaverbrook, who was present at all my conversations with Mr. Bonar Law on the subject of the conduct of the War from this time onward until the reconstruction of the Government, I was persuaded to give up the idea of resignation. I also consulted a very old and always a very good friend of mine, the late Sir Edward Russell (afterwards Lord Russell) of the *Liverpool Post*. I sent my memorandum on to him, but he advised against resignation. Mr. Bonar Law urged that if I resigned and joined Carson in criticism it would make his position in the Government quite intolerable. He also would have to retire. Thus we should break up the national unity. I therefore decided not to send in my memorandum, and to postpone for the time my intention of leaving the Government. I accepted the War Office with considerable misgivings, partly on the ground of general War policy and partly because I disliked working in fetters.

On 6th July, 1916, therefore, Mr. Asquith, who had been once again in temporary charge of the War Office pending the appointment of Lord Kitchener's successor, handed it over to me.

I was at the War Office for only five months—too short a time to effect much change in its internal organisation and policy, particularly since the Chief of Staff, Sir William Robertson, regarded any effort to exercise authority on my part as an impingement upon his special powers, so he thrust out all his prickles whenever he suspected I might be about to attempt any rash civilian interference with the sanctities of military matters. The two chief tasks which I was able to carry out during my brief tenure—tasks of which I give some account in following sections—were the tidying up of the appalling muddle in Mesopotamia, and the reconstruction of the Transport system on the Western Front. I also stirred up recruiting in the Empire outside these islands.

In these problems, which I inherited with my new office, I claim to have achieved a good measure of success. In the case of another inherited problem I was less happy. This was the matter of a military mission to Russia. I had from time to time since the War began pressed the Government to establish closer relations between the Western Allies and Russia. I was anxious not only to secure a more effective co-ordination between East and West, but also to find out what could be done towards re-equipping and thus reorganising the Russian Armies.

Lord Kitchener was on his way to Russia when he lost his life. It was a mission of extreme urgency, for the critical state of affairs in that allied country could hardly be exaggerated, and if she were to be saved from collapse it was vital that we in the West should come to a good understanding with her on matters of strategy, finance, and equipment supply.

Lord Kitchener had pre-eminently possessed the right qualifications for this mission. Now that he was gone, it became a question of finding someone suitable to replace him.

The obvious and in fact inevitable person for this mission was Sir William Robertson. As Chief of the Imperial General Staff he possessed the necessary status, prestige and qualifications. The only conceivable alternative would have been General Haig, the Commander-in-Chief, who clearly could not be spared from France in the middle of a great offensive. True, Robertson was not an authority on finance, but this could be got over by sending Lord Reading with him to deal with questions of that nature which needed to be settled.

Robertson made difficulties. The Somme offensive was in full blast, and he was very busy with the arrangements it involved. Time slipped by, and when we reached the latter part of September I felt it was imperative to bring matters to a head; for Archangel was ice-bound in winter, and winter would soon be here.

Accordingly I wrote the following letter to Mr. Asquith: —

CONFIDENTIAL.

" War Office,
26th September, 1916.

My dear Prime Minister,

Before you come to a final decision on the suggestion that I made to you this morning, as I attach very great importance to something being done on those lines, I should like to put before you once more the considerations which convinced me that action on this matter is essential. I have thought so for some time.

1.   The tone of some of the communications from Petrograd indicates a good deal of irritation against us in Russian official, and specially in Russian military circles.

2.   The Germanophile influences have been considerably strengthened in the Russian Government by recent changes. Our friends have disappeared one by one and there is no man now of any influence in the Russian Bureaucracy who can be said to be favourable towards this country.

3.   The Russians, like all peasant peoples, are very suspicious of a trading and financial community. They always imagine that we are trying to get the better of them in a bargain. The mere fact that their suspicion is a ridiculous one to a business man does not in the least affect the peasant mind. They have undoubtedly got it into their heads that we are anxious to make money out of them. This suspicion must be removed.

4.   It is not a question of terms but of atmosphere. The Russian is a simple and, I think, a good fellow, and once we win his trust there will be no difficulty in doing business with him. We must therefore take some striking action which would clear away these suspicious vapours that obscure the real issues. I therefore urge the importance of sending immediately to Russia emissaries of high standing with full powers to clear up the situation. It is a misfortune that Bark and Bylaeff left before an agreement was arrived at. But that is past.

5.   Whoever is sent must not merely possess authority, but must be known by the Russians to be a person or persons of high standing and influence in this country. I would strongly urge that Sir William Robertson and Lord Reading be asked to go. As to Sir William Robertson, his standing here is known to the military authorities in Russia, and for the moment they are the only people who count in Russia. The bureaucrats are poor creatures. He could discuss with General Alexeieff the military dispositions for next year. It is important these two men should meet. Up to the present the Russians have never conferred with the Western Powers as to military plans. Men like General Gilinski, who represented the Russian Armies in Paris, are worse than of no account; and I am afraid that if there is a second Chantilly conference Alexeieff either cannot or will not send anyone who will have full power to decide the outlines of the next campaign. The eastern generals probably concentrate their minds too exclusively on the east, and I am not sure that the western generals are not inclined to commit a similar error by limiting their views too much to the countries where their forces are operating. It would be a good thing for both General Robertson and for General Alexeieff that they

should interchange views, and the decision arrived at by these two great soldiers after such an interchange might very well be decisive.

As for Lord Reading, he has the high standing and the necessary diplomatic gifts and the knowledge of finance which would enable him successfully to achieve an understanding with Russia.

I am afraid of the present misunderstanding developing into strained relations. It would probably not produce a rupture during the progress of the War, but it would certainly have a very sinister influence upon the peace negotiations.

Ever sincerely,
D. LLOYD GEORGE.

P.S.—There has already been a delay of some months in ordering essential military material for Russia, and I am apprehensive that Russian generals will attribute failures—due to their own shortcomings—to our delay in furnishing them with financial assistance."

My proposal in regard to Sir William Robertson was shattered against the rock of personal suspicions. He was already predisposed to imagine that I would welcome his absence from the War Office, and there were those in the Cabinet who were resolutely hostile to anything I did or suggested, who deliberately encouraged Robertson to refuse the proposed mission. Indeed, one of them subsequently admitted that he had advised Robertson not to go. As a consequence, I received on the next day this letter from the C.I.G.S.: —

" War Office.
27/9/16.
6.15 p.m.

Dear Mr. Lloyd George,

The Prime Minister has just sent for me to discuss the Russian visit. I have thought it well over since you spoke to me this morning and have concluded that it is impossible for me to make the visit without losing entire control over the War, and this at an important time. I quite realise the force of what you say, but if I went I should be away for at least a month and that is much too long if I am to keep my hand on the many problems we are dealing with.

I am honestly very sorry not to be able to fall in with your proposal, and as I told the P.M., if I am asked to go—I shall go, but my opinion is that I ought *not* to go, if I am of any use as C.I.G.S.

Callwell got on well when he went. He would be better than no one!

Q

Believe me, I am sorry, but I must tell you what I feel about the necessity for my remaining at my post.

Yours very truly,

W. R. ROBERTSON."

With this refusal the proposed mission to Russia collapsed, and our chance of coming to a real understanding with our great Ally in the east was lost until it was too late to save Russia from her final collapse.

Such news as came through to us during the autumn of 1916 from Russia showed what a fatal blunder the abandonment of the mission was proving. All the omens were pointing to a breakdown of the Russian military effort and to a separate peace with Germany. At the end of July, Sazonow, faithfully pro-Ally, had been intrigued out of the Russian Foreign Ministry and been replaced by Sturmer, who was suspected, not without reason, of pro-German leanings. The King of Sweden (who was pro-German in sympathy) had remarked to the British Ambassador at Stockholm. on hearing this news, that there would be peace between Russia and Germany in two months! Though this prophecy was unfulfilled, it was based on a true insight into the trend of affairs in Russia.

Sir George Buchanan, the British Ambassador in Petrograd, mentioned in a private letter to Lord Charles Beresford on 17th October the prevalence of rumours of a separate peace, which Sturmer had officially denied, and reported the growth of a pro-German sentiment in influential circles. In a further letter of 28th October he stressed the progress which pro-German and anti-British propaganda was making, and added: " The losses which Russia has suffered in this war are so colossal that the whole country is in mourning; and so many lives have been uselessly sacrificed during the recent unsuccessful attacks against Kovel and other places that the impression seems to be gaining ground with many people that it is useless going on, more especially as Russia, unlike Great Britain, has nothing to gain by prolonging the war . . . with the people becoming every day more discontented and with a man like Sturmer at the head of the Government, I cannot help feeling anxious."

On 30th November, Lord Rhondda sent me a series of memoranda written by a British officer stationed at Archangel. recording his impression gleaned on a visit to Petrograd and Moscow. He, too, was impressed with the strength of German propaganda and war weariness among the mass of the nation. " From the highest to the lowest all are of opinion that the spirit of the Russian populace in the big cities of late has fallen very greatly," he wrote. " The chief cause, of course, of this change in national *morale* is the extreme difficulty of getting the first necessities of life, even at any price, and the now universal necessity of standing in long queues in the big towns to get a small supply of such articles as milk, black and white bread, butter and/or cheese, sugar, tea and coffee, meat, fish, etc. . . . These queues form an excellent field of operations for agents of German propaganda, where it is subtly hinted and often even openly asserted by people standing waiting their turn that all this misery is merely being suffered for the aggrandisement of England. . . ."

Then came the following prophetic sentences: —

". . . The next three months are the critical period. . . . Either the Government will yield or there will be a *coup d'état*, or, if neither of these things happen, Russia will have to stop fighting and make peace, with disastrous results."

This informant urged that measures of counter-propaganda should be initiated with the utmost dispatch. "It is only with the most assiduous and patient nursing that the Russian Government and people can be led through another one or two years of war and hardship, and no effort or comparatively trifling expense should be spared in achieving this. . . ."

But the warning was too late. The ice had already closed round Archangel. Before it melted again in the spring, Russia had crashed into revolution, and all hope of reinforcing her as an Allied Power was at an end.

CHAPTER XXVII

SIR WILLIAM ROBERTSON

SIR WILLIAM ROBERTSON was one of the enigmas of the War. He was not a great soldier, but that he possessed an outstanding personality is beyond question. The fact that there was such a wide diversity of opinion and such an acute controversy as to his gifts and character is sufficient proof that he was no common man. No one in so exclusive a profession as the Army, where social prestige and accomplishment count for so much, could have risen from the humblest upbringing and the lowliest rank to the topmost heights which he occupied unless he possessed talents well above his fellows. He was industrious, steady, intelligent; all the administrative tasks entrusted to him, whether as ranker, N.C.O., or commissioned officer, he discharged competently and with distinction. He was an excellent organiser. He had, during his military career, few opportunities, if any, of leading men in the field. His experience had been of an administrative kind, and here he was a conspicuous success. In that respect amongst all the generals, he was second only to Sir John Cowans. He had other qualities which made for speedy promotion in the Army. He was cautious and discreet. His massive reticence made a deep impression on all whose duty it was to seek his opinion.

A laconic sentence, or often a mere grunt which might signify anything, was all that he vouchsafed in answer to the most anxious searcher after truth on our military position. He was non-committal but he was sternly orthodox. Such mistakes therefore as he committed were all of the negative kind, and as these were always in accordance with Army regulations and traditions they counted in his favour and helped his promotion. He understood the Army better than any of his rivals.*

Such men always get on in any vocation. These qualities of

* Extract from *Times* obituary leading article: " . . . he was not a genius, except in CARLYLE's definition. There was no meteoric brilliance about him; his imagination was commonplace. . . . That is the true lesson of ROBERTSON's career. Genius dazzles by its splendour; but it is possible to see this man exactly as he was, to watch each of the struggles which he made, and to understand completely the reasons why he triumphed. There is excuse in genius for failure to emulate it. ROBERTSON's career offers no excuse. What he did any man or boy of ordinary attainments can do also, provided that he is willing to make the necessary sacrifices of immediate leisure and comfort."

circumspection in judgment and speech lead even shrewd and experienced observers of all sorts and conditions of men to infer that there is a vast mental hinterland unexplored and unrevealed. Mr. Asquith declared Robertson to be "the greatest strategist of the day." That he most certainly was not. But his oracular monosyllables and grunts misled much abler men than himself. Of his abilities I have already spoken. Some of his limitations I have indicated. His mind was sound but commonplace. He was cautious to the point of timidity. There lay his strength—that also accounted for his drawbacks. A general who takes no risks or leaves them to others never won a difficult campaign.

When I first met him he had reached a very considerable position in the military hierarchy. He was Chief of the Staff to the Commander-in-Chief of the Expeditionary Force in France. I was certainly impressed at my first acquaintance with him. I saw a good deal of him later on in the War and I came gradually to understand his powers and his limitations.

He had a profound and disturbing suspicion of all foreigners; if I may use a fruit grower's vocabulary, Robertson had the canker of xenophobia in his very sap and that vitiated the quality of his product. In a war conducted by an alliance of several nations it was essential to victory that there should be a sound and broad interpretation of the policy of the single front. In the order of his distrust came Frenchmen, first and deepest of all, then Italians, Serbians, Greeks, Celts, and last of all—if at all—Germans. The Austrians had no existence for him except in his arithmetical tables. They were not near the Western Front and did not otherwise obtrude their hostile presence into his strategical conceptions. The French always irritated him and brought out all his stubbornness. That is why they called him " General Non-non "; that represented his first impulse towards all their requests and proposals. Briand once said to me: " Rob-berrt-son says ' Non ' before he has heard what your proposal is about."

Of the Germans he had a very high opinion and no dislike. In 1916, when the German Army was making its stubborn defence of the slush on the Somme plateau, he said to me: " If we and the Boche were together, we would have beaten the whole lot of them long ago." When the fighting was at its worst he did not hesitate to express his opinion in a discussion on Peace Terms, that a strong Germany in Central Europe was vital to the preservation of Peace. His memorandum on that subject rose in parts to the heights of statesmanship. After a week's reflection on his own temerity he withdrew the memorandum and cancelled it. He would have been much more effective as a politician than as a soldier. Since he has already passed away I can express this opinion without inflicting the hurt it would inevitably have caused him.

I shall have a good deal to say later on as to his fitness for the position of Chief of the Imperial General Staff. I do not believe he ever visualised the full significance and responsibility of that great position. His function ought to have been that of Chief Military Adviser to the Cabinet on the War as a whole. Sir Douglas Haig, Sir Archibald Murray, Sir John Maxwell, General Milne and General Maude were all sectional generals, and their minds were bound to be concentrated in the main, if not entirely, upon the problem of defeating the army immediately in front of them, but the C.I.G.S. ought to have realised that it was his duty to supervise and to co-ordinate efforts on all the battlefields. He came into full authority when the British contribution to the War in men, material, money and ships had grown to vast dimensions and was still growing. We were therefore entitled not indeed to impose our ideas upon the Allies or to dictate to them, but to impress and insist much more than we did. Our chief failure in the first three campaigns of the War was in co-ordination of forces and resources, in a full realisation of what the united front meant strategically. Robertson rendered no help in overcoming this calamitous defect. From the moment he became C.I.G.S. he hindered and thwarted at every turn every effort to concentrate and distribute the aggregate power of the Allies in such a way as to achieve the surest and speediest results. I felt profoundly that in this respect he completely failed the statesmen whom he derided, but ought to have guided.

Sir Douglas Haig was a stronger man. I doubt whether he was abler than Robertson, but he had better fighting qualities. He was a man of more indomitable will and courage. He was also Robertson's senior; that counts in every profession but most of all in the Army and Navy. Other qualifications being fairly equal, seniority has always the say. That is why, whenever I saw these two men together, I felt that Haig dominated, over-awed and almost bullied his junior. Robertson was not endowed with that intrepidity in thought and action that makes great generals.

There was a rigidity about Robertson's physical movements which gave an indication of his lack of mental suppleness and adaptability. He did not argue, he shrank from being involved in argument and he hated contention; one reason being that he was very sensitive about any challenge to his personal or official dignity in word or deed. When the Woolwich workers were making some trouble on a question of time or wages, Dr. Addison invited Sir William Robertson to address them on the urgency of their work. He thought that a few words from so distinguished a soldier might appease them. When, however, the two reached the hall they found it filled with a raging and noisy crowd who hurled questions at the visitors without respect to stars or stripes. The Chief of the Imperial Staff was offended at that kind of reception. He felt his dignity would be impaired by arguing with a tumult, so he declined to speak and left the meeting to Dr. Addison.

He rarely intervened in Council and I never heard him take much part in discussion with Allied generals. At these conferences between the soldiers and sailors of the Allies, Robertson usually sat at the table in gruff silence. His protests were frequent, but generally inarticulate. He thoroughly disapproved of Foch, Nivelle, Joffre, and Lyautey, but he never condescended to dispute with them. He seemed bored, if not overpowered by the voluble confidence of the French generals. When I attended the Rome Conference in 1917, M. Briand and General Lyautey, who was then Secretary of State for War in France, travelled by the same train. Late at night Lyautey sent for Sir William Robertson and myself to his saloon. He had a map of Palestine in front of him, and from this he proceeded to deliver a very lengthy lecture on the strategy of a campaign for the conquest of Jerusalem. Robertson never uttered a word of approval or dissent; he let out an occasional grunt, and when Lyautey had concluded his address, he turned to me and said: "Has he finished?" I told him I thought he had. We got up, and on our way back to the British carriage he said to me: "That fellow won't last long." Nor did he, for his demission ensued in a very few weeks.

Robertson's appearance gave no idea of the essential geniality and kindliness of the man. In repose his facial expression was sullen, if not rather morose; in conversation he melted and often became entertaining, so long as you did not venture on a topic on which he disagreed with you. In that case he found refuge in glumness.

He could be full of fun. I recollect returning from a visit to Paris with him and Lord Kitchener. In the train there was a good deal of pleasant chaff interchanged between us. Lord Kitchener was giving an account of his house down in Kent to which he was very attached. He complained, however, that there was no water in the particular valley in which he had built his residence, but it added to his grievance that there was plenty of water in the valleys on either side. Robertson said: "Then why don't you make a tunnel from one of these valleys to draw water into your own?" This idea amused the sapper.

Personally I was attracted by Robertson and would have liked to have been able to work with him to the very end. That is a story I must tell in later chapters.

CHAPTER XXVIII

TRANSPORT

SIR DOUGLAS HAIG once told Sir Eric Geddes that the problem of warfare consisted of "three M's": Men, Munitions, Movement. I tell elsewhere in this story the way men were supplied to our military authorities by civilian organisers, and the use or misuse that was made of them; I have shown how those same authorities proved unable to organise the production of their munitions, and had to remit this task to politicians and men of business. Now I have to show how the professional soldiers who fought so valiantly in the stricken area also found themselves unable to cope with the vast problem of Movement which this unprecedented war set before them, and how here again disaster was narrowly averted by the aid of the civilian expert. I am not arraigning the professional soldier, but only the supercilious folly miles behind the shell area which stigmatised all civilian aid in the construction or direction of the war machine as unwarranted interference by ignorant amateurs.

It is of course hardly surprising, when one recalls the gigantic scope of the transport problem—the millions of men with their equipment, baggage, horses, etc., which had to be moved to and from France and from one front to another; their colossal daily supplies of food, fodder, ammunition, tools, trench warfare supplies; medical and surgical stores and evacuation of wounded—that elderly officers who had reached seniority after years of service under the rather rigid conventions of a small army, and with no practical experience of traffic on a large and continuous scale, would not necessarily be competent to work out the best method of dealing with this vast tangle of unanticipated transport. It required an exceptional experience which they had never obtained, and exceptional organising ability which the process of their selection could not guarantee.

Quite early in the work of the Ministry of Munitions I encountered this failure of the military to organise unprecedented transport, and that no further away than within the walls of Woolwich Arsenal. When I took over Woolwich in August, 1915, and I put Mr. Vincent Raven in charge of it, he found himself responsible for a bewildering range of factories and departments, occupying an area of about $3\frac{1}{2}$ miles long by $2\frac{1}{2}$ miles wide, with about 150 miles of internal railway track for bringing in and distributing its supplies of raw material and evacuating its output. There was not enough rolling stock. The system was so confused that it was impossible to get the raw material into the Arsenal, to get the finished goods out, or to move stuff efficiently from place to place within the Arsenal itself. Traffic was hopelessly congested. He had to get a special expert in from one of the railway companies to take charge, and organise the system of transport. He speedily got things on to an efficient footing.

But the real crux of the transport problem was the connecting links between the French ports and the front line. On this side, the movement of goods and men in Britain, and their dispatch to the French coast, were organised by our own highly efficient railway chiefs and shipping services. Once landed in France, they came on the French railway system, and were badgered and disorganised by inexpert officers who were trying to wring from it services on a scale hitherto unconceived. As might have been expected, the result was confusion, congestion and delay.

While I was Minister of Munitions I sent Geddes over to France on one occasion, with the permission of the War Office, to look into some matter of the recovery and transport of salvage. The account he gave me on his return of the transport situation was so disquieting that I suggested to Lord Kitchener that he should be sent to make an investigation and report, with a view to its better organisation. But Lord Kitchener held the opinion that these were purely military matters, into the sanctity of which no profane civilian must be allowed to intrude. He was by this time suffering from that growing inertia and ossification of the mind which so gravely impaired his usefulness during his last months of office.

Shortly before I left the Ministry of Munitions it was reported to me from France that there was a shortage of ammunition. On enquiry I found that this was in no way due to failure on our part to produce it. In fact our munition factories were becoming choked up with completed output because the base depots in France were too congested to receive it.

On the day on which the death of Lord Kitchener was reported, Sir Eric Geddes, whose special work had been so much hampered by the failure in transport facilities, came to see me on the subject of transport. It appeared that in reply to a request from the War Office for an estimate as to output of artillery ammunition from 1st July onwards, the figure of 1,000,000 rounds per week had been given. Of the possibility of this production the War Office was frankly sceptical, and stated that even if it were produced it could not be conveyed either across the Channel or to the front owing to the congested state of the ports and roads, and that in any event the guns could not fire it. In view of the fact that the last advance estimate of the Ministry had been exactly fulfilled, and in view of all our efforts to produce

Q*

what the Army wanted, this attitude was, to say the least of it, some-what exasperating.

As soon as I became Secretary of State for War in July, 1916, I sent through Lord Derby, who was then my Under-Secretary, a request to Sir Douglas Haig that he should invite Sir Eric Geddes to go over and look into the matter of transport. But my suggestion was not favourably received. The day after I learnt this I was going over myself to France to visit the whole of the front from Verdun to Flanders. When I reached Paris I saw Lord Esher, who was located there in his usual post of general adviser to everybody and liaison officer between everybody and anybody—a most useful kind of person if he possesses tact, discernment, and experience. Lord Esher had these qualities in a superlative degree. He was a friendly and helpful personage with a great knowledge of military things and people. I told him all my misgivings about transport and Haig's polite snub to Derby. I said that I had sent Derby because I thought he was a special favourite of the Commander-in-Chief! He did not confirm that impression and said: "Go there yourself and talk quite frankly about the whole position. Talk to Haig himself about it and refuse to be referred to his staff. Your only difficulty will be that although Haig is not a good judge of men he stands by them with stubborn loyalty to all, whatever their quality. But if you can show him that essential supplies are being kept from his army during the progress of a great battle, he will listen and look into the matter." I took his advice, drove straight to G.H.Q. and stayed the night at Sir Douglas Haig's château. He received me with great cordiality, and gave me the usual sanguine estimate of the progress and prospects of the Somme offensive. Casualties were omitted from the narrative. When I approached him on the subject of transport I decided that it would be better not to discuss merits or details, but to ask him to see Sir Eric Geddes and afford him an opportunity for seeing the transport arrangements and reporting to him on their condition. To this suggestion he assented with alacrity, as it enabled him to get out of what might turn into a disagreeable discussion with the new Secretary of State for War. I was equally pleased because I felt assured that he would now treat the proposal for a change not as an arraignment of his organisation of the war front but as a method of helping him at a critical moment. With his agreement I wired Sir Eric Geddes an invitation to pay a visit to G.H.Q. and inspect transport arrange-ments.

Sir Eric went over and spent two days there. He was treated, need-less to say, with perfect courtesy. At the end of the time the Commander-in-Chief asked him if he had seen everything, and Geddes answered that he had seen enough to think about, but did not know what to think yet. He stayed a few days longer, but then had to tell Haig that he had been shown nothing which the ordinary distinguished tourist would not have been shown; and that what he wanted was a month, in which time he would analyse the problem and produce a report and programme.

Very fortunately, Sir Eric Geddes and Sir Douglas Haig had by this time taken warmly to each other. Sir Douglas later on stated that he " recognised in him the very qualities which the army in the field required." The upshot was that the Commander-in-Chief invited the railway expert to come and spend a month making a thorough investigation and evolving a programme for the transport system. Sir Eric went as a civilian, with a small expert civilian staff to assist him. There never was a more efficient group. He also took with him Sir George Beharrell and General Mance, D.D.M. at the War Office, whom I lent him for the purpose, and Sir Philip Nash, who with Beharrell had been working under Geddes in the Ministry of Munitions. In France he further added to his staff General Freeland, who was on the staff of the Director of Railways at G.H.Q. With these assistants he prepared a programme of transport improvement, including a light railway system for serving the forward areas behind the front line.

On Sir Eric's return I appointed him Director of Military Railways at the War Office. This brought me to my first conflict with the military members of the Army Council. The appointment had to be sanctioned by the Council. One of the generals sitting around the table, speaking obviously on behalf of the rest, protested against a civilian appointment which overrode or circumscribed the authority of experienced and respected generals already discharging these functions to everybody's satisfaction. I challenged this statement and submitted facts which proved serious confusion and congestion, from the ports to Amiens, at Amiens, and from Amiens to the front. Sir William Robertson sat glum during the discussions. Ultimately the appointment was sanctioned. The military members met and decided to send me a formal written protest. Immediately I received it I summoned another meeting of the Army Council and asked the protestors to state their case. The same spokesman repeated his arguments—the rest were silent and once more the appointment was confirmed. The following morning Sir John Cowans came to see me. He looked a little shy and embarrassed. He told me the military members of the Council had met and drawn up a document which they had asked him to present to me. He put on his great horn spectacles and drew a foolscap paper from his pocket. I stopped him and asked him whether it had anything to do with the Geddes appointment, and when he answered in the affirmative I told him that this matter was finally settled and I declined to re-open it. He smiled and said " I thought you would say so. This paper is therefore of no use." He then tore it up and laughed. Thus ended my first encounter with the military members. I got on much better with them afterwards.

No sooner had Geddes taken up his post than Sir Douglas Haig wired that he wanted Geddes to join his staff in France as Director-General of Transportation. This created a difficult situation, for I did not want to lose him, in view of the important transport reforms I wished him to inaugurate at the War Office, and Geddes himself was by no means eager to go to France, knowing as he did what bitter jealousy of the interloper would be felt by some of the staff officers who had hitherto had charge of transport there. However, General Butler, who had come over from the Commander-in-Chief as a special emissary to secure the services of Geddes in France, was so insistent and persuasive that we eventually made a compromise. It was agreed that Sir Eric should hold the two positions simultaneously; while remaining Director of Military Railways, he should also become Director-General of Transportation in France, and thus be in a position to place his railway experience and remarkable gifts of organisation alike at the service of the War Office and the Expeditionary Force. He had two experienced railway managers as deputies, Sir Guy Granet at the War Office and Sir Philip Nash at G.H.Q. in France.

There was the inevitable and anticipated disgruntlement in some quarters among the staff at G.H.Q. over this appointment. Certain indignant generals tendered their resignations. They started a rumour—only too readily believed in some quarters—that I was up to the politicians' trick of forcing unwanted civilians on the Army, and interfering with the military authorities.

To dispose finally of the suggestion that I exercised my authority to force Sir Douglas Haig to dismiss a competent military staff in order to substitute civilians who knew nothing of war conditions, I would like to quote a letter written to Sir Eric by the Commander-in-Chief: —

"General Headquarters of British
Army in France,
Friday, September 22, 1916.

My dear Geddes,
Butler has told me of his interview with you, and I am very pleased to think that you are prepared to join me here and help in beating the Germans for the good of the Empire.

I should be grateful if you would come over and see me in order that there may be no misunderstanding as to the conditions on which you are prepared to help.

After full consideration of the organisation which you proposed to me on your last visit, I am most willing and anxious that you should take over complete charge of Transportation services of the Army in France. That is to say that you would have under your control: —

(a) Broad gauge railways.
(b) Narrow gauge railways.
(c) Inland water transport.
(d) Roads.

and that whilst working under instructions from my Q.M.G. you will have direct access to me, and will be in the closest touch with me and my General Staff in order to know our plans so as to look ahead *in time* and provide for our future needs. . . .

Looking forward to seeing you,
Believe me,
Yours very truly,
D. HAIG."

The appointment also called forth the following exchange of letters between the Commander-in-Chief and myself: —

"War Office,
27th September, 1916.

My dear General,
Geddes has told me that you have asked him to become your Chief Executive Officer for Transportation in France. I had as you know already appointed him to a similar position in this country. I have told him that I would approve his undertaking complete responsibility for the work upon both sides of the Channel if you wish him to do so. The main thing, to my mind, is that he should be given a very free hand and the personal support of yourself and myself. If you decide to appoint him on your Staff I hope you will find it possible to make these conditions so far as France is concerned. I am doing so in England. He will have direct access to me and then I shall be able to take a close personal interest in supporting the full development of your transportation policy.

Yours sincerely,
D. LLOYD GEORGE.
General Sir Douglas Haig, G.C.B., etc."

The General's reply was as follows: —

"General Headquarters,
British Armies in France,
1st October, 1916.

My dear Mr. Lloyd George,
I thank you for your letter of the 27th September. I am writing officially to the War Office on the subject of Geddes' appointment, but reserving various details for further discussion here with my Quartermaster-General and Inspector-General of Communications.

It is my intention to give Geddes as free a hand as possible and to give him my personal support, but it is essential that changes shall be made gradually and without upsetting the existing organisation, which has done excellent work under very difficult conditions and has never failed me up to date.

Yours very truly,
D. HAIG."

Within a month Sir Eric had established his headquarters for the B.E.F. Transport at a little place three miles from Montreuil, called Monthouis, and before long destined to become famous under the soubriquet of " Geddesburg." From this centre Geddes organised the improved transport system which functioned so splendidly during the latter part of the War.

For a man of Sir Eric's railway experience the problem was not a very difficult one. It called chiefly for expert knowledge in the handling of traffic and the capacity to think on an adequate scale and then act promptly. The military transport authorities had been trying all along to " make do " with a totally insufficient transport system. The French railways in the area had been placed at their disposal, and over these and over French country roads, neither of which had been designed to bear a tithe of such weight and volume of traffic, they were trying to move their troops and stores. Naturally the machine broke down. There was an efficient service from depot or factory in Britain up to the French port. But the assembling yards behind the ports were the point of greatest weakness, having become a real bottle-neck which strangled the traffic flow. When the goods finally got past and on to the railheads, which were placed perhaps as much as fifteen miles behind the front line, they had to be conveyed forward this distance over broken-down roads which were simultaneously being used for movement of troops.

Putting experienced railway men in charge of the assembling yards helped to relieve the congestion there. But the first big innovation which Sir Eric undertook was the construction of light narrow-gauge railways in the forward areas to move supplies from the broad-gauge railheads up to the line. Till this time there were no light railways at all. He framed a programme for an eventual 1,000 miles of light railway with rolling-stock to correspond. The first stage in the execution of that programme involved an order for 1,000 miles of light steel rails, and one stormy autumn night I was awakened in the small hours at the Hotel Crillon, where I was staying during a visit to France, by a dispatch rider bringing Sir Eric's report setting out the proposal for this requisition. I read and initialled it, and it was rushed back to " Geddesburg " in time for Beharrell to fly with it to Boulogne and catch the 9 o'clock boat in the morning. He arrived in London and dismayed Sir Ernest Moir with the size of the requisition. But Sir Ernest duly produced the goods, and by June, 1917, the whole 1,000 miles of light railway were complete. The dimensions of the task may be judged when I say that the 1,000 miles of narrow-gauge track involved 60,000 tons of steel for rails and sleepers, apart from the requirements of rolling stock. I may add here that in the autumn of 1917 a further 900 miles of light railway were ordered, and that up to the end of the War the total length supplied reached well over 4,000 miles.

The congestion behind the ports in France could only be removed by increasing the capacity of the standard-gauge lines to clear the imported goods away. Sir Eric made arrangements with Sir Ernest Moir about the provision of supplies for this purpose.

At the end of November he put forward his programme for additional standard-gauge lines. Hitherto the Army had relied mainly on the existing French lines, and though in the two years 1915-16 Britain had supplied the French Government with over 150 locomotives and 2,300 tons of railway material for maintenance of its railways, very little had been done to supplement the existing system with any British military railway additions. Sir Eric's new programme was for 1,200 miles of standard-gauge line, 300 new large main-line locomotives, and about 9,000 wagons. Sir Douglas Haig backed this up by paying a personal visit to this country at the beginning of December, and on 12th December wrote asking for means to carry out large schemes of doubling lines and building new lines, connecting lines, depots and extensions.

When I say that 1,200 miles of standard-gauge track involved 160,000 tons of steel, or 6,000 tons a week for six months, it will be seen that Sir Eric was not afraid to "think big." The support accorded to him by the Commander-in-Chief shows also that he had taught G.H.Q. to share his outlook. By June, 1917, nearly all this huge order had been completed, and a requisition for a further 1,000 miles had been received.

With the expansion of the railways, the congestion at the ports was reduced. It was possible to clear the quays and speed up the discharge of cargoes when the bottle-neck beyond had been broadened.

The roads were another vital link in the transport system. They are, of course, the first requisite for organised military operations, a fact of which the Romans were well aware when they constructed their great military highways. Throughout the War the roads of France were subject to terrific strain, and in the forward area, before the light railways were constructed, they were the only means of movement for both troops and stores. Of course, they got knocked to pieces, and for some time no proper effort was made to keep them in repair.

Sir Eric Geddes made arrangements for the systematic repair and construction of roadways. The stone for them was mainly quarried in France. The work was done to a large extent by prisoners of war.

Before leaving the subject of roads, I should like to pay a tribute to the fine work which Sir Henry Maybury did in organising this branch of our transport facilities. On the formation of the Transportation Department at " Geddesburg," Sir Henry Maybury was brought over to take charge of the road construction work, the maintenance of the existing roads, and building of new ones, particularly where the front moved forward. The mobility of our road transport in the latter part of the War was due in a high degree to his efforts.*

Closely connected with the transport developments was the recruitment of the Chinese Auxiliary Corps by Sir Eric Geddes, who sent an officer to China to recruit 15,000 Chinese labourers for work in France, out of whom some 6,000 were required for work on the railways and 1,000 for inland water transport, the others being employed at various tasks on the road, railheads, dumps, etc.† They were immensely powerful fellows, and it was no uncommon spectacle to see one of the Chinese pick up a balk of timber or a bundle of corrugated iron

---

* To illustrate the dimensions of motor transport used by the Army, I quote the following figures showing the total numbers of mechanical transport vehicles acquired by the War Office from the outbreak of War to 1st September, 1916, and the numbers supplied by the Ministry of Munitions between the latter date and the end of December, 1918 : —

(a) Lorries: heavy and light:

Acquired by War Office from every source before 1/9/16	21,705	
Supplied by M. of M. from 1/9/16 to Dec., 1918	37,785	
Total		59,490

(b) Cars, vans and ambulances:

Acquired by War Office, etc.	9,630	
Supplied by M. of M., etc.	24,170	
Total		33,800

(c) Steam wagons:

Acquired by War Office, etc.	440	
Supplied by M. of M., etc.	714	
Total		1,154

(d) Tractors:

Acquired by War Office, etc.	936	
Supplied by M. of M., etc.	2,505	
Total		3,441

(e) Motor cycles:

Acquired by War Office, etc.	18,750	
Supplied by M. of M., etc.	22,300	
Total		41,050

* These figures are, of course, exclusive of the motor vehicles supplied to our Allies.

† I am told that when I was asked to sanction the recruitment of "Chinese labour" for the British Army in France, I replied, "For Heaven's sake don't give it that name. What about Chinese Auxiliary Corps?" The former appellation would have recalled an unpleasant political controversy still fresh in party memory on both sides.

sheets weighing three or four hundredweight, and walk off with it as calmly as if it weighed only as many stone!

At times, of course, these Chinese coolies came under aerial bombing or long-distance shelling. That did not greatly perturb them; they were far less nervous under fire than the British West Indian Auxiliaries, who were similarly engaged on Labour Corps duties. But it tended to disorganise their work in another way, because if they suffered any fatal casualties, they would all break off work to attend the funeral, and neither threats nor cajolery had the least effect on them, nor would bombing or shelling by the enemy scatter their cortège, until the obsequies had been duly completed.

The whole story of British achievement in the sphere of transport during the War has never yet been told. It would be well worth telling in detail, and would reflect very high credit on those who were responsible for its development, most of all on Sir Eric Geddes. The following extracts from Sir Douglas Haig's final dispatch, while they exhibit some remarkable reticences about certain points in the story, pay a merited tribute to the "civilian experts" whose advice I persuaded him to consider in 1916:—

"The successful co-ordination and economic use of all the various kinds of transportation requires most systematic management, based on deep thought and previous experience. So great was the work entailed in the handling of the vast quantities, of which some few examples are given above, so complex did the machinery of transport become and so important was it that the highest state of efficiency should be maintained, that in the autumn of 1916 *I was forced to adopt an entirely new system for running our lines of communication.** The appointment of Inspector-General of Communications was abolished, and the services previously directed by that officer were brought under the immediate control of the Adjutant-General, the Quartermaster-General, and the Director-General of Transportation. The last-mentioned was a new office created with a separate staff composed for the greater part of civilian experts to deal specifically with transportation questions. . . .

The Director-General of Transportation's branch was formed under the brilliant direction of Major-General Sir Eric Geddes during the autumn of 1916, as above stated. To the large number of skilled and experienced civilians included by him on his staff, drawn from the railway companies of Great Britain and the Dominions, the Army is deeply indebted for the general excellence of our transportation services."

* My italics. D. Ll. G.

CHAPTER XXIX

THE MESOPOTAMIA MUDDLE

THERE are three reasons why I incorporate a chapter on the Mesopotamia scandal in my reminiscences of the War. One is that I
opposed the initiation of the campaign. I quote the following minute
from the War Council held on February 24th, 1915: —

> " Mr. Lloyd George suggested that the Mesopotamia Expedition
> was merely a side issue. The Turks knew how far-reaching the
> effects of a disaster there would be and would spare no efforts to
> bring it about. The Mesopotamia force ought, in his opinion, to
> be withdrawn and concentrated on the Dardanelles."

The second is that when I became Secretary for War on 6th July,
1916, the first urgent task which I found awaiting my attention was
the problem of dealing with the mess and muddle of the British
Expedition to Mesopotamia. My last reason for telling it as part of
my War story is that it is a perfect example of what military administration is capable of if entirely freed from civilian " interference."
It was an ideal professional soldiers' campaign lacking even a
minimum of supervision from the meddlesome politician. Tradition
places the Garden of Eden in the land between the Euphrates and the
Tigris. In this blissful enclosure there reappeared in 1916 the
Paradise of the Brass Hat. He reigned alone in unfettered and unrestricted sway over this garden for nearly two years. There was no
serpent or consort to mislead or meddle with him. Where there were
any politicians roaming about they were as meek as any beast in the
ancient Garden. He ran his Eden alone. Let us see what kind of a
Paradise he produced.

It is a gruesome story of tragedy and suffering resulting from incompetence and slovenly carelessness on the part of the responsible
military authorities. Attempts had been made to smother up the
story through a campaign of secrecy and deliberate misrepresentation,
but despite these efforts enough had leaked out early in 1916 to make
it clear that strong action on the part of the Home Government was
demanded.

The history of the expedition up to that date can be briefly outlined
as follows. Towards the close of September, 1914, it became evident
that Turkey was likely to join the enemy powers. This made it at
once important to take steps for safeguarding the oil supplies in the

Persian Gulf, which were owned by the Anglo-Persian Oil Company, a concern in which the Government had become large shareholders as a means of ensuring supplies of oil fuel for the Navy.

Troops were at the time being dispatched from India to France, and the Imperial Government—through Lord Crewe, who was then Secretary of State for India—arranged with the Government of India for one brigade to be diverted to the Persian Gulf, to occupy the island of Abadan at the mouth of the Euphrates, and protect the oil tanks and pipe-lines. This force was duly sent, and landed on 23rd October, 1914.

Within a fortnight after this, on 5th November, 1914, war was declared on Turkey. Thereupon two fresh brigades were dispatched to Mesopotamia, and on 22nd November the town of Basra was captured and occupied. Basra was the seaport of Mesopotamia, and was on the west bank of the Shatt-el-Arab (the wide joint stream of the Tigris and Euphrates) about 70 miles up river from the open sea.

This expedition, though sent by arrangement with the British Government at home, and subject to the general agreement whereby all expenses of the Indian Expeditionary Forces beyond their ordinary cost of maintenance should be borne by Imperial Funds, was in respect of its administration under the sole control and responsibility of the Indian Army authorities.

Under threat of Turkish attacks, the Indian Government reluctantly sent another brigade in February, and when the danger to the force grew more acute they were peremptorily ordered in March to send a fourth. Meantime the expedition had extended its area in December by capturing the town of Kurna, where the Tigris and Euphrates join, 50 miles above Basra. It had thus occupied the whole length of the Shatt-el-Arab.

The Indian Government decided on 1st April, without obtaining the consent of the India Office at home, to organise the expedition as an army corps. They sent two more brigades to complete a second division, and appointed General Nixon to be Commander-in-Chief of the force. He was instructed to make plans for occupying the whole of the Basra Vilayet, and eventually advancing on Baghdad.

The oil-field lay to the east of the Shatt-el-Arab, up a tributary, the River Karun, and the pipeline ran down its left bank to the island of Abadan. On 19th April the Home Government asked the force to move against the Turks in this region. General Nixon asked on the same day for more forces, which were refused by India. The Home Government concurred, and added a warning against extensive operations, saying, "Any proposal involving possible demands for reinforcements of undue extension is to be deprecated. . . . Our present position is strategically a sound one and we cannot at present afford to take risks by extending it unduly. In Mesopotamia a safe game must be played."

General Nixon then sent part of his force, under General Gorringe, up the Karun river, and the other part under General Townshend, to capture Amara, 90 miles up the Tigris, getting a last-minute sanction from the British Government. Both operations were successful, and on 3rd June Amara was taken. Then, in boiling heat, an advance was made up the Euphrates to Nasariyeh, 68 miles beyond Kurna. The Indian Government now became eager for more progress, and got the consent of Sir Austen Chamberlain, who was then Indian Secretary, for Townshend to advance on Kut, 150 miles up the Tigris beyond Amara. Kut-el-Amara was entered after severe fighting on 29th September, 1915.

In November, 1914, the idea of an eventual advance on Baghdad had been turned down both by the India Office and by the Viceroy of India, who gave strong reasons against it. But subsequent successes had led the Indian Government to favour the project, and they sought permission from the Home Government for General Nixon to carry out his plan for this advance. On 6th October, 1915, it was definitely vetoed by Sir Austen Chamberlain, but later he relented to the point of saying that if the General Staff approved and thought the operation feasible, with the aid of two fresh divisions which might presently be placed at the disposal of the Mesopotamian force, the India Office would be prepared to consider it. The Indian General Staff, also after some hesitation, agreed that with two fresh divisions Baghdad could be taken and held. In the end General Nixon told General Townshend to go ahead and capture Baghdad with the tired men he had at his disposal, on the strength of the hope that presently another two divisions would arrive in Mesopotamia.

Townshend advanced as far as Ctesiphon, a few miles from Baghdad, where he found the enemy strongly entrenched, and numerically equal or superior to his own exhausted troops. After a fierce fight the British forces retired, and had to retreat down the river, compelled by lack of supplies and medical accommodation for casualties, and fighting a series of rearguard actions till they reached Kut, which they prepared to hold until relieved and reinforced by the further troops which were expected. More than 30 per cent. of the force had been killed or wounded.

General Townshend reached Kut on 3rd December, where he was told by the military authorities to defend himself till relieved. By 7th December the town was fully invested by the Turks. After suffering severely in attempts to take it by storm they settled down to beleaguer it.

The remainder of the British forces hastily improvised efforts to relieve the town. They were reinforced by the two promised divisions from France. These were Indian divisions, already severely punished in the French fighting, and they arrived piecemeal during December at Basra, where 12,000 troops were immobilised through lack of transport to take them to the front. The attempts of the Tigris force to relieve General Townshend were heavily defeated. They made some progress in their attacks on the beleaguering lines, but owing to lack of reinforcements they abandoned the attempt to break through. Ultimately, on 29th April, 1916, after having gallantly defended the town for 147 days, Townshend's brave men were starved into surrender.

Long before this tragic climax, it had become clear that the expedition was being hopelessly mismanaged in some way or other, and early in February, 1916, the War Office took charge of the expedition. The forces there were, however, parts of the Indian Army, and immediately under the Indian General Staff in Simla. It was not until July, 1916, when I went to the War Office, that the administration of matters connected with the expedition was transferred to the control of the Home Government.

This transfer was my first step towards clearing up the muddle. My second was to promote the appointment of a Commission to make an investigation into the muddle and its causes. This Commission was set up in August, 1916, and issued its report on 17th May, 1917. The report was signed by seven of the eight Commissioners, while Commander J. Wedgwood put in a separate report, substantially agreeing with the other, but emphasising more forcibly certain aspects of the blunders and errors which had been committed, particularly by the Viceroy and Commander-in-Chief in India.

The facts revealed by this Commission's report cast a baleful light upon the mismanagement, stupidity, criminal neglect and amazing incompetence of the military authorities who were responsible for the organisation of the expedition, and on the horrible and unnecessary suffering of the gallant men who were sent to failure and defeat through the blunders of those in charge.

The General Staff in India knew perfectly well the nature of the country to which the force was being sent, and the kind of equipment which would obviously need to be supplied to it. Mesopotamia is a flat, alluvial tract, largely covered by floods in the wet season, while in the summer the rivers dwindled to very shallow streams. There are no proper roads, and water transport was the principal means of moving either men or supplies. It is a country of torrid heat in summer, though the nights throughout a considerable part of the year are cold, and during the winter and spring the country is subject to cold winds and icy storms. It was a primitive and backward country, some distance by sea from the nearest civilised base.

Obviously, therefore, the first essential for sending any expedition to Mesopotamia was to ensure that it was very well found; that it had an ample supply of suitable river boats for its transports; that clothing and food should be suited to the conditions of the country; that medical equipment, especially for the wounded and the sick, should be above the average, to meet the dangers of a sterile and disease-ridden land; that provision was made for establishing a well-equipped base at the port of Basra; and that arrangements for reinforcements should be carefully planned and promptly executed.

Every single one of these obvious duties was not merely done badly, but left undone to the point of incredibility. In the opening months of the War the Indian Government showed an extraordinary tardiness in rendering any help at all to the Empire in its struggle. Only under strong pressure would it send a single soldier to the front, and despite its enormous population it declared itself incapable of recruiting substantial additional forces. It would not spend an extra pice on the War; indeed, in the Budget debate of March, 1915, at Simla, a member boasted that although it was a War Budget, military expenditure had not been increased, and was, in fact, below the original estimate. The Indian troops which came to France came under the control of the British authorities; but those which were sent to Mesopotamia were entirely in the hands of the reluctant and parsimonious authorities at Simla, and were stinted and starved of every kind of equipment and support. " Every general who appeared before us agreed," said the Commissioners, " that the Mesopotamia Expedition was badly equipped."

It was short of artillery, particularly of heavy guns. The Indian Military Authorities do not appear to have thought of asking for any. It was not till December, 1915, when the ill-starred attack on Baghdad had been already attempted and failed, and General Townshend was beleaguered in Kut, that the first request was received for heavy guns for Mesopotamia, and not till 26th May, 1916, that India sent a definite statement of its requirements for these weapons.

Even as late as the spring of 1916 the expedition was deficient in many things which India could have supplied, such as wire-cutters, rockets, Véry lights, water-carts, tents, mosquito nets, sun-helmets, bombs, medical supplies, and even blankets and clothing. The Commander-in-Chief in India excused himself before the Commission by saying that some of these articles had not been heard of before the War, at least in India. But they had not been supplied to this expedition when the War had been in progress 18 months. Even the Turks were using Véry lights in Mesopotamia before our troops had any.

Despite the severities of the weather at certain seasons, the military authorities proposed at first to leave the provision of warm clothing for the troops entirely to private benevolence, sending them out with nothing but " shorts " and tropical clothing. The Viceroy himself protested against this.

There were no aeroplanes at all for the first six months, though the need for them in that wide, roadless land was obvious. For this failure the authorities at home must share the blame.

But it is when we come to the question of river transport that the blundering and incompetence of the military authorities is seen in its full functioning. So long as the expedition was confined in its objectives to the original landing on the island of Abadan, or the port of Basra, it was mainly dependent on ocean-going transport. But from the moment when, in December, 1914, it advanced, with the approval of the authorities at Simla, up river to Kurna, special river transport became a vital necessity, and with each further advance, which lengthened the line up the river, the need for transport vessels increased.

As early as 23rd November, 1914, after the capture of Basra, General Barrett was advised by Commander Hamilton, R.I.M., who knew the Tigris intimately, to apply at once for 12 special steamers, as they would have to be built to an unusual pattern, and would take 12 months to construct. But the General and his staff did not think the matter urgent, and did nothing about it till in January they were asked by India what further transport they needed. He then asked for seven steamers and two lighters. In February he asked for four tugs. These were obtained in India in March, and sent out; but when in May General Nixon took over, he found that they were useless for the hot weather, when the river ran low. He asked for vessels drawing not more than 3 feet or 3 feet 6 inches.

After delays in India, this request was ultimately incorporated in a requisition telegraphed to the India Office on 4th August, 1915. Nothing was done till confirmation in writing turned up in September. Then the officials at the India Office made inquiry of the firm recommended to them for this work, but rather than pay them a commission amounting to one-third of one per cent. for supervising the execution of the order they turned to their expert naval architect, who without special knowledge of the conditions of the Tigris, proceeded to secure them the building of vessels differing in a number of respects from the type ordered—vessels which were sent out in sections between April and December, 1916. It may be briefly stated that on account of the alterations of the pattern these boats were useless for the purpose of up-river transport; that the fact that they had to be assembled at Basra meant considerable further delay after they reached Mesopotamia; and that owing to lack of facilities for shipbuilding at Basra, and the large size of some of the sections, they were very difficult to handle—particularly as no drawings, descriptions or instructions came with them. Some sections sank in 30 feet of water, and the rest had to be towed to Bombay to be erected there. The Commission remarks:—

"More inept proceedings than those connected with the purchase and shipment of river craft in England in 1915 and early in 1916 would be hard to find."

When in October, 1915, General Nixon learnt that the paddle-steamers wanted would take a year to build he asked for stop-gap boats from India. The Indian authorities replied as they had done previously in June, that no suitable tugs were available. A month later they admitted that there were 13 available. The Commission gives a picture of the circumlocution and red tape which created the long delays before any request from Mesopotamia got even a negative reply. "Correspondence was usually conducted between the G.O.C. in Mesopotamia and the Chief of the Staff in Simla or Delhi. From the latter officer, anything about river craft would be transmitted to the Quartermaster-General, who would thereafter communicate what he thought necessary to Captain Lumsden, R.N., the Director of the Royal Indian Marine at Bombay." How that officer spent his time is thus described by the Commission: —

> "The Director of the Royal Indian Marine was not granted—at any rate did not exercise—any initiative in maritime or nautical matters. . . . The time of the Director and Senior Officers of the Indian Marine is much taken up with mere office or desk work. The amount of writing which they have to get through—or at all events do get through—can only be described as enormous. . . . The Director of the Royal Indian Marine gave to the Commission a list of the duties, the discharge of which he considered rendered it impossible for him to visit Mesopotamia and see for himself the actual state of things there. Most of the duties specified required neither maritime experience nor nautical knowledge, and could have been performed by any alert business man, even though he may never have been on blue water in his life."

The report, in fact, makes several references to the fact that the Indian officials never went to look at things for themselves, and when they were told of conditions, refused to pay attention to the reports. Worse, they blankly misreported the facts. "So much out of touch was Simla with the actual situation in Mesopotamia that we find the Indian General Staff, in 'appreciations' in June and September, 1915, definitely stating that the expedition was well supplied with river craft, and using this among their arguments for the advance to Baghdad."

The lack of river transport up to the spring of 1916 was a direct cause of the failure of military operations carried out by the troops with the utmost bravery. On account of the shortage it took nearly two months to concentrate troops and supplies for the advance from Amara to Kut, and the advance to Baghdad was fatally delayed through the same cause. It seems almost certain that, but for the shortage of river transport, the Turkish Army would have been destroyed between Amara and Ctesiphon; and the evidence shows conclusively, according to the Commission, that shortage of river transport was the chief cause of the failure to relieve Kut.

Since the vital importance of such transport was clearly understood both in India and at home, it is natural to ask what on earth possessed the military authorities to allow the advance up the Tigris in face of the shortage. The report of the Commission brings out that General Nixon, the commander on the spot, when he found the Indian authorities unable or unwilling to provide the needed transport, was optimistically ready to try his luck with what he had; and the Indian authorities themselves, having failed to provide what they must have known was necessary, made no effort to impress the gravity of the shortage on the India Office at home. This Office was allowed to get the impression that all was well, an impression perpetuated by a typically official incident. General Nixon's appeal for more vessels, sent to the India Office by the Indian Government, was not laid before the Secretary of State. The Military Branch of the India Office sent it on to the Stores Branch as an indent; and though it was forwarded to the War Office, no letter was sent drawing attention to the shortage of transport it revealed. Thus military officials both in India and in London suppressed or ignored facts which, had they been known by either the War Council or the Cabinet, would have prevented the granting of consent to the ill-fated advance on Baghdad.

Allied to the failure to furnish river transport was the neglect to develop wharfage and storage facilities at Basra.

The boats available had their usefulness heavily reduced through this failure. General Gorringe stated that "no improvement in the unloading wharves for ships was made until December, 1915 . . . although the accommodation was bad and congested for stores of every kind being unloaded." To the physical drawbacks was added the incompetence of the military officials. The Commission reports that delays to steamers were at first occasioned, not so much by inability to get cargoes out into lighters, as by inability or unwillingness of the military departments ashore to receive it rapidly.

"It is clear that management of the traffic of a port and discharge of cargo was not work to which officers of the Royal Indian Marine had previously been accustomed. . . . Men with these qualifications were known to be employed in one or other of the great Indian and Burmese river ports. Their advice was not asked for; and their assistance was not utilised until more than a year after the landing of the expedition in Mesopotamia when conditions in Basra had become serious."

In January, 1916, the Indian Government at last sent an expert civilian, Sir George Buchanan, formerly in charge of the Port of Rangoon, to become Director-General of Basra and reorganise its traffic and facilities. Characteristically, they omitted to define his status and duties; and General Nixon proceeded to limit and circumscribe these in such a way that Sir George Buchanan found it impossible to carry on, and soon returned to India. In his report to Simla he said: —

> " I found it difficult to realise that we had been in occupation of Basra for a year, as the arrangements for the landing and storing of goods of every description were of the most primitive order, and in the absence of roads, the whole area was a huge quagmire. To a newcomer appearances were such that troops and stores might have been landed, for the first time, the previous week. . . . The military expedition to Basra is, I believe, unique, inasmuch as in no previous case has such an enormous force been landed and maintained without an adequately prepared base."

But if the neglect of transport by the military authorities was directly responsible for the failure and defeat of the expedition, their neglect of medical equipment turned disaster into horror.

Tales of the atrocities resulting from inadequate provision for the wounded and sick were so widespread that even Sir Beauchamp Duff, the Commander-in-Chief of the Army in India, felt himself compelled in March, 1916, to set up a Commission to inquire into the matter. Their report was, however, such a sickening exposure of official negligence and incompetence that the Indian Government would not publish it. The Mesopotamia Commission appointed by the Home Government had this report before them, and published it as an appendix to their own report. It was known as the " Vincent-Bingley " Report, as Sir William Vincent and General Bingley were the chief members responsible for it.

The evidence of both reports is that the expedition was systematically starved by the Indian military authorities in regard to every vital medical provision, and that protests were stifled and outside offers of help refused.

The standard of the Indian Army in this respect was low to begin with. A witness from the Indian Medical Service told the Commission: " I doubt whether you gentlemen would consider that the Sepoys' Hospitals in peace-time India are hospitals at all." Sir Alfred Keogh, Director-General of Army Medical Services at the War Office, said: —

> " I have no hesitation whatever in saying that the medical arrangements connected with the Army in India have been for years and years most disgraceful. . . . Anything more disgraceful than the carelessness and want of attention with regard to the sick soldier in India it is impossible to imagine."

But if things in India were bad, they were far worse in Mesopotamia. The expedition was sent out with a medical establishment, even according to its organisation orders, lower than that laid down for a frontier campaign; and " the actual amount of medical personnel in Mesopotamia was during long periods far below even this meagre scale."

There was at times a serious shortage of essential drugs. Necessary appliances for the hospitals were scanty or altogether lacking. Often there was no ice. For months there were no electric fans. There were not enough bandages, blankets, bed-pans, and splints. Even when the wounded got to the military hospital at Bombay it was to find there an appalling state of neglect—no X-ray apparatus, a lack of splints and surgical appliances, a shortage of doctors, surgeons, nurses, and attendants.

The doctors and ambulance staffs with the expedition performed miracles of heroic work, but there were very few of them. At the first battle of Kut some of the fighting units were without stretcher bearers, and wounded men were left on the field of battle all night, some of them being stripped, mutilated, and killed by the Arabs.

No wheeled transport for seriously wounded cases was sent out. Instead, a number of riding mules were supplied! The Commissioners say: " We have no evidence that these riding mules were ever used by the wounded, though their presence on one occasion in a very restive state is recorded by a witness. They are obviously useless for serious cases."

In default of wheeled ambulances, the medical officers were forced to move the more seriously wounded in springless army transport carts, drawn by mules, ponies, or bullocks. The A.D.M.S., 3rd Division, said that this cart, "which is without springs, has no cover to give protection against rain or the direct rays of the sun; and the bottom of which consists of bars of iron which, even when liberally covered with mattresses or other padding, renders the placing of a wounded man, especially cases of fracture, in such a conveyance, a practice which can only be designated as barbarous and cruel."

In some cases, we learn, dead bodies were used as cushions on these carts, in default of any other means of padding them.

But it is when we come to the transport of wounded and sick men down the river to Basra that the story reaches its culminating horror. There were no river steamers at all fitted as medical transports, nor any personnel to attend to casualties on the journey. Use had to be made of the scanty river transport employed in bringing men, stores and animals up stream, and as congestion grew it became impossible to clean or disinfect these boats in any way before sending the wounded, thickly packed, in them, down to Basra, and detailing from the scanty and overworked field ambulance staffs a few men to accompany them—too few to give proper attention or even to feed them.

" Wounds which required dressing and re-dressing were not attended to, and the condition of many of the patients who travelled by these steamers was, when they reached Basra, deplorable. There the wounds of many were found to be in a septic condition, and in urgent need of re-dressing. In some cases bed sores had developed, more than one patient arrived soaked in fæces and urine, and in a few cases wounds were found to contain maggots."

The Commission quote a description, by Major Carter, I.M.S., which I cannot repeat without apologising for its repulsive horror, of how the wounded, after Ctesiphon, arrived in Basra. Yet it is necessary for us to face frankly the record of what actually happened to a number of valiant men who fought for Britain and her Empire in the Great War. Our soldiers had not merely to read of, but to suffer this. Here is the account : —

" I was standing on the bridge [of the hospital ship *Varela* from Bombay] in the evening when the *Medjidieh* arrived. She had two steel barges without any protection against the rain, as far as I can remember. As this ship with two barges came up to us I saw that she was absolutely packed, and the barges too, with men. The barges were slipped, and the *Medjidieh* was brought alongside the *Varela*. When she was about 300 or 400 yards off it looked as if she was festooned with ropes. The stench when she was close was quite definite, and I found that what I mistook for ropes were dried stalactites of human fæces. The patients were so huddled and crowded together in the ship that they could not perform the offices of nature clear of the edge of the ship, and the whole of the ship's side was covered with stalactites of human fæces. This is what I then saw. A certain number of men were standing and kneeling on the immediate perimeter of the ship. Then we found a mass of men huddled up anyhow—some with blankets and some without. They were lying in a pool of dysentery about 30 feet square. They were covered with dysentery and dejecta generally from head to foot. With regard to the first man I examined . . . . [I omit a still more terrible passage of the description] . . . . The man had a fractured thigh, and his thigh was perforated in five or six places. He had apparently been writhing about on the deck of the ship. Many cases were almost as bad. There were a certain number of cases of terribly bad bed sores. In my report I describe mercilessly to the Government of India how I found men with their limbs splinted with wood strips from ' Johnny Walker' whisky boxes, ' Bhoosa' wire, and that sort of thing."

" Were they British or Indian?"

" British and Indian mixed."

This state of affairs was thus described by the G.O.C. of the expedition : —

" Wounded satisfactorily disposed of. Many likely to recover in country comfortably placed in hospitals at Amara and Basra. Those for invaliding are being placed direct on two hospital ships that were ready at Basra on arrival of river boats. General condition of wounded very satisfactory. Medical arrangements under circumstances of considerable difficulty worked splendidly."

What about Major Carter's report to the Indian military authorities? The Commission gives the following account of its reception: —" He [Major Carter] was treated with great rudeness. Surgeon-General Hathaway, in writing to the D.M.S. in India on this subject, says: 'The Army Commander, realising the injustice, ordered the D.A. and Q.M.G. and myself to deal with him [Major Carter] with reference to his objectionable remarks.' And General Cowper, then D.A. and Q.M.G., told us: ' I threatened to put him under arrest, and I said that I would get his hospital ship taken away from him for a meddlesome, interfering faddist.' " General Cowper was passing on treatment he had himself received, for the Commander-in-Chief in India, Sir Beauchamp Duff, had threatened to dismiss him for sending to India too insistent demands as to the need for River Transport.

Not only would the authorities do nothing themselves; they would let no one do anything to help them. On 11th August, 1915, the Secretary for India wired the Viceroy with an offer from the Lord-Lieutenant of Hampshire to raise funds for the sick and wounded soldiers in Mesopotamia, and send out doctors, nurses, medicines, and hospital comforts. After consulting the Commander-in-Chief, the Viceroy answered that money was ample and sufficient for supplying comforts for sick and wounded in Mesopotamia and in India; that everything necessary was being done, and that his Government had arranged for doctors and nurses. Electric fans were offered by the Madras Fund in December, 1914, for installation in the hospitals at Basra, but by the middle of 1915 none had been actually installed. The British Red Cross Society cabled General Nixon to accept two petrol-driven motor-launches. The offer was repeated on 28th December, and the reply was: —

" Nothing required at present. If anything needed in future will not hesitate to ask you."

This was just after the total breakdown of medical services following the battle of Ctesiphon.

I need not particularise further the failures of the military authorities to deal with other medical and sanitary issues; the insufficient and inappropriate food they supplied, which led by 1915 to an outbreak of scurvy among the troops, and a much more serious outbreak the following spring; the neglect of water supply, so that the troops were reduced to drinking from the nearest river, and an

outbreak of cholera resulted.   The report of the Commission makes
it clear that on every hand there was utter failure to make the most
elementary provision for the obvious needs of the expedition.   In
their " Findings," they remark: —

> " Looking at the facts, which from the first must have been
> apparent to any administrator, military or civilian, who gave a few
> minutes' consideration to the map and to the conditions in
> Mesopotamia, the want of foresight and provision for the most
> fundamental needs of the expedition reflects discredit upon the
> organising aptitude of all the authorities concerned."

I need not refer to the way in which the military authorities in India
starved the expedition of drafts and reinforcements—although they
were in charge of a country of 315,000,000 people, of whom 50,000,000
belonged to fighting races.   But one amazing incident deserves mention.   When in October, 1915, the advance on Baghdad was in
prospect, and the need for reinforcements to support the force there
was urgent, the Imperial Authorities asked the Indian Government
to provide a division temporarily, as the two divisions from France
might not get there in time.   "With the intention of evading this
liability," says the Report, "the Indian Government resorted to procedure which, to say the least of it, was disingenuous."   There were,
in fact, certain artillery batteries, cavalry regiments, and infantry
brigades which could be spared in India, but the Home Government
was not informed of this, and the reason given in a minute from the
Military Secretary of Sir Beauchamp Duff to the Viceroy's Military
Secretary ran as follows: —

> ". . . It is proposed by the Chief that the force he has named
> should be assembled . . . for eventualities, but that the Home
> Government should not be informed of this. . . . The Home
> Government are very anxious that Baghdad should be taken, and
> they will send us the required force if we hold out, but they will
> give us nothing if the least sign of willingness to find reinforcements
> is shown by us."

So the Viceroy cabled on 17th October: —

> ". . . In no case could I undertake to supply from India, even
> temporarily, a further force of the strength of a division."

The Indian Government, as Commander Wedgwood remarks,
" held out " while Serbia was being overrun, and while our last man
was being put in at Loos.

It is hardly necessary to add that the Commission passed severe
censures upon the Commander-in-Chief in India, Sir Beauchamp
Duff, and the Viceroy, Lord Hardinge; on the Surgeon-General, the
Director of Medical Services, the Indian Marine, and the Commanding Officer in Mesopotamia, General Nixon.   It further condemned

the whole military system of administration as " cumbrous and inept " and recommended its drastic reform.

When I was appointed Secretary of State for War in July, 1916, my first task was to take in hand the Mesopotamian situation. The most urgent call was for improved transport and medical arrangements. It was my good fortune to secure the assistance of the Q.M.G., Sir John Cowans, a man whom I have always considered to be the most capable soldier thrown up by the War in our Army. I shall never forget the quiet efficiency with which he detailed the steps that he thought should be taken. He had no hesitation in utilising experienced civilian assistance and some of the ablest of his transport officers in the Barge department were promoted civilians. All that could be done from this end was put in hand and pressed through without delay and there were no further scandals in the administration of the Mesopotamian Army.

The Commission also stated that " it was not until London took over the sole charge that there was any marked improvement in the management of the campaign. The improvement and success since effected are a striking illustration of the all-importance of unity of control in time of war." A number of references are made through the report to the better state of things which had supervened since July, 1916.

I feel that I cannot conclude this rather gruesome chapter without quoting a first-rate example of official circumlocution. It might serve a useful purpose to insert it here as a warning.

The Report of the Mesopotamian Commission gives a graphic description of the cumbrous procedure and circumlocution which at that time hedged round any proposal to make provision for the needs of the Army. It was supplied by Mr. Brunyate, Financial Secretary to the Indian Government, and for some years Financial Adviser to the Commander-in-Chief and Military Member of Council. When asked to give a concrete case of how a paper relating to a proposal for army equipment would pass through the two departments, he replied : —

" The Quartermaster-General, it may be supposed, wishes to have more mules. Probably before putting forward the proposal at all he sees the Commander-in-Chief personally as Commander-in-Chief and ascertains from him that he is willing to have that proposal ventilated. He then writes a note stating his facts, probably supported by a note from the Director of the Army Remount Department, makes a definite recommendation, estimates the cost, and marks his note to the Army Department of the Government of India. The office clerks of the Army Department note on the case, the Assistant Secretary notes, the Deputy Secretary may note, and it reaches the Army Secretary—we will call him General Holloway, though he is not actually Army Secretary now. He criticises the proposal if he thinks fit . . . the office of the Financial Adviser then note upon it . . . the clerks in the Finance Adviser's office note, the Assistant or Deputy Financial Adviser notes, now Mr. Fell. Mr. Fell may be prepared at once to accept the proposal on behalf of the Finance Department, and may intimate that he does not intend to refer it to the Finance Member. The file then goes back to the Army Secretary, and in that case he at once arranges for the necessary orders to be issued to give effect to the Quartermaster-General's proposal, unless he thinks the case of sufficient importance to refer it to the Army Member.

Such reference will, of course, practically always be required if the proposal is one requiring the sanction of the Secretary of State. In that case the Army Secretary would take the Army Member's orders at this stage, and a dispatch to the Secretary of State would then be drafted in the Army Department. . . . Or again, Mr. Fell, when the case first reached him, might have criticised the proposal, and indicated a desire to see it modified or rejected. In that case the file would still go back to the Army Secretary, and he would doubtless at that stage take the orders of the Army Member unless before doing so he wished to have the opinion of the Quartermaster-General on the criticisms and suggestions which had been made in the military finance branch. Mr. Fell, when criticising the proposal, would probably have indicated whether he intended to refer the case eventually to the Finance Member. Thus when the Army Secretary brought these criticisms before the Army Member, the latter would know that if he decided to override the Financial Adviser's criticisms, he might have to face opposition from the Finance Member. The Army Member would then pass his orders. If he adhered to the scheme as put forward by the Quartermaster-General and the Army Department he would record a note to that effect. The file would then go back to the Financial Adviser, and the latter would not note again, but would submit the case to the Finance Member. If the Finance Member decided not to press the objections raised by Mr. Fell, the proposal would become a fully accepted proposal, and orders would be issued for putting it into effect. If, however, the Finance Member definitely objected to the scheme, the case would then go back to Mr. Fell for return to the Army Secretary for re-submission to the Army Member. The Army Member might then defer to the Finance Member's objection, in which case the whole proposal would be dropped with the Army Member's concurrence, though a reluctant concurrence. If, however, the Army Member, in spite of the Finance Member's objections, considered that the proposal was a necessary one, he would intimate to the Army Secretary that the case should be referred to His Excellency the Viceroy, under our Rules of Business, which prescribe that when two Members of Council differ the case must be referred for the orders of the Viceroy. The Army Secretary would then lay the case before the Viceroy. The latter might very possibly indicate a personal opinion that, in the circumstances, as a particular case, he thought it perhaps desirable that the views of the Army Member should be deferred to, and any expression of the Viceroy's wish in an ordinary case is very frequently—I might almost say generally—deferred to. Or the Viceroy might, pursuing the ordinary procedure under our Statutory Rules of Business, simply instruct the Army Secretary that the case was to be brought up in Council the following week. It would then be discussed in Council, the Army Secretary being present, but not taking any part in the discussion, and would be settled by the views of the majority of the Council."

Asked how long a disputed case might take, he replied:—

" At the best a disputed proposal would, I think, ordinarily take a good many weeks. I cannot put it more exactly than that, but a great deal depends on whether the responsible secretary takes a grip of the case and prevents it being constantly remitted backwards and forwards between the Financial Adviser on the one side and the Administrative Authority, the Quartermaster-General, or whoever he may be, on the other, inviting each in turn to reply to the other's rejoinders and criticisms. Where a case was not taken hold of and put to an end, I have known it very lamentably protracted from this cause. . . ."

This fantastic picture is not a page from some Dickensian work of fiction. It is a sober account by a highly responsible official of the actual procedure adopted up to 1916 by the military authorities at Simla—procedure to which any request for vitally necessary supplies for the Mesopotamian Expeditionary Force would be subjected. It helps to explain the tragedy which befell that gallant company.

As Sir John Cowans was the General Officer who undertook the reorganisation of the transport system in Mesopotamia, and as his work was a triumphant success, it would not be out of place here to give my impressions of this genial and competent soldier. The first time that I recollect seeing Sir John Cowans—" Jack " Cowans as he was known to all his numerous friends—was at the first meeting of the Munitions Committee which was set up at the end of 1914. We met at the War Office, in the Secretary of State's room, and when the discussion on the supply of munitions had come to an end, and our interviews with General von Donop and others were over, Lord Kitchener suggested that we might like to see the man who was responsible for the other war supplies—the Quartermaster-General. General Cowans was sent for, and my first impression was that of a large, rather ungainly, awkward and weather-beaten man with a

R

stolid face and shrewd eyes.   He did not in the least resemble my
idea of a Staff General.   He had rather the visage and demeanour
of a successful corn merchant in an agricultural town.   He sat down
without a glimmer of expression on his face, and when asked for
particulars as to food supplies for the Army, he slowly and clumsily
pulled out a shabby spectacle case and extracted a pair of horn-
rimmed glasses.   When these were adjusted he pulled out of his
pocket a worn note-book that bore a distinct resemblance to a laundry
book, and casually gave us extracts from the notes therein for the
answers.   Then the clothing—another book.   We listened and
gradually realised that we were being given a lucid summary of the
organisation of supplies which was so completely satisfactory that
when Lord Kitchener inquired of us whether we wanted to put any
questions, we all felt there was nothing left to ask.   This perfunctory
soldier surprised me with his quiet, unostentatious efficiency.   It was
borne in upon the Committee that here was a man who understood
organisation—that he was an organiser to his finger tips.   When I
came to know him better I realised that under his rough exterior
and   stolid   look   there   was   a   simple   and   kindly   nature   and
inexhaustible fund of good humour and joviality.   Once you knew
him it took little to awaken the twinkle in his eye and to provoke
his hearty, noisy, infectious laugh.

With an appearance of being extraordinarily casual, Cowans was
an excellent business man.   His own department was perfectly
ordered, and he himself was thoroughly acquainted with all the
workings of it.   He discharged his duties throughout the four and a
half years of the War in such a way as to give complete satisfaction
to everybody concerned, soldiers and civilians.   Whatever doubts and
grumbles there were about the deficiencies and shortcomings of other
war leaders, there never was a murmur from any quarter as to the
efficiency with which Sir John Cowans did his work.   That is more
than can be said about any other prominent figure in the War,
military or civil.

I have already described the appalling state of affairs in
Mesopotamia when Cowans took the job in hand.   Quickly, with
almost incredible speed, the state of affairs changed completely.
Without fuss and apparently without effort he straightened things
out and no more was heard of scandals in Mesopotamia.

When as Secretary for War I came to grips with the Army Council
because I insisted upon putting civilians into jobs which soldiers had
hitherto been responsible for, it was Cowans who was sent as representative of the irate generals to put their protest before me.   He
was certainly the best person for the job as far as I was concerned,
for his efficiency and good humour made him an acceptable mediator.
You could not quarrel or get angry with Jack Cowans.   He smiled
wrath away.

CHAPTER XXX

THE KNOCK-OUT BLOW

THE latter half of 1916 saw a succession of sporadic and untraceable attempts in certain quarters to bring about an inconclusive peace. Kites were flown and hints broadcast in Holland, in Spain, at the Vatican, in Sweden, and the U.S.A. There was good reason to think that some at least of these movements were being stimulated by German agents, as this was a propitious moment for securing favourable terms for the Central Powers. In the early months of the War, Germany with her elaborately prepared and highly efficient military equipment and organisation had pressed her attack upon the Allied Powers, who were far less skilfully directed, less adequately equipped, and, in the case of the British forces, only just beginning to improvise their military resources. The tide of German conquest had now reached its height, but there was a good deal in the military and naval situation to engender misgiving and even despair of a clear, unmistakable victory being secured on either side.

The uneasy stirring of this peace talk brought to the fore the question of the aims with which we were pursuing the War, and the terms on which we hoped to end it. In August, 1916, the matter was raised in the War Committee, and Sir William Robertson, amongst others, was asked by the Prime Minister to prepare a memorandum setting forth the views of the General Staff on the peace terms desirable from the military point of view. Sir William Robertson's memorandum, dated 31st August, 1916, is in many respects a very remarkable document to have been written in the circumstances of the time. It reads: —

" 1. Although the end of the War is yet by no means in sight, negotiations for peace, in some form or other, may arise any day, and unless we are prepared for them we may find ourselves at a great disadvantage, not only as compared with our enemy but also as compared with our Allies. It is not unlikely that M. Briand already possesses very decided views on the subject, carefully worked out for him under his general direction by the clever people who serve him, and who do not appear on the surface of political life. At a hastily summoned council we should have no chance against him, armed with a definite policy to which he may beforehand, and unknown to us, have committed the Russians and perhaps other Powers of the Entente. If this should happen, the Germans might take advantage of it to drive in a wedge between us and the other Entente Powers, with the result that we might find ourselves without support in those claims which we may be compelled to make, more especially in regard to the disposal of the captured German colonies. We need therefore to decide, without loss of time, as to what our policy is to be; then place it before the Entente Powers and ascertain in return what are their aims, and so endeavour to arrive at a clear understanding before we meet our enemies in conference.

2. For centuries past—though unfortunately by no means continuously—our policy has been to help to maintain the balance between the Continental Powers which have always been divided by their interests and sympathies into opposing groups. At one time the centre of gravity has been in Madrid, at another in Vienna, at another in Paris, and at another in St. Petersburg. We have thwarted, or helped to thwart, each and every Power in turn which has aspired to Continental predominance; and concurrently as a consequence we have enlarged our own sphere of imperial ascendancy. As part of this traditional policy we have aimed at maintaining British maritime supremacy, and at keeping a weak Power in possession of the Low Countries. In more recent years a new preponderance has been allowed to grow up, of which the centre of gravity has been in Berlin, and the result of it is the present War.

3. It is submitted that the basis of peace negotiations must be the three principles for which we have so often fought in the past and for which we have been compelled to fight now, namely: —

  (a) The maintenance of the balance of power in Europe;
  (b) The maintenance of British maritime supremacy; and
  (c) The maintenance of a weak Power in the Low Countries.

4. If and when these general principles, and such others as are deemed necessary, are accepted by His Majesty's Government it will be possible to formulate the conditions upon which, and upon which only, we would be prepared to negotiate. No useful purpose would be served by discussing these conditions until the general principles have been settled, but some of the many questions demanding examination may be mentioned by way of showing how important it is to commence investigation with as little delay as possible. It may be added that this paper is written mainly from a military standpoint, and in this connection it cannot be too often remembered that the conditions upon which peace is concluded will govern, or at any rate ought to govern, the size and nature of the army subsequently required by us.

5. If the balance of power in Europe is to be maintained it follows that the existence of a strong Central European Power is essential, and that such a State must be Teutonic, as a Slav nation, the only other alternative, would always lean towards Russia, which would accordingly obtain a preponderant position and so destroy the very principle which we desire to uphold. On the other hand, as Germany is the chief European competitor with us on the sea, it would be advantageous to make such terms of peace as would check the development of her navy and of her mercantile marine. In other words, it would be to the interests of the British Empire to leave Germany reasonably strong on land, but to weaken her at sea. The full extent to which His Majesty's Government have already been committed is not known to the General Staff, but apparently it is the intention to break up Austria-Hungary. By the Roumanian Political Convention a large part of Eastern Hungary will be transferred to Roumania; Italy will no doubt insist on retaining Trieste with Istria and some of the neighbouring districts; and Serbia is to be given part at least of Herzegovina, Bosnia and Slavonia. The chief problems to be determined are the disposal of Austria proper, of the Magyar district of Hungary, of the Northern Slav provinces of Bohemia, Moravia and Galicia and finally, whether there shall be access to the Adriatic from the north otherwise than through Italian or Serbian territory. It is clear that all these provinces cannot become independent States. Galicia may be absorbed in a new Polish Kingdom, but Bohemia and Moravia on the one side and Hungary on the other will be difficult of disposal. Acting on the principle of maintaining a strong Germany, it might be advantageous if Austria proper were incorporated in that Empire, more especially as thereby ten million South Germans would be brought in as a counterpoise to Prussia. The other alternative, which has the advantage of settling the question of the disposal of the various provinces, is to maintain a diminished Austria-Hungary, and in that case an Adriatic port, Fiume for choice, should be allotted to it. This new Austria-Hungary would very probably form a very close union with Germany, but such a union might be not altogether to our disadvantage on land as limiting the power of Russia and the Slav States, and on sea as preventing the Mediterranean from becoming a French and Italian lake.

6. As regards the western boundaries of Germany we will presumably be obliged to agree to the wishes of the French with regard to Alsace and Lorraine. Belgium must be restored to her pre-war condition, and it may be desirable that the Grand Duchy of Luxembourg should be added to her territories. It would be advantageous if Belgium could be given free access from the sea to Antwerp by transferring to her that part of Seeland which lies

south of the Scheldt.   In this case Holland might be given compensation in East Friesland and in the East Frisian Islands.

7.   On the north it is to be wished that the whole of Schleswig and possibly a part of Holstein should be restored to Denmark. From a naval point of view it would be of the highest importance to take away from Germany the Kiel Canal—which might be internationalised—the Harbour of Kiel, the North Frisian Islands, and the eastern shores of the Heligoland Bight.   These questions, as all others of a naval nature, are of course matters for the Admiralty to advise upon.

8.   On the east the boundaries of Germany will depend on those that may be given to Poland.   A difficulty in the way of creating this new State is to provide it with a sea port.   The Poles themselves are desirous of having Dantzig, and state, in support of this claim, that 60 per cent. of the population of West Prussia is Polish.   It would, however, scarcely seem feasible in any circumstances to cut off East Prussia from Germany, and it is hard to believe that Germany will ever be so crushed as to consent to the transfer of Posen to Poland, unless the latter were to form a State of the German Empire under a German Prince, a contingency which presumably could only occur in the event of a German victory.   As regards Poland, we shall probably be obliged to conform to Russian wishes.

9.   Bulgaria may either secede from the Central Powers and be allowed to retain her existing territories, plus the uncontested zone of Macedonia, or she may fight on to the end.   In the latter case, if and when Russia is established in Constantinople, it is possible that she may try to annex Bulgaria, and eventually to link it up with Bessarabia by wresting the Dobrudja from Roumania.

10.   The principal suggestions here made for examination are that Germany should be reduced on the west and north by the cession to other Powers of parts of Alsace and Lorraine, East Friesland, Schleswig, and part of Holstein; that there should be some rectification of frontier due to the creation of Poland; and that in the south she should be strengthened either by the incorporation of Austria proper, or by a close union with a much diminished Austria-Hungary; and that her naval power should be shaken by taking away from her the Kiel Canal and various districts on the North Sea and Baltic which are of great maritime importance.

11.   It is apparently the intention to break up the Turkish Empire by handing over Constantinople and the Straits to Russia, and by dividing up Mesopotamia, Syria, and parts of Asia Minor. This intention does not affect the question of the future boundaries of Germany in Europe, but it is of importance as preventing German development in the Near East.

12.   In Asia outside the Turkish Empire, our main concern is with Persia, and there seems no reason why any agreement that it may be necessary to make with Russia concerning that country should be discussed at the Peace Conference.

13.   Our future relations with our Allies demand as close consideration as our relations with our enemies.   What is our policy to be towards the French in Salonika, towards the Italians and French in Albania, towards the Italians in Asia Minor, towards the Russians in the Balkans, and towards the Slav world generally in connection with the creation of Poland?   It is well to remember that the present grouping of the Powers is not a permanency, and indeed it may continue but a very short time after the War is over.

14.   With regard to her colonies, Germany will have lost the whole of them when the campaign in German East Africa has been completed.   They are: —

Kiauchau
Togoland
The Cameroons
German South-West Africa
German East Africa
German New Guinea
The Bismarck Archipelago
The Caroline, Marshall, Marianne, Solomon and Samoan Islands, in the Pacific.

Germany is certain to make strenuous efforts to recover all or most of these Colonies in order that she may keep her " place in the sun " and preserve at least the semblance of a position as a world power.   She is therefore likely to put forward tempting bargains to those Powers who are not interested in order that pressure may be brought to bear upon those Powers who are interested to relinquish their claims.   We alone are interested in all these Colonies, and France only in the Cameroons, Belgium in East Africa, and Japan in Kiauchau and the Northern Pacific Islands.   It is easy to see therefore that if the cession of a portion of, say, Poland to Russia, or of Alsace-Lorraine to France, or even the complete evacuation of Belgium is made conditional by Germany upon our giving up Togoland, South-West and East Africa, and the Southern Pacific Islands, we may be placed in a difficult position.

15.   Kiauchau, the Marianne, Caroline and Marshall Islands have been occupied by, and are being administered by, the Japanese, and Japan is unlikely to release her hold on them without a substantial *quid pro quo,* which it will not be easy to find.

16.   The Samoan Islands were occupied by, and are now

administered by, the Government of New Zealand, which is likely to attach a high sentimental value to this, the first conquest of a young people. The same applies to German New Guinea, the Bismarck Archipelago and the Solomon Islands, which were occupied by and are now in the hands of the Australian Government, who have the further inducement to keep what they have got, that these islands form a valuable buffer between the mainland and possible Japanese encroachment.

17. In Africa the difficulties are even greater. The Union of South Africa, with the experience of this war behind it, is unlikely to tolerate the neighbourhood of a great foreign power. They have conquered German South-West Africa with their own resources, and taken a leading part in the campaign in East Africa. We are, therefore, likely to enter the Peace Conference with Togoland as the only possession which we can use freely for the purpose of bargaining.

18. The many problems which the future disposal of the German Colonies involve require very full consideration, and no time should be lost in obtaining the views of the Dominions, and in deciding on the attitude to be adopted in regard to the other Entente Powers.

19. Another question requiring discussion and settlement, as far as possible, is that of enemy proposal for an armistice pending negotiations for peace. The existence of the Entente blockade makes it extremely difficult to suggest any equitable terms on which an armistice could be arranged. From the point of view of the Entente the maintenance of the blockade during the armistice is absolutely essential, as otherwise the Central Powers would be able to provision themselves during the armistice and would consequently be in a much better position to recommence hostilities if the negotiations for peace were to collapse. The enemy would no doubt strongly oppose a maintenance of the blockade because it would progressively weaken him every day that it continued, with the result that at the end of the armistice he would be in a worse position than at the commencement. But we may hope that during the same period his position would, if there were no armistice, become worse, and we cannot allow him to reap an advantage from an armistice which he would not obtain if there were no armistice. In fact we need not concern ourselves with him. The last thing Germany would do, in similar circumstances, would be to give the least consideration to the difficulties of her enemy. Moreover, our desire will be to conclude the negotiations as quickly as possible, whereas the removal of the blockade will almost certainly tend to lengthen them indefinitely.

20. There seem, therefore, to be three courses which require consideration: —

(a) Refuse an armistice altogether and continue fighting during peace negotiations or until the enemy surrenders unconditionally.

(b) Limit the armistice to land and air operations; maritime operations, whether submarine or otherwise, being continued.

(c) Agree to some kind of rationing policy during the armistice, calculated to leave the Central Powers in the same economic position at the close as at the beginning of the armistice.

21. All three courses have their objections. As regards (a) it would not be easy to conduct peace negotiations while active operations were in progress, as the constant fluctuations in the fighting might have a corresponding influence on the negotiations. It must also be remembered that the negotiations would necessarily take a long time as so many different Powers are concerned, to say nothing of the conflicting interests and large areas involved.

22. On the other hand it will be difficult to draft satisfactory terms for an armistice even if it is confined to land and air operations alone, for unless the terms are most precise and can anticipate all possible contingencies, constant complaints will be made as to infringements of its conditions and innumerable disputes may in this way arise. Further, if it were decided to grant an armistice as in (b), and submarine attacks on passenger and merchant vessels were continued, the Conference proceedings might become embittered and a settlement rendered the more difficult. Course (c) is not recommended. The more hungry the enemy is kept the better, and after all he probably has enough to live upon. Also, it would be difficult to arrange a scale of rations that would be acceptable to all parties.

23. It is quite evident that the question is beset by numerous difficulties and therefore its examination is the more urgent. On the whole it seems hardly possible to refuse an armistice, but it is necessary that we should have some definite guarantees of good faith, and therefore it is suggested that the granting of an armistice should at least be made conditional on: —

(a) The immediate withdrawal of all enemy troops inside their pre-war frontiers;

(b) Immediate release of all prisoners of war held by the enemy;

(c) Tentative surrender of a certain portion of the enemy fleet.

W. R. ROBERTSON, General,
War Office,   Chief of the Imperial General Staff.
31st August, 1916."

Apart from the interest of this document as setting out the ideas of the military authorities upon the territorial measures that should

R*

be taken to limit the perils of a recurrence of the German menace, it is of value in that it reflects the expectation current at the time that peace negotiations might not be far distant on the horizon.

There were, however, marked differences in the attitude adopted by various influential people to this prospect. Many who had entered the War reluctantly felt that once it had been forced upon us, it would be a real disaster if peace were made before it had been demonstrated clearly that no military machine, however perfect, could prevail in the end against the roused conscience of civilisation. But this view was by no means fully appreciated and shared in all quarters. In face of our dubious military position and unsatisfactory outlook, there were those who felt attracted towards the possibility of a prompt if inconclusive peace.

The third campaign of the War was now drawing to a close and the Allies seemed further than ever from achieving a favourable determination of the issue. At the end of the first campaign Belgium had been almost entirely occupied by the enemy; a large and important section of Northern France had also been overrun by the Germans, and even after the retreat from the Marne ten of the richest provinces of France remained in enemy occupation. At the end of the second year's campaign Serbia had fallen entirely into the hands of the Central Powers, Bulgaria with its brave army had joined the enemy and thousands of square miles of Russian territory had been conquered and were adding to the resources of the enemy in food, timber and labour.

By the end of the third summer Roumania had been crushed and most of its territory, including its capital, was in enemy occupation. Invaluable reserves of oil and corn were added to the enemy stores of essential supply. The Balkans were thus almost entirely in the hands of the Central Powers, for whose munitions the road to Constantinople had been cleared. Turkey had been resuscitated and was making a formidable contribution to the military strength of its allies. She was holding up at one point or another hundreds of thousands of British and French troops. We had been driven by Turkish forces out of the Dardanelles, and a British army had surrendered to the Turks in Mesopotamia. In the west, attempts made with colossal losses to release the fierce grip of the German Army on the soil of France had not succeeded in producing any tangible result. The Germans had been hammered by the most formidable artillery ever mobilised on a battlefield and they had suffered severely, and had to abandon some territory, but their casualties were not comparable with those inflicted on the French and notably on the British Army, and the territorial gain was insignificant, whether computed in superficies or strategy. The German attack on Verdun had failed, but the French had even there lost considerably more men than the Germans.

The French nation was bleeding at every pore, and no one could visit France without feeling that although the courage of this gallant people was undaunted and its spirit unbroken, its ardour was being quenched in the blood of its sons. Official reports from Italy were far from encouraging. The Italian people were by no means as united in their decision to enter the War as the other belligerents. Their inadequately equipped troops had since May, 1915, performed prodigies of valour and triumphs of engineering skill in scaling fortresses drilled and blasted out of the great mountains that lowered over the Italian plains; but progress had been slow, and losses had been heavy. Recently, there had been a serious setback. The Cabinet were informed early in November by Sir Rennell Rodd, our Ambassador in Rome, upon the accuracy of whose reports on the Italian position we all placed implicit confidence, that—

> " there were already in Italy certain symptoms of war weariness and discontent at the protraction of the struggle. Great Britain is represented as the only country anxious to prolong the struggle *à outrance* for her own ends. It would be wrong to pretend that there exists here the same grim determination to carry through as prevails in France and in the British Empire."

The Russian armies were broken and quite unable to offer any effective resistance to the German attack, and although their position in respect of ammunition and rifles was supposed to have improved during the year it was quite clear that their equipment would not enable them to stand up much longer to the formidable artillery at the disposal of Hindenburg's armies. Ten thousand tons of ammunition stacked at Archangel had, either through carelessness or treachery, been blown up. The whole administration was slack, incompetent, and drenched with corruption. No wonder that the Russian people were seething with discontent. The peasantry were permeated with sullen disaffection. The workers in the towns were becoming more difficult and insubordinate. Strikes multiplied and street demonstrations were becoming a menacing feature.. The soldiers had ceased to believe in the possibility of victory, and whether they were called upon to advance or to resist they obeyed mechanically, but their response lacked spirit or confidence. Discipline alone held them in the trenches. Food everywhere throughout Russia was becoming scarce. Revolution was only a question of time. It was taken for granted on all hands. Although we were assured by our representative in Russia that it would not occur until the War was over, the Allies could not rely upon a population saturated with a spirit of disgust with its Government to go on risking precious lives at the behest and for the sake of an autocracy which no longer commanded respect, and which in fact had become universally despised among all classes high and low. There were hopes that Russian resistance might last long enough to hold up a considerable proportion of the Central Powers' Armies until the Allies on the Western and Italian Fronts had at last achieved the long-expected " break through." But that hope was becoming increasingly precarious and in the event it proved to be illusory. A complete collapse of the Russian resistance meant two or three million German and Austrian troops, with their formidable train of artillery, released for the Western and Italian Fronts, to attack an exhausted France and discouraged Italy.

There was another impending peril which threatened the very life of Britain—the sinking of our merchant ships by enemy submarines. The German Admiralty had set itself the task of increasing its submarine fleet fourfold in numbers. The increase in size and power of these elusive vessels of destruction was more menacing than the augmentation in their numbers. It meant that the area of attack was widened. The newer types could travel into the ocean and hunt far and wide for their prey. The difficulties of organising effective protection were thereby considerably enhanced. The output of the German yards was multiplying at an alarming rate, and the figures of our losses leapt up steeply week by week. The defence was by no means equal to the assault. It had to fight an invisible foe—an enemy who left no spoor behind, but who destroyed and then disappeared, pursuing his course in the trackless depths, unseen, unseeable, and untraceable, leaving nothing behind to indicate direction or distance.

The following table shows the rate at which British merchant vessels were being sunk by submarines during 1916: —

Date.		No.		Tonnage.
January, 1916	...	5	...	62,288
February ,,	...	7	...	75,860
March ,,	...	19	...	99,089
April ,,	...	37	...	141,193
May ,,	...	12	...	64,251
June ,,	...	11	...	36,976
July ,,	...	21	...	82,432
August ,,	...	22	...	43,354
September ,,	...	34	...	104,572
October ,,	...	41	...	176,248
November ,,	...	42	...	168,809
December ,,	...	36	...	182,292

This is how the position appeared at that time to Lord Robert Cecil, who was then an influential member of the Cabinet: —

" One thing is clear. Our situation is grave. It is certain that unless the utmost national effort is made it may become desperate, particularly in the matter of shipping. The position in Allied countries is even more serious. France is within measurable distance of exhaustion. The political outlook in Italy is menacing. Her finance is tottering. In Russia there is great discouragement. She has long been on the verge of revolution. Even her man-power seems coming near its limits."

This was a situation that must necessarily invite doubt in the stoutest hearts and recruit patriotic and humanitarian sentiment to the side of immediate peace. But for reasons which I give later on I felt that any attempt to make peace at a time when the Germans were at the climax of strength and achievement, whilst we were only just beginning to mobilise our full power, would necessarily be unsatisfactory and inconclusive.

The attitude of France towards any peace overtures at this stage was one of uncompromising hostility, despite the gloom of the outlook. It was set out very clearly at a sitting of the French Chamber in a speech of exceptional power by the Prime Minister, M. Briand. A Socialist by the name of M. Brizon had delivered a speech on 19th September, 1916, in the course of which he dwelt upon the losses of France and ended by asking if France had not suffered enough, and whether she could not now negotiate peace. M. Briand in reply delivered one of the most eloquent speeches of his life. I quote an extract from that speech. When he sat down he received from the Chamber what is said to be " such an ovation as has never been accorded to a Prime Minister," and the House by 421 votes to 26 ordered the speech to be placarded throughout France. It may therefore be assumed that it represented the determined and even fierce resistance of the country which had suffered most from the War to any premature efforts to make peace.

" Look at your country, M. Brizon. It has been violently attacked. It stands for something in the world as a propagator of those ideas which have done work for the world's progress. When your country, which has for two years had the honour to be champion of right, has stayed the invader, and defends the whole world, when its blood flows, you say, ' Negotiate peace.' What a challenge, what an outrage to the memory of our dead! [Loud cheers, and a shout. ' debout les morts! '] What, M. Brizon! Ten of your country's provinces are invaded. Our old men and women and children have been carried off. They bear their misery bravely, awaiting deliverance at your hands. Is it then that you come to us saying, ' Negotiate, go and ask for peace '? You little know France if you imagine that she can accept economy of milliards, or even of blood in such humiliating circumstances. What peace would you get for France? It would be a peace of war. If you wish that peace should shine upon the world, M. Brizon, if you wish the idea of liberty and justice to prevail, ask for victory, and not for the peace obtainable to-day, for that peace would be humiliating and dishonouring. There is not a Frenchman who can possibly desire it."

On the other hand Germany had her troubles. A blockade had been tightly drawn around the Central Powers, while on the other hand the Allies had developed very extensive arrangements for securing their own essential supplies. Austria and Turkey were broken reeds. Germany could not lean her hopes too heavily upon them. In Britain the work of the Ministry of Munitions was now bearing copious fruit, and the adoption of national service was securing hundreds of thousands of men for our armies.

It was natural, therefore, that Germany should be ready to welcome and foster suggestions from any quarter urging an early peace settlement, while her strength remained intact and her position on the War map lent colour to the suggestion that she was substantially a victorious Power. Rumours indeed reached us that her emissaries in the United States were angling for intervention by President Wilson with a view to an early and favourable peace.

The President himself would not have been without his own reasons for being attracted by the suggestion of proposing such an intervention. The Presidential election was at hand—it was due at the beginning of November—and there was the very large and influential German-American vote to consider. He was, moreover, standing on his reputation as the man who had kept America out of the War, and anything he could do to reduce the very real danger —a danger which not long after took concrete form—that America would after all be drawn into the conflict, would obviously help his election campaign. The moment was, however, in my view utterly inappropriate for the discussion of any peace terms which would be remotely satisfactory to the Allies. I will not pretend that my opinion was shared by all members of the British Cabinet. There were those among them who had grave doubts about the military position and the outlook for our shipping, our food supplies, and financial reserves. Lord Grey, Lord Lansdowne, Mr. M'Kenna, and Mr. Runciman in particular were obviously uneasy about the prospect. They had misgivings as to the possibility of continuing the War beyond Christmas, 1916. It has become clear from statements which have since been published that a similar impression was widely held abroad.

I felt it vitally important to throw out a sharp challenge to the defeatest spirit which was working from foreign quarters to bring about an inconclusive peace, and which appeared to find an echo even in some responsible quarters in our own country.

I was no friend to war. It was only with the utmost reluctance that I had at the last minute agreed to the ultimatum of Britain. My pacifist attitude was very well known, and had it not been for

Germany's violation of Belgian neutrality, I should up to the last have refused to remain in a Cabinet which implicated the country in war with all its carnage and organised barbarism. But once having entered on the War, I was no less resolute to pursue it until at least the object of our sacrifice had been achieved. It was not merely a question of abiding by the Shakespearian counsel: —

> " Beware
> Of entrance to a quarrel: but being in
> Bear't that the opposed may beware of thee."

A conference under existing conditions might have involved a peace which would have been a virtual and practical abandonment of the cause which compelled us to take up arms.

Accordingly, copying an example which had been set shortly before by Lord Grey himself, I granted, on 28th September, 1916, an interview to an American correspondent—in this case Mr. Roy W. Howard, the President of the United Press of America—in which I outlined my views as to the attitude this country and her Allies should adopt towards any talk of an immediate peace.

I began by pointing out that Britain had only now got into her stride in her war effort, and was justifiably suspicious of any suggestion that President Wilson should choose this moment to " butt in " with a proposal to stop the War before we could achieve victory. " There had been no such intervention when we were being hammered through the first two years, as yet untrained and ill-equipped. Our men had taken their punishment without squealing. They had held grimly on while the winning Germans talked of annexing Belgium and Poland as their spoils of victory, and of making it a fight to a finish with England."

" The whole world—including neutrals of the highest purposes and humanitarians with the best of motives—must know that there can be no outside interference at this stage. Britain asked no intervention when she was unprepared to fight. She will tolerate none now that she is prepared, until the Prussian military despotism is broken beyond repair."

It was idle for people now to deplore the horror of continued conflict, when their pity had not moved them to stop it while British troops were being gassed, and exposed to an overpowering attack that used ten shells to their one.

" But in the British determination to carry the fight to a decisive finish there is something more than the natural demand for vengeance. The inhumanity and pitilessness of the fighting that must come before a lasting peace is possible is not comparable with the cruelty that would be involved in stopping the War while there remains the possibility of civilisation again being menaced frcn the same quarter. Peace now or at any time before the final and complete elimination of this menace is unthinkable. No man and no nation with the slightest understanding of the temper of the citizen army of Britons, which took its terrible hammering without a whine, or a grumble, will attempt to call a halt now."

"But how long do you figure this can and must go on?" I was asked.

"There is neither clock nor calendar in the British Army to-day," was my reply. "Time is the least vital factor. Only the result counts—not the time consumed in achieving it. It took England 20 years to defeat Napoleon, and the first 15 of those years were black with British defeat. It will not take 20 years to win this war, but whatever time is required, it will be done.

"And I say this, recognising that we have only begun to win. There is no disposition on our side to fix the hour of ultimate victory after the first success. We have no delusion that the War is nearing an end. We have not the slightest doubt as to *how* it is to end."

"But what of France?" I was asked. "Is there the same determination there to stick to the end; the same idea of fighting until peace terms can be dictated by Germany's enemies?"

"The world at large has not yet begun to appreciate the magnificence, the nobility, the wonder of France," I replied. "I had the answer to your inquiry given me a few days ago by a noble Frenchwoman. This woman had given four sons—she had one more left to give to France. In the course of my talk with her I asked if she did not think the struggle had gone far enough. Her reply, without a moment's hesitation, was: 'The fight will never have gone far enough until it shall have made a repetition of this horror impossible.' That mother was voicing the spirit of France. Yes, France will stick to the end."

I pointed to the defence of Verdun as evidence of French staying power. While the British were buoyed up by a sporting spirit, the French were burning with an unquenchable patriotism. The motto of the Allies was "Never again!" I was myself fresh from a visit to the battlefields, and the ghastliness I had witnessed was something which must never be re-enacted. The War must make that certain.

This was the substance of my interview, which was given very wide currency, and was discussed in every country. The "Policy of a Knock-Out Blow," as it was called, caused great exasperation, not only to the Central Powers (as witnessed by the constant reference to it in their Press and in the speeches of their politicians), but even to several of my colleagues in the British Cabinet, who, if not exactly pacifists, were leaning towards an early peace of accommodation. Several of my colleagues regarded the interview as provocative, and many held that it did not accurately represent the attitude of the Government towards the idea of an immediate peace.

It was not long before I discovered that this interview had caused a great deal of perturbation and animadversion amongst the members of the Cabinet. I received the following letter from Lord Grey: —

"29th September, 1916.

My dear Lloyd George,

The more I think of it the more I am apprehensive of the possible effect of the warning to Wilson in your interview, and I want to explain why this is so.

1. Briand's speech, and I think steps taken in Washington, has made any further warning to Wilson unnecessary for the present.

2. We shall now be held responsible in America for warning Wilson off the course. He will now point to your words as the reason why he can do nothing, and this will tend to bring him and Bethmann-Hollweg together.

3. Wilson will be more disposed to put upon us the pressure that Congress has urged him to put, which may be very inconvenient.

4. The extreme submarine warfare will be precipitated by Germany, who will tell Wilson that as he can do nothing because of us, Germany must use every means against us. Wilson and his supporters will be less inclined than before to resent submarine warfare against us.

5. It has always been my view that until the Allies were sure of victory the door should be kept open for Wilson's mediation. It is now closed for ever as far as we are concerned.

I am still anxious about the effect of submarine warfare.

I hope you won't think me captious in questioning one point in our interview of which the rest not only draws my assent but my admiration. I may be quite wrong in my view, but a public warning to the President of the United States is an important step, and I wish I had had an opportunity of putting these considerations before you and discussing them with you.

No answer needed now as nothing more can be done till we see the effect.

Yours sincerely,

GREY OF F."

To this I replied: —

"October 2, 1916.

My dear Grey,

Thanks for your letter. I wonder whether you are still of the same opinion after reading M.I.I.'s secret information? Have you seen it?

Spring-Rice's telegram 2943 seems to be also very significant.

If the hands of Wilson had been forced—and there is every indication that the Germans and Irish co-operation could do so—then we should be in a very tight place. Any cessation of hostilities now would be a disaster; and although we could always refuse or put up impossible terms, it is much better that we should not be placed in that predicament. *You* could not have warned off the United States without doing it formally. I could commit a serviceable indiscretion; you could not. It would ruin you; I am inoculated!

. . . In so far as callous impenitence will allow me, I am genuinely sorry for adding one dram to your cup of anxieties.

Ever sincerely,

D. LLOYD GEORGE."

Lord Grey committed himself to a series of forecasts in this letter all of which were falsified by the event. He predicted that it would encourage Wilson to " do nothing and would tend to bring him and Bethmann-Hollweg together." A few months later, when I was Prime Minister, Wilson broke off diplomatic relations with Germany, and a few weeks after doing so entered into the War on the side of the Allies. Grey predicted that another result of my letter might be an increase in the pressure which the President would bring to bear upon us. That also turned out to be an unrealised apprehension. He foresaw that my interview would precipitate an extreme submarine warfare by Germany, and that President Wilson as a result of it would be less inclined to resent submarine warfare against us. Germany had decided at the beginning of 1916 to increase fourfold the number and potency of her submarines. At the end of August she had already launched a large number of these new, more powerful craft. And so far from Wilson and his supporters being less inclined than before to resent submarine warfare, it was the intensification and extension of the submarine campaign that provoked America to declare war against Germany early in 1917.

As to Grey's prediction that the door against Wilson's mediation would, as a result of my interview, be " closed for ever as far as we are concerned," two or three months later President Wilson issued his famous Peace Note.

It is, however, significant of Lord Grey's frame of mind at this time that he seemed to have a doubt as to the victory of the Allies—and that he was relying as a means of escape from the consequences of defeat upon the mediation of the President of the United States.

How little Lord Grey's estimate of the probable effect of my interview corresponded with reality is made clear by the reports which came to hand from our Ambassador in the United States, Sir C. Spring-Rice. In a telegram to the Foreign Secretary, dated 4th October, 1916, Spring-Rice said: —

" I am informed from a very reliable source that the President has no intention of making peace proposals. The Secretary of State for War's statement has had a great effect.

I have also reason to believe that action will not be taken on the Retaliatory Clauses. . . ."

He followed this up with a letter dated 6th October, 1916, in which he wrote : —

" Mr. Lloyd George's statement, which had an immense and instantaneous effect in this country, put a stop to the peace rumours which for some time have been prevalent here. It seems generally acknowledged now that the President has no intention of offering his mediation at any rate in the near future."

The letter also said that the American Government was maintaining uncompromising opposition to Germany in regard to any extension of the submarine campaign, and explained that the peace rumours emanating from German sources were being used by them to assist their deals on the stock market.

" The publication of a peace rumour is at once followed by a general decline on the Stock Exchange, and the authoritative quarter which launches such a rumour is in excellent position to profit by its power."

In a later telegram, dated 20th October, 1916, Sir C. Spring-Rice reported: " Lloyd George's interview had the most excellent effect here." There is in fact no evidence that my " Knock-Out Blow " interview did anything to injure our cause in the States. On the contrary, it steadied opinion there and helped to increase the sympathy felt with us in our desperate fight.

CHAPTER XXXI

THE LANSDOWNE PEACE MOVE

Should we make or encourage peace overtures whilst the issue of the War was still in doubt and the enemy had good reason to claim that he had won on points? The British Cabinet was brought by the intervention of one of its most respected members to a searching and considered examination of the question.

The type of partisan pacifist who maintains that an honourable and satisfactory peace could have been negotiated long before November, 1918, is generally anxious to cast the whole of the blame for prolonging the War on the Coalition that came into existence at the end of 1916. In order to sustain their criticism they assume that 1917 afforded the first real opportunity for making peace. The discussions which took place in the Asquith Cabinet on the desirability of encouraging peace overtures and the decision arrived at by the Cabinet are either unknown to these critics or are wilfully ignored by them.

The first serious peace movement in Europe started immediately after the termination of the sanguinary battle of 1916. The horrible and futile carnage of the Somme following on the ghastly losses of Verdun had sent a thrill of horror through all the belligerent lands and there was a distinct movement for an interchange of views as to the possibility of a settlement.

In the middle of November Lord Lansdowne startled the Cabinet by a memorandum which he circulated amongst members with the consent of the Prime Minister. It was written the day before Mr. Asquith and I left England for the Paris Conference, and was in the hands of members of the Cabinet on our return. This bold document frankly suggested doubts as to the possibility of victory. It was at least courageous, and proved that he at any rate was quite alive to the perils of the Allied situation. It was clear that Lord Lansdowne thought a condition of stalemate had been reached and that there was no prospect of any improvement.

The text of this memorandum was as follows: —

" The members of the War Committee were asked by the Prime Minister some weeks ago to express their views as to the terms upon which peace might be concluded. I do not know whether there has been a general response to this invitation, but the only reply which I have seen is one written last month by the First Lord of the Admiralty, in which he deals at some length with the problems which might have to be discussed at any Peace Conference. Mr. Balfour observes truly that these questions cannot be profitably examined except upon an agreed hypothesis as to the military position of the combatants at the end of the War, and he proceeds to assume, though merely for the sake of argument, that the Central Powers, either through defeat or exhaustion, have to accept the terms imposed upon them by the Allies.

I venture to suggest that the attention of the War Committee might with advantage be directed to a somewhat different problem, and that they should be invited to give us their opinion as to our present prospects of being able to 'dictate' the kind of terms which we should all like to impose upon our enemies if we were in a position to do so.

We are agreed as to the goal, but we do not know how far we have really travelled towards it, or how much nearer to it we are likely to find ourselves even if the War be prolonged for, say, another year. What will that year have cost us? How much better will our position be at the end of it? Shall we even then be strong enough to 'dictate' terms?

It seems to me almost impossible to overrate the importance of these considerations, because it is clear that our diplomacy must be governed by an accurate appreciation of them.

We have obtained within the last few days from the different Departments of the Government a good deal of information as to the situation, naval, military and economic. It is far from reassuring.

From the President of the Board of Trade we received on the 26th October a most interesting and carefully compiled memorandum tending to show the daily growing shortage of tonnage and its consequences. Mr. Runciman comes to the conclusion that our shipbuilding is not keeping pace with our losses, and that, although the number of our vessels is down, the demands on our tonnage are not diminished. We must look forward to depending more and more on neutral ships, but we can be under no illusions as to the precarious nature of that resource. I do not think I exaggerate when I describe this most important document as profoundly disquieting. But in a later memorandum, dated 9th November, the President paints the picture in still gloomier colours, and anticipates, on the advice of his experts, 'a complete breakdown in shipping . . . much sooner than June, 1917.'

The President of the Board of Agriculture has recently presented to the Cabinet his report on Food Prospects in 1917. That report goes to show that there is a world's deficit in bread-stuffs, that the price of bread is likely to go higher, that there had been a general failure of the potato crop, that the supply of fish is expected to be 64 per cent. below the normal, that there is considerable difficulty in regard to the supply of feeding-stuffs, that the difficulties of cultivation steadily increase, that land is likely to go derelict, the yield to decline, and the number of live-stock to diminish greatly.

Lord Crawford's later note, dated 9th November, on Home Food Supplies, shows that these anticipations were not unduly pessi-mistic. The position has, he tells us, become much worse, and, owing to the inroads made upon the agricultural population by the demands of the Army, it is in some parts of the country ' no longer a question of maintaining a moderate standard of cultiva-tion, but whether cultivation will cease.'

Turning to our naval and military resources, we have a report from the First Lord of the Admiralty, dated 14th October, from which we learn that, in spite of the tremendous efforts which we have made, the size of our Home Fleets is still insufficient, that we have nearly reached the limit of immediate production in the matter of capital ships, that we have not got nearly enough destroyers to meet our needs for escort and anti-submarine work, that we shall certainly not have enough for our Allies, and that the position in regard to light cruisers is not much better. From the same report we may infer that the submarine difficulty is becoming acute, and that, in spite of all our efforts, it seems impossible to provide an effectual rejoinder to it. The increasing size of the enemy submarines, the strength of their construction (which will apparently oblige us to re-arm our merchantmen with a heavier gun), and their activity in all parts of the world, point to the same conclusion.

The papers which we have from time to time received from the General Staff and from the War Committee prove that in the matter of man-power we are nearing the end of our tether. The last report of the Man-Power Distribution Board seems, in particu-lar, to sound a grave note of warning. The unexhausted supply of men is, they tell us, now very restricted, and the number avail-able can only be added to by a still further depletion of industry. In the meanwhile Ireland still declines to add to the available supply the 150,000 men who would be obtainable from that country, and I am not aware that any serious attempt is to be made to secure them.

All these seem to me to be very serious factors in the calculation which it is our duty to make. It will be replied, and no doubt truly, that the Central Powers are feeling the pressure of the War not less acutely than we feel it, and I hope we shall also be told that our staying powers are greater than theirs; but, even if this be so, it is none the less our duty to consider, after a careful review of the facts, what our plight and the plight of the civilised world will be after another year, or, as we are sometimes told, two or three more years of a struggle as exhausting as that in which we are engaged. No one for a moment believes that we are going to lose the War; but what is our chance of winning it in such a manner, and within such limits of time, as will enable us to beat our enemy to the ground and impose upon him the kind of terms which we so freely discuss?

I do not suppose for an instant that there is any weakening in the spirit of the people of this country, and I should hope, although I do not feel absolute confidence on the subject, that the same might be said of our Allies, but neither in their interests nor in ours can it be desirable that the War should be prolonged, unless it can be shown that we can bring it to an effectual conclusion within a reasonable space of time.

What does the prolongation of the War mean?

Our own casualties already amount to over 1,100,000. We have had 15,000 officers killed, not including those who are missing. There is no reason to suppose that, as the force at the front in the different theatres of war increases, the casualties will increase at a slower rate. We are slowly but surely killing off the best of the male population of these islands. The figures representing the casualties of our Allies are not before me. The total must be appalling.

The financial burden which we have already accumulated is almost incalculable. We are adding to it at the rate of over £5,000,000 per day. Generations will have to come and go before the country recovers from the loss which it has sustained in human beings, and from the financial ruin and the destruction of the means of production which are taking place.

All this it is no doubt our duty to bear, but only if it can be shown that the sacrifice will have its reward. If it is to be made in vain, if the additional year, or two years, or three years, finds us still unable to dictate terms, the War with its nameless horrors will have been needlessly prolonged, and the responsibility of those who needlessly prolong such a War is not less than that of those who needlessly provoke it.

A thorough stocktaking, first by each Ally of his own resources, present and prospective, and next by the Allies, or at all events by the leading Allies, in confidential consultation, seems indispensable. Not until such a stocktaking has taken place will each Ally be able to decide which of his desiderata are indispensable, and whether he might not be prepared to accept less than 20s. in the £ in consideration of prompt payment. Not until it has taken place will the Allies as a body be able to determine the broad outline of their policy or the attitude which they ought to assume towards those who talk to them of peace.

I think Sir William Robertson must have had some such stock-taking in his mind when he wrote the remarkable paper which was circulated to the Cabinet on the 31st August. In that paper he expressed his belief that negotiations for peace in some form or other might arise any day, and he urged that ' we need therefore to decide without loss of time what our policy is to be, then place it before the Entente Powers, and ascertain in return what are their aims, and so endeavour to arrive at a clear understanding before we meet our enemies in conference.' The idea may, for all I know, have been acted on already.

Many of us, however, must of late have asked ourselves how this war is ever to be brought to an end. If we are told that the deliberate conclusion of the Government is that it must be fought until Germany has been beaten to the ground and sues for peace on any terms which we are pleased to accord to her, my only observation would be that we ought to know something of the data upon which this conclusion has been reached. To many of us it seems as if the prospect of a ' knock-out ' was, to say the least of it, remote. Our forces and those of France have shown a splendid gallantry on the Western Front, and have made sub-stantial advances; but is it believed that these, any more than those made in 1915 with equally high hopes and accompanied by not less cruel losses, will really enable us to ' break through '? Can we afford to go on paying the same sort of price for the same sort of gains?

Judging from the comments supplied by the General Staff, I should doubt whether the Italian offensive, however successful, is likely to have a decisive effect.

At Salonika we are entangled in an extraordinarily difficult enterprise, forced upon us, against our better judgment, by our Allies, and valuable only because it occupies enemy troops who would otherwise be fighting the Russians and the Roumanians. On the Russian and Roumanian frontiers we shall be fortunate if we avoid a disaster, which at one moment seemed imminent. General Brussiloff's language is inspiring, but is it really justified by the facts? The history of the Russian operations has been very chequered, and we shall never, I am afraid, be free from the danger of miscarriages owing to defective strategy, to failure of supplies, to corruption in high places, or to incidents such as the disastrous explosion which has just lost us 10,000 tons of munitions at Archangel.

Again, are we quite sure that, regarded as political rather than military assets, our Allies are entirely to be depended upon? There have been occasions upon which political complications have threatened to affect the military situation in France. I quote the following sentences from a letter written a few days ago by a very shrewd Frenchman: ' Rappelez-vous bien que la Démocratie française n'est pas menée par son gouvernement; c'est elle qui le mène; un courant d'opinion publique en faveur de la cessation de la guerre pourrait être irrésistible. . . . Au feu, le soldat français se battra toujours comme un héros; derrière, sa famille pourra bien dire: en voilà assez!' Italy is always troublesome and exacting. Sir Rennell Rodd, in a dispatch dated the 4th November, asks us to take note of the fact that there are already in Italy 'certain symptoms of war weariness and discouragement at the protraction of the struggle. . . . Great Britain is represented as the only country anxious to prolong the struggle à outrance for her own ends. . . . It would be wrong to pretend that there exists here the same grim determination to carry through as prevails in France and the British Empire.' The domestic situation in Russia is far from reassuring. There have been alarming disorders both at Moscow and in Petrograd. Russia has had five Ministers of the Interior in twelve months, and the fifth is described as being by no means secure in his seat.

Our difficulties with the neutrals are, again, not likely to diminish. It is highly creditable to the Foreign Office that during the last two years we have escaped a breakdown of our blockade policy, which, in spite of continual obstruction and bad faith, has produced excellent results; but we have been within an ace of grave complications with Sweden and the United States. As time goes on the neutrals are likely to become more and more restive and intolerant of the belligerents, whose right to go on disturbing the peace of the civilised world they will refuse to admit.

I may be asked whether I have any practical suggestion to offer, and I admit the difficulty of replying. But is it not true that, unless the apprehensions which I have sketched can be shown, after such an investigation as I have suggested, to be groundless, we ought at any rate not to discourage any movement, no matter where originating, in favour of an interchange of views as to the possibility of a settlement? There are many indications that the germs of such a movement are already in existence. One cannot dismiss as unworthy of attention the well-substantiated reports which have come to us from time to time upon this subject from Belgian, Scandinavian, Japanese and Russian sources, or such circumstantial stories as those told in Sir Esmé Howard's dispatch of the 24th August as to the meeting held at Prince Lichnowsky's house, and in Lord Eustace Percy's memorandum as to the intimations made by the Rector of the Berlin University. The debates in the Reichstag show that the pacifist groups are active and outspoken. From all sides come accounts of the impatience of the civil population and their passionate yearning for peace.

It seems to me quite inconceivable that during the winter we shall not be sounded by someone as to our readiness to discuss

terms of peace or proposals for an armistice. Are we prepared
with our reply? Lord Crawford has dealt with the question of
an armistice. I am not sure that I agree with some of his suggestions, but I am sure that he is right in holding that
an unconditional refusal would be inadmissible.

As to peace terms, I hope we shall adhere steadfastly to the main
principle laid down by the Prime Minister in the speech which he
summed up by a declaration that we could agree to no peace which
did not afford adequate reparation for the past and adequate
security for the future, but the outline was broadly sketched and
might be filled up in many different ways. The same may be said
of the not less admirable statement which he has just made at the
Guildhall, and of the temperate speeches which the Secretary of
State for Foreign Affairs has from time to time delivered.

But it is unfortunate that, in spite of these utterances, it should
be possible to represent us and our Allies as committed to a policy
partly vindictive and partly selfish, and so irreconcilably committed to that policy that we should regard as unfriendly any attempt,
however sincere, to extricate us from the *impasse*. The interview
given by the Secretary of State for War in September last to an
American correspondent has produced an impression which it
will not be easy to efface. There may have been circumstances
of which I am unaware, connected perhaps with the Presidential
election, which made it necessary to announce that at the
particular moment any intervention, however well meant, would
be distasteful to us or inopportune. He said, indeed, that ‘ the
world must know that there can be no outside interference *at this
stage* ’—a very momentous limitation. For surely it cannot be
our intention, no matter how long the War lasts, no matter what
the strain on our resources, to maintain this attitude, or to declare,
as M. Briand declared about the same time, that for us, too, ‘ the
word peace is a sacrilege.’ Let our naval, military and economic
advisers tell us frankly whether they are satisfied that the knock-out
blow can and will be delivered. The Secretary of State’s formula
holds the field, and will do so until something else is put in its
place. Whether it is to hold the field, and, if not, what that something else should be, ought surely to depend upon their answer,
and that again upon the result of the careful stocktaking, domestic
and international, which, I hope, is already taking place.—L.

November 13, 1916.”

“ The above note had been written before the discussion, which
took place at to-day’s Cabinet, from which we learned that the War
Committee had already decided to take important steps in the
direction which I have ventured to indicate.—L.

November 13, 1916.”

Coming from a statesman of Lord Lansdowne's position and ante-cedents, this document made a deep impression. No one could accuse him of being a mere " pacifist." He was the author of the Entente Cordiale in 1904. He was an unflinching advocate of the policy of standing by all the implications of that fateful Treaty.

Before the Cabinet came to any conclusions on the Lansdowne memorandum, the Prime Minister invited the opinions of the military and naval authorities on the suggestion of a possible stalemate. The Chief of Staff, Sir William Robertson, truculently repudiated such a possibility. Ultimate victory was assured the Allies, provided the advice of the War Office was obediently followed in every particular and its demands patriotically fulfilled in every detail. There must be more men and material hurled at the enemy, and the hurling must be done exclusively on the Western Front. It was made quite clear that there would be still heavier casualties than those already suffered. From that Sir William Robertson did not shrink, but this further slaughter of British lives must occur in France and Flanders and not elsewhere.

Sir Douglas Haig put in a memorandum on similar lines. In this note, which Sir William Robertson appended to his answer to the Lansdowne memorandum, the Commander-in-Chief stresses the difficulties of maintaining any offensive in France during the winter, but points out that the conditions of which he complains represent only the normal situation at that time of the year. On the other side of the picture, the Germans had been badly defeated on the Somme, and their casualties had been undoubtedly heavy—far heavier than those of the Allies. Their *morale* had been lowered seriously. Indeed, he reached the conclusion that—

" an appreciable proportion of the German soldiers are now practically beaten men, ready to surrender if they could find opportunity, thoroughly tired of the War, and hopeless of eventual success."

The Allied troops, on the other hand, were all confident of victory.

" It is true that the amount of ground gained is not great. That is nothing. Our proved ability to get the enemy to move at all from his defensive positions was the valuable result of the fighting."

Sir Douglas Haig further said that he regarded the prospects of success on the Western Front in 1917 as most favourable. For this, however, he wanted many more troops, and an ample supply of munitions—of which " the enormous quantities required have been furnished this year with unfailing regularity." More aircraft, more road and railway material, etc., were also wanted.   Given these supplies, he and his army were confident of being able to achieve ultimate victory.   From the memoranda put in by the Chief of the Imperial Staff and the Commander-in-Chief there could be no doubt as to military opinion about our prospects.

Lord Grey's contribution was characteristic.   His position as Foreign Secretary was pivotal when it came to a question of making peace or continuing war.   We all anxiously awaited his guidance. He was the most departmental of Ministers, and had always been buried in his office, with hardly a thought for anything else.   He scarcely ever expressed any opinion on any Cabinet questions outside his own department.   His aloofness was monumental.   He had a habit—entirely his own—of drafting his dispatches at the Cabinet table whilst discussions were proceeding on home affairs.   This lofty detachment he carried into the War Cabinets.   In the discussion bearing on the most effective methods of prosecuting the War he had little to say or suggest.   Having been forced to declare the War from which he had failed to save his country, it was for others to direct it and find the means for its successful prosecution.   But here was a question pre-eminently affecting his department.   Should any peace approaches be encouraged or entertained?   The initiative had been taken by one of his immediate predecessors at the Foreign Office— Lord Lansdowne.

In spite of the confidence manifested by the military authorities, Lord Grey expressed his misgivings as to the effect of the submarine campaign, and said he thought it had not been mastered and for the present seemed to be getting more and more beyond our control.   He went so far as to say, however, that as long as the military and naval authorities considered that the position of the Allies was likely to improve, even though it might not result in the ultimate and com- plete defeat of Germany, it would be premature to make peace. Should it at any future time become evident that the Allies could not improve further their position, they should proceed forthwith to make the best peace terms they could.

Ever non-committal and hesitating, he neither associated himself with Lord Lansdowne nor did he dissent from his views.   He neither approved nor disapproved.   Whatever the decision or the event his intervention would conform to either.   Was he in favour of the Lansdowne thesis?   If it were turned down and its author and his supporters were taunted with faintheartedness, no one could fairly quote one sentence of unequivocal commendation from Lord Grey. On the other hand, if either then or later Lord Lansdowne's brave memorandum were justified, then no one could say that Lord Grey had offered any hostile criticism to its purport.

Sir William Robertson in his memorandum had arraigned the Foreign Secretary's diplomacy both before and during the War and had ascribed to its feebleness most of our misfortunes. The attack occupied one short paragraph in Sir W. Robertson's contribution. Lord Grey devoted pages to an explanation and defence of his failures —his failures to avoid war; to keep Turkey out of the War; to secure the timely help of Greece; and to lure Bulgaria on to our side. He had done everything of which diplomacy was capable without adequate military support. The failure was military and not diplomatic. All very interesting, but having no bearing on the momentous issue raised by Lord Lansdowne—whether it was better to make peace now or to fight on in the hope that we might be in a better position later on to dictate terms.

It is rather surprising that no constructive suggestions for peace were ever put forward by him either now or at any time. If he gave any thought to the terms of peace which he had in his mind as the end and aim of the War he never favoured his colleagues with his ideas. The only concrete proposals as to peace terms submitted to the Asquith Cabinet came from another pen. It was shortly before the Lansdowne discussions that the Government for the first time had submitted to its judgment any categorical, concrete and comprehensive scheme of a peace settlement. This was the document, to which reference has already been made, which came from the pen of Mr. Balfour, then First Lord of the Admiralty. It is a truly remarkable document and will bear careful perusal. The sentences in which he refuses to commit himself to any expression of opinion as to the possibility of future wars are ominous, coming from such an experienced statesman and so clear and penetrating an intellect. Apart from that it is the first time any statesman of the first rank committed himself to a written forecast of the conditions of peace.

"THE PEACE SETTLEMENT IN EUROPE
Memorandum by Mr. Balfour

The Prime Minister asked the Members of the War Committee to express their views on the peace settlement; and the present paper is an attempt—a very tentative and halting attempt—to comply with this request.

Even the most tentative suggestions must, however, proceed upon some hypothesis with regard to the military position of the combatants at the end of the War. What this will be no human being can foresee with any assurance. But inasmuch as it is convenient to proceed upon a hypothesis which is clear and determinate, I shall assume in what follows, though merely for the sake of argument, that the Central Powers, either through defeat or exhaustion, have to accept the terms imposed upon them by the Allies.

Let me add this further preliminary observation. The number

of questions which will have to be discussed at any Peace Conference is obviously very large. In what follows I desire to do no more than to offer some stray reflections upon the most important group of these questions—that which is concerned with the redistribution of population in the European area. By this limitation will be excluded not merely such subjects as the restriction of armaments, the freedom of the seas and the revision of international law, but also Heligoland, the Kiel Canal, strategic modifications of frontiers,* and the extra-European problems connected with Asia Minor and Germany's Colonial Empire.

On some of these subjects I may perhaps trouble the Committee at a later date.

The principal object of the War is the attainment of a durable peace, and I submit that the best way of securing this is by the double method of diminishing the area from which the Central Powers can draw the men and money required for a policy of aggression, while at the same time rendering a policy of aggression less attractive by rearranging the map of Europe in closer agreement with what we rather vaguely call ' the principle of nationality.'

The second of these methods, if successfully applied, would secure many objects which are universally desired by the Allies. It would give Belgium her independence, restore Alsace and Lorraine to France, provide some kind of home rule for Poland, extend the frontiers of Italy, and establish a Greater Serbia and a Greater Roumania in South-East Europe; I should greatly like to see it applied in Bohemia also. To Bohemia, Germanic civilisation is profoundly distasteful. The Czechs have been waging war against it for some generations, and waging it under grave difficulties with much success. Whether an independent Bohemia would be strong enough to hold her own, from a military as well as from a commercial point of view, against Teutonic domination —surrounded as she is at present entirely by German influences— I do not know; but I am sure the question deserves very careful consideration. If the change is possible it should be made.†

Now, a map of Europe so modified would not only carry out the second of the two methods of preserving peace which I have described above, but would also help to carry out the first. The resources of men and money on which the Central Powers could draw for purposes of aggressive warfare would be greatly diminished. Alsace-Lorraine, Austrian Poland, with, possibly, parts of German Poland, Transylvania, Italian Austria, Bosnia

---

* Of course such strategic modifications might involve transfers of populations, which could not properly be described as negligible. But their object would not be to acquire territory, but to increase security by making frontiers more defensible.

† I presume that arrangements will be made by which the frontier of Bohemia would, to some small extent at least, become coterminous with the New Poland.

and Herzegovina would cease to be recruiting grounds for supplying German or Austrian Armies; and the men of military age thus withdrawn from the Central Armies would be added to the nations with which the Central Powers are now at war; thus, as it were, counting two on a division.

The populations thus transferred would, I suppose, be more than 20 millions. I take no account in this argument of the non-Italian population which Italy will no doubt obtain if the Allies are successful; nor do I discuss the uncontested zone coveted by Bulgaria. If the principle of nationality be rigidly applied, I suppose that, without doubt, Bulgaria ought to have it. Whether she deserves it, and whether, in view of Serbian sentiment we can give it to her, is quite another question.

I conceive that this general scheme is, broadly speaking, what public opinion in this country would desire to see carried out. The point on which there might be most difference of opinion would perhaps be the fate of Poland—since the fate of Constantinople and the Banat is already settled so far as the Allies can settle it. Almost the only thing on which Russia and Germany seem to be agreed is that the status of Poland should be altered by the War, and that, while receiving some measure of autonomy, it should remain dependent upon one of its two great neighbours. But as to what the limits of the new Poland should be, and on which of its two great neighbours it is to be dependent, there is, it need hardly be said, a fundamental divergence of opinion between Petrograd and Berlin.

Looking at the Polish question from a purely British point of view, I should like to see the new State include not merely Russian Poland, but as much of Austria and German Poland as possible. This, of course, is in strict accord with the two principles laid down earlier in the paper. But I should *not* like to see the old Kingdom of Poland restored. I should fear that the new Poland would suffer from the diseases through which the old Poland perished; that it would be a theatre of perpetual intrigues between Germany and Russia; and that its existence, so far from promoting the cause of European peace, would be a perpetual occasion of European strife.

Moreover, even if such a Poland were capable of playing the part of an efficient buffer State (which I doubt), I am not sure that a buffer State between Germany and Russia would be any advantage to Western Europe. If Germany were relieved of all fear of pressure from Russia, and were at liberty to turn her whole strength towards developing her western ambitions, France and Britain might be the sufferers; and I am not by any means confident that cutting off Russia from her western neighbours might not divert her interests towards the Far East to an extent which

British statesmen could not view without some misgivings. The more Russia is made a European rather than an Asiatic Power, the better for everybody.

I therefore conclude that the solution of the Polish question which would best suit our interests would be the constitution of a Poland endowed with a large measure of autonomy, while remaining an integral part of the Russian Empire—the new State or province to include not only all Russian Poland, but also Austria's and (part at least of) Prussia's share in the plunder of the ancient kingdom.

Personally I should like to see the Danish portions of Schleswig-Holstein, filched by Prussia and Austria from Denmark in 1863, again restored to their former owner. But Denmark would hardly accept the gift unless it was accompanied by some form of territorial guarantee which she would think effective; and even then the memory of Belgium might act as a deterrent. But the question should be seriously considered. I ought, parenthetically, to add that unfortunately the region through which the Kiel Canal passes is German both in language and sentiment.

So far I have indicated the kind of changes which I should like to see attempted when peace comes to be discussed. But there are some projects advocated by those who believe in the complete victory of the Allies which I regard with great suspicion. Among these perhaps the most important are the projects for breaking up or reconstituting the German Empire. If I had my way, I should rule out any attempt to touch the internal affairs either of Germany or of Austria. It may be that, under the stress of defeat, ancient jealousies—forgotten in the hour of victory—will revive. South may be divided from North, Roman Catholic from Protestant, Württemberg, Bavaria and Saxony from Prussia, or from each other. A revolution may upset the Hohenzollerns, and a new Germany may arise on the ruins of militarism.

Any or all of these things are possible, but I would certainly deprecate any attempt on the part of the victorious enemy to bring them about. One of the few recorded attempts to crush militarism in a defeated State was Napoleon's attempt to destroy the Prussian Army after Jena. No attempt was ever less successful. As everybody knows, Napoleon's policy compelled Prussia to contrive the military system which has created modern Germany. It may be—I hope it will be—in the power of the Allies to strip Germany of much of her non-German territory; but, whatever be the limits of the new Germany, I hope no attempt will be made to control or modify her internal policy. The motto of the Allies should be ' Germany for the Germans—but only Germany.'

This formula, however, even if it be accepted, does not solve the problem of Central Europe. It says nothing, for example, of the future relations between Germany and Austria. I should myself desire to see the Dual Monarchy maintained, shorn indeed of a large portion of its Slav, Italian, and Roumanian territories, but still essentially consisting of Austria and Hungary. If this were to occur, we should have in the future, as we have had in the past, a German Empire and an Austrian Empire side by side and probably kept in close alliance—political if not also economic— for purposes of mutual protection. Other possibilities, however, have to be considered. The result of the War may be the complete break-up of the Dual Monarchy; and if the Dual Monarchy breaks up, it is reasonable to suppose that the German portion of it would coalesce with the German Empire, leaving Hungary either isolated or dependent. Apparently such a change would create a great German-speaking State more formidable than Germany before the War; and this may be, in fact, what would happen. On the other hand, it must be remembered that such a change would profoundly modify the position of Prussia. The Roman Catholics and South German elements would become overwhelmingly strong; and if the driving force behind German aggression be due, as most observers think, to Prussian organisation and Prussian traditions, the change might in its ultimate effect be a defeat for German militarism.

But I do not disguise from myself either that the dangers of such a Teutonic reorganisation are considerable, or that the likelihood of its occurring may be increased if the result of the War is to convince the German-speaking peoples that their only hope of national greatness lies in their consenting to forget all causes of difference and welding themselves into a single powerful State. Those who think the future must necessarily resemble the past may perhaps be disposed to remind us that for the five centuries preceding the Bismarckian era the political tendencies prevailing in Germany have been, on the whole, centrifugal and separatist. They will argue that this inveterate tradition, interrupted though it has been for forty-five years by a united and triumphant Germany, nevertheless represents the real tendencies of the race; and that to this tradition it will revert after a war for which Prussian policy and a Prussian dynasty have been responsible.

Personally, I am inclined to doubt this conclusion, plausible as it seems; nor do I believe that anything which we and our Allies can accomplish will prevent the Germanic Powers, either united by alliance or fused into a single State, from remaining wealthy, populous, and potentially formidable.

For this reason I do not share the fears of those who think that the triumph of the Slav countries is likely to menace German pre-dominance in Central Europe. When we remember that the Slav populations are divided by language, religion and government;

that they fought each other four years ago; that they are fighting each other at this very moment; that the only one among them which can count as a Great Power is Russia; and that Russia, according to most observers, is likely to be torn by revolutionary struggles as soon as the pressure of war is removed; when (I say) we remember these things, we shall probably be disposed to think that the Germanic States will be very well able to take care of themselves, whatever be the terms of peace to which they may have to submit.

This is a fact (if it indeed be a fact) which is sometimes ignored. Many of those who speculate about the future of Europe seem to fear that Germany will be so weakened by the War that the balance of Power will be utterly upset, and Britain will be left face to face with some other Great Power striving in its turn for universal dominance. I doubt this. In any case it seems to me quite clear that, measured by population, Germany—and still more, Germany in alliance with Austria—will be more than a match for France alone, however much we give to France, and however much we take from the Central States. If, therefore, Europe after the War is to be an armed camp, the peace of the world will depend, as heretofore, on defensive alliances formed by those who desire to retain their possessions against those who desire to increase them. In that event the Entente is likely to be maintained. Germany may suffer a spiritual conversion; Russia may break up; France and Britain may be rendered powerless by labour troubles; universal bankruptcy may destroy universal armaments; international courts may secure international peace; the horrors of 1914, 1915, 1916, and 1917 may render the very thought of war disgusting to all mankind. On these subjects it is vain to speculate. All I would for the moment insist on is that the greatest territorial losses which the Allies can or ought to inflict on the Central Powers will leave them powerful both for defence and offence. Whatever trouble Russia may give us in Mesopotamia, Persia and Afghanistan, I do not think she will attempt the domination of Europe, still less succeed in securing it.

There are two subsidiary points on which I may say a word before concluding—rights of way and indemnities. If the shores of the Adriatic are in Italian hands, if Salonika is in Greek hands, how are we going to provide the Central Powers with commercial access to the Mediterranean and the South? That they should not be denied such access seems to be fairly clear. It is one thing to cut off Germany from her megalo-maniacal designs upon Asia Minor, Mesopotamia, Persia, and India; it is quite another to put the commerce of Austria-Hungary with the Eastern Mediterranean and the Suez Canal at the mercy of the States which lie between it and the sea. There could, it seems to me, be no more powerful incentive to new wars. Some method of guaranteeing to States which have no convenient seaboard the free flow of commerce through selected channels is therefore urgently required. I have had no time to give to the subject, but I have sometimes idly wondered whether the treaties which apply to navigable rivers flowing through different States might not—with the necessary modifications—be applied also to ports and railways.

My last topic is war indemnities. I have, for the sake of argument, assumed that the success of the Allies is going to be complete. On this assumption—ought indemnities to be demanded?

Germany has never made any secret of her intention of beggaring her enemies and reducing them, if she got the power, to complete commercial subservience. My own inclination would be strongly against imitating Germany's behaviour in 1871 and imposing a commercial treaty on my opponents for my own advantage. Such treaties are needlessly humiliating, even when they are not onerous. When they are, they are sure, sooner or later, to be broken.

But there are two things I should like to do, and which in the interests of international morality I think ought to be done. I think the Central Powers should be made to pay for the damage they have done in Belgium, Northern France, and Serbia; and I think they ought to surrender shipping equivalent in amount to that which they have sent to the bottom in the course of their submarine warfare. These are charges which it should be within their power to meet; and if within their power to meet, then certainly within our right to demand. Whether more can or ought to be exacted is a point on which I feel incompetent to give an opinion; but it may be worth remembering that to take territories from the German or Austrian Empires free of debt, is in effect to increase the burdens on the States from which they are taken, and to relieve the burden on the States to which they are added.

A. J. B.

Oct. 4, 1916."

Mr. Henderson, one of the ablest and most influential of Labour leaders, at this time publicly as well as in private, threw in the whole weight of his great influence with organised labour against " a premature peace." His words are worth quoting: —

" The War has gone on too long for some of the people of this country. It is possible that in the military situation of the case we may become war-weary, and I want to warn everyone of the danger of a premature peace. I am as strong for peace as any man or woman can be, but I must be satisfied that the peace we expect places us, above any doubt, beyond the recurrence of such a catastrophe. . . . We are in the War, and to talk about peace with all the most unscrupulous military forces against us would be a step to having the whole thing fought over again. That would not be ending the War by a permanent peace. A peace under such conditions, with Belgium and France, Serbia and Roumania, in the condition they are! No! We want not a dishonourable peace, but a lasting, permanent peace, peace based upon national right and national honour, and I say these two words in spite of the fact that one of my own colleagues has described them as platitudes."

This speech fairly expressed the view I also took at the time as to the mistake of encouraging peace overtures until the military situation had considerably improved.

Another member of the Government whose attachment to the cause of peace is above suspicion, Lord Robert Cecil, came to the conclusion that in view of the military estimates of our prospects: —

" A peace now could only be disastrous. At the best we could not hope for more than the *status quo* with a great increase in the German power in Eastern Europe. Moreover, this peace would be known by the Germans to have been forced upon us by their submarines, and our insular position would be recognised as increasing instead of diminishing our vulnerability. No one can contemplate our future ten years after a peace on such conditions without profound misgiving. I feel, therefore, that we are bound to continue the War."

He then proceeds, in the memorandum from which I am quoting, to make certain practical suggestions as to the organisation of the nation. Lord Robert Cecil's memorandum has a further interest because it contains a review of the military position at that date by a very able observer: —

" Whether we agree with Lord Lansdowne's conclusions or not, one thing is clear. Our situation is grave. It is certain that unless the utmost national effort is made it may become desperate, particularly in the matter of shipping. The position in Allied countries is even more serious. France is within measurable distance of exhaustion. The political outlook in Italy is menacing. Her finance is tottering. In Russia there is great discouragement. She has long been on the verge of revolution. Even her man-power seems coming near its limits.

On the other hand, our enemies, though badly injured, are not disabled. The economic position of Germany may or may not be alarming. It is certainly not yet desperate. No certain information as to her supplies is available. There is no trustworthy ground for thinking that she is starving, although she may be—very possibly she is—in want of other necessaries, such as wool, cotton, lubricating oils, rubber, which will hamper and diminish her military strength, and there is great political discontent. In Austria the position is probably worse."

The Prime Minister, having, according to his wont, carefully gathered or received opinions amongst his colleagues without attempting to influence them, decided ultimately that the time had not yet arrived for peace feelers. No member of the Cabinet expressed his dissent from this conclusion.

I have given a fairly exhaustive account of the Lansdowne episode because I am anxious to demonstrate that the Governments that conducted the War never lost sight of the importance of seizing any favourable opportunity that might offer itself to make an honourable peace. The Lansdowne discussions have also their special value because they are the first occasion on which any of the belligerent Governments courageously faced the possibility that peace might have to be considered without victory. The Asquith Government examined the whole position with great care and came to the unanimous conclusion that to enter into peace negotiations with Germany before inflicting a complete defeat upon her armies, would be disastrous. The principle of President Wilson's subsequent dictum in favour of peace without victory was thus carefully studied and emphatically repudiated in advance by the Asquith Government. What is more to the point, when one considers the kind of criticism levelled at the Government of 1917, is the conclusion come to by the Asquith Administration that without acknowledgment of defeat on the part of the Central Powers overtures of peace should not be encouraged, as they would settle none of the issues raised by this colossal struggle, and might and probably would be dangerous to the *morale* and solidarity of the Allies.

Mr. Asquith himself gave no countenance to a timorous or defeatist attitude. A fortnight after my " knock-out blow " interview had been published, he delivered, on 11th October, 1916, a speech in the House of Commons, in the course of which he said:—

" The strain which the War imposes on ourselves and our Allies, the hardships which we freely admit it involves on some of those who are not directly concerned in the struggle, the upheaval of trade, the devastation of territory, the loss of irreplaceable lives— this long and sombre procession of cruelty and suffering, lighted up as it is by deathless examples of heroism and chivalry, cannot be allowed to end in some patched-up, precarious, dishonouring compromise, masquerading under the name of Peace. No one desires to prolong for a single unnecessary day the tragic spectacle of bloodshed and destruction, but we owe it to those who have given their lives for us, the flower of our youth, the hope and promise of our future, that their supreme sacrifice shall not have been in vain. The ends of the Allies are well known; they have been frequently and precisely stated. They are not selfish ends, they are not vindictive ends, but they require that there shall be adequate reparation for the past and adequate security for the future. On their achievement we in this country honestly believe depend the best hopes of humanity."

Here we had a fine and firm resolve expressed in the splendid eloquence of which Mr. Asquith was a master. The fact that his eldest son Mr. Raymond Asquith, a young man of great brilliance and promise, had fallen in action a few weeks before the delivery of this speech, gave tragic force to this passage.

Hardly less emphatic was a statement made less than a fortnight later by Lord Grey. It is indeed somewhat curious to note that while Prince Max of Baden in his " Memoirs " describes Germany watching through the late autumn of 1916 what it regarded as the approach of a " trial of strength between Lloyd George and Lord Grey," for and against the policy of the "knock-out blow," Lord Grey himself, speaking on 23rd October to a gathering at the Hotel Cecil, was declaring : —

" There must be no end to this war, no peace except a peace which is going to ensure that the nations of Europe live in the future free from that shadow and in the open light of freedom. For that we are contending. It is our determination, which the progress of the War but deepens, in common with our Allies, to continue the War till we have made it certain that the Allies in common shall have achieved the success which must, and ought, to be theirs, till they have secured the future peace of the whole continent of Europe, till they have made it clear that all the sacrifices we have made shall not have been made in vain."

These valiant words lend little colour to the rumour which for some reason or other was then evidently widespread, not only in this country but even more throughout Central Europe, that Lord Grey was one of those who were angling for an inconclusive peace.

Can anyone doubt now, on a calm review of the position, that Mr. Asquith and his colleagues were right in the conclusion to which they came? Could we have made a peace at that time which would not have recognised Germany as a victor? Could we have made it at any time before the final breakdown of Germany's prowess? Would Germany have agreed to restore the complete independence of Belgium? Even if she consented to evacuate Belgium, would she have agreed to impose no military and commercial conditions which would have meant the practical incorporation of Belgium in the sphere of German domination and military and trading expansion? All the evidence is in the negative. The few far-seeing German statesmen who foresaw the perils which encircled the Fatherland and were anxious that peace should be made whilst the German military power was intact, never ceased to urge the German Chancellor to make an unequivocal statement about the full restoration of Belgium. Their efforts and urgent appeals were in vain right up to the final collapse. Prince Max of Baden, who later on became Chancellor, pointed out to the German leaders that even so pronounced a pacifist as Mr. Ramsay MacDonald, speaking in the House of Commons in the spring of 1916, had insisted that a declaration by Germany of her intention to restore a complete Belgian sovereignty and every " portion of it " was a condition precedent of any peace settlement. That declaration never came.

Would Austria have given up her conquests in Serbia? Would there have been no terms imposed as to the fortification of the Serbian capital, which would have left Serbia helplessly at the mercy of Austria, and thus reduced her to a state of vassalage to the Austrian Empire? Would no part of Serbian territory have been carved out to requite Czar Ferdinand's loyal rapacity? Then what about the Baltic provinces of Russia and Russian Poland? Would Germany have given up all her marvellous conquests in Russia and added nothing to her territories in that quarter? A suggestion that Alsace-Lorraine be restored to France as a condition of peace would have been greeted throughout the Fatherland with a Teutonic guffaw. France at the end of 1916 was certainly not in a position to ask for more than the restoration of the German conquests of 1914. Even then were the German industrialists prepared to give up the Briey mines? All the contemporary evidence points the other way. Apart from that there was not one chance in a million that peace negotiations could produce a settlement in the east or west satisfactory to the most moderate Allied statesman.

Would real disarmament have been any part of a 1916 peace? Would Germany have consented to dismantle the redoubtable military machine that had placed her in such a commanding position in the world? And if Germany did not disarm, no other country could have afforded to do so. To quote again the words then used by a statesman whose name is a guarantee for pacific intentions—Lord Robert Cecil—" A peace now could only be disastrous. At best we could not hope for more than the *status quo* with a great increase in the German Power in Central Europe." The only result would have been a bigger Germany, better armed, confident that her armies were unbeatable in the field even by overwhelming numbers, and with a military staff which had learned how war under modern conditions could be best and most effectively conducted.

It is often said now by men who are seeking busily to find fault with those who shouldered the terrible responsibilities of decision in the War, that no harm would have been done had the Allies taken the initiative in approaching the Central Powers with a view to the Convocation of a Peace Conference in 1916, even if such a conference failed. It is urged that if Germany and Austria made unreasonable conditions the Allied populations would have firmly supported their representatives in rejecting these terms and would then have continued the fight with renewed zeal and conviction. Would they? If Germany had offered to withdraw all her forces from Northern France and from Belgium, merely imposing certain conditions in the case of Belgium as to the uses of the ports of Belgium and as to the dismantlement of her frontier fortresses, could the Allied Governments have roused once more the spirit of 1914 to the pitch of facing for more than two years the horrible losses of the preceding two and a half years, merely in order to restore Alsace-Lorraine to France or to hand back Courland and other conquered territories to the incompetent hands of Russian autocracy? The inhabitants of these lands are no more Russian than they are German. Once the carnage of war had stopped, would Britain have consented to renew it and send her sons to fight other bloody battles like the Somme in order to restore the useless fortifications of Belgrade, or to rescue some obscure vilayet in Macedonia from the clutches of the Bulgarian king? At any rate, the risk that nations would have accepted any humiliations inflicted upon foreigners, rather than send millions more of their own kinsmen to the wholesale slaughter of modern warfare, were too great for those who looked forward to the permanent triumph of international right, justice and peace as a result of the sacrifices of this generation. We should have met at the Congress a Germany which had victoriously held up Europe for two and a half years, shattered completely the power of three of her enemies, Russia, Roumania and Serbia, and was still in occupation of the territory of two more, and had successfully defied every effort to dislodge her hold on her conquests. The best that could be hoped for would be a completely liberated France and Belgium, with a Germany swollen through its eastern conquests by scores of thousands of square miles and tens of millions of population. With a war so ended we should have been confronted with a triumphant Prussian militarism which had demonstrated its invincibility in the field against overwhelming odds in numbers, material and wealth. Mr. Asquith and his Cabinet were emphatically right in refusing to assent to the Lansdowne proposition. Had they done so, even if they had secured the adhesion of France, it could not have ended in a great and workable peace. France would not have agreed readily to make any overtures, because no peace possible at that time would have satisfied her essential conditions—the restoration of her lost provinces and reparation for her damaged towns and villages. Italy would have been fooled, for she had banked on Allied success for the redemption of the Italian valleys in the Austrian Empire, and notwithstanding her heavy losses she would have had nothing out of any peace settlement which was attainable in 1916. It would have been said that Britain was anxious for peace and was prepared to sell her Allies to attain it. Such an impression would have had a shattering effect on Allied *morale*—east and west. The failure to make peace or a refusal by France to follow a peace initiative from Britain would have distracted and divided opinion in America, at the moment when opinion in that great country was being driven rapidly in our direction by the reckless and indiscriminate methods of the submarine campaign.

CHAPTER XXXII

THE MILITARY POSITION AT THE END OF THE 1916 CAMPAIGN

IF we were resolved to continue the War, it was vital that we should fight in a way that would give us a reasonable chance of achieving victory. But when I surveyed the outlook both on land and sea in the closing months of 1916, I saw the gravest grounds for disquietude. There was as yet little sign that the efforts and sacrifices we had made were leading us towards a victorious conclusion; and the information which came either to the War Office or to the Admiralty was by no means reassuring.

In October, 1916, at one of the stilted and formal morning interviews which the Chief of the Imperial Staff in the course of his duty accorded to me as his civilian chief, after he had exhausted a few secondary and trivial matters upon which he had gone through the form of consulting me, I probed him as to the position on the Somme, the terrible casualties, and the insignificant gains. He returned the familiar answers to the effect that the German losses were greater than ours, that the Germans were gradually being worn down, and their *morale* shaken by constant defeat and retreat. All the same it struck me that his answer was not given with the usual rigid confidence. I then asked him whether he would mind telling me whether he had formed any views as to how this sanguinary conflict was to be brought to a successful end. For the time being the question took him aback, and he looked like a general in full dress who thought to himself "This is one of those fool questions that ignorant civilians always fire at you, and they must not be encouraged." He just mumbled something about "Attrition." I asked him whether he would mind giving me a memorandum on the subject. In due course it was written, and here is a summary of it: —

The Western Front is still held to be the main theatre of operations for the British forces.

As to the secondary theatres: In Mesopotamia the British force is improving its position, and will be in a condition to meet any effort the Turks can make against us by the time they are ready to attack. In Egypt there is similar reason to expect that the Western Front against the Senussi will be safe by the end of the year, and arrangements complete for an advance on the east into the Sinai desert. At

Salonika the Allied forces have held the Bulgarian-German Armies. General Milne has asked for a reinforcement of 15 divisions and heavy artillery to achieve a victory on the Macedonian front, but the C.I.G.S. considers such a transfer from the main theatre of the Western Front undesirable. He thinks the only decisive campaign in the Balkans this winter must be on the Roumanian front. He regrets that the Allies have agreed to send reinforcements of 39,000 rifles to Macedonia.

In German East Africa we hold the coast line, and have driven the German forces into the unhealthy interior.

On the Western Front we are now superior to the Germans in numbers, in aircraft, in artillery, and probably to some extent also in the supply of ammunition. The effect of the Somme offensive has been to unsettle the enemy and weaken their *morale*. They are not actually demoralised, and we cannot expect them to collapse, but their prospects are worse than ours when we were being subjected to similar assault in 1914, as they have not behind them the undeveloped resources we had then. So our relative superiority is growing greater every day. But the C.I.G.S. holds that we must keep up the western pressure, as if the Central Powers can transfer more of their troops to the east the result will be disastrous. He gives figures to show the extent to which such transfers have taken place in the last five months. Since 1st June, the German forces have increased by $27\frac{1}{2}$ divisions, most of which have been added to the Eastern Front, where the number of battalions has risen (between 1st June and 23rd October) by 221, while on the west it has been reduced by 74.

He then goes on to show how we have increased our mechanical strength on the Western Front. The following figures show the growth of British artillery in France.

	1st Jan. 1916.	End Oct. 1916.
Field guns	1,938	3,060
Howitzers & heavy guns ...	785	1,879
Daily income of ammunition ...	30,000 rds.	210,000 rds.

Howitzers and heavy guns would number over 2,000 by the end of the year, and the increase in machine-guns, trench mortars, etc., has been on a corresponding scale. But in man-power the Army in France is 80,000 below establishment, and should be reinforced. There should be a further comb-out, and the Home Defence Force should be reduced after the Navy had been induced to make more effective arrangements to prevent invasion. The greatest possible force should be available in France by the spring of 1917.

The Entente Powers are suffering from bad communications and defective co-operation, apart from France and England. The value of the Entente troops of Roumania, Belgium, Serbia, Portugal and

Russia is low—in the case of Russia through lack of equipment. The enemy troops are more mobile and have a moral superiority. The duration of the War depends on the staying power of Germany's allies. Austria and Turkey are growing exhausted, and Bulgaria is weakened by its previous wars. Germany is, however, fighting with undiminished vigour, and can continue the War for as yet an indefinite period. But her supplies of food would become very short in another six months.

The C.I.G.S.'s conclusion was that the end of the War could not yet be predicted. We must be prepared to put our whole effort, tighten the blockade, rally every available man, and face still greater strain and sacrifice, to secure the peace we desired.

Sir William Robertson ended his memorandum with a table setting out the estimated numbers of troops and of still available reserves at the disposal respectively of the Allies and of the Central Powers. It is worth studying, for it contains ominous figures upon which I comment later on. The following is a summary of this table: —

	Entente Armies, including troops in home territory, and excluding coloured troops.	Reserves still available.
British	3,517,000	?
French	2,978,000	775,000
Russian	4,767,000	6,500,000
Italian	1,676,000	1,250,000
Roumanian	590,000	380,000
Belgian	128,000	10,000
Serbian	117,000	22,000
Portuguese	65,000	
	13,838,000	8,937,000

Enemy Forces.

German	5,470,000	2,000,000
Austro-Hungarian ...	2,750,000	800,000
Turkish	500,000	300,000
Bulgarian	400,000	112,000
	9,120,000	3,212,000

The C.I.G.S.'s picture did not present a cheerful outlook. We could now hold our own against the Turks in Mesopotamia and Egypt—but nothing more just yet. At Salonika we could stand up to the Bulgarians if they attacked, but we were in no position to attack them. On the Western Front we were doing better. We were shaking the German *morale*. His solitary proof of it was disturbing. Several German divisions had fled from the western battlefield to the east. Why? Not because they were beaten but because they felt they could hold their own in the west with 74 fewer battalions. What a commentary on the smashing triumphs of the Somme!

The statistical table showed that so far as existing effectives and reserves at any rate were concerned, we had an overwhelming majority of men compared with the enemy powers. But our superiority in numbers depended entirely on Russia and Roumania remaining effectively in the War. That was becoming increasingly problematical. Once they were eliminated the numerical superiority passed over to the enemy countries. Equality of numbers then would only be attainable by a further heavy drain on our man-power. It was an ominous fact that of the 13,838,000 Allied troops, 5,357,000 were Russian and Roumanian; and of the reserves 6,880,000 were Russian and Roumanian. Roumania, with her 970,000, was about to disappear from the Allied schedule. Russia, with her 11,000,000, was to follow soon after. As to the general military position I have summarised it in a preceding chapter. It was not encouraging.

The conviction was borne in upon me that a much more serious effort must be made to co-ordinate the Allied efforts in east and west; Sir William Robertson admitted the Allied weakness in that respect. In thinking this matter over I made up my mind to have a confidential talk with the Prime Minister about the situation, and I accordingly invited him to come round one evening to dinner at my house.

The invitation was accepted and the dinner duly took place. Besides Mr. Asquith there were present Lord Crewe, Lord Grey, Mr. Balfour, Lord Curzon and, I think, Lord Lansdowne. I laid before them my views as to the seriousness of the situation and as to the steps which should be taken. Mr. Asquith heard me sympathetically and recommended me to bring the matter forward for discussion at the next meeting of the War Committee.

This meeting took place on 3rd November, 1916, and, in anticipation of it, I secured from Sir William Robertson a further statement, which I reproduce here, setting out his views as to the probable end of the War: —

" 1. You tell me the War Committee wish to have my opinion with respect to the probable duration of the War, and I must at once confess that I feel it very difficult to express any opinion which can usefully be relied upon. Hindenburg is alleged to have stated recently that no man can foresee the end of the War, and I certainly cannot. This inability to forecast events is not peculiar to this war, but is more or less common to all wars. It is, in fact, greatly accentuated in the present war, both by the colossal scale of the War and the conditions under which it is waged. Never before, for instance, have such large questions of international finance and commerce been involved.

2. Further, we are not fighting for some comparatively minor object which we might hope to attain after giving the enemy a sound beating, but we are to continue the War ' until the military domination of Prussia is wholly and finally destroyed.'

3. The question you ask me is by no means merely, or even mainly, a military one. For example, I am ignorant of: —

(a) Probable solidarity of the Allies and of enemy countries.

(b) Social and economic conditions in the enemy countries.

(c) Comparative staying power in money and commerce of the two opposing sides.

(d) Possible submarine developments.

(e) The power of our Navy to keep open sea communications and preserve adequate mercantile marine for the supply of ourselves, our Allies, and the Allied Armies overseas.

(f) Advantages and disadvantages which may accrue from Allied diplomacy.

4. The staying power in men counts for very much, but I do not know what men we ourselves are capable of putting into the field, or when they can be put there. Nor do I think, for reasons explained in my paper of the 26th ultimo,* that in the case of the other belligerents any really useful purpose would be served by attempting to find the answer to your question by the manipulation of figures. In the first place the figures we use are to a great extent guess-work. Secondly, although the Entente have on paper more men than the enemy, they cannot be nearly so easily liquidated in practice. Russia is corrupt, badly armed and administered, and will not improve her communications; Italy refused to move men from her own country; Roumania is in retreat. Finally, Germany's interior position and complete control over the policy and operations of the Central Powers give her an advantage worth many hundreds of thousands of men.

5. On the Western Front we and the French have been steadily gaining a moral and material ascendency over the enemy, and as regards ourselves it is still within our power to put more men and more guns and munitions into the field. If we do this, and if we do not fritter away our efforts in non-vital theatres, and if Russia can be supplied with a reasonable amount of heavy artillery and other necessary war material, we may hope that in the future the pressure upon the enemy on both fronts will not be less severe than it has been in the past. How long we can continue to apply this pressure, and when we may expect to derive decisive results from it are questions which mainly depend upon the factors

* Summarised on pages 537-38.

mentioned in para. 3. It also depends upon the strategy of the Entente, over which my control is very limited. I am, therefore, quite unable to form any opinion as to when the end of the War may be, but I think we shall be well advised not to expect the end at any rate before the summer of 1918. How long it may go on afterwards I cannot even guess. One thing is quite certain, as I have many times said during the present year, and that is that we cannot hope for a conclusion in our favour unless and until we make full and appropriate use of all our resources. We have not yet taken the steps to do this and we ought to take them at once. I referred to some of them in the final paragraph of my paper of the 26th ultimo, and I may add here that we must: —

Have a full day's work from every man and woman.

Make all possible use of foreign labour.

Check present waste and extravagance in the national life.

Become as self-supporting as possible.

Clearly explain to the nation the grave nature of the task in front of us.

Secure a control over the War in all its aspects equivalent to the contribution we are making towards it. (I emphasised this in January last, but little, if any, improvement has been effected.)

W.R.R.

C.I.G.S.

November 3, 1916."

Basing myself upon this document, I made a statement at the War Committee, of which I give the following extracts from the summary contained in its minutes: —

" Mr. Lloyd George . . . read to the War Committee a minute by the Chief of the Imperial General Staff, dated the 3rd November, 1916, regarding the probable duration of the War.

Mr. Lloyd George said that this was one of the most serious documents on the War that he had read. We were not getting on with the War. We were now at the end of the third campaign of the War, yet the enemy had recovered the initiative. He had in his occupation more territory than ever before, and he had still some four millions of reserves. At no point had the Allies achieved a definite clean success. . . .

How then, Mr. Lloyd George asked, is the War to be brought to an end?"

I then summarised the facts of the Allied military position in terms which were subsequently embodied in the memorandum which appears later.

The minute then goes on : —

"So far as the public was concerned, the responsibility for the conduct of the War attaches to the politicians, and more especially to the Cabinet Ministers who compose the War Committee. The public will forgive anything except inaction and drift. He urged that the politicians responsible for the conduct of the War in the principal Allied countries, ought to meet together to take stock of the situation. In the first place, the representatives of France, Italy, and Great Britain should confer together. . . .

He suggested that the first object of the Conference should be to insist that West should confer with East. . . .

Mr. Lloyd George concluded by urging : —

1. A small conference composed of two ministers each from France, Italy, and this country.

2. A military conference to take place subsequently in the East, which should be attended by the principal generals from the West, preferably Generals Robertson, Joffre, Castelnau and Cadorna."

In the discussion which followed, so the minutes state, a general agreement was expressed with the tenor of my remarks, though they were criticised by some members as unduly pessimistic in regard to the general situation of the Allies.

It was generally agreed that the offensive on the Somme, if continued next year, was not likely to lead to decisive results, and that the losses might make too heavy a drain on our resources, having regard to the results to be anticipated. We decided, therefore, to examine whether a decision might not be reached in another theatre. As a preliminary step my proposals were approved in principle, and it was left to Lord Grey and myself to draft a telegram to Paris and one to Rome with regard to the proposed conference in Paris.

The War Committee agreed that before the meeting of the military conference at Chantilly, arranged for 15th November, it was essential that there should be consultation between the heads of the principal Allied Governments, in order to take stock of the situation and of the broad principles of policy and strategy that should decide the next phase of the campaign and the operations next year. They considered that the question should be first discussed by the statesmen, who had the real and ultimate responsibility for the whole conduct of affairs, and that the presence of expert advisers at this stage of the conference would be undesirable. They regarded a large conference as useless and suggested that it should be limited to two statesmen each from this country, France, and Italy, the British representatives being the Prime Minister and myself. The difficulty about Russian representation appeared insuperable, as no one could take the place of the Emperor and his chief political and military advisers, who could not leave Russia at present.

The War Committee further agreed that, if the Paris Conference arrived at important conclusions these should be discussed with Russia, and that this could probably best be done by sending representatives of the Allies to Russia, where they could be received by the Emperor, and confer with the chief persons who, under the Emperor, directed policy and strategy. Without a visit to Russia, no final agreement affecting both West and East could be adopted, and in no other way than a visit to Russia could full consultation and effective discussion be assured.

It was arranged that Lord Grey and I should concert a telegram to Paris and Rome on these lines.

The military conference at Chantilly, to which reference is made in the above quotations from the War Committee minutes, was one that had already been arranged to take place in November between representatives of the military staffs of the Allied Armies. While there would be obvious advantages in arranging our conference of statesmen at a time when we could have these military authorities available for consultation, it seemed no less important to claim priority for the political conference, since, as was pointed out at our Committee, we were the authority ultimately responsible for decisions.

At the next meeting of the War Committee, on 7th November, it transpired that there appeared to be some difference of opinion among our Allies as to the proposal for a further conference in Russia. Italy was dubious about the possibility of sending representatives to such a conference. Further, it seemed that the military chiefs were proposing to hold their meeting at Chantilly a week before the Paris conference could be held, and this I considered to be undesirable; for as I pointed out to the Committee, there would be a tendency among the generals to commit themselves at this conference as to their strategical views, before the responsible heads of the Governments had been able to reach a decision as to what they felt it necessary to take in hand in the way of preliminary consultation with our Eastern Allies, and there might be difficulty subsequently in inducing the generals to modify or reconsider their opinions.

A telegram was accordingly dispatched on that day to Rome and Paris in the following terms: —

" We are of opinion that the only way to secure effective consultation on the future conduct of the War ensuring the best co-operation in east and west and the co-ordination which is essential to success, is for a conference to be held in Russia and preferably at the Russian General Headquarters if the Emperor would allow it.

We regard conference at Paris as preliminary to conferring on the spot in Russia and the main object at Paris should be to arrange this. To postpone consultation at Paris as suggested by Italy would involve very considerable delay. The Prime Minister and Secretary of State for War will, therefore, go to Paris on Monday in order to have informal conversation with M. Briand on Tuesday, the day which he has chosen. After this we hope it will be agreed to ask the Russian Government to fix a conference in Russia at the earliest possible date at which Great Britain, France and Italy should be represented. We consider that the conference to be of any use must be small in numbers and be in Russia. The other Allies can be called into conference subsequently at Paris if need be.

Meanwhile we urge that military conference at Chantilly should be postponed for a week. We think it would serve no useful purpose till the considerations which we wish to put before M. Briand have been examined and without these considerations before it the conference at Chantilly might be committed to conclusions that it would be necessary to revise."

The views here expressed were ultimately agreed to by our Allies, and the Paris conference was arranged to take place on Wednesday and Thursday, 15th and 16th November, 1916; but General Joffre refused to postpone the military conference at Chantilly, and it was held on the same date as the Inter-Allied conference. In the event it dominated and to a large extent stultified the political conference. The soldiers successfully torpedoed our efforts to secure a joint examination by soldiers and statesmen from the east and west, of the strategy of the Allies for the campaign of 1917. The disastrous military offensives of that year were hatched at Chantilly by the generals, and their selfish action in precipitating momentous decisions without consultation was largely responsible for failure to avert the Russian crash.

In preparation for this Paris conference I drafted a statement setting out my view of the military situation, and of the need for a further conference in Russia to co-ordinate the Allied efforts in east and west. This statement was revised and very extensively abridged by Mr. Asquith, and the condensed version of it, rendered into French, was taken by us to Paris. I give below a copy of this document, re-inserting, in italics, the principal passages in my original draft which were blue pencilled by Mr. Asquith from the memorandum as laid by him before M. Briand. The omissions were due not so much to disagreement about the accuracy of the statement as to the Prime Minister's reluctance to append his signature to a document which the French might regard as critical of the higher commands in both countries. In effect he took all the sting out of the document.

" The time has come for the Allies, in their innermost counsels, to look the facts of the situation in the face. The war environment is always peopled with illusions, many of them deliberately fostered in order to keep up the spirit of the combatants, many others created by the electric atmosphere engendered by all great wars.

We are at the turning-point of the campaign. *Upon the decisions we take now will depend the ultimate issue. In 1914-15-16 we could afford to blunder without throwing away the chance of final victory. If we take the wrong turning in 1917, I do not believe that our fortunes can be retrieved.* The situation is undoubtedly grave.

We are approaching the end of the third campaign. After months of hard fighting we have made no appreciable impression on the strongholds of our enemies. On land they hold all their conquests, with hardly any diminution in the area of the conquered territories. At sea they are more formidable and destructive than they have ever been since the commencement of the War. On land they have recovered initiative which some months ago they lost. Our new ally, Roumania, whose irruption into the field on our side was *confidently predicted by one of the highest military authorities* to mark the end of Austria, is now fighting for very life on her own soil, and *is barely holding her own with the help of Russia. Nearly 50 per cent. of the army with which she entered the field has already been put out of action. She has been deprived of hundreds of square miles of her territory and* the German forces are within 20 miles of the richest oil wells in Europe.

At sea, the British, Allied and neutral shipping, on which depends not merely the active co-operation of England in the alliance, but the very life of the English people, its food, its munitions, and those of its Allies, is being destroyed at an alarmingly increasing rate.

On land, what is the prospect? We were confidently assured in February, 1915, by a high military authority that in a few months' time the Germanic federation would have exhausted its reserves. This is the end of 1916. The Germans since June have added twenty-seven new formations to their gigantic armies; this week they have added another. Their army has increased since June by 300,000 and our military advisers, after careful investigation of the facts, now inform us that the reserves of man-power available for Germany and her allies exceed 3,000,000 men, without reckoning the additional 1,000,000 of young men who march every year into military age.*

As to the blockade, Germany will be saved from famine, and

* Lord Kitchener.

will even be able to make headway against every difficulty, so far as its most essential war needs are concerned, if it succeeded in securing the Roumanian cornfields. On the Somme, the Allies have achieved a succession of brilliant victories, but what has been the result of these operations? What were the results which the Somme offensive was designed to provide?

1.   To draw closer the bonds of the Franco-British Alliance. That has been achieved beyond all doubt.

2.   To raise the siege of Verdun. We have succeeded there.

3.   To break through the German lines and roll the enemy back to the Meuse. Here we were not successful.

3a.   *The capture of some important strategic position then held by the enemy and the occupation of which by the Allies would have placed him at a serious disadvantage in the next push —something comparable to what the capture of Verdun would have been for the Germans. That object has failed.*

4.   To divert great forces from the Eastern Front so as to enable the Russian offensive on that front to succeed. The movement of enemy troops has been the other way. *Since the Somme offensive began, nineteen divisions have left the West for the East, and as a result, the* Russian offensive, which started so brilliantly in the spring, and from which so much was hoped, has been stopped, and has given place to complete immobility.

Another object has been recently added to the occupation of such a number of German divisions as to make it impossible for the Germans to concentrate such forces on Roumania as would crush that country. That event is still doubtful. All we know is that Germany has as many troops and guns there as the difficult terrain will permit.

The most brilliant success scored by the Allies this year has been the recapture of the Verdun forts by a single *coup de main,* without great losses to the assailants. This is a feat of arms, the planning and execution of which displayed the highest qualities of generalship. In barely fifteen days the French Army completely wiped out the results of the grim and costly German attacks, which have gone on for eight months. In consequence, the western line is a little more favourable to the Allies than it was at the end of 1915. *If anyone this time last year had ventured to predict the actual position to-day he would have been denounced as a morbid and malignant pessimist.*

We must now take such measures as will prevent the situation next year from being only a repetition, if not an aggravation, of the present situation. Time is no longer in our favour.

The outstanding features of the conduct of the War which gave me the greatest concern as to the future are twofold:—

1.   That in the main decisions taken during the last three campaigns every military estimate of what could be accomplished with the resources at our disposal has not only been mistaken, but conspicuously falsified by events.

2.   That the same mistakes are repeated time after time without any reference to the disastrous experience gained by the failure of the preceding ones.

Let us take the campaign of 1915 as an example. This campaign was ruined by two obsessions.

The first was that the Germans intended a great attack on the Western Front.

As a matter of fact their great attack was on the East and South-East.

The second was that by frontal attack, backed up by such artillery preparation as the Allies were then capable of, their forces would break through the German lines. This mistake was committed at Neuve Chapelle, repeated at Artois, Festubert, Loos, and Champagne. When the attack failed to accomplish its full purpose, it was always thought to be due to the absence of something which could easily be supplied if a second attack of the same kind were made. Then when the second failed, it was said that it came very near success, and that a few more guns or more divisions of infantry would have ensured complete triumph.

The failure to conceive what was possible and what was not under present conditions of warfare was responsible for the failure of the experiments, which were repeated each time with greater forces, and consequently ended each time in enormously greater losses. Still the same old obsession has taken a firmer grip than ever of the military brain.

There is no fundamental difference in the character of any of these attacks. There is no essentially novel form of strategy or attack introduced.

The nearest approach to a new resource or device has been the employment of the tanks, and that came from entirely non-military sources.

Another example of the failure to estimate the real obstacles in the path of victory was the Dardanelles. The military attack on Gallipoli was entirely conceived and planned by soldiers, and the greatest soldier amongst them told me shortly before the attack that Gallipoli would be carried with the forces then at the General's command with losses not exceeding 5,000. How lamentably the military diagnosis failed is now a matter of history, but in each succeeding attack there was the same under-estimate of obstacles, the same conviction that we could butt through by throwing great masses of men and guns on the enemy lines as though we were fighting in the eighteenth century and not in the twentieth.

I hold in the history of 1915 the case of Serbia to be the most unpardonable and, I fear, the most irreparable of all the Allied failures. We realise now how important it was for us to block the German road to the east. We could have cut off their supplies. We should have given the German people the sense of being hemmed in, and what would have been more destructive to their morale than the consciousness of that fact? We could have won Bulgaria and organised a great Balkanic Federation with a reserve of 2,000,000 fighting men, which we could have gradually equipped and made formidable armies out of for attacking the Germanic Powers on their southern flank. We could have encircled the Powers in a ring of flame. Turkey, with very little ammunition and hardly any power to manufacture it, would soon have collapsed from sheer exhaustion. This could have been accomplished by the timely occupation of the Vardar Valley with half the forces which are now in Salonika, and a third of the men who fell in fruitless and fatuous attacks on German barbed-wire entanglements in the Western campaigns of 1915. Instead of this, what has happened? The German road to the east is open from Belgrade to Baghdad; she is supplied with corn, cotton, coffee, tea, copper, and, what is still more important, with first-class fighting men. These facts have given her people new hope. Bulgaria is equipped, Turkey is reorganised; Greece is overawed with a third of her people hostile to the Allies; Serbia is destroyed; Roumania is fighting for her life. An attempt was made to occupy the Vardar Valley in November, 1915. We realised at last how vital it was to seize the bridge to the east. But it was then too late. The Balkans, which might have been an asset, are now a heavy burden.

In 1916 we have repeated in the case of Roumania the fatal error of 1915 in the case of Serbia. The volcanic energy which Russia has displayed in retrieving the blunder made may yet redeem the situation. Nevertheless, it was a blunder of the most inexplicable character. What are the facts? We all knew exactly what the Roumanian equipment consisted of. We knew that the Roumanian Army had no heavy guns, and that her supply of ammunition even for field-guns was quite unequal to the stress of a sustained attack or defence. As long as the Austrian Armies were engaged elsewhere Roumania might be all right; but our military advisers must have known that if the Germans chose to withdraw their forces from the attack on Verdun and send a few of their *reserve divisions to Roumania, Roumanian guns and ammunition were quite unequal to facing such a concentration.   This, however, does not seem to have been foreseen by any of the advisers of the Allies; at least, no one seems to have made any provision against this contingency.   Either no Government contemplated it as possible, or each Government thought it was the business of the other to make plans for meeting that eventuality.   It was only after the German attack had developed that the Allies improvised hurried expeditions to rescue Roumania from her doom.   It is no exaggeration to say that Roumania may be the turning-point of the campaign.   If the Germans fail there it will be the greatest disaster inflicted upon them.   Afterwards it will only be a question of time. But should Germany succeed I hesitate to think what the effect will be on the fortunes of the campaign.   Eight hundred thousand men who constitute excellent fighting material if well equipped will have been thrown away.*   The Germans' stores, much depleted, will be stocked with great quantities of oil and corn, which will place the Central Powers above any anxiety in these two important respects—and yet no one seems to have thought it his particular duty to prepare a plan which would bring such triumph to the Allies if it succeeded, and which would certainly avert a possible disaster of the first magnitude to their cause.   And this is the third year of a campaign which has seen many muddles of the same sort committed through this fatal lack of co-operation and forethought.*

The Salonika expedition is another illustration of the two fatal defects which have pursued the Entente—tardiness and lack of co-operation.   The Salonika expedition launched in time would have saved Serbia and given us the Balkans.   At best all that can be said for it now is that it is holding 250,000 Bulgarians and Turks with a force which is nominally at any rate double that number. Why so many Bulgarians should think it necessary to confront it I am at a loss to know.   General Milne's figures show that the aggregate number of Allied rifles available do not very much exceed 100,000.   The equipment in guns and in transport of these troops is ludicrously inadequate even for the modest rôle which it is supposed to play. Neither General Foch nor Sir Douglas Haig would ever dream of attacking the tiniest Somme village defended by a single German regiment with the guns and ammunition General Sarrail and General Milne have at their disposal for the storming of over 200 miles of the strongest positions in Europe held by over 200,000 of the finest infantry.   The ammunition of the two combined forces would hardly last out a couple of days in a Somme bombardment.   No wonder when the Roumanians came

---

* Sir William Robertson's memorandum placed the Roumanian effectives and reserves at 970,000 men.

to discover the depleted condition of our ammunition they con-
cluded that we had not altogether kept the spirit of the bargain
into which we had entered with them. The whole state of the
Salonika Army gives the impression that the generals in command
had as a matter of policy been deprived of every temptation to
make too effective a use of the armies under their control. It is
true that we have recently sent large reinforcements of men and a
few batteries of heavy guns, and a further stock of ammunition.
If they had been dispatched two months ago—and it is just as
difficult to spare them now as it was then—General Sarrail might
have really threatened the Bulgarian flank on the Monastir side
and compelled them to withdraw perhaps a couple of divisions
from the Roumanian Front in order to save Macedonia. Sarrail
failed for lack of transport, lack of troops, lack of guns, and what
the Roumanian and Russian public know now about this, the
French and British public will know soon.

The history of our dealings with Greece is a dreary picture of
paralysing indecision. The Greek people are with us, and have
indicated their sympathies repeatedly by their votes, but the King
is now, and always has been, the Kaiser's friend and the Entente's
foe. He has never missed an opportunity of serving the former
and selling the latter. He gave valuable information to the
enemy as to our troops, our positions, our intentions, and our
movements. Under our very eyes, with our troops looking on, he
handed over an important strategic position like Fort Ruppel to
the enemy—a fort which it would take us thousands of valuable
lives to storm. He gave the Germans a whole division of infantry
and most valuable mountain guns. He has fooled us all round the
ring and made us the laughing stock of the East whilst we were
writing lawyer's letters to his military advisers.

It is only by a relentless scrutiny of our shortcomings in the past
to find out wherein we have failed that we can hope to avoid failure
in the future. Our first duty is to calmly face the facts of the
situation, however painful, and to acknowledge, at any rate to
ourselves, and in our own councils wherein we are responsible for
the unsatisfactory conditions with which we are now confronted.
To attempt to ignore them or to gloss them over amongst ourselves
is a sure guarantee of disaster. I quite realise the importance of
keeping up the public faith in victory, and that it is not always
necessary to call the attention of the people to the dangers and
defects of our position; but in the War Councils of the Allies the
facts must be exposed as they really are, and, unless this is done,
someone must take the public into his confidence and give the
people a chance of saving themselves before it is too late.

But so far as the British Government can judge, the operations
in the west, if continued on the present footing, hold out no hope

of our inflicting on the German armies in 1917 a defeat sufficiently crushing to put an end to the War, unless we are able to reinforce them by much greater efforts in the other theatres of war.

The position in the southern theatre does not offer any much greater hope of a decisive success. It is true that the Italian Army, by means of a campaign admirably conceived and well carried out, has made appreciable progress and gained considerable victories. All the same, trench warfare generally predominates on this front, and one can see no dawning of a day of big results.

On the Eastern Front the Russian attack, starting under such happy auspices, has been brought to a full stop, and it is clear that on the principal Russian Fronts there will be great difficulties to overcome before serious progress can be made.

As we have already said, the entry of Roumania on to the scene did not produce the decisive results which had been hoped for, and if the situation in this theatre is a little less grave than it has been, it continues, none the less, to be an object of serious preoccupation for the Allies. As we foresaw, the difficulty of communications by land and sea has prevented a decisive success on the Salonika front. The greater part of the Bulgarian Army, it is true, has been held there, and on the flanks there are slight advances to record. All the same, these operations do not allow us to count on a decisive success in that region, unless the operations are combined with others on other fronts in such a way as to divert a considerable part of the forces opposed to us. Even in that case, the lack of roads and railways will hold up our advance, which would, in any case, be difficult in face of the resistance awaiting us.

The effect of our inability to obtain a decisive result on the Salonika front is that the Central Powers still keep open the route which leads them to their objectives in the East.

What is the prospect in front of us? What is our policy? *Has anyone mapped out a road to victory? If he has, I have not yet been privileged to see that document. Words will not win. We must have a definite plan. I have only heard of one.* People talk of hammering, and of a war of attrition. The success of hammering depends entirely upon whether you are making a greater impression on the barrier or the hammer. The success of a war of attrition depends upon the time it takes, and who can last out the longest. In examining the chances of success of a war of attrition, certain essential factors must always be present to the mind.

The first is the reserve man-power of the Central Powers and their allies. Our General Staff places these reserves at three or four millions. They reckon in addition that each year a million young men become available for service.

We shall be wise not to conclude that even these appalling figures exhaust the man-power of the enemy. Polish conscription may well give him between 500,000 and 1,000,000 men. Prisoners, Polish and Lettish labour, are constantly releasing young men from essential trades. The German military leaders are also clearly giving a good deal of attention and thought to the substitution of machine power for man-power. They believe that owing to the perfection of their machinery they can reduce the numbers of their infantry men by several thousand in each division, and they have one considerable advantage over the Entente, that being in possession of enemy ground, they can gradually give way, selling land dearly as they retreat without any serious damage to their military position. This last point is illustrated by the difference between the fighting on the Somme and the fighting at Verdun. The French Army could not retreat five miles at Verdun without giving up something of considerable strategical value and of infinitely greater moral importance. They were consequently bound to defend every kilometre at the most appalling cost. On the other hand, the Germans could give up 5, 10, even 20 kilometres on the Somme without surrendering any point of much strategic or moral importance.* The only thing that matters to them is that in reconquering French or Russian territory their enemies should pay more for its capture than it cost them in its defence.

Another factor, if we wish to measure the chances of a war of attrition, is the effect of the submarine campaign against our merchant shipping. The importance of this cannot be exaggerated. Undoubtedly during the last few weeks the destruction of Allied and neutral tonnage has taken on alarming proportions, and unless effective steps can be taken to check it, the consequences may be of the most serious character to the armies of the Allies. Our success depends so much upon our maintaining the unchallenged supremacy of the sea that if we fail to protect our transports and our supplies, it will be impossible for Great Britain to maintain her present forces either in the east or the west. It will become equally impossible for France and Italy, Russia or ourselves to keep up the present supply of munitions. We feel confident of being able to defeat this latest and most pernicious development of the German submarine attack, but it would be idle to pretend that it does not fill us with serious anxiety, when we contemplate the prospect of a campaign lasting over a period of years.

The difficulties which we have experienced in making payment for our purchases from abroad must be as present to the minds of French statesmen as to ourselves. Our dependence upon America

---

* This they did in the spring of 1917, thereby disarranging the whole of the Nivelle plans.

is growing for food, raw material and munitions. We are rapidly exhausting the securities negotiable in America. If victory shone on our banners our difficulties would disappear. *Success means credit: financiers never hesitate to lend to a prosperous concern: but business which is lumbering along amidst great difficulties and which is making no headway in spite of enormous expenditure will find the banks gradually closing their books against it.* The fall of Roumania would have a serious effect on our American credit. On the other hand, if Roumania succeeded in resisting the tide of invasion then the victories of Verdun and our advance on the Somme would have their maximum effect, and the Americans would open their purses and send us their merchandise. The problem of finance is the problem of victory . . . *not debatable victory, but unchallengeable victory; not victory won here countered by disaster there.*

Another consideration to be taken into account is the morale *of the four nations behind the armies. As the War drags its weary and bloodstained path, the sacrifices and the sufferings must necessarily increase; the casualties will become heavier, and the gloom cast by the appalling losses over the homes of the country will become darker and deeper. Then food will become scarcer and costlier, the burdens of taxation will be heavier.' Efforts will be made perhaps by powerful neutrals to patch up peace on what would appear to be specious terms, and there is a real danger that large masses of people, worn out by the constant strain, may listen to well-intentioned but mistaken pacificators; and, last of all, there is the danger, which one hardly likes to contemplate but which is ever present in our minds, of one of the four great Allies being offered terms which seem better than an indefinite prolongation of the horrors of war. No alliance has ever borne the strain of a protracted war without breaking. These are considerations which it would be well for us to bear in mind when we are urged to depend upon attrition as the sole means of bringing this terrible war to an end.*

What, then, is our suggestion? It is that the responsible military and political leaders of the four great Allied nations should for the first time since the commencement of the War meet together to discuss the situation and to formulate their policy or strategy. The responsible leaders of the Central Powers and their Allies are constantly meeting to discuss plans, to devise new plans, to revise old ones. The real military leaders of Russia never had five minutes' conversation with the military leaders of the West. Such communications as I have read between them indicate a good deal of divergence in essential points of strategy. Take, for instance, General Alexeieff's despatches on the Balkans. These are questions not merely of strategy, but of equipment, which have never yet

*been discussed by the Higher Commands at the various confer-
ences. I do not regard discussion about Russia with General
Jillinski, or even General Palitzine, as an interchange of views
between East and West. History will mock at us for our neglect
to insist upon a meeting of the responsible military and political
leaders of the various fronts for three whole campaigns. The whole
policy of the Allies ought to be co-ordinated; there ought to be a
complete understanding between the East and West. Surely
Generals Joffre and Robertson have something to say about their
experiences in the West which it would be worth General
Alexeieff's while to hear. On the other hand, General Alexeieff
must have had a good deal of experience and must have learned
many lessons which it would be valuable for his Western colleagues
to hear something of. There is no other business which would
have been conducted for three years without some sort of interchange of opinions between the men that matter in the direction
of affairs. If a conference is decided upon, it would be a farce
to send anyone there except the men who matter; the men who
represent France, Russia, Italy, and Britain must not merely be
men of the highest capacity, they must also be men whose decisions
could practically be accepted, not because they have been tied
down by their instructions and therefore cannot assent to anything
which their colleagues or superiors had not already given previous
assent to, but accepted because of the high positions which the
representatives hold.*

What, then, is our proposition? We have shown above all the
importance of the rôle played in the present war by Roumania and
the Balkan countries. We have shown that the conquest of
Roumania would furnish the enemy with very considerable
resources of man-power, and would be an incalculable aid to the
re-establishment of their economic equilibrium. On the other
hand, we have shown that the elimination of Bulgaria would
complete the encirclement of the Central Empires, would isolate
Turkey, which would then be compelled to die of exhaustion, and
would bring the Entente Powers markedly nearer to final
victory.

Although these advantages are so evident that they justify the
greatest efforts for the achievement, we do not hide from ourselves the considerable difficulties to be anticipated. Our military
advisers have more than once explained to our Government and to
the French Government how difficult and uncertain every operation must be that is based on Salonika.

Our proposition is that the statesmen and generals of the great
Western Powers should confer with the statesmen and generals of
the Eastern Front, taking for their programme the examination
of the situation in its entirety, and more particularly the military

situation in the east. The object of the conference must be to determine what it is possible to do on the Eastern Front, and what is the nature and importance of the help which the west ought to give to the east for those operations which are judged to be necessary. Moreover, the statesmen and generals of the west ought to explain clearly to the statesmen and generals of the east the limits which are imposed on our possible effort in the Salonika region. In Russia, since the dismissal of M. Sasonoff, there are only two men who can speak with authority; the Emperor and General Alexeieff. At the present moment it is impossible for either of these to come to the west. That is why—and we insist on this point—it is of capital importance that generals and statesmen competent to represent the Western Powers with the fullest authority should go to Russia as promptly as possible in order to discuss these questions, the interest of which is vital for the conduct of the War."

A meeting of the Cabinet was held on Monday, 13th November, and on the following morning the Prime Minister and I proceeded to Paris accompanied by Sir Maurice Hankey. He had arranged to have a private conversation with M. Briand on the morning of 15th November before the Allied Conference opened that afternoon, with a view to placing before him confidentially the opinions of the British War Cabinet. This private meeting was fixed for the Quai d'Orsay at 10.30 a.m. on 15th November. When Mr. Asquith, Sir Maurice Hankey and I arrived we found there was no M. Briand. We were informed that the *President de Conseil* had been unexpectedly detained at a meeting of one of the Committees of the *Chambre des Députés* to which he had been suddenly summoned, but that he expected to arrive soon. We waited for another half an hour and then came another message that he had found it impossible to get away, but that we might expect him in another quarter of an hour. Then Sir Maurice Hankey learnt from an amused official that the Chairman of this Committee was M. Clemenceau, and that he was subjecting the French Premier to a fierce cross-examination on certain unsatisfactory aspects and episodes in the conduct of the War and that M. Briand was having a very *difficile* time. We then realised that M. Briand was detained by circumstances over which he had not the least control, and that one of the circumstances was the redoubtable " Tiger " over whom no one had any control.

Another three-quarters of an hour passed and M. Briand hurried into the room looking flustered, unhappy and altogether rather badly mauled. We learnt that he had escaped the ruthless claws of the great political cat this time, but with difficulty, and only by the exercise of every fibre and sinew of his renowned dexterity and suppleness. He was not, however, in a state of mind which would enable him to give cool and concentrated attention to our memorandum. We felt that the conditions were not propitious for a calm examination of the military position. The problems raised needed all the concentration and composure which every member of that small gathering could command. However, after an interchange of the usual civilities and conventional inquiries Mr. Asquith explained the purpose of the informal meeting he had sought. He pulled out of his pocket the memorandum and read it, or rather rushed through it, without emphasis or pause. M. Briand, whilst preserving the pose of a courteous and attentive listener, was evidently too ruffled and distracted to take in ideas at such a speed. He asked Mr. Asquith to leave a copy and promised to study it all with great care before the afternoon meeting. That was all, and then we shook hands and Mr. Asquith and I drove off to the Hotel Crillon, feeling like men whose proposals, to which weeks of thought and debate had been given, had been received with civil torpidity. Here was the country that had so far sustained the most serious damage in the War and had the enemy in occupation and control of its finest provinces, and yet there seemed no evidence of any racking pre-occupation on the part of its leaders with the problems of liberation. That was the burden of M. Clemenceau's satire, and I felt that there was some justification for his bitterness. No man has a greater admiration for M. Briand's gifts, but as a War Minister he was much too easy-going. My mind inevitably travelled on to contemplate the obvious similarity between French and British leadership. Both Mr. Asquith and M. Briand were men of rare intellectual gifts, but unfortunately they both lacked driving power. Once again we were captained by men who were distinguished figures on the bridge in normal weather; skilful navigators in ordinary storms, but not qualified for command in the most raging typhoon that ever swept the seas. France as well as Britain were both led by men devoid of vigour and initiative. Yet the fortunes of the Alliance depended upon their leadership.

The first session of the Inter-Allied Conference from which so much was hoped took place that afternoon. The importance of these meetings is shown by the list of those attending, which included, for the British Government, Mr. Asquith and myself, accompanied by Lord Bertie and Sir Maurice Hankey; for the French Government, M. Briand, President of the Council and Minister for Foreign Affairs, Admiral Lacaze, Minister of Marine, with M. de Margerie, Director of Political and Commercial Affairs at Quai d'Orsay; for Russia, M. Isvolsky, Ambassador in Paris; for Italy, Signor Carcano, Minister of the Treasury, Senator Tittoni, Minister of State, and the Marquis Salvago Raggi, Ambassador in Paris.

The President of the Council (M. Briand), after welcoming those present, made a characteristic speech, eloquent but inconclusive, the minute of which I quote verbatim.

" M. Briand recalled that at the moment when the former Conference of March, 1916, met, the whole of Europe was still suffering from the anguish caused by the attack on Verdun. The advance made in the last days of February by the German Armies had given rise to the keenest apprehension; but the Allies on that occasion reviewed the situation in all its aspects, and co-ordinated their efforts, and as a result of that co-ordination they had been able to carry out an offensive which had already given satisfactory results, and of which one of the first consequences had been to relieve Verdun.

At the same time the Russian Armies had taken the offensive on their side, and one of the effects of these operations had been to relieve the congestion on the Italian Front, and to allow our Allies to score a brilliant revenge against the Austrians.

The results obtained, however satisfactory they might be, were not, strictly speaking, decisive, but they had at least the consequence of removing the initiative in the field from the Germans and transferring it to the Allied troops. But that was not enough to bring victory.

The War was about to enter upon a serious—one might say a decisive—phase, and the Allies would have to close their ranks in order to bring the War to a speedy end by achieving a final victory over their enemies, since the patience of the nations could not be indefinitely submitted to such an ordeal.

Before discussing this problem, a question of principle arose: What ought to be the attitude of the Governments towards the General Staffs; whatever might be their confidence in the General Staff—a confidence indeed fully justified—ought the Governments to abandon absolutely to them the conduct of operations?

The French Government did not think so. It held, on the contrary, that it was the Governments which, since they bore the whole responsibility for the conduct of the War, should take the initiative in regard to operations, it being always understood that the execution of the plan adopted should be left to the military authorities, who had the means to carry it out.

If there was agreement on this point, the moment would seem to have come for the Government to envisage the direction which it would be desirable to give to the War. On that very day the delegates of the General Staffs were studying at Chantilly the elements of the problem, and their labours would be of great service in enabling the Governments to take a decision in full cognisance of the circumstances.

What struck the Premier first of all when studying the situation on the basis of the documents furnished by the military authorities and carefully checked by General Headquarters, was the fact that the Allies had altogether at their disposal effectives superior by at least 50 per cent. to those which the combined strength of the Germans, Austrians, Bulgarians and Turks could put against them. That was a consideration well calculated to give courage and to justify an absolute confidence in final victory.

These hopes showed a still firmer foundation, added M. Briand, if the present fighting value of the armies were compared. While our troops had not only lost nothing of their attacking qualities, but on the contrary had never ceased to improve, as the success of our last Anglo-French offensive on the Somme had demonstrated, the soldiers of the German Army were far from possessing to-day, even among their officers, the same qualities as at the time of their formidable attack on Verdun.*

Furthermore, the Allied situation from the point of view of munitions was growing stronger and stronger every day.

Such considerations should not, however, be allowed to lull our courage to sleep, or make us lose sight of the great goal we had to reach. They should, on the contrary, stimulate our ardour, encourage us to intensify our efforts, and make us understand the great advantages which we have reaped from putting into the common store our strength and our resources.

And now, what course of action ought we to adopt on all fronts? It was on this point that it would seem worth while to deliberate, in order to discover the swiftest solution of the War. The French Government considered, and its opinion would doubtless be shared by the military authorities, that it was absolutely necessary to manifest an incessant activity on all fronts. This activity could not bring about a decisive result all at once, but it was indispensable in order to retain the initiative in the Allies' hands. The offensives of the armies of General Brussiloff and General Lechnisky had frankly not been decisive, but they had enabled the Russians to take 400,000 prisoners and disorganise the Austrian Army.† On its front, the Italian Army had dealt the Austrian Army terrible blows, which had greatly weakened it; while on our front our valiant troops and those of our friends and Allies the English, had undertaken an offensive which had already had happy consequences which were familiar to his hearers.

All these operations, without being decisive had had the effect of preventing our enemies from continuing the tactics of which we had been the victims at the outbreak of war, and from dealing us blows, first on one front, and then on the other. Since our activity had shown itself everywhere, the Austro-German Armies had been everywhere condemned to act on the defensive. Let that

* A few weeks later the 50 per cent. superiority had already disappeared, and the mutiny in the French Army did not quite bear out M. Briand's claim as to the superior " attacking qualities " of the Allied troops.

† The greater numbers of Russian and Roumanian prisoners captured by the Central Powers are not mentioned.

lesson profit us and encourage us to keep on! But what operations could be undertaken in winter? The French Government considered, and it had made its views on this subject known to its Allies, that it was in the Balkans that the most effective efforts could be put forth. What, in fact, was Germany doing?

Pressed on all sides, it was not hesitating to violate the rights of nations in an attempt to procure new reserves of men in Poland. It was said that it could find in this way 300,000 or 400,000 men. Suppose these figures correct, would it not take several months more to train these new recruits and make soldiers of them? Were we going to wait without doing anything until Germany and Austria were able to use these troops against us? Would it not be much more worth while to make straight away an effort to stop, or at all events to render useless this violation of the rights of nations?

But what could be done? Let us ask ourselves. *It seemed to him indispensable to try by energetic action in the Dobrudja and against Sofia to put Bulgaria out of action, and thereby Turkey.*

That effort was not impossible, and he thought that Russia would be disposed to make it, if we could second her action by an offensive on the Salonika Front. There could not be for the army of the east any question of undertaking an operation of large scope. The narrowness of its base rendered this task almost impossible. But it could, for instance, continue its pressure on the German-Bulgarian Armies, and try to recapture Monastir.

The Salonika Army, although inadequately supplied with men, had at all events carried out the promise made to Roumania to immobilise the Bulgarian Armies on its front. Since the entrance of Roumania into the picture, not a single Bulgarian soldier had been able to leave the Salonika Front to take part in operations against our new Ally. That in itself was an appreciable result, *but it was necessary for those operations to continue so as to free Roumania, and at the same time the activity of the Allied Armies must be intensified on all the other fronts.*

If Bulgaria and Turkey were put out of action before the end of the winter, public opinion in Germany and Austria would certainly be demoralised, and next spring we should be able to deal our enemies decisive blows.

That was how the French Government saw the course of the War. If the Allied Governments were in agreement with it in deciding that it was the Governments which should take in hand the general conduct of the War, and if they shared its way of looking at things, he had the firm conviction that we should be able next year to obtain decisive results.

We had come to a grave hour—maybe to a critical hour, if there was wobbling in the decisions of the Allies and a dispersal of their efforts.

T

' I have shown you the goal that we wish to reach,' said the President of the Council in conclusion. ' It is worth our while to give it serious study, for if we adopt a definite solution, we shall have rendered a signal service to the cause which we support.' "

It was then the turn of the British Prime Minister to urge upon the conference the definite proposal set forth in our memorandum. The minute of the Conference continues: —

" Mr. Asquith thanked M. Briand, in the name of the British Government, for the eloquent words he had just uttered. But, added the Prime Minister, to attain the goal which has been indicated with such precision, it will be needful for statesmen and generals from the Great Powers of the west to proceed to Russia to confer with the Russian statesmen and generals, to determine what it is possible to do on the Eastern Front, and what is the nature and the importance of the help which the Western Powers can render to Russia and Roumania, to bring to a favourable issue those operations which are considered necessary. This conference would have for its object the examining of the situation in its entirety, and more particularly the military situation in the east. It is necessary that this meeting should take place as soon as possible, and that the statesmen charged to represent the Western Powers should have full authority to discuss the grave problems on which the conduct of the War depends.

The British Prime Minister was of the opinion, that it was not the military authorities but rather the Governments which ought to undertake responsibility for the political and strategical conduct of the War, and he proposed that the representatives of the Powers met here to-day should forthwith, and *without prejudice in any respect to the conclusion of the conference which would be held in Russia,* enter on an engagement to submit themselves to the decisions of this Assembly.

The Chief Italian Delegate thought, like M. Briand, that as the Governments had the responsibility of power, it was to them that the right belonged of deciding the conduct of the War, but he was of opinion that no decision ought to be definitely fixed before there had been consultation with the competent military authorities. With this reservation, M. Carcano entirely associated himself with the point of view of the French Government. The Minister of the Treasury pointed out at the same time that he was in this expressing only a personal opinion, and that he did not think himself authorised to enter on an engagment in the name of the Royal Government. He would wish to refer the matter to the President of the Council, who had been unable through sickness to be present at the conference, but with whom the final decision rested.

M. Briand pointed out that at present they were concerned only with an exchange of views between the delegates of the Allied Powers, and that the solutions arrived at by them did not bind their Governments, and were only taken *ad referendum*. It could not indeed be otherwise, since it was a question of summoning a conference in Russia, the principal theatre of war during the winter, to discuss these problems there and take the necessary decisions.

M. Tittoni declared that the Italian Government had been in agreement with the French Government since the coming into power of M. Briand in considering that the Balkan theatre was that in which the War would reach its decision. But when it was a case of discussing in what manner the Allies ought to concert their efforts to attain a definite result, it was evident that they would have to discuss in the first place among themselves the conditions of the joint military and financial co-operation.

The President of the Council did not disagree with this, but he pointed out that it was necessary for the Governments to take into their hands the direction of the War. The front on which operations were taking place was so extended that it was difficult to embrace with a single glance, *and there was no army chief who would not be tempted—it was human nature—to consider the front on which he was in command as the most important, just as each soldier did—hence the necessity for the Governments to be the arbiters of operations.* Our enemies had shown that they would not hesitate, even at the risk of a sacrifice of *amour propre*, to keep in view only the end to be reached. Did they not, the moment that Roumania entered on the scene, give up the pursuit of their attack on Verdun, despite even a dynastic interest therein, to transfer their principle effort to the Balkans?

That example should not be lost on us. *It was not a question of obtaining a success at one point or at another, but of envisaging the final result, and of co-ordinating our effort to obtain as soon as possible the ultimate victory.*

The Russian Ambassador, although without instructions and without special powers, undertook to state that the proposal to hold a conference of the Allies in Russia would be met with the liveliest sympathy on the part of His Majesty and his Government. M. Isvolsky added that he personally considered that it was the Governments, and not the Staffs, which ought to have the direction of the War, but that question did not arise in Russia, since the Emperor was at once the supreme head of the armies and of the Government.

As to the question of the principal theatre of operations during the winter it was clear from all communications received from Russia that the Imperial Government and everyone in Russia were well aware of the capital importance of the operations in the Balkans.

M. Briand noted with satisfaction that all the delegates were agreed in principle in recognising that the Eastern Front would be during the winter the principal theatre of operations. Since that was the case, and while leaving to the conference which would be held in Russia the task of deciding what should be done by the Russian and Roumanian Governments, we could examine straight away to what extent these efforts could be seconded by the army in the east.

Mr. Lloyd George noted with satisfaction that all the delegates had approved in principle the proposition of the British Government for summoning a conference in Russia to decide on the general conduct of the War, and that they were in agreement as to the necessity of adopting a common line of action.

' But that is not enough,' added Mr. Lloyd George. ' *We must not rest content with taking these decisions. We have still to see that they are carried out.* After having decided on the Salonika expedition, the English and French Governments entrusted its execution to persons who were not perhaps sufficiently convinced of the importance of this front, and have not given sufficient attention to it to know whether the effectives were adequate, whether the transport was well organised, and in particular whether the artillery corresponded to the needs of the operations. Certain military authorities had said, it is true, that heavy artillery could not be utilised in this theatre on account of the bad state of the roads and of the topographical conditions; but the Germans have shown us the contrary in the Carpathians. *When Governments have taken a decision, they ought to see that it is carried out.*

' The goal towards which our efforts ought to be directed has been indicated with much eloquence by the President of the Council. It is a matter of encircling Germany more and more every day, of cutting its communications with the East, of hindering the formation of new armies.

' To get there, we shall have to unite all our resources. One cannot in fact avoid the thought that the magnificent offensive of the Russian Armies, despite the valour of the troops and the skill of the generals, has not perhaps yielded all that was hoped for, solely because of the inadequacy of heavy artillery on the Eastern Front. These armies ought then to be given the cannon and the munitions of which they stand in need, and that without waiting until the French, English and Italian Armies have been furnished with all the material that is necessary to them. We have got to help Russia and Roumania, not by taking from the surplus of our production, but by drawing if it must be upon what is necessary for ourselves, for it would be a shortsighted policy not to put these armies straight away into a position to fulfil the task which falls upon them.'

Mr. Lloyd George proposed, in consequence, that the Assembly should adopt the following resolutions: —

1. The three Governments of France, Italy and Great Britain undertake to participate in a political and military conference which shall be held in Russia as soon as possible.

Each Government will send to this conference, as its representatives, statesmen and officers of high rank, possessing full authority to speak in the name of their respective Governments.

2. The aim of the conference will be to examine the political and military situation in all its aspects, and in particular to fix the nature and the importance of the military effort which the Allies ought to carry out in the east during 1917. The object of the conference shall be at the same time to estimate the importance of the help which ought to be provided by France, Italy and Great Britain, to Russia and Roumania, in order to enable these Powers to carry out the operations which shall have been decided on.

3. The Governments represented at the present conference shall enter into an engagement to furnish in the fullest possible measure to their Allies the full military equipment asked for by the conference, which will be held in Russia, even if this should result in a certain slowing down in the equipment of their own armies, and Russia shall on its side enter into an engagement to conform to the decisions adopted by this conference.

This last phrase does not in any way imply that the conference will impose certain conditions on Russia, it simply means that Russia will take the necessary steps to enable her to make use as promptly as possible, and with all the desired intensity of the resources put at her disposal by the Allies. It turned out that 300 pieces of heavy artillery sent to Russia at the beginning of the year could not be used until a quite recent date through lack of artillery-men to serve them.

M. Tittoni, after stating that the Italian delegates could only take part in these deliberations *ad referendum*, asked permission to tell the meeting the reflections which Mr. Lloyd George's proposition suggested to him. One could not doubt, said he, the good will of the Italian Government; its solidarity with the Allies was whole and entire; but he did not want to rest content with theoretical formulas, and was trying to do practical work. Now, it was no use hiding the fact that the realisation of the programme advanced by the President of the Council and by Mr. Lloyd

George would come crashing against difficulties independent of the good will of men. He had to speak freely.

Now, for the Italian Government, one of the principal difficulties at the present moment was the financial question, and that was one of the reasons for the journey of the Minister of the Treasury. The question of exchange was becoming almost acute, since, less rich than France and England, Italy was experiencing great difficulties in meeting its payments to foreign countries. Of course, the Italian Government was ready to make every possible effort, but it was necessary for its Allies to come to its aid as well with the help it might require from the financial aspect.

So far as concerned the operations at Salonika, the Senator of the Kingdom of Italy could only express his personal opinion, this question being chiefly within the competence of the military authorities; but he was convinced that the Italian Government would be ready to make the effort asked of it, if it had the assurance that the Russo-Roumanian pressure would be so powerful and continuous that it would be impossible for the Austro-Germans to withdraw troops from the Balkans in order to send them to one of the other fronts. If this condition was not fulfilled, the Allies would be running a great risk in weakening the French, English and Italian Fronts, to any extent, however slight. *An intensification of the effort at Salonika would seem useless, if it were not the consequence and the complement of a great Russo-Roumanian effort.*

It should not be lost sight of that to realise this effort many difficulties would have to be surmounted, not only difficulties of a military order, but economic and financial difficulties as well. It would not be sufficient to send troops; we must also be able to ensure their transport; their artillery supplies, and the provisioning under all heads. The question of the reinforcement of the Eastern Army thus presented very great difficulties.

M. Briand remarked that when the Allies envisaged a plan of campaign, it was, of course, understood to be subject to the reserve that what proves impossible should be abandoned, and that it was precisely the object of the conferences then being held, and of that which would take place in Russia to discover the steps to be taken to secure unity of action on all fronts, regard being had to the resources and the means of each of the Allies.

It would, for instance, be impossible to ask France—which had ten departments invaded, which had mobilised more than 6,000,000 men, which had taken part in the operations in the Dardanelles and at Salonika, and had gone at the outset to the aid of Serbia—it would be impossible to ask her for a greater effort in men. *But if France were asked for artillery, machine-guns, munitions, and if it were in her power to furnish them, she would give them at once.* France had already given a good deal of war material to her Allies, but she was ready to intensify still further her production if this was possible.

The Allies ought to try and fill up the gaps wherever they appeared. If one country was embarrassed in regard to effectives, the others ought to come to her help; if there was another in a difficult financial situation, it was their duty to try to give her the resources which she needed. *In the grave circumstances through which we were passing, all our resources must be pooled without making it a question of* amour propre. That was how the French Government, and assuredly also all the Allied Governments, understood the conduct of the War."

The remainder of the session was devoted to a consideration of the position in Greece. With regard to this country the discussions were confined mainly to the question of the recognition of M. Venizelos's Government. A new factor, which was brought out by M. Briand, was that the King, in his conversations with M. Benazet, had made some remarkable promises. He had said that he was ready to withdraw his troops from Thessaly on condition that the territory evacuated was not occupied by Venizelist troops. He had also offered to give us the whole of the Greek material of war, and even to put his fleet at our disposal. M. Briand said that, if this offer were accepted, the Allies would obtain the use of 200 mountain guns, with 1,000 rounds a gun, as well as a vast amount of other war material.

Mr. Asquith pointed out that if one of the conditions of the King's offer to M. Benazet was the abandonment of M. Venizelos his proposals would have to be rejected. He explained at considerable length the sympathy and respect felt in England for M. Venizelos, and urged that the ideal solution was the reconciliation of the King with M. Venizelos, and that our policy should be directed towards that. He also urged the desirability of the official recognition of the Venizelist Government, particularly owing to the anomalous position of the Venizelist troops, and the danger they ran of not being accorded belligerent rights.

M. Briand did not dispute the desirability of reconciliation between King Constantine and M. Venizelos, and said that in France public opinion was as favourable to M. Venizelos as it is in England. Public opinion, however, he added, was not aware of the difficulties.

The general opinion of the conference was not in favour of the recognition of M. Venizelos at present. It was pointed out that, in order to obtain belligerent rights, it was necessary that the enemy, no less than the Allied Governments, should recognise M. Venizelos.

It was generally agreed, however, that the Allies should not let any opportunity pass to support M. Venizelos and his friends, and to protect them wherever necessary. The friends of the Entente, as

M. Briand said, must not be the victims of their favourable sentiments towards the Allies.

The question was left much where it stood, and no resolution was passed. M. Briand finally summed up the discussion as follows: —

" So the Allies may expect a development which does not seem as though it could be delayed much longer, and which should be of a nature to give them satisfaction; but it still goes without saying that if the King or his Government were to adopt measures against M. Venizelos and his friends, the Allies would intervene immediately with all necessary vigour to defend the great Greek patriot, who has always shown himself favourable to their cause."

Thus ended the first day's conference. Before our meeting on the afternoon of the next day, the military chiefs at Chantilly had completed their deliberations, and had agreed upon a programme which bears evident marks of having been settled for them in advance by the French Headquarters Staff, and which ran as follows: —

" General Headquarters of the
French Armies,
Staff Office, 16th November, 1916.

The members of the Conference give their approval to a plan of action by the Coalition, as it has been defined in the memorandum which has been submitted to them, a plan having for its object to give a decisive character to the campaigns of 1917. They adopt, in consequence, the following resolutions: —

1.

(a) During the winter of 1916-17, the offensive operations now being engaged in shall be pursued to the full extent compatible with the climatic conditions on each front.

(b) In order to be as much as possible in readiness to face every new situation, and especially in order to prevent the enemy from recapturing in any way the initiative of operations, the armies of the Coalition shall be ready to undertake joint offensives from the first fortnight of February, 1917, with all the means at their disposal.

(c) From the time when the armies are ready to attack, the Commanders-in-Chief shall adapt their respective conduct to suit the situation of the moment.

(d) If circumstances do not prevent it, the joint offensives carried out with all the means which each army can bring into play, shall be unloosed on all the fronts as soon as they can be synchronised* to dates which shall be fixed by common accord between the Commanders-in-Chief.

* It is admitted that synchronisation will be realised if there does not elapse a delay of more than three weeks between the initial dates of the offensives released on the various fronts.

(*e*) With a view to realising all accord necessary between these diverse hypotheses, the Commanders-in-Chief shall not cease to maintain a close contact with each other.

2. ON THE BALKAN FRONT

(*a*) The Coalition shall seek to put Bulgaria out of action as soon as possible. The desire of the Russian High Command is to continue and intensify with this object the operations in hand.

(*b*) Against Bulgaria the Russo-Roumanian forces shall act from the north, and the Allied Army at Salonika from the south, the action of these two groups of forces being closely combined, so as to obtain a decision on one or other front of action, following the development of operations.

(*c*) The Allied Army of the East shall have its effectives raised as soon as possible to 23 divisions. This figure for effectives corresponds on the one hand to the number of troops which can be manœuvred and supplied with provisions in the theatre of operations in question, and on the other hand to the contingents which can be spared from the Western theatres of operations. With the object of attaining this effective force the British Government will raise without delay its forces to seven divisions, the French Government to six divisions; the Italian Government, having been informed of the intentions definitely affirmed by the Russian High Command, shall be requested to raise to three divisions the Italian forces at Salonika.

(*d*) The Allied Army of the East shall be carefully maintained at the full complement of its effectives.

3. SECONDARY THEATRES OF OPERATIONS

On all secondary fronts, actions aiming at the immobilisation of the enemy forces shall be pursued with means as reduced as possible, in order to reserve the maximum forces for the principal theatres.

4. MUTUAL SUPPORT

(*a*) The members of the Conference renew the undertaking for mutual assistance adopted by the Conference on 5th December, 1915, and fully observed by all throughout the course of the present year, that is to say: —

If one of the Powers is attacked, the others shall come immediately to its help to the full limit of their resources, whether indirectly by attacks which the armies not assaulted by the enemy will unloose upon prepared zones, or directly by the dispatch of forces between theatres of operations linked by easy communications.

(*b*) In readiness for this latter eventuality, studies of transport and of the employment of combined forces shall be undertaken between the French, English, and Italian Headquarters Staffs.

5. MAINTAINING THE EFFECTIVES OF THE SERBIAN ARMY

The effectives of the Serbian Army shall be maintained by voluntary enrolments of prisoners of Serbian race, in the hands of Italy and Russia, to the full extent and with all the precautions determined by these two Powers.

Signed by the Representatives of the Commanders-in-Chief of the Allied Armies present at this Conference and designated below : —

For Belgium : —
General Wielemans, Chief of the General Staff of the Belgian Army.

WIELEMANS.

For Great Britain :
General Sir W. Robertson, Chief of the Imperial General Staff of the British Armies.

W. ROBERTSON.

General Sir Douglas Haig, Commander-in-Chief of the British Armies in France.

DOUGLAS HAIG.

For Italy : —
General Porro, Chief of the General Staff of the Italian Army.

PORRO.

For Roumania : —
Colonel Rudeano, Chief of the Roumanian Military Mission at the French G.H.Q.

RUDEANO.

For Russia : —
General Palitzine, representative of His Majesty, the Commander-in-Chief of the Russian Troops, and the Chief of the Russian Military Mission.

PALITZINE.

For Serbia : —
General Rachitch, delegate of the Serbian Army at the French G.H.Q.

RACHITCH.

For France : —
General Joffre, Commander-in-Chief of the French Armies.

JOFFRE."

Accordingly, at our meeting on Thursday, afternoon, 16th November, the representatives of the Allied Governments were joined by the leading generals (Joffre, Robertson, Haig, and Porro), whose report formed the agenda for our discussion, and whose conclusions limited and for practical purposes defined our action. I extract the following passages from the minutes of this session.

After M. Briand, with Mr. Asquith's support, had proposed that for the moment no more could be done than to approve the Chantilly resolutions *ad referendum* to the Petrograd Conference to which the plan of Eastern operations had been referred, I intervened as follows: —

" Mr. Lloyd George wanted to know how the figure of 23 Divisions was arrived at. According to the information supplied, there were only 19—7 English, 6 French, 3 Italian, and 3 Serbian, the effectives in the Serbian Army amounting, according to the information supplied by General Milne, to about 36,000 rifles, which only equalled three divisions on the basis of the standard of the Allied Powers.

General Joffre explained that there was a Russian Division, and that the Serbian Army was counted as six divisions.

Mr. Lloyd George expressed his astonishment at this valuation, and pointed out that the Serb effectives were being reduced all the time. The Serbian soldiers fought with a courage which could not be praised highly enough, but the Serbian Army had no reserves, and its losses were rather high. It was for that reason that he only reckoned there to be three divisions of effectives in that army.

Admiral Lacaze recalled that 140,000 Serbians had been transported from Corfu to Salonika.

General Joffre added that this figure of 23 divisions was the maximum that the Salonika theatre of operations would permit of employment. We could only deal with practical propositions. Besides, to raise the effectives of the Army of the East to this figure would take a good deal more time yet, *for if there were at our disposal a sufficient number of boats, there were still lacking the railways and necessary facilities to enable us to utilise a more numerous army.** This meant that we must immediately intensify the activity at Salonika, and for that it would be preferable to send there one division straight away, rather than to send two or three in January or February.

Mr. Lloyd George asked on what information the opinion was based that this figure of 23 divisions was the maximum that could be used at Salonika, and whether this attitude was shared by the generals commanding the East.

General Joffre replied that this advice was the result of calculations made at General Headquarters.

* The British War Council decided to take steps for this purpose in January, 1915, but the military authorities entirely ignored the decision. See Vol. I, page 235.

General Robertson announced that the British Government had received a *report from General Milne in which he declared that the possibility of utilising thirty divisions at Salonika could only be contemplated if the means of communication, the roads, and railways, could be expanded, and if two new ports could be brought into service.*

General Joffre explained that the military authorities had had to base themselves on the existing state of affairs, *because it would take not less than 12 or 18 months to construct the roads and railways needed to enable thirty divisions to manœuvre.* Replying to Mr. Lloyd George he said that no report had been received from General Sarrail.*

M. Briand pointed out that it was by taking for their basis the position as it stands with its present possibilities that the General Staffs had been led to consider that 23 divisions represented the maximum of what could be absorbed and used this winter on the Salonika Front. That was not to say that they could not, by constructing new roads and new railways, use more important effectives, but that the General Staffs had primarily had in view the realisation as early as possible of the objective set before them —namely the conquest of Monastir, and along all the rest of the front a continuous action designed to retain the enemy forces so as to prevent the Bulgarians from sending troops to the Roumanian Front.

General Joffre added that *the means of communication were not yet sufficient, and before being able to utilise the effectives that had just been spoken of, locomotives and waggons would have to be sent for the Greek railways.*

Mr. Lloyd George paid a tribute to the remarkable skill of the Italian engineers, especially over country of such a character, and wondered whether the Allies could not approach the Cabinet at Rome to ask them for help in this task.

General Porro stated that if necessary the Italian Government would be quite ready to send engineer officers to construct railways in Greece. *He added that the reports from General Pettiti confirmed all that General Joffre had said about the lack of means of communication and about the bad state of the roads, which were almost unusable.*

General Joffre *explained that the roads were so bad that half the fighting troops were being used in maintaining them.*

Mr. Asquith expressed pleasure at the assurance given by General Porro. He considered indeed that Italy could not render a more important service than that of improving the lines of communication in the Balkans.

General Joffre remarked that if the Army of the East had not

* He was Commander-in-Chief of the Salonika Expedition. Decisions had been arrived at without any previous consultation with, or even report from him.

yet reached Monastir, that was largely due to the difficulty of transport of men and materials in those regions, and indeed to the all but impossibility of revictualling them in certain cases. *The first thing to do was to construct roads and railways:* but it must not be lost sight of that, to the extent to which the army advanced, the engineers and workmen would have to make new railways for it. Progress would thus be necessarily very slow, *and that was why the military authorities considered that not more than 23 divisions could be used on the Salonika Front,* and preferred to retain the effectives that were at their disposal for the Western Front.

M. Briand thought the question should be dealt with by stages. For the moment the concern was that the expeditionary corps should be able to realise its objective on the Monastir side, and hold the Bulgarian troops on its front.

If, later on, after the construction of new railways and improvement of the means of communications, it appeared that the expeditionary corps could absorb new troops, the French Government, and no doubt also the other Governments, would be ready to send the necessary troops.

The President of the Council pointed out, in passing, that the conclusions of the military conference were in agreement with the views exchanged on the previous day between the delegates of the Powers. The conclusion of the work of the General Staffs confirmed the importance of intensifying operations in the east, so as to put out of action Bulgaria and Turkey. These conclusions were only adopted, it need hardly be repeated, *ad referendum,* but each group of delegates could forthwith inform its Government, and support at the Petrograd Conference the resolutions which had been proposed.

The President of the Council asked the delegates of the Powers to register the conclusions of the General Staffs while waiting for the possibility of going to meet the Russian Government and get them approved there in definite form."

After this the Italian Representatives gave an interesting account of the economic and financial state of affairs in Italy and its connection with the military situation. They emphasised the vital need of imports and raw materials if the *morale* of the Italian army and people, which remained high, was to be maintained. They described the difficulty of a country whose exports had shrunk to small dimensions, owing to war conditions, in paying for imports unless further financial assistance was forthcoming. Mr. Asquith, while pointing out that our own position was far from easy, promised to examine with the utmost good will any proposals the Italian Government could make for the improvement of the situation, and M. Briand gave a similar undertaking. If the Allies wished to be victorious, he said, it was essential that they should put all their resources into the common stock. Some had reserves of men, others produced a superabundance of war material, others again could dispose of important financial resources. But if the Allies established a balance of their general situation it would be easy for them, or at least possible, to fill up the gaps which might exist by one or the other.

In regard to Poland the Conference discussed the text of a protest to be made by the Allied Governments against the creation by the Central Powers of a Kingdom of Poland.

The text of the draft originally proposed was purely negative in character, merely consisting of a protest, on the grounds of international law, against the German action. Mr. Asquith pressed very strongly that it should not be purely negative in character, but should contain a reference to the promises made by the Grand Duke in regard to Poland in August, 1914.

It will be obvious from the records I have here produced that this conference, on which so much store had been set, turned out from the point of view of securing a genuine examination of the military position and strategy, by a gathering at which both soldiers and statesmen were represented, to be little better than a complete farce. M. Briand's opening speech at the Wednesday afternoon session was characteristic of his strength and weakness—eloquent in phrase, inconclusive in decision—strong in statement, feeble in action. The Allies, he explained, were superior in numbers, equipment and valour to their dispirited foes. We must energise these superior forces of the Allies and promote such a co-ordination of effort as would overwhelm the inferior armies of the enemy. The only danger was that the patience of the Allied nations would be worn out. So we must attack on all sides with all our strength. Our resources were common, so must be the front. The Balkans were the point upon which this united strength should be concentrated in the coming months. He envisaged such energetic action from the Salonika base against Sofia as would free Roumania and put Bulgaria and Turkey out of action before the winter. He pointed the result of this enterprise with a broad brush dipped in radiant colours—public opinion in Germany and Austria would certainly be demoralised, and next spring we should be able to deal our enemies a decisive blow. And he ended up with the proposal of a local operation for the capture of Monastir, a feat achieved later on by the broken army of Serbia alone. He also laid it down in precise terms that the statesmen of the Alliance must make clear to the Chantilly warriors that the strategy and direction came from Governments and not from staffs, and that it was for the latter merely to carry out the instructions framed at the political conference. At that very moment M. Briand had obviously agreed in advance to accept General Joffre's plans which went no further than Monastir! The idea of breaking through the

Bulgarian lines in order to extend effective aid to Roumania was in fact abandoned in the very speech wherein it was advocated with resounding rhetoric.

As for the document submitted to the second session by the generals, setting out their decisions at Chantilly, it was an intimation that the military leaders regarded the determination of the lines of the campaign for 1917 to be a matter for which they had the primary responsibility. To this attitude they adhered in spite of an elaborate appearance of deference to the wishes of the Government. The 1917 campaign was theirs with all its disasters. It repeated all the bloody stupidities of 1915 and 1916 and extinguished finally the *morale* of the Russian Armies, already shaken but not irretrievably shattered. It also temporarily broke the spirit of the French and Italian and British Armies.

The proposal for the conference of responsible political and military leaders to be held immediately on Russian soil to settle the future plans of the Allies was completely ignored by the generals. They had agreed to their plans at Chantilly and they had no intention of allowing General Alexeieff to alter them. Signor Tittoni's objection to agreeing to the meeting, except *ad referendum* to a sick Prime Minister, helped the generals to avoid committing themselves to a conference. As to Salonika they made a concession to civilian obtuseness. An attack was to be staged in that quarter at an early date, but it must be done as cheaply as possible. The stupid politicians must be deluded into the belief that it was a serious operation with a view to crumpling up Bulgaria—a preposterous piece of deception to any one who had made any study of the comparative strength or numbers, equipment and position of the combatants on that front. The generals knew that they had no intention of pressing the attack beyond Monastir. The storming of the Balkans they knew too well was far beyond the power of the badly equipped Salonika Army. But the strength of the Salonika force must be exaggerated for civilian ears. It was, or soon would be, an army of 23 divisions brought up to effective strength. They juggled and shuffled with " divisions " when they knew they were only sham divisions. As a matter of fact it was the equivalent of barely ten divisions, and no effort was contemplated to increase its numbers in offensive efficacy. In the matter of artillery and transport it was hopelessly below the standard of the Western Front. When their attention was called to the inadequacy of the forces, Generals Joffre and Robertson urged that the transport facilities were so defective that you could not feed a larger number of troops, let alone carry the necessary ammunition for more cannon. It would take 12 to 18 months to improve these facilities. The Expeditionary Force had already been at Salonika for that period and these improvements had not been attempted. As I have previously said, a decision had been arrived at by the British War Council as far back as January, 1915, to take immediate steps to increase transport facilities between Salonika and Serbia. Lord Kitchener promised to take the matter in hand at once. Here, at the end of 1916, a campaign which our military advisers considered essential to restore our failures in South-Eastern Europe, could not be attempted because the port, rail and road transport were so inefficient that no effective attack could be staged. It came out in one of the military reports that half the troops were occupied not in fighting but in road repairing. General Milne reported that with 33 divisions the Bulgarian Army could be beaten. Had the necessary 33 divisions been landed, backed by a powerful artillery, what a difference it would have made to the course of events! Bulgaria, now getting tired of the War, would have been eliminated. The Bulgarian peasantry never cared for the side they were forced by their King to take. The road to Roumania would have been reached. The Russian Armies and those of the west would have joined hands. Turkey would have been cut off from the source of her supplies. More heart and spirit would have been given to the depressed and disaffected Russian soldiers. The Revolution would have been further postponed. Austria would have been enveloped on the east, the south and the west and would have fallen to pieces. 1917 might have seen the end of the War. What a difference that would have made to the world!

I left the conference feeling that after all nothing more would be done except to repeat the old fatuous tactics of hammering away with human flesh and sinews at the strongest fortresses of the enemy. If Russia and Roumania fell out, there was nothing more that could be done.

When Mr. Asquith, Sir Maurice Hankey and I returned to the hotel and Mr. Asquith, after a short and perfunctory conversation, retired to his usual rest before dinner, Sir Maurice and I went for a walk together to talk matters over.

We both felt that nothing in the way of a change in the conduct of the War had been accomplished and that in the absence of some dramatic *coup* things would go on as before until we slid into inevitable catastrophe. We felt that if either Russia or Italy collapsed or if the submarine losses could not be checked, the balance of advantage in favour of the Allies would be lost and would pass over to the enemy. I was in favour of an immediate resignation to rouse Allied opinion to the actualities of the position. To this Sir Maurice was opposed until some other means of effecting a change in the War direction had first been attempted. I can recall that as we passed the Vendôme Column, Sir Maurice paused and said "You ought to insist on a small War Committee being set up for the day-to-day conduct of the War, with full powers. It must be independent of the Cabinet. It must keep in close touch with the P.M., but the

Committee ought to be in continuous session, and the P.M., as Head of the Government, could not manage that. He has a very heavy job in looking after the Cabinet and attending to Parliament and home affairs. He is a bit tired, too, after all he has gone through in the last two and a half years. The Chairman must be a man of unimpaired energy and great driving power." We both agreed that it was important that Mr. Asquith should continue to be Prime Minister. His great prestige and his unrivalled authority in the House of Commons would be assets which were regarded as indispensable. It was decided, therefore, that on my return to England I should place the proposition before the Prime Minister; but that before I did so it would be best to sound Bonar Law, whose good will and approval it was essential to secure. I wired from Paris to Lord Beaverbrook, asking him to arrange a meeting between Bonar Law and myself the following evening.

CHAPTER XXXIII

THE FOOD POSITION

BY the autumn of 1916 the food position was becoming increasingly alarming and grave, and its handling by the Government was a most conspicuous example of its hesitancies. The increasing shortage of shipping made the food position doubly grave, dependent as we were upon ships for most of our food supplies. As far back as September, 1915, Lord Selborne, in a memorandum which he submitted to the Cabinet, had urged that "we should appoint another committee of the Cabinet to consider the whole question of the food supply of the nation for the next 18 months." In this document he had pleaded the value of an increased wheat production. "It is only about a month," he wrote, "since the Chancellor of the Exchequer [Mr. M'Kenna] showed an invincible repugnance to encourage the growth of wheat in England by offering the farmers a guarantee. It is possible to increase the production of food in the United Kingdom by voluntary effort, but a guarantee of the price of wheat would be by far the most effective measure which the Government would take for that purpose." On 10th March, 1916, I raised this issue anew by urging on the War Committee that the aim we ought to keep in view in the matter of food supplies was that this country should as far as possible be self-contained. To this end the Board of Agriculture ought to be armed with drastic powers to improve the production of food so as to reduce our dependence on imports. Every possible acre ought to be cultivated against the prospective extension of the submarine campaign. I suggested the utilisation of machinery on a large scale. The plan, however, must be a *national* one.

On 23rd March, 1916, I spoke again on the same subject in connection with the problem of the shortage of ships.

In the War Committee of 31st October, 1916, the Prime Minister had read a letter from the Commander-in-Chief of the Grand Fleet, who "expressed misgivings regarding the danger to the cause of the Allies from submarine attacks on merchant shipping, *which must be expected to increase in the spring, when the enemy would have more submarines.*" It was known that in this opinion the Admiralty were in complete agreement with the Commander-in-Chief. Lord Crawford was now Minister of Agriculture, and had circulated to the members of the Committee an urgent document showing the seriousness of the situation; and how the outlook grew more difficult as time went on. He pointed out that *our stocks of wheat and flour at that moment (30th October) amounted to four months' consumption, and that there was a world deficit of wheat.* The probable wheat *requirements of importing countries during the 12 months ending 1st September, 1917, were 72,000,000 quarters, while the total available supplies were estimated at 63,000,000.*

The freight space required to carry the necessary imports of grain and feeding stuffs in the eight months, November-June was 8,981,000 shipping tons. The potato crop, too, had failed in England, as in Germany and France. The forecasts indicated a shortage of some 1,800,000 tons (or 24 per cent.) as compared with 1915. Moreover, the crop was diseased and a shortage of seed potatoes was possible. Fish supplies were some 64 per cent. below normal, and the prices had risen from 100 to 400 per cent. The feeding of live stock was causing anxiety, as foodstuffs were costly and labour scarce.

Lord Crawford stressed the desirability of establishing some central food department to supervise and co-ordinate the varied relations of the State with the import, purchase and distribution of food. The whole field and the general prospects might be suitably submitted to the continuing and comprehensive survey of the central body. (This suggestion had now been before the Committee for at least seven months, but no advance had been made nor decision taken.)

Lord Crawford ended his memorandum by the statement *that not before August, 1917 (i.e., when the harvest of 1917 had been gathered in) would war policy be free to dissociate itself from the influence of home food supply.*

I supported Lord Crawford whole-heartedly in his efforts to obtain a decision as regard the food supply, and on 10th November I circulated a short memorandum embodying a few concrete suggestions which I thought would materially help in solving the food problem. These were as follows: —

" That someone—who shall not be a member of the Ministry—be immediately appointed to organise the food supplies, including purchase, production, distribution and prices.

That he should be equipped with all the necessary legislative, administrative and financial powers to enable him to utilise to the full the food-producing capacity of the United Kingdom.

That *inter alia* he should direct his attention to:

1. Securing adequate supplies of food, especially from home sources;

2. Keeping prices down.

3. Increasing the acreage of land in this country which produces cereals, potatoes, vegetables, and other food products;

4. The mobilisation and utilisation to the full and in the best way of

(a) All the available mechanical appliances for the cultivation of the soil;

(b) The manufacturing capacity of this country and the United States for the output of machinery for cultivation;

(c) The skilled agricultural labour of the country;

(d) The unskilled male and female labour capacity of the country for agricultural purposes;

5. The utilisation for animal fattening of the enormous waste of food products now consigned to the refuse heaps in the great towns.

War Office, November 10th, 1916."

The same day (10th November) there was a meeting of the War Committee, at which the question of shipping shortage was discussed. The President of the Board of Trade, in the course of his statement, said that the Wheat Commission were at present unable to find 40 free vessels for the essential service of conveying the Australian wheat supplies. *The conclusion that he drew was that a complete breakdown in shipping would come before June, 1917.*

On 13th November, the War Committee met to discuss the food position again. They had before them Lord Crawford's memorandum. The President of the Board of Agriculture, with the clarity and suavity which he always commands, urged his case. He gave a sketch of the immediate and prospective outlook as regards food. He pointed out that land was going out of cultivation, that labour was scarce. The harvest this year, he said, had been less by half a quarter per acre than had been anticipated, which was equal to a reduction from 12 to 10 weeks' supply. He was apprehensive of next year's harvest unless immediate steps were taken. He again urged the necessity for a Central Food Controlling Authority. I realised that if the submarine menace were not checked (and there seemed at that moment no expectancy that anything could prevent it from increasing in gravity) the War as far as we were concerned might end in starvation for this country. It was now months since the proposition of a central authority had been put before the Government, but we seemed to be no nearer achieving it. I therefore pressed at this meeting for the appointment of a Central Authority (which I had also insisted upon in my memorandum of 10th November). I urged, however, *that the President should have real authority with complete control subject only to the War Committee. I considered, moreover, that the person appointed should not be a Minister of the Crown, as his time would largely be taken up with answering questions in Parliament. He need only attend the War Committee whenever he wanted a decision of first-class importance. Above all,*

I impressed upon the Committee that the appointment should be made at once. The actual difference between 10 and 12 might seem to be small, but in point of fact it was very serious. I therefore begged the Prime Minister to treat the necessity of obtaining a man to control all food supplies as one of immediate urgency. I said that I attached great importance to machinery and cultivation. I saw no reason why every village in the country should not be self-supporting, just as it was when I was a boy.

The President of the Board of Trade pointed out that nearly all the statutory powers required to carry out my proposals already existed in the Defence of the Realm Act, and that he had recently circulated to the Cabinet new regulations under the Act of a most drastic kind.

In spite of these " full powers " and " drastic regulations," the Government had not sanctioned the measures suggested by the Minister for Agriculture and no progress was being made with the increase of home production.

The War Committee approved of my proposal for a Food Controller, in principle, subject to the right man being found to control the great organisation contemplated.

There were enough provisos in this last paragraph to prevent any action being taken immediately. As a matter fact, no food controller was appointed under Mr. Asquith's Premiership.

On 16th November, the First Sea Lord of the Admiralty and the Chief of the Admiralty War Staff circulated a note to the Cabinet stressing the increasing gravity of the submarine danger. They concluded the note with the following words : —

" The increasing danger to our supplies from the enemy's submarines has recently become so much more evident through their ruthless attacks on neutral shipping as to make this question need more serious reconsideration *before it is too late.*"

But no immediate decision was taken. The accumulation of problems requiring urgent attention had indeed become so great that there seemed to be no time for any one of them to be properly thrashed out and a decision to be arrived at. On 22nd November, the matter was still in abeyance. The question of shipping and food supply was reaching a crisis, and the President of the Board of Trade circulated a memorandum complaining that nothing had been decided at the Cabinet meeting on 10th November, and calling attention again to the urgency of the matter from the point of view of tonnage. On the same day the Wheat Commission sent a communication (the memorandum of the President may have been written as a result of this), urging the provision of further tonnage for food supplies. " So far from adding," they said, " to the reserves in the country, the shipments during the last fortnight to arrive this year have been nearly 200,000 quarters a week less than requirements, and all the information of the Commission points to the conclusion that this low rate of shipment will be continued until a further supply of tramp tonnage has arrived for loading in the Northern Range."

On the same day (22nd November) the Shipping Control Committee met and discussed the tonnage situation in relation to the serious position of the wheat supply in this country.

They reported: "The Committee are informed that the stocks of wheat are running down; that we are living from hand to mouth. In London there are only two days' supplies, and London has therefore to be fed by rail from other ports. In Bristol there are only two weeks' supplies. . . .

"The Wheat Commission have purchased 700,000 quarters in North America, *but there are no steamers to bring the wheat to England.*

"In normal circumstances there would be ships ' coming free ' in the Mediterranean after discharge of coal." These ships, however, owing to war conditions, would not become available for four months, and the wheat position was dangerously acute.

On 23rd November (the next day) three Ministers (the President of the Board of Trade, Lord Curzon, and the President of the Board of Agriculture) raised, as a matter of great urgency, our present and prospective critical situation in regard to grain supplies. They brought in support the letter from the Wheat Commission and the report of the Shipping Control Committee; and the President of the Board of Agriculture pointed out that we were *consuming 200,000 quarters a week more than we were receiving; that every week we were buying sufficient wheat for 15 days' consumption, but were unable to ship it; and that if the wheat we had purchased were not brought forward it would diminish our power to purchase.*

It was decided that a conference should be held that afternoon between the Admiralty, Shipping Control Committee, and President of the Board of Trade, and that they should report next day to the War Committee.

In spite of these urgent messages showing the critical position of our food supplies none of the plans suggested either by the Ministry of Agriculture or myself for dealing with the situation were put into operation during the lifetime of the First Coalition. A paralysis of will seemed to have seized the Government. Whatever the subject, it was impossible to get a move on. I am not sure that this palsy did not account for the unanimity of the Cabinet on the question of rejecting overtures for Peace. These would have meant action. The pacifist element were easily persuaded to do nothing. The Government was getting into that nervous condition where they could neither wage war nor negotiate peace.

CHAPTER XXXIV

A CABINET OF INDECISION

It is hard for me to convey an adequate picture of the sense of frustration and tangled impotence which oppressed me during those closing months of 1916. There are nightmares in which one welters amid a web of fettering strands and obstacles, and watches, wide-eyed, some doom approaching against which the strangled throat cannot force a sound of protest or appeal. The ineffectiveness and irresolution of our leadership in those dark weeks bred something of this nightmare feeling.

There was at this time a whole series of developments and problems which were being paltered with or shelved. Some of the wider issues of general policy I have already described. Firm handling of them was vital to our prospects of success, and I grew increasingly convinced that it was my duty as a responsible Minister to dispel this miasma of indecision and force these matters to a definite issue, even at the risk of resignation from the Ministry and a subsequent public exposure of the ineptitude of the Allied war direction. I have also told of the way in which two or three important questions were dealt with, and these afford an illustration of the general method of procedure adopted by the Government in an emergency. One of them was the neglect to take competent strong measures to protect our merchant ships against submarine raiders. The alarming rate at which our ships were being sunk was rapidly increasing. The October sinkings had been nearly 70 per cent. above those of September, and the Admiralty wrung their hands in despair when reporting fresh disasters at our meetings, but offered no hope that they could grapple successfully with the rapidly developing catastrophe. Then there was our failure to take steps to co-ordinate our strategy with our Russian Ally —a failure intensified by the refusal of Sir William Robertson, backed and instigated by a member of the War Committee—to represent this country at the proposed Russian Conference. His refusal dealt a death blow to our prospects of saving our Ally from collapse and concerting our military strategy with her. It was prompted by a groundless apprehension that the whole idea was a manœuvre to shift him from his position in the War Office, and that the methods of the intrigue by which he had supplanted Lord Kitchener were to be practised in turn on himself—that Robertson, in fact, was to be

581

"kitchenered" out of his position of high authority.   This point of view was pressed upon him by a prominent Cabinet Minister and he was only too ready to listen.   It is idle to vow that I had no such purpose in view, and that I had always urged a more authoritative touch between east and west than that which was represented by the appearance at our conference of Russian generals, for whom their own army had no use at home.   Those who are capable of such baseness in a great crisis will readily believe that others meditated it.   I was pressing on my colleagues what I sincerely believed was the best course in the interest of my country.   However, Sir William Robertson would not go and the Prime Minister was not prepared to order him to go.   At that time there was no military substitute of sufficient authority.   Sir Douglas Haig could not be sent.   He was so committed by ideas and loyalty to the front for which he was responsible that he could hardly be expected to review impartially the battlefield as a whole.   Sir Henry Wilson was thoroughly disliked and distrusted by the Prime Minister.   So that when Sir William Robertson declined to undertake the mission it dealt a sinister blow at the whole project.

The situation in regard to aeroplanes was another of the vital issues which were being muddled and mishandled in a fashion all too symptomatic of the methods of the Government.   At that time we had already been discussing for weeks the question of aeroplane production.   There was a wasteful rivalry going on between the Army and Navy on the subject.   Certain works had been captured by the Navy that ought to be assisting in increasing the much-needed output for the Army.   On the Western Front the Germans had regained superiority, especially in attacking and raiding machines, and the military chiefs were clamouring for more aeroplanes of these types.

The Cabinet debates on this issue were so protracted that judgment upon it was never delivered during the lifetime of the Asquith Coalition.   The question of responsibility for the manufacture of aeroplanes was raised by Mr. E. S. Montagu on behalf of the Ministry of Munitions in September, 1916.   Mr. Montagu was anxious that his Ministry should undertake the manufacture of all the aeroplanes required by both the Army and the Navy.   In a memorandum to the Cabinet, he pointed out that: —

"The present organisation, under which the supply of aircraft material is the concern of two bodies—the War Office and the Admiralty—acting under the general supervision of a third—the Air Board—and in constant and inevitable competition with a fourth—the Ministry of Munitions—appears to me to be one for which no arguments can be adduced, and which cannot be expected to obtain satisfactory results.   In my opinion it is necessary at once to adopt one of two plans—either to set up a new Supply Department responsible for the entire supply of both Air Services, or to entrust the task of obtaining that supply to the Ministry of Munitions, which was created to meet a situation in regard to munitions similar to that which now appears to exist in regard to aircraft."

The Aviation Board had been set up with a view to co-ordinating the efforts of both Army and Navy. Over this Board Lord Curzon presided. He was strongly opposed to Mr. Montagu's scheme. He admitted that: —

"At this moment a source of urgent anxiety to General Trenchard lies in the appearance on the German Front of two new machines better in certain respects than any which we now possess there. It is not the *number* of these available that concerns him, but the fact of their superiority."

But he claimed that: —

" We are developing fresh engines and fresh aeroplanes which we believe will surpass the recent German production. But the question at issue is, will our machines in fact be superior and will they be developed in time?"

He was clearly of the opinion that a new department should be set up which would have sole and complete control over the production and to a certain extent, the direction of all machinery for aerial warfare.

When Lord Curzon put forward his plan on these lines, he was in turn challenged by Mr. Balfour in a very caustic and amusing memorandum. To this Lord Curzon replied in suitable terms. It was clear that if the controversy did not conduce to the provision of aeroplanes it at least provided excellent entertainment for those who were privileged to read these documents and to hear the discussions. The pleadings took some time. First, the statement of claim by Lord Curzon. Time must be given for the First Lord of the Admiralty to file his defence, then there was a rebutter and surrebutter. An interpleader by the Ministry of Munitions. Then at last the case was set down for trial.

I have a melancholy recollection of Cabinet Committee discussions at this period. The aeroplane case was always first in the list after the usual preliminary reports from the Army and the Navy. Lord Crawford's urgent memorandum on the food position should have come next, and shipping also would have to be discussed, but with such skilled protagonists as Mr. Balfour, Lord Curzon, and Mr. Montagu the time was generally occupied in thrashing out the merits and demerits of the conflicting claims championed by these trained dialecticians. When in despair of conciliating the antagonistic proposals the Prime Minister had a habit of turning round to the mantelpiece to see whether any temporary relief from his perplexities was indicated by the position of the hands on the clock. We all knew what that meant. He was making for a postponement of further discussion to the next meeting. Lord Crawford put in a despairing cry for a few minutes' consideration before lunch of his anxieties about the food of the nation. He pointed out each time that the position was steadily getting worse, that consumption was exceeding supply at a time of the year when the process ought to be reversed. On the other hand, the Prime Minister would point out that it was clear from the hour which had been reached that there was no time left for the discussion of so grave a problem. There was nothing left for Lord Crawford but to plead for a special meeting to consider his difficulties. That meeting never took place in the lifetime of that Administration. At our next meeting came again the aeroplane case (part heard). At the last meeting ever held we all thought that a decision had been arrived at, but as we were dispersing, I saw Lord Curzon standing alongside the Prime Minister and challenging that fact. Mr. Asquith surrendered and said that the case would have to be re-argued at the next meeting. When the next Cabinet meeting took place in Downing Street it was under a different Government.

CHAPTER XXXV

THE CRISIS: DECEMBER 1916

THE upshot of our November peace discussions in the Cabinet had been the decision of the Government not to make peace until the fortunes of the Allies were unchallengeably better than those of the Central Powers. But this decision made it incumbent upon them to take the necessary steps to improve those fortunes before the patience of the Allied nations became exhausted. We had not only to resolve on the prosecution of the War to the utmost limit of our resources, but to take steps to utilise those resources to the best advantage, and especially to see that the great combined strength of all the Allies should not be dissipated and wasted through lack of co-ordinated effort. We had also to make sure that one of the most powerful of the Allies should not retire out of the struggle in a spirit of despair.

At the Paris Conference, M. Briand had pointed to the possibility of exhaustion as one of the perils of the situation. As a matter of fact, we were only a few weeks off the popular uprising in Russia against continuing the sacrifices of the War. Yet in face of this near-ing danger there was manifest among our leaders no clearness of vision as to their course, no firmness of leadership and no promptitude or boldness of decision. Their disposition was to leave all vital questions to the Military, Naval or Civilian Organisation in charge of some special war activity, and I felt in my bones that unless some new energy and inspiration were injected into the War direction, we should before long drift into irretrievable disaster. I therefore came to the conclusion that I must act without further delay.

Having regard to the political forces in Parliament, I realised that it was essential that I should carry with me two men—Mr. Bonar Law and Sir Edward Carson. Standing alone I could only bring pressure to bear upon Parliament, and through Parliament upon the Govern-ment, by means of a popular agitation conducted with the support of a section of the Press. This would necessarily take time, and might have the effect of discouraging and demoralising public opinion. Russia a few weeks later proved the danger of producing a sense of disillusion-ment in the public mind, even by justifiable and necessary criticism. It would have reacted on the Army, whose ardour had been tem-porarily damped by the Somme mud—even more than by the Somme carnage. It was therefore essential that if a change was to be effected in the direction of our war activities it should be achieved with as little disturbance and public agitation as possible.

Of Sir Edward Carson I had seen a good deal through the patriotic good offices of a friend and supporter of his, Sir Arthur Lee—now Lord Lee of Fareham. Sir Edward Carson was convinced that the War was being badly muddled. His few months in the Coalition Cabinet, with its Serbian collapse, its Dardanelles fiasco, and the bloody futilities of our strategy in France and Flanders had the result of deepening his distrust of the Prime Minister's capacity to direct the War. His view was that all the disasters which had befallen the Allies could have been averted but for the Prime Minister's slackness. Mr. Bonar Law on the other hand, having the Scotsman's natural respect for brains, was a great admirer of the Prime Minister, and it took him many months' experience of his obvious tardiness, indecision, and lack of drive in action to come to the conclusion that whatever Mr. Asquith's mental equipment—and of that neither of us had any doubt—he did not possess the qualities that make a great War Minister.

The story of my negotiations with Mr. Bonar Law and Lord Carson has already been told by Lord Beaverbrook in his fascinating book on "Politicians and the War." It is frankly told not from my point of view, but as a vindication of Mr. Bonar Law. Making an allowance for that honourable personal bias, I am prepared on the main facts to accept his narrative. As between Mr. Asquith and myself he is clearly unbiased. He has no personal interest in either of us.

Sir Edward Carson was for pushing Mr. Asquith out of the Premiership. He argued that any shifts like a War Committee, whatever its composition, must necessarily fail so long as the chief responsibility and authority was vested in Mr. Asquith. Certain Ministers whom he named would be constantly at his ear and poisoning him against the new committee, and postponing, modifying, and thwarting its decisions. Mr. Bonar Law was emphatically of the opinion that it was desirable for the sake of preserving the national unity that Mr. Asquith should retain his position of Prime Minister. He dreaded anything like a split in the Cabinet at such a juncture. He was also apprehensive that there might be a division in his own Party if Mr. Asquith were driven out of the Premiership. Most of the Tory Ministers were devoted adherents of Mr. Asquith's leadership in the War. I was also in favour of retaining Mr. Asquith as Prime Minister provided he left the new committee full and unfettered powers to direct the War. It is rather significant that at this stage not one of us (except Sir Edward Carson) contemplated Mr. Asquith's retirement and consequently there was nothing said at any of our interviews as to his possible successor. I wish to confirm Lord Beaverbrook's statement that Lord Northcliffe was never, at any stage, brought into our consultations.   He had taken sides with Sir William Robertson against me on my criticism of the military chiefs for the prolongation of the Somme fighting and the failure to avert the Roumanian collapse.   He had threatened to attack me in his papers if I continued " to interfere with the soldiers."   When he saw that something was going on he made an effort to resume friendly relations.   But he was not only left out of the negotiations, but as far as I know he was not informed as to what was actually taking place.

After a good deal of conferring and debating between Mr. Bonar Law, Sir Edward Carson, Lord Beaverbrook and myself, I drew up the following memorandum for submission to the Prime Minister: —

" 1st December, 1916.

1.   That the War Committee consist of three members—two of whom must be the First Lord of the Admiralty and the Secretary of State for War, who should have in their offices deputies capable of attending to and deciding all departmental business, and a third Minister without portfolio.   One of the three to be Chairman.

2.   That the War Committee shall have full powers, subject to the supreme control of the Prime Minister, to direct all questions connected with the War.

3.   The Prime Minister in his discretion to have the power to refer any question to the Cabinet.

4.   Unless the Cabinet on reference by the Prime Minister reverses decision of the War Committee, that decision to be carried out by the Department concerned.

5.   The War Committee to have the power to invite any Minister, and to summon the expert advisers and officers of any Department to its meetings."

I showed it to Lord Derby who fully approved of its terms.

I then took it to Mr. Asquith, having first of all explained to him fully the reasons that had prompted me to come to the conclusions embodied in my memorandum.   He promised to think it over and let me know his views later on in the day.   In the evening I received from him the following letter: —

" 10 Downing Street.
1st December, 1916.

My dear Lloyd George,

I have now had time to reflect on our conversation this morning, and to study your memorandum.

Though I do not altogether share your dark estimate, and forecast of the situation, actual and prospective, I am in complete agreement that we have reached a critical situation in the War, and that our own methods of procedure, with the experience which we have gained during the last few months, call for reconsideration and revision.

The two main defects of the War Committee, which has done excellent work, are (1) that its numbers are too large; (2) that there is delay, evasion, and often obstruction, on the part of the Departments in giving effect to its decision. I might with good reason add (3) that it is often kept in ignorance by the Departments of information, essential and even vital, of a technical kind, upon the problems that come before it, and (4) that it is overcharged with duties, many of subordinate bodies.

The result is that I am clearly of opinion that the War Committee should be reconstituted, and its relations to and authority over the Departments be more clearly defined and more effectively asserted.

I come now to your specific proposals. In my opinion, whatever changes are made in the composition or functions of the War Committee, the Prime Minister must be its Chairman. He cannot be relegated to the position of an arbiter in the background or a referee to the Cabinet.

In regard to its composition, I agree that the War Secretary and the First Lord of the Admiralty are necessary members. I am inclined to add to the same category the Minister of Munitions. There should be another member, either without portfolio, or charged only with comparatively light departmental duties. One of the members should be appointed Vice-Chairman.

I purposely do not in this letter discuss the delicate and difficult question of personnel.

The committee should, as far as possible, sit *de die in diem*, and have full power to see that its decisions (subject to appeal to the Cabinet) are carried out promptly and effectively by the Departments.

The reconstitution of the War Committee should be accompanied by the setting up of a Committee of National Organisation to deal with the purely domestic side of war problems. It should have executive powers within its own domain.

The Cabinet would in all cases have ultimate authority.

Yours always sincerely,
H. H. ASQUITH."

The reply was entirely unsatisfactory. The Prime Minister's counter proposal would effect no improvement and hardly any change in the position as it stood. The Prime Minister was to preside over the Committee and any Ministers dissatisfied with any of its decisions were entitled to appeal to the Cabinet before any steps were taken to carry them out. Then what about the Committee of National Organisation which was to be set up quite independently of the War Committee to deal with the purely domestic side of War problems?

(1) Would food production and distribution be relegated to it?
(2) What about shipping and ship-building?
(3) Would the question of man-power be left to it?

If these questions were taken out of the cognisance and authority of the War Committee it would have a more limited scope and less power than the existing body of that name. I felt convinced that Mr. Asquith was resolved not to agree to any change in the War direction. I therefore decided to act without further loss of time and I wrote to Mr. Bonar Law as follows: —

> " War Office,
> Whitehall, S.W.
> 2nd December, 1916.
>
> My dear Bonar,
> I enclose copy of P.M.'s letter.
> The life of the country depends on resolute action by you now.
> Yours ever,
> D. Lloyd George."

I had seen Mr. Bonar Law late on Friday evening and it was decided that we should go forward with our plan of reorganisation whatever the consequences. On Saturday and Sunday Mr. Bonar Law was entangled in a series of clumsy manœuvres in which his Conservative colleagues were engaged. They had lost confidence in Asquith, but they did not want me. They disliked Carson and had no fanatical belief in Bonar Law. What were the poor fellows to do? They had no clear idea themselves. The story is told in detail by Lord Beaver-brook. Much of what he relates I learnt for the first time when I read his book. I could make no further progress until Mr. Bonar Law knew exactly where he stood in reference to the other leaders of his Party. However, on Sunday afternoon I was asked by the Prime Minister's secretary—Sir Maurice Bonham Carter—to come up from the country to talk things over with his Chief, who was returning from Walmer Castle specially with that object. At the interview which ensued Mr. Asquith and I discussed the whole situation in the friendliest spirit and ultimately came to a complete understanding. The terms of that arrangement are given by Mr. Asquith in the letter he wrote me the following morning. As soon as the agreement was reached he sent for Mr. Bonar Law to inform him of the " complete agreement " arrived at. I met Mr. Bonar Law on my way out. The Prime Minister and I were to meet on Monday to discuss the personnel of the new committee. On that question I anticipated no insuperable difficulty. The Monday meeting never came off and I was never privileged to meet Mr. Asquith as Prime Minister again.

In the Monday morning papers there appeared the following announcement: —

" The Prime Minister, with a view to the most active prosecution of the War, had decided to advise His Majesty the King to consent to a reconstruction of the Government."

Some time in the course of the morning I received the following letter from the Prime Minister: —

> " 10, Downing Street, S.W.
> 4th December, 1916.
>
> My dear Lloyd George,
> Such productions as the first leading article in to-day's *Times*, showing the infinite possibilities for misunderstanding and mis-representation of such an arrangement as we considered yesterday, made me at least doubtful as to its feasibility. Unless the impression is at once corrected that I am being relegated to the position of an irresponsible spectator of the War, I cannot go on.
> The suggested arrangement was to the following effect: The Prime Minister to have supreme and effective control of war policy.
> The agenda of the War Committee will be submitted to him; its Chairman will report to him daily; he can direct it to consider particular topics or proposals; and all its conclusions will be subject to his approval or veto. He can, of course, at his own discretion attend meetings of the Committee.
>
> Yours sincerely,
> H. H. Asquith."

When I read that letter I felt the Prime Minister had completely changed his tone. There was none of the cordiality and friendliness which had characterised our Sunday conversation. I had not seen *The Times* article of which he complained, and I certainly had no responsibility for it. I had not communicated any information as to the negotiations which were going on with Mr. Asquith or the agreement arrived at with him, to the proprietor or editor of that paper, either directly or indirectly.* I was frankly too pleased with the idea that a break had been averted on terms which gave some chance of putting new energy into our war activities to do anything that would imperil the completion of the new arrangement. I replied: —

> " War Office,
> Whitehall, S.W.
> December 4, 1916.
>
> My dear Prime Minister,
> I have not seen *The Times* article. But I hope you will not attach undue importance to these effusions. I have had these misrepresentations to put up with for months. Northcliffe frankly

---

* Lord Beaverbrook makes this quite clear in his narrative of these events. *Vide* " Politicians and the War."

wants a smash. Derby and I do not. Northcliffe would like to make this and any other rearrangement under your Premiership impossible. Derby and I attach great importance to your retaining your present position—effectively. I cannot restrain, or, I fear, influence Northcliffe. I fully accept in letter and in spirit your summary of the suggested arrangement—subject, of course, to personnel.

Ever sincerely,
D. Lloyd George."

During that Monday I pressed for my promised appointment with the Prime Minister. I was constantly put off by his secretaries. At last I was promised an interview at six o'clock. That interview was never accorded. Here is a facsimile of a note sent in by my private secretary, late in the afternoon to me in my room at the War Office: —

" War Office,
Whitehall, S.W.

Bonham Carter says that the Prime Minister does not think he will trouble you to come over to-night. He is going to write."

Meanwhile the Prime Minister was engaged in a series of interviews with all my colleagues (Liberal and Conservative) who were hostile to the new Committee. He even summoned a formal meeting of all the Liberal Members of the Cabinet to discuss the situation. It was to take place at the hour fixed for my interview. Mr. Arthur Henderson was also invited to attend. I received no invitation to attend that meeting to explain my position, although I was still a member of the Cabinet and had done nothing to forfeit my right to be summoned to a conference of the Liberal Section. My last act had been to agree with the Prime Minister on the very issue which was to be discussed at the meeting.

On Tuesday morning I received the following letter from the Prime Minister: —

" 10, Downing Street, S.W.
December 4, 1916.

My dear Lloyd George,

Thank you for your letter of this morning.

The King gave me to-day authority to ask and accept the resignations of all my colleagues, and to form a new Government on such lines as I should submit to him. I start, therefore, with a clean slate.

The first question which I have to consider is the constitution of the new War Committee.

After full consideration of the matter in all its aspects, I have come decidedly to the conclusion that it is not possible that such a Committee could be made workable and effective without the Prime Minister as its Chairman. I quite agree that it will be

U

necessary for him, in view of the other calls upon his time and energy, to delegate from time to time the chairmanship to another Minister as his representative and *locum tenens*; but (if he is to retain the authority, which corresponds to his responsibility, as Prime Minister) he must continue to be, as he always has been, its permanent President.   I am satisfied, on reflection, that any other arrangement (such, for instance, as the one which I indicated to you in my letter of to-day) would be found in experience impracticable, and incompatible with the retention of the Prime Minister's final and supreme control.

The other question, which you have raised, relates to the personnel of the Committee.   Here again, after deliberate consideration, I find myself unable to agree with some of your suggestions.

I think we both agree that the First Lord of the Admiralty must, of necessity, be a member of the Committee.

I cannot (as I told you yesterday) be a party to any suggestion that Mr. Balfour should be displaced.   The technical side of the Board of Admiralty has been reconstituted, with Sir John Jellicoe as First Sea Lord.   I believe Mr. Balfour to be, under existing conditions, the necessary head of the Board.

I must add that Sir Edward Carson (for whom, personally, and in every other way, I have the greatest regard) is not, from the only point of view which is significant to me (namely, the most effective prosecution of the War), the man best qualified among my colleagues, present and past, to be a member of the War Committee.

I have only to say, in conclusion, that I am strongly of opinion that the War Committee (without any disparagement of the existing Committee, which, in my judgment, is a most efficient body, and has done, and is doing, invaluable work) ought to be reduced in number; so that it can sit more frequently, and overtake more easily the daily problems with which it has to deal. But in any reconstruction of the Committee, such as I have, and have for some time past had, in view, the governing consideration, to my mind, is the special capacity of the men who are to sit on it for the work which it has to do.

That is a question which I must reserve for myself to decide.

Yours very sincerely,

H. H. Asquith."

The letter was a complete repudiation of the agreement he had entered into with me on Sunday and confirmed in writing on Monday. He had reached his decision to go back on his word without giving me an opportunity of further discussion with him.   He saw all the critics.   He resolutely refused to see me although he had promised to do so.   Had I gone back on my word I know the nature of the comment that would have been passed on me by those who worked with frenzy to persuade Mr. Asquith to break faith. How it would have fitted into that legend of distrust which they so assiduously worked up for years, and which seems to be their sole article of unwavering faith!

I therefore felt bound to send him the following reply: —

> "War Office,
> Whitehall, S.W.
> December 5, 1916.

My dear Prime Minister,

I have received your letter with some surprise. On Friday I made proposals which involved not merely your retention of the Premiership, but the supreme control of the War, whilst the executive functions, subject to that supreme control, were left to others. I thought you then received these suggestions favourably. In fact, you yourself proposed that I should be the chairman of this Executive Committee, although, as you know, I never put forward that demand. On Saturday you wrote me a letter in which you completely went back on that proposition. You sent for me on Sunday and put before me other proposals; these proposals you embodied in a letter to me written on Monday: —

> 'The Prime Minister to have supreme and effective control of war policy;
> The Agenda of the War Committee will be submitted to him; its chairman will report to him daily; he can direct it to consider particular topics or proposals and all its conclusions will be subject to his approval or veto. He can, of course, at his own discretion attend meetings of the Committee.'

These proposals safeguarded your position and power as Prime Minister in every particular. I immediately wrote you accepting them ' in letter and in spirit.' It is true that on Sunday I expressed views as to the constitution of the Committee, but these were for discussion. To-day you have gone back on your own proposals.

I have striven my utmost to cure the obvious defects of the War Committee without overthrowing the Government. As you are aware, on several occasions during the last two years I have deemed it my duty to express profound dissatisfaction with the Government's method of conducting the War. Many a time, with the road to victory open in front of us, we have delayed and hesitated whilst the enemy were erecting barriers that finally checked the approach. There has been delay, hesitation, lack of forethought and vision. I have endeavoured repeatedly to warn the Government of the dangers, both verbally and in written memoranda and letters, which I crave your leave now to publish if my action is challenged; but I have either failed to secure decisions or I have secured them when it was too late to avert the evils. The latest illustration is our lamentable failure to give timely support to Roumania.

I have more than once asked to be released from my responsibility for a policy with which I was in thorough disagreement, but at your urgent personal request I remained in the Government. I realise that when the country is in peril of a great war, Ministers have not the same freedom to resign on disagreement. At the same time I have always felt—and felt deeply—that I was in a false position inasmuch as I could never defend in a whole-hearted manner the action of a Government of which I was a member. We have thrown away opportunity after opportunity, and I am convinced, after deep and anxious reflection, that it is my duty to leave the Government in order to inform the people of the real condition of affairs, and to give them an opportunity, before it is too late, to save their native land from a disaster which is inevitable if the present methods are longer persisted in. As all delay is fatal in war, I place my office without further parley at your disposal.

It is with great personal regret that I have come to this conclusion. In spite of mean and unworthy insinuations to the contrary—insinuations which I fear are always inevitable in the case of men who hold prominent but not primary positions in any administration—I have felt a strong personal attachment to you as my Chief. As you yourself said on Sunday, we have acted together for ten years and never had a quarrel, although we have had many a grave difference on questions of policy. You have treated me with great courtesy and kindness; for all that I thank you. Nothing would have induced me to part now except an overwhelming sense that the course of action which has been pursued has put the country—and not merely the country, but throughout the world, the principles for which you and I have always stood throughout our political lives—in the greatest peril that has ever overtaken them.

As I am fully conscious of the importance of preserving national unity, I propose to give your Government complete support in the vigorous prosecution of the War; but unity without action is nothing but futile carnage, and I cannot be responsible for that. Vigour and vision are the supreme need at this hour.

Yours sincerely,

D. LLOYD GEORGE."

His reply and the further correspondence that ensued will explain the progress of events that terminated the life of the Asquith Coalition.

" 10 Downing Street, S.W.

December 5, 1916.

My dear Lloyd George.

I need not tell you that I have read your letter of to-day with much regret.

I do not comment upon it for the moment, except to say that I cannot wholly accept your account of what passed between us in regard to my connection with the War Committee. In particular, you have omitted to quote the first and most material part of my letter of yesterday.

Yours very sincerely,

H. H. ASQUITH."

" In the meantime, I feel sure that you will see the obvious necessity in the public interest of not publishing at this moment any part of our correspondence."

" War Office, Whitehall, S.W.

December 5, 1916.

My dear Prime Minister,

I cannot announce my resignation without assigning the reason. Your request that I should not publish the correspondence that led up to and necessitated it places me therefore in an embarrassing and unfair position. I must give reasons for the grave step I have taken. If you forbid publication of the correspondence, do you object to my stating in another form my version of the causes that led to my resigning?

Yours sincerely,

D. LLOYD GEORGE."

" As to the first part of your letter, the publication of the letters would cover the whole ground."

" 10, Downing Street, S.W.

December 5, 1916.

My dear Lloyd George,

It may make a difference to you (in reply to your last letter) if I tell you at once that I have tendered my resignation to the King.

In any case, I should deprecate in the public interest the publication in its present form at this moment of your letters to me of this morning.

Of course, I have neither the power nor the wish to prevent your stating in some other form the causes which have led you to take the step which you have taken.

Yours very sincerely,

H. H. ASQUITH."

On Mr. Asquith's resignation, Mr. Bonar Law was summoned by the King and entrusted with the task of forming an Administration. His first suggestion to the Sovereign was that he should summon some of the leading figures in the recent discussions with Mr. Balfour and Mr. Henderson to Buckingham Palace to see whether it was not possible to avoid any break in the unity of the nation by constituting a National Government under the leadership of Mr. Balfour. It is now a matter of history how we expressed our readiness to serve under Mr. Balfour—all of us except Mr. Asquith, who asked indignantly " What is the proposal? That I who have held first place for eight years should be asked to take a secondary position." This broke up the conference. Mr. Asquith subsequently refused to serve in a Bonar Law Administration. Mr. Bonar Law then declined to undertake the responsibility of forming a Ministry and recommended the King to send for me. This course he took in spite of the advice given him to the contrary by Mr. Balfour, Sir Edward Carson, and myself. I neither sought nor desired the Premiership. I knew that in the circumstances my elevation to that position would be skilfully misrepresented. I also knew that a War Committee in a Bonar Law Administration from which the obstructive elements had been kept out, had an excellent chance of working smoothly and effectively, and I felt confident that Mr. Bonar Law would give me a free hand and extend to me the support of a loyal chief, which was all I desired. However, Mr. Bonar Law refused to listen to our combined entreaties, and I had to undertake the terrible responsibility of Premiership in a muddled war, with at least half my own party and more than half the Labour Party bitterly hostile, and a considerable section of the Tory Party—including most of their leaders—suspicious and distrustful.

I surveyed the possibilities. I was assured of the support of something under one half the Liberal Members in the House. Every Conservative Minister in the Government, except Mr. Bonar Law, and as I subsequently discovered, Mr. Balfour, was hostile to my Premiership. The attitude of Labour was doubtful, but not altogether antagonistic. I was satisfied that I would receive the active co-operation of Mr. Bonar Law and Sir Edward Carson (much the most influential leaders in the Conservative Party as far as its rank and file was concerned) and Lord Milner—who carried great weight with the Tory intelligentsia and Die-Hards (not by any means identical groups). If I secured the adhesion of Mr. Balfour I felt that I could risk the opposition of the other Conservative mandarins. I felt he had neither the energy, initiative, nor the administrative gifts requisite for the position of First Lord of the Admiralty at such a critical moment. His elimination from the Admiralty was an unwritten demand I had submitted to Mr. Asquith. Mr. Balfour had been told by Mr. Asquith of the adverse view I had formed of his administration of the Navy, and of my request for his removal. Nevertheless, I have since discovered that he supported my demand for a change in the War direction and refused to join in a reconstruction of the Ministry under Mr. Asquith.

As he said in letters written at the time to the Prime Minister, after he had been informed of my objection to his retaining Office at the Admiralty: " We cannot, I think, go on in the old way. I still think (a) that the break-up of the Government by the retirement of Lloyd

George would be a misfortune; (*b*) that the experiment of giving him a free hand with the day-to-day work of the War Committee is worth trying; and (*c*) that there is no use trying it except on terms which would enable him to work under conditions which in his own opinion promise the best results." He ended by insisting that his resignation should be accepted and " that a fair trial should be given to the new War Council à la George."

I knew nothing of these letters at the time. I only knew that I tried to get Mr. Balfour out of the Admiralty and that as this disagreeable fact would in all probability be communicated to him, an approach to him under these conditions was not very hopeful. I confess that I underrated the passionate attachment to his country which burnt under that calm, indifferent, and apparently frigid exterior.

Mr. Balfour was then ill in bed. Mr. Bonar Law undertook to sound him. He went to offer him the post of Foreign Secretary. He accepted it without any of the hesitations and portentous declarations of his patriotic duty which smaller and less sincere men might have indulged in—and later on did. But as Mr. Bonar Law was leaving, Mr. Balfour suddenly turned to him and said: " Would you mind telling me why Lloyd George was so anxious to get me out of the Admiralty?" Mr. Bonar Law answered with his usual bluntness: " You had better ask him yourself."

Quite recently I discovered that my objections to his retaining office at the Admiralty were a source of hurtful perplexity to him up to his last days. He thought I resented the report he issued to the Press of the much debated battle of Jutland. That report undoubtedly conveyed the impression even to friendly minds that the victory was debatable. My reasons for thinking he was not the best selection for the Admiralty had no reference to this episode. The First Lord during a Great War ought to be a man of exhaustless industry and therefore of great physical energy and reserve. It was an office that called for unceasing attention to detail. It meant long hours, early and late. Mr. Balfour was obviously unsuitable for such a post.

As I have mentioned previously, the story of the first five days of December, 1916, and of the efforts I made to bring about a new system in the direction of war—efforts which, quite contrary to my intention, culminated in a change of Government and the retirement of Mr. Asquith—has already been told very graphically and in considerable detail by Lord Beaverbrook in the second volume of his " Politicians and the War." His account presents the story from the point of view of himself and of Mr. Bonar Law. Naturally, the events were seen by me at the time from a somewhat different angle, but there is no difference of substance between us as to the main features and stages of that crisis.

There was a tragic bitterness about the situation which developed through those days, and which forced a cleavage between me and colleagues with most of whom I had for long years been working in the happiest and most fruitful collaboration—a cleavage later on aggravated and perpetuated by the malice of petty-minded men with baneful effects on the future political development of our country. But even at the worst it had its brighter aspects. One was that it brought Mr. Bonar Law and myself into a close partnership, and laid the foundations of a mutual understanding and real friendship which is one of the happiest of my political memories.

From the moment I was invited by the King to form a Government I was so overwhelmed with urgent affairs, which brooked no delay, that I found no opportunity for presenting to the public my reasons for the course of action which ended in the downfall of the Asquith Administration. It was not merely the time occupied in the actual formation of the Government. That took a few days of interviewing, negotiating and adjusting. And here I would like to pay a tribute to the tact, the wisdom and loyalty with which both Mr. Bonar Law and I were assisted in this difficult and even dangerous task by Sir Edmund Talbot (now Lord FitzAlan). He smoothed many difficulties and probably averted many indiscretions.

The moment the Government was formed there were many pressing matters to attend to which ought to have been settled many months ago. The campaign for 1917 had already been settled before I became Prime Minister. But there were many urgent questions which demanded immediate decision and prompt action. The production of aeroplanes—the food supplies of the country—the protection of our ships and the development of ship-building—the better mobilisation of the man-power of this country—the mission to Russia, too long delayed—the German peace move—and afterwards President Wilson's peace notes; these constituted but a part of the calls upon the attention of the War Cabinet. In these circumstances Mr. Bonar Law and I could not enter into a controversy upon the causes that led to the recent crisis. Apart from that consideration, we came to the conclusion that it was not desirable to have discussions upon personal matters which might endanger the national unity and imperil national co-operation. Neither of us therefore issued any statement on the subject. Had we done so we knew we could not have left it there, as we should have been bound to reply to inevitable criticisms and comments from those who were now freed from the cares and burden of office and who had more time, and, as it turned out, more inclination to dwell upon these things.

As far as Mr. Bonar Law was concerned the decision was probably the right one. But there is no doubt that my influence in the Liberal Party suffered severely from my neglect to put my case before opinions had hardened and prejudices had been created. Misrepresentations were soon broadcast throughout the land, and time was given for them to strike root in the soil, and when I regained leisure it was too late to eradicate them. Most of this work was done privately at confidential gatherings of Liberal associations throughout the country. Missionaries were dispatched from Headquarters at Abingdon Street to every district to spread tendentious reports of the origin, motives and methods of the crisis. At secret conclaves much could be said which the presence of a newspaper reporter would have checked. Some salient facts were suppressed; others were distorted, and when I resumed my political activities after the War was over, I was amazed at the beliefs that were current as to what had really happened. When I asked Mr. Asquith for permission to publish the correspondence, he had, as is shown in the above correspondence, refused to accede to my request on public grounds. I was rather surprised to find, when he came to address Liberal Members a few days after his resignation and to explain to them why he resigned, that he summarised some of the passages from his own letters and actually quoted some in full, whilst he omitted altogether to communicate to his hearers the statements I made in reply. His reason for doing so was: —

" I will not read his letter because it is private; it was written very confidentially."

He did not think it necessary in the interest of fair play to explain that I had asked him for permission to publish my letter, and that he had refused. He conveyed the impression to them that the Sunday agreement was not an agreement at all, but merely a proposal for further discussion. He never informed them that he told Mr. Bonar Law after our Sunday interview that he and I had agreed on terms, and that the only question left for further debate was that of personnel; that he had made the same statement that very evening to Mr. Montagu and to Lord Reading. He never informed the meeting that on Monday I had repeatedly asked to see him and that he had declined to give me an interview, nor did he inform them of the important fact that a meeting of all the Liberal Members of the Cabinet had been summoned on Monday night to consider the position and that I had not been invited to attend the meeting. He withheld from them the fact that at a conference at Buckingham Palace presided over by the King he had refused to serve in a National Ministry under the Premiership of Mr. Balfour, although Mr. Bonar Law, Mr. Henderson, and myself were quite prepared to do so. Nor did he tell them that when Mr. Bonar Law was entrusted with the task of forming a National Government he had refused, after consultation with his Liberal colleagues, to join it. It was obvious that, if these vital facts had been communicated to those Members who had assembled at the Reform Club, they would have taken a different view of the transaction. Unfortunately, we allowed a very one-sided statement to go by default, and the truncated statement, because it was unchallenged,

u*

was accepted by the majority of Liberals in the country as a fair account of what had happened.

I will only give one example of the kind of thing which influenced Liberals against me at that time. Here is a speech delivered by Mr. Runciman to his constituents immediately after he left office: —

> "In re-forming the Government the present Prime Minister invited his Unionist colleagues to rejoin him. He invited the Labour Party to join him, and he gave an invitation to one Liberal Minister. I was not that one. I have been asked by my constituents already why I did not join the new Government. I can only make the simple reply that it was impossible to accept an invitation which I had not received."*

Surely there never has been a better example of *suppressio veri*. Had Mr. Runciman told his constituents that he was one of those who had agreed at the meeting of Liberal Ministers on Monday night not to take office under anyone except Mr. Asquith, and that at the meeting when that decision was reached the question of my Premiership was discussed as the alternative; had he informed them that he was one of those who advised Mr. Asquith not to serve under any other Premier, quite a different impression would have been conveyed to the minds of his electors. He clearly wished them to believe that whereas I was inviting Conservative and Labour men to join my Government, I wantonly and deliberately ruled out all my former colleagues except one.

* How busy I was may be inferred from the fact that I read the speeches of Mr. Asquith and Mr. Runciman for the first time when I came to write this story.